WAR WITHOUT END

D0109810

WAR WITHOUT END

*Israelis, Palestinians, and the
Struggle for a Promised Land*

Anton La Guardia

*Too long a sacrifice
Can make a stone of the heart*
W. B. Yeats

Thomas Dunne Books

St. Martin's Griffin

New York

THOMAS DUNNE BOOKS.
An imprint of St. Martin's Press.

WAR WITHOUT END. Copyright © 2001, 2003 by Anton La Guardia. All rights reserved. Printed in the United States of America. No part of this book may be used or reproduced in any manner whatsoever without written permission except in the case of brief quotations embodied in critical articles or reviews. For information, address St. Martin's Press, 175 Fifth Avenue, New York, N.Y. 10010.

www.stmartins.com

Library of Congress Cataloging-in-Publication Data

La Guardia, Anton.
    War without end : Israelis, Palestinians, and the struggle for a promised land / Anton La Guardia.
        p. cm.
    Updated ed. of: Holy Land, unholy war : Israelis and Palestinians. Great Britain : John Murray, 2001.
    ISBN 0-312-27669-9 (hc)
    ISBN 0-312-31633-X (pbk)
    1. Arab-Israeli conflict. 2. Arab-Israeli conflict—1993—Influence. 3. National characterisitcs, Israeli. 4. Jews—Israel—Identity. 5. Palestinian Arabs—Ethnic identity. 6. Zionism. I. La Guardia, Anton. Holy land, unholy war. II. Title.

DS119.7.L243 2003
956.9405—dc21   2003041288

First published in Great Britain by John Murray (Publishers) Ltd, under the title Holy Land, Unholy War: Israelis and Palestinians.

First St. Martin's Griffin Edition: May 2003

10 9 8 7 6 5 4 3 2 1

To Jane Ksenia

My beloved spake, and said unto me,
Rise up, my love, my fair one, and come away

Song of Solomon

Contents

Illustrations

28. A Palestinian boy stones an Israeli tank
29. An armed Jewish settler takes his child for a stroll in Hebron
30. Would-be Islamic suicide bombers at a Hamas rally
31. Palestinian workers queue for work in Israel
32. Photographers record Israel's withdrawal from Lebanon

MAPS

The author and publisher would like to thank the following for permission to reproduce illustrations: Plates 2 and 25, Milner Moshe, Israel Government Press Office; 3, 4, 5, 22, 23, 26, 27, 28, 29, 30, 31 and 32, Associated Press; 6, 8, 10 and 18, Institute for Palestine Studies, Washington, DC; 7, 9, 11 and 24, Central Zionist Archives, Jerusalem; 12 and 13, Hulton Getty; 14, Israel Government Press Office, Jerusalem; 15, Ilan Bruner, Israel Government Press Office, Jerusalem; 16, *The New York Times*; 17, Kibbutz Lohamei ha-Getaot; 19, Kluger Zoltan, Israel Government Press Office, Jerusalem; 20, UNRWA photo/Myrtle Winter Chaumeny; 21, UNRWA photo/George Nehmeh.

Preface

THE PACE OF events in the Middle East is the foreign correspondent's blessing, and the book-writer's curse. I have experienced both in the past decade.

The outbursts of violence, the sudden breakthroughs in peace negotiations and the volatility of Israeli politics make for a constant flow of dramatic news stories. They also make it extremely difficult to write a book.

I first arrived in Jerusalem as a "fireman" to cover the Gulf War for *The Daily Telegraph* in 1990. My temporary assignment lasted an exhilarating seven years, having been extended repeatedly by the need to cover major events—the Madrid peace conference of 1991, the election of 1992 that brought Yitzhak Rabin to power, the Oslo accords of 1993 and the start of Palestinian autonomy, the suicide bombing campaign by Islamic militants, the aftermath of the assassination of Rabin in 1995 and so on.

By the time I left Jerusalem I thought I was ready to take a broader view. "A book on the Middle East?" my colleagues asked, with a tone of commiseration. "How can you write a book when the story keeps changing?"

As they predicted, I found myself frequently having to rip up passages to take account of major developments—the election of Ehud Barak, the Israeli army's withdrawal from south Lebanon and the rush for a permanent peace agreement. Just when I thought I had neatly encapsulated the situation, the Al-Aqsa Intifada exploded.

As I embarked on another re-write, jettisoning material that was now out of date, I realized that the Intifada is a milestone—a place from which to consider the tumultuous road to Palestinian statehood, the experiment in Palestinian autonomy, and the forces that destroyed this attempt at "peace."

I have tried to paint a cultural portrait of Israelis and Palestinians, seeking to explain the elements of history, religion and culture—the symbols of identity—that make up these two peoples. It is not a political chronicle of the twists and turns in the "peace process." Nevertheless, it is frustrating to try to paint a subject that constantly fidgets, changes pose, pulls faces and adopts new costumes. Like any portrait, the parts that I highlight in detail and those that I brush in with swift strokes are a subjective choice, yet I hope that the canvas captures something of the essential nature of these two peoples who resemble each other in many ways, yet are so irreconcilably different.

I have argued that the response of visitors to Israel and Palestine over the past century has said as much about the observer as about the country itself. I should therefore declare myself: I was born in Rome, and I am a lapsed Roman Catholic.

This book would not have been possible without the help, enthusiasm and talent of my researcher and translator in Jerusalem, Carol Sutherland. She has been a mine of knowledge on even the most esoteric of subjects, and has that journalist's instinct for the telling detail and the compelling story. I could not have hoped for better in her lucid translations into English.

During my years in Jerusalem, Kim Weiss, the *Daily Telegraph's* assistant, was indefatigable in providing a stream of up-to-date information about the world I was reporting. Ohad Gozani, the newspaper's correspondent in Tel Aviv, was an instant databank of knowledge on Israel and an early warning system for breaking news stories. What cumulative experience I have acquired about Israel has come, in no small part, through their work and friendship.

Likewise, Said al-Ghazali and Nihaya Kawasmi were my indispensable eyes and ears on Palestinian society, reporting, translating and helping me to interpret complex events as Palestinians moved convulsively toward statehood. They were always ready to head out into the West Bank and Gaza Strip at a moment's notice, even in the most trying of times.

Sergei Makarov and his wife, Elena, introduced me to Russian society in Israel, while Rana Wassel in Beirut provided essential research in the refugee camps in Lebanon. Thank you to Mimi Ash in Jerusalem for her efficient picture research.

I am particularly indebted to the following for reading the manuscript and suggesting improvements at different stages of preparation: Nicholas Goldberg, a fellow journalist; Alec Russell, Foreign Editor of *The Daily Telegraph*; Said Aburish, the author of several books on the Middle East; and Dr. Emanuele Ottolenghi of St. Antony's

College, Oxford. I appreciate the kindness of others who have read all or part of the manuscript.

I would like to thank the following, in no particular order, for their suggestions and assistance in planning and researching the book. Jerome Murphy O'Connor, David Rosen, Nabil Feidy, Albert Agazarian, Massimo Torrefranca, Tzvika Dror, the staff at the Warsaw Ghetto Fighters' Museum and the Rishon Le-Zion Museum, Daniel Ben-Simon, Tom Segev, David Horowitz, Ze'ev Chafets, Yossi Klein Halevi, Sahira Dirbas, Michal Peleg, Daoud Kuttab, Saud Abu Ramadan, Muhammad Dawwas, Hayyan Juabeh, Dan Wakin, Esteban Alterman, the Khalil Sakakini Centre in Ramallah, AKUM (The Society of Authors, Composers & Music Publishers in Israel), and the United Nations Relief and Works Agency (UNRWA).

Many, many others have had a hand in this book—whether consciously or not—in interviews, debates, and conversations I have had over the years that I wandered the Middle East. They are too many to name, but their omission does not diminish my appreciation for the time they have given me.

My employers at *The Daily Telegraph* made it all possible by sending me to Jerusalem in the first place, and keeping me there much longer than I expected. My thanks to the former editor, Max Hastings, and the former foreign editors, Nigel Wade, Patrick Bishop, and Stephen Robinson.

I am grateful to Charles Moore, the newspaper's current editor, who allowed me to take time off to begin writing the book between my postings in Jerusalem and Johannesburg.

The Yad Ben-Tzvi library in Jerusalem has been exceptionally helpful in providing guidance for relevant books. The library at the Hebrew University has given invaluable assistance. The Zionist Federation library in Johannesburg was very helpful as I hunted for Israeli sources in a beautiful but troubled land where the concerns of the Middle East are very distant.

The archives of *Ha'aretz*, the *Jerusalem Post* and *Israel News Today* (a daily translation service of the Hebrew press and broadcasts) have been vital tools.

Roddy Murray has provided excellent maps.

I am most grateful to Grant McIntyre, my editor at John Murray, for his enthusiasm—and infinite patience—in overseeing this book as I carted my boxes of research material from one continent to another and struggled to fit book-writing around the demands of news.

I very much appreciate the inspired job that Beth Humphries has done in tightening, correcting—and improving—this manuscript. The repetitions, mistakes and blunders that remain are all mine.

My deepest gratitude and love are reserved for my wife, Jane, who has put up with the project as if it were another member of our family, and endured the loss of weekends and holidays for the past three years. She discussed my ever-changing ideas for the structure of the book, watched me procrastinate over tiny points of detail and helped shape drafts of chapters when they were still too disjointed to present to anybody. My daughters Gemma and Alexandra—in that state of blissful innocence where they still ask "what is war?"—have been too young to understand why their father spent so long "in the office" tapping on a keyboard instead of helping them with their alphabet. This book is dedicated to them too.

Note on Transliteration and Terminology

When the publishers of T. E. Lawrence's *Revolt in the Desert* queried the many conflicts in his spelling of Arabic names, the man known as "Lawrence of Arabia" wrote back: "There are some 'scientific systems' of transliteration, helpful to people who know enough Arabic not to need helping, but a washout for the world. I spell my names anyhow, to show what a rot the systems are."

Semitic languages like Arabic and Hebrew are based on a consonantal system that derives words from three-letter roots. The vowel sounds are usually implied by the context, and there are sounds such as the pharyngeal *'ayin* that simply do not exist in western languages. Any transliteration is by necessity an approximation. To the horror of academic purists, I have adopted no particular system. Where possible, I have spelled proper names in accordance with the preference of the individuals in question. Otherwise, I have used spellings that seem best to reflect current pronunciation, yet are simple enough to be recognizable to English-speaking readers. With well-known words, figures and places, I have used spellings that are most familiar in British or American newspapers. There is no reason, however, to maintain outdated spellings such as Moslem and Mohammed, when Muslim and Muhammad are perfectly acceptable and more faithful to the original. I have tried to identify particles such as the definite article *ha-* in Hebrew and *al-* in *Arabic*—writing ha-Cohen rather than Hacohen, and Izz al-Din rather than Izzedin. There are no capital letters in Hebrew or Arabic, so their use in transliteration is entirely a matter of preference. I recognize in advance that there are many inconsistencies.

All terminology in the Arab–Israeli conflict is loaded with political meaning. I have usually used the word "Palestine" as a historical and geographical reference to the country during the time of the British mandate and earlier, but I have at times used it also in the context of how Palestinians and their supporters call the country. I have often used "Arabs" and "Palestinians" interchangeably, without seeking to pass comment on when the Arabs of Palestine began to see themselves as Palestinians. Israel includes both Arabs and Jews, but I have usually used the term "Israelis" to mean Israeli Jews. When speaking of the Arab citizens of Israel, I have used "Israeli Arabs" and "Israeli Palestinians" interchangeably even though there is a constant debate over these names. I hope my readers will forgive these shorthand labels.

Acknowledgments

I have mentioned the sources of quotations wherever possible, without disrupting the flow of what is supposed to be a narrative rather than an academic book and without encumbering the text with endless footnotes. I have given a fairly full bibliography at the end to help those wishing to refer to the sources.

I would like to thank the following, in no special order, for permission to quote material used in this book: Tom Segev, for permission to use material from two of his books, *1949: The First Israelis* and *The Seventh Million*; Hala al-Sakakini, for the use of excerpts from the diary of her late father, Khalil al-Sakakini, *Such Am I, O World*, and her own memoirs, *Jerusalem and I*; Salma Khadra Jayyusi and Columbia University Press, for the use of several poems and other material in *Anthology of Modern Palestinian Literature*; Eitan Szenes, for the use of the poem, "Walk to Caesarea," by Hanna Szenes; The International Committee of the Red Cross, for Jacques de Reynier's reports on the Deir Yassin massacre; Kibbutz Degania Aleph for the use of Joseph Baratz' memoirs, *A Village by the Jordan: The Story of Degania*; *The Journal of Mediterranean Studies*, University of Malta, for the use of excerpts from "Arab Folksongs and Palestinian Identity," an article by Abdellatif Barghouthi of Bir Zeit University; A. Chahine & Fils, Beirut, for use of the lyrics of Fairuz' song *Zahrat al-Madayin*; Abdallah al-Udhari and Saqi Books, London, for the use of verses from the collection of poetry, *Victims of a Map*, including the poem,

"We Travel Like Other People" by Mahmoud Darwish; Histadrut Ivrit of America, New York, for the use of verses from *City of Slaughter* by Haim Nahman Bialik; Random House, Inc, New York, for the use of *The Diaries of Theodor Herzl*; The Jewish Agency, Jerusalem, for the use of material from *The Goodly Heritage* by Avraham Yaari; A.P. Watt Ltd. for the use of material from Yeats' poem, "Easter 1916"; Arthur Hertzberg for material from *The Zionist Idea*; Hannah Amichai, for the use of Yehuda Amichai's poems "Ecology of Jerusalem" and "Suicide Attempts of Jerusalem"; Yaakov Rotblit, for the use of *Shir ha-Shalom* (*Song of Peace*); The Orion Publishing Group Ltd., London, for use of Moshe Dayan's *Story of My Life*; Neville Mandel for the use of material on early Arab responses from *The Arabs and Zionism before World War I*, quoted on pp. 101–2; Erez Biton for the use of verses from "A Moroccan Offering" in *Minha Maroka'it*; The Penguin Group (UK) for use of *The Koran*, translated by N. J. Daewood.; The Jabotinsky Institute, Tel Aviv, for use of Jabotinsky's writing; and Green & Heaton, for use of Yael Dayan's books, *My Father, His Daughter*, and *Israel Journal: June 1967*.

Every effort has been made to contact copyright holders, and the author apologizes for any omissions, which he will be pleased to rectify at the earliest opportunity.

Foreword to the American Edition

AFTER the atrocities carried out by Osama bin Laden's Islamic suicide squads on September 11, 2001, many bewildered Americans asked themselves: "Why do they hate us?"

The answer to this simple question is complex and incomplete. It has to do with the crisis within Islam, the memory of the golden age of Arab civilization and anger at its modern decay, the clash of tradition with western modernity, the poverty amid oil wealth, illegitimacy of Arab rulers, political oppression, the legacy of colonialism and many more reasons.

And somewhere prominently near the top of the list of any explanation is the word "Israel" and America's role in protecting the Jewish state. This is not the only motive for which many Arabs hate America, nor even the main reason. Even if Israel did not exist, America would be deeply involved in the Arab world by virtue of two accidents of nature—the geography that permitted the construction of the Suez Canal, and the geology that brought the bounty of oil in the Gulf.

Nevertheless, survival of the Jewish state symbolizes, for many Arabs, everything that they believe is wrong with their universe—cowardly and corrupt leaders, oppressive but incompetent armed forces, and fragmentation of the Arab and Islamic nation. In short, a state of weakness that allows foreigners to take Arab land with impunity. The word most used by Arabs when speaking about their relations with the West is "humiliation," and nothing is more humiliating than the way Israel has repulsed one Arab army after another over the past five decades.

With the outbreak of the Al-Aqsa Intifada—the Palestinian armed uprising that started in September 2000—anti-American emotions across the Arab and Islamic world have been inflamed by images of the conflict beamed by satellite television stations across the Arab world. In the popular Arab mind, Israel is shooting Palestinians using American guns and is shielded by American power, while the Arab watches impotently.

Osama bin Laden may like to evoke the suffering of Palestine, but the September 11 attacks are not directly linked to the Arab-Israeli dispute. Bin Laden had declared war on America long before the Intifada had started, primarily in response to the deployment of American troops in his native Saudi Arabia where they are deemed to be desecrating the land of the Prophet Muhammad. What's more, the American presence in the Gulf has nothing to do with Israel; it is the result of Iraq's invasion of Kuwait. But in the accumulation of grudges, America's support for Israel and America's containment of Iraq by sanctions and military strikes are evidence of the same vast plot to dominate the Arabs.

America was not always regarded as the great Satan. The Arab world was colonized by Britain and France, not America. It was the Soviet bloc that provided the first weapons to the new-born Israel. It was President Dwight Eisenhower who told Israel, Britain, and France to withdraw from Egyptian territory after the fiasco of their military intervention in the Suez crisis of 1956.

Yet today America is seen to embody several identities: as heir of European imperialism, defender of the Jewish intruders, protector of corrupt Arab leaders, controller of the economic system that extorts cheap oil, and source of depraved social habits that corrupt Muslim youth.

This is the deep current of anger that Osama bin Laden seeks to exploit. To Bin Laden's admirers, the September 11 attacks were an act to redeem Arab and Muslim honor after years of subjugation. In his first appearance on a propaganda video released after September 11, Bin Laden stood in his military fatigues and boasted: "Here is America struck by God Almighty in one of its vital organs, so that its greatest buildings are destroyed. Grace and gratitude to God. America has been filled with horror from north to south and east to west, and thanks be to God that what America is tasting now is only a copy of what we have tasted. Our Islamic nation has been tasting the same for more than 80 years, of humiliation and disgrace, its sons killed and their blood spilled, its sanctities desecrated."

Bin Laden issued his video through his favorite Arab satellite television station, Al-Jazeera, the closest thing to an independent Arab television station. Its extraordinary power is a testament to Arabs' thirst for information.

In a region where most Arabs are excluded from power, and where official pronouncements are not to be trusted, the world is often interpreted through the rumor mill and conspiracy theories. The belief in great foreign plots and unseen forces helps to explain why the Arab and Muslim nation appears to be so debilitated, and shift responsibility away from the failures of Arab leadership. Enter European anti-Semitism, whose notions of Jewish plots to dominate the world can help explain Israel's survival in a sea of Arabs.

Across the Muslim world, the Protocols of the Elders of Zion, a tsarist forgery purporting to detail a conspiracy by Jews to seize control of the world, have become embedded into ideological theories propounded by both Islamists and Arab nationalists.

After the horrible events of September 11, 2001, it did not take long for a terrible lie to be born that the Jews, not Muslims, were behind the destruction of the World Trade Center and the other outrages in America. Within days of the September 11 attacks, the myth emerged that 4,000 Jews had deliberately stayed away from the World Trade Center after being tipped off by the Mossad to stay at home. This story, which appeared to originate with militant Islamic groups in Pakistan and was then popularized by Hezbollah in Lebanon, spread with astonishing speed. Newspaper columnists picked it up, Arab ministers repeated it and sheikhs amplified it until it became established fact.

For many people across the Arab and Islamic world, it all fits into a pattern of world Jewish domination: Who benefits most from the attacks being blamed on Muslims? Israel. Why are the newspapers and television not reporting this fact? Because the Jews control the media. In an unintended compliment to the Jews, there is the claim that only the Mossad could have executed such a complex operation. Plots, evil conspiracies, global domination—this is the language of the enraged and the powerless.

If Osama bin Laden were to be captured or killed, the Islamist fervor in the Arab world is unlikely to diminish. Others will take up the cause of holy war, with the rallying cry of liberating Palestine and defeating Israel and America.

This book is an attempt to describe the nature of Israel and Palestine, the symbolism they represent, the mirror histories of their people, and the extraordinary power that this tiny country exerts across the globe.

The book was first published in Britain in the summer of 2001, and has been updated to take account of the events of the repercussions of September 11 on the conflict between Israel and the Palestinians. It originally appeared under the title of *Holy Land, Unholy War: Israelis and Palestinians.* This was changed at the insistence of my American publishers, who at first wanted the book to be called *The Israelis.* In the intense argument over the issue, my publishers demanded the simple catchiness of their title while I insisted that the name should reflect the fact that this is a land of two people, whose lives are inextricably intertwined.

I would like to express my gratitude to Thomas Dunne for accommodating to my stubbornness. I am also indebted to Sean Desmond for overseeing the production of this updated edition, and for putting up with my repeated requests for more time to make changes.

Alan Philps, my successor as the *Daily Telegraph*'s correspondent in Jerusalem, was ever ready to offer his experience and insights on how events have evolved. I would like to thank my father, Luciano La Guardia, and step-mother, Maria-Pia, for their love and warm hospitality in Umbria during the preparation of this edition and for their support throughout this project.

London, February 18, 2002

Foreword to the American Paperback Edition

THE HOLY LAND has long been a place of violence, but rarely has the blood of innocents been spilled so casually as during the middle months of 2002. Anybody who witnessed at first hand the hopes of peace in 1993, and the difficult attempt to turn them into reality, can only feel heartbroken at the way Israelis and Palestinians have dragged each other down another rung of hellish violence.

I returned to Jerusalem at the end of March 2002, just in time to watch Israel sweep through the cities of the West Bank, smash through Yasser Arafat's headquarters in Ramallah and lay siege to gunmen who had taken refuge in the Church of the Nativity in Bethlehem.

The people and places of the country were familiar, save for a few new buildings, but the character and spirit were utterly transformed. Strolling out for a coffee in the semi-deserted streets near the office in Jerusalem felt like a death-defying stunt. Going for hummus and kebab in Bethlehem, a fifteen-minute jaunt in my days in the Middle East, was simply impossible. When I last went to Bethlehem, there were Israeli tanks creaking past my favorite restaurant, Abu Shanab, a simple place run by a man with a fabulous handlebar moustache.

While the people of Jerusalem and Bethlehem tried to keep out of sight and out of harm's way, the faces of the dead were everywhere. There were pictures of Palestinian martyrs on posters peeling off the walls of Palestinian cities, portraits of dead soldiers on Israeli television, newspaper photographs of ordinary Israelis wiped out in suicide attacks and valedictory video messages of the bombers themselves.

As I write this update, the United States is gathering its mighty military machine for a seemingly inevitable war to depose Saddam Hussein. One can only guess at how it may unfold and how events in Baghdad will affect Israelis and Palestinians; my hope is that the Bush administration will seize the opportunity of victory in Iraq—if that is what emerges—to turn its attention to the festering hatred in the

Holy Land. The dispute cannot be reduced to just to an issue of terrorism, important as it may be. The question of Israel and Palestine is also a question of dispossession.

For this updated edition, I am particularly indebted to my colleagues at the *Daily Telegraph* who live in the region or have reported it. Alan Philps, Ohad Gozani and David Blair have generously allowed me to use accounts of events that they witnessed during the tumultuous period of March–May 2002. The assistance of Said Ghazzali and Kim Weiss was, as always, indispensable. They and many others have helped to keep me up to date with events and interpret them.

I am grateful to Alec Russell, Foreign Editor at the *Daily Telegraph*, who sent me out to cover events unfolding in the Middle East at a pivotal time.

The patience of my wife, Jane, has been stretched to the limit as I have embarked on another in the seemingly endless succession of updates for this book in the past year. My love for her, however, has no limits. My daughters, Gemma and Alexandra, are sadly beginning to understand that bad things happen in Jerusalem when they hear the radio bulletins. I hope they will one day be able to see the elusive peace of Jerusalem, peace within her walls and prosperity within her palaces.

London, 5 February 2003

The Middle East

MEDITERRANEAN SEA

Beirut

SYRIA

LEBANON

Damascus

GOLAN HEIGHTS

ISRAEL

Amman

Tel Aviv

Jerusalem

IRAQ

GAZA STRIP

WEST BANK

Cairo

JORDAN

Suez Canal

Eilat

EGYPT

Sinai

SAUDI ARABIA

100 miles

The changing shape of Israel and Palestine

British mandate 1920

British mandate after 1921

UN partition plan 1947

Jewish state
Arab state
International

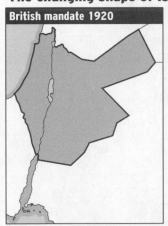

Armistice lines 1949-67

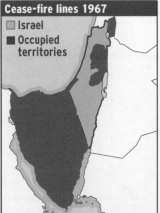

Cease-fire lines 1967

Israel
Occupied territories

Israel today

Israel
Occupied territories

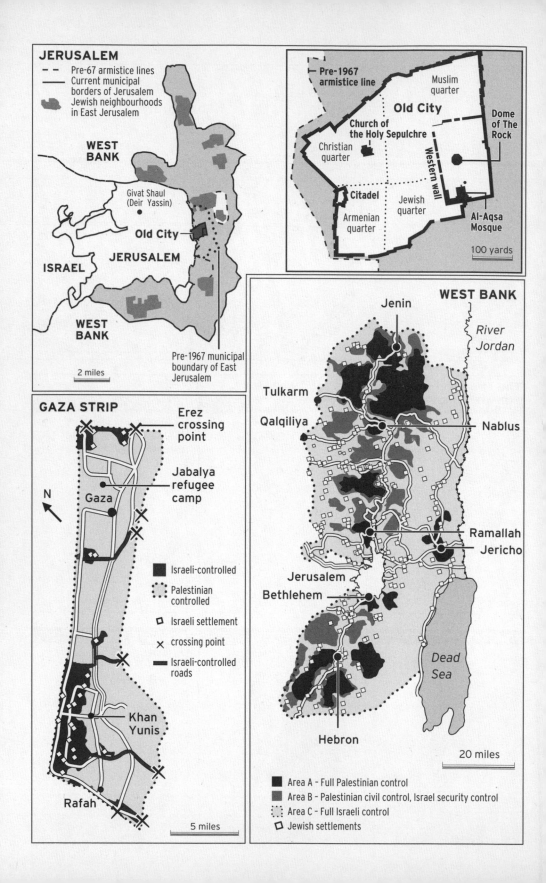

JERUSALEM

- – – Pre-67 armistice lines
- —— Current municipal borders of Jerusalem
- ▪ Jewish neighbourhoods in East Jerusalem

WEST BANK

Givat Shaul (Deir Yassin)

Old City

JERUSALEM

ISRAEL

WEST BANK

2 miles

Pre-1967 municipal boundary of East Jerusalem

– Pre-1967 armistice line

Muslim quarter

Old City

Church of the Holy Sepulchre

Christian quarter

Western wall

Jewish quarter

Dome of The Rock

Citadel

Armenian quarter

Al-Aqsa Mosque

100 yards

GAZA STRIP

Erez crossing point

Jabalya refugee camp

Gaza

N

■ Israeli-controlled
▫ Palestinian controlled
◇ Israeli settlement
✕ crossing point
■ Israeli-controlled roads

Khan Yunis

Rafah

5 miles

WEST BANK

Jenin

River Jordan

Tulkarm

Qalqiliya

Nablus

Ramallah

Jericho

Jerusalem

Bethlehem

Dead Sea

Hebron

20 miles

■ Area A – Full Palestinian control
■ Area B – Palestinian civil control, Israel security control
▫ Area C – Full Israeli control
◇ Jewish settlements

Israel and the Occupied Territories

MEDITERRANEAN SEA

LEBANON

Metulla

Damascus

Kiryat Shmona

DEMILITARISED ZONE

Kibbutz Lohamei ha-Getaot

GOLAN HEIGHTS

Acre

Sea of Galilee

Haifa

SYRIA

Tiberias

Nazareth

Afula

Kibbutz Degania

River Jordan

WEST BANK

Nablus

Tel Aviv

Ramla

Amman

Ramallah

Rishon Le-Zion

Jericho

Jerusalem

Bethlehem

JORDAN

Gaza City

Sderot

Hebron

Dead Sea

GAZA STRIP

Beersheba

Dimona

ISRAEL

EGYPT

SINAI

40 miles

Eilat

A Small Country with a Big History

A T THE check-in for El Al flights at Ben-Gurion airport, there is a young woman who sends passengers into separate queues for the security grilling. Jews one way and non-Jews the other, clean and unclean like a modern Noah's Ark. The Hebrew speakers slip through effortlessly after some cursory questioning. The rest usually wait in line to face an interrogation ranging from the routine to the insolent. Are you carrying a package for anyone? Do you know any people in Israel? What are their names? Do you travel to the West Bank? Do you have any Arab friends? What are their names? And on and on.

Despite the perfunctory "I'm sorry for the inconvenience," this is designed to be an unpleasant experience. It is meant to probe the identity of the passenger, prod and poke at the traveler's story. "So you are a journalist? Do you have anything to prove it? Please turn on your computer and show me something you have written." Sometimes the interrogator goes away, and another one comes back to start all over again. Mind games. I was once asked, in all serious-ness: "You are not Jewish, so why are you visiting Israel?" There are no qualms here about "profiling," ethnic or otherwise. Foreign women traveling on their own receive particularly close scrutiny, ever since Nizar Hindawi, a Jordanian working for Syrian intelligence, sent his pregnant Irish girlfriend on to an El Al flight without telling her he had hidden a Semtex bomb in the false bottom of her bag. An alert El Al guard spotted the device, saving the lives of 375 people that day in April 1986.

Even abroad, when you walk up to the El Al counter you already walk into the bit of Israel, sensing the ever-present threat of terrorism and war that Israel lives under. In some western European countries, an Israeli security officer sits next to the driver of the bus taking passengers from the terminal to the aircraft. Other agents are already deployed on the tarmac, protecting the access steps or leading a sniffer dog over the luggage. Sometimes an armored car shadows Israel-bound aircraft as they taxi to the runway. Every El Al flight has armed guards and bulletproof cockpits.

Before September 11, 2001, this kind of overbearing security was an annoyance that a traveler had to accept as part of the unique Israel travel experience, like watching women soldiers with guns on the streets of Jerusalem or hearing the sonic boom and rattle of fighter jets over the Old City of Jerusalem. After the attacks on America Israeli-style may be the future of all international air travel.

When the world saw how Islamic suicide squads armed with just knives had hijacked four airliners and turned them into flying bombs on America's cities, the sense of shock in Israel was mixed with a feeling of reassurance that "it would never have been allowed to happen here." What had once been for many Israelis a longing for the relaxed normality of life in America turned to incredulity at the laxness of U.S. attitudes to airline safety. Israel's army of security experts—retired army and intelligence agents—analyzed the events: had the hijackers tried to attack an Israeli plane, they would probably not even have reached the check-in counter; if they had managed to get on to the aircraft, they would have been stopped by the armed guards; and if by a miracle they had managed to take over the cockpit, they would have been shot down by the Israeli air force before they got anywhere near a major city. For once El Al's advertising pitch, telling Israelis that "no other airline goes as far to ensure your safety as your national airline" and "El Al flies on safe routes over friendly nations" did not sound like the brave boast of an airline carrying a debilitating security burden.

The initial impression of Israel is not just of an embattled people obsessed with security, but of a particularly youthful people. Those charged with ensuring safety at Ben-Gurion are scarcely of college age, often young women in their early twenties fresh out of national service. You can easily identify the guard on an El Al flight: it's the young man with short-cropped hair sitting awkwardly in business class looking as if he borrowed his father's jacket.

At Ben-Gurion airport the visitor gets a glimpse of the paradoxes of Israel—a democracy that has been at war for more than half a century, a Jewish state that claims to give equal rights for its Arab minority, a refuge for the Jews whose creation has left millions of

Palestinians in exiles. Inconvenient and irritating as the Israel travel experience may be for the western traveler, it is a humiliation for a Palestinian who, upon arrival or departure at Ben-Gurion is taken off to a separate room for intense screening and searches. An American or other foreign passport is no protection. International frontiers, checkpoints, airports and harbors—whether in Israel, the rest of the world or even in "brotherly" Arab countries—are invariably places of dread for Palestinians. Their lack of homeland is reason for instant suspicion. If they ever tried to forget they were Palestinians, they are reminded of it at frontiers.

Foreigners everywhere they go, they are subject to the whims and prejudices of their hosts or occupiers. After the 1991 Gulf War, Palestinians were expelled *en masse* from Kuwait after the Palestinian leader Yasser Arafat declared his support for Iraq's President Saddam Hussein. In 1993 and 1994, hundreds of Palestinians were expelled from Libya and left stranded for weeks on the border with Egypt, which refused to admit them.

The creation of Israel brought to rest the image of the Wandering Jew. Now it is the Palestinian who restlessly roams the world. The experience is described time and time again in Palestinian literature. "We travel like other people, but we return to nowhere," wrote the poet Mahmoud Darwish. In another poem, *Diary of a Palestinian Wound*, the writer protests: "My country is not a suitcase."

If the suitcase encapsulates dispossession for Palestinians, it is a symbol of fulfillment and renewal for the Jews who have made their way to Israel over the past half-century. It represents independence, freedom from persecution, and a fresh start. The black-and-white pictures of Moroccan Jews arriving in new towns with large square suitcases on their shoulders are images of a heroic age. The photographs of Ethiopian Jews arriving in Israel holding little white bundles speak of a state that thinks of itself as a place of refuge for Jews from the remotest corners of the world.

Ben-Gurion airport is where hundreds of thousands of hope-filled Jewish immigrants first come into contact with Israel. Through here come the old and the young, the secular and the religious—each to claim the promise of a piece of Zion. Under Israel's Law of Return any person with a Jewish grandparent has the right to settle in Israel and claim citizenship. But the "Right of Return" is stubbornly denied to an Arab who, decades after being evicted from Palestine, still holds the keys to his house and the deeds to his land in any of the hundreds of Arab villages destroyed at the time of Israel's creation.

Ben-Gurion airport should be a staging point between Europe and the Far East, a great global entrepôt, a Singapore of the Levant. Instead it is a dead end, blocked off by a solid wall of Arab hostility. Until the peace agreement with Jordan in 1994, no airliners from Israel flew eastward. Even now, to get beyond Amman, you have to take a long detour, either south past Yemen, or north over Turkey. Most of Israel's direct neighbors may as well inhabit a different planet. From Ben-Gurion airport it is easier to travel to Nepal than to Syria, and faster to fly some 5,700 miles to New York than to find a way of reaching Beirut 130 miles away. The only Israelis who fly to Lebanon ride in the cockpit of an F-16 or a Cobra attack helicopter.

Ben-Gurion airport's luggage hall is bedecked with loud neon advertisements boasting of the advantages of a certain hotel or credit card. Still, Israel cannot resist giving a nationalist message even to this banality. A large appliqué depicts lines of people streaming toward a walled city on a hill—an idealized Jerusalem—with a quotation in Hebrew of Jeremiah's prophecy: "Thy children shall come again to their own border" (Jer. 31: 17).

The largest wall is taken up by a luminous montage of images of Zionist achievements: pictures of tractors, industrial machinery, soldiers, Jewish immigrants arriving in the Promised Land, and a portrait of David Ben-Gurion, Israel's first Prime Minister. The image of Theodor Herzl, the father of modern Zionism, is circled by a neon light, a saintly halo.

The road from the airport feeds into Israel's main six-lane highway leading west to Tel Aviv, the modern metropolis, and east to Jerusalem, the historic capital. All along this artery there are symbols of the changes which Zionism has brought to the land; the memorials to the battles for the road to Jerusalem in 1948 and the signs to Lod and Ramla, (the former Arab capital of Palestine in the eighth century) whose Arab populations either fled or were evicted by Jewish forces.

Neat orange orchards are protected from the wind by lines of elegant cypress trees. Most of these were once cultivated by Arabs and now they belong to Jews. The Jaffa orange, made famous by Arab merchants at the end of the nineteenth century, has become a symbol of modern Israel.

A visiting Jew may feel a surge of pride at these sights. He sees that the "sick" land, as Herzl once described Palestine, is bountiful through the diligence of the Jews. The land of milk and honey is restored. For the passing Palestinian, who finds that the fruit of his forefathers' labor has been expropriated, and that the evidence of passage of his people has been almost totally obliterated from the landscape, this is, in the words of the Palestinian author Ghassan Kanafani, "the land of sad oranges."

*

The creation of Israel was, by any definition, an extraordinary event. Not only did Jews survive through the centuries of diaspora, in itself an historical anomaly, but they also mustered the strength to infiltrate a land already settled by another civilization and conquer it.

There was nothing inevitable about the emergence of Israel. It was born at a fleeting moment in history when the stars were favorably aligned. Palestine was carved out of the carcass of the Ottoman empire before Arab nationalism could gather its full force. It was created by an act of British colonialism at a time when empire-building was already going out of fashion. The settling of North America and southern Africa by Europeans stretches back to the seventeenth century, yet the Zionist takeover of Palestine took just a few decades to complete. The embryonic Jewish state was shielded by British imperial arms, which put down repeated Arab uprisings and turned back the Nazis at El-Alamein. This allowed the Jews to develop their institutions to the point where they were strong enough to hound out their former British protectors soon after the end of the Second World War. Since the United Nations voted to create a Jewish state (and an Arab state) in a rare instance of agreement between the United States and the Soviet Union in 1947, a few million Jews have held out against scores of millions of Arabs.

A popular Israeli joke asks: "Why did Moses wander in the wilderness for forty years?" Answer: "Because he was looking for the only place in the Middle East where there is no oil." Yet this semiparched country with negligible natural resources has developed a far more sophisticated economy than has been created by even the wealthiest of oil sheikhdoms, and enjoys a standard of living comparable to that of many western European countries.

So outlandish was the notion of a Jewish state when Theodor Herzl proposed it in his seminal pamphlet of 1896, *Der Judenstaat*, (The Jewish State), that he was derided by his contemporaries as insane, a false Messiah, an operetta general and, as one of his newspaper office colleagues put it, "the Jewish Jules Verne." The work was feverishly written after the trial of Captain Alfred Dreyfus, a French officer arrested on trumped-up charges of betraying military secrets to Germany. Based in Paris as correspondent for Vienna's influential *Neue Freie Presse*, Herzl heard the French crowd's shout of "Death to the Jews." He decided that anti-Semitism was an incurable evil that would follow Jews wherever they sought refuge, preventing all attempts at assimilation into host societies. The only solution to the oppression of Jews in Europe was Jewish sovereignty.

> We are one people—our enemies have made us one without our consent, as repeatedly happens in history. Distress binds us together, and, thus united, we suddenly discover our strength. Yes, we are strong enough to form a State, and, indeed, a model state.

It was not a new idea; the plea for the restoration of Jews to the Promised Land has long formed part of the daily Jewish prayers. The novelty lay in the means by which statehood would be achieved—by negotiation with the great powers and the mobilization of Jewish capital. Moreover, its proponent was not a religious visionary but a thoroughly assimilated Jew.

Herzl thought Jewish independence would be forged by harnessing the new technology of steam power and electricity to provide the means for an organized mass migration. Jewish statehood, he said, would enhance the well-being of the world.

For Herzl, it did not much matter where the state would be. "Let the sovereignty be granted us over a portion of the globe large enough to satisfy the rightful requirements of a nation; the rest we shall manage ourselves," he wrote. He suggested two possibilities: Palestine, "our ever-memorable historic home," or Argentina, "one of the most fertile countries in the world." With time he would also consider Cyprus, Sinai, and even Africa—anything to provide a shelter for persecuted Jews.

Yet once the idea of statehood had caught the imagination of Jews, it could only be realized in Palestine. Herzl discovered that any attempt to settle anywhere but the Promised Land would tear the Zionist movement apart. After 2,000 years of exile, Jews were not about to end their dreams of restoration in Uganda, as the British government had once proposed to Herzl. Only Palestine had been "promised" by God.

The first Zionist congress in Basle in 1897 was a piece of political theater, with members arriving dressed in black suits and top hats. The meeting passed a deliberately vague declaration stating that "The aim of Zionism is to create for the Jewish people a homestead in

Palestine secured by public law." Herzl was hailed as a king. A few days later, he confided to his diary an astonishingly bold prediction, and a remarkably accurate one:

> If I were to sum up the congress in a word—which I shall take care not to publish—it would be this: At Basle I founded the Jewish State. If I said this aloud today, I would be answered by universal laughter. In five years perhaps, and certainly in fifty years, everyone will perceive this.

The Balfour Declaration, Britain's promise to establish a Jewish national home in Palestine, was issued 20 years later. The State of Israel was born in the heat of war on May 14, 1948, fifty-one years after the Basle congress, with a declaration read by David Ben-Gurion who stood beneath a portrait of the brooding figure of Herzl.

Herzl himself visited Palestine just once. A year after the Basle congress, he sailed to Constantinople for an audience with the German Kaiser, Wilhelm II, who was making a political "pilgrimage" to gain influence in the Ottoman empire. After an encouraging initial private meeting, Herzl sailed ahead of the imperial party to Jaffa and prepared to present an official Zionist deputation to the Kaiser in Jerusalem. Wilhelm II may have been briefly enamored of the Zionist idea as a means of extending German influence in the Near East at the expense of the British. But by the time he received Herzl's delegation in Jerusalem he had already dropped the idea of a German protectorate in Palestine, not least because it was stubbornly resisted by his Turkish ally, Sultan Abdel-Hamid II. Herzl spent ten days in Palestine and left in a hurry on board an orange freighter, fearing the Turkish authorities would arrest him or even have him assassinated.

In 1902, Herzl published a novel called *Altneuland* (Old-New Land). The book may be stiff in style, but it still makes fascinating reading today. It features a lovelorn Viennese Jew who escapes to a desert island for twenty years, and returns in astonishment to find that Palestine is flourishing under the settlement of Jews, as a utopian "New Society." The book immortalized the motto: "If you will it, it is no fable." It is a well-used technique of Israeli comedy to imagine what Herzl would have thought were he to return and witness modern Israel. Would he be proud, distressed or simply confused? Herzl set an exacting standard: his Jewish state should not only be a refuge for Jews, but also a model for all humanity of how a tolerant and enlightened society can be built. Israel should be, in the words of Isaiah, "a light unto the nations."

To his followers, Herzl, with his jet-black beard and proud stance, was a modern-day prophet, a new Moses who would lead the Jews once more to the Promised Land. Like Moses, Herzl died before the Jews could take Palestine. He passed away in 1904, at the age of 44, after prolonged heart disease. In accordance with Herzl's dying wish to be buried by the Jewish people in Palestine, his remains were exhumed the following year and reburied on top of a hill in Jerusalem bearing his name, Mount Herzl.

In one sense, Herzl was tragically prescient. Anti-Semitism in Europe, he believed, could only get worse, although even he could not have guessed that his beloved Germany would exploit the power of industrialization to conduct a genocide of Jews. On a slope of Mount Herzl Israel has erected its memorial to the six million Jewish victims of the Nazis, Yad Vashem, an almost obligatory ceremonial stop for visiting dignitaries.

What Herzl did not foresee, or refused to consider, was the appalling price that Palestinians would pay for the resolution of Europe's Jewish problem on Arab soil. Herzl thought the Arabs would eagerly welcome the prosperity which the Jewish colonizers would bring. Instead, the State of Israel was forged in the fire of a war that drove out more than four-fifths of the Arab population from the territories the Jews conquered.

Next to Herzl's grave lies the main military cemetery, where fresh graves for the casualties of the ceaseless Arab-Israeli conflict are continually being dug. And near Mount Herzl are the ruins of the village of Deir Yassin, where reports of a massacre of Arabs by Jewish forces in 1948 accelerated the Palestinians' exodus.

Herzl, then, is not only the prophet of Zionism, but also the accidental forefather of the Palestinian national movement. Palestinians may argue about exactly when the Arabs of Palestine came to think of their primary identity as "Palestinian," but there is no doubt that the clash with Zionism and the mass exodus of Arabs in 1948 crystallized their national consciousness.

Israel has lived by the sword ever since its birth. It prides itself on being a country of warriors. The conflict has also produced the symbols of the Palestinian guerrilla and the Palestinian child stone-thrower. The souvenir store at Ben-Gurion airport offers videos on the Jewish state's military successes. The *keffiyeh*, the checkered headscarf of the traditional Palestinian peasant, has metamorphosed into an item of revolutionary Marxist chic, worn by left-wing students at campuses across Europe. Bought in the Jerusalem souk, countless of these headscarves are packed by tourists as souvenirs.

Over the decades of struggle, the Palestinians have fought, rioted, hijacked, and bombed their way back into western conscience, from which they had been banished for decades. Remembrance of the Holocaust of the Jews has intensified in Europe and America, but there is also a realization that Palestinians need a country of their own. That country is not Lebanon or Jordan, but a piece of historic Palestine.

Many Israelis, exhausted by war and conflict, have reached the same conclusion. In a process that political scientists call "post-Zionism,"—in which Israeli patriotism is less blinding,—Israelis have slowly and painfully reexamined their national myths, their selective history and even the impact of the Holocaust. No longer do Israelis argue that there is no such thing as a Palestinian people. The Oslo peace accords signed in Washington in September 1993 were an attempt gradually to partition Palestine once more into an Arab and a Jewish state. The eruption of the the *Al-Aqsa Intifada*, roughly translated as the "Al-Aqsa Mosque Uprising," in October 2000—part riot and part war—is a reminder that more than a century of Arab–Israeli conflict is far from resolved. The Palestinians do not yet have a state they feel gives them justice as a people, and the Israelis do not have peace. The Jewish Question may have been solved by the creation of Israel. The Question of Palestine remains an open sore.

★

Few can be indifferent to the country between the Mediterranean and the Jordan River. Israel . . . Palestine . . . the Holy Land . . . the Promised Land . . . the Land of Milk and Honey. Whatever the appellation, it instantly summons up images, memories, snatches of newspaper headlines, a passage from the Bible, a Koranic verse, a poem, a song, or a hymn.

The place may set your soul resonating with its spiritual energy, or it may jangle your conscience. You may be seduced by the people, or grow to detest them. The visitor may embark on a trip of theological and archaeological discovery, or mock the politics of religious superstition. The student of current affairs may wish to meet a real Zionist pioneer or witness the suffering and struggle of Palestinian revolutionaries. Too much has happened here for anyone to be indifferent.

On one trip to Israel some years ago, as my aircraft crossed the

shore over Tel Aviv and the jumble of solar heaters on the roof of
every building reflected the sun like a carpet of broken mirrors, the
Israeli passengers broke into spontaneous applause and a raucous rendition of *Heveinu Shalom Aleichem*—a song of celebration whose
words mean "We have brought you peace." Moments later, as we
touched down at Ben-Gurion, Christian pilgrims filled the air with
an emotional hymn to the land trodden by Jesus. Even in the air, the
ancient land can exert its mystical power.

Once I was seated next to an Italian Roman Catholic priest who,
with no prompting on my part, insisted on expounding his views on
Israel. He showed off his rudimentary Hebrew by mouthing the
instructions to operate the door of the emergency exit. "Hebrew is
the language which God spoke. It's like meeting a beautiful woman.
If you speak her language, it's more interesting," explained the celi-
bate cleric. While recognizing a Hebrew-speaking God, he was in no
doubt that the Christianity derived from Jesus' teaching—not
Judaism—was the true divine revelation.

He went on, with a tone of awe, "Israel is a very organized country. Just imagine, the Jews held out against all the millions of Arabs
and the rest of the Muslim world on their own," and then he shook
his head, "But the Jews are too proud. All the terrible things that the
Germans did to them, they are doing it to the Arabs." The Jews were
superheroes and super-evil, the chosen people and eternal sinners.

Everything in Israel and Palestine is larger than life. This is a sliver
of a country—no more than 75 miles wide by 260 long, with a population of five million Jews and about four million Palestinians in
both Israel and the occupied territories. Yet it commands the devotion of one billion Muslims, 1.7 billion Christians and some 13 million Jews around the world.

"The word Palestine always brought to my mind a vague sugges-
tion of a country as large as the United States. I do not know why,
but such was the case," wrote Mark Twain in *Innocents Abroad*. "I sup-
pose it was because I could not conceive of a small country having so
large a history."

Twain arrived in 1867 on the first pleasure trip to Palestine, the
precursor of today's bus tours of holy sites. He crossed the Atlantic on
the side-wheel steamship, the *Quaker City*, with a group of about 150
Americans. The tour included the main cities of Europe, the Holy
Land, and Egypt. His account of the trip was immensely popular for
its irreverent tone. "Oriental scenes look best in steel engravings," he
wrote, "I cannot be imposed upon anymore by that picture of the

Queen of Sheba visiting Solomon. I shall say to myself, 'You look fine, Madam, but your feet are not clean and you smell like a camel.' "

Most contemporary books about the Holy Land, thought Twain, reflected the creed of the authors who set out to find a "Protestant Palestine" or a "Baptist Palestine."

> Honest as these men's intentions may have been, they were full of partialities and prejudices, they entered the country with their verdicts already prepared, and they could no more write dispassionately and impartially about it than they could about their own wives and children.

Twain's visit was part of a new western obsession with Palestine. Thousands of travelers made their way to Palestine in the nineteenth century, attracted by the late Ottoman empire's more liberal political climate, propelled by the growing spirit of inquiry and carried by the power of steamships. Arrival in Palestine was mostly by ship at the Arab port of Jaffa.

Gazing down at this little port today it is difficult to imagine that nature has so poorly endowed one of history's most venerable harbors. Palestine's shore consists largely of miles of dunes created by sand borne from the Nile. It is bereft of inlets or safe anchorages, and the rocky outcrop of Jaffa with its chain of reefs offers a rare but imperfect natural breakwater against the storms. In rough weather, ships often found it impossible to land their cargos for weeks at a time.

Steamships had to anchor half a mile or more off shore. Loading and unloading was a laborious adventure carried out by Arab dockers in unsteady rowing boats. Negotiating the narrow passage through the rocks in a heavy swell was often a chilling experience. "Jaffa is celebrated for at least two things: its excellent oranges and its infamous landing," noted one British traveler, Sir Frederick Treves, in 1912.

Jaffa was founded, according to some classical accounts, even before the Flood. The Greeks believed that its treacherous rocks are where the beautiful Andromeda was chained as a sacrifice to the sea monster and was saved by Perseus, who turned the water purple with the blood of the beast. The origin of the name may be *yafa*, the Hebrew for beautiful. The Arabs, too, were struck by Jaffa's beauty. They called it "The Bride of the Sea."

Jaffa was an ancient staging post on the coastal plain of Palestine, the historic land bridge between Africa and Asia. A route known as the Horus Road by the Egyptians and as the Via Maris (Way of the Sea) by the Romans connected the civilizations in Egypt and Mesopotamia. There were no easy alternatives; the plain was sandwiched between the sea and a line of mountains forming the biblical heartland known as Judea and Samaria. Farther inland was the deep and arid chasm of the Jordan Valley, and then the arc of deserts stretching from Sinai to Arabia, Iraq and Syria.

The narrowness of this coastal route has determined much of Palestine's eventful history. Armies have campaigned along the highway from the time of the Pharaohs to Richard the Lion Heart, Napoleon and Allenby. Jaffa's name appears for the first time in the list of Canaanite cities captured in 1468 B.C.E. by Thutmose III, arguably the greatest Egyptian Pharaoh. In the centuries after Egyptian rule came the Philistines, Assyrians, Babylonians, Persians, Greeks, Jews, Romans, Byzantines, Arabs, Turks, French, and the British.

Here, the Bible tells us, King Solomon brought the cedars from Lebanon which were taken up to Jerusalem to build the first permanent temple to the God of the Israelites. It was in Jaffa, according to the New Testament, that Peter brought Tabitha back from the dead. And it was in Jaffa that the Zionist settlers first landed and set out to build the metropolis—Tel Aviv, the "first Hebrew city" of modern times—that has swallowed up the original port.

At the dawn of the twentieth century, Jaffa was the largest Arab city in Palestine, and its pathetic harbor the third busiest in the eastern Mediterranean, after such venerable trading posts as Alexandria and Beirut. The Jaffa orange began to be shipped in major quantities to Britain in the 1870s, eclipsing traditional exports including wheat, olive oil, and soap. By the start of the twentieth century, some 5,000 tourists and about 15,000 pilgrims were passing through Jaffa every year. Although welcomed, the westerners were still known as *franj*, or "Franks," the old Arab appellation for the Crusaders.

The visitors left behind a bulging library of travelers' tales. About 2,000 works, some of them consisting of several volumes, were written in just eight decades between 1800 and 1878. In contrast, about 1,500 manuscripts survive from the whole of the preceding 15 centuries. The outpouring of literature concentrated on biblical history, and had little to say about contemporary Palestine.

The country was seen through lenses tinted by the past. The present, by definition, was a state of fallen grace and misery; evidence of the curse of God.

Some of the best-loved images of Palestine are the exotic lithographs made in 1839 by the Scottish artist, David Roberts. Queen Victoria and the archbishops of York and Canterbury were among the first buyers of his prints. Even today, Roberts's biblical and archaeological landscapes are a prized gift for anyone who has spent any time in the region. These images are so familiar that it takes a while to notice the distortions and artistic liberties; the mountains are too lofty and the cliffs too dramatic. The antiquities are too mighty, the Arab figures too picturesque and the faithful too devout to be real. His picture of Jaffa seen from the beach, for instance, depicts the mound as much more impressive than it really is. A nonexistent range of hills has been conjured as a backdrop in the south to lend dramatic perspective. A group of Jews—the only Jews to appear in Roberts's prints—is seen negotiating with Arabs for passage back to Poland. Two Arab women are sitting beside them, with implausibly low-cut dresses revealing their necks and shoulders beneath severe black veils.

Photography arrived in the Holy Land at the same time as Roberts, within months of the invention of the daguerreotype. The new art, which had at first to be improved with artistic touches to make it more palatable, quickly became a thriving industry producing a vast number of images of biblical themes.

Palestine with its religious images is always filtered by the mind's eye; the devout are overcome by stepping on the soil where Abraham, King David, and Jesus once trod, the rationalist is amused by the dubious superstitions, while the military man can lose himself in reliving famous sieges and military campaigns.

For Jews, arrival in Jaffa was the first painful reminder of the loss of Eretz Israel, the Land of Israel, and its sorry state since the exile of the Jews. The rabbis said Jews should rend their shirts three times in Palestine—upon seeing the cities of Judah, again when they arrive at Jerusalem, and a third time when they come before the ruins of the temple. To Herzl, coming ashore at Jaffa, the place consisted of "poverty and misery and heat in gay colors."

Most Christian visitors walked around filled with romantic visions of the past; the shepherd with a headscarf would immediately evoke the memory of Jesus' birth while the sight of the Sea of Galilee might bring to mind the words of the Sermon on the Mount. Thomas Cook capitalized on the new interest in the Levant by organizing his "Eastern Tours" in 1869. Cook soon dominated the tourist market in Palestine, providing selected guides, landing boats at Jaffa, tents, horses, western food including English ham and Yorkshire bacon, all at fixed prices. Cook could not offer all comforts, however. Most of his customers were poor riders—"unaccustomed to the back of the horse as to that of an ostrich," said one observer—despite the English saddles which Cook imported.

The guidebooks of the period are lively, opinionated and bigoted. Explicitly and implicitly, the visitor is told to keep aloof from the local rabble. One of the earliest guides was issued in 1858 by John Murray, the publisher of this book. It informs readers that the dress and manners of the inhabitants "are all primitive," the Arabs are "illiterate and ignorant of all Frank inventions," yet the poor exhibit a pleasing "native dignity" in their hospitality. Muslims, it says, are "proud, fanatical and illiterate," and the upper classes "both physically and mentally feeble, owing to the effects of polygamy, early marriages and degrading vices." It suggests that the visitor should carry a revolver visibly on his hip, as well as the tourist's paraphernalia of a notebook, field glasses, and a measuring tape. The best protection against the withering heat and sun, it states categorically, is wool rather than linen, with some kind of veil worn beneath a hat.

The Baedeker guide to Palestine and Syria of 1898 tells readers: "Travelers will scarcely be inclined to adopt Oriental costume: to do so without considerable familiarity with the language would only expose one to ridicule." It warns visitors against giving money to beggars and informs them that "bargaining is the universal custom." A set of Arabic phrases to help haggle in the bazaar is helpfully provided. The book advises sternly: "Intimate acquaintance with Orientals is also to be avoided. . . . Beneath the interminable protestations of friendship with which the traveler is overwhelmed lurks in most cases the demon of cupidity."

These guidebooks are products of their time, an age of European dominance when westerners were convinced of their superiority. The books and tours of Palestine made the landscape of the Holy Land ever more familiar to Europeans and rekindled dreams of the gallant Crusades. Each political crisis in the East provoked a new round of demands in Europe that Palestine be reconquered for Christendom, or at the very least be absorbed culturally under a "peaceful Crusade." Protestant England was awash in visions of the imminent advent of the End of Days, the essential precursor of which was the return of the Jews to the Holy Land and their conversion to Christianity. The great powers competed for influence by building religious and educational institutions, and extending consular protection over minorities such as Christian sects, Jews, and the Druze.

From the 1860s, calls to colonize Palestine became ever louder. The advocates of European settlement argued that the Arab inhabitants should either be subdued by military force, gathered into reservations or turned into a servile class of "hewers of wood and drawers of water."

Jaffa became a magnet for visionaries, cranks, and philanthropists, who started buying up farmland in the surrounding plain. Water was plentiful, the soil was fertile, there was easy access to the port and railway, and foreign consuls could raise their protective umbrella around them. A group of 43 American families belonging to the Church of the Messiah, an offshoot of the Mormons, arrived in Palestine in 1866 to make the land ready for the Second Coming of Christ. They brought prefabricated buildings, as well as the first modern farm machinery in Palestine. The venture lasted about a year before collapsing amid hardship, bureaucratic obstacles, and personal recrimination.

In 1868, the first of a movement of former Lutherans calling themselves the Temple Society, who believed that the German "people of God" had an inviolable right to possess the Holy Land, settled in Haifa. Soon they spread to the Jaffa area where they took over, among other properties, the plot and homes abandoned by the American colonizers. At their height, there were some 1,200 Templers scattered in various communities and the movement prospered until the outbreak of the Second World War, when its members were interned by the British. A neighborhood of Jerusalem founded by the Templers is still commonly known as the "German Colony."

A steady trickle of Jews had always come to Palestine to lead a life of piety in the holy cities of Jerusalem, Hebron, and Tiberias. When the first of a new breed of secularized Jewish settlers from eastern Europe arrived in 1882, following a wave of pogroms in southern Russia, most Arabs must have regarded them as little different to the other groups of bizarre foreigners filled with strange utopian visions. But these settlers, fired by the crankish idea of reestablishing the Jewish commonwealth, did not leave. They conquered the land.

2

One God, Many Religions

THE HEBREW TERM for traveling to Jerusalem and the Promised Land is *aliyah*—"ascent." The road to Jerusalem is indeed a physical ascent, and a steep one at that. Israelis also use *aliyah* to mean a spiritual uplifting. Zionism maintains that for a Jew to move to Israel is the highest form of self-expression, and one who leaves Israel is inevitably committing the sin of *yeridah* or "descent."

I have always felt a touch of elation about the drive up to Jerusalem, even on the most rushed or exhausting of days. The mountains of Judea rise sharply from the coastal plain. Plowed fields suddenly give way to rocky slopes with planted forests of cypress and pines. The road seems to be sucked into the fastness of the rock as it enters a narrow gulley.

Nature's fortified gateway to Jerusalem is called Sha'ar ha-Gai but it is still known by many people by the earlier Arab name of Bab al-Wad. The rusted hulks of destroyed armored cars litter the side of the road as a memorial to the struggle by the embryonic Jewish state to lift the Arab siege of Jerusalem. The first symbols of the Holy City are images not of ancient religion, but of modern warfare.

Early travelers on their way to Jerusalem remembered the struggle between David and Goliath which the Bible says took place in nearby foothills. At Bab al-Wad, the contemporary visitor is asked to view Israel's conflict with the Arabs as a similar struggle against the Arab Goliath.

There is a quickening of the pulse as you crawl over each rise, and fall down each valley. Every hilltop is like the rung of an otherworldly ladder up to Jerusalem. The air becomes thinner, crisper.

It brings to mind the words of "Jerusalem of Gold," a slow, melancholic folk tune composed just weeks before the Six Day War of 1967 that remains one of the best-loved songs in Israel. It speaks of a city that dwells alone, with a wall in its heart, a city of gold, copper, and lights, and evokes the Jews' return to Jerusalem. Until that time the road from Tel Aviv led to a dead end: an anti-sniper wall along Jerusalem's ceasefire line between Israeli and Jordanian forces. The war "united" the two halves of the city under Israeli rule. The beloved Zion of Jewish daily prayers and the Israeli national anthem was back in the hands of the Jews.

For Palestinians, the defeat of 1967 compounded the "catastrophe" of the creation of Israel in 1948. All of the old British mandate territory of Palestine had fallen to the Israelis; hardly an inch of the homeland was under Arab, let alone Palestinian, rule. It was the Palestinians' turn to mourn for Jerusalem. *Zahrat al-Madayin* ("The Flower of Cities") a lament by the Lebanese-born Fairuz, one of the Arab world's greatest living singers, most successfully captured the emotions of Palestinians. It is an almost operatic piece, its passages moving from mourning, to anger, to the hope that Arabs will reconquer Jerusalem, to the blast of victorious trumpets and finally to the vision of peace restored to the suffering city.

> Justice fell at the gates
> When Jerusalem fell, love retreated and war settled in the hearts of
>   the world [. . .]
> You, O Jordan River will wash my face with your sacred waters
> And you, O Jordan River, will wipe away the footmarks of the
>   barbarians
> The spreading anger
> Is coming
> More fear
> Is coming . . . The House is ours
> Jerusalem is ours.

Three simple words, "Jerusalem is ours," distill the essence of a century of strife between Arabs and Jews.

Jerusalem creeps upon you quietly. There is no grand vista. The first glimpse of the holy city is of a mantle of concrete slipping down from a ridge of hills above the road, eating up the forested slopes. Jerusalem is a huge building site. Cranes are as common as church towers and minarets. Constantly expanding in the race to preserve the Jewish demographic majority, Jerusalem's face is continually being remodeled, leaving gashed hillsides as scars.

The Old City crouches coyly behind the modern urban landscape. Visitors have to thread their way through the drab commercial district, past a conference hall, hotels, the bus station, office buildings—until they run unexpectedly into the walls built by Suleiman the Magnificent. You can barely make out the monuments behind this veil of stone; like Roberts's images of oriental women, there is only a coquettish hint of the hidden delights in the glimpses of the golden Dome of the Rock and the charcoal-gray cupola of the Holy Sepulcher. When you find an unencumbered view of the Old City from the terraces of the Mount of Olives or Talpiot, you feel like David gaping down at the naked Bathsheba.

The accounts of foreign visitors to Jerusalem are filled with the startled impressions of their authors. Theodor Herzl first glimpsed the Zion of Jewish prayers through a haze of malarial fever in 1898: "In spite of my weariness, Jerusalem and its grand moonlit contours made a deep impression on me. The silhouette of the fortress of Zion, the citadel of David—magnificent!"

By the light of day, however, Herzl was repelled by the physical decay. Of the Western Wall, he wrote: "A deeper emotion refuses to come, because that place is pervaded by hideous, wretched, speculative beggary." Even as he schemed to convince the German Kaiser to prize Palestine away from the Ottomans and turn it over to the Jews, Herzl was busy planning how he would rebuild the city. He wrote in his diary:

> When I remember thee in days to come, O Jerusalem, it will not be with pleasure. The musty deposits of two thousand years of inhumanity, intolerance, and uncleanliness lie in the foul-smelling alleys. . . . If we ever get Jerusalem and if I am still able to do anything actively at that time, I would begin by cleaning it up. I would clear out everything that is not something sacred, set up workers' homes outside the city, empty the nests of filth and tear them down, burn the secular ruins and transfer the bazaars elsewhere.

For days Herzl gave himself to his architectural fancies. He would turn Jerusalem into one of the most beautiful cities in the world, with only religious sites left inside the Old City and a modern, green city spread over the hills nearby. Looking down from the Mount of

Olives, he was inspired not by the legends of David and Solomon, but by the grandeur of Rome, capital of the empire which destroyed the Jewish temple. "Great moments. What couldn't be made of this countryside!" his diary reads. "A city like Rome, and the Mount of Olives would furnish a panorama like the Janiculum."

Herman Melville, visiting Palestine in 1857, wrote glumly in his diary: "Judea is one accumulation of stones—Stony mountains & stony plains; stony torrents & stony roads; stony walls & stony fields; stony houses & stony tombs; stony eyes & stony hearts." He thought that the Jews in the Old City lived "like flies in an empty skull."

Modern psychiatrists have diagnosed a mental illness known as the "Jerusalem Syndrome." They explain how otherwise normal visitors, disoriented by the dissonance between the Jerusalem of their minds and the real city on the ground, fall prey to delusions, hear voices, and imagine themselves to be biblical figures.

When I first arrived as a journalist in 1990, at the start of the crisis over Iraq's invasion of Kuwait, I felt daunted by the weight of Jerusalem's history which I had only half learned as a child and which now bore down with full force on the events I had been sent to report. As a boy dragged to church, I had imagined Jerusalem as an ethereal, legendary place, a kind of Atlantis or Shangri-La. Belief in Jerusalem seemed to be a matter of faith, like belief in the Resurrection. But at dawn, as my taxi drove along a deserted Jaffa Road, I was confronted by a concrete, real city with shops, signs in Hebrew, and litter. Even the presence of traffic lights seemed bizarre in God's city. The very ordinariness was disconcerting. At the Mahane Yehuda market, the buildings crowded tighter together on the city's main artery. I studied the stone houses with red tiled roofs. They were of familiar shape, perhaps a bit more heavily set than buildings in Europe and with an oriental shape to the windows, but this was undeniably a western city. I had been to more strange and exotic places before, but in the morning twilight, none felt more mysterious than Jerusalem.

★

The Jewish sages said that the world has ten portions of beauty, of which nine grace Jerusalem; ten portions of suffering, of which nine afflict Jerusalem; ten portions of wisdom, of which nine exalt Jerusalem, and ten portions of godlessness, of which nine disgrace Jerusalem.

In early rabbinical times, when this aphorism was composed, there

was already a sense of love and hate, a dichotomy between the heavenly and earthly Jerusalem, between the sublime reverence the city
inspires, and the jealousy which faith provokes among imperfect
mortals.

For the prophets of the Hebrew Bible, the magnitude of Jerusalem's
holiness is such that its sins seemed equally vast. Jerusalem acquired a
schizophrenic mystical personality, sublime and satanic. Isaiah, Jeremiah and the other prophets described the city as a bride and a har-
lot, a mother and a widow, faithful to God and a murderess. God,
they prophesied, would send down cataclysmic destruction, but
would restore Jerusalem to pristine purity and righteousness, and its
inhabitants would forever honor a new covenant with God.

With time, especially in the turbulent period leading to the Roman
destruction of the temple and afterward, these apocalyptic notions
sharpened into a vision of two separate Jerusalems: the earthly one
and the heavenly city waiting to descend to earth upon God's command. The restoration of a new Jerusalem was intimately bound up
with the idea of a Messiah, a righteous king descended from David
who would liberate the Jews from the yoke of occupation. This was
later elaborated into variations on the theme of a semidivine being
who would restore Israel, gather the exiles and rule over an era of
eternal peace. All this would be preceded by a period of war, plague,
destruction, and cosmic disturbance.

The dual identity of Jerusalem, surmised later mystical rabbis, is
coded in the very name of Hebrew Jerusalem, *Yerushalayim*, because
the *-ayim* ending in Hebrew means a pair, such as *einayim* "eyes" or
raglayim "legs."

Medieval Arab chroniclers perceived a similar mixed identity. Al-
Muqaddasi, a native of the city, described Jerusalem as "a golden bowl
filled with scorpions." He waxed lyrical about the bounty of the land
which does not need irrigation and the piety of Jerusalem's inhabitants. Yet al-Muqaddasi also complained that the baths of Jerusalem
were the filthiest he had come across, the taxes were heavy and the
city was devoid of learned men. "Everywhere the Christians and Jews
have the upper hand," he grumbled.

This split personality seems predestined by geography. Jerusalem
stands on the watershed of the Judean Hills, the dividing line
between desert to the east and lush woodland to the west, the vast-
ness of the sea on one side, and the endless aridness on the other. The
Old City is surrounded on three sides by taller hills: the Mount of
Olives with its churches and mosques, Mount Scopus with the cubist

architecture of the Hebrew University and the ridge of the new city dominated by the King David Hotel. Through a break in the eastern line the sun-bleached floor of the Jordan Valley is visible far below. From the southern hill of Abu Tor, the city almost seems to be airborne, nestled in a large bowl hovering in midair.

The Old City rises on a ridge between two ravines, the Kidron Valley and the Hinnom. Jewish tradition says the first is the Valley of Jehoshaphat, where Judgment Day will take place and the righteous will go to the Garden of Eden. Its slopes are covered with the ancient graveyards of Muslims, Christians, and Jews who want to be first in line. The other valley is Gehenna, synonymous with Hell and eternal torment because of the bloodcurdling child-sacrifices to Moloch which Jeremiah said were practiced there. Jerusalem is not so much two cities as one, suspended between heaven and earth, between heaven and hell.

Little has changed. Jerusalem is a starkly beautiful, but profoundly flawed city. From the balcony of my home in Abu Tor, I have watched the city's white limestone blush through a range of shades, according to the mood of the sky. The expanse of stone seems capable of displaying as many emotions as the sea. Jerusalem gleams blinding white at noon in summer, washes with gold, ocher, and pink at sunset, and becomes dusty yellow when the hazy desert wind known as the *Khamsin* blows from the east. In winter, storm clouds from the sea curl over the ridge of Jerusalem, a canopy of steel-gray rushing overhead.

The gilded orb of the Dome of the Rock glimmers on a base of turquoise ceramics raised above the scattered blocks and domes of the Old City. It is a jewel set ostentatiously on the rocky finger of Jerusalem.

But look below the Old City, outside the walls, and the land is dry and scabrous with the poor and neglected Arab neighborhoods of Silwan, Al-Tur, and Ras al-Amud. The Arab and Jewish halves of the city, reunited in 1967, now are joined only by the force of Israeli arms. The eternal capital of Israel is a beacon to Jews around the world, who are invited to make it their home, while Jerusalem's Arab inhabitants are treated as foreigners in their own city.

The old dividing line between Arab East and Jewish West Jerusalem runs down the street where I lived for seven years. The barbed-wire fences and minefields have long gone, even if some of the houses still bear the scars of sniper fire across the ceasefire line. More than a quarter of a century after the frontier was eliminated, it remains etched in the mind of the city's inhabitants. Palestinians live on one side of the street, Israelis on the other. These reluctant neighbors exchange only the most cursory greetings as they pass each other. The tarmac is colonized by Arab children, and Jewish mothers quickly march their offspring past the urchins who, unlike the Jewish kids, do not have a decent park in their half of the neighborhood. Not once have I seen Jewish and Palestinian children play together.

From my window, the old frontier can easily be traced into the distance. The Jewish neighborhoods enjoy more spacious and elegant buildings, the streets are well lit and the gardens generously watered. The Arab areas are shabby, dusty, and dark. Few Israelis venture into East Jerusalem. To most Jews half of the "united" city is, to all intents and purposes, another country.

Periodically, down my street come squads of soldiers and groups of Israeli teenagers accompanied by armed guards to survey the legendary deeds of their forefathers. Arab children disappear until they have passed, only to reappear behind the group. In this proverbial city of peace, military transport vehicles move tanks and howitzers through streets to outlying bases. Since the start of the new Palestinian uprising, tanks and machine-gunners in the Jewish neighborhood of Gilo, on the edge of East Jerusalem, have periodically traded fire with Palestinians across the valley in the West Bank town of Beit Jala.

In the 3,000-odd years between the story of King David's capture of Jerusalem and the city's unification by Israel, Jerusalem has been subjected to at least 50 sieges, sacks, captures, and changes of ownership. The city is surrounded by army checkpoints, the main gathering places are permanently patrolled, and at times of particular tension soldiers are even posted at bus stops. Guns are routinely carried by a significant number of Israelis along with the other accoutrements of daily life, like mobile telephones, beepers, or workmen's tools.

Jerusalem is a city of explosions. Car alarms are set off by the crack of sonic booms radiating from military aircraft overhead. A duller thud with a longer echo indicates the carnage of a Palestinian bomb. Every few weeks, the night sky reverberates with the flash and boom of fireworks to celebrate an arts festival or the anniversary of an Israeli military victory. In the dead of night, the ground rumbles with the distant pounding of artillery.

Other tribal sounds drift through my window at weekends. At dusk on Friday, sirens wail through the city to announce the beginning of the Sabbath, and a hush falls over West Jerusalem. The call to prayer of a hundred mosques rising up five times a day from the valley in the east suddenly seems magnified, a hundred plaintive voices creating a pulsing sound, like cicadas. The peal of bells from the churches on Mount Zion carries farther on the Sabbath. In the summer nights between the end of the first Palestinian uprising in 1993 and the start of the second one in 2000, the over-amplified rhythm of an Arabic band announced the betrothal of a Palestinian couple. At the end of the Sabbath on Saturday night a Jewish wedding hall would compete, with a rock version of Hasidic music. "Messiah! Messiah! Messiah! Ay-yay-ya-ya-ya-yay!"

Pilgrims come to Jerusalem to seek communion with God and are assaulted at every turn by souvenir hawkers. The Arab merchants in the souk of the Old City are delightfully eclectic in the wares they sell: menorahs for Jews, olive-wood crosses and rosaries for Christians and, for the political pilgrim, macabre T-shirts with a picture of a sub-machine-gun and the words "Uzi Does It."

The Old City of Jerusalem is a poor advertisement for the brotherhood of man. Its alleys are the focus of narrow ethnic and religious politics. The quarters are split along sectarian lines—Jewish, Muslim, Christian, and Armenian—with countless competing subdenominations all praying to the same One God.

Each sect has a uniform. In Jerusalem, religion has created a city of hats. Every conceivable form of headwear makes its appearance to identify the wearer to fellow humans, if not to God. There are the black hats made of felt or extravagant fur worn by Ultraorthodox Jews. Snow rarely falls in Jerusalem, so in the winter rains these have to be covered with plastic bags. The knitted skullcaps of modern religious nationalist Jews come in varying shapes, sizes, and patterns to specify exactly how patriotic and how pious the wearer sees himself as being. Jews gathered at the Western Wall covered with the white *tallit* (prayer shawl) are like an otherworldly congregation.

Palestinians, especially older men, favor the checkered *keffiyeh* headscarf, in its red or black variety. Arab women usually cover themselves in plain white. The *keffiyeh* is a remarkably flexible article, serving to protect from the sun or the cold. Young Palestinians wrap their heads in it to avoid identification during riots or to protect themselves from tear gas. At Damascus Gate, the center of Palestinian life, the green berets of the Israeli border police jut out in the swirling stream of covered Arab heads.

The wine-red fez, or *tarboush*, still makes an appearance, particularly on the heads of the kavasses, Ottoman-era bodyguards for for-

eign dignitaries whose role is now ceremonial, mainly the opening of
a path in crowds during Christian processions. Armenian priests wear
sinister black hoods; the Franciscans, brown. At Easter the tourists
wear baseball caps, straw hats, and the occasional crown of thorns.
The outrageously large Turkish turbans—which can be seen in
Roberts's paintings and prompted one guidebook to quip that "some
inhabitants seem to wear most of their wardrobe on their heads"—
have disappeared, alas.

All this would be a quaint, picturesque scene, if each creed did not
claim for itself the absolute Truth. God here is not One, not even
Three but a multitude. Jerusalem is a Babel of faiths. The prism of the
human mind has refracted the light of a single God into a bewildering number of gaudy colors.

*

Jerusalem is, above all, a city of memory, or rather selective memory.
It lives as much in the past as in the present.

The dispute between Israelis and Palestinians over land and statehood, is as much a conflict over history. Arabs, Jews, and Christians
have each ruled Jerusalem exclusively, and each side seeks to highlight its own glorious era while ignoring the others' claims. From the
same common tapestry of history Israelis extract blue and white to
create an Israeli flag, while the Palestinians use the Arab colors of
black, red, green, and white. It boils down in part to the bare question: "Who was here first?"

The Jews claim an unbroken line to the ancient Israelites. The
Palestinians go one better by maintaining ultimate descent from the
Israelites' Semitic predecessors, the Canaanites, and the Israelites' ene-
mies on the coastal plain, the Philistines, who gave their name to
"Palestine." Moreover, Arabs have lived in the country for more than
1,300 years.

The names of Jerusalem—the Hebrew *Yerushalayim* and the Arabic
Al-Quds—are politically charged. Jerusalem first enters written history as a curse. It is mentioned as "Rushalimum" in the so-called
Execration Texts, nineteenth-century B.C.E. pottery bearing the
names of the Canaanite cities and rulers deemed hostile to Egypt.
These were smashed to cast an ill spell upon the foes. It is mentioned
as "Salem" early in the Bible as the place where Abraham receives a
blessing from Melchizedek.

Jerusalem's origin as a holy city begins with a patch of rock
exposed to the winnowing wind. This, according to the Bible, was

the threshing floor of Araunah the Jebusite, perhaps the last ruler of Jerusalem before it was conquered by David immediately after he was crowned king of the newly united Israelite kingdom. The Bible says God sent a plague from the coast to punish David for taking a census. The destruction stopped only when an angel appeared on Araunah's threshing floor. David built an altar on the spot. He bought it from Araunah for 50 shekels of silver (600 shekels of gold, according to another biblical account), and turned down the Jebusite's offer to give away the place, complete with oxen and wheat for sacrifice. The Bible maintains that because David's hands were bloodied by war, God entrusted David's son, Solomon, with building a permanent temple here to house the Ark of the Covenant.

Archaeologists place David's golden reign around the year 1,000 B.C.E., but in the absence of corroborating evidence, some experts are starting to question whether David and Solomon ever existed. True or not, the story occupies a central position in Jewish thought. So important is the threshing floor that it was called the "Foundation Stone" by rabbinical sages. Here the Ark rested in the Holy of Holies, the inner sanctum of the temple which only the High Priest could enter once a year, on Yom Kippur. Jews and Christians believe this is where Abraham bound his son Isaac for sacrifice.

By prophetic times, Jerusalem and the Children of Israel had become synonymous. The agonies of the people of Israel were the tears of the "daughters of Zion." Israelite worship was centered on the temple in Jerusalem. Animals were continually butchered and offered up as sacrifices to God, and three times a year Jews were enjoined to make the pilgrimage to the temple. It was during the Passover festival that Jesus came to the temple, which had been rebuilt and vastly expanded by Herod. His preaching, including the expulsion of the dealers and the prophecy that the temple would be destroyed, incurred the wrath of the priestly authorities and soon precipitated his execution by the Romans.

The two destructions of the temple, first by the Babylonians in 587–586 B.C.E. and then by the Romans in 70 C.E., are the defining moments in Jewish history. According to Jewish tradition, both tragedies took place on Tisha B'Av, the ninth day of the month of Av in the Jewish calendar, a date that is observed as a day of fasting and mourning. Countless other tragedies are attributed to this mystically cursed date, such as the expulsion of Jews from Spain in 1492.

The epochs of Jewish history are marked by the destruction of the

temples. The First Temple Period ends with the deportation of part
of the people from the kingdom of Judah to Babylon. After the fall
of Babylon to the Persians, Cyrus the Great allowed the return of
the Jewish "remnant" who, under Nehemiah and Ezra, rebuilt the
temple. In the Second Temple era a new form of Judaism emerged
from the half-century of exile. This began the transition from tem-
ple-centered worship to a more spiritual, moral religion based on
the written word and the change from "Israelite" or "Hebrew" to
"Jew."

Bereft of their temple and state, the Babylonian exiles turned to
their writings. Scribes, rather than temple priests, became a vital force
of cohesion. In all probability, the exiles established the first synagogues as places of communal worship and reading of scriptures. The
responsibility for faithfulness to God moved from rulers to the individual. If God had ceased to smile upon Israel, then his command-
ments must be respected more diligently. Sabbath observance, in
particular, became a paramount obligation and intermarriage with
pagans was forbidden.

The exiles consolidated theological notions such as the cosmic
struggle between good and evil, the idea of judgment after death and
the expectation of a divinely anointed savior who would come at the
end of time. The tribal monotheism of Israel become more universal
in character, even though Israel remained the chosen people. God
was no longer simply greater than other gods but the absolute single
God, and world events were part of His master plan. In time, the
prophets said, Israel's message would spread to the gentile world, and
would become a "light unto the nations."

The arrival of Alexander the Great's armies in 332 B.C.E. initiated
the great clash between Judaism and Hellenism that would stretch for
centuries through the rule of Alexander's successors, the Romans and
the Byzantines, until the advent of Arab rule.

The Maccabees led the Jews in a successful revolt against their
enfeebled Greek overlords in Syria who desecrated the temple.
Rebellion against the might of Rome, however, ended in tragic failure in 70 C.E.. Josephus Flavius, the Jewish-Roman historian,
recounted the last moments of the House of God:

> While the holy house was on fire, everything was plundered that
> came to hand, and ten thousand of those that were caught were slain;
> nor was there commiseration of any age, or any reverence of gravity;
> but children and old men, and profane persons, and priests, were all

slain in the same manner. [. . .] The flame was also carried a long way, and made an echo, together with the groans of those that were slain; and because the hill was high, and the works at the temple were very great, one would have thought the whole city was on fire. Nor can one imagine any thing either greater or more terrible than this noise.

The revolt was extinguished in 73 C.E. when the Romans captured the last Jewish fortress at Masada, on the shore of the Dead Sea. According to Josephus' celebrated account, the defenders committed suicide rather than be enslaved by the Romans. It was a final act of defiance and fanaticism, "an example which shall at once cause their astonishment at our death, and their admiration at our hardiness." The Masada story later became a central element in Zionist myth-building, with Israeli soldiers brought to the fortress to pledge to defend the restored Jewish state.

The temple was never rebuilt. On Titus' arch in Rome, a marble relief shows legionnaires carting away its menorah. The temple tax, levied on every Jew in the empire, was henceforth paid into Roman coffers. The embers of revolt still flared periodically. A chain of Jewish uprisings broke out throughout the empire when Trajan vainly attempted to conquer Mesopotamia and extend his empire to the Persian Gulf. His successor Hadrian made peace with the Parthians, but was faced with a second war in Judea in 132–135 C.E., led by Simeon Bar-Kochba; this was put down. Hadrian banned Jews from Jerusalem and surrounding areas, and outlawed circumcision and the public teaching of the Torah. The district was renamed Syria Palestina and the refounding of Jerusalem as the Roman colony of Aelia Capitolina was hastened.

This tumultuous conflict with Rome marked the parting of ways between embattled Jews and gentile Christians. Jews, who had formed about 10 percent of the population of the empire, were persecuted. The Christians eventually won over the Emperor Constantine and Christianity became the empire's religion. Judaism, shattered by the loss of its religious and political leadership, became a diaspora religion in its own land. The trauma of the first destruction and exile by the Babylonians had already laid the foundations for a religion that would survive without the temple. Now, after the expulsion from Jerusalem, Judaism dedicated itself to prayer, charity, study, and strict observance of Jewish ordinances under the leadership of rabbis who interpreted religious law.

The sages finalized the text of the Bible and codified the centuries of oral law into the Mishnah at the beginning of the third century. Two separate compilations of commentaries on the Mishnah, known as the Talmud, were completed in Palestine and in Babylonia by around 500 C.E.. More layers of commentaries, interpretations and new rulings would follow, to create a body of law known as the *halacha*. This would help preserve Jewish identity through the succeeding centuries by creating a wall of regulations that insulated Jews from assimilation by gentiles. It would also create a body of Jews who could be singled out as "strangers" and scapegoats.

The memory of the ruined temple bound Jews together throughout the centuries of exile. Appeals for the restoration of the temple became and remain part of the daily prayers. Many of the temple rituals were transferred to the synagogues, which were built facing the site of the temple and inspired by its ground plan. The temple became a symbol of redemption for the Jewish people, and a pillar in preserving collective identity. The lament of the Babylonian exiles now was more relevant than ever, and has remained among the most enduring expressions of longing for Jerusalem:

By the rivers of Babylon, there we sat down, yea, we wept, when we remembered Zion.

We hanged our harps upon the willows in the midst thereof.

For there they that carried us away captive required of us a song: and they that wasted us required of us mirth, saying, Sing us one of the songs of Zion.

How shall we sing the Lord's song in a strange land?

If I forget thee, O Jerusalem, let my right hand forget her cunning.

If I do not remember thee, let my tongue cleave to the roof of my mouth; if I prefer not Jerusalem above my chief joy.

Remember, O Lord, the children of Edom in the day of Jerusalem; who said, Raze it, raze it, even to the foundation thereof.

O daughter of Babylon, who art to be destroyed; happy shall he be, that rewardeth thee as thou hast served us.

Happy shall he be, that taketh, and dasheth thy little ones against the stones. (Psalm 137)

The early verses of this psalm are universally quoted in Israel as expressions of love and beauty, while the final bloodthirsty stanzas are tactfully dropped as inappropriate in the modern age.

When the Jews drifted back to Jerusalem, they venerated the remaining ruins of the temple. By Ottoman times, the western retaining wall became known by Western travelers as the "Place of Wailing" and subsequently as the "Wailing Wall." Guidebooks of the nineteenth century described how Jews would weep before the massive stonework, crying:

> O God, the heathen are come into thine inheritance; thy holy temple have they defiled; they have laid Jerusalem on heaps [. . .] We are become a reproach to our neighbors, a scorn and derision to them that are round about us. How long, Lord? wilt thou be angry forever? shall thy jealousy burn like fire? (Psalm 79:1, 4–5).

The transformation of Palestine into a Christian holy land begins with the Emperor Constantine's conversion to Christianity. After the Council of Nicea in 325, Constantine embarked on a massive program of church-building in Palestine. He ordered Jerusalem's notables to erect a church on the site of Jesus' death and crucifixion: "by an abundant and unsparing expenditure they should secure the completion of the work on a scale of noble and ample magnificence."

The site of Jesus' crucifixion and burial, said Eusebius, the fourth-century Bishop of Caesarea and chronicler of the early Church, had first been a rubbish heap, then a pagan temple: "a gloomy shrine of lifeless idols to the impure spirit whom they call Venus." The stone and timbers of the pagan temple were scattered in distant sites, as was the earth that had covered the burial cave. As the workmen dug down, "beneath the covering of earth, appeared, immediately, and contrary to all expectation, the venerable and hallowed monument of our Savior's resurrection," said Eusebius in *The Life of Constantine*.

Eusebius does not support legends that the Holy Sepulchre was discovered by Constantine's mother, Helena. (She is identified by old British chronicles as the daughter of the British king Coel, the reputed inspiration for the Mother Goose rhyme, "Old King Cole was a merry old soul . . .") Helena, the story goes, starved a rabbi until he identified the secret location of the Holy Sepulchre. Three crosses were found and, according to different traditions, the True Cross was identified by using it either to raise a dead man or to heal a sick woman. Helena is also credited with dedicating the churches of the Nativity in Bethlehem and of the Ascension on the Mount of Olives.

Jews were banned once more from the city, but the accession of the pagan Emperor Julian brought a brief respite. Work on rebuilding the Jewish temple began in 363, but Christian accounts say it was prevented by a miraculous earthquake that set fire to the building.

The death of Julian put an end to the project. Christian pilgrimages to the holy places gathered pace.

The wars between Byzantium and Persia saw the Persians take Jerusalem in 614 with the help of Jewish allies. The Persians destroyed most churches and briefly handed over the city to the Jews, but later restored it to Christians and allowed the churches to be rebuilt. The Byzantine Emperor Heraclius recaptured Jerusalem in 629.

The wars had exhausted both empires, and within a few years both fell to the forces of Islam that exploded out of Arabia. Jerusalem had been, for Islam, the first *qibla*, or direction of prayer, before Muslims turned toward Mecca. Muslims present their capture of Jerusalem in 638 as an exemplary demonstration of a peaceful and respectful conquest, rarely seen in the Holy City.

The pious second Caliph of Islam, Omar Ibn al-Khattab, gave a guarantee of religious freedom and respect for holy sites and allowed 200 Jewish families to settle in Jerusalem after they had been excluded by the Byzantines. According to one Arab account, Omar was greeted by the Patriarch Sophronius and was shown the holy sites. Omar declined an invitation to pray at the Holy Sepulchre, declaring: "If I had prayed in the church it would have been lost to you, for the Believers would have taken it, saying: Omar prayed here."

He then asked to see the Temple Mount, the "mosque of David" as he called it, and was shocked to find that it had been turned into a dung heap by the Christians. The rubbish was piled half-way up the doors, so that he was forced to crawl to reach the temple platform. Omar set a personal example by clearing the rubbish into his camel-hair tunic. According to one chronicler, he had the first al-Aqsa mosque built at the southern end of the platform deliberately so that Muslims would face only Mecca, rather than both Mecca and the rock that juts out from near the center of the platform. *Al-Sakhra*, or "The Rock," is regarded as the departure point for the Prophet Muhammad's Night Journey, while for many Jews and Christians it is the likely site of Abraham's sacrifice and of the Holy of Holies of the Jewish temple. The complex of mosques and shrines on the former temple platform came to be known as the Haram al-Sharif, the Noble Sanctuary.

The Dome of the Rock, the masterpiece of Islamic architecture, was erected to enshrine the rock in 691. It remains the most distinctive and beautiful monument in Jerusalem, even though it is ostensibly secondary to the main Al-Aqsa mosque. The geometry of a dome supported on an octagonal drum is meant to symbolize the transition from earth to Heaven, a distant announcement of paradise itself. The building is also a symbol of Islam superseding previous religions, appropriating the holy enclosure of Jews and castigating the errors of Christian dogma in the Koranic inscriptions which decorate the shrine:

> People of the Book, do not transgress the bounds of your religion. Speak nothing but the truth about Allah. The Messiah, Jesus the son of Mary, was no more than Allah's apostle and His Word which He conveyed to Mary: a spirit from Him. So believe in Allah and His apostles and do not say: "Three." Forbear, and it shall be better for you. Allah is but one God. Allah forbid that He should have a son! (4: 171)

The unstable Fatimid Caliph Al-Hakim, although born of a Christian mother, broke with Islamic tradition of tolerance for the "People of the Book," as Muslims call Jews and Christians, by ordering the destruction of the Holy Sepulchre in 1009. The wreckers attacked the revered rock tomb of Christ until debris covered the meager remains. Al-Hakim tried to force Jews and Christians to convert to Islam. He soon locked horns even with the Muslims, by claiming to be a divine incarnation and having his name substituted for that of God in Friday prayers. Amid Muslim riots, the edicts against Jews and Christians were lifted just as abruptly as they had been imposed. Muslims were banned from fasting on Ramadan or going on the Haj pilgrimage. Al-Hakim sank into his madness, and one night in 1021 rode out of Cairo alone and was never seen again. As a final bizarre epilogue, Al-Hakim became the inspiration for the breakaway and secretive Druze sect who survive in Syria, Lebanon and Israel. They believe that the Caliph did not die but was taken up into Heaven. The Holy Sepulchre was restored with funds from the Byzantine emperor, but on a much smaller scale. Constantine's main basilica and atrium were abandoned.

To the cry of "God Wills It," Christians rallied to Pope Urban II's call in 1095 for a crusade to liberate the Holy Land from the "infidel" Muslims. The army of pilgrims and knights arrived, against all odds, at the gates of Jerusalem in 1099 and conquered the city with a massacre of Muslim and Jewish inhabitants. The contemporary chronicler Fulcher of Chartres described the slaughter:

> On the top of Solomon's Temple, to which they had climbed in fleeing, many were shot to death with arrows and cast down headlong from the roof. Within this Temple about ten thousand were

beheaded. If you had been there, your feet would have been stained up to the ankles with the blood of the slain. What more shall I tell? Not one of them was allowed to live. They did not spare the women and children.

The carnage of the Crusades would forever embitter relations between Islam and Christianity. The fanaticism rekindled the idea of *jihad*, or holy war, among Muslims. The Crusaders turned the Dome of the Rock into a church, while the larger Al-Aqsa mosque nearby served as the residence of the Crusader king of Jerusalem and then the headquarters of the military order known as the Templars.

Salah al-Din, better known in the West as Saladin, the foe of Richard the Lion Heart, fatally weakened the Crusaders at the Battle of Hattin in 1187 and retook Jerusalem. Unlike the Crusaders, the Muslims carried out no murder or looting. Most of the Christians were set free unharmed or allowed to leave upon payment of a ransom. Those who were not ransomed were sold into slavery. "How many well-guarded women were profaned, how many queens were ruled, and nubile girls married, and noble women given away . . ." wrote the Muslim historian, Imad al-Din. Saladin rededicated the Dome of the Rock and the Al-Aqsa mosque, and the Holy Sepulchre was opened to pilgrims within days.

For more than eight centuries, despite many upheavals, Jerusalem remained under Muslim rule. Then, at the end of 1917, Turkish troops retreated in the face of the British army advancing up from Egypt. On December 9, the elderly mayor of Jerusalem, Hussein Bey al-Husseini, took a white bedsheet from a mission hospital and set out to surrender the city. He found two startled soldiers who were foraging for supplies. They alerted two sergeants, who in turn set out to find a senior officer who could take delivery of the city. The process took so long, it is said, that the mayor caught a chill and died of pneumonia three weeks later.

★

The holy geography of Jerusalem has remained almost unchanged since Saladin's time: Muslims on the Haram al-Sharif, Jews outside its retaining walls, and Christians at the Holy Sepulchre. But within these boundaries, there has been ample opportunity for conflict.

Chronic rivalry between Christian denominations in the Holy Sepulchre ensured that the keys to the church remain to this day in the hands of Muslim guardians, appointed at least since the time of Saladin. Wajeed Nusseibeh is often to be seen sitting on a wooden bench at the entrance to the church, looking mildly bored. He seeks to supplement his honorific role by offering his services as a uniquely qualified tourist guide. Every night at eight o'clock, he or one of his representatives pulls the heavy wooden leaves shut, climbs up a ladder to fasten the iron fetters across the door and passes the ladder through a small window to the monks within. They stay locked in until the arcane procedure is reversed before dawn the next morning. It is an anachronistic role more than eight decades after the end of Muslim rule in Palestine. "If the Greeks or the Latins had the key, it would create a problem. It would mean the church was owned by one or other denomination. It's simpler to give it to a Muslim, who is neutral," explained Nusseibeh. "Muslims accept Jesus as a prophet and respect Christianity. Our Prophet Muhammad even married a Christian woman."

The guardianship, says Nusseibeh, was given to his ancestors who accompanied the Caliph Omar to Jerusalem. However, the job was subsequently divided between the Nusseibehs and another Muslim family, the Judehs, probably after Saladin retook the city. As a result, the Judehs now hold the keys to the entrance and hand them over daily to the Nusseibehs, who open and close the doors. "I hold the keys on behalf of the Sultan," declared Abdel-Kader Judeh, brimming with pride at his noble ancestry; reputedly he is descended directly from the Prophet Muhammad himself.

The churches say they allow the guardians to remain as a bit of folklore. But they know that any attempt to reclaim the keys could undermine the delicate structure of the *Status Quo*, an informal set of rules freezing the balance of power within the hallowed precinct to the situation in 1757. The absurdly complex and imprecise Ottoman code sets out the rights and privileges of each community and the ownership of every part of the church, down to the last candle-holder, icon, and rusty nail. Yet none of the subsequent rulers—Britain, Jordan, or Israel—has dared tamper with the Status Quo for fear of causing religious chaos.

In 1929 a British administrative officer glumly described the prevailing "spirit of distrust and suspicion and the attitude of intractability in all matters." He explained: "The right to repair a roof or floor implies the right to an exclusive possession on the part of the restorers. Again, the right to hang a lamp or picture or to change a lamp or picture is a recognition of exclusive possession of a pillar or wall. The right of other communities to cense at a chapel implies that the proprietorship is not absolute."

By its very nature, the Status Quo requires constant reaffirmation of each community's rights, and perpetual alertness in case of infringement by others. A privilege, once lost, may never be recovered.

These disputes were once the stuff of international diplomacy. A power struggle between France and Russia for domination of the church and other holy sites was a factor in the outbreak of the Crimean War in 1853. Today tensions are under greater control, but can still surface. The dissonant Latin hymns, ancient Coptic chants, mysterious invocations in Aramaic and the pealing of Greek bells still sound like tribal war signals. In the early 1990s, Greek and Armenian monks came to blows in Bethlehem's Church of the Nativity because of a dispute over who should clean a lintel.

Rivalry has also meant that the restoration of the Holy Sepulchre, damaged by fire in 1808 and an earthquake in 1927, has made slow progress. The dome above the tomb, designed to admit a serene shaft of light from its center as in Rome's Pantheon, was blighted by scaffolding for more than two decades until the sides agreed on how it should be decorated. Icons, cherubs, and mosaics were rejected by one side or other, and the parties finally settled for neutral golden rays. Girders holding together the shrine around the tomb, known as the Edicule, remain in place since the days of British rule because of disagreements over how to restore it.

The two Muslim guardians keep a diplomatic silence on the disputes of Christians, but are not immune to what the Victorian painter Edward Lear called the "Jerusalem squabblepoison." Abdel-Kader Judeh believes his title carries the greater honor. "My family has the keys in the name of the Sultan," he points out. Not so, retorts Wajeed Nusseibeh. "Without us nobody can enter the church."

European interference in the church has all but disappeared. Instead, international scheming has involved the Arabs in power struggles over influence at the Haram al-Sharif. The main rivalry has been between the Palestinian leader Yasser Arafat and Jordan's late King Hussein. Others, too, have played the great game for the shrine, such as the late King Hassan of Morocco, for long the head of the Arab League's Jerusalem Committee, and Saudi Arabia's King Fahd, already Custodian of the Two Holy Places, Mecca and Medina.

These jealousies became most apparent in 1991 over the question of urgently needed repairs to the Dome of the Rock, after a botched restoration in 1964. The dome, made of golden sheets of anodized aluminium, leaked from the start, endangering the structure and mosaics beneath. At the end of the 1991 Gulf War, Saudi Arabia offered to pay for the repairs, prompting King Hussein, the self-appointed guardian of Islamic shrines in Jerusalem, to sell a villa in Britain to raise the funds so that Jordan could secure the honor. A resplendent new dome was unveiled in 1994, made of copper sheets gilded with 24-carat gold. The restorers admitted that until the 1960s the dome had been made of somber lead. But gold had now become the established color, a shining symbol of the Muslim presence. Even the Israelis associated the Dome of the Rock with gold through the song, "Jerusalem of Gold."

Along with guardianship of the shrine, King Hussein inherited the resentment of Palestinian nationalists, rarely sympathetic to his Hashemite dynasty's moderate stand in the Arab–Israeli conflict. Two marble inscriptions extolling King Hussein's restoration work were smashed, while the Palestinian leader Yasser Arafat successfully imposed his own choice of Mufti, the supreme Muslim religious authority, over the Jordanian appointee. As a boy in 1951, King Hussein watched the murder of his grandfather, King Abdallah, by a lone Palestinian gunman at the entrance of the Al-Aqsa mosque, where a bullet hole is still visible on one of the polished white marble columns.

The Wailing (now Western) Wall, for its part, is not free of controversy even under Israeli rule. A constant source of friction between Muslims and Jews during the British Mandate, it is now the subject of a power struggle between Orthodox rabbis, who control worship at the wall, and more liberal streams trying to carve out a place for themselves at Judaism's holiest shrine. Fights periodically break out between outraged Ultraorthodox men and their foes, ranging from women seeking equal prayer rights to Reform and Conservative Jews who want the right to worship at the wall.

The small women's area at the site is separated by a screen from the men's section. But according to religious law, women must cover their arms and legs, must not read from Torah scrolls and must not be heard praying because, according to Jewish tradition, "a woman's voice is indecent." Feminists seeking to challenge the restrictions, some of them wearing the *tallit* prayer shawls and skullcaps usually reserved for men, have had chairs thrown at them. During one Feast of Shavuot, a group of Conservative Jews trying to pray were jostled, spat at, and complained they had bags of excrement thrown at them.

★

The holy power that emanates from Jerusalem warps the cosmos in even stranger ways than a black hole.

Some Jewish sages said the Foundation Stone, or *Even Shetiyah*, is the base of the world, a cosmic pillar. This is the center of the world, according to Jewish tradition. (Christians place the center point in the middle of the Church of the Holy Sepulchre.) The sages said the Foundation Stone was thrown into the primeval waters by God, and the world grew out of it. To others the stone was the "navel," from which the world grew like an embryo. One Jewish tradition is that the world rests on a whale, with the rock on the center of its back. A Muslim account claims that all the "rivers and clouds, vapors and winds come from under the Holy Rock in Jerusalem."

Muslims say the rock was originally taken from the Garden of Eden and according to one version, the holy Ka'bah in Mecca will be joined to it on Resurrection day. Today the visitor is shown the indentation where Muhammad left a footprint, the grooves where the angel Gabriel held down the rock to stop it rising to Heaven with the Prophet, and a reliquary containing the hairs of Muhammad's beard. Christian pilgrims during the Crusades similarly reported seeing Jesus' footprint. Another tradition is that an opening in the cave beneath *Al-Sakhra* in the Dome of the Rock leads to the "Well of Souls," Hell itself.

At the Holy Sepulchre, a glass pane shows the rock of Golgotha rent asunder by an earthquake when Jesus was crucified. Adam's skull is said by some legends to be buried within it, so that Jesus' redemptive blood seeped over it and brought Adam to life. A sixth-century visitor known simply as the Piacenza Pilgrim reported that when the True Cross is brought out for veneration in the church, "a star appears in the sky, and comes over the place where they lay the cross." Little flasks of oil are brought out to be blessed, and when they touch the wood, "the oil instantly bubbles over, and unless it is closed very quickly, it all spills out."

The Western Wall, *Ha-Kotel ha-Ma'aravi*, or simply the *Kotel*, is said to be the permanent home of the *Shekhinah*, the woman-like embodiment of the divine presence. On the Ninth of Av, it is said, a white dove perches on the wall and weeps over the destruction of the temple. As recently as 1940, as the Nazis were slaughtering Jews in Europe, tears are reported to have oozed from the *Kotel*.

Places of veneration do not respect physical rules. The holiest shrine in Judaism began life as the eastern wall, then moved to the southern wall and finally came to rest at today's Western Wall. Al-Buraq, the Prophet Muhammad's steed who carried him to Jerusalem on his Night Journey, appears to be a restless beast. An Israeli study maintains that the wall where he alighted has also moved around: it is now fixed at the Western Wall to deny Jews an exclusive claim.

For Christians, Abraham's sacrificial altar was for a while transposed to the Holy Sepulchre, only to return later to the Dome of the Rock. Over the centuries, the Way of the Cross has taken many different routes across the city. The current Via Dolorosa, so painfully and earnestly paced by pilgrims, has little to do with Jesus' last footsteps to the crucifixion. Christ, archaeologists believe, did not come from the east to Calvary, as the current Via Dolorosa suggests, but probably from the west.

The seventeenth-century cabbalist rabbi Abraham Azulai claimed that a sort of holy ozone hole had opened in the spheres of Heaven above Jerusalem and Palestine to allow God's divine power to pass through. As a result, Jerusalem was particularly suitable for prophecy. The city has a hot line to Heaven. Jewish sages likened it to praying directly before God's throne. For Muslims a prayer in Jerusalem is worth 500 elsewhere. Medieval Christian pilgrims were convinced that praying at the shrines of Jerusalem earned a sinner enough indulgences to last a lifetime.

Jews today jam little pieces of paper containing prayers and supplications to God into the Western Wall. You can even fax and e-mail your prayer to the *Kotel* from abroad, and the rabbis promise the greatest discretion in placing the messages between Herod's vast stone blocks.

Time does strange things in Jerusalem. The date of the Muslim feast of Ramadan, traditionally set according to a Jordanian timetable, now depends on the vagaries of Palestinian foreign relations, which sometimes call for the feast to be aligned with Saudi sightings of the new moon.

When Israel changes its clocks to and from summer time, Palestinians switch clocks on a different day in a show of independence. The result is that one often shows up for appointments with Palestinians either indecently early or embarrassingly late. The same political commemoration, such as the anniversary of Israel's founding, is marked on different days by Israelis and Palestinians, who use the Jewish and the western Gregorian calendar respectively. The pilgrim has to check whether Easter ceremonies take place according to Israeli, Palestinian, or solar time. Moreover, the Eastern and Western Churches celebrate Easter according to different calendars.

Not surprisingly, Jerusalem is more than generously endowed with places of prayer. One count found that in 1994 there were 1,072 synagogues, 59 mosques, 65 churches, and 72 convents. At any given moment, some part of Jerusalem will be at work, at rest, in conflict, or at prayer. "The air over Jerusalem is saturated with prayers and dream," wrote the late Israeli poet Yehuda Amichai. "Like the air over industrial cities, it's hard to breathe."

In the prayers of Jews, Muslims, and Christians, there is a special request for peace. All punctuate their prayers with the expression "Amen," "So be it." The word is used boisterously in the synagogue response, in a matter-of-fact fashion in the churches, and in a long collective chant during Muslim prayers. This is the limit of a common language of faith in Jerusalem.

★

Spring is a crazy, intense, and eccentric time when the religious passions of Jerusalem are awakened by nature. God's ear is subjected to intense demands in this season, which sees a promiscuity of religious feasts: Passover, Easter, and the Muslim pilgrimage festival of Nebi Musa fall within weeks, often days, of each other. Even the tiny Samaritan community comes out to celebrate its nighttime Passover sacrifice on the blustery summit of Mount Gerizim. As Islamic feasts wander through the solar year, the feast of sacrifice, 'Id al-Adha, joined the other spring rites in 1998.

These celebrations are all intimately connected, and often deliberately in opposition. Easter evolved out of Passover with the message that Jesus' teaching and death supersede the religion of the Old Testament. The Nebi Musa pilgrimage from Jerusalem to the reputed tomb of Moses in the desert was established to provide a Muslim counterweight to the Christians who would swamp Jerusalem at Easter. The Samaritans continue to slaughter animals at Passover, implicitly challenging the Jewish belief that sacrifices can take place only when the temple is rebuilt. Muslims also sacrifice animals. 'Id al-Adha commemorates Abraham's readiness to sacrifice his son, not Isaac as Jews maintain but Ishmael, and not in Jerusalem but in Mecca. Each religion is a distorted reflection of the others, as if seen in a fairground hall of mirrors. In some places the features can be recognized, in others they are grotesquely stretched while other parts are shrunk until they virtually disappear.

Sir Ronald Storrs, the first British military governor of Jerusalem, described the dread with which the first Easter was awaited by the new rulers in 1918:

> Eastertide, the culmination of the Christian year, is almost throughout the world a season when, if only for three days, the death of strife becomes the victory of peace. Easter in the Holy Land, and most of all in the Holy City, had meant for generations the sharpening of daggers and the trebling of garrisons. [. . .] These three preponderating events [Passover, Easter, and Nebi Musa] of the three Religions, summon into Jerusalem, together with the genuinely pious, hordes of the politically and criminally turbulent, in the very crisis of the riotous Easter Spring.

The religious holiday season remains, under Israeli rule, a time of heightened alert. The security cordon dividing Jerusalem from the West Bank is strengthened. West Bank residents are often kept out of Jerusalem entirely during Passover. Herzl, in *The Jewish State*, had envisioned the Jewish state posting ceremonial guards around Christian holy places. "This guard of honor would be the great symbol of the solution of the Jewish Question after eighteen centuries of Jewish suffering." He did not mention Muslim sites. In the modern state of Israel, security forces do a lot more guarding than honoring at the holy sanctuaries. They do not wear colorful uniforms but sweat-stained flak-jackets; soldiers do not hold aloft ceremonial standards, but rather nervously grip their truncheons, tear-gas launchers, and rifles. The crackle of police radios echoes though the alleys instead of brass bands.

Jerusalem is crammed with humanity. From the four corners of the world flock Christians: Russians, Cypriots, Indonesians, Americans, and many more. Passover is one of the main pilgrimage feasts for Jews, who pour into the city from around Israel and the Diaspora. Muslims seem to have the right idea: they head out of the city for the openness of the hills of Nebi Musa.

Each group sees only its own Jerusalem. Jews sing their way to the Western Wall brimming with pride at the sight of the Israeli colors flying from every other building. Christians trudge up the Via Dolorosa, sing hymns through the souk and prostrate themselves at

Calvary filled with visions of Jesus. Some reenact the Passion dressed as Roman soldiers with plastic swords, and a wide-eyed Jesus carrying a cross with red paint streaming from his crown of thorns. A woman with a loudspeaker shouts at the bemused Arab store owners: "See what you have done to him. Why have you done this?"

During the spring festivals in Jerusalem, one sees how Judaism, Christianity, and Islam, all monotheistic religions which conceive of God as the supreme moral being, have retained real or symbolic attachment to the earliest form of worship: animal sacrifice. The symbol of the paschal lamb at the Passover table, the notion of Jesus himself as the supreme sacrifice to God, the slitting of the throats of animals by Samaritans on Mount Gerizim and the homes of Muslims on 'Id al-Adha—all these recall the ancient notion that God's favor of life must be purchased with blood.

In the days of the temple, tens of thousands of animals were slaughtered by families at Passover. One Roman account quoted by the fifteenth-century Jewish writer, Solomon ibn Verga, relates that so many animals were brought to Jerusalem that "the grass was not seen any longer, and everything was turned white, by reason of the white color of the wool."

This assault of rituals, ceremonies, and sacrifices is difficult to reconcile with the simple notion of a single God: God is one, but man invented many religions.

★

Passover in Jerusalem is a bewildering time for the uninitiated foreigner. The week-long Feast of Unleavened Bread commemorates the Exodus of the Children of Israel from bondage in Egypt and the emergence of the Israelites as a separate people. It is also a festival of inscrutable Jewish dietary law.

Israel lives by the unique rhythm of the Jewish calendar. Christmas is nonexistent, the western New Year's Day is an ordinary day without the groggy mist of hangovers, while the country grinds to a virtual halt during the interminable succession of feasts in the autumn.

Passover is a national, all-encompassing event. Supermarket shelves are suddenly wrapped in large sheets of paper to hide away any products suspected of containing *hametz*, or "leavened bread." That means almost everything: no pasta, biscuits, cookies, flour, breakfast cereals, crackers, croissants. In religious households even animals are subjected to a leaven-free diet. Products must be stamped with the magic words *kasher le-pessach*, kosher for Passover, if they are to compete during the festive season. A foreigner needs a well-honed sense of chutzpah to tear away a corner of the wrapping, reach inside for a tin of baked beans and present it at the checkout counter.

Israelis munch through prodigious quantities of *matzah*, unleavened bread which usually comes in the form of sheets of dry, saltless crackers.

You cannot escape *matzah*. Restaurants' menus are decimated by the ban on *hametz*. The entire nation is denied its staple of bread and hummus. There is no couscous in Moroccan restaurants, no spaghetti in Italian eateries. Moreover, Ashkenazi Jews may not eat pulses. Burger chains make do with *matzah* buns. *Matzah* pizza looks as if it has been baked on cardboard, and the holiday pastries are the consistency of damp sawdust.

Many restaurants simply give up and close down for the week. Ordinary bread, even the flat pitta, can only be found among the Arabs in East Jerusalem. But since the latest Intifada has pretty well eliminated that avenue, many Israelis guiltily hoard bread at home to eat it away from prying eyes. Others take a holiday and travel to Europe, Turkey, America. Tens of thousands join a counter-Exodus to Sinai, where Moses and the Israelites wandered in the wilderness for forty years before entering the Promised Land.

After one *matzah*-filled day, I repaired to the five-star King David Hotel. I knew better than to order a sandwich, so I opted for an early gin and tonic. "Sorry, sir. It's Passover," said the waiter, raising his eyebrows at yet another ignorant foreigner. Gin does not even closely resemble bread, leavened or not. But as a product made from fermented grains, the rabbis insist it has that indefinable, noxious, all-pervading quality of leaven.

The injunction to eat unleavened bread is contained in the Book of Exodus: "Seven days shall ye eat unleavened bread; even the first day shall ye put away leaven out of your houses: for whosoever eateth leavened bread from the first day until the seventh day, that soul shall be cut off from Israel." (Exod. 12:15). Simple enough: no leavened bread for a week.

Leavened dough is defined as the flour of five species of grain— wheat, barley, spelt, rye, and oats—which has been mixed with water for the length of time it takes a man to walk a Roman mile: 18 minutes. But because of the risk that a Jew may sin inadvertently, the rabbis have created the closest thing in Jewish law to an impregnable fortress. Firstly, Ashkenazi rabbis expanded the definition of *hametz* to include rice, millet, beans, pulses, maize, and peanuts. Then they ruled that even a bit of leaven, such as a drop of water falling on a bag of flour, would irredeemably contaminate anything that came into contact with it. Finally, any grain product that is not carefully monitored and certified as unleavened *matzah* by a rabbinical inspector is suspect and is forbidden. In rabbinical writings, leaven became a metaphor for corruption and impurity, a notion adopted by the New Testament writers who spoke of purging "the leaven of malice and wickedness."

This kind of triple-fastening of the rules is an important link in the religious fence which the rabbis have sought to erect to keep "Israel separate from the heathen." The attempt to preserve the law and Jewish identity, however, creates any number of problems. One year, for example, a rabbi called on the devout not to drink tap water on Passover because Arabs dropped sandwiches in the Sea of Galilee, Israel's main reservoir, polluting the whole of the country's water supply with *hametz*.

Manufacturers show their inventiveness in designing a range of products that are "Kosher for Passover" yet similar to the old leavened versions. There are Kosher for Passover lipsticks, ice-creams, chocolate wafers, nut bars, and hamburger buns. There are special Kosher for Passover cleaning materials that will not contaminate homes as frazzled housewives scrub frantically to get rid of the very last crumb of stale bread.

Those with stocks of *hametz* resort to the legal fiction of temporarily "selling" their leavened bread to a non-Jew. The prize for oddity must go to the solemn ceremony in which the State of Israel, represented by the Ashkenazi and Sephardi chief rabbis, as well as the Finance Minister, in all seriousness sell off the country's *hametz* to an Arab. One year Ahmed Moghrabi, a lawyer in East Jerusalem, briefly became Israel's biggest property owner. After producing a down payment of NIS 20,000 (Israeli shekels: about £4,000 sterling), he shook the traditional velvet scarf to seal the agreement and formally took possession of all grain owned by government ministries and state-owned companies and their subsidiaries, whether on land, ships, or air, in Israel or abroad. His property included products made with grains, like bread, biscuits, beer, wines, whiskey, cosmetics, and non-essential pharmaceuticals. Horses, oxen, cattle, and chickens which were fed on grains were part of his empire.

At the end of Passover, Mr. Moghrabi announced that he no longer wanted to exercise his option, and he was refunded his money. The selling of *hametz* is probably the one and only time an Arab is given a central role in the functioning of the Israeli state. It should be noted that Jewish Law, which has created this loophole, warns sternly that "the transaction shall not be considered a mere jest, but should be effected according to the true manner of merchants." In 1995, the rabbis stopped selling to Mr. Moghrabi because they had the shocking suspicion that his mother was Jewish, which under Jewish law makes him a Jew and nullifies his *hametz* contract.

★

The Passover meal, the seder, is the most important family occasion in the Jewish calendar. It is a time when Jews collectively reassert their identity. The ritual of the seder, every piece of food, every song and hymn, is a symbolic act, a pillar in the edifice of institutionalized remembrance which has preserved Jews through the centuries. Nurturing the memory of the past is a daily task for Jews; at Passover it is turned into an art form.

Passover is supposed to be a commemoration of freedom, but it is better described as a celebration of survival. The reading of the Haggadah—the retelling of the Exodus story, of God's promise of the Land of Canaan, his blessings and the plagues inflicted on Pharaoh, the reciting of psalms and singing of songs of thanksgiving—has remained largely unchanged for centuries. It is not just a religious morality tale, but an ancestral history; Jews feel they have a direct tribal bloodline to the Israelites who fled Egypt, and beyond to Abraham, Isaac, and Jacob. The Haggadah declares that "In every single generation, it is a man's duty to think of himself as one of those who came out of Egypt."

The celebration of Passover in Jerusalem has a unique resonance. For centuries, in communities scattered from South America to China, Jews have not only celebrated the redemption of the past but have also prayed for the imminent restoration of Jews to the Promised Land, with the words of the Haggadah:

> O Thou pure One, who dwellest in heaven, raise up the assembly of Thy people innumerable! Shortly lead them—called the plant of Thy vine—in freedom to Zion with a joyful shout. Next year in Jerusalem rebuilt!

For a Jew to be able to recite these words as a free person in Jerusalem is the fulfilment of a millennial desire. For Jews, the creation of Israel is a modern miracle, the consummation of God's promise, long in coming, but here at last. The covenant with Abraham remains eternally valid.

Passover is intricately bound up with the idea of the Promised Land; it marks the Exodus from Egypt and the first celebration by Joshua and the Israelites after crossing the Jordan River. Jews were instinctively Zionists before Herzl turned the idea into a modern political movement. In *Altneuland*, Herzl's heroes celebrate Passover on the shores of the Sea of Galilee and the seder is the setting for the revelation of how the "New Society" which the Jews have created in Palestine was first founded. He presents a modern Haggadah for a modern Exodus, not a rush to flee Pharaoh and a succession of plagues, but a well-organized arrival with the willing consent of the Turks, who are blessed with tribute from the grateful and prosperous Jews.

At any Passover table in Israel you witness the extraordinary variety that the ingathering of Jews has produced. One year I celebrated at the home of Dennis Diamond in Jerusalem. An interior decorator and writer, he was born in South Africa before emigrating to Israel in the 1970s. His daughter had brought her Russian-born boyfriend, who had made *aliyah* to Israel only two years earlier. The other guests were the British-born Rabbi David Rosen, his wife and three daughters. Rosen had studied in an Ultraorthodox yeshiva in Jerusalem, but escaped its closed world by joining the Israeli army, a supreme act of impiety for the ultrareligious. He served as Chief Rabbi of Cape Town and later of Ireland, before returning to Israel.

My wife and I were the two non-Jews at the table. In temple times foreigners were not allowed to partake of the paschal lamb, according to the injunction in Exodus (12:43): "This is the ordinance of the Passover: There shall no stranger eat thereof." The destruction of the temple has, if nothing else, allowed non-Jews to attend the seder.

Rabbi Rosen held up the plate with the ritual food: an egg, representing the festival offering in the temple; horseradish, used as the bitter herb which Jews are enjoined to eat as a reminder of their slavery; a sprig of parsley which is dipped into salt water in remembrance of the Israelites' tears; and *haroset*, a sweet paste of almonds, fruit, and wine recalling the mortar which the Israelite slaves worked. Rabbi Rosen was vegetarian, so the *zeroa*, usually a roasted shankbone symbolizing the paschal lamb sacrifice, was replaced by a roasted mushroom.

So much tragedy has befallen the Jews that even a happy feast like

Passover has a melancholy air about it. Rabbi Rosen held up the three sheets of *matzah* and recited the opening words of the Haggadah in Aramaic:

> "This is the bread of affliction which our fathers did eat in Egypt. Let all who hunger come and eat. Let all who are in need come and partake of the paschal lamb! This year we are here; Next year—in the Land of Israel! This year we are slaves; Next year—free men!"

There was an orange on the seder plate, an act of protest against traditionalist Orthodox rabbis who refuse to ordain women on the grounds that "a woman at the pulpit is like an orange on a Passover plate." We soon reached the passage about the "Four Sons," Judaism being an unabashedly male-centered religion. Rosen had only daughters. "I had daughters so that I could avoid the circumcision," quipped Rosen. They had become indistinguishable from Israeli-born sabras; one was studying art history at university, the other served as a training instructor in the Israeli army, and the third was at secondary school.

We drank the traditional four cups of wine and the *matzah* was blessed: "Blessed are Thou, Lord our God, King of the Universe, who brings forth bread from the earth. . . ." The wine, the bread, and the blessing. Memories of countless church services of my youth came back to me: ". . . took Bread; and when he had given thanks, he brake it, and gave it to his disciples, saying, Take, eat, this is my Body which is given for you: Do this in remembrance of me . . . this is my Blood of the New Testament, which is shed for you. . . ." I had never understood the Eucharist as a Jewish ceremony until I came to Israel. To me, Jesus' familiar words were a sort of farewell speech, a ceremony which he had improvised on the spot. The Jewishness of Jesus had been, to me, no more than folklore. The Passion could have taken place anywhere in the Roman world. By coincidence it happened in Palestine. Now, seen in its Jewish context, the sight of a Roman Catholic priest standing at the altar in his robes, holding up the little round host and dipping it into wine seems like a parody, a mockery of the faithful. None of the relatives who marched me to church in my youth, I am sure, had any concept of the Jewish Passover that Jesus was commemorating with his twelve disciples—twelve, not eleven, because twelve represents the twelve tribes of Israel.

The first Christians celebrated Easter as a Jewish Passover meal. They observed the Sabbath and worshipped at the temple. But as gentiles entered the Church under the influence of Saint Paul, Christianity began to part ways with Judaism and quickly became a purely gentile religion after the destruction of the temple. The date of Easter was made to fall on a Sunday to mark its separation from Passover.

As Christianity absorbed Greek philosophy, it also tapped into a rich vein of Greek anti-Semitism. One of the first recorded diatribes against Jews was spread by Manetho, the third-century B.C.E. Greek-Egyptian historian, who claimed that the Jews were descended from a group of 80,000 "lepers and impure people" who revolted against Egypt.

According to the first-century rhetorician Apion, quoted by Josephus, the historian of the Jewish revolt against Rome, the Jews would yearly kidnap a Greek man, fatten him up in their inviolable temple, then "lead him into a certain wood, and kill him, and sacrifice with their accustomed solemnities, and taste his entrails, and take an oath upon this sacrificing a Greek, that they would ever be at enmity with the Greeks."

The kernel of this accusation would merge centuries later with the imagery of Jesus' blood and the notion of Jewish deicide at Passover to create a superstitious brew known as the blood libel—the belief that Jews sacrificed a Christian, usually a child, to mix the blood with the Passover bread. The first such accusation took place in Norwich in 1144 when a boy called William was said to have disappeared. The blood libel spread to France, Spain, Germany, and farther east, often surfacing at the time of Easter and Passover. It provoked massacres and expulsions of Jews despite attempts by some popes and emperors to put an end to the cruel accusations. Carried by missionaries, it surfaced in Damascus in 1840. The Nazis used the blood libel in full force for their anti-Semitic propaganda.

For centuries, the Passover feast of freedom became a feast of dread. A recurrent theme of Jewish literature is the narrow escape of families from mobs fired by the blood libel. "Not one persecutor only has risen to destroy us; but in every generation there are those who rise to destroy us," says the Haggadah. "But the Holy One, blessed is He, always saves us from their hands."

At our Passover meal, Rosen wore a white robe known as a *kittel*. It is supposed to be a festive dress, but Rosen gave it an additional somber meaning: "The kittel was worn like a funeral shroud. Passover was such a dangerous time that Jews prepared to go to their deaths."

Toward the end of the seder a fifth cup of wine was poured for the Prophet Elijah, the precursor of the Messiah and protector of Jews.

The door was opened for Elijah, a tradition which, Rosen explained, seeks to show gentiles that Jews "have nothing to hide." One illustrated Haggadah at the table showed Elijah's fist. smashing down the Nazis. We recited the words of vengeance:

> "Pour out Thy wrath upon the nations that do not know Thee, and on the kingdoms that do not call on Thy name. For they have devoured Jacob and laid waste his dwelling place. Pour out Thy indignation upon them, and let Thy fierce anger overtake them. Pursue them with wrath and destroy them, from beneath the heavens of the Lord."

Rosen is as liberal as they come in the orthodox world. He read this portion as "Pour out Thy compassion upon the nations that do not know Thee...."

A key figure in interfaith dialogue with Christians, Rosen argues that the degree of anti-gentile sentiments among Jews depends on the degree of oppression by gentiles, the *goyim*. But more than half a century after the creation of the State of Israel, it becomes more difficult to accept this as a sufficient explanation for the seam of intolerance within Jewish tradition; its interpretation of God as a sectarian deity, its view of the world as separated into Jews and heathens, the depiction of gentiles as enemies and oppressors, the expressions of vengeance such as "Pour out Thy wrath," and the daily prayers against heretics with the passage:

"Blessed are thou, Lord, our God, King of the universe, for not having made me a *goy* . . . for not having made me a slave . . . for not having made me a woman." Rabbis try to put a kindly interpretation on this passage, but to be called a *goy* in Israel is an insult. Powerful rabbis in Israel still debate issues such as the circumstances in which a Jew may violate the Sabbath to save the life of a *goy*. Most Israeli Jews would not marry a gentile, and even if they tried it would not be allowed by the rabbis. For two people of different religions to marry, one partner must convert or the couple must wed abroad.

Since the end of the Second World War, Western churches have made strides in seeking reconciliation with Jews. Roman Catholics have removed the term "Perfidious Jew" from the Easter liturgy, the Jewishness of Jesus has been acknowledged, anti-Semitism has been condemned as a sin against God's creation of man in His image, and the Vatican has established diplomatic relations with Israel despite the resistance of the Palestinian Arabs among its flock. Holding the whip hand, Christians rightly had to do the lion's share of reexamining their beliefs, particularly after the Holocaust. In Israel today, however, one struggles to find Orthodox rabbis making an equivalent reevaluation of their perceptions of gentiles. Reform and Conservative movements have tried to formulate a modern set of Jewish beliefs, but they are shut out of public life in Israel, where the Orthodox establishment regards them as little better than *goyim*.

During my years in Israel I have only occasionally encountered racism directed specifically at me, although I witnessed it abundantly heaped on others, particularly Arabs. In contrast, I have received much warmth, such as from my Passover host who gave each of his guests a written message. Mine read: "The guest who feasts with you might perchance be one of the Angels who feasted with Abraham."

★

The Holy Fire is one of the most ancient and yet most pagan of Christian celebrations, a frenzied, ecstatic, and at times violent gathering. It is the high point of the year for the Eastern churches, far more important than Christmas. It is an annual miracle that allows the dwindling community of Christian Arabs in Palestine to feel they still stand taller than the wealthier Western churches.

The devotion of the Eastern churches is what makes the Holy Sepulchre come alive. The conjunction of religious fervor and the ever-present physical danger of crushing, riot, or fire has created a menacing excitement every time I have attended the ceremony.

On the Saturday before Easter Sunday, according to the Eastern calendar, the Holy Fire is said to come down from Heaven to Christ's tomb, where the Greek Patriarch waits to receive it and pass it out to the faithful.

The crowds of Palestinian Christians, supplemented by pilgrims from Greece, Cyprus, Egypt, and Russia, begin to gather from early morning, sometimes staying overnight on Good Friday. Old ladies dressed in black pour water or perfume on the pink slab at the entrance where, it is believed, the body of Jesus was anointed before burial. The liquid, thus saturated with holiness, is soaked back up with a sponge or handkerchief and stored in a bottle to be sprinkled at home, or drunk as a remedy. Some women even rub new underwear over the stone, ready to wear on their funeral day. (Travelers of the nineteenth century complained that pilgrims would turn the church into a brothel in the belief that a child begotten in its precincts would be blessed for the rest of its life.)

By late morning, the tumultuous mass is packed into every cranny of the church. The scaffolding used for the interminable repairs bows dangerously under the weight of young lads who climb up for a better view. The crowd is carefully segregated: Greeks on the right, Armenians, Copts, and other smaller denominations squeezed to the left. Stewards struggle to keep open a passage from the entrance to the elaborate carbuncle which encloses the tomb.

The holiest shrine in Christendom is far from an imposing sight. It is dark, cramped, more like a monk's grotto than the lofty cathedrals of Europe. It is hidden in the souk, its main entrance like the fire exit of a dilapidated cinema. The interior of the church is cluttered with the mosaics, lamps, icons, and sacred pictures of the denominations competing to stake out their slice of territory. Herman Melville's notes had little good to say: "The Holy Sepulchre (No Jews allowed in Church of H.S.)—ruined dome—confused and half-ruinous pile . . . terraces of mouldy grottos, tombs & shrines. Smells like a dead-house." Jerome Murphy O'Connor, author of *The Holy Land*, the unsurpassed archaeological guide to the region, writes: "The frailty of humanity is nowhere more apparent than here; it epitomises the human condition. The empty who come to be filled will leave desolate [. . .] ."

Yet I would not have it any other way. The architecture fits its setting, creating a dark, brooding atmosphere appropriate to the fallen state of Christianity in the Holy Land. Its jumble is like the musty home of a demented pensioner who has kept every kitsch relic of a past life even while the walls of the house are crumbling. There are remains of a lost age: the little crosses carved into the walls by past pilgrims, the sliced and reused columns of Constantine's church and the sword of Godfrey de Bouillon, the first Crusader king. The very ugliness of the church has the fascination of a medieval gargoyle, and the same sense of fear-filled primitive mystery.

In the restless wait, pilgrims hold up bunches of 33 candles, symbolizing the years of Jesus' life. Young men dance on the shoulders of friends and rattle drums to an intricate Arabic beat, chanting: "*Hada qaber saidna!*"—"This is the tomb of our Lord!" It has the same fierce rhythm and cadence of the songs of the Palestinian revolt, and the Israeli police officers charged with keeping order look uncomfortable, tense, before the hostile crowd. At the turn of the century, favorite chants included lines such as "O Jews, O Jews, We are the blood of Christ, You are the blood of monkeys," or "O Jews, O Jews! Your feast is the feast of apes." Occasionally scuffles break out with

Israeli police, but just as frequently the mask of Palestinian brother-hood is dropped and the fight is between Greek and Armenian Christians.

A bit of rough and tumble is part of the pleasure of the Holy Fire. This is football hooliganism in the cloak of religious fervor, and over the centuries events have more than once spun out of control. Turkish soldiers regularly used to search the pilgrims for hidden cudgels and knives. Perhaps the bloodiest incident took place in 1834, as described by the English traveler Robert Curzon:

> The soldiers with their bayonets killed numbers of fainting wretches and the walls were spattered with blood and brains of men who had been felled like oxen, with the butt of the soldiers' muskets. Everyone struggled to defend himself [and] in the melee all who fell were immediately trampled to death by the rest [. . .] I saw full four hundred people dead and living, heaped promiscuously one upon the other, in some places about five feet high.

The climax of the ceremony is heralded by the arrival of the Greek Orthodox Patriarch. He receives dignitaries in the Greek chapel, then dresses in a riot of white and gold and circles the tomb three times with a train of chanting clergy. He finally stops before the entrance to the tomb, which has been sealed with a heap of wax and is guarded by Greek and Armenian clergy. The Patriarch enters with an Armenian bishop, who must wait in an antechamber while the Patriarch alone enters the little tomb. After a suitable dramatic pause to allow the crowd to fall into an expectant hush, a porthole on the side of the tomb glows orange. A thunderous roar resounds within the dome, and hundreds of eager hands press toward the flame which is offered from the tomb. The fire passes from candle to candle, spreading through the crowd like a blazing oil slick, encircling the tomb, spilling through the narrow passages and pouring out through the entrance. Flaming tapers are thrust into your face, wax drips on your clothes and there is the acrid smell and sizzle of singed hair. A cloud of smoke floats upward, soon obscuring the sea of light. Young men link hands to create passages for runners to rush the fire to their respective chapels. In bygone times, a ship would wait in Haifa to receive the fire and take it to Russia.

The origins of the Holy Fire are unknown. Some detect the influence of the Zoroastrian fire ritual, others an echo of the orgiastic spring rites of Dionysus. One of the earliest references to the Holy

Fire is by a ninth-century pilgrim known as Bernard the Monk, who said "an angel comes and kindles the light in the lamps which hang above the sepulchre." The twelfth-century Russian abbot, Daniel, wrote: "The Holy Light is not like any earthly fire for it shines in a different and wonderful way and its flame is red like cinnabar and it shines in a way which is quite indescribable."

The Holy Fire is regarded as a yearly reminder of the central miracle of Christ's resurrection. Jesus here is an eastern Christian: he performs his miracles at the times appointed by the Orthodox church year. The Crusaders celebrated the Holy Fire, but according to Daniel, only the lamps of the Eastern churches were lit. Those placed by the "Frankish" Roman Catholics were disdainfully ignored by God.

The Roman Catholic Church once subscribed to the Holy Fire but later rejected its authenticity. Watching the ceremony impassively from the Latin gallery, one Roman Catholic priest quipped: "The real reason for the fire is the friction between the Greek and the Armenian bishops inside the tomb."

★

The Dome of the Rock glows warmly with the first rays of dawn glinting over the Mount of Olives. On the great plaza of the Haram al-Sharif the faithful rush to take their places as the muezzin calls them to prayer for the start of 'Id al-Adha, the feast of sacrifice, which marks the culmination of Haj pilgrimage to Mecca. Even the singing birds seem to join in the appeal as they turn and glide between the cypress trees.

A chant rumbles from the congregation. It includes part of the Shehadah, the central Muslim declaration of faith, delivered in the slow, relentless incantation typical of this feast: *Allahu Akbar. Allahu Akbar. La ilaha illa-llah* . . . "God is Great. God is Great. There is no God but God . . ." The voice of the multitude filters into the alleys of the Old City, as Palestinian radio, broadcasting the prayer live, seeps out of open windows. In the distance, church bells clang to their own liturgical timetable.

The preacher reminds Muslims to sacrifice an animal in obedience to God and as a reminder of how Abraham's faith won the redemption of Ishmael. They must be generous to the poor, the maimed, orphans, and the womenfolk. It is a strange sermon to non-Muslim ears, because Jews and Christians place Abraham's would-be sacrifice in this precise spot, beneath the Dome of the Rock, but the Muslims praying here believe it happened far away, in Mecca. Islam, declaring itself the final revelation, has remoulded Jewish and Christian traditions, accusing their followers of falsifying God's message.

> Some of the People of the Book wish to mislead you; but they mislead none but themselves, though they may not perceive it. People of the Book! Why do you deny Allah's revelations when you know they are true? People of the Book! Why do you confound the true with the false, and knowingly hide the truth? (Koran 3:65–71)

Islam believes it is the pure faith of Abraham. Solomon, Moses, and Jesus were prophets, but the Jews and Christians disobeyed their teaching. Christian doctrines of the divinity of Jesus and the Trinity are treated as deliberate distortions, as is the story of Jesus' death by crucifixion. In Muslim tradition the crucifixion was either an illusion, or God substituted another man for Jesus on the cross.

In Muhammad's time, as today, the unbelievers, the *kafirun*, are perceived to be eternally plotting against Islam. In historic times the struggle was against the Christians, the Crusades and, later, against western imperialism. Now it is against the Jews.

The concept of a supernatural, Messiah-like savior is not especially strong in Islam. Instead Arabs, in particular Palestinians, have developed a heightened longing for an earthly savior who would restore the unity of Islam and expel the foreigners: a new Saladin to defeat the new (Jewish) Crusaders. "Keep loyal to the faith, and Allah will grant you a great leader who will restore the dignity of the Muslims," said the imam during his sermon on 'Id al-Adha.

The Haram al-Sharif, which until the Ottoman liberalization in the nineteenth century was forbidden to non-Muslims, remains off limits on Fridays. Over the years I have scrambled countless times over the rooftops of the Old City, dodging Israeli policemen and begging forgiveness of families, to find a perch on the wall overlooking the faithful. My trips have usually been a wasted effort in terms of journalism—outbreaks of violence in Jerusalem can rarely be predicted—but I have never regretted the hours passed watching the devotions below me. A full-capacity gathering for Muslim prayers is a majestic scene.

The Haram al-Sharif succeeds in exuding serenity even when jammed with tens of thousands of worshippers. Its open plaza offers relief from the closed, winding paths of the Old City. Its monuments stand out, uncluttered by other buildings. The sight of serried ranks of men bowing to the ground as a single body is a simple yet powerful declaration of the unity of Islam before God.

At the end of the prayer, the Muslim faithful stream out quickly, merging with a group of Italian nuns praying on the Via Dolorosa, armed with cameras and bibles. According to the tradition of paying homage to the dead on major feast days, the crowd makes for a graveyard that lies in front of a curious sealed double gate leading to the Haram al-Sharif. This has been the subject of conflicting legends, including the claims that either Elijah or Jesus will enter the city through here at the End of Days. Muslims are accused (by Christians and Jews) of digging the graveyard in this spot to prevent the Messiah from returning because contact with a cemetery would ritually defile him. Its location, however, has much more to do with the fact that Muslims, like Jews and Christians, place Judgment Day in the ravine below, the Kidron Valley. Islamic tradition says that a sword, narrow bridge, or line will appear between the Haram al-Sharif and the Mount of Olives. The believers will pass safely, while sinners will fall below into the fire of Gehenna.

The relatives of a recently deceased woman offered coffee and sweets to passers-by. Mourning among Palestinians is a very public affair; tradition says that when a Muslim sees a funeral passing by, he should join the procession, read *Al-Fatiha*, the opening verse of the Koran, or perhaps even lend a hand to carry the body for a stretch.

Many placed palm fronds on graves, a symbol of life in the desert which substitutes for flowers in western cemeteries. The royally elegant palm is carried by the Jews during the autumn festival of Sukkot, or the Feast of Tabernacles, and has been adopted by Christians for Palm Sunday. It was a symbol of Judea, and after the Romans crushed the First Revolt, they minted coins depicting a Jewish woman mourning under a palm, watched by a legionnaire, with the inscription JUDAEA CAPTA.

The Muslim Quarter at the time of 'Id al-Adha covers up its glum, embittered face with a veil of cheer. The homes of those who have departed on the Haj are made ready for their imminent return. The façade is painted brilliant white, with multicolored stencilled pictures of the Ka'bah in Mecca, the Dome of the Rock, Islamic crescents, flowers, the name of Allah and a congratulatory message for the pilgrim, henceforth to be addressed with the title "*Haj.*"

The municipality no longer permits animal slaughter in the Old City, but many families manage to smuggle in their beasts. They are often killed by a volunteer butcher, who recites a prayer before slitting the animal's throat. Once the blood has fully drained, compressed air is forced beneath the pelt to separate it from the flesh. The dead beast puffs out like a balloon and its legs straighten. Within minutes the carcass is prepared. One-third will be eaten by the family, another third will be given to relatives and the remainder will be donated to the poor.

Muslims devised feasts such as 'Id al-Adha as a means of redistributing wealth long before Marxism. Alms-giving is a central tenet of Islam and the mosques become the center of a network to collect donations to buy animals and feed needy families. Like Passover, 'Id al-Adha is a festival of the family, or rather the clan. Muslims spend much of the three days of holiday visiting relatives, bringing money to women who have married out of the family and gifts to children.

There is hardly a single Palestinian family that has not been torn apart; relatives have either fled abroad, been deported, or been prevented by Israeli bureaucracy from returning. Travel for a Palestinian is a travail, even at the best of times. A ring of permanent Israeli military checkpoints prevents West Bankers from visiting families in East Jerusalem. Movement in and out of the Gaza Strip is all but impossible. Palestinians adapt as best they can; a member of the family is deputed to travel to Jordan to visit married sisters, or Jerusalemites make the effort to travel out to the West Bank.

For Palestinians, every holiday is a reminder that they are still under occupation, without a homeland; they are, as Jews might put it, still slaves of Pharaoh. In these circumstances, religion becomes the vehicle of protest.

★

In the days of Turkish rule, when there were no internal borders in the Levant, the great flow of pilgrims returning from the Haj often took a detour through Jerusalem. This was the *zyara*, or "visit," and on the road up from the Jordan Valley, the pilgrims would stop at a domed complex in the desert known as Nebi Musa, where Muslims believe Moses was buried. It was part pilgrimage site and part caravanserai.

Here, after the Muslim reconquest of Jerusalem from the Crusaders, Saladin created a new Islamic shrine to counterbalance the weight of Christian visitors to Jerusalem. (Some accounts say it was Sultan Baybars about a century later.) Unlike other Muslim festivals that creep through the seasons, the week-long Nebi Musa celebrations were deliberately timed to coincide with the Orthodox Holy Week, in order to keep a large body of loyal Muslims ready to overcome any subversion by Christians. So the one unique Palestinian gathering was born as a political challenge to foreigners. Claude Regnier Conder, a British army officer, recalled the menacing scene in 1875:

> parties of wild fanatical Muslims paraded the streets of Jerusalem, bearing green banners surmounted with the crescent and inscribed with Arabic texts. A bodyguard armed with battle-axes, spears and long brass-bound guns accompanied each flag, and a couple of big drums with cymbals followed.

The British, when they first arrived in Palestine, did not grasp the subversive potential of Nebi Musa. Sir Ronald Storrs was seduced into thinking that it was "normally a blameless (if rather pointless) event, consisting of a week's sticky holiday by the Dead Sea, with mild feasting, booths of fruit and sweets, and shows ranging from an indelicate variant of Punch and Judy to the circumcision of anxious little boys before a gaping assembly of proud relations." He even provided a British military band to accompany the procession.

Two years after Britain's conquest of Jerusalem, Nebi Musa became the flashpoint of the first major Palestinian riot against British sponsorship of Zionism. It took British forces three days in April 1920 to put down the violence that left several Jews and Arabs dead and hundreds wounded in Jerusalem.

It is no coincidence that in the heat of the political struggle over the future of Jerusalem, the Palestinians have recently revived Nebi Musa. For some years during Israeli rule, the site of Nebi Musa had been given over to a sheikh trying to rehabilitate drug addicts.

In 1998, Sufi mystics stood in a circle, dancing to the jarring sounds of cymbals and drums beneath a forest of large flags decorated with Koranic verses. Stalls sold food, drink, colored eggs, cheap children's toys (guns are a favorite). Family groups were spread out among the bushes, sheltering from the sun under bright tents and sizzling meat on portable grills. Folklore stopped here. The rest was politics.

Inside the white-domed edifice, the Palestinian Authority organized a rally to sing the praises of the *Rais*, or President, Yasser Arafat. Abu Ammar, as he is known, was extolled as the new Saladin in speech after speech. Arafat is not the only claimant to the mantle of Saladin; in Tikrit, President Saddam Hussein's birthplace in Iraq, officials give out booklets depicting Saddam being anointed by Saladin, also a son of the town. The Syrians, meanwhile, have possession of Saladin's burial place in Damascus and have recently restored the tomb near the Omayyad mosque. The legendary humility of Saladin has long been forgotten by the kings and life presidents of the modern Arab world; the noble warrior has been replaced by petty oppressors, while the charger has become the black-tinted Mercedes.

A few dozen men moved from the heat and speeches into a mosque off the main courtyard; the prayer leader was all but drowned out by the razzmatazz outside. The shrine itself, the tomb of Moses covered in Islamic green velvet, is housed in a small room adjoining the mosque.

The Mufti of Jerusalem, Ekrima al-Sabri squatted near the front. "The shrine is not necessarily the real grave, but it is a symbol," he explained. "According to our historical narration, Moses did not enter Palestine." The traditional site of Mount Nebo, where Moses gazed at the Promised Land before dying, lies on a ridge on the opposite side of the Jordan Valley, but according to Deuteronomy, "no man knoweth of his sepulchre unto this day."

"In Islam there is no separation between religion and politics," said the Mufti. "Nebi Musa symbolizes the liberation of Jerusalem from the occupation of the *franj* (Crusaders). It was at the same time as Easter so that the Crusaders would not take advantage of the feast to attack the Holy Land." But why, I asked, should Muslims keep up the tradition when the Crusaders are long gone? "There are no Crusaders, but there is still the West. The West has replaced the Crusaders, and the West supports Israel in its occupation of our country. We consider this another form of Crusader war."

Palestine, for Muslims, is a *waqf*, or Islamic endowment, a sacred possession given in perpetuity. There can never be another sovereignty, and Muslims are duty-bound to fight Israel. "Jews can live here as citizens, but not as rulers," said Al-Sabri.

Islam regards Moses as a preeminent prophet. So what about God's pledge to give the Promised Land to Jews? The Jews, said Al-Sabri, forfeited their right by rejecting God's first order to enter the Promised Land. According to the Book of Numbers, the spies sent to scout the land reported that it "is a land that eateth up the inhabitants thereof; and all the people that we saw in it are men of a great stature. And there we saw the giants . . ." (Num. 13: 32–3).

The Bible and Koran say that, for their disbelief, the Israelites were condemned to wander the wilderness for 40 years. Moses too was forbidden from entering the Promised Land, and died at its threshold. According to Al-Sabri's interpretation of Islam, "God's promise was cancelled. What we have now is the result of the Balfour Declaration, not God's promise. Britain planted Israel here, and the United States is helping Israel."

The Koran accuses both Jews and Christians of failing to listen to God's word, defying the Prophet Muhammad, refusing to accept the new-old faith of Islam and making of it "a jest and pastime." Jews were singled out as accursed:

> You will find that the most implacable of men in their enmity to the faithful are the Jews and the pagans, and that the nearest in affection to them are those who say: "We are Christians." That is because there are priests and monks among them, and because they are free from pride. (5:82)

Still, for most of the centuries of persecution in Christendom, the lands of Islam offered a refuge for Jews until the early years of Zionism, when those fleeing pogroms in Russia made their way to Turkish-ruled Palestine. Like Christians, Jews were "People of the Book" to be treated as *dhimmi*, a status that combined protection with second-class citizenship and a special poll tax. The yellow badge originated in medieval Baghdad. Jews were discriminated against, but rarely persecuted violently.

Judaism and Islam have much in common. They are both religions regulating all aspects of life, rather than just questions of personal faith. They are arguably more strictly monotheistic than Christianity, denying the doctrine of the Trinity, and both impose dietary laws. They devised similar systems of religious jurisprudence. The rabbis' *responsa* were similar in tone to the sheikhs' *fatwa*. In Byzantine and Crusader times, the Jews generally took the side of the Muslims.

The advent of Zionism overturned this mutual tolerance, and Palestinians responded with a double-edged ideological sword, idealizing the Islamic period of coexistence with Jews, while dusting down and reworking the old Islamic polemics against Judaism.

Although Arab historians make clear that Omar Ibn al-Khattab knew he was building the first Al-Aqsa mosque on part of the platform where the Jewish temple had stood, contemporary Muslim leaders vehemently deny there was ever any temple beneath the Al-Aqsa mosque or the Dome of the Rock. The Mufti was adamant: "There is no connection between Al-Aqsa and the temple. It is an illusion."

Al-Sabri admits there was a Jewish temple in Jerusalem, but claims that nobody knows where it is. Why not the Haram al-Sharif, as the Jews and every archaeologist maintain? Al-Sabri offered his clinching argument: "God ordered this mosque to be built. God is just; He would not have built it at the expense of another religion."

★

On the summit of Mount Gerizim, the Samaritans gathered at dusk around a narrow trough, reciting their holy verses in a lost language. The full moon glowed in the east over Jordan. Restless with anticipation, children held down sheep, one for each family. They were dressed in white robes and red fezzes, and were shod incongruously in trainers, boots or slippers.

With a crescendo of the ancestral chant, the sheep were turned over on to their backs and sacrificial knives were slipped through their throats. The animals kicked meekly for a few minutes, until the last flux of life drained out. The men rose with glazed eyes, smearing blood on the foreheads of relatives nearby to the resounding cheer of the audience. The carcasses were skinned and cleaned, impaled on wooden stakes and finally lowered to cook slowly in oven pits dug in the ground.

After the religiously charged atmosphere of Jerusalem, the bloody ritual of the Samaritan Passover sacrifice has the appealing quality of being devoid of political ramifications. It can be enjoyed as a living fossil. The ceremony is one of the few occasions when both Israelis and Palestinians usually stand cordially together, even at times of tension.

The traditional account is that the Samaritans are a remnant of the ten "lost tribes" of the destroyed northern kingdom of Israel; for Palestinians they are harmless "Palestinian Jews" to be protected, demonstrating that Palestinians are not anti-Semitic, only anti-Zionist. The Samaritans enjoy the right to become Israeli citizens, and to have their own representative in the Palestinian legislative council. It is a uniquely privileged position for a tiny community that was once a breath away from extinction.

The Samaritans, made famous by Jesus' parable of the Good Samaritan, were suppressed at different times by Jews, Christians, and Muslims. At the start of British rule in Palestine, they numbered just 146 souls clinging around their holy Mount Gerizim. By 1998 they had expanded to 604.

Upon the creation of Israel, the Samaritans split their bets. Part of the community settled in the new Jewish state, while the rest remained in Nablus, at the foot of Mount Gerizim, under Jordanian rule. Israel's capture of the West Bank in 1967, a disaster for Arabs, was a blessing for Samaritans who were able to reestablish contact between the halves of their people. But the 1993 peace accords between Israel and the Palestinians, which began a process of repartitioning the West Bank, brought the renewed prospect of separation. Samaritans have started a lonely lobby of American and British officials to ensure that their interests are taken into consideration. The Samaritans, said Binyamin Tsedaka, editor of the Samaritan newsletter, "must walk between the raindrops" of Israel, Jordan, and the Palestinians.

The Samaritan sacrifice at Passover is the foundation of the sect's belief. The belief in the holiness of Mount Gerizim is at the core of the long polemic between Samaritans and Jews. Most of the sacred events which Jews place on Mount Moriah in Jerusalem, such as Abraham's preparation to sacrifice Isaac, the Samaritans attribute to Mount Gerizim. Here the Samaritans built a rival temple.

The Bible identifies the mountain as a symbol of God's blessing, opposite the cursed Mount Ebal. In the deep valley between the mountains stands Nablus, close to the site of the biblical Shechem, the natural gateway to Palestine where the Bible says Abraham first entered the land of Canaan and Joseph was buried.

The Bible portrays the Samaritans as a polluted, mixed breed of Israelites and outside settlers brought in by the Assyrians after they destroyed the kingdom of Israel. While adopting the Israelite religion, the Bible writers said, the Samaritans continued to "serve graven images."

The Samaritans say it is the Jews who are the backsliders, while the Samaritans are the true Children of Israel. The Jews, they claim, broke away in the days of the Judges, when the High Priest Eli established a new cultic shrine at Shiloh. The Samaritans recognize only their version of the Torah, the first five books of the Bible, as holy scriptures. Far from having watered down the true Israelite faith, the Samaritans say they observe even more stringent regulations on ritual purity than the Jews. Their name, say the Samaritans, does not derive from the name of Samaria (Hebrew: Shomron) region where they lived, but from *shomerim*, the "keepers" of the true faith.

"We are the most ancient religion in the world," the late High Priest, Yosef Ben Ab-Hisda Ha'abta'ai, told me in Nablus when I met him shortly before he died at the age of 79. By the Samaritans' reckoning, he was the 124th high priest in a distinguished line dating back to the biblical Ithamar, son of Aaron and nephew of Moses.

Here were a people who could, in theory, dispute Israel's ownership of the land on the Jews' own ground of religious argument. But history is written by winners; not losers. "The Jews were smart, but the Samaritans were not," confided one of the High Priest's colleagues, Hosni Wasef. "When attacked, the Jews ran away and scattered. Samaritans believed that the mountain is holy and stayed here. Whenever there was a war, our numbers kept decreasing."

The High Priest bemoaned the Samaritans' main existential problem: an overabundance of men. The sect's members traditionally married among themselves, but necessity forced the sect to allow their young men to take Jewish wives. Samaritan women, however, may not leave the fold. "If a Samaritan woman leaves she can be punished by stoning until she dies. But we don't have the power to impose the penalty, so she is merely excluded from the community and nobody talks to her," said the High Priest.

The Samaritans claim to own the oldest document in the world, a Torah scroll dating from the entry of the Israelites into Canaan, a contention disputed by experts. In 1995, two ancient scrolls were stolen from the Samaritan synagogue in Nablus. The thieves at first demanded a ransom of $7 million and then lowered it to $2 million. They took blindfolded Samaritan representatives through the streets of Amman to view the stolen scriptures. But the community is too poor to pay, and the efforts of Israeli, Jordanian, and Palestinian officials have so far failed to turn up the criminals or the scrolls.

The High Priest was still perturbed by the theft. "We have no power, except to pray to God to guide the ones who took them to bring them back." As I left, he solemnly reminded me of the story of the Samaritan woman who gave Jesus water at Jacob's Well (John 4:9). He added: "It is a debt which every Christian must pay back."

One of the few sources of income for the Samaritans in Nablus is gained from acting as unofficial fortune-tellers and sorcerers for Palestinians. A surprising number of people come to the Samaritans to try to solve their problems, obtain charms, and cast curses upon their enemies. It may be a reputation born from the belief that any people who can survive for so long in such wretched conditions must possess magic powers. Samaritans claim the secret of divining the future was handed down from Joseph, who interpreted Pharaoh's dream and predicted the famine that would grip Egypt.

The High Priest professed neutrality between the Israelis and

Palestinians, but admitted to a fondness for the former Jordanian rulers. King Hussein, he recalled, found jobs for all the Samaritans.

"We are weak; we are small," said the High Priest. "If we support the Palestinians it would not help them. If we support the Israelis it would not help them. We concern ourselves with practicing our religion."

3

Every Man Under His Vine

THE WINERY OF Rishon Le-Zion is an oddity. Standing at a major intersection in the center of Israel's fourth-largest city, the somber brick edifice looks more like a Victorian factory than a French *château*. There are no graceful vineyards to be seen anywhere: they were ripped up long ago to make way for urban sprawl. Today the grapes are grown on the hills farther inland and brought to the Carmel Mizrahi winery. As the village of Rishon Le-Zion expanded into a city, the winery was left stranded in the midst of rows upon rows of charmless concrete blocks of flats.

Carmel's winemakers perform their task of aging and blending the vintages enveloped in the delicate bouquet of motorcar fumes seeping over the outside walls. In the cavernous cellars, dug to keep the fermenting juices cool in their large vats, a guide whispered to me in a solemn tone: "Tradition says we cannot speak loudly because the wine is resting." The wine, it seems, has become accustomed to the rumble of traffic on nearby Herzl Street.

It was a quick tour of the plant, because many of the production facilities were out of bounds, to preserve the all-important kosher stamp. "The whole process is controlled by Orthodox Jews," explained my guide. "We must cook the wine at 55 or 60 degrees centigrade, and we are not allowed to eat in the winery. Every seven years, we must let the vineyards rest."

Carmel is the largest winery in Israel. Although newer and more prestigious vintages have emerged elsewhere in the country, Carmel is a national institution. When Israeli Jews gather to celebrate Passover and chant "Next Year in Jerusalem," many do so over Carmel wine. Even in the Diaspora, the four cups of wine representing the four expressions of redemption in Exodus will often be poured out of a bottle of Carmel. The presence of an Israeli wine at the seder table is living proof that the longed-for ingathering of the exiles is indeed under way.

Carmel wine is as much a symbol of Zionist enterprise as the Jaffa orange or the Uzi submachine-gun. The winery was built by Baron Edmond de Rothschild to provide an economic base for early settlements, including Rishon Le-Zion, which in 1882 was the first community to be founded by Zionist immigrants.

The love and regard with which the baron is held in Rishon Le-Zion and the rest of Israel is not entirely reciprocated by some of his descendants. A few years ago, a guide told me, the Carmel winery brought out a new collection of higher-quality wines but was forced to drop the word "Rothschild" from the label after objections from French members of the family who feared it would harm the reputation of their own fine Bordeaux wines.

In its time, the winery was said to be the second largest in the world. Its vintages were sold mainly to diaspora Jews under exotic labels such as *Vins des Côteaux de Judée*, and even won prizes in Paris at the turn of the century. Indeed, Herzl had optimistically predicted in *Altneuland* that the soil of Palestine would one day produce fine wines and cigars. Viticulture, and the baron's munificence, allowed these settlers to fulfil the prophecy that "they shall sit every man under his vine and under his fig tree" (Micah 4: 4).

The baron at first did not want his philanthropy to be publicized and became known simply as *Ha-Nadiv ha-Yadua*, the "Well-Known Benefactor." He soon took several other settlements under his wing, and the development of Jewish colonies in Palestine would become the largest expression of his philanthropy, surpassing his financing of the Louvre in Paris. It was such nurture which allowed the fledgling colonies to survive, beginning an unbroken tradition of wealthy diaspora Jews supporting Zionist endeavors. "Without me, the Zionists could have done nothing; but without the Zionists, my work would have been dead," the baron said in his later years.

Diaspora Jews provide tens of millions of dollars a year to Israel. All over the country, park benches, municipal buildings, hospitals, and even individual ambulances bear the names of their donors. The name of the main square in Jerusalem was effectively sold to the Safra banking family in return for a $10 million donation for the city's new municipal offices. Strangely, there is little tradition of charity within Israel itself.

Rishon Le-Zion, "First in Zion," refers to the Book of Isaiah's herald of "good tidings" for Jerusalem (Isa. 41: 27). The city, moreover, was home to the first Hebrew kindergarten and elementary school, the first Hebrew orchestra and, initially, the Jewish National Fund. The town claims to be the place where the Israeli flag was first flown and where the national anthem was set to music. In modern Israel, however, Rishon Le-Zion has lost its prominence to Jerusalem, the spiritual and political capital; to Tel Aviv, the business and cultural heartland; and Haifa, the industrial core of Israel and the country's main harbor. Rishon Le-Zion is now merely a satellite town in Tel Aviv's metropolitan sprawl.

It is a pleasant enough city, with a charming central park outside the winery that includes an avenue lined with palms from the Canary Islands, the remains of an agricultural station where early settlers experimented with crops such as tobacco, cotton, mulberry, almonds, and eucalyptus. At one end of the main artery, inevitably called Rothschild Street, stands the great synagogue, built as a "warehouse" to deceive suspicious Turkish officials. Its façade displays a simple elegance rarely matched in Israeli architecture. A few of the first settlers' sandstone homes are still standing, some in a state of disrepair, others lovingly restored as a museum.

Not everybody is pleased with the city's development. Coming out of the municipal archive armed with the memoirs of one of Rishon Le-Zion's founders, Aharon Mordechai Freiman, I ran into the author's great-granddaughter, Miriam Atzmon, who still lived in one of the original houses. She radiated that mixture of hardness and sadness that is so common to Israeli women.

"Rishon Le-Zion has changed incredibly since I was a child. Everyone used to know everyone else," she explained. "But then came the immigrants from Morocco and Yemen, and now you have the Russians. The city has become too big and noisy." Her complaint was, in Zionist terms, a curse of abundance—too many Jews, too much development. For the founders, the arrival of the smallest trickle of Jews from the remote corners of the world was not a cause of annoyance, but of wonder. Her great-grandfather's memoirs, an often ponderous account of the first 25 years of the community, filled with statistics on agricultural production, suddenly come to life when describing the arrival of newcomers:

Hundreds of young families, poor or wealthy, are setting out for the Holy Land, to work it and to guard it, to earn their daily bread peaceably by the sweat of their brow by working the land of their estate. [. . .] It is only the sacred ideal, to bring the land of our forefathers back to life and raise it from its humiliation—this alone unites these [people] who are distant from and strange to one another, and so new communities are being born in Eretz Israel. We see how great is the strength of the sacred notion of settling the Land of Israel.

★

The story of Rishon Le-Zion, and that of modern Israel, begins a world away from the Mediterranean shores of Palestine. It starts in Russia.

In the nineteenth century, roughly half of the Jews in the world lived in Russia's so-called Pale of Settlement, a large swathe of territory running roughly from the Baltic to the Black Sea. The winds of European enlightenment and Jewish emancipation were being felt in Russia, though more feebly and with more turbulent crosscurrents than in western Europe. Jews were beginning to pull away from the passive and secluded traditionalism of the rabbis to pursue a secular education, seeking to join the stream of world thought.

The impact of the industrial revolution was propelling secularized Jews to both extremes of the spectrum. They were to be found prominently among both capitalists and socialist revolutionaries. Moreover, ideas of modern nationalism inspired by the successes of Italians, Germans, and Greeks stirred the long-held messianic longing for a return to the Land of Israel.

Two rabbis, Yehuda Alkalai and Tzvi Hirsch Kalischer, separately challenged the belief that Jews should wait patiently for the Messiah to gather them back to the land of their forefathers.

Alkalai, born in Sarajevo in 1798, was appointed rabbi to the town of Semlin, in Serbia, in 1825. There he saw how the Greeks had won their independence from Turkey, while other nationalities in the Balkans were also rising up against their Ottoman overlords. In 1839 he started to publish a succession of semimystical pamphlets calling for a large-scale return. Like Jacob, who bought a parcel of land near Shechem, Jewish magnates should rent the Land of Israel from the Sultan of Turkey. He advocated restoration of the Hebrew language and the creation of an assembly of elders to lead the community.

By extracting the mystical numerical secrets supposedly embedded in the biblical text, Alkalai concluded that at least 22,000 Jews should return to the Holy Land "as a necessary preparation for a descent of the Divine Presence among us." He organized small circles of followers as far away as London and settled in Palestine as an example to others, but his efforts had little impact. However, his followers included Herzl's grandfather, Simon Loeb Herzl, who may have planted a seed of the return in the mind of the future father of Zionism.

At around the same time in the Polish-speaking city of Thorn, in East Prussia, Kalischer was witnessing the Poles' struggle for independence from Russia. In 1836, he wrote to a member of the Rothschild dynasty that the redemption will not come by divine intervention, but "by human effort and the will of governments." In 1862, he completed his principal work, *Drishat Zion* ("Seeking Zion"), which argued:

> The Almighty, Blessed be His Name, will not suddenly descend from on high and command His people to go forth. He will not send the Messiah from heaven in a twinkling of an eye, to sound the great trumpet for the scattered of Israel and gather them into Jerusalem. He will not surround the Holy City with a wall of fire or cause the Holy Temple to descend from the Heavens. [. . .] On the contrary, the Redemption will begin by awakening support among the philanthropists and by gaining the consent of the nations to the gathering of some of the scattered of Israel into the Holy Land.

Kalischer advocated the creation of agricultural colonies and was instrumental in pressing the Alliance Israélite Universelle, a French Jewish institution of philanthropy, to provide the initial subsidy to found the Jewish agricultural school of Mikveh Israel, "Hope of Israel," on the outskirts of Jaffa in 1870.

In the same year as the publication of *Drishat Zion*, in the cosmopolitan environment of Paris, Moshe Hess, a socialist intellectual who associated with Karl Marx and Friedrich Engels, had just rediscovered his Jewish roots. Born of an Orthodox family in Cologne in 1821, Hess abandoned his faith and married a prostitute, in part to atone for the sins of bourgeois society. In his book, *Rome and Jerusalem*, published in 1862, he declared: "After twenty years of estrangement I have returned to my people. Once again I am sharing in its festivals of joy and days of sorrow, in its hopes and memories."

Hess, outraged by a blood libel against Jews which had surfaced in Damascus in 1840, steadily abandoned his belief that Jews and other people would become subsumed into a single humanity. Nations, he now thought, had unique traits and missions to fulfil. Jews, he said, "shall always remain strangers among the nations" and he believed that:

A great calling is reserved for the Jews: to be a living channel of communication between the continents. You shall be the bearers of civilization to peoples who are still inexperienced and their teachers in the European sciences, to which your race has contributed so much. You shall be the mediators between Europe and far Asia, opening the roads that lead to India and China—those unknown regions which must ultimately be opened to civilization. You will come to the land of your fathers decorated with the crown of age-long martyrdom, and there, finally, you will be completely healed from all your ills!

Rome and Jerusalem prefigured many Zionist doctrines but the book found no English translator for fifty years. Alkalai, Kalischer, and Hess, in their different ways, were crying in the wilderness. They wrote in the heyday of liberalism, when the outlook for Jews throughout Europe seemed bright. The early Zionist writers tried to pull Jews toward the ancient land. But for Zionism to capture the popular imagination, Jews would have to be pushed by the resurgence of anti-Semitism.

★

On the first of March, 1881, Tsar Alexander finally ran out of luck. After surviving several assassination attempts by anarchists—including attempts to shoot him, derail his train, and even blow up the Winter Palace in St. Petersburg—the Tsar was killed by a bomb thrown at his carriage. Power passed from the reforming Tsar, who had emancipated the serfs and lifted some of the burdens on Jews, to his son, Alexander III, who promptly rolled back his father's liberal reforms.

A campaign of subjugation of all non-Russian nationalities, with particular attention to the Jews, ensued. The bombers were arrested: some bore Jewish names. Anti-Jewish riots broke out in several towns of southern Russia, where Jews were most assimilated into the Russian culture. The violence consisted mainly of looting, but there were some instances of murder and rape. Similar violence broke out the following year. The indifference, even sympathy for the mobs, of the Tsarist authorities as well as Russian intellectuals shocked many of the modernizing Jews, who had dared to believe that the oppression of the Middle Ages was ending. The Russian word for these communal riots, *pogrom*, or "devastation," became part of the political vocabulary. A series of anti-Jewish decrees known as the "May Laws," passed in 1882, closed off rural areas to Jews and curtailed their numbers in schools and universities, while Jews were driven out of the professions.

Russian Jews were at a turning point. Moshe Leib Lilienblum, a teacher in a yeshiva who lost his religious faith and became a socialist, spent two days in a cellar cowering from the Russian mobs. It was a revelation which made him abandon the Haskalah (the Jewish "Enlightenment" that sought to merge secular studies with Hebrew romanticism) and with it the belief in the power of modern culture to improve the lot of Jews in Russian society. Saying "all my ideals left me in a flash," he dedicated himself to Zionism. In his diary, he recounted his experience of the unrest in Odessa in 1881: "I am glad I have suffered. At least once in my life I have had the opportunity of feeling what my ancestors felt every day of their lives."

The following year Leo Pinsker, a distinguished physician in Odessa who fought with the Russian army during the Crimean War, also lost faith in Russian tolerance. In his pamphlet, *Auto-Emancipation*, he argued that anti-Semitism was an incurable illness. Judaism and anti-Semitism were inseparable.

> Among the living nations of the earth the Jews occupy the position of a nation long since dead. [. . .] This ghost-like apparition of a people without any unity or organization, without land or other bond of union, no longer alive, and yet moving about among the living—this eerie form scarcely paralleled in history, unlike anything that preceded or followed it, could not fail to make a strange impression upon the imagination of the nations.

To escape persecution, Jews must find a country, anywhere in the world, where they could have asylum. Pinsker's work captured the emotions of the moment. It galvanized the disparate Jewish Zionist study circles known as *Hovevei Zion*, or "Lovers of Zion." Modeled on other European nationalist movements, these semi-secret groups emerged in the late 1870s and offered courses in Hebrew language and Jewish history. Others organized self-defense groups.

In 1884 Pinsker convened the founding conference of the Lovers of Zion, who established their central offices in Odessa and sought to encourage practical settlement in Palestine. Among the delegates to the conference was Natan Birnbaum, who in 1890 first coined the word "Zionism," a term based on the poetic name for Jerusalem, to describe the political movement for the establishment of a Jewish state.

Theodor Herzl, a 22-year-old law student in Vienna at the time of the Jewish upheavals in Russia, was blissfully ignorant of Pinsker or any other Zionist writings. A frustrated playwright and dandy, he carried an ebony-handled stick. As a boy he had fantasized about building the Panama Canal. Now he felt twinges of anger at the anti-Semitism which was budding in the West. In 1883 he resigned from Albia, a German student society, when its members rowdily endorsed Wagner's anti-Semitism at a memorial meeting to mark the composer's death in Venice.

It would take several more years to shake Herzl out of his complacency and convince him that anti-Semitism could not be eradicated from Europe, not even from republican France. Within a year of the 1895 Dreyfus scandal, Herzl published *The Jewish State*, calling for an organized mass emigration of Jews from Europe to a new state.

Herzl read Leo Pinsker's *Auto-Emancipation* for the first time just before *The Jewish State* was about to be distributed. Startled by the "dumbfounding agreement" with his own work, he noted, "it is a good thing I knew nothing of it—or perhaps I might have abandoned my own undertaking."

Chaim Weizmann, the first President of Israel, who was then a Russian student in Berlin, recalled that the very term, "the Jewish state," "came like a bolt from the blue." Weizmann wrote that "fundamentally, *The Jewish State* contained not a single new idea for us," but Russian Jews were captivated by Herzl's personality. "What has given greatness to his name is Herzl's role as a man of action, as the founder of the Zionist Congress, and as an example of daring and devotion," noted Weizmann.

The pogroms of 1881–82 set in motion a vast movement of Jews seeking to escape poverty and discrimination. Between 1881 and the outbreak of the First World War in 1914, a total of some 2.75 million Jews are estimated to have migrated, mostly from Russia, but also from the eastern regions of Austria-Hungary and Romania. The vast majority went to the United States where they accounted for about 11 percent of immigrants. In 1894, the Tsar's chief adviser, Konstantin Pobedonostsev, explained how the Jewish problem would be solved: "One third will die out. One third will leave the country and one third will be completely dissolved in the surrounding population."

The new exodus had started from the land of affliction in Russia, but for most Jews the Promised Land was America, not the Land of Israel. Only a small proportion—about 2–3 percent of the migrants—went to the ancestral land, the fourth-favorite destination after the United States, Canada, and Argentina. For all the intellectual ferment, Zionist ideals had clearly not had much practical effect on the Jews of eastern Europe.

Between 55,000 and 70,000 Jews settled in Palestine in two waves, known in Israeli history as the First Aliyah and the Second Aliyah. It was the largest influx of Jews to the Holy Land since the expulsion from Spain in 1492. Many early immigrants went to the traditional holy cities to lead a life of religious dedication. Many others reemigrated, disappointed by the physical and economic hardships of living in Palestine. The remaining group were the hard core of pioneers who created the new Jewish agricultural colonies: the founding fathers of Israel who became the stuff of Zionist legend.

They are the giants of Israel's past, even if in their time they were virtual unknowns. As in the Homeric epics, their deeds have been romanticized to create a bygone age of heroic innocence, merging the raw adventure of the pioneers in the New World with the ancient longing for the restoration of Israel nearly 2,000 years after the destruction of the temple by Titus' legions.

★

For Zalman David Levontin, a bank clerk in Kremenchug, in what is now the Ukraine, a personal affront at a hotel in Kharkov in April 1881 changed the course of his life. A hotel attendant told him bluntly he could not extend his stay. "Sorry, sir. I cannot permit you to stay here, the orders of the Chief of Police regarding Jews are very firm," Levontin recalled in his memoirs.

The 25-year-old Levontin boarded a train home, unable to forget the incident. "Questions began to scuttle round inside me and demand solution," he wrote in his diary. "What makes Kharkov so holy and what is my crime that I have been forced to leave the city at night before I could finish my business there? Why can this heavy, pot-bellied man sitting here opposite me in the railway carriage stay in the hotel in Kharkov as long as he likes, and why am I less than him—less even than the drunken servant in the hotel?"

When he got out at a station for a breath of fresh air, he heard fellow passengers discussing a pogrom at Yelizavetgrad (later Kirovograd), the first in the wave of anti-Jewish violence which started that year. He felt that "salt has been rubbed into the wounds of my heart." Back on the train, Russians discussed the pogrom approvingly.

Arriving home, news reached the Jewish community of violence spreading to other towns. Many Jews decided they must leave, but, Levontin said, they were divided over whether to go to the "land of liberty and freedom" in America, or to Palestine and "pitch our tents among the sons of Shem, in that country where we were born and became a people."

Even as a boy Levontin, the son of a Hasidic family who was nevertheless tutored privately in secular studies and languages, wondered why freed American slaves had been able to establish Liberia in their African homeland but Jews could not recreate their ancient kingdom. He once suggested in a Hebrew newspaper that 50 families should found a settlement in Palestine to "lay a cornerstone for the settlement of the Land of Israel." Now he resolved to take action.

Levontin founded an association of 15 families which agreed to move to the Holy Land. Levontin was chosen to go to Palestine to scout a suitable plot of land, and the others would follow. He created a similar group in Kharkov, where Jews were about to declare a fast—a traditional plea for mercy in times of trouble—to appeal for help from "Israel's Rock and Redeemer."

Armed with letters of introduction and filled with hope, he set off for the Holy Land at his own expense. His ship dropped anchor off Jaffa in the spring of 1882. He was astounded to discover that he could not find, as he had expected, any like-minded Jews.

It is said that Levontin used to seek recruits by standing on the docks at Jaffa and shouting *Shalom Aleichem* to arriving passengers. If any replied *Aleichem Shalom*, thus identifying themselves as Jews, he would try to persuade them to join his project. Visiting Jerusalem, he was upset by the constant religious infighting in which "quarrels and squabbles are borne heavenwards by the blasts of the shofar" and decided to return to Jaffa, "far from the battlegrounds of the zealots." The mutual antagonism of Zionists and the religious establishment was already apparent.

Levontin, now joined by Yosef Feinberg, the son of wealthy parents, who studied chemistry at Swiss and German universities, tried at first to buy land in the Gaza area, deeming it cheaper and an easier place to establish a large settlement. They met Christoph Hoffmann, leader of the Templers, and learned of the countless difficulties the German Christian sect had endured in setting up its four separate communities in Palestine.

By the summer, after a number of failed transactions, Levontin and his small band of supporters found a tract of land south of the village of Beit Dajan, in an area known as Ein Kara. Levontin was reluctant to buy it, fearing that it lacked water despite its biblical association: at En-hakkore, "The Spring of the One Who Called," God had brought forth a spring to quench the thirst of Samson after he had slain a thousand Philistines with the jawbone of an ass (Judges 15: 18). However, Levontin yielded before the enthusiasm of his comrades.

With his group, Levontin took half of the roughly 3,000-dunam acquisition (approx. 670 acres), while the other half was bought by his uncle, Tzvi, who gave his share to six poor families on generous terms. The settlers drew up their objectives in verbose articles of association. These included pledges "to serve as an example to our Israelite brothers who come to lay claim to the Holy Land," "to rebuild the ruins of our nation," "to walk in the way of our Torah," and to observe religious requirements concerning living in the Land of Israel. The members, initially a cooperative, vowed "to do their utmost to do away with silk clothes and all manner of jewelery, even on the Sabbath and holidays, and to forgo all luxury which wastes the money of Israel."

At the end of July 1882, about half a dozen of the group set out with two horses and a cart loaded with tents and other essential equipment. "In sacred awe and gaiety of spirit we left the town of Jaffa and set forth for our estate," recalled Levontin, who arrived first. That evening, as he waited at the top of the hillock where Rishon Le-Zion's Great Synagogue now stands, he lay down on his coat and contemplated the stars. He was seized by elation and doubts at the same time.

> I recalled heroic Samson who fought the Philistines here and who smote them with the jaw-bone, I remembered the blood of my forefathers which had been spilt here, and on whose graves I had perhaps spread my overcoat. I felt a great love for the place, the love of a son, long exiled from his father, who has finally returned home, only to find his father absent. Tears ran from my eyes, and my soul and my heart turned over within me. This was my home and resting place, my cradle, the cradle of my childhood—I felt this even in the dead of night. But my brothers—where were my brothers? Would the day dawn when they would come from the ends of the earth? [. . .] What

strength would I have to devote myself to this idea when my pockets were empty? Could a hand, till now accustomed only to holding a pen and calculating profit and loss, now guide a plow and extract a living from the soil, for myself, for my wife and my children? Was I to sacrifice those dearest to me on the altar of this ideal? Did I have the right to do so—and if I did, would it benefit anyone?

Levontin's servant interrupted this train of thought. He pointed to some bedouin tents in the distance and said: "When you build your houses and settle here [. . .] dozens of horsemen will come in the dark of night [. . .] to plunder and murder." Levontin replied that the Jews would not stand idly by:

We have come here to enjoy the rights of this country, which does not discriminate between its inhabitants, and if anyone should wickedly show us his fists, then we'll show him that we too have fists, and rifles and daggers and spears.

*

Amos Elon's classic portrait of the country *The Israelis—Founders and Sons*, published in 1971, portrays the first settlers as naïve romantics, "innocents at home" who were only dimly aware of the presence of Arabs and ignorant of their potential hostility. Palestine was, according to a common dictum, "a land without a people for a people without a land." From Levontin's own account, however, it is apparent that on the first day of the first Zionist settlement the Jews already sensed that they would have to fight to stay on the land.

Levontin kept his land-buying mission a secret from Arabs. And when the Turkish authorities banned settlement by Jews, the transaction for Ain Kara was made in the name of the British Vice-consul in Jaffa, Haim Amzalak, a Sephardi Jew from Gibraltar.

The Ottoman empire was acutely sensitive to foreign scheming in Palestine. From the reports of its diplomats, the Sublime Porte (the Ottoman government) was far from ignorant of the stirring Jewish nationalism. In the catalogues of the Ottoman foreign ministry, researchers have found a file entitled: "Situation of the Jews; Question of their immigration into Turkey: 1881." Even before the start of the First Aliyah, the Ottoman government had decided that Jews could settle in scattered groups throughout the empire, but *not* in Palestine.

It tried, ineffectively, to impose entry restrictions and ban the sale of land to Jewish settlers. Having engaged in four wars with Russia in the nineteenth century alone, the Sublime Porte was naturally wary of a large influx of Russian immigrants, Jewish or otherwise.

This was the era of the Capitulations, when European powers infringed upon Ottoman sovereignty by taking upon themselves the task of protecting foreigners and minorities such as Roman Catholics, Orthodox Jews, and Druze through their consuls. Palestine was being built, settled, measured, and excavated by a myriad of foreigners. The last thing the Sultan needed was the implantation of another nationalist minority in the bosom of the empire after the loss of the European provinces in a succession of national uprisings and wars, as well as Britain's take-over of Egypt.

The Porte had been approached directly at various times in the past with schemes for the settlement of Jews in its domains, such as the plan presented in 1879 by the British writer and traveler, Laurence Oliphant, to create a Jewish enclave on the east bank of the River Jordan. In 1882, Oliphant again tried to win the authorities in Constantinople over to his scheme, raising hopes among a group of lovers of Zion. They were known as *Bilu*, a Hebrew acronym for the first words of the biblical exhortation in Isaiah, "O house of Jacob, come ye, and let us walk (in the light of the Lord)" (Isa. 2: 5). Bilu members set out for Palestine in the summer of 1882, shortly after Levontin.

When part of the contingent, numbering just 14 souls, set sail from Constantinople for Jaffa, the Porte issued orders to its governor in Jerusalem forbidding Russian, Romanian, and Bulgarian Jews from landing at Jaffa or Haifa—a restriction which settlers could usually overcome by distributing baksheesh to local officials. Some of the *Biluim* trained at the Mikveh Israel agricultural school, then joined Levontin at Rishon Le-Zion as hired laborers. With time, the *Biluim* would found their own settlements.

Zeev Dubnow, a Bilu member living in Jerusalem, wrote to his brother in 1882: "The ultimate aim is to build up this land of Israel and restore to the Jews the political independence that has been taken from them for the past two thousand years. [. . .] The Jews, with weapons in their hands if necessary, will announce with a loud voice that they are masters in their ancient land."

Arabs were hired to build the first houses of Rishon Le-Zion, and the Jewish newcomers startled their Arab neighbors by using camels to pull a cart to carry water from the village of Beit Dajan. Soon relations with the Arabs were put to the test. When Arabs were found grazing their flocks on the colony's fields, Levontin gathered half a dozen armed men and rode out to confront the "trespassers," capturing two Arabs and five animals.

The threat to send the Arab shepherds to Jaffa for trial apparently brought a guarantee from the elders of the nearby village of Sarafand that such incidents would not be repeated. By this firm action, said Levontin, "we suffered no farther loss from that day on [. . .] and our brothers live in peace and amity with their Arab neighbors."

Perhaps so. But Haim Hisin, a Bilu settler, recalled that within a few months at Rishon Le-Zion, intellectual pursuits faded away and "we were now better at wielding our fists than the pen."

Within five years of the creation of Rishon Le-Zion, nine Jewish colonies had been founded. Disputes with Arabs, large and small, cropped up almost everywhere. In 1886, for instance, in Petach Tikva a drawn-out dispute over pasture land turned violent when Arab peasants attacked the colony, killing a woman and injuring five others.

Were these "passing incidents" and ordinary "banditry," as Israeli writers have long maintained? Or were they the first stirrings of Arab resistance to the encroachment of foreigners? The difficulty in trying to reconstruct events of the late nineteenth century is that the Jewish newcomers, aware that they had embarked on a historical mission and inspired by the biblical tradition of preserving the memory of sacred events, were vigorous writers of letters and diaries, while there is a dearth of first-hand Arab accounts of the period.

The Jewish settlers left countless stories of their hopes and hardships. Aharon Freiman, in his account of the first years of Rishon Le-Zion, quotes the biblical injunction about the importance of memory: "Remember the days of old, consider the years of many generations: ask thy father, and he will shew thee; thy elders, and they will tell thee." The settlers frequently wrote in a wooden style, not helped by the limitations of Hebrew in the early phase of its revival, but such defects were more than made up for by their immediacy: for example the story of one of the first people to be killed in Rishon Le-Zion. The local *mikveh*, or Jewish ritual bath, doubled as the colony's bath-house. On Thursdays a large rock, which was heated over burning coals for four days, would be rolled into the water to warm it up. One day, however, a woman blinded by the steam slipped and fell into the boiling water and, despite being treated with egg whites, died from her burns within days.

The largely illiterate Arab peasants left few written records and Arab governments, in general, have not opened up their state archives. Oral traditions are by now colored by the hindsight of a century of conflict with Zionism and decades of nationalist myth-making. The Arabs of the period are an anonymous, voiceless mass, easily dismissed with broad generalizations by the propagandists of Zionism and the prejudices of European travelers. The field of Palestinian studies, moreover, has been dominated by Israeli and Jewish scholars, while Palestinian academics have only recently started to make up the lost ground. Even they concede that most basic reference works on Ottoman Palestine—the period when Palestinian nationalist identity began to emerge, at least among Arab intellectuals—have been written by Israelis.

If in 1882 Arabs in Palestine had not yet developed a sense of nationalism in the modern sense of the word, they were conscious of a special quality of the Holy Land. There was a budding local patriotism. Devotional books, known as *Fada'il al-Quds* or "Merits of Jerusalem," extolled the virtues of the Holy City and the surrounding towns. Saladin's expulsion of the Crusaders from Jerusalem remained a proud and vivid memory, while the legacy of the Crusades created a deep wariness of Europeans, who were generally regarded with a mixture of suspicion and awe.

Backward, oppressed, malarial as it may have been, Palestine in the nineteenth century was certainly not empty. After the pacification of the countryside in the middle decades of the century, Arab peasants had started to come down from the relative safety of their mountain villages into the coastal plain. By the time Levontin landed in Jaffa, the population of Palestine was expanding rapidly, from about 350,000 in 1865 to about 470,000 in 1882. The Jewish population numbered around 24,000.

Economic activity was developing quickly as the Levant joined the world economy. For a country that was often described as half-dead, ruined and cursed, Palestine managed to export considerable agricultural surpluses—wheat, barley, sesame, olive oil, soap, fruit and vegetables and, especially in the latter decades of the century, Jaffa oranges. The region's most important export markets were France, England, Italy, and Egypt. The pilgrim trade, moreover, brought revenue and established a local service industry.

Ahad Ha'am, the champion of a form of Zionism which gave priority to Hebrew cultural revival over immediate and haphazard settlement, published a trenchant account of the state of the Jewish colonies in 1891. In *Truth from the Land of Israel* he wrote:

> We abroad are used to believing that Eretz Israel is now almost totally desolate, a desert that is not sowed, and that anyone who wishes to purchase land there may come and purchase as much as he desires. But in truth this is not the case. Throughout the country it is difficult to find fields that are not sowed. . . . But, if the time should come when our brothers' life in the Land of Israel develops to such an extent that it encroaches in any degree upon the lives of the Arabs, they will not give way easily.

The Tanzimat reforms of 1839–76, which sought to modernize the Ottoman empire, also led to changes in land tenure which allowed the wealthy families of Arab "notables" to acquire large estates in the coastal plain and valleys. It was mainly these estates that the Zionist movement would steadily acquire.

The Zionists had the greatest difficulty in establishing a presence in the mountainous historical heartland of Judea and Samaria, the present-day West Bank, where Arab peasant villagers retained control of their land under a communal system of ownership known as *musha*. British administrators saw this small-scale farming as an obstacle to modern agricultural development, but in the long term it preserved the hill region as a core of Arab presence on the land.

The establishment of Jewish settlements upset traditional Arab patterns of land usage whereby villagers, for instance, enjoyed customary grazing rights on land which was not formally owned by them. With time, the sale of land by absentee Arab landlords to Jews meant the dislocation of a growing number of Arab tenant farmers, whose plight fired the emerging nationalism of educated Arabs in the cities. As early as 1870, Arabs in the village of Yazur protested about the sale of land to Mikveh Israel.

The idea of an empty land ready for Jewish colonization was not so much a question of innocence as of European chauvinism. The "invisibility" of the Arabs was self-serving. Palestine at the time of the first Zionist settlement was not empty of people, but of people deemed worthy by Europeans of controlling their own country.

The second half of the nineteenth century may have been springtime for nations in Europe, but elsewhere it was still an age of empire. At the time of the founding of Rishon Le-Zion, the scramble for

Africa was only just starting, the Russian empire was reaching its high point of expansion into Asia, and the Ottoman empire was being carved up. The frontier in the American interior was just disappearing.

It was in this climate that Herzl sought to secure a charter for Jewish colonization guaranteed by one or other imperial European power. His record of his experiences during his visit to the Jewish colonies in Palestine is telling of the perceptions of the period. His delegation was met near Rishon Le-Zion by a cavalcade of Jews singing Hebrew songs. They had come from the nearby settlement of Rehovot. The visitors were impressed, recounted Herzl: "We had tears in our eyes when we saw those fleet, daring horsemen, and the proof that our young clothes-peddlers can be thus transformed. Hedad! [Hurrah!] They cried, and dashed away across the fields on their little Arab horses. I was reminded of the Far West cowboys of the American plains whom I once saw in Paris."

However, the colony's early ideals of communal life had to be jettisoned in favor of Baron Rothschild's strict economic criteria. "Fear of Monsieur le Baron hovers over all of them. The poor colonists have swapped one fear for another," wrote Herzl. He was given a frank assessment by the physician of the colony:

> Fever! All of the colonies suffer from fever. Only large-scale drainage operations and the elimination of swamps, he said, could make the country habitable. This is also my view and intention. It will cost billions, but create billions of new wealth! Such Arabs as are immune from fever might be employed to do the work.

Such was Herzl's only thought for the Arabs of Palestine: they would become, like the ancient Gibeonites of the Bible, the hewers of wood and drawers of water. The following year, Herzl received one of the first recorded Arab protests through the Chief Rabbi of Paris, Zadok Kahn. It was a letter from Yusuf Diya al-Khalidi, a veteran liberal member of the first Ottoman parliament.

Zionism was, in theory, a just idea, he agreed. "My God, historically it is certainly your country," he wrote. But the reality was that Palestine was an integral part of the Ottoman empire and was venerated by hundreds of millions of non-Jews. Their opposition was inevitable. "By what right do the Jews demand it for themselves?" He said wealth could not purchase Palestine, "which can only be taken over by the force of cannons and warships," and predicted a popular movement against Jews which the Ottoman government would not be able to quell. He concluded: "For the sake of God, leave Palestine in peace."

Herzl wrote back, assuring the notable that Jews did not wish to remove Arabs. On the contrary, the arrival of Jews would make the Arabs richer. "Their well-being and private wealth will increase through the importation of ours," said Herzl, in an argument that remains current to this day.

Herzl should have known better, and probably did. In *The Jewish State*, he argued against step-by-step settlement of the sort started by the First Aliyah.

> An infiltration is bound to end badly. It continues till the inevitable moment when the native population feels itself threatened, and forces the government to stop a further influx of Jews. Immigration is consequently futile unless we have the sovereign right to continue such immigration.

In short, the Jews needed to secure sovereignty first in order to overcome Arab resistance. They needed not only the force of will, but the force of a state. When Herzl made his first approach to Abdel-Hamid II in 1896, offering through an intermediary to pay off the Ottoman debt in return for the right to settle in Palestine, the Sultan sent back the prophetic response:

> The Jews may spare their millions. When my Empire is divided, perhaps they will get Palestine for nothing. But only our corpse can be divided. I will never consent to a vivisection.

★

At the same time as Levontin and his fellow settlers were pitching their tents at Rishon Le-Zion, another experiment in Jewish national revival was about to take place in Jerusalem. Ben-Zion Ben-Yehuda was born in a dark room close to the site of the ancient Temple Mount. The firstborn of Eliezer Ben-Yehuda, the pioneer in the revival of the Hebrew language, Ben-Zion was the first child of modern times to grow up with Hebrew as his only language. The child, his father insisted, was to hear no "foreign sounds."

The rebirth of Hebrew from a semi-forgotten sacred language of scripture into a modern vernacular was as fantastic a notion as the Rishon Le-Zion settlers' plan to restore the Jewish people to Ottoman Palestine. For Ben-Yehuda, the conjunction of the founding of Rishon Le-Zion and the birth of the first Hebrew child was a powerful, almost mystical symbol of regeneration. The consumptive Ben-Yehuda displayed as much single-minded zeal in this linguistic challenge as any of the pioneers clearing the swamps.

It was a harsh imposition on his children. Ben-Zion's stepsister, Dola, later recalled in the Israeli television documentary series, *Pillar of Fire*:

> It was as if we were under house arrest. We were not allowed to go out into the streets and speak to strange children. And what happened when the eldest child turned four or five? A cat and a dog were brought home for us. The dog was male, the cat female, and the eldest child could speak to the dog in the masculine and to the cat in the feminine . . . these were our first friends, the first Hebrew-speaking animals for two thousand years.

Eliezer Ben-Yehuda, born Eliezer Perlman in the Lithuanian town of Luzhky, was educated in a traditional yeshiva and fell under the spell of Rabbi Joseph Blucker of Plotzk, a secret adherent of the Haskalah enlightenment who exposed the boy to secular subjects. The leaders of the Haskalah had advocated the use of biblical Hebrew as a vehicle to spread modern learning among traditional Jews in Europe. At the age of 13, Ben-Yehuda was given a Hebrew translation of the novel, *Robinson Crusoe*. It would change his life and, with time, the course of Jewish history.

Ben-Yehuda's nationalist spirit was fired by the Russian–Turkish War of 1877–78 over Bulgarian demands for independence from Ottoman rule. He recalled in the introduction to his life's work, a Hebrew dictionary comprising all the words used and often forgotten: "During this time, suddenly—it was as if the heavens opened and a light shone forth—a pure and gleaming ray flashed before my eyes, and a mighty inner voice called in my ears. Israel's Rebirth on the Soil of the Fathers!" He left Russia to study medicine in Paris, hoping to make a living as a doctor in Palestine. In an article published in the Vienna-based Hebrew language newspaper, *Ha-Shahar*, he argued for the creation of a Jewish spiritual center in the Land of Israel. He signed the article "E. Ben-Yehuda" meaning "Son of Judea."

Ben-Yehuda at first dismissed the claim that Jews did not count as a nation because they lacked a common spoken language, citing the example of multilingual Switzerland, but he later changed views. "Just as the Jews cannot really become a living nation other than through their returning to their ancestral land, so too, they are not able to become a living nation other than through their returning to their ancestral language," he wrote.

Hebrew started to die out as the spoken language of Jews even before the Christian era, when the Jews of the Near East adopted Aramaic. However, even after the destruction of the temple by the Romans, Hebrew survived in religious literature, poetry, and as a lingua franca among the dispersed communities, the equivalent of Latin in the medieval world and classical Arabic among the spoken dialects of the Arab world.

For the traditionalist Jewish communities of eastern Europe, Hebrew was a sacred language, not one for everyday use. For the most part it was reserved for men who studied in the yeshivas, while the language of daily communication was Yiddish, a Jewish variant of medieval German written in Hebrew letters. Unlike settlement in Palestine, which was subject to a host of political factors, Ben-Yehuda thought that reviving Hebrew as a spoken language was simply a question of "the will of the community." Testing his idea on a friend at a café on the Boulevard Montmartre, he noted, "The astonishing sounds of this dead, ancient, and oriental language mingled with the din of the gay sounds of the vibrant, lovely, and rich French language."

Sick with tuberculosis, Ben-Yehuda went to recover in Algiers, where he had to speak Hebrew to make himself understood by other Jews. He fell in love with the oriental "Sephardi" pronunciation which he believed was closer to the original sound of Hebrew. Returning to Europe, he was joined in Vienna by the love of his Russian youth, Deborah Jonas. The couple set off for Palestine in 1881. Sailing down the Danube, Ben-Yehuda recalled how he began speaking to his bride-to-be in Hebrew:

Her vocabulary increased by the hour. As we passed through the Iron Gate, I was so awed by the sight that I could not help exclaiming: "Ma yafe hamakom hazeh (How beautiful this place is)." My wife, who only a day or two previously had not known a word of Hebrew, rejoined: "Be-emet yafe zeh hamakom (Indeed, this place is beautiful)." Those were the first words uttered by a woman in our age in the course of a secular conversation in Hebrew as a living, spoken tongue.

As the ship sailed down the Syrian coast, more and more Arab passengers came on board. Their presence was like a cold shower on Ben-Yehuda's romantic notions of returning to the land of the Bible.

> I was suddenly seized with a depressing sense of fear. I felt that they considered themselves the masters of what was once the land of my ancestors and that I, the descendant of those ancestors, was coming there as a stranger [. . .]! I was suddenly broken, and regrets seemed to well up within me [. . .]

A similar sense of dread struck him as he landed in Jaffa, which Ben-Yehuda found distressingly Arab in character, but the depression started to lift at a Jewish inn where the owner spoke to him in Hebrew. In Jerusalem, Ben-Yehuda joined the staff of *Ha-Havatzelet*, a weekly Hebrew pamphlet catering mainly to Orthodox Jews then living in Palestine; later he founded *Ha-Tzvi*. He was in many ways the originator of modern Hebrew journalism, introducing a secular tone and European style of presentation.

Living in poverty, and seeking to adapt to the piety and appearance of his Jewish neighbors, he grew a beard and sidelocks, while his wife, whom he married in Cairo, agreed to wear a *sheytl*, or wig. Ben-Yehuda formally dropped his name of Perlman, and took Ottoman citizenship under the name Eliezer Ben-Yehuda. With this symbolic act, he inspired the tradition that Jews arriving in the Land of Israel should drop their diaspora names and create a new Hebrew identity.

The Orthodox community began to suspect Ben-Yehuda's commitment to Jewish tradition. Upset by his attacks on the *halukkah* system of philanthropy to support religious communities, his sacrilege in using Hebrew as a secular tongue and his advocacy of profane Jewish manual labor in agricultural settlements, they took their revenge in 1894. The religious establishment denounced Ben-Yehuda to the Turkish authorities for an article containing the phrase "let us gather strength and go forward." This, they told the Ottomans, amounted to a call to arms. Ben-Yehuda was formally ostracized by the rabbis and the Turks threw him in prison. He was sentenced to a year in jail for sedition but, helped by pressure from Baron Edmond de Rothschild, the conviction was overturned on appeal. His newspaper, *Ha-Tzvi*, remained banned for some months.

It was during this period of enforced inactivity that he began to work on his dictionary. Originally conceived as a small booklet, this turned into an opus of 17 volumes, completed only after his death. It is arranged more like a thesaurus than a dictionary, so that words of similar nature are grouped together—e.g. all words relating to "tree." This was designed to make it easier for an aspiring Hebrew speaker to find the correct word for an idea he or she could not describe. There are elaborate references to similar words in other Semitic languages, especially Arabic, and translations into French, German, and English.

Hebrew, said Ben-Yehuda, was a hamstrung language. The loftiest thoughts had to be expressed in simple terms. He even had to invent the word for "dictionary"—*millon*, derived from the Hebrew for "word" *milla*. He popularized his new words in the pages of his newspapers and even his fiercest critics, he noted, had started to use them.

Ben-Yehuda was riding the swell of a wave of Hebrew revival. Soon after arriving in Jerusalem, he was offered a job teaching "Hebrew in Hebrew" at a school run by the Alliance Israélite Universelle and among his earliest disciples were the members of Bilu.

Rishon Le-Zion became the first of the new Jewish communities where Hebrew took root, largely through the work of David Yudelovitch, a member of Bilu and headmaster of the village school from 1887. Every subject was taught in Hebrew, despite the opposition of the baron's officials who at first promoted French. Yudelovitch recalled:

> I devoted myself to the fight to make Hebrew the language of the boys and girls in the school, out of doors, in their homes and everywhere. It was a difficult task for several reasons. [. . .] The Hebrew language that was to be revived was poor. It lacked words for common articles and concepts like towels, sleeve, seriousness, plate, handkerchief, interesting, postal order, egoism, trip, progress, date, pin, interview, mobilization, apathy, and many others evolved during the succeeding half-century. We were only semi-articulate; and sometimes a foreign word was bound to creep in to explain something.

Herzl thought the Jewish state should be a polyglot country. In *Altneuland*, theaters staged productions in German, English, French, Italian, and Spanish. "Who among us has sufficient acquaintance with Hebrew to ask for a railway ticket in that language?" he asked. The more militant Hebrew revivalists went as far as tearing up Yiddish newspapers and disrupting meetings conducted in anything but Hebrew.

Their victory was not assured until the eve of the First World War.

In what came to be known as the "Language War," advocates of Hebrew in 1914 forced the Hilfsverein der Deutschen Juden (Relief Organization of German Jews), which sponsored most of the teachers in the Jewish community through a network of 50 schools, to back down from plans to make German the language of teaching at the new Haifa Technical Institute (the Technion). The institution was supposed to be a monument to German culture in the Orient, particularly because Hebrew was hopelessly short of technical terms.

Ben-Yehuda was apoplectic at this plan, warning the Hilfsverein that "blood will flow in the streets." Teachers at the Hilfsverein schools went on strike and students demonstrated outside the German consulate in Jerusalem. In February 1914, the Technion relented and agreed to teach all courses in Hebrew. When Britain conquered Palestine and pledged to create a Jewish national home, it recognized Hebrew as one of the official languages, alongside English and Arabic. Ben-Yehuda's dream was becoming reality. Subsequent waves of immigrants would periodically try to retain their "languages of the ghetto," but ultimately succumbed to Hebrew.

Hebrew's vocabulary may still lack the range of adjectives, adverbs, and synonyms of English. But for most Israeli children, it is the only language they will ever master completely. Just a few decades ago, Hebrew was often spoken with reverential correctness, as an educated German might speak English with punctilious grammar and old-fashioned colloquialisms. The speeches of the founding generation politicians such as David Ben-Gurion today sound stilted. Hebrew is a language of the street, replete with class and ethnic distinctions. Its popular slang is constantly evolving with the infusion of new words and expressions.

Hebrew is the mortar holding together Israel's disparate ethnic groups. Tuition for new immigrants is heavily subsidized by the state. Special newspapers are published in simple language, with the diacritical marks to indicate how the vowels should be pronounced. Radio stations, too, broadcast programs in simplified vocabulary. Hebrew is a powerful link to a common past, a symbol of ancient nationhood reinforced by the physical evidence of Hebrew inscriptions and parchments uncovered by archaeologists. The cost is the loss of cultural diversity: the heritage of two millennia of existence across the world has been deliberately dissolved in the melting pot of Hebrew-Israeli culture.

Ben-Yehuda had wanted to mine the Arabic language, with its common Semitic roots, to revitalize Hebrew. But subsequent architects of the Hebrew language knew little Arabic, and as Arabs were perceived increasingly as the enemy, they preferred to borrow from European languages if they could not derive a substitute from a Hebrew root. For example the Hebrew for "neutrality" is *netraliyyut*, instead of Ben-Yehuda's suggested *hiyyud*, from the Arabic *hiyad*. Arabic, according to Hebrew experts, has contributed only a few score words to standard Hebrew, compared with thousands of Aramaic terms. Some of the choice swear-words, however, are taken from Arabic's fine range of insults.

Ben-Yehuda succeeded in making East European immigrants drop the Ashkenazi pronunciation of the yeshivas and the giants of Haskalah literature, in favor of the oriental Sephardi pronunciation. However the first settlers, with their Yiddish and Russian-honed pronunciation, never mastered the most distinctive sounds of the Levant. The result is that the full-blown oriental pronunciation so admired by Ben-Yehuda as the closest to the cadence of biblical Hebrew is regarded, especially by Israelis of European stock, as the low-class accent of poor immigrants from the Arab world. Many a Sephardi Jew seeking social advancement has tried hard to abandon the oriental pronunciation.

The Academy of the Hebrew Language, *Ha-Akademia la-Lashon ha-Ivrit*, born out of the Hebrew Language Committee founded by Ben-Yehuda in 1890, produces a constant stream of new words— from *meshivon* for "answering machine" to *ya'efet* for "jet lag." Its telephones buzz with dozens of queries a day from MPs, journalists, and lovers of crossword puzzles. The academy tries to resist foreign imports but its very title—*Ha-Akademia*—is a non-Hebrew loan word.

Many of the words created in the last century have been abandoned. A contemporary reader is frequently left dumbfounded by the mysterious terms used by the newspapers of the 1890s. In other cases, words have changed meaning. The daily *Ha-Or* suggested in 1892 the word *ziyun* for "risk," a word which today is slang for "sex." In pre-state days, *zayn* meant "weapon" but today means "penis." An old pioneering song with the momentous lyrics of "*Yehudi, zayn kah!*"— "Jew, seize your weapon!"—today causes uncontrollable hilarity.

Hebrew can be magnanimous in victory. Today it is the old Jewish tongues such as Yiddish and Ladino, so despised by Ben-Yehuda as "jargon," that are being lovingly nurtured by those fearing the complete loss of a venerable heritage. The main influence on Hebrew today comes from English, both because of the legacy of the British

Mandate, and because of the all-pervading influence of American culture. On Ben-Yehuda Street in Jerusalem, English can be heard as commonly as Hebrew. English has chic value. For the well-heeled and educated, it is a vital component of a child's education. English makes Israelis citizens of the world, and cabinet ministers are ridiculed if they cannot hold their own against world leaders in English.

Russian left its influence on Hebrew, for instance, in words with the diminutive suffix *-chik* and another suffix *-nik*, indicating belonging to a party or group, e.g. *kibbutznik* (belonging to a kibbutz) or *likudnik* (belonging to the Likud party). It is making a comeback with the arrival of some 600,000 Jews from eastern Europe in the 1990s and the founding of several Russian-language newspapers. In some towns, you are more likely to get an answer if you ask for street directions in Russian than in Hebrew. Still, the chances are that Russian will dissolve into the Hebrew melting pot within a generation.

★

A rusted Syrian tank lies half buried at the entrance to Kibbutz Degania, its tracks slowly melting into the soil.

In this placid pastoral setting of sleek cypresses and effusive eucalyptus trees, of lush banana plantations and riotous bougainvillaeas, with leisure boats rocking gently on the Sea of Galilee, it is difficult to imagine Degania as a frontier settlement or as a battleground of the first Arab–Israeli war.

It was here in 1948 that the defenders of Degania, many of them little older than children, turned back a Syrian armored column. The leading tank was halted with nothing more than a Molotov cocktail thrown at pointblank range, and it has been left as a trophy at the spot where it was destroyed.

The fighting in Degania was a defining moment in Israeli history. It is the Jewish version of the Battle of Britain, when the sheer grit of the few held off invasion by a more powerful enemy. The survival of Degania helped to save the infant Jewish state from being throttled at birth, and to define its borders. The tank is more than a reminder of valor in war; it is a tribute to a whole system of communal values begun at Degania, the "Mother of the Kibbutzim." The kibbutz was, in its time, a kind of secular Jewish religion. Its adherents believed in the power of communal life based on socialist principles to reform Jews who were seen to have fallen into a state of wretchedness, confusion, and uncertainty during their centuries in the *galut*, or Exile.

Toiling on the land, not the Talmud, was seen as the means of personal salvation and national redemption.

The "religion of labor" produced the Jewish pioneer: a new man who was strong, proud, devoted to the land, and a fearless warrior who spoke the Hebrew of his biblical ancestors. With its mixture of social enlightenment and military prowess, the kibbutz was Athens and Sparta rolled into one.

Border kibbutzim such as Degania have for decades embodied all that was considered noble in Israel: their members created the model of egalitarian living, they redeemed the land by sweat and ingenuity, and defended their possessions with determination. They were living proof that socialism could be created voluntarily, without coercion by the state, without gulags for dissidents and without sacrificing democratic norms.

The image of the Jew as a meek pen-pusher or petty trader was supposed to have been banished forever by the new role model of the sabra, or native-born Israeli. The word *sabra* derives from the name of the native prickly pear and is a metaphor for a person who is tough and prickly on the outside, but soft and sweet within.

The new Jew returned to nature in his forefathers' land; not just returned to nature but tamed it, draining malarial swamps, clearing fields of boulders, reforesting the mountains, and channeling irrigation water according to his will to make the desert bloom. He also cast off the ghetto of the mind, abjuring the centuries-old rabbinical traditions and rediscovering the heroes of the Hebrew Bible—vain, murderous, deceitful, and philandering as they were. The Bible was a national history book and an ethical inspiration, but the Talmudic learning which sustained Jewish identity in the Diaspora was now a part of the "old" existence to be discarded.

The kibbutzniks rewrote the Passover Haggadah, reworking the traditional Exodus story using events from contemporary Israel and readings from modern Hebrew literature. The tales of celebrated sages, such as Rabbi Akiva who was buried in the city of Tiberias near Degania, were sometimes replaced by accounts of kibbutz life. Other Jewish religious festivals were reinterpreted to emphasize their origins in the ancient Jewish agricultural cycles.

As the incubator of Israel's army, the kibbutz movement entrenched the doctrine that settlements are an essential and symbiotic part of defense strategy—settlements provided security and laid a claim to the land, while the armed forces, in turn, helped to build settlements. The camaraderie and cohesiveness engendered by kibbutz life was regarded as a vital ingredient in the superior fighting spirit. Throughout Israel's wars, kibbutz members have made up a disproportionate share of the officer corps, and suffered a disproportionate number of casualties.

The Labor Zionist movement in general, and the kibbutzim in particular, created Israel's modern heroes. Moshe Dayan, perhaps the most recognizable general, was one of the first children born in Degania, although his family later moved to a less rigid cooperative, known as *moshav*, in Nahalal. Motti Hod, commander of the air force during the Six Day War—whose pilots destroyed the Egyptian air force on the ground and effectively won the war in the first morning of fighting—is another famous son of Degania. For Dayan, Degania was the modern embodiment of the spirit of the biblical patriarchs who walked alone, carrying "a new faith, a new nation, a new land."

Kibbutzniks never accounted for more than about 7 percent of the Jewish population, but in the formative years of the Zionist endeavor they constituted a distinct elite, a kind of socialist-inspired aristocratic caste of east European Ashkenazi origin. Their values became the dominant ethos for the rest of the country.

"Today many of our best people are kibbutzniks. From this group come the majority of our officers," wrote David Ben-Gurion in the 1960s. "Although in the nation, the kibbutzim constitute a minor element, their contribution to the economy is enormous, out of all proportion to their size." When he retired, Ben-Gurion settled in Kibbutz Sdeh Boker in the Negev Desert, seeking by his personal example to convince others to populate the southern wilderness. The kibbutz, he believed, was "a social experiment from which peoples everywhere can take inspiration and ideas."

Especially in the 1960s and 1970s, thousands of non-Jewish foreigners would spend their summers as volunteers on the kibbutzim, offering their labor and receiving in exchange what they hoped would be the spiritually uplifting experience of kibbutz life, not to mention the prospect of an affair with a flesh-and-blood Israeli pioneer.

The kibbutz was responsible for Israel's informality in dress—shorts and sandals. It also inspired the traditional songs of Israel, odes to the beauty of the land and its bounty, or laments for friends who have passed away. Not for Israel the bombastic blasting of brass and the crashing of drums and cymbals which other countries have adopted as their national anthems. Instead, at times of national trauma, such as a particularly bloodthirsty bombing, it is the melancholy eastern European folk melodies with their pastoral lyrics that interrupt the radio programs.

Israel's national dance, the hora, in which participants hold hands in a circle and take steps in unison, was consciously adapted from Balkan folk dances to symbolize unity and equality. Group sessions of folk songs and dance remain a popular pastime, although they are giving ground to computer games and television. The "Negev Lullaby," a well-known song, evokes the pioneering days:

> The wind, the wind over our house
> The star hides its light
> Father out there is plowing our fields
> Sleep, sleep, son
>
> —Why is he plowing at night
> Instead of putting me to bed?
> —Our land, son, takes up all our time
> Sleep son, sleep son [. . .]
>
> If he is plowing the fields of the valley
> Why does he need a pistol and a Sten [gun]?
> —Without weapons no furrow will run deep
> Sleep son, sleep son

Today this picture of the revered farmer-soldiers of the kibbutz is in steep decline. The socialist elite that founded the state and guided it for decades is increasingly impotent. The heroic characters who populated novels such as Leon Uris's *Exodus* have given way to angst-ridden personalities in the books of Amos Oz. The kibbutzim are suffering an ideological and financial crisis, and in many cases they are literally bankrupt.

At the same time, the prestige of the army has been sullied by a succession of military errors, a more critical view of its Israeli history, problems of morale and a general sense of fatigue with the conflict. The troubles of the kibbutz and the army are, in many ways, intertwined; they are a reflection of a new Israel that is losing the ideological certainties of the past but remains divided and confused over the future. Malaise infects a period that is commonly described as "post-Zionist."

In part, the old pioneering and military elites are victims of their own success. Israel's early victories may not have achieved a full peace with the Arabs, but the Jewish state today is infinitely more secure than it was in 1948. Its economy, too, has prospered. Amid greater security and wealth, the collective "We" of Israeli folk songs has given way to the "Me" of personal ambition. Young Israelis are no longer interested in the austere agricultural life, but want the thrills of western consumerism.

The impact of the near disaster of the 1973 war against Egypt and Syria and the ill-fated invasion of Lebanon in 1982 contributed to an economic crisis which accelerated the dismantling of Israel's socialist-inspired economy, with the kibbutz as its shaky centerpiece. In the 1980s the government moved to rein in Israel's hyperinflation, then running at a peak of nearly 500 percent per annum, by sharply raising interest rates. Many kibbutzim were buried beneath an insurmountable mountain of debt, incurred by reckless spending, inept business ventures, and failed speculation in the capitalist nerve center, the stock market. Kibbutzniks discovered that their state-building task of claiming remote areas and guarding the frontiers now placed them far from Israel's economic heartland. Moreover, the defeat of the Labor party in 1977 robbed the kibbutzim of political patronage and all manner of hidden government subsidies which might have helped them ride the storm.

The economic difficulties caused social strains. Kibbutzniks could no longer turn a blind eye to slackers in their midst, and could no longer rely on the amateurish management which saw factories sprouting among their orange groves and fields of grain. Worst of all, young kibbutzniks, the very people once held up as models of pioneering virtues, left the communal settlements in alarming numbers. The kibbutzim have lost about 6 percent of their population in as many years. Communal settlements are no longer the source of Israel's leaders; increasingly they are becoming old age homes, places of memory.

The fate of the Hula Valley, in the upper reaches of the Jordan River, stands as a metaphor for the plight of the pioneering generation. The draining of the valley's swamps after the creation of the state was hailed by Ben-Gurion as an historic achievement by Israel's kibbutz pioneers to reclaim farmland and rid the area of malaria. But the peat soil dried out and lost fertility. It created dust storms and was the source of fires. The ground subsided by two meters, and nitrates polluted the Sea of Galilee downstream. In the mid-1990s, the Israeli government decided to reflood part of the valley to expand the wetlands habitat for birds migrating between Europe and Africa.

Tourism, not farming, is the new economic promise for the troubled kibbutzim in the Galilee.

The late Likud Prime Minister, Menachem Begin, could once win electoral points by denouncing the "millionaire kibbutzniks," but such barbs today would have no impact. To a growing number of Israelis, the once-venerated kibbutz has become an irrelevance.

True, the kibbutz is remarkable for having survived the circumstances of its creation. Many kibbutzim are now being run by a third generation of members. But the movement is being forced to adapt or die, and former bastions of socialism throughout the country are succumbing to sacrilegious free market reforms such as differential salaries, individual responsibility for paying bills and private ownership of property. A few stubbornly retain the old ideals, but many more are selling off the land. The acres which the founders labored so hard to make productive are being turned into industrial zones, shopping centers or even, in prime real estate locations, into private villas for the wealthy.

★

A majestic cypress towers above the carefully tended lawn of Degania. It is known as the "Tree of the State of Israel" and was planted in 1948. In a young country like Israel, few trees have grown to this size.

The lawns, open gardens, and tree-lined alleys of Degania lend it a country-club atmosphere. It boasts a large swimming pool and tennis courts. But even in relatively well-off kibbutzim such as Degania, members' accommodation remains simple, even spartan.

Yona "Yoya" Shapiro, daughter of one of the kibbutz's founders, has lived in the shadow of the Tree of the State of Israel for nearly four decades and has watched the kibbutz develop with the passing of the seasons. A feisty 76, she showed little enthusiasm for the social revolution sweeping Degania when I met her at her home, little larger than a hut.

Through the years, Yoya worked in the vegetable garden, as a cook in the communal kitchen, in the laundry, and as a seamstress. "I have what I want. I am satisfied with what I have. For me, any change would be a change for the worse," she explained. "The young think differently. I am not young anymore, and I cannot tell them how to lead their lives."

At the age of 25, with a rifle in hand, she fought in the trenches in 1948 to defend Degania against the Syrians. She still remembers the tank breaking through the perimeter fence. "We were opposite the tank, maybe twenty to twenty-five meters away. But I was sure we were going to stop them. I never saw it in any other way. I thought 'We have to stop them, otherwise Degania will cease to exist,'" she recalled. "We fired at them whenever we saw them, but it did not help. They kept coming. Bullets came into the pillbox and killed the girl next to me. But suddenly, the Syrians turned around on the main road and went back."

The children of the kibbutz had been given simple military training at an early age, cleaning weapons and learning to hide them from British search parties. Occasionally, the children would be taken into the surrounding countryside and left to find their own way home. As a young woman, Yoya said, the pleasures of life were simple—sitting together, singing and dancing. The television age which has helped to create the global village has only contributed to breaking up the fellowship of the kibbutz.

All meals in Degania were eaten together in the dining room, the focal point of the community. Unlike other kibbutzim, Degania never inflicted on children the practice of making them live communally in "Children's Houses" rather than with their parents. The kibbutz allocated jobs and distributed money according to the perceived needs of each member. It decided how much each person could spend on clothing or food, or whether a child should go to university.

There was an endearing side to such strictures. Until the 1950s and beyond, a money box was left open for anyone to draw funds, and members would jot down the amount they had taken in a notebook. Equality also carried its pain, such as the obligation to hand over to the kibbutz any money earned outside the community. Yoya's husband, Allan, an American-born lawyer and journalist, recalled once receiving a four-figure dollar check for an article he had written for the *New York Times*. "I looked at the check for a day or two, and then handed it over to the treasurer," he said, sighing.

All this is disappearing. The kibbutz had once taken upon itself the task of providing for its members as it deemed appropriate, but now a growing share of Degania's expenditure is left to members. The personal "budgets"—nobody yet dares call them "salaries"—now cover all sorts of items that were once supplied directly by the kibbutz, such as clothing, shoes, and utilities bills. Although it was a dilution of kibbutz philosophy, Allan admitted that wastage has been visibly reduced.

The dining room has closed for evening meals except for the eve of the Sabbath and other holidays. Worse, the dining room service has been privatized, and members must swipe a computer debit card to "pay" for their meals. This in a movement where members once argued fiercely over the most trivial issues of communal living: can long benches be replaced with individual chairs, or would this be an intolerable bourgeois heresy? Should members own their own clothes, or should they share all items, including underwear? Are women allowed to wear lipstick?

Most of Degania's income is from an industrial tools factory that employs kibbutz members and outsiders in roughly equal numbers. The rest comes from members employed outside the kibbutz who remit their income, and from what little is left of the kibbutz's farming. Even on the land, the very foundation of the "religion of labor," the kibbutz now employs Thai wage laborers. The kibbutz, seeking to turn diaspora Jews into heroic peasants, has produced an increasingly bourgeois generation for whom it is difficult to provide stimulating jobs.

In contrast with many other kibbutzim, Degania claims to be holding on to its young people, and its population remains stable. But Yoya's son, Ron, was among those who had little desire to become a kibbutz farmer or tool worker. Instead the university education which the kibbutz granted him has pulled him away from the land to become a lawyer. Degania can now boast the first kibbutz-trained judge, but after painful deliberation, Judge Ron Shapiro formally left the kibbutz shortly before being appointed to the bench.

He would be the pride of many an Israeli mother, but not Yoya. "I told my son when he went to study law that if my parents were to come out of their graves they would be disappointed. They would say that studying law is not being a farmer," she remembered, adding with a touch of bitterness: "At that time I did not know he would leave Degania."

★

The establishment of Degania is recounted by Yoya's late father, Yosef Baratz, in a booklet entitled *A Village by the Jordan*. The tale begins, again, in Russia. Baratz describes the village of his birth in the Ukraine, the mounting troubles faced by Jews under Tsarist rule, and his family's move to Kishinev. His father, Zeidet, ran a general store which, he recalled, "somehow always smelled of mint, boot-leather, and candle-wax." He later opened an inn.

Kishinev was a place where the Tsar sent Russian revolutionaries into exile. The merging of socialist politics with budding Jewish nationalism made it an early center of Zionist activity. At Passover in 1903, the Jewish quarter of Kishinev was sacked at the start of a new wave of anti-Semitic violence. The pogroms were, once more, manipulated by the Tsarist authorities in reaction to the revolutionary agitation in which many Jews were prominent. The violence in Kishinev left 45 dead and hundreds injured, prompting Haim Nahman Bialik, who would become Israel's national poet, to compose "The City of Slaughter," a poem still studied by Israeli schoolchildren:

> Arise and go now to the city of slaughter;
> Into its courtyard wind thy way;
> There with thine own hand touch, and with the eyes of thine head;
> Behold on tree, on stone, on fence, on mural clay,
> The spattered blood and dried brains of the dead.

The Kishinev pogrom was the prelude to another outburst of riotous killings that accompanied the revolutionary upheavals of the last years of Tsarist rule. The violence against Jews, which peaked in 1905, and the collapse of the reforms that briefly ushered in a representative parliament, caused another and much larger wave of Jewish emigration from Russia.

In the face of this violence, Herzl presented the Zionist movement with a British plan to establish a Jewish colony in part of Uganda. He recommended this as a temporary expedient to save Jews from the misery in Russia and as an apprenticeship for eventual statehood in Palestine. The idea caused uproar in the Zionist movement, particularly among eastern European delegates, including Chaim Weizmann, who were adamant that Africa could never be the Promised Land. In the end Herzl abandoned the Uganda scheme. He died in 1904 and the movement, bereft of its leader, concentrated on supporting practical Zionism.

The immigrants arriving in Palestine at the time came to be known as the Second Aliyah. Unlike the previous settlers more than two decades earlier, these new arrivals were imbued with revolutionary socialist ideals and were more politically organized. This was the generation of the Labor Zionists, who moulded nationalist aspirations with Marxist doctrine. They founded the kibbutzim, the first Jewish forces and, ultimately, the State of Israel.

Yosef Baratz had decided in late 1906 to settle in Palestine despite the objections of his parents. At the age of 15 he boarded a ship crammed with Russian Christian pilgrims carrying whole sides of pork. "I had never been so close to people eating pig before," recalled Baratz.

The chain of Jewish settlements already founded in Palestine since 1882 allowed the new immigrants to subsist by wandering from one temporary laboring job to another. Baratz made friends with other newcomers in Jaffa, and a group set out for Rishon Le-Zion (whose wine they were familiar with from Passover meals in Russia) to meet the legendary *Biluim* who helped to found the community. It was to be a disappointing encounter, as he wrote in his book:

We thought that to talk with the Biluim we would have to wait until sunset—we imagined a village like in Russia—hens pecking on the road, children shouting by the river, and not a soul in sight while the sun is high and all the peasants are in the fields. But what was this? We were in a pretty street of neat brick houses with red tiled roofs; from one of them came the tinkling of a piano. The street was full of people strolling up and down. We couldn't believe our eyes. We asked:
    "Who are these?"
    "Biluim."
    "And who does the work?"
    "Arabs."
    "And what do the Jews do?"
    "They're managers, supervisors."
    It was a great shock to us. I said to myself: "This isn't what we've come for," and I could see that the others were disappointed as well.

The established Jewish colonists were equally suspicious of the new arrivals, considering them to be either insolent socialist trouble-makers or, at best, weaker than the Arabs as laborers. Baratz worked in the colony of Rehovot before being sent to Jerusalem by Ha-Poel ha-Tza'ir, the right wing of the Labor Zionist movement, to learn stonemasonry. His hands, although toughened in the fields, were so raw from the hammering that he could not hold a piece of bread. "Those first weeks in Jerusalem were terrible," recalled Baratz. "I had been given a hut among some olive trees; every night I would creep under the trees and cry—I was afraid that I would not hold out and I was lonely and my fingers ached."

He took on a job posing nude at the newly created Bezalel art school in Jerusalem, hardly the occupation for a would-be pioneer, but the money was a welcome addition to the pool of earnings he shared with three friends. Baratz went on to work in Jaffa, where the city of Tel Aviv was being built, and then to the new community of Atlit. The lone Jew among hundreds of Arab laborers, he recalled the howling of Arabs who were treated for malaria by being bled from a cut on the ear.

He moved on to Zichron Yaakov, one of the early Rothschild colonies and a way-station for pioneers moving from Jaffa toward the opportunities opening up farther north in the Galilee. Here the conflict between the old and the new settlers' rival visions for the future of the new Jewish settlement in Palestine was apparent. In Petach Tikva in 1905, the older generation of farmers boycotted the pioneers, or *halutzim*, after they had been caught dancing with young women. Two years later, the newcomers organized a strike at the Rishon Le-Zion winery.

The newcomers often banded together to share their meager incomes and find mutual solidarity in a forbidding environment. Cooperative arrangements emerged as much from necessity as from ideology. Many would-be pioneers despaired and returned home. Some killed themselves. David Gruen, a 20-year-old engineering student better known as David Ben-Gurion arrived in Jaffa in 1906 and was advised by doctors to leave after succumbing to malaria in the vineyards of Rishon Le-Zion.

An outlet for the restless energies of the pioneers was provided by the new lands being opened up for settlement. The Jewish National Fund (JNF) of the Zionist movement was beginning to buy tracts of land in Palestine "for the eternal possession of the Jewish people," using donations from Jews in the Diaspora. These included a large plot at Kinneret on the shores of the Sea of Galilee. In 1908, encouraged by a more liberal climate following the Young Turks' revolution, the Zionist Organization opened an office in Jaffa under Arthur Ruppin, a German-trained economist. The immigrants of the Second Aliyah, he thought, were the elite of eastern European youth. They were "models of industry and devotion to their work," though given to overemotionalism and frequent indiscipline.

The farm at Kinneret had been run along traditional lines, with a manager presiding over hired Jewish workers. Soon the laborers resented the manager's domineering "bourgeois" style and considered his high salary a waste of money. Ruppin fired both manager and workers and started anew, but the farm continued to make losses. As an experiment, Ruppin agreed to allow a group of seven workers to work an inaccessible part of the land as an autonomous cooperative, in return for a high share of earnings. Their tract on the far side of the Jordan River was known by its Arab name of Umm Juni. It turned a profit within a year and, with the viability of cooperative farming demonstrated, the first group of farmers moved on, replaced in 1910 by a commune of workers in Hadera. The group was based around a core of pioneers from Romny, in the Ukraine. They were joined by Baratz and his future wife, Miriam, who startled the men-folk by her ability to work in the fields. The 12 members of this commune, or *kevutza*, were the founding fathers of Degania.

The kevutza renamed the farm Degania, or "Cornflower," after the wild flowers which bloomed in the fields in spring. At first they lived in mud huts. Baratz recalled:

> We arrived in summer. It was very hot down there, two hundred meters below sea level. The air buzzed with mosquitoes and it lay heavy and close between the hills. The flat valley was like a hot plate, the heat pressed on it. Everything was burned brown. The river was a trickle. But when the rains came, it flooded the land and when the waters withdrew they left swamps and mud. For months on end we were cut off by mud.

At Umm Juni, the pioneers laid the foundations of the kibbutz. The members of the commune resolved to live with neither masters nor slaves, in a climate of mutual caring and in spiritual balance with nature. Baratz wrote:

> We talked a terrible lot of theory, yet it wasn't theory we were concerned with exactly: we were looking for a practical answer to our needs and we were trying to find out what it was that the land was asking of us. For what had happened while we were in exile? The land had lost its fertility and it seemed to us that we ourselves, divorced from it, had become barren in spirit. Now we must give it our strength and it would give us back our creativeness.

Similar ideas were adopted by other pioneers, and by 1914 there were 11 groups. After the First World War, the model was adapted to create a much larger type of collective community, with hundreds of members instead of a few dozen, which would be called a "kibbutz." These were to be communal villages rather than the extended family of Degania. The first kibbutz was founded at Ein Harod in 1921. By the time the State of Israel was born, with the differentiation between a *kevutza* and a kibbutz rapidly disappearing, there were 149 communal farms. These grew to more than 260 communities today.

The pioneers at Degania were deeply influenced by the Zionist writer, A.D. Gordon. Inspired by Tolstoy's glorification of the Russian peasant as the repository of wisdom and by his call for a simple, self-sufficient life, Gordon articulated a philosophy of Zionism which became known as the "religion of labor." Acting on his own belief, at the ripe age of 48 he made his way to Palestine. Gordon disagreed with the more hard-line Labor Zionists, who in his view wrongly tried to reorganize society rather than the human spirit.

Beer Borochov, the chief ideologist of the Poalei Zion, or "Workers of Zion" movement, shoehorned Marxist doctrine into Zionist ideas, producing a jargon-filled "scientific" argument that Zionist settlement in Palestine was not only desirable, but inevitable. He said that the Jews, as a landless minority distant from the tools of production, could not organize to struggle against the exploiters: only in its own land could a Jewish working class be created in order to fight for social revolution. Jewish colonization of Palestine would take place not because Jews desired to return to their ancestral Jewish soil, but for objective economic reasons: it was the ideal underdeveloped land where revolutionary energies could find outlet.

Socialist slogans were adapted to Zionism. "Jewish workers of all countries unite . . ." said one Poalei Zion proclamation. Bourgeois Jews went to Palestine (without Borochov) deliberately to create a Jewish peasant class which could then fight the class struggle. The result was odd scenes of Jews plowing fields or picking oranges by day, and earnestly discussing political theory and Russian novels by night.

Amid all the sloganeering and hair-splitting debates on the socialist revolution among a bewildering variety of factions, the interests of the toiling Arab peasant, dislocated by the influx of Jews, were almost entirely ignored. The immigrants of the Second Aliyah were largely united behind the idea of building the country with their own rather than Arab hands. The "conquest" of the land must be accompanied by the "conquest" of labor; that is, the replacement of Arab workers by Jewish pioneers. Many argued that Jews should not "exploit" Arabs, and should therefore have nothing to do with them. Whether out of such misplaced altruism, or out of naked self-interest, the "conquest of labor" aggravated the mounting resentment of Arabs, who saw their country flooded with Jewish immigrants who made little secret of wanting to found a Jewish state in the heart of the Arab world.

Herzl had conceived of Zionism as a means of weaning Jews away from socialist agitation. Instead, the new wave of immigrants carried socialism with them to Zion. On the shores of the Sea of Galilee, which in *Altneuland* Herzl had imagined as overlooked by a Jewish Côte d'Azur of elegant villas, there emerged instead a ring of model socialist farms.

Degania's experiment in creating a new utopian social order created internal frictions almost as soon as it started. Rivalries emerged between the core of founders and newer members, notably Shmuel Dayan, father of the future general. The son of an itinerant peddler from the Ukrainian town of Zhashkov, Shmuel Dayan had made his way to Palestine after reading a famous appeal for pioneers issued by Joseph Vitkin, a schoolmaster in the Galilee: "Awake, O youth of Israel! Come to the aid of your people. Your people lies in agony. Rush to its side. Band together; discipline yourselves for life or death; forget all the precious bonds of your childhood; leave them behind without a shadow of regret [...]."

There were disputes over the status of women, over the anarchic pilfering of common food stores and even over accommodating the requirements of vegetarians in the group. There was a heated arguments over whether the pioneers should move on from Degania or create a settled community.

Yosef and Miriam Baratz were the first couple to be married at Degania. It was, recalled the groom, the event of the year among the pioneers. Guests came from around the Galilee, and from as far away as Tel Aviv, a two-day trip. The birth of the Baratzes' first son, Gideon, caused renewed difficulties. The *kevutza* had long discussed how children should be brought up, but the arrival of Gideon had upset their elaborate theories of communal life. Miriam would bring the child into the cowshed, where he would be licked by the cattle and covered by flies while she worked.

Shmuel Dayan was upset that she had "set up a private kitchen" to be with her child in the evenings. He noted in his memoirs: "This was a tremendous blow to the kibbutz and its ideology. Members who spent their hours of rest apart from their comrades were cut off from the most important affairs."

By the autumn of 1914, he had proposed a vow of abstinence, suggesting that members "be allowed to marry only five years after the settlement established itself economically and consolidated itself socially." Within weeks, however, Dayan himself became the first to break the vow when he discovered that his fiancée, Dvorah, had become pregnant. The wedding posed new questions. The couple debated whether to have a traditional religious ceremony, to the merriment of their comrades. On the wedding day, carts were sent out to fetch wine and a *shochet*, a ritual slaughterer, to substitute for a rabbi and officiate at the ceremony under a canopy on the banks of the Jordan River. Their first son, Moshe, was born on May 4, 1915, at the height of the First World War.

It was a time of trial for the Jews of Palestine, many of whom had been deported from the coastal cities, while all communities in Palestine were ravaged by disease, food shortages, and the requisitions of the Turkish army. But for the Degania settlers, a new dawn for Zionism was about to break with the advent of British rule in 1917.

*

At midnight on Tuesday, November 27, 1917, Khalil al-Sakakini heard a soft knock on the door of his home in the Katamon neighborhood in Jerusalem. Standing there was an anxious Jewish acquaintance, Alter Levin, a minor poet and insurance agent, asking for refuge. As an American citizen, he had been ordered to surrender himself to the Ottoman authorities. Anyone who failed to do so would be considered a spy, as would anyone sheltering an American.

With British troops closing in, "the rumble of artillery around Jerusalem was like the roll of thunder," recalled Al-Sakakini. The Arab nationalist educator and writer, who had already expressed his dismay at the penetration of Jewish settlers into Palestine, wondered what to do. His diary records:

> If I accept him, I'm a traitor to my government; and if I refuse him, I'm a traitor to my language [i.e. Arab identity] . . . I told myself that he wasn't appealing simply to me for refuge, but to my whole people as represented in me. He was appealing to the literature expressed in my language, before the coming of Islam and after it. He was appealing to that ancient Bedouin who sheltered a hyena fleeing from its pursuers and entering his tent. And I should add that he had bestowed a great honor on me by coming to me for refuge. . . .

Al-Sakakini, then 39 years old, agreed to hide Levin. But a week later, just when he had begun to feel safe, there was another late-night knock on the door. The police had tracked Levin down by arresting and beating a Jewish woman: Levin had asked her to smuggle kosher food to him. A dismayed Al-Sakakini wrote: "Man, why didn't you eat our food, God forgive you? If you thought our food was impure, then we must be impure too, because we eat impure things. So how could you take refuge with us? Oh, religions! Oh, foolish minds, rather! How many victims have you claimed!"

Levin and Al-Sakakini were led away, convinced they would be executed. But in the chaos of Jerusalem in the last days of Ottoman rule, they languished for two days in the prison of the Russian compound, and were then marched to Jericho and Amman with the retreating Turkish troops. They were put on a train for Damascus, where Al-Sakakini spent 40 days in jail with Levin before being released. In his diary, Al-Sakakini makes clear the anger he felt toward his cell-mate, but politeness forbade him from revealing his resentment.

In August 1918, Al-Sakakini fled Damascus to join the forces of the Arab Revolt that were advancing alongside the British, but could not return to Jerusalem until January 1919. Levin, too, was eventually able to return. When the two men met, wrote Al-Sakakini, Levin would "incline his head to honor me, because I had risked my life and sheltered him." In 1933, Levin committed suicide, apparently because his business was in trouble.

Such Am I, O World, the diary of Al-Sakakini, is one of the few personal accounts of the formative period of Palestinian resistance to Zionism, illustrating the shattering of Arab nationalist hopes, the sharpening of Palestinian identity, and the growing despair and militancy of Palestinians as they watched their land being bought up and settled by Jewish immigrants.

Al-Sakakini, born in Jerusalem in 1878 and exiled to Cairo where he died in 1953, was one of the foremost intellectuals of his generation. He introduced modern teaching methods to Palestine and founded schools in the belief that education was the key to reviving Arab national identity. In 1909 he founded the noted Al-Dusturiyyah school, noted for its nationalist ethos. Under British rule he was a moving force behind the Muslim–Christian Associations that sought to unify Arabs and articulated opposition to Zionism in the early years of British rule. Like many Arab nationalists, he at first distinguished between a Jewish national movement and Jews as individuals. In February 1914, three years before his arrest with Levin, Al-Sakakini records that he had been teaching his pupils at his Al-Dusturiyyah school (the first Arab national school in Jerusalem) about Zionism.

"If I hate the Zionist movement, it is only because it is attempting to found its existence and independence on the destruction of others. [. . .] It is as if it is trying to achieve independence by stealth and to steal it by wiles," he noted. A few days later, he highlighted the danger that a Zionist conquest of Palestine would sever Egypt and North Africa from the rest of the Arab world. But there was also some grudging admiration for the dedication of the Jewish immigrants, which he thought unmatched by the Arabs. In 1914, Al-Sakakini wrote that the Arabs needed their own Baron Rothschild.

Al-Sakakini was by no means alone in expressing alarm at the infiltration of Jewish settlers. The same Young Turk revolution of 1908 that allowed the JNF to move its land acquisition operations to Palestine and create Degania also allowed Arabs, particularly the urban elite, to voice their opposition.

Resentment of Zionism came in many guises—there were those who feared the fragmentation of the empire, those who saw a threat to "Palestine," and those like Al-Sakakini who saw Zionism as a danger to Arab national awakening. Then there were those who feared economic competition, those who protested about the dispossession of the peasants and those motivated by pan-Islamic sentiment. There were also those who still regarded Zionism as either innocuous or even of benefit.

In 1905, Negib Azoury, a Maronite Christian who had served in Jerusalem as an Ottoman official and later moved to Paris, penned an Arab nationalist manifesto entitled *Le Réveil de la Nation Arabe*, a work permeated with European anti-Semitism. Even though it had little impact in its time, it became something of a prophetic warning.

> Two important phenomena, of the same nature but opposed, which have still not drawn anyone's attention, are emerging at this moment in Asiatic Turkey. They are the awakening of the Arab nation and the latent effort of the Jews to reconstitute on a very large scale the ancient kingdom of Israel. Both these movements are destined to fight each other continually until one of them wins.

The title of one prominent Arab newspaper founded in Jaffa in 1911, *Filastin* (Palestine), encapsulated the budding local patriotism. *Al-Mufid*, another newspaper, bemoaned the emigration of Arabs to America while Jews flooded the country. In 1913, Sheikh Suleiman al-Taji had the first known anti-Zionist poem published in *Filastin*, a piece that lambasted the meekness of the Ottoman government. It started:

> Jews, sons of clinking gold, stop your deceit;
> We shall not be cheated into bartering away our country!

In 1914, some nationalists were advocating violence to stop Jewish immigration. Haqqi Bey al-Azm, a political leader who had earlier advocated an entente between Arab nationalists and Zionists, now argued that the Ottoman government was helping the Zionists, who would conquer the land as far as the Euphrates. He wrote: "By employing means of threats and persecution [. . .] by pushing the Arab population into destroying their farms and setting fire to their colonies, by forming gangs to execute these projects, then perhaps the [Zionists] will emigrate to save their lives."

The elements that would make up Palestinian nationalism are already discernible before the end of Ottoman rule. But it would take the acceleration of Zionist settlement and the growth of Jewish "national" institutions under the tutelage of British colonizers to push Palestinians into active opposition.

The proportion of Jews in Palestine, about 9 percent at the start of the First World War, rose to about 18 percent in the census of 1931 and about 30 percent at the start of the Second World War. The first to come after the defeat of Turkey were the Russian pioneers of the Third Aliyah, then middle-class urban Polish Jews of the Fourth Aliyah and, just before the Second World War, the wealthy German Jews of the Fifth Aliyah. The settlement of Jews was a gradual but relentless approach that went under the name of "another dunam, another goat."

"The situation in the country goes from bad to worse," Al-Sakakini wrote to his son, Sari, in 1933. "Every day the ships deposit hundreds of Jewish immigrants and every day another large piece of land is sold. The people act haphazardly in their attempt to forestall danger, or rather, they are concerning themselves with other things, or sleeping. They have surrendered to despair. [. . .] The Jews and the British know that the Arab nation is divided and at odds with itself, that it's weak, poor, and ignorant, and so they are taking advantage of the opportunity to put their policy into practice [. . .]."

Like many nationalists, Al-Sakakini did not at first favor independence. "If Palestine is separated its fate will necessarily be that it will become Jewish [...] or pass into [the hands of] a foreign government, on the grounds that Palestine is not fit for autonomy because of the great ignorance and religious zealotry of her people," he wrote in 1919. But the collapse of the dream of a Greater Syria, when French troops occupied Damascus in 1920, forced Palestinians to concentrate on saving Palestine.

Al-Sakakini was only too aware of the weaknesses of his own people. He attempted to overcome religious differences, but confided his despair at the tribalism of the Muslim who believes that "the interests of his family take precedence over all other interests." In a letter to his son in the 1930s he bemoaned the infighting and ineffectiveness of Arab political meetings: "They are like the poet who, when told that the enemy was at the gates with horses and men, replied: 'I shall write a poem against them,' as if a satirical poem could repulse dangers."

In 1920, Al-Sakakini wrote in his diary that he was disgusted by the anti-Jewish violence after the Nebi Musa festival of 1920 in which Muslims shouted "The religion of Muhammad arose by the sword." By 1933, however, his diary expresses admiration for Palestinians' growing rebelliousness.

The Jews are panic-stricken, seeing a people armed only with their shoes attacking machine guns and mounted soldiers, bringing the soldiers down from the horses and trampling them. If they can do this with no organization and no weapons in their hands, what would things be like if they were organized and armed, or if the entire Arab world were to take part in the coming revolts?

4

The Hundred Years War

THE PASSAGE TO manhood for most Israeli boys takes just a few hours. It begins with tearful farewells from their parents and ends up with the boys sitting half-bewildered at a military base outside Tel Aviv, having traded their jeans for fatigues. One moment they are spotty teenagers leaving home for the first time, the next they are soldiers in the mighty Israel Defense Forces (IDF), the shield of the Jewish state, the most powerful army in what is already a highly militarized region.

The bar mitzvah, at age 13 is the initiation rite to Jewish manhood; military service, at age 18, is the price of admission to Israeli citizenship. The path to army life begins at Bakum, the "Induction and Placement Base" known by its Hebrew acronym as "the Bakum," a shabby former British army barracks where the recruits are assigned to their units and take the initial bureaucratic steps to enlistment. A heavy burden is placed on these teenagers: they are told the survival of their country in the face of implacable enemies depends on their abilities. Unlike most western European countries, where conscripts only play at being soldiers, many Israeli boys are likely to come under live fire, and some will die.

At one reception center next to the Bakum, I looked at the faces of the boys, some excited by the adventure of the army, others embarrassed by the fussing of their parents, some standing proud and others looking glum. Some had girlfriends who came to see them off, others would learn more about sex and relationships while in uniform. Women soldiers mingled with the crowds to offer advice and solace, and to deal with problem cases. "There are a lot of people who do not come when they are supposed to," said one. "Then the police go out and look for them." Another explained: "It's horrible. You're not at home, you cannot do things your way. You are just one of many. You are not special anymore."

Flashbulbs illuminated family groups in every corner. In the background, a crackling voice announced through a loudspeaker the departure of the next contingent. With each call, a group made its way to a waiting bus. A few minutes later, the bus was gone and well-wishers shuffled back. Fathers fought back tears and mothers wailed openly. For many parents, this is the moment when their mental clocks begin a countdown of the years, months, and days their children have left to serve. One writer has called the ritual of the young being sent to the army "Isaac's Sacrifice," in which parents willingly give up their sons to the all-powerful, all-knowing state.

Binyamin Itzik came to Israel from Yemen as a child with his parents in 1922. He had just seen off his second son, Ori. "Our parents fought in 1948 and they thought it would be the last war," he said. "I fought in 1967 and thought it would be the last war. We have to see what will happen."

One mother, Pnina Tzur, who had just said good-bye to her son Assaf, was still shaking with emotion. She said: "He was born at the time of the peace agreement with Egypt. I was hoping that by the time he turned 18, he would not have to go to the army. It's part of life in Israel to say goodbye to your child. It's hard but I accept it."

At the Bakum itself, enlistment seemed at times to be a preparation for death. Soldiers had their upper and lower teeth photographed and gave prints from all ten fingers, information vital to identifying their bodies should they be killed. The conveyor belt of procedures included vaccinations, banking arrangements, crash courses in donning gas masks, and the fitting of new uniforms.

Under Israel's system of long conscription (a minimum of three years for men) and extensive reserve duty (yearly service of up to two months or more for some in combat units), a country of five million Jews can at short notice field a trained army of about half a million soldiers, more powerful than the armed forces of most western European countries. The former Chief of Staff, Yigael Yadin, liked to say: "Every Israeli citizen is a soldier on eleven months' annual leave."

The vision of Israelis selflessly and bravely taking up arms to defend their country has changed of late, amid evidence of falling morale and increasing cases of Israelis, both young and old, shirking military duty. But even in an age of disillusionment, the army remains the single most important institution in Israeli life. It seeps into every corner of society. It is, in many ways, a state within a state, a body entrusted not only with the nation's defense but also with nation building itself. Its ranks are supposed to be a melting pot for disparate communities of immigrants, the place where Russians and Moroccans become Israelis; a great social leveler where professors serve as reserve soldiers and take orders from their students. In its early years the army established settlements, built roads, helped with the harvest and sent its soldiers to teach Hebrew to new immigrants. The army radio station still enjoys greater popularity than the state broadcaster.

Officers and men undergo basic training together, and promotion is decided on performance and the assessment of other soldiers. The friendships forged in the army can last a lifetime. Reservists usually serve in the same units with the same fellow soldiers year after year, and the bonds of military comradeship form an important part of one's social connections in civilian life. They are a great source of *proteksiya*, or patronage. A good stint in the army, especially service in elite units such as the air force or the *sayeret matkal* commandos, is an important advantage in later life. For many recruits, the choice of what to do during army service is considered as carefully as their studies. The question a young job-seeker is most likely to be asked is: "What did you do in the army?"

The IDF is a young army, with frequent changes of blood. In the 1950s Dayan was Chief of Staff at 38 and Yadin had been given the job at just 32. The age brackets have crept upward over the decades, with the age of the Chief of Staff now hovering around 50. But Israeli officers are still expected to find a second job in civilian life at the end of their military career.

Women nominally serve 21 months as soldiers, but in practice a large proportion are exempted and of the rest many are demobilized early. For all the images of women serving in the trenches in 1948, and the frequent sight of women carrying rifles slung across their backs, soldiering in Israel remains a man's job. Most Israeli women soldiers are put to work making coffee and shuffling papers for male officers. They are supposed to lend a nurturing touch to the men around them, and many have a miserable time fending off unwanted sexual advances from senior officers. Many of the women are better educated than the men they serve with. As the army has slowly opened up more noncombat disciplines to women, particularly gifted girls may now repair weapons, work in communications, and serve with anti-aircraft defense units. Curiously, women are used as instructors in infantry, artillery, and armor units—teaching men how to fight in a battlefield from which they are excluded. The army was pleasantly surprised to find that men trained harder and complained less when being instructed by a female sergeant. In late 1998, after strong pressure from women's activists, the first Israeli female F-16 pilot graduated from flight training school. But for the most part, the army's attitude to gender issues is still summed up by the dictum: "The best men to the cockpits, and the best women to the pilots."

Decades of bloodshed, privation, and sacrifice have made of Israel a macho and often harsh society. "Tears, here, don't soften the eyes. They only polish the hardness of faces, like rock," wrote the late poet Yehuda Amichai. But the relentless military casualties have not yet hardened Israelis to their own losses. There are nearly 1,000 war memorials in Israel, large and small, made of stone or jagged metal, bombastic or modestly touching. According to one estimate published in the Hebrew daily, *Ha'aretz*, there is a memorial for every 17 fallen Israeli soldiers, compared to the ratio of about one for every 10,000 soldiers killed in the battlefields of Europe.

Israel is a small country and casualties are felt close to home. On Israel's buses, the cacophony of the passengers dissipates into a respectful hush when the news comes on. Anything more than a handful of dead will bring on mourning music. During my years in the Middle East, these melodies often beat the army censor and alerted journalists that something had happened.

The sequence of official observances mirrors Israel's genesis: Holocaust Day, Memorial Day, and Independence Day represent the Jews' emergence from the ashes of genocide in Europe, the blood sacrifice in the battlefields of Palestine, and finally the reward of sovereignty. It makes for an extreme swing of mood, one moment mournful and then, at dusk on the eve of Independence Day, jubilation.

Amid the revelry, however, one still senses the lingering fear of being swamped in an Arab sea. Every year on Independence Day newspapers publish the latest demographic figures as if they were some kind of report card. Is the Jewish population increasing fast enough to keep up with the Arabs? Is immigration up or down? In April 1999 the vital statistics were: Israel's population of 6.1 million included 4.8 million Jews and 1.3 million non-Jews (not counting Palestinians in the West Bank and Gaza Strip). This represented an increase of 2.3 percent on the previous year. Israel accounted for 36 percent of the world's Jewish population of 13.1 million, a sixfold increase since 1948. There are more than 250 million Arabs.

★

Theodor Herzl believed that the Jewish state would, at a stroke, relieve Jews from oppression, cure the gentile oppressors of their anti-Semitism, and rejuvenate the Levant. So perfect was his solution, so self-evident its benefits to all concerned, that the state would have little need for armed force.

In *The Jewish State*, Herzl wrote that the polity would be neutral, although its army would be equipped with "every requisite of modern warfare." In his memoirs, he daydreamed more about the ceremonial uniforms of the future Jewish cavalry than about any battles it might have to fight. By the time he wrote *Altneuland*, Herzl had done away with the military altogether. Members of the New Society were required only to give two years of community service, and the most martial of activities were "athletic and rifle clubs."

In reality, Israel has not known a day of peace, and has lived formally in a state of emergency since its creation. The army has become the supreme national institution, the quintessential embodiment of Israeli values. For David Ben-Gurion, it was "a unique expression of our Israeli personality." The country still prides itself on being a nation of warriors second to none in the world. The author Amos Oz described Israelis as a race of "circumcised Cossacks."

Israel is among the top ten international arms exporters, and its ex-soldiers are eagerly hired as bodyguards, military consultants, and advisers around the world. Computer games allow nerds to pretend they are Israeli air force pilots. T-shirts on sale in Jerusalem's souvenir stores in the Old City are printed with a picture of an F-16 fighter and the words: "Don't worry America. Israel is behind you."

Ben-Gurion liked to say that miracles were part of government planning in Israel. He was tickled by a joke about two Israeli ministers discussing the country's budget problems. One says: "We must declare war on the United States!" The other gives him a bemused look. "Yes," explains the first. "After we lose the Americans will spend billions to rehabilitate us just as they did with Germany and Japan." The second minister shakes his head and asks: "What if we win?"

By 1907, with the arrival of the Second Aliyah, Jews in Palestine formed a secret self-defense group to repulse the growing number of attacks on Jewish communities. It called itself Bar-Giora, after a leader of the Great Revolt against the Romans, and adopted the motto: "In blood and fire Judah fell; in blood and fire shall Judah arise." Its members believed that the new Jews should not only reclaim the land by the sweat of their brows, but defend their possessions on their own. No longer would they hire Arabs or Circassians as guards.

The group expanded and renamed itself *Ha-Shomer*, The Guard. The members of this embryonic army cut strange figures. They aped the oriental dress and manners of the very Arabs and Circassians whom they sought to replace, complete with flowing robes, headscarves, and curved knives. They wore bandoliers of bullets strapped across their chests, and became noted horsemen. Their number included a few women. Within three years, Ha-Shomer took over the protection of seven colonies, including Rishon Le-Zion.

Israel is the product of war. In the First World War, Turkey allied herself to Germany and the Austro-Hungarian empire—an ill-fated gamble that hastened the final dismemberment of the "Sick Man of Europe." In the carve-up of the empire, Britain took a band of territory from Jaffa to Baghdad and created the borders of the modern entity called Palestine.

On November 2, 1917, with British armies advancing into southern Palestine from Egypt, the Foreign Secretary Arthur James Balfour wrote a brief but momentous letter to Lord Rothschild, a scion of British Jewry. The Balfour Declaration, as it has been known ever since, said:

> His Majesty's Government view with favour the establishment in Palestine of a national home for the Jewish people, and will use their best endeavours to facilitate the achievement of this object, it being clearly understood that nothing shall be done which may prejudice the civil and religious rights of existing non-Jewish communities in Palestine, or the rights and political status enjoyed by Jews in any other country.

A month later, General Sir Edmund Allenby entered Jerusalem, not on horseback but on foot, like a pilgrim. One Jewish bystander thought he looked like the Messiah.

"A terrible beauty is born," said W. B. Yeats of Ireland's Easter Rising of 1916. A year later, in Palestine, another terrible beauty was being fashioned.

The Balfour Declaration was a deliberately ambiguous statement.

What would be the borders of the "national home"? Was it to be a state, as the Zionists had first understood the term? And how was the protection of the civil and religious rights of non-Jews to be reconciled with it?

Popular lore has it that the Balfour Declaration was Lloyd George's reward to the Zionist leader Chaim Weizmann, a professional chemist, for his help in devising a new industrial method to produce acetone, a vital solvent needed in the manufacture of munitions, which were in desperately short supply in the early years of the war. Weizmann certainly made powerful friends, but Britain was motivated by complex considerations. They included the need to protect the Suez Canal and the desire to secure a land route to India; the attempt to harness the supposed power of world Jewry for the Allied cause; the prestige of Britain returning to the Holy Land more than six centuries after the last Crusaders had been expelled from Acre; and a peculiarly British form of gentile Zionism which believed that the return of the Jews to Palestine would presage the return of Jesus. Later, British policy in the Middle East would be counterbalanced by the budding realization of the importance of petroleum in Arab countries, especially after Winston Churchill converted the navy from coal to oil in 1911.

With the arrival of the British, the pre-war Ha-Shomer guards were disbanded, and replaced by a larger militia known as the Hagana, under the control of the Histadrut trade union federation, which doubled as a kind of Jewish government. The Hagana was the immediate predecessor of the Israeli army, and its founders included members of the Jewish Legion, a unit of the British army.

The symbol of the Israel Defense Forces is a sword with an olive branch twined around it. But Israel, born in the fire of battle in 1948, has lived by the sword ever since. The olive branch has thrown out a few leaves, but no roots. Israel's conflicts—the 1948 War of Independence, the 1956 Sinai Campaign, the 1967 Six Day War, the 1973 Yom Kippur War, the 1982 invasion of Lebanon, the Palestinian Intifada, the 1991 Gulf War, and the second Palestinian Intifada of 2000—are the most important signposts of its history.

Israel leads a schizophrenic existence. It inhabits parallel worlds, like the earthly and heavenly Jerusalems of the Jewish sages. It is both victim and aggressor, underdog and bully, deeply insecure and supremely arrogant, a democracy and an abuser of human rights. The Israelis can one moment argue that Arab countries present a mortal threat to Israel, and the next threaten to blow up their capitals into dust.

When Israel fights Arab states it presents itself as an enlightened society struggling to survive, "a small country in a bad neighborhood"; it wraps itself in the mantle of the biblical David. But when Israel turns against the Palestinians, it becomes Goliath. Appropriately, the most vivid image of the years of the mass Palestinian uprisings of 1987 and 2000 was the sight of Palestinians using a simple sling to hurl stones at Israeli soldiers armed with automatic weapons. The Israeli–Arab conflict is a struggle of two minorities. Israel is regarded as a foreign body within the bosom of the Arab world, while Palestinians in Israel and the occupied territories are treated as a hostile presence in the body of Jewish Israel. All this has had a corrosive effect on the morale of the army, and its standing in society. Once revered by all, the army has become fair game for criticism. Still, it is the one Israeli institution to enjoy a degree of consensus in a society riven by ideological, religious, and ethnic disputes. For all the talk of "post-Zionist" disenchantment, Israelis are still impressed by, if not enamored with, the army's top brass.

The appointment of a new Chief of Staff is followed as closely as any political contest, and involves just as much back-biting. Generals often migrate to the political arena, where security credentials remain an invaluable asset. Popular generals are shamelessly courted by political parties. Countless senior officers are appointed to top government jobs, if not to the government itself, after retirement.

General elections look like contests between army officers. In the prime ministerial contest of February 2001, Ariel Sharon, the controversial former major-general and defense minister, beat the incumbent Ehud Barak, a former Chief of Staff. In the election of 1999, four political parties were led by former generals. The list of past prime ministers includes the assassinated Yitzhak Rabin, a former Chief of Staff, and, although not regular soldiers, two "fighting fathers" of the right-wing underground, Menachem Begin and Yitzhak Shamir.

In a country with a surfeit of famous, larger-than-life generals, Moshe Dayan is still one of the best known, if only because of the black patch strapped across his left eye. His successes and failures, his moments of vision and shortsightedness, his dashing heroism and arrogance, all reflect the vicissitudes of Israel and of its army. His eyepatch is a metaphor for Israel. One eye filled with vision and the other hopelessly blind.

*

"My name Moshe was born in sorrow," wrote Moshe Dayan in his autobiography. "It had been inscribed a year before on a solitary tombstone in an olive grove in Degania, where the Jordan River flows out of the southern end of the Sea of Galilee. It marked the first grave in this fledgling settlement [. . .]."

Dayan was named after Moshe Barsky, an 18-year-old settler at Degania who had been ambushed by Bedouin in November 1913. He put up a fight and was shot in the back. His body was found with a shoe and a staff on his head, which the Jewish settlers took as a deliberate sign of vengeance, presumably because he had killed or wounded one of his assailants. According to Dayan the murder was not political, but another case of the lawlessness which plagued the land. It was not until he was in his late teens that he understood the political significance of a string of Arab riots and uprisings in 1920, 1921, 1929, and 1936.

Britain tried to assuage Arab resistance by progressively scaling back the scope for Zionist ambitions. It soon began to limit Jewish immigration and made clear early on that it had no intention of allowing Palestine to become "as Jewish as England is English." In 1921, Britain lopped off the eastern part of Palestine—from the Jordan River to the border with Iraq—to create Transjordan. Zionist hopes were further frustrated by the loss of the Litani River and the Golan Heights when Palestine's border was demarcated in the early 1920s.

The ambiguous and contradictory promises made by Britain to its various allies—France, the Hashemites, and the Zionists—quickly came unstuck. With the assent of his erstwhile British allies, the Hashemite Prince Faisal, who had led the Arab Revolt against Turkish rule with the help of the British officer, T. E. Lawrence, was expelled from Damascus by French forces in July 1920. Syria and Lebanon were placed under a French mandate, while Britain was entrusted with the mandates to rule Palestine and Iraq. Faisal would be enthroned as king in Baghdad, while his brother, Abdallah, was enthroned in Transjordan.

The year 1920, which saw the hopes of Arab unity and independence destroyed, came to be known as *Al-Nakba*, or "The Catastrophe" (a term later adopted for the dispersal of Palestinians in 1948). Palestinians, many of whom had dreamed of a Greater Syria, would turn their energies toward a specifically Palestinian struggle. It was part of a wave of postwar turmoil in the wider Arab world, including riots in Egypt in 1919, the defeat of the Hashemites in Arabia by the puritanical followers of Ibn Saud in the same year, and an uprising in Iraq in 1920.

The troubles produced Israel's first war hero, Yosef Trumpeldor, who was killed defending the settlement of Tel Hai close to Syria in April 1920. Every Israeli schoolchild learns of Trumpeldor's rousing last words: *Ein davar. Tov lamut be'ad artzenu* ("Never mind. It is good to die for our country"). More recently, however, iconoclasts have suggested that his final utterances were, in fact, some choice curses in Russian.

The point at which Arab resentment of Zionist encroachment developed into a separate Palestinian national consciousness is the subject of heated debate among academics. In *Palestinian Identity*, the Palestinian academic, Rashid Khalidi, finds the first glints of nationalist identity among the literate notables in Ottoman days. The sense of nationhood then gradually spread wider with the shock of the First World War, the losing struggles against the British and the Zionists, and finally crystallized with the trauma of dispossession and dispersion in 1948.

Dayan writes that he did not become aware of a nationalist resistance until 1932, when a bomb was thrown into the hut of the Dayan family's neighbors. The attack had been perpetrated by followers of an Islamic preacher from Haifa, Sheikh Izz al-Din al-Qassam. Discovering that his Arab friends admired the Sheikh's movement, Dayan realized for the first time that there was a "deep national and religious chasm that separated the Arabs from the Jews who were fulfilling the ideals of Zionism."

Sheikh Izz al-Din, whose name inspired Palestinian suicide bombers of the 1990s, was killed with a band of followers by British forces in 1935. This provided only a short respite; the sheikh's attacks were the prelude to a three-year Arab uprising which came to be known as the Arab Revolt. It began with a riot in Jaffa in April 1936, followed by the declaration of a general strike. Armed attacks ensued, not just against Jews, but also against the British, who were seen as the protectors of Zionism, and against members of the Arab ruling class considered to be collaborators.

The rebels took control for a while of towns such as Nablus, Bethlehem, and Ramallah and, briefly, even the Old City of Jerusalem. Faced with a common enemy, the Hagana was drawn into cooperation with Britain to put down the revolt. A lasting influence on the Hagana was the unofficial cooperation with the special night squads set up by an eccentric English captain, Orde Wingate, a brilliant, unconventional fighter and, for a British officer, an unusually ardent believer in Zionism. He considered himself an honorary member of the Hagana and was known as "The Friend." After a long night's march, recalled Dayan, "Wingate would sit in a corner stark naked, reading the Bible and munching raw onions as though they were the most luscious pears." Eventually promoted to a general, Wingate was killed in an air crash in 1944 after commanding the Chindits, a guerrilla-style force which fought the Japanese in the jungles of Burma.

By 1939 the British had all but put down the Arab Revolt with stern measures such as the demolition of villages and parts of Jaffa, as well as using Arab civilians as human shields against attacks by armed bands. The Palestinian leadership was exiled, and Haj Amin al-Husseini, the Mufti of Jerusalem, escaped to Syria.

In 1937 the Peel Committee proposed partitioning the remaining part of Palestine into a Jewish and an Arab state with an "exchange of populations." Some Jewish leaders grudgingly accepted the proposal, but sought to determine the border by extending the Jewish presence. The Hagana not only defended Jewish settlements, but now also built them. Beginning in 1936 and for the following 11 years, more than 100 overnight "tower and stockade" settlements were erected.

With the approach of the Second World War, Britain feared losing support in the Arab world and in 1939 issued a White Paper which severely curtailed Jewish immigration for five years, even for those seeking to escape Nazi persecution. Thereafter, further immigration would be dependent on Arab consent, effectively an Arab veto. The British also held out the promise of independence for a majority Arab state within ten years. This amounted to the end of the Jewish dream of statehood, but even these concessions were not enough for the exiled Mufti, who allied himself with Hitler.

The White Paper abruptly broke the entente between Britain and the Jewish community, known as the *Yishuv* or "Settlement." It was the Jews' turn to riot and go on strike against the British. The Jewish militias began to organize ships carrying illegal Jewish immigrants. The relationship between Britain and the Jews was pregnant with contradictions, never more so than during the war. In the spring of 1941, with Britain's position in the Middle East threatened by a massive German pincer from Greece and North Africa, there was a second honeymoon of military cooperation between Britain and the Yishuv. After years spent waging a war of shooting and bombing against Arabs and later against the British, the breakaway Etzel movement, or *Irgun Tzva'i Le'umi* ("National Military Organization," known as the "Irgun") declared a ceasefire. This led to the creation of a new splinter group, *Lehi* (*Lohamei Herut Israel*, Fighters for the Freedom of Israel, known as the Stern Gang), whose hatred of Britain was so intense that at one point it even sought an alliance with the Nazis. Both these groups, regarded by the British as terrorists, would produce Israeli prime ministers.

Some 26,000 Jews in Palestine volunteered to serve in the British army. The Hagana, meanwhile, mobilized its own permanent nine-company underground strike force, known as the *Palmach*, a Hebrew abbreviation of "assault companies." Its members participated in British commando operations as saboteurs or as guides and intelligence agents. Some were parachuted behind enemy lines in Europe.

Dayan commanded a reconnaissance unit which preceded the Allied invasion of Vichy-held Syria and Lebanon and was wounded during a skirmish with French troops. "The story of the Hagana's participation in the invasion of Syria might never have been remembered, even as a footnote to history, had it not been for the fact that on the same night . . . Moshe Dayan lost his eye," wrote Yitzhak Rabin in his memoirs.

With Rommel's Afrika Korps bearing down on British-held Egypt, the Hagana and Britain devised an improbable plan to turn the Carmel range into a Jewish redoubt that would hold out against the invading German army. Some Jews were determined to go down fighting in a new Masada. But after the German rout at Al-Alamein in October 1942, the threat to Palestine receded. Britain again feared inflaming Arab passions, and closed down the Palmach's training bases.

In early 1944, with the horror of the Nazi Holocaust of the Jews increasingly apparent, Etzel and Lehi unleashed a new offensive against the British. They blew up government and police offices, raided British armories for weapons and assassinated Lord Moyne, a British minister of state for the Middle East. Churchill, the leading pro-Zionist of the British government, spoke of "new gangsters worthy of Nazi Germany." David Ben-Gurion ordered the Hagana to help Britain crush the armed revolt. It was a period known as the *saison* or hunting season, when the Hagana kidnaped members of the underground and handed them over to the British.

But after the end of the war, when Britain's newly elected Labor party repudiated its pro-Zionist platform, the Hagana joined the dissidents. The Jewish militias unleashed wholesale attacks on bridges, railways, police stations, and airfields. Illegal ships carrying refugees from Europe tried to run the British naval blockade, and those caught were interned in Cyprus. Britain poured 100,000 troops into Palestine but time and again, Britain's position was weakened by pathetic scenes of British soldiers manhandling survivors of the gas chambers.

In July 1946 the King David Hotel in Jerusalem, which housed much of the British administration, was blown up by Etzel. The blast killed 41 Arabs, 28 Britons, 17 Jews and five others. As the violence intensified, Etzel staged a spectacular attack on the old Crusader fortress at Acre, freeing more than 200 prisoners. The British administration hanged three Etzel men who had been captured, prompting the group to execute two kidnaped British servicemen.

In February 1947, Britain threw up its hands and asked the United Nations to decide what should be done with Palestine. In November of that year, the General Assembly voted for Palestine to be partitioned into a Jewish and an Arab state, with Jerusalem as an international city. The scene of Jews gathered around their radio sets to follow the vote is one of the enduring images of the period: "Afghanistan, No; Argentina, Abstain; Australia, Yes. . . ." The partition resolution was passed: 33 voted in favor, including the United States and the Soviet Union, 10 against, mostly from Arab and Muslim states, and there were 10 abstentions, including Britain. The Jews' right to statehood had been endorsed by the world. Dayan wrote: "We were happy that night, and we danced . . . we danced—but we knew that ahead of us lay the battlefield."

★

The "War of Independence," as Israel calls its first war with the Arabs, is really two separate wars: the scramble for territory between Jews and Arabs in Palestine as the British withdrew from the country, and the full-scale conflict between the newborn state of Israel and the surrounding Arab countries.

Incidents broke out almost immediately after the U.N. partition vote, with rioting escalating to sniping and bombs, and eventually local fights for cities, remote Jewish outposts and, above all, the roads. The fiercest fight was for the road to Jerusalem. The Hagana steadily gained the upper hand and on the eve of independence it created a continuous area of Jewish control, including the main coastal cities of Jaffa, Haifa, and Acre, and large parts of the Galilee, including Tiberias and Safed.

As waves of Palestinian refugees streamed out of Jewish-controlled areas, the new Israel improved its strategic position just in time to face the onslaught of the invading armies of Egypt, Transjordan, Iraq, Syria, and Lebanon. General Sir Alan Cunningham, the last British High Commissioner, sailed from Haifa. Ben-Gurion proclaimed the independence of the Jewish state. There had been proposals that the country be called "Zion," "The Jewish State," "Judea," "The Land of Israel," and "Ever," from the word *ivri*, meaning Hebrew. In the end the leaders of the Yishuv settled on "State of Israel."

Israel was, on paper, heavily outnumbered by the Arab forces. But in the field the sides were roughly matched because many of the Arab armies were operating at the end of long lines of communication, had to keep back large parts of their forces to ensure security at home and lacked real commitment. In terms of equipment, however, the Israeli forces were critically under strength at the start of the Arab states' offensive. The three weeks between the Arab invasion and the first truce, of 11 June, were a desperate struggle for survival.

The first crisis came on the Jordan River, in Dayan's birthplace of Degania. A Syrian armored brigade took two kibbutzim nearby and the frontline positions in the neighboring kibbutzim of Degania A and B were being shelled. A delegation from Degania pleaded with Ben-Gurion for reinforcements, but all he could give them was the loan for one day of four antiquated 65mm field guns mockingly called "Napoleonchiks"—and Moshe Dayan. Dayan had the defenders rearrange their disposition, and they stopped the Syrian tanks at the gates of Degania. At the eleventh hour, the Napoleonchiks were in position and opened fire. The Syrians retreated in disarray, and never attempted another attack on the area. Dayan was struck by their lack of fighting spirit, noting that they had fled "like birds in the corn field, when we chase them by banging on empty cans."

Still, by the time the first ceasefire came into effect, the Egyptians had advanced to within about 30 miles of Tel Aviv and linked up with the Arab Legion in the southern outskirts of Jerusalem. The Transjordanians had once again severed the main road to Jerusalem (but the Israelis managed to cut a new "Burma Road" through the mountains) and, more important, captured the Jewish Quarter of the Old City.

Hostilities resumed for 10 days in early July. Resupplied by Czechoslovakia, Israel broke Egypt's lines in the northern Negev and captured a swathe of Lower Galilee, including Nazareth. Jerusalem was effectively partitioned between Israel and Transjordan.

The U.N. mediator, Count Folke Bernadotte, was assassinated in Jerusalem by Lehi in September, and the war resumed the following month. Israel took Beersheba, leaving an Egyptian brigade surrounded at Faluja. The besieged force included an intelligence officer, Major Gamal Abdel-Nasser, who would later take power in Egypt and become the symbol of Arab nationalism. The whole of the Galilee was taken, and Israeli troops spilled into Lebanon and Sinai.

The armistice agreement with Egypt was signed in Rhodes in February 1949. Lebanon, Transjordan, and Syria followed Egypt in signing armistice accords. There were tantalizing glimpses of peace in behind-the-scenes maneuvering, but the conditions were either unacceptable to a victorious Israel (Egypt demanded control of the Negev), or the Arab leaders could not muster the necessary political support. King Abdallah of Jordan seems to have colluded with Israel to prevent the creation of a Palestinian state. His forces limited themselves mainly to holding territory in the West Bank rather than attempting seriously to attack Israel. Ben-Gurion, in turn, rejected demands that Israel should capture the central highlands, saying it was time to end the war and concentrate on building the country. Abdallah secretly concluded an accord with Israel which would have given him a land corridor between the West Bank and Gaza Strip, but never ratified it.

The readiness to accommodate the Jewish state, a continuation of the contacts established by his brother Faisal with Zionist leaders in 1917, would later cost Abdallah his life: he was assassinated by a Palestinian at the Al-Aqsa mosque in 1951. But his pragmatism, so reviled by many of his contemporaries, preserved the West Bank and the Old City of Jerusalem in Arab hands for nearly two decades, laying the foundation for later Palestinian claims to the territory.

The War of Independence has long been portrayed in Israel as a miraculous victory against overwhelming odds. More recent work by historians argues, however, that Israel enjoyed numerical superiority over its enemies in the battlefield for most of the war. Israel benefited from the fact that it operated within internal lines of communication and enjoyed a single command. It displayed mobility and the ability to fight at night, and knew how to concentrate forces for major assaults. Above all, Israel's fighting spirit was intensified by the knowledge that the state had its back to the Mediterranean. The Israeli army's ranks were swelled by refugees arriving from Europe, and by experienced soldiers, including foreign volunteers, demobilized from Allied armies. Ultimately, said the historian Benny Morris, the stronger side won.

Israel won about a third more territory than it had been allocated

under the U.N. partition plan. It provided a refuge for the traumatized survivors of the Nazi Holocaust, but about 700,000 Palestinian
refugees—most of the Arabs in Israeli territory—were driven out,
never to return. The end of the war was in many ways an unsatisfac-
tory outcome for all sides. Israel formed—and still forms—a Jewish
dagger in the heart of the Arab world, severing Egypt and North
Africa from the Fertile Crescent and the Arabian peninsula. For
Arabs, its very existence is a humiliation, a new Crusader state.

Israelis, for their part, bemoaned the loss of Jewish holy sites,
including the Western Wall, in the West Bank. Military planners worried about the vulnerability of the borders, including the nine-mile-
wide "narrow waist" between the West Bank and the Mediterranean.
The main concentration of Israeli population in the coastal plain was
within range of Arab artillery.

Israel's territory, wrote Yigal Allon, the former Palmach commander, in *The Making of Israel's Army*, "was much less than it was
within her military capacity to achieve, and much less than was necessary for her defense against farther threats from the same enemies."
A "Second Round" was long anticipated. A children's war game of
the same name appeared in the shops.

★

The Six Day War of 1967 is regarded by Israelis as their finest
moment. Hardly anybody remembers the six-day war of 1956, when
Israeli forces broke through Egypt's defenses in Sinai in a dress
rehearsal for the decisive war eleven years later.

Israel's Sinai campaign was part of an ill-fated conspiracy to give
Britain and France a pretext to "separate the forces" and seize back
the Suez Canal, which had been privatized by Gamal Abdel-Nasser.
Israel cast itself in the role of aggressor, but in return sought western
support to take over the eastern Sinai coast to ensure freedom of
shipping through the blockaded Straits of Tiran, Israel's own "Suez
Canal." All three hoped Nasser would be toppled.

At the time, Israel's Sinai campaign was regarded as an extraordinary feat of arms, comparable to Hannibal's crossing of the Alps.
Tourists, archaeologists, and countless other academics swept in
behind the armies in search of evidence of the Exodus story. "This is
neither legend nor dream, my friends," said the words to one contemporary song. "This is the people of Israel face to face with Mount
Sinai." Ben-Gurion spoke dreamily of establishing the "Third Kingdom of Israel."

In 1956, the United States was a superpower but not yet the steadfast ally of Israel that it would become. President Dwight Eisenhower, citing the breach of the United Nations charter and seeking Arab support to contain the Soviet Union, forced Britain and France to withdraw from the Canal Zone. The following year the Israelis retreated after receiving assurances of freedom of shipping and the curbing of cross-border attacks from the Gaza Strip.

The 1950s were the years when Israel laid down its main military doctrines. It was, in the words of Yigal Allon, an island without the strategic advantage of being surrounded by sea. Early on, Israel decided that it could not maintain large standing armed forces. It created the system of a small permanent force consisting of a skeleton of career officers and technicians, especially in the air force, and a body of conscripts. In times of crisis, the bulk of the army would be made up of trained reserve soldiers. But given Israel's lack of strategic depth, and the minimum of two days required to mobilize its reserves, Israel would be vulnerable to surprise attack. Good intelligence was of paramount importance.

In 1950, Yigal Yadin, then Chief of Staff, expounded what still are the cardinal rules of Israeli warfare. He emphasized the importance of the morale of the country, unity of command, and age-old principles such as surprise, mobility, concentration of force, and the indirect approach. At the root of Israel's doctrine was the realization that the Jewish state could not sustain long wars of attrition: it must fight short, sharp, and decisive wars. The aim would be to shift the battle to enemy territory at the earliest opportunity. The need for speed was underlined by the belief that international diplomacy would favor the oil-rich Arabs and would quickly try to limit Israeli gains. Israel's defense, therefore, was to be based on a policy of blitzkrieg.

Land forces would constitute the military backbone, increasingly reliant on armor. The air force was at the time tasked with protecting the skies over Israel and lending tactical support to the army, with no strategic bombing arm. The navy was comparatively small, dedicated mainly to coastal defense.

The policy of heavy retribution for attacks by Palestinian guerrillas, or *fedayin*, was established, with mixed results. A special force, Unit 101, was set up to carry out the reprisals. Its unkempt volunteers, hand-picked by the combative Major Ariel Sharon (who became notorious over the 1982 invasion of Lebanon and was elected Prime Minister in 2001), carried out a campaign of murderously effective raids.

Having fretted about the Israelis' lack of fighting abilities in the early years of the state, Dayan, serving as Head of Operations, now had to worry about the excesses of Unit 101. Controversies over the killing of Arab civilians in reprisals—especially the killing in 1953 of 69 people, mostly women and children, during demolition of the Jordanian village of Kibya—prompted new orders to attack only military positions.

Unit 101 was merged with the paratroop battalion to create a full brigade under Sharon, and by being seen successfully taking on Arab military positions, the red berets basked in public adulation. The paras, said Ben-Gurion, were a "hothouse for heroes."

Dayan held to the notion that dead and wounded men were not to be abandoned on the battlefield, at almost any cost. In 1954, the paratroopers staged several raids into enemy territory to kidnap Jordanian soldiers and successfully exchanged them for a captured Israeli fighter. The same tactic has been tried, so far with little success and at the cost of strong international criticism, in trying to secure the release of Ron Arad, an Israeli navigator captured by Lebanese Shi'ite militia after his plane was shot down over Lebanon in 1986. Israel kidnaped the Lebanese Shi'ite cleric, Sheikh Abdel-Karim Obeid, in 1989, and another Shi'ite leader, Mustafa Dirani, in 1994 but years later, Arad's whereabouts are unknown. In October 2000, Lebanon's Hizbollah movement infiltrated the border and kidnaped three Israeli soldiers, knowing the value that Israel places on the recovery of its servicemen. In 1985, for example, Israel freed some 1,000 Palestinian security prisoners in exchange for six soldiers captured in Lebanon.

★

In April 1967 an Israeli tractor attempted to work a disputed field, drawing Syrian artillery fire on Kibbutz Gadot. The Syrian positions were out of range of Israel's tanks, and the air force was called into action. Israel shot down six Syrian aircraft which had been scrambled to challenge them and pursued their prey all the way to Damascus.

The countdown to the Six Day War had begun, although Israeli planners may not have known it. Egypt, the most powerful country in the Arab world, was embroiled in the civil war in Yemen, and Israel assumed the Syrians would not move without Egyptian support.

Tension on the northern border, already raised by Israel's use of demilitarized zones, was heightened by skirmishes over the division of the waters of the Jordan River between Israel, Syria, and Jordan. In

1964, Israel completed its National Water Carrier, a network of concrete pipes and tunnels, to bring water from the Sea of Galilee to the southern parts of the country. In response, Syria started work on canals to divert the sources of the Jordan River. Israel staged incidents in order to knock out the Syrian earth-moving equipment, and these often escalated into mini-battles involving tanks, artillery, and aircraft.

The exact sequence of events which led to war may never be known. Martin van Creveld, the military historian, argues in *The Sword and the Olive* that many senior officers in the IDF were spoiling for a fight and wanted to provoke the increasingly radical Syrian government into war. On the Arab side, he surmised, an unspoken reason for Nasser's ill-conceived rush to war may have been his desire to stop Israel from completing the development of nuclear weapons.

In the first half of May, the Soviet Union fed intelligence reports to Egypt of an Israeli build-up along the Syrian frontier. Nasser, despite Israeli denials, disengaged from Yemen with alacrity and ostentatiously poured troops into Sinai, ordering UN troops out of the area. Egyptian troops reoccupied Sharm al-Sheikh. The blockade on the Straits of Tiran, which Israel had declared in 1957 would be a *casus belli*, was reimposed.

By the end of May Jordan had signed a mutual defense pact with Egypt. Iraq joined a few days later. Arab leaders proclaimed that they would reconquer Palestine once and for all.

As Israeli ministers tried to find a diplomatic solution, the generals demanded that Israel take immediate military action to prevent the Egyptians from reinforcing their positions. In an atmosphere of popular fear of another Holocaust, graves were dug in public parks in anticipation of massive casualties. Chief of Staff Rabin collapsed from apparent nervous exhaustion on May 23 and, according to the contested version given by the then Chief of Operations Ezer Weizman, offered to give up the command. At the height of Israel's military crisis, Israel's most senior officer lay sedated for nearly two days.

The Israeli public, largely ignorant of how powerful the IDF had become, grew even more alarmed by the apparent prevarication of the Prime Minister, Levi Eshkol, who faltered and stumbled through a televised address. Instead of calming Israelis, he gave the impression that the nation was rudderless.

Under pressure, the Prime Minister agreed to create a government of national unity. He dismissed calls to hand power back to Ben-Gurion. Instead, he succumbed to strident demands that Dayan, then retired from the army and out of the cabinet, be appointed defense minister. "It took the entry of eighty thousand Egyptian troops into Sinai to get me back into the government," Dayan commented.

H-hour was set for 0745 on June 5. Israeli aircraft had earlier taken off in staggered formation over the Mediterranean, and struck simultaneously at nine air bases after the Egyptian predawn patrols had landed for their morning breaks. Only 12 aircraft had been left to defend Israeli skies. Acting on excellent intelligence, Israel destroyed nearly 300 aircraft in the next three hours. Three-quarters of the Egyptian air force were left burning and by 1100 hours Weizman could be heard shouting that the war had already been won. The Israeli air force was free to wreak similar damage on the Jordanian and Syrian air forces, which had joined the hostilities.

With air superiority assured, the task on the ground was easier. The Gaza Strip and the fortress-like defenses guarding the access routes to the northern Sinai were penetrated by the second day with a series of outflanking maneuvers and attacks through terrain deemed impassable.

Jordan ignored Israel's appeals to stay out of the war—King Hussein later admitted that he had been misled by Egyptian propaganda claims that they were winning a stunning victory—and Israeli paratroopers triumphantly entered the Old City through the Lion's Gate on the third day of the war. The rest of the West Bank had fallen by nightfall.

Yael Dayan, the daughter of the defense minister and a successful emerging author, had returned from Athens to rejoin the army. She was posted to the military spokesman's unit, attached to a task force on the southern front commanded by Ariel Sharon. Her war diary, published as *Israel Journal: June 1967*, recounts the moment troops in Sinai heard of the fall of Jerusalem. "The news was cried out and the convoy was lit [struck] as if by lightning. The 'something' had happened. It was not a conquest but liberation . . . it was the long route of our people, from Moses to the paratrooper who first touched the sacred wall. We were suddenly not defending a frontier, a settlement, a decade, we were part of something that was larger."

On the fourth day of the war, the Israelis reached the Suez Canal. With Egypt and Jordan requesting a ceasefire, Rabin went to sleep that night thinking the war was over. He was woken at 7 A.M. to hear that Dayan had just ordered an assault against the Syrians on the Golan Heights. The defense minister had at first rejected demands by northern communities to take action against Syria, which had limited itself to fighting local skirmishes. But Dayan changed his mind because Syria had agreed to a ceasefire during the night, a decision seen as removing the threat of Soviet intervention had Israel opened a new front. The Syrians initially put up stiff resistance. But by the next day, the Israelis had taken Kuneitra (which Herzl had once seen as a great railway entrepôt between Europe and Asia) as the Syrians redeployed their troops northward to defend Damascus. For all the words written about the vital strategic importance of the Golan Heights, its conquest was an afterthought. The main purpose, wrote Dayan, was to put Israeli settlements out of Syrian artillery range and "show the Syrians that they could not continue to harass us with impunity."

Israel's victory was won by mastery of the skies, and by its ability to switch its forces from one front to another. It essentially fought three separate battles in quick succession against Egypt, Jordan, and Syria. Israeli soldiers' ferocious blitzkrieg was driven by the belief that they were fighting to stop a new Holocaust.

The conquest of territory was a poisoned chalice. Israel had become a mini-empire, occupying a sullen and resentful Palestinian population in the West Bank. On the first day of war, Dayan had told the nation on radio: "Soldiers of Israel, we have no aims of conquest." In the aftermath of victory, however, the Israeli government was ambivalent about the return of captured territory. "The war is over; now we are waiting for a phone call from Hussein," Dayan told the BBC. The call did not come.

★

Yael Dayan records how, a few days after the end of the Six Day War, she sat with her father on a bridge over the Suez Canal at Kantara. They dangled their feet over the still waters, and as a couple of bloated corpses floated past, her father said: "It must be unbearable to be part of a defeated army." Just a few years later, Moshe Dayan would come close to experiencing that deepest gloom. The euphoria of 1967 would give way to the disillusionment of 1973.

The humiliation of the Arabs in 1967 did not bring them to the peace table, as some Israeli leaders had assumed, but increased their public defiance. The Arab summit in Khartoum in September 1967 issued what became known as the Three No's: No peace with Israel, No negotiations with Israel, and No recognition of Israel.

Israel's new borders were more defensible and afforded the army greater strategic depth. The Suez Canal, said Dayan, was "one of the best anti-tank ditches available." An invader from the east would have to ford the Jordan River and climb some 3,000 feet up the mountains in the West Bank before reaching Jerusalem. In the north, the Syrians no longer overlooked the Sea of Galilee. Instead, the Israelis were on the plain leading to Damascus. The victorious doctrine of striking the first blow and fighting the war on the enemy's territory gave way to a defensive posture—and hubris.

Israel and the Arab states were fully drawn into the Cold War. Israel rearmed with better and more plentiful weapons from the United States, while the Arabs quickly rebuilt their forces with the assistance of the Soviet Union. Military incidents multiplied after 1969, when Egypt declared that it no longer recognized the ceasefire, and escalated into a campaign of increasingly severe border clashes dubbed the "War of Attrition."

Israel built a vast defensive network of fortresses on the water's edge of the Suez Canal known as the Bar-Lev line, but these would soon prove to be as ineffective as the Maginot line. Israeli commando counterraids were daring and often brilliant—at one point in 1969 the Israelis carted off an entire Soviet-built radar installation. The air force bombed civilian and military installations deep inside Egypt, faced the new generation of Soviet anti-aircraft missiles, and sometimes fought dogfights with aircraft flown by Soviet pilots. By 1970 the fighting had escalated to the extent that the superpowers acted to impose a ceasefire.

Nasser died in September 1970 and was succeeded by Anwar al-Sadat, who in 1972 expelled all Soviet advisers. The move put Israel even more at ease; the Egyptians were deemed to be too incompetent to operate their sophisticated arsenal on their own. Sadat's "Year of Decision" in 1971 came and went. In 1973 the IDF boasted that "our situation has never been better" and in September, just days before the start of the Yom Kippur War, the army was studying proposals to cut national service from three years to two and a half.

At 1400 hours on October 6, Egypt and Syria unleashed a coordinated surprise attack across the Suez Canal and on the Golan Heights. The onslaught "came as a surprise, though it was not unexpected," wrote Dayan, with a certain evasiveness. Earlier in the year, Dayan had told the army to be ready for a war by the summer. But on the eve of the actual conflict, the army had been lulled into believing that Egyptian troop movements were just a regular military exercise. Syria's mobilization was interpreted as a precaution against a possible *Israeli* attack. Israel had gradually reinforced its positions in response to the deployments on the other side, but always reluctant to cripple its economy by sending its full reserves to the front, it was not fully mobilized when war broke out.

Israel was trapped by the "concept" that the Arabs were not ready for war. No amount of evidence on the ground—including a secret warning from Jordan's King Hussein ten days before the war that Egypt and Syria were likely to attack—could shake Israel out of its complacency. It did not understand that Sadat would consider launching a limited war to gain political advantage. On the morning of the war, Prime Minister Golda Meir ordered full mobilization but rejected demands by some commanders for a preemptive strike against enemy airfields and air defenses for fear of alienating international opinion. The timing of the attack on Yom Kippur, the holiest day of the Jewish year, has long been held as proof of the Arabs' perfidy. In fact, it meant that Israeli reserve soldiers could be easily found at home or at synagogue and mobilized quickly through Israel's deserted streets.

At the time of the Egyptian attack, Israeli tanks on the canal were outnumbered by about ten to one. On the water's edge, the Israelis had 450 soldiers and three tanks on a front line some 100 miles long. In the first minute of the Egyptian attack, fortified positions on the Bar-Lev line came under massive bombardment and the first wave of about 8,000 Egyptian infantrymen crossed the canal on rubber dinghies, demolished the earthen ramparts with high-pressure jets of water, and dug in to repel Israeli counterattacks. Israeli aircraft tried to hit the Egyptian pontoon bridges, but encountered heavy fire from a dense network of anti-aircraft defenses.

The tanks of the wrong-footed Israelis were picked off by anti-tank missiles. By the following morning all the fortresses had either fallen or were surrounded by the Egyptians swarming across the Canal. These static defenses had turned into traps for the Israelis, forcing them to try to rescue the besieged defenders and fight at the water's edge rather than farther back, out of range of the anti-aircraft missiles. When reserves counterattacked on the third day, they were thrown into battle in a confused and piecemeal fashion. Arab soldiers could no longer be scattered by "banging on empty cans."

The Suez Canal front stabilized on October 10 as the Egyptians dug in, to the fury of the Syrians and the relief of the Israelis, who could concentrate on the critical northern front. Here the Israelis were again heavily outnumbered and on the fourth day, October 9, the situation had become desperate. The 7th Armored Brigade, down to just seven tanks, was about to withdraw when the Syrians miraculously broke off the attack.

The turnaround in fortunes is attributed in Israeli military lore to the exploits of Lt. Col. "Yossi," who rushed home from his honeymoon in the Himalayas and set out to the front with an improvised force of 13 repaired tanks. Surprised, the Syrians came to a standstill and their rear echelons were seen to retreat, followed by the forward tanks. But it had also been reported in the American press that Dayan, facing defeat, threatened nuclear retaliation. By October 11 the Israelis had regained their positions on the Golan. They counterattacked and ended the war with additional territory beyond the ceasefire line of 1967.

With the Syrians now appealing for help, on the 14th the Egyptians launched one of the largest armored battles in history, with some 2,000 tanks locked in fighting along the entire front. This time the Israelis were better prepared. The Egyptians were more exposed as they emerged from the cover of their anti-aircraft missiles and their attack was beaten off.

It was the turning point of the war. The Israelis pressed their advantage the following night by crossing the Canal through a "seam" between two Egyptian armies in an operation masterminded by Ariel Sharon. Sweeping north and south along the rear of the Egyptians, the Israelis attacked the anti-aircraft defenses from the ground and encircled the Egyptian Third Army. It was saved by a U.N. ceasefire that came into force on October 22. The Egyptians were left holding two major bridgeheads on the eastern bank of the Suez Canal, and the Israeli forces holding a swathe of territory on the western bank and a seemingly open road to Cairo.

Fighting did not stop until two days later, after the United States and Soviet Union, which both actively resupplied their clients, rattled their sabers at each other in the most serious superpower confrontation since the Cuban missile crisis. The United States had prevented a victory by Soviet arms, and, with Henry Kissinger's subsequent shuttle mission, established itself as the driving force in Middle East diplomacy. The cost, however, was the first oil shock. Between October and December 1973 the price of oil quadrupled as Arab producers raised prices, cut production, and imposed embargoes against countries sympathetic to Israel, such as the United States and the Netherlands. The western world was split. The roles during the Suez crisis were reversed. Now it was countries such as France and Britain which sought to mollify the Arabs, and the United States which schemed with Israel.

Israel's ability to snatch victory from the initial disaster was, arguably, a vindication of its military prowess. But the Yom Kippur War was almost as great a trauma as the Six Day War had been for the Arabs. For Israelis and Arabs alike, its significance was that the myth of Israeli invincibility was demolished.

The October War, as Arabs call it, is remembered as a great victory which was stolen from them by American intervention. In Cairo's October War Museum, visitors are seated on a stage which revolves within a large diorama reconstructing different phases of the crossing of the Suez Canal. There are explosions and flashes of light. The Star of David lies tattered on the ground as Egyptians are shown reconquering their lost lands. Inevitably, perhaps, the story of how the war ended in the near annihilation of the Third Army is left untold.

In Israel, the euphoria of 1967 gave way to the disenchantment of 1973. Dayan, the hero of the Six Day War, became the scapegoat of the Yom Kippur War. Families of dead soldiers shouted "murderer" at him. In the search for those responsible for Israel's lack of military preparedness, the official Agranat commission of inquiry forced the resignation of the Chief of Intelligence, the CO Southern Command, and the Chief of Staff. Dayan was exonerated, proving himself to be Israel's paramount "Minister for Survival." The Labor party was re-elected to power in December 1973 with a reduced majority, but under pressure from the country and the party itself, Golda Meir resigned in April 1974.

Yitzhak Rabin, the hero of 1967 who, as ambassador to Washington in 1973, was unsullied by the failures of the Yom Kippur War, took over. The Labor party, in power for more than a quarter of a century, had been mortally wounded and Rabin lasted just three years. In 1977, social discontent, declining economic standards, and disillusion with the Labor establishment propelled to power the right-wing Likud party under Menachem Begin, the former leader of the Etzel underground movement. To his surprise, Dayan was appointed Foreign Minister in Begin's government.

The war was the turning point in the desultory peace talks. Egypt had overcome the humiliation of 1967 and any agreement could be presented as the outcome of military valor. Israel realized, in the most painful way possible, that it could not live by the sword indefinitely. In late 1974 and early 1975, Kissinger mediated the Disengagement Agreements with both Egypt and Syria, in which Israel, despite winning the war, conceded territory. This included areas captured in 1967, such as Kuneitra on the Golan. The town was demolished by the departing Israelis in a fit of pique and has been left in ruins ever since by the Syrians as a symbol of Israeli wickedness.

A UN force was appointed to patrol areas where military forces were limited in strength. The Suez Canal was reopened. A more substantial second Interim Agreement between Israel and Egypt was concluded in September 1975, and Israel withdrew to the eastern side of the strategic Sinai passes, where American early-warning stations were set up.

These were the first tentative steps toward a peace treaty with Egypt. In November 1977, Sadat struck out on his own. He made a startling offer to visit Jerusalem and speak to the Knesset. It was a theatrical political act which surprised Israel and the United States, and outraged the Arab world. Sadat's emotion-filled visit to Jerusalem was not reciprocated by a similar grand Israeli gesture. But after months of grinding U.S.-mediated negotiations, Israel and Egypt signed the Camp David accords in September 1978. After several crises, the full Israeli–Egyptian peace treaty was sealed in Washington in March 1979. Sadat was ostracized in the Arab world, and, like Jordan's King Abdallah before him, he was assassinated in 1981 for having dared to make peace with the Zionist enemy.

Dayan had once said he would rather have "Sharm al-Sheikh without peace than peace without Sharm al-Sheikh" in order to secure the vital Straits of Tiran. But the peace treaty obliged Israel to withdraw gradually from the whole of Sinai, including its settlements close to the Gaza Strip. Full diplomatic relations and unimpeded passage by Israeli ships through the Suez Canal were assured. The two sides promised to make a good-faith attempt to reach an agreement on Palestinian autonomy in the occupied West Bank and Gaza Strip.

The Israeli–Egyptian treaty soon turned into a "cold peace," formally correct but lacking any spirit of reconciliation. Egypt was isolated in the Arab world, and disillusioned by the autonomy talks that were going nowhere. Dayan resigned in October 1979 because of Begin's intransigence over the West Bank and Gaza Strip, and he was soon followed by the defense minister, Ezer Weizman.

Dayan's health, already battered by the loss of his eye and a narrow escape in an archaeological accident, declined visibly after he underwent surgery for cancer of the colon in 1979. He died on October 16, 1981, at Tel Ha-Shomer hospital. In a poem attached to his will, Dayan expressed an essentially gloomy perspective on Israel's fate.

Israel's model farmer-soldier, a serial adulterer, and plunderer of archaeological sites, wrote to his family: "Only two things could I do/Sow, plow and reap the wheat/and fight back against the guns threatening our home./Let each of you cultivate our ancestors' land, and have the sword within reach above your bed. And at the end of your days, bring it down and give it to your children."

★

Israel's sword became ever heavier, but ever blunter. The Yom Kippur War prompted the country to embark on a rapid military expansion to try to avoid being overwhelmed again by sheer numbers. Even fully mobilized, the Israelis had only about a third of the number of soldiers deployed by Egypt and Syria in 1973. Thereafter, the total size of the IDF grew from about 300,000 to about 540,000 in 1982.

Generous American aid, which became even more generous after Israel made peace with Egypt, allowed Israel to overhaul its equipment with the full range of modern American weapons, from F-15 fighters to EC-2 Hawkeye airborne electronic warfare aircraft. Israel also developed a variety of home-built armaments, including the small light-triggered Uzi submachine-gun and the mighty Merkava tank (hailed as one of the best in the world), as well as an array of nuclear weapons with the missiles to carry them. Israel's reach extended to Uganda, where its special forces carried by Hercules aircraft staged the extraordinary rescue of 104 Israeli and foreign hostages in Entebbe in 1976, and to Iraq, where F-15 and F-16 aircraft bombed Saddam Hussein's nuclear reactor in 1981.

The corpulent Ariel Sharon, Dayan's favorite general, took over as defense minister in 1981. "The minister of defense appeared to personify the new IDF; perhaps no longer lean, it was definitely mean," wrote van Creveld in *The Sword and the Olive*. "However, in this case as in so many others the outcome of hubris was tragedy. In June 1982 the mighty military machine Israel had built was destined to be thrown away in the one country, and against the one opponent, where it stood no chance and was foredoomed to defeat."

Sharon's decision to wade into Lebanon's civil war was perhaps Israel's greatest military folly. Sharon seized on the attempted assassination of the Israeli ambassador to London, Shlomo Argov, by the dissident Abu Nidal faction as a pretext to hurl the army at the PLO. The declared aim was to push the PLO's guns and its handful of decrepit Soviet tanks 40 kilometers north of its border, putting Israeli communities out of the range of Palestinian artillery and Katyusha rockets. Whether by force of military circumstances (as Sharon claims), or by secret design (as the son of the then Prime Minister Begin alleges), the Israelis pushed much farther north and encircled Beirut.

There they linked up with the embattled Christian Maronite militias, the Phalangists, with whom they had maintained clandestine relations in their civil war against the alliance of Muslim leftists, Palestinians, and Syrians. The Israelis battled with Syrian forces in the Bekaa Valley and, in a spectacular air campaign, shot down about 100 Syrian planes (around one-fifth of its air force) and destroyed the Syrian anti-aircraft system in Lebanon, with insignificant losses to Israel.

Operation Peace for Galilee turned into an improbable attempt to redraw the political map of the Middle East. The idea was to install the sympathetic Phalangist leader Bashir Gemayel as President in Lebanon. He would sign a peace treaty with Israel, evict the Syrian forces and destroy the PLO's military infrastructure in Lebanon. This, in turn, would establish a new power balance in the region to the point where the Palestinians might try to set up their state in Jordan.

This grand design, however, was to go horribly wrong. After a two-month siege and cruel bombardment of Beirut, the Israelis finally forced the PLO and Syrian forces to evacuate the city under the supervision of American, French, and Italian troops. At the same time, Bashir Gemayel was elected President. So far, so good. But on September 14, 1982, Gemayel was killed by a bomb, almost certainly planted by Syrian agents. Israeli forces moved to take over mainly Muslim West Beirut the following day, supposedly to maintain order, for the first time entering the capital of an Arab country. A day later, Phalangist militias, thirsting for revenge, turned on their Palestinian enemies and swarmed into the Palestinian refugee camps of Sabra and Shatila. They were supposed to "mop up" PLO fighters on behalf of the Israelis, but once inside, the Phalangists carried out a three-day massacre of civilians, including women and children. Estimates for the number of dead range from 500 to 3,500. The Israelis were at the gates to the camps, and at one point even provided illumination for the Phalangists.

Begin was seemingly untroubled by the international outrage. "Goyim are killing goyim, and the world is trying to hang the Jews for the crime," declared Begin. But a large section of the Israeli public—supportive at first of the operation but increasingly troubled by the rising casualties—was shocked by the association of their army with the atrocity. Up to 400,000 protesters poured into central Tel Aviv. The public consensus which the army had enjoyed in Israel was finally shattered. Lebanon was not a fight for survival but a misadventure. It could not be presented as a war of *eyn brera*, "no choice."

Reluctantly the government set up a commission of inquiry, which forced the resignation of the head of Military Intelligence, Major-General Yehoshua Saguy, and criticized Begin and the foreign minister, Yitzhak Shamir. The strongest finding was directed at Sharon for "having disregarded the prospect of acts of vengeance and bloodshed by the Phalangists" and "for not ordering appropriate measures for preventing or reducing the chances of a massacre." Begin, however, refused to sack Sharon, and merely stripped him of his defense portfolio.

Bashir's brother, Amin, was elected President, and the following May he signed a peace treaty with Israel. It was a stillborn agreement which Gemayel repudiated nine months later, under pressure from Syria. As the civil war intensified, the Israelis pulled back from the outskirts of Beirut to the Awali River to try to limit their mounting casualties. In the process, however, they exposed dozens of Christian villages to attack which U.S. warships, shelling from the sea, could not prevent.

A new foe emerged from the Lebanese hornets' nest that Israel had stirred: *Hizbollah*, the "Party of God," a radical Islamic Shi'ite movement inspired by the Iranian revolution. Hizbollah adopted the tactic of suicide car bombings, killing 241 U.S. Marines in Beirut and 30 Israeli soldiers in Tire at the end of 1983.

On September 15, 1983, Begin stunned his cabinet by announcing his resignation. "I cannot go on any longer," he said. It is generally assumed that the daily antiwar protests outside his window had demoralized the Prime Minister. Yitzhak Shamir, a leader of the Lehi underground movement, was chosen to replace Begin. He led Likud into the 1984 elections, which resulted in a tie between Likud and Labor. A national unity government was formed in which Shimon Peres, the Labor leader, became Prime Minister for the first two-year rotation. With more than 650 Israeli soldiers killed, he ended the agony by withdrawing the army in January 1985 to a narrow "security zone," a buffer zone up to nine miles wide patrolled by the Israelis and their client militia, the South Lebanon Army. "After we get the IDF out of Lebanon, we will have to get Lebanon out of the IDF," was a common dictum of the 1980s. The old songs of the army's bravery and comradeship gave way to a bitter parody of a famous children's song: "Come down to us, airplane/Take us to Lebanon/ We'll fight for Sharon/And we'll come home in a coffin."

The crippling blow to the PLO's military infrastructure in Lebanon did not, however, remove the problem of Palestinian nationalism. In fact, it probably helped to bring it closer to home for the Israelis. With the collapse of the dream of liberation from abroad, either by PLO fighters in Lebanon or by the armies of the Arab countries, Palestinians in the West Bank and Gaza Strip began to look inward. Throughout 1987 there was a sharp increase in demonstrations and riots by Palestinians, punctuated by guerrilla attacks. On December 8, 1987, four Gazan workers were killed in a traffic accident. The rumor quickly spread that they had been deliberately murdered by Israelis. The Gaza Strip broke out in riots, which quickly spread to the West Bank. The mass uprising, known as the *Intifada*, or "shaking off," was born.

The Israeli government, and even the PLO, did not understand the significance of the protests which had erupted, almost out of the blue. The uprising raged for the best part of five years before petering out in the early 1990s. The Intifada was a broad campaign of daily riots, strikes, and boycotts. The incidents ranged from spray-painting slogans and stoning Israeli soldiers to murdering alleged collaborators. Eventually, it turned into an armed struggle. The Intifada was often more damaging to Palestinians than to Israelis, but it created a powerful sense of national awakening and moved the center of gravity of Palestinian politics to the West Bank and Gaza Strip. Israelis, for their part, were jolted out of the delusion that Palestinians had come to terms with an "enlightened" occupation.

★

The Yom Kippur War made Israelis question the competence of their army and government, the Lebanon War made them doubt its morality, and the Intifada made them accept the futility of trying to deny the existence of Palestinians as a separate people.

The daily scenes of soldiers shooting stone-throwers was a deeply disquieting, if not revolting, spectacle for many Israelis. When Yitzhak Rabin, defense minister in the unity government, called on soldiers to "break their bones," many did just that in front of television cameras. The most powerful armed forces in the Middle East, the embodiment of everything that was considered noble in Zionism—an army of "humanists and fighters," as Ben-Gurion had put it—was reduced to chasing, beating, and shooting poverty-stricken Arab children through the slums of Gaza. The callousness of military occupation, the legalized torture carried out by the Shin Bet (the domestic intelligence service) and the squalor of the Palestinian refugee camps prompted many Israelis to reexamine their justification for holding on to the occupied territories. The stone-throwers did not present a mortal threat to Israel, and the occupation seemed only to corrupt Israeli society. A significant number of soldiers, usually reservists, refused to serve in Lebanon or the occupied territories. Dozens were given jail terms for their insubordination; many others were simply allowed to stay at home discreetly.

Historians, writers, film-makers, journalists and many others—mainly secular Israelis on the left of the political spectrum—began to challenge the certainties, dogmas, and myths of the past in a process labeled "post-Zionism" (a term which first appeared in the 1960s). Idols such as Ben-Gurion, Moshe Dayan, and Trumpeldor were hammered. The War of Independence, Masada, Ha-Tikva (the national anthem), and even the Holocaust were reexamined in a harsh and critical new light. Archaeology, too, whose findings had largely supported the traditional accounts of the Israelites' conquest of the Promised Land, was subjected to greater scrutiny, with doubts raised about the authenticity of, among others, David and Solomon. Self-righteousness gave way to self-doubt. Instead of holding itself up as an example to humanity, Israel is now feverishly absorbing the latest trends from the West. Many Israelis are exhausted by wars and no longer want to be a nation of heroes; they want to enjoy the material pleasures of life in a more "normal" country integrated with the western world.

Israel's military power ensured the state's survival, but peace and stability could not be preserved without coming to terms with Palestinian nationalism. Its much-vaunted deterrent power came into question during the 1991 Gulf War when Israel was attacked by dozens of Scud missiles tipped with conventional warheads. Despite Prime Minister Yitzhak Shamir's veiled threats to retaliate with nuclear weapons if necessary, the Israeli army could only sit back in frustration and watch the American-led allies pound Baghdad's forces.

In the late 1980s and early 1990s, a substantial number of Israelis began to think about the unthinkable—negotiations with the PLO and some kind of Palestinian state in the West Bank and Gaza Strip. In other words, they had come full circle back to the idea of partition, first proposed by the United Nations in 1947. The peace movement agitated for Israel's withdrawal from the West Bank and Gaza Strip. This reassessment was helped by a turn toward moderation by the PLO, which articulated ever more clearly the idea of a two-state solution instead of the illusion of annihilating Israel. By 1992, such ideas had become mainstream in the center-left. Yitzhak Rabin, the former general, was elected on the promise to make peace with the Palestinians and the other Arabs while maintaining security.

Among the new members of parliament was Yael Dayan, the eldest of Moshe Dayan's three children and the third generation of her family to serve in the Knesset. She was already a prominent peace campaigner. She criticized Rabin for deporting 400 Palestinian Islamic activists in late 1992. While Moshe Dayan wanted Israelis to live and work up to the edge of Israel's dangerous borders, his daughter said they were perfectly sensible in fleeing Tel Aviv during the Scud missile attacks. In early 1993 Yael flew to Tunis to meet with Yasser Arafat. She declared him to be not the incarnation of Hitler, as many Israelis thought, but a "symbol of peace and compromise."

She outraged her party at the time, but within a few months the Labor government signed the Oslo peace accords with the PLO that allowed Arafat to establish a Palestinian "authority" in Gaza and the West Bank city of Jericho. At the ceremony at the White House in September 1993, there was nothing like the exuberant Carter–Begin–Sadat triple handshake on the South Lawn. President Bill Clinton stood back to let the sides shake hands. Arafat beamed like a boy in a toyshop, while Rabin looked as if he had just swallowed cod liver oil. His foreign minister Shimon Peres, the main architect of the accords, took Arafat's hand with gravitas, as if he were Israel's Prime Minister. Later, Peres's book on the Oslo process would bear a photograph depicting Clinton, Peres, and Arafat on the cover, with Rabin—whose long-standing rivalry with Peres was the stuff of Labor party legend—cropped out. Within a year, King Hussein of Jordan made peace too, not wanting the Palestinians to get too far ahead of him.

The historic compromise with the Palestinians brought to a brutal climax the divisions among Israelis. Where a substantial portion of secular Jews were drifting toward "post-Zionism," the other half of Israel was becoming increasingly nationalist and religious, zealously attached to the notion of settling the biblical heartland of "Judea and Samaria." Now it was the turn of ultranationalists to refuse to serve in the army. Many saw leftists like Yael Dayan as the enemy. She had offended their religious sensibilities by gestures such as ostentatiously going to the beach on Yom Kippur, calling King David a homosexual in a Knesset speech, and demanding the right for women to pray in a non-Orthodox manner at the Western Wall.

As the Left abandoned Zionist myths, the Right adopted the old pioneering symbols of the Labor Zionism—settlement, army service, and the fascination with archaeology—and brewed them with a religious militancy reminiscent of Islamic radicalism. As secular Israelis become disenchanted with the army, nationalist-religious yeshiva students are now some of the most dedicated Israeli troops. Kibbutzniks still dominate the highest echelons, but according to Israeli media reports, religious Israelis, wearing their trademark knitted yarmulkes, now make up almost half the company-grade officers in combat units. Many commentators have begun to question whether these soldiers would remain loyal to the government if it came into conflict with rabbinical authorities, say on the question of evacuating Jewish settlements in the West Bank.

Israelis have developed a contradictory attitude to the IDF. They worry about the periodic evidence of falling standards and morale, yet they are increasingly reluctant to sacrifice themselves to serve in the army. Youngsters' motivation, measured by the willingness of school-leavers to join combat units, dropped sharply in the mid-1990s, to the alarm of the High Command. Elite units, such as the air force and the paratroopers, still enjoy an overabundance of volunteers, but there is scant interest in the less prestigious units.

It is becoming easier to avoid army service, and there is less shame in draft-dodging. Nearly half of all Israelis of army age do not serve at all, for a variety of reasons; exempted categories include Arabs, or Orthodox Jews studying in yeshivas, or those not deemed to be physically or mentally fit.

Moshe Dayan's great-nephew, the rock star Aviv Geffen, openly admitted that he avoided army service by threatening suicide if he were enlisted. This has had little impact on his success among teenage fans, who regularly send his records to the top of the charts. Wearing heavy mascara and gloomy black clothes, Geffen is the antithesis of the tanned, neat-cropped, and square-jawed model of sabra manhood. He sees himself as the spokesman of the angst-ridden "screwed up generation" of Israelis. Despite criticism of his draft-dodging, he was invited to perform at the fateful rally where Yitzhak Rabin was killed in 1995. Geffen's song about a dead friend, "Cry for You," became the prayer of mourning for a secular generation of teenagers traumatized by the murder.

Among older Israelis there is a distinct reluctance to give up time for reserve duty. Most of the burden falls on a relatively small proportion of those eligible. Such glaring imbalance in what is supposed to be universal military service creates bitter resentment among those who still sacrifice their time, careers, and even their lives. Many reservists simply refuse their summonses. This is not to say that Israelis are not patriotic; they simply don't want to be taken for *freierim*, or suckers.

Even commando units, whose ranks have produced a disproportionate number of Israeli generals, seem to have lost the secret touch displayed in masterly operations such as the Entebbe rescue. In 1992, five members of the then-secret *Sayeret Matkal*, Israel's equivalent of the SAS, were killed when a dry run for an assassination attempt went wrong. Conflicting reports said the target was Iraq's President Saddam Hussein, or perhaps the leader of Lebanon's Hizbollah movement, Sheikh Hassan Nasrallah. But whoever the intended victim, the operation was abandoned and Israel's generals promptly turned on each other, seeking to avoid responsibility.

The once-fabled Mossad intelligence service—the fearsome "long arm" of Israel which kidnaped the Nazi leader Adolf Eichmann in Argentina in 1960 and scoured the world to assassinate Palestinian leaders—was made to look little better than the Keystone Cops after a series of bungled operations in the late 1990s.

In September 1997, two Mossad agents staged a bizarre attempt to kill Khaled Meshal, a political leader of Hamas, the militant Palestinian group responsible for a succession of suicide bombings in Israel. The idea was to brush past Meshal and spray him with a secret poisonous spray. Not only was the notion of carrying out a hit in Amman, the capital of one of the few friendly Arab states, ill-conceived, but the execution was hopelessly flawed. The two agents, carrying fake Canadian passports, were caught after a street brawl with Meshal's driver. Israel was forced to ransom its jailed agents by providing an antidote to save Meshal's life and releasing Hamas's spiritual leader, Sheikh Ahmad Yassin. Worse news came three months later, when it emerged that Yehuda Gil, one of the Mossad's most respected field operators, had been submitting fake reports about Syria for more than two decades. His deception, which could have been culled from Graham Greene's *Our Man in Havana*, included reports that

Damascus was mobilizing troops on the Golan Heights, and precipitated a war alert in 1996.

Mishaps were not unknown even in the mythological age of the Israeli armed forces. Then they were covered up with the collusion of a compliant press. Today the failures of the security establishment are revealed and publicized in a society that no longer accepts the old blanket of official secrecy and no longer treats its generals and spies as demigods.

★

Salah Ta'mari vividly remembers the fateful day in June 1967 when he tuned in to the BBC. Instead of the great victories claimed by Arab state radio stations, he heard the voice of Moshe Dayan speaking from the Old City of Jerusalem, which had just fallen to the Israelis.

It was, recalled Ta'mari, a moment of shock and disbelief, the turning point of his life. The last portion of Palestine was lost. The Arabs had failed; Gamal Abdel-Nasser's pan-Arabism, which had mesmerized a whole generation, proved to be hollow. The Palestinians could rely only on themselves. "Our world was turned upside down. Our dreams were shattered in just a few hours," explained Ta'mari. I dropped out of Cairo University in my final year and picked up a gun. I became a full-timer in Al-Asifa, the military wing of Fatah. Had things not gone the way they did in 1967 I would never have thought of joining the military. I wanted to stay in Bethlehem where I lived. I wanted to become a teacher, a writer maybe. Most of us who picked up a gun were more an intelligentsia in khaki than primitive people who did not know any better."

I first met Ta'mari on the windswept slopes of Jabal Abu Ghneim, a wooded hill on the boundary of Israeli-controlled Jerusalem and Bethlehem, as he led what in those years were still peaceful demonstrations against Israel's construction of the new Jewish neighborhood of Har Homa.

Tall and retaining rugged good looks as he pushed 60, Ta'mari, a senior PLO military commander in Jordan and Lebanon, was now a political activist. After more than three decades in exile, Ta'mari returned to the West Bank with Arafat's entourage after the Oslo accords. He had been excluded from the official Fatah list in the 1996 Palestinian council elections but ran as an independent and topped the list for Bethlehem.

Week after week, he would lead marches of protesters from Bethlehem up the hill to Jebal Abu Ghneim to demonstrate Palestinians' frustration at the "Judaization" of Jerusalem, and settlement expansion in general. "As children we used to play on this hill," he would explain. It was an ultimately forlorn and failed effort, however. Despite international opprobrium, Israel sent in the bulldozers to carve up the wooded hill. Yet the protest singled Ta'mari out as one of the few genuinely charismatic PLO figures in the West Bank, a man ready to lead on the ground rather than issue verbose condemnations or spend his days behind an expensively appointed desk.

Ta'mari was already a leader of renown. In the foreword to *The Little Drummer Girl*, John Le Carré extols Ta'mari's courage and thanks him for "having shown me the Palestinian heart." Aharon Barnea, the former Arab affairs correspondent for Israel Radio, and his wife Amalia, wrote *Mine Enemy*, an account of their fascination and friendship with Ta'mari after his capture by the Israelis in Lebanon. To this day, Ta'mari maintains, Barnea is his only real Israeli friend. With the outbreak of the Al-Aqsa Intifada, however, he seems to have been eclipsed by more militant activists.

Ta'mari, born Asad Suleiman Hassan, hails from the large Bedouin tribe of the Ta'mara who live near the ruins of Herodion. His *nom de guerre*, Salah Ta'mari, is derived from Saladin (Salah al-Din, who reconquered Jerusalem from the Crusaders).

His political consciousness was formed in Manger Square in Bethlehem, which was already a mixed Christian–Muslim town in his childhood. There, as a boy of five, he saw Palestinian refugees fleeing the fighting in the first Arab–Israeli war. In the 1950s, residents gathered in the square to donate funds for the Algerian revolution, with women taking off their jewelery for the cause. Fired by Arab nationalism, in 1955 he joined older students in demonstrating against the U.S.-inspired Baghdad Pact, a pro-western regional alliance stretching from Pakistan to Turkey to contain the Soviet Union. Jordanian police opened fire, killing four of Ta'mari's friends. "That day we were baptized in fire and rose to adulthood," he explained. A year later, he was rudely evicted from the square by policemen preparing for the arrival of Jordan's Queen Dina. "I hated her," recalled Ta'mari, not realizing at the time that she would one day become his wife.

In 1963 Ta'mari went to university in Cairo, where he studied English literature and became general secretary of the Union of Palestinian Students, the only legal Palestinian organization at the time. It had previously been led by a quixotic engineering student called Yasser Arafat. In 1953, Arafat had made one of his first tentative steps on the political stage with a theatrical petition, written in blood, telling Egypt's leadership: "Don't Forget Palestine."

Ta'mari attended the founding conference of the Palestine Liberation Organization at the Ambassador Hotel, in Jordanian-controlled East Jerusalem in May 1964. The organization had been set up by the Arab League, at the behest of Egypt's President Nasser, to represent the interests of all Palestinians. For many, it was a moment of great excitement, even though the PLO was, in its original incarnation, a toothless body led by the lawyer and diplomat, Ahmad Shukayri.

Yasser Arafat formed his "Fatah" group (an acronym meaning "Conquest" derived by reversing the initials of Palestine Liberation Movement) in 1959 with a small group of friends in Kuwait, where he was working as an engineer in the emirate's public works department. They established a small publication, *Filastinuna*, "Our Palestine," which demanded the liberation of Palestine, criticized Arab regimes for their failure to act, and called on Palestinians to take up arms. Fatah believed that the lessons of the armed struggle that evicted the French from Algeria could be applied to Palestine, but its ideas ran counter to the prevailing belief that Arab ranks must first be united before they could undertake the liberation of Palestine.

Fatah made preliminary contacts with fellow revolutionaries in Europe, Algeria, China, and even secured an encounter with Che Guevara. But Fatah remained a relatively obscure group, with few funds or weapons, despite its enthusiastic preaching of the need for a people's war against Zionism. Its early cross-border attacks in 1965 were a puny affair. The first raid was stopped by the Lebanese authorities, notwithstanding a portentous leaflet announcing that "our revolutionary vanguard has issued forth." Fatah's first "martyr" was killed not by the Israelis but by Jordanian border guards.

The armed campaign, designed in part to provoke a new Arab-Israeli war, drew a hostile response from many Arab governments. Some saw the insurgents as agents of Communism; Egypt denounced them as part of a wily plot by western and Zionist forces to give Israel a pretext to attack the Arabs. Yet the attacks began to catch the imagination of some Arabs, and leaders opened up their purses. Saudi leaders, in particular, were impressed by the past connections of Arafat and other leaders of Fatah with the Muslim Brotherhood, a movement for Islamic revival. But Syria, which had sponsored the early Fatah operations, soon turned against Arafat and arrested him in Damascus in 1966.

Palestinian revolutionaries were quickly discovering that they would not only have to fight the Zionists; they would also have to maneuver in the treacherous waters of Arab politics. Sometimes the rivalries between Arab regimes would provide the Palestinians with important opportunities; at other times they would present a more dangerous threat than even the Israeli armed forces.

The Six Day War transformed the map of Palestinian politics. At a meeting with Arafat, George Habash, at that time a young Palestinian activist, said disconsolately: "Everything is lost." Arafat made an extraordinary reply: "George, you are wrong," he said. "This is not the end. It's the beginning."

The humiliation of the Arabs by Israel was the opportunity for Palestinians to assert an independent voice. Nasser's Arab nationalism was crushed. Within days of the war ending, Fatah's leaders met in Damascus and resolved to continue the armed struggle. Arafat and his followers slipped through Israeli lines and infiltrated the West Bank, seeking to set up secret guerrilla cells along the lines of Maoist doctrine that a revolutionary should be able to operate among his people "like a fish in water."

Most of the West Bank, however, was too stunned by the occupation to consider rising up in arms against the Israelis. After about a year marked mainly by failures, Fatah changed tactics and tried instead to mount hit-and-run attacks from outside Israel's borders. Its defiant action had a galvanizing effect on demoralized Palestinians. Volunteers and funds began to flow into the proliferating Palestinian groups, each vying with the others to announce heroic military deeds, whether real, inflated, or fictitious. Arab governments were gradually sucked into the conflict, opening their borders and coffers to the Palestinian revolutionaries.

On March 18, 1968, an Israeli bus struck a mine left by Palestinian fighters in the south of the country. A doctor and instructor accompanying the party of high school students were killed, while several teenagers were injured. It was the 38th Fatah operation in little more than three months. The Israelis decided it was time to teach the Palestinians an exemplary lesson. Arafat's showdown with Israel had arrived.

★

The Palestinian revolutionaries had read the manuals on guerrilla tactics, such as the aphorism of the North Vietnamese military leader, Vo Nguyen Giap. "Is the enemy strong? One avoids him. Is the enemy weak? One attacks him." After the Six Day War, the Israelis were undoubtedly strong. But the Palestinians, knowing the Israelis were going to attack, decided to make a stand at their main headquarters in Jordan, Karameh. They were breaking all the rules of guerrilla warfare, but Fatah had a vital political point to make.

"It is up to us, now, to provide an example for the Arab world in general and for the Palestinian people in particular," Ta'mari told a meeting of Fatah commanders. "If we remain and fight, we may be able to convince the world that we are not merely 'terrorists' but fighting men, ready to sacrifice their lives for their country. If we abandon the battlefield from the beginning, it will be a blow to our image."

At dawn on March 21 the Israelis dropped warning leaflets over Karameh. Their paratroopers could not be landed in time because of fog, and could not cut off escape routes before Yasser Arafat slipped away on a motorcycle. The paratroopers unexpectedly came under fire from George Habash's men hiding in caves, while the main force faced the nasty surprise of heavy fire from Jordanian units. Moreover, Fatah forced the Israelis to take Karameh street by street. In the end, the Israelis destroyed the town, killed 120 Fatah men and took a similar number prisoner. But the Israelis lost 28 dead before finally extricating themselves, abandoning some casualties and equipment in the field. Ta'mari survived by sheltering under a table in a house as Israeli sappers blew up the building.

Karameh immediately became a byword for valor in Palestinian mythology. Less than a year after the combined Arab armies were overwhelmed by the Israelis in the Six Day War, the Palestinian fighters had held their ground against a superior enemy. The revolutionary guerrillas took over the Palestine Liberation Organization, swept away its leader, Ahmed Shukayri and the "generation of defeat," and rewrote the charter to declare: "Armed struggle is the only way to liberate Palestine." Arafat became the leader of the PLO, and the second historic leader of the Palestinians after Haj Amin al-Husseini.

Karameh was not a victory in battle, but survival against overwhelming odds. It placed Palestinians back on the political map of the Middle East. The guerrilla campaign was never really an attempt to reconquer Palestine: it was a statement of the existence of Palestinians as a dispossessed people.

The armed struggle became a near-religion for exiled Palestinians, keeping alive the hope that one day they would return home. It gave them a sense that they still could control their destiny. Thousands of Palestinians, many of them abandoning their studies, enthusiastically volunteered to join the revolution. The governments of a hitherto demoralized Arab world bestowed their patronage and largesse on the new heroes. King Hussein of Jordan declared, after Karameh: "we are all *fedayin*."

But two years later, power was slipping from the monarch's hands to the myriad Palestinian revolutionary groups, whose members swaggered with their weapons through the streets of Amman, hung Marxist banners on mosques and began a campaign of hijackings and kidnappings. Palestinians spoke openly of taking over the country as part of Palestine.

The inevitable confrontation came in September 1970. King Hussein ordered his army to crush the Palestinians and thousands died in the civil war that came to be known as "Black September." Syrian forces threatened to intervene on the side of the Palestinians, but were stopped by Jordanian tanks, while Israel mobilized its troops to warn Damascus off the adventure. The Israelis found themselves in the strange position of taking in Palestinian fighters escaping the king's forces.

At the height of the battles in Amman, Ta'mari married Dina Abdel-Hamid, who had been divorced by King Hussein after a short marriage. The defeated Palestinians vented their fury on the world with a wave of international terrorism under the code-name "Black September." Its first targets were King Hussein's regime, but the operations spread to include the hostage-taking and killing of Israeli athletes at the 1972 Olympic Games in Munich. At the same time, the upheaval, caused by the Yom Kippur War, the shock of the Arab oil embargo, and the growing support of Third World countries brought important diplomatic successes for Arafat. In a political propaganda coup, he was invited to address the U.N. General Assembly in 1974.

The PLO rebuilt its forces in Lebanon but accelerated the country's slide toward civil war. With the Israeli invasion of Lebanon, the PLO was forced to leave Beirut. As he boarded his ship, Arafat told his incredulous audience: "We are going to Jerusalem."

Ta'mari had surrendered to the Israelis in Sidon, and soon established himself as the leader of prison protests in Israel's Ansar camp. In *Arab and Jew, Broken Spirits in the Promised Land*, David Shipler, the former correspondent for the *New York Times*, describes Ta'mari as a cynical and facile Palestinian propagandist. Meeting him during a visit to Ansar, he felt outraged by the sight of prisoners chanting "Ansar is Auschwitz."

Languishing in exile in Tunis, the PLO was given a new lease on life by the Palestinian Intifada, which caught the PLO, as well as the Israelis and the rest of the world, by surprise. Palestinians brought their grievances once more to the daily television bulletins. In 1988, the PLO proclaimed its nonexistent state and Arafat set about a new diplomatic initiative in which he recognized Israel's right to exist and, to widespread skepticism, publicly renounced terrorism. In Arafat's broken English, it came out as renouncing "tourism."

The U.S. opened a formal dialogue with the PLO, but in 1990, Arafat almost wrecked the PLO by supporting Saddam Hussein in his invasion of Kuwait, suggesting that the Palestinians were in the "same trench" as the Iraqis. Saddam's offer to withdraw from Kuwait once Israel withdrew from the occupied territories turned him into a false messiah of the Palestinians. But Arafat bet on the wrong horse. When Saddam's army was forced out by an international alliance led by the United States the PLO's vital flow of funds from Gulf oil states was cut off. Hundreds of thousands of Palestinians were thrown out of liberated Kuwait, the birthplace of Arafat's Fatah movement.

Yet the Gulf War was the starting point for a political process that has brought Mr. Arafat to the brink of establishing a small, but real state. The Americans dragged the Israeli Prime Minister, Yitzhak Shamir, to the 1991 Madrid peace conference. It was the political price for Arab support in the war against Iraq, but the Prime Minister later let slip that he would have dragged out the talks for ten years if necessary but he was voted out the following year.

It was Israel's Prime Minister Yitzhak Rabin who threw a lifeline to Arafat. The election of a Labor government in Israel in 1992 paved the way for the Oslo accords the following year. The agreement called for a five-year period of interim autonomy and was closely modeled on the 1978 Camp David accords between Israel and Egypt, once bitterly reviled by the Palestinians. The essential new ingredient that made it palatable to Arafat was that Israel formally recognized the PLO as its negotiating partner.

For all the years of armed struggle, Palestinians have few, if any, military heroes in the usual sense of the word. Their history is not one of proud victories, but of heroic failures. There are no Dayans, Rabins, or Sharons for a movement that has not won a conventional battle or liberated any Palestinian territory by force of arms.

The Palestinian anthem, "My Homeland, My Homeland" is based on a Fatah song, "Commando, Commando." Yet there are no men of obvious military prowess among the Palestinian leadership. Palestinians see themselves not, like the Israelis, as a nation of extraordinary fighters, but as a nation of martyrs.

"Behold the martyr's body . . ." wrote the poet Abdel-Rahim Mahmoud in the first half of the twentieth century:

> . . . sprawled on sands, attacked by vultures,
> his blood tinting the earth crimson,
> haunting northern breezes with its scent.
> His radiant brow covered with dust
> only seems more luminous.
> The smile on his lips
> mocks this earthly life,
> and his dreams of eternity
> shape blissful visions.
> I swear this is how men SHOULD die . . .

Many of the most popular Palestinian figures today have served time in Israeli jails. By definition they were losers, but the heroic Palestinian is one who has extracted some kind of symbolic victory out of defeat. Survival against the odds has been the greatest achievement of the Palestinian movement.

Sitting in an office in Bethlehem in 1998, I asked Ta'mari whether the fighting, bloodshed and pain had all been worth while. First of all, he said, learning to use a weapon was essential to Palestinians' survival. The question of military training for children had been taboo until 1976, when Christian militias massacred thousands of Palestinians at the Tel al-Zaatar refugee camp. After that, even children had to become fighters.

"Everybody above the age of 14 got military training to defend their refugee camp," said Ta'mari. "At Sabra and Shatila we had a huge youth camp. We had established one of the best musical bands, and they were slaughtered during the massacre. But the youth in the military squad survived."

Secondly, the years of bombs and guerrilla attacks had a political purpose. "The armed struggle," said Ta'mari, "is the young man's way of drawing attention to his plight, especially when one is overwhelmed by propaganda that turns white into black and black into white. Sometimes you cannot bear to watch televisions because of how grotesque our image appears. You just scream and pull your hair. Young Palestinians yelled by planting bombs. Sometimes planting a bomb is easier than going through the agony of explaining to some stupid American or European that Palestinians have legitimate rights.

"The fact that we are here is proof that we made the world hear us. The fact that countries in the world recognized the PLO is proof that we were right."

When I saw Ta'mari in 1998, Palestinian euphoria at the diplomatic breakthrough had already given way to weariness over the drudgery of negotiation, and disillusionment with the corruption, authoritarian practices, and sheer ineptness of Arafat's Palestinian Authority. "Maybe we overromanticized the whole thing. When it comes down to it, it's not so romantic dealing with sewage, taxation, salaries, and unemployment," mused Ta'mari.

Ta'mari spoke slowly, searching the ceiling for the right words. Oslo, he said, is still riddled with injustice. "You do not know how difficult and tough it is to bargain over the land where you were born and spent your childhood. They are bargaining with you over something that is your very being; it's like asking you to amputate your arm or your toe. The fact that we agreed to Oslo does not mean they were right. We are under huge pressure. We want to make our children avoid what we went through."

The two-state solution is, in Ta'mari's view, itself an interim step. "I have not abandoned my dream of a democratic state in all of Palestine where Palestinians—Jews and non-Jews—will live together."

Ta'mari has developed a reputation as a "constructive" critic of the Palestinian Authority. He complained of the inefficiency and laziness of the administrators, but clearly still had deep respect for Arafat himself. Ta'mari sounded a warning, which I disregarded at the time, that Arafat's commitment to peaceful means was conditional. The war was far from over. "The minute he loses faith in this agreement, Arafat does not lack the courage to say 'the agreement is finished, and we are no longer abiding by it,'" said Ta'mari. "He has great courage, both in war and in peace."

★

Metulla is one of the oldest Jewish settlements in Israel, at the end of a finger of territory jutting into Lebanon. Its little houses of dark stone and red tiles give it a European look, or at least a distinctly non-Israeli appearance. Its sports center boasts an ice skating rink that is the envy of the rest of the country. It belies its position as a strategic settlement on Israel's turbulent frontier with Lebanon, Israel's own mini-Vietnam. I have often been struck by Israelis' ability to lead a life of outward normality in a chronic security crisis. I had been to Metulla many times to cover Israel's long-running conflict in Lebanon. This time I was heading beyond the "Good Fence" and into the euphemistically named "Security Zone."

Our military convoy formed up in a field below Metulla. There were about 30 soldiers gathered around the commander, a bearded major who looked more like a teacher than a combat officer. His briefing was a long lecture on all the things that could go wrong on our short journey to rotate soldiers on an artillery base.

"We have received intelligence reports on the possibility of a car bomb attack by Hizbollah," he began. "We do not know exactly where. We have to be careful. It might be a Mercedes or a BMW. If a car tries to join our convoy, stop it in any way. Push it out or shoot at it."

And then: "There has been fog in the last few days. Hizbollah may have managed to plant roadside bombs. If the first vehicle is hit, the others must stop. If the bomb is in the middle of the convoy, those in front go forward and those behind reverse. If a car is hit, do not volunteer to help. We have special procedures. There might be other bombs in the area. . . . If there is shelling from mortars or machine-gun fire from a distance, keep moving forward to change your position . . ."

Pointing out that I was not armed, the major appointed two soldiers to protect me and went on: "If they try to kidnap a soldier you have to stop them by every possible means, even if you have to shoot the soldier. It will be worse if he is kidnaped." He made it sound as if a simple operation to supply a base was a death-defying feat. The army has changed. This was not the swashbuckling army of a "plucky little country"; this was an army terrified of casualties.

We were counted, and a soldier went around with a felt pen writing identifying letters on each person's hand. We were already being prepared for death. "Don't worry," said Aviv, the driver of the Humvee I would be riding. "He likes to frighten us more than necessary." The Humvee, he noted proudly, was the safest vehicle in the convoy.

As we lumbered across the border, there was a beguiling air of normality in this war zone. Lebanese farmers worked the black earth in the plain of Marjayoun. We passed houses of gray cement breeze-blocks and even a place calling itself the Paradise Hotel. Everyone in the convoy was scrutinizing the hills and rocks for signs of trouble. A BMW came toward us and was waved over to the side. It was difficult to say who was more nervous: the soldiers fearing a car bomb, or the occupants of the car fearing they would be shot as suspected car bombers. As we approached the artillery position, we were met by a tank ready to give covering fire should the convoy be attacked at this vulnerable point.

The base was abuzz with activity as the newcomers took off their flak jackets and helmets and other soldiers prepared to go home. The 155-mm howitzers in the center of the compound, surrounded by piles of shells, were quiet for the moment. These guns spat out their shells almost every day but the gunners could not see what they were firing at. A house, a hill, a road—it's just a distant coordinate on a map. Firepower was the mainstay of Israel's tactics in south Lebanon. There were, of course, ambushes, patrols, and air surveillance. But artillery and air strikes are the safest response (for Israelis) to Hizbollah attacks on outposts held by the IDF or its allied militia, the South Lebanon Army (SLA).

Lebanon has been the proxy battleground for Israel's war with Syria. Where the Golan Heights is the quietest of Israel's borders, Syria has encouraged Hizbollah to take on the Israelis in South Lebanon. The Syrians, say Israeli experts, "will fight Israel down to the last Lebanese." While Israel and Syria conducted on-off negotiations over the Golan, Lebanon has been a kind of Chinese torture for the Israelis. A steady trickle of minor casualties which, over a prolonged period, turned into torment for much of the country. Israel could not defeat Hizbollah. It could only hold its positions and try to limit its losses. Hizbollah operated on its home territory and enjoyed popular acceptance as a movement fighting to liberate occupied Lebanese soil. Moreover, it was supplied by Iran through Syria. If Lebanese civilians were killed, Hizbollah reserved the right to retaliate with Katyusha rockets against Israeli towns.

In 1993 and in 1996, Israel tried to change the "rules of the game" with massive and systematic bombardment of south Lebanon. The point was not so much to eradicate the small bands of Hizbollah fighters as to create a flight of hundreds of thousands of refugees northward. The idea was to threaten Beirut's fragile effort at reconstruction and eventually exert pressure on Lebanon's Syrian masters to restrain Hizbollah. Dropping prodigious amounts of high explosive on a country was bound to end in tragedy, and it did. On April 18, 1996, in the midst of a 16-day bombardment, Israeli shells hit a compound of United Nations peace-keepers in the village of Qana, killing about 100 Lebanese refugees who had sheltered under the protection of the blue flag. The Israeli government twisted this way and that. The IDF said it had no idea there were refugees in the U.N. camp, and had been trying to hit a group of Hizbollah fighters nearby. It claimed the carnage was caused by a slight cartographic error.

"When I heard about Qana I felt pretty bad, but you learn to live with it," said one 19-year-old soldier I met at the artillery base. "It's forgotten pretty quickly," chipped in another.

Modern gunnery is not foolproof: one soldier admitted once missing his target by up to a mile. A far more pressing and annoying issue for these Israeli soldiers was the question of draft-dodgers. Nearly everybody had a friend who had managed to wriggle out of serving in the army. The most detested were the yeshiva students, who "hide" behind their Torah scrolls.

Hizbollah is a more formidable, more organized and more dedicated foe than the Palestinian groups ever had been. True to its policy of liberating Lebanese soil, it did not attempt Palestinian-style cross-border raids, although there is little doubt that it could have penetrated the frontier. Its targets were military, weakening Israel's claim to be fighting "terrorists."

Hizbollah fired machine-guns and mortars at fortified outposts, placed remote-controlled bombs to ambush convoys and patrols and even found the weak points in the legendary armor of the Merkava tank. It was often privy to high-quality intelligence on Israeli movements from sources within the SLA. It was also a savvy propagandist, taking video cameras on operations and broadcasting on its private television station battlefield footage of its successes, such as planting its flag on the ramparts of Israeli positions. Hizbollah inflicted, on average, between 20 and 30 fatalities a year on the Israelis. In April 1999 it claimed its most important scalp when it killed Major-General Erez Gerstein, the head of the IDF's euphemistically named "liaison unit" with the SLA, along with two other soldiers and an Israeli radio reporter with a roadside bomb in the Security Zone.

To the army's embarrassment, the entanglement in Lebanon brought out the opposition of the Jewish Mother, a more awkward rival than Hizbollah. The Jewish Mother no longer gives up her children to the army, but wants them safely at home. The "Four Mothers" movement was born when two helicopters ferrying troops to Lebanon crashed at night in northern Israel in February 1997, killing 73 servicemen. The incident was an eye-opener for four women whose sons were serving in Lebanon. As they saw it, the crash happened because Israel was resupplying its bases by helicopter at night, and that was because many of the roads were too dangerous for convoys. The time had come to leave Lebanon and defend Israel from within its own borders. The fact that the movement started in northern Israel, among the very communities that the army is supposed to be protecting by its presence in Lebanon, gave it greater impact. While opposed by many Israelis, including other women, the "Four Mothers" movement quickly grew into a country-wide protest which the government could not ignore.

The debate crossed party lines. Even Ariel Sharon, who threw Israel into the morass in the first place and for years chastised the Labor party for withdrawing to the Security Zone in 1985, proposed plans for a phased unilateral withdrawal from the Security Zone. By the late 1990s the question was no longer whether Israel should withdraw, but when and how.

Until the end, the soldiers in south Lebanon tried to put on a brave face. "Everybody wants to kill Hizbollah," said Captain Erez Meirovitch. "On the other hand, you try to bring everybody home safely. I don't know which I want more." Erez (the Israelis still prefer to use first names) commanded a company just inside Israel's frontier with Lebanon. His troops were responsible for patrolling a section of the border fence and securing a sector of the Security Zone. He was 23 years old and soft-spoken. When I met him in 1998, he had stayed on in the army beyond his standard term of national service. It was his sixth year in uniform, and his fourth tour of Lebanon. Erez went on: "I prefer to serve in Lebanon than in the territories [the West Bank and Gaza Strip]. Here you have an enemy; in the territories you don't know who your enemy is. And here you know you can shoot anybody carrying a gun."

I sat with Erez on the rampart, looking into Lebanon. Part of the sector was called "Little Vietnam." The antenna from an Israeli position rose up amid the hills in the distance. How did he feel about the debate raging in Israel over whether to remain in Lebanon? "As a commander I tell my soldiers that it's our mission and we have to do it. But the soldiers go home to their parents. Three days later they come back with all kinds of things in their heads." He complained of receiving endless queries from anxious parents. "I changed my telephone number because I always had mothers and parents calling me with stupid questions. Why is my son crying? What are you doing to him?"

The overall commander of the Galilee division, responsible for security on Israel's northern border, was a strange apparition. Brigadier-General Ephraim "Effi" Fein, who now goes by the surname Eitam, was strongly built and sported a thick black beard. His eyes had a steeliness about them. If he had not been wearing the IDF insignia he could have been mistaken for a Hizbollah fighter. In a sense it was appropriate that Eitam should be charged with fighting a fundamentalist Islamic movement, because he himself, as one of the very few Orthodox Jews in the senior ranks of the army, was part of the broad national-religious movement in Israel.

As the commander of the Givati Brigade, he avoided prosecution for an incident in which his soldiers beat to death a Palestinian after receiving orders to use clubs to break the bones of rioters they had caught. In 2001, Eitam resigned after failing to be promoted and lambasted the government's peace policy. Like so many other military commanders before him, he pursued a political career and carved out a position on the extreme Right of the Israeli spectrum.

When I met him in 1998, at a time when he was still constrained by army rules in what he could say, Eitam was proud of being the most senior religious officer in Israel. The country was at the end of the period of the "hegemony of liberalism," in which individual rights were being taken to extremes and the family vilified. Now religious Jews were taking elite positions, and would help Israeli society "take a more balanced view of its national identity." Effi was not always observant. He was born a secular kibbutznik. Effi lived in Kibbutz Ein Gev, jammed between the Sea of Galilee and the base of the Golan Heights. At the age of four, he knew how to roll his blanket and run into underground tunnels to take cover from Syrian shelling. The Golan, he recalled, was called the "mountain of blood and fire."

"Hizbollah," he admitted, "is quite an impressive force by the standards of the guerrilla forces we have known in the Middle East. But if you compare it to the IRA or the Vietcong then it is not that impressive."

The key problem with a unilateral withdrawal was that it would demonstrate weakness, and that would be a fatal mistake. "We are not fighting to gain territory, but to gain time. Every day, every hour, every minute which passes, we gain time for the politicians. I believe it is a process of letting the energy burn out of the conflict. I am very optimistic. Look at Egypt and Jordan. Our job is to fight back and convince the other side that hostile activities will bring them only to a dead end. If we give up, if we withdraw, if we go out on our knees, then it will never stop."

Effi's words carried the intensity of a missionary's. They were, essentially, a restatement of Vladimir Jabotinsky's vision, as long ago as 1923, that the Jews could never hope to be accepted voluntarily in the Arab world. All natives have resisted colonizers, from the time of Joshua's crossing of the Jordan to the taming of the American West. The only answer was to erect an "iron wall" of Jewish soldiers, and wait for a day in the future when the Arabs would grudgingly come to terms with the Jewish presence and produce a more moderate leadership. He wrote:

As long as the Arabs feel that there is the least hope of getting rid of us, they will refuse to give up this hope in return for either kind words or for bread and butter, because they are not a rabble, but a living people. And when a living people yields in matters of such a vital character it is only when there is no longer any hope of getting rid of us, because they can make no breach in the iron wall.

In Lebanon, though, the iron wall was badly rusted and weakened. After years of sterile debate it was the Labor Prime Minister, Ehud Barak, who took the decision to end the agony. The man who had made his fame as a commando assassinating Palestinian leaders in Beirut, ordered the army to withdraw from the Security Zone at the end of May 2000. Under cover of night, Israeli tanks churned their way back across the international border. As explosions lit up the night sky where Israeli sappers had left demolition charges to destroy their old positions, soldiers gave broad grins, held up Israeli flags and flashed victory signs. Jewish mothers sighed with relief. The Palestinians watched, and learned the lesson that Israel cannot stand casualties.

Within a few months of the departure from Lebanon, the Al-Aqsa Intifada broke out. Some of the Israeli soldiers who had flashed their V-for-Victory signs as they left Lebanon were then killed or wounded in the occupied territories.

5

Victims of Victims

ABRILLIANT WHITE cone rises from the orange groves beside the coastal road north of Acre. It resembles a smokestack, or perhaps a modern version of a Mesopotamian spiral ziggurat.

This peculiar structure is Yad Layeled, a memorial to the Jewish children killed in the Nazi Holocaust. It stands next to an old Turkish aqueduct, deliberately juxtaposing a carrier of life-giving water with a symbol of death. The architectural tension is heightened by the spiral ramp, which does not lead upward to celestial communion with the heavens, but downward into the darkness of the earth.

The children who visit here first sit in the luminous interior of the cone, decorated with stained-glass images based on the drawings of children from the Theresienstadt concentration camp. The exhibits swallow them inexorably into the vortex, along passages suffused with the voices of children of the past and video recordings of elderly survivors recounting their experiences as children. The young visitors weave through a reconstruction of the ghettos, then slide down rail tracks recalling the train journey to the death camps. Like the victims, the children never see the next stage; they never see what lies around the bend until they finally arrive in a dark pit with an eternal flame for those killed in the Holocaust.

Yad Layeled is the newest addition to the museum and documentation center of Kibbutz Lohamei ha-Getaot, the Ghetto Fighters' kibbutz, founded by veterans of the 1943 Warsaw Ghetto uprising against the Nazis. The members intended not only to participate in the pioneering task of building the new state by joining a kibbutz, but also to be a living memorial to the six million Jews who perished in the *Shoah*, the "Catastrophe," as the Holocaust is known in Israel.

There is a second history, though, which is not told in the galleries and seminar rooms of Kibbutz Lohamei ha-Getaot. It is the story of the Arab village of Al-Sumayriyya, whose inhabitants were evicted from the land now occupied by the kibbutz. Al-Sumayriyya was conquered by the Israeli army on May 14, 1948, just a few hours before David Ben-Gurion pronounced Israel's independence. Within days, Israeli army sappers had reduced it to rubble to ensure that its 800-odd inhabitants would not return. Most of the villagers fled across the northern border to Lebanon, and a few managed to stay in other Arab villages in what was to become Israel. None have ever been allowed to return to their lands.

The ruins of Al-Sumayriyya lie just a few hundred yards away from Yad Layeled. The arched doorway of the demolished village mosque is barely visible through the wild grass and bushes of prickly pear cactuses. Al-Sumayriyya is one of more than 400 Arab villages in Israel that were destroyed during the exodus of Palestinian refugees known as *Al-Nakba*, or "The Catastrophe."

The story of Palestine and Israel is one of tragedy upon more tragedy. The suffering of Jews in the Holocaust has been followed by the suffering of the Palestinians thrown out of their homeland. The United Nations' decision to carve out a Jewish state was motivated in large part by sympathy for the devastation inflicted on European Jews; the war for the creation of the Jewish state led in turn to the uprooting of more than 700,000 Arabs from their homes. The settling of Jewish refugees from Europe, some of whom were taken directly to fight in the front lines of the first Arab–Israeli war, was paralleled by the departure of Arab refugees. Many Holocaust victims simply moved into vacated Arab houses. The wandering Jew found a home, while the homeless Palestinians still wander the Middle East.

One need not equate the two miseries. The extermination of the Shoah belongs to a different universe of evil to the dispossession of Palestinians in the Nakba. For all the awful things that happened in the decades of conflict, the Jews did not gas Palestinians. Yet the two tragedies are inextricably entwined. They are part of the same mosaic of conflict over Palestine. If the Jews were victims of the Nazis, the Palestinians are in many ways the victims of the victims. For each side, the trauma is a defining moment in its history, and the memory of the tragedy lies at the core of national identity. It makes for an

often somber, resentful and dark mood—sometimes just melancholic—charged with self-righteous indignation. The open wounds
leave little space for self-deprecating humor.

For the past half-century of the Israeli–Arab dispute, each side has
minimized, ignored, or distorted the other side's pain to deny its right
to exist as a people. In the struggle for Palestine, Israelis and Palestinians have not only fought over who has the oldest claim to the land,
but have also argued over who has suffered the most.

To many Israelis, the Palestinians' readiness to kill has turned them
into the modern embodiment of the Nazis. In 1982, after the IDF's
destruction of Arafat's headquarters in Beirut, Prime Minister Menachem Begin wrote to U.S. President Ronald Reagan saying he felt
as if he had sent the Israeli army into Berlin to destroy Hitler in his
bunker.

Palestinians have usually regarded the Holocaust as a propaganda
tool used to deny them their own national aspirations. They have var-
iously denied that the Holocaust ever happened, or claimed its scale
was vastly exaggerated ("Six thousand, maybe, but not six million")
or harnessed the horror as a rhetorical weapon to accuse the Israelis
of behaving like Nazis in their treatment of Palestinians.

Article 20 of the now-dormant charter of the Palestine Liberation
Organization, drafted in 1968, states: "Claims of historical or religious
ties of Jews with Palestine are incompatible with the facts of history
and the true conception of what constitutes statehood. Judaism,
being a religion, is not an independent nationality. Nor do Jews constitute a single nation with an identity of its own; they are citizens of
the states to which they belong."

The Israeli Prime Minister Golda Meir put it bluntly in 1969:
"There was no such thing as Palestinians. When was there an independent Palestinian people with a Palestinian state? It was not as
though . . . we came and threw them out and took their country
away from them. They did not exist." In the 1978 Camp David
accords, Menachem Begin included a side-letter specifying that he
understood the terms "Palestinians" and "Palestinian people" to mean
merely "the Arabs of Eretz Israel."

At the Madrid peace conference in 1991, Palestinians were not
allowed to attend as a separate delegation, because of Israeli objections. Instead, they were part of the Jordanian team. Still, Haider
Abdel-Shafi, the chief Palestinian delegate, was permitted to make his
own speech. He stood before the conference while the world

watched, and made what is perhaps the most articulate and dignified Palestinian declaration of nationhood:

> We, the people of Palestine, stand before you in the fullness of our pain, our pride, and our anticipation, for we have long harbored a yearning for peace and a dream of justice and freedom. For too long, the Palestinian people have gone unheeded, silenced and denied— our identity negated by political expediency, our rightful struggle against injustice maligned, and our present existence subsumed by the past tragedy of another people. It is time for us to narrate our own story. . . .

In his truculent rebuttal, the Israeli Prime Minister, Yitzhak Shamir, all but shrugged off the "Palestinian-Arab" plea for recognition.

> The Palestinian-Arab spokesman made a valiant effort at recounting the sufferings of his people. But let me say that twisting history and perversion of fact will not earn them the sympathy which they strive to acquire. Was it not Palestinians who rejected every peace proposal since the beginning of the century and responded by violence? Was it not Palestinians who produced a leader who collaborated with the Nazis in the extermination of Jews during the Holocaust?

The political architecture of peace, no matter how carefully the future borders are laid out, no matter how craftily the leaders finesse the questions of settlements and Jerusalem, no matter how much money the world pledges to support the "peace process," cannot be complete without each side recognizing the other's agony, and abandoning the notion that it alone is the victim of history.

★

Apart from Yad Layeled and the other buildings related to the Holocaust memorial, there is little else in Kibbutz Lohamei ha-Getaot to indicate the burden of the nightmare which it carries. The houses are well spaced out in neat gardens. There is a common dining room, a playground, a swimming pool, a cowshed, a factory, and a guest house. Children and old people live a life of measured industriousness.

Avraham and Esther Tzoref looked like a veteran kibbutz couple anywhere in Israel. Their home was decorated with cheerful watercolors. Although 75 years old, Avraham was built like a barrel and had strong hands. He wore a short-sleeved shirt and shorts. Esther, six years his junior, had a pleasant round face and was attired in a floral dress.

This picture of contented normality was deliberately created and maintained for decades. Both Avraham and Esther came to Israel having narrowly survived the Holocaust and, after they met in their new country and were married, they decided not to burden their children with the past. For years they had not even told each other of their experiences. Their silence was partly by choice, and partly the result of the indifference of many Israelis to the suffering of Holocaust survivors during the early years of the state.

It was not until 1984, when the kibbutz published a collection of testimonies of members who had survived the Holocaust, that the Tzorefs' children learned the details of their parents' ordeal in Europe. "I told them about the cold and the clothes we wore, but I never told them the difficult things," said Avraham. He had agreed to be interviewed because he feared it would be his last chance to tell his story.

The stories of Avraham and Esther are contained in *Testimonies of Survival*, a collection of 96 kibbutz members' personal accounts of the Holocaust. These are not biographies but recollections. The dates and names of places are often missing or left vague. There are many loose ends and unanswered questions. The essence of the stories is the will to live and the twists of fate.

Avraham was one of nine children living in the town of Janovo in Lithuania. Tzoref is the Hebrew rendition of Avraham's former surname, Goldschmidt. His father had been a soldier in the Tsar's army and then the Red Army. The family was splintered. His father was "fanatically religious" and ignored domestic affairs. But Avraham turned away from Judaism and joined the Communist youth league, the Komsomol, while his brother Avshalom became a Zionist and moved to Palestine in 1934.

When Hitler launched Operation Barbarossa against his erstwhile Soviet allies in the summer of 1941, Avraham's family was caught by the speed of the German advance and took refuge in a synagogue in Kovno. But Lithuanian militias, acting on orders from the SS Einsatzgruppen, or "special duty groups," soon gathered them along with thousands of Jews in Seventh Fort, part of Kovno's fortress. Between 6,000 and 7,000 were shot dead at the beginning of July. Among the victims was Avraham's father. The ghetto was established the following month. The Germans carried out repeated *Aktionen*—raids to gather, deport, and murder Jews—in the first months of the ghetto's existence. After one raid, Avraham ran back to the synagogue where his family had been staying, and found that his mother, siblings and other relatives had been taken away. "Death. They're dead," reads the account in *Testimonies of Survival*. "I, Avramel, am left alone. The next day a rumor went round that those who had been deported would be brought back. I found a pan. I gathered some scraps of food, a crust of bread. I make a sort of stew. I heat it up. I wait. It gets cold. I wait. So it goes on for four or five days. I sit beside the pan with the stew in it, and wait for them to come back. Because when they come back, they're sure to be hungry. . . ."

There was another *Aktion* in October, when the Germans rounded up young people for deportation. An aunt saved Avraham, then 17, by dressing him up in a long overcoat to make him look like an adult, and claiming that he was her husband. Avraham was later sent to a series of forced labor camps. His only clothes were camp pajamas. He had no shoes. He recalled "The pursuit of every scrap of food. I work and keep my eyes on the German, watching to see when he finishes his meal, waiting for him to throw something away that none of any of the other prisoners notice. Then, just like a starved dog, I fall upon the scraps."

After liberation by the Red Army, Avraham's brother, Meir, who had also survived, went back home to look for his wife and baby whom he had left on the steps of a monastery. Avraham, too, decided to go back, but then heard that Jewish refugees were being sent to Siberia, so he decided to make for Palestine instead, where he met Esther on a kibbutz.

Esther was one of three children born to a self-employed black-smith in the Polish hamlet of Druysk, east of Vilna (Vilnius). Her older brother, Israel, fled to the Soviet Union when the war broke out in September 1939. In the partition of Poland between the Germans and the Soviets, the Red Army occupied her village. In the vacuum left by the retreating Soviets, there were riots and pogroms against Jews in the village. Some of the Jews formed self-defense groups to fight back. In those chaotic days, she said, most people (including some Jews) were waiting for the Germans to come and restore order.

Eventually the Jews were moved into a ghetto by the Germans, but it was poorly guarded and they could sneak out to barter goods for food. Months later, her family was deported to the ghetto in

Vilna. For the first time they heard about the mass executions of Jews at Ponary, near Vilna, from a relative who had escaped. "Extermination, what's that? We thought she had lost her mind," said Esther in her published testimony.

Esther's family was moved from one forced labor camp to another in Estonia. Esther, by now about 15 and tall enough to pass for an adult, escaped the forced separation of children from their parents. One day they heard screaming from the children's hut and saw the Germans loading the children on to trucks to take them away. Among them was Esther's six-year-old sister, Miriam. She later managed to send a note back with one of the male workers. It had been written by a friend. "Dear Mummy, don't worry. I wash myself and I wash my hair. Mummy, I'm well. . . ."

Esther, passing herself off as an adult, had to work as one, breaking rocks with a pick. She recalled the cold huts, the ragged clothes and, above all, the miserable rations. Her parents were found unfit for work and led outside the camp. Esther heard gunshots and knew they had been killed. "Inside me, something had stopped. Everything was a blur. [. . .] Everything was lost in the numbness which had descended on me."

With the Red Army advancing in the East, Esther was deported westward, to the Stutthof concentration camp near Danzig, where prisoners were stripped naked for roll call and had to stand next to piles of the dead and dying. She was part of a group of women who used their cups of coffee to wash themselves. In the bitter struggle to survive, she recalled, the prisoners "were losing their humanity . . . stealing from one another, resorting to despicable tricks to ensure that someone else, not themselves, would be selected" for deportation.

She was sent on another forced march toward the heart of Germany. With only a slice of bread to eat every three days and eating snow for water, Esther collapsed. She was left in a pigsty in a German village with 23 other women. Eventually the women realized that the Germans had gone, and the strongest crawled out to find scraps of food from rubbish heaps.

Soldiers of the Red Army burst in and thought the women were dead. "When they realize what they are seeing, they burst into tears. Soldiers stand around us and cry. Something I thought had gone forever wells up in me, and I burst into tears. [. . .] One of the women staggers to her feet and goes over to the Red Army soldier and embraces him. She lifts up her arms and hugs him. She clings on to him, to the soldier, she hangs on to him. She has stopped moving. She has died with her arms round his neck. [...] It was the 15th of March 1945. I was not yet 17 years old."

Esther decided to put the past behind her, to start afresh in Palestine and "build something new." Already before emigrating from Europe, she had joined the nucleus of a future kibbutz. The members sang pioneer songs, danced, and learned Hebrew.

Avraham, for his part, agreed to go to a kibbutz because he felt "like an old man, tired of life." For the seven months that he sat in a British detention camp in Cyprus for illegal immigrants, Avraham thought hard about how he would tell his relatives in Palestine how the family had been killed by the Germans in Lithuania.

He arrived in Palestine in the summer of 1947, at the age of 20, and went to stay with his brother, Avshalom, who had emigrated before the war and lived on Kibbutz Ginossar. Two months passed, but his brother never asked about the family. It was, Avraham felt at the time, the worst thing that could have happened to him. He recalled: "My brother was busy. He had his family. I waited for us to sit and cry together about our family. I did not have a chance to tell my story."

Avraham gave talks about the Holocaust to groups of Israelis, such as soldiers or teachers. He would describe the events in general, but not his personal experience. On one occasion, he recalled, a soldier asked him why the Jews did not fight back, then got up and walked out of the room. On another, a teacher asked why he endured the humiliation, why not throw himself at the fence and commit suicide? "I told her a 17-year-old boy wants to live," said Avraham. "I wanted to live so I could come here and tell you what happened."

The Holocaust was a collective trauma of the Jews, but for years the stories of personal agony were only told in whispers. Israel as a whole was obsessed with its own heroism and wanted to hear only of the exploits of the soldiers and pioneers. Few people wanted to know about the weakness of Jews who were sent "like lambs to the slaughter." Many native-born Israelis assumed that survivors had lived by corruption or ruthlessness. Tzvika Dror, who compiled the interviews with survivors at Kibbutz Lohamei ha-Getaot, was shocked when a former prime minister told him: "Tzvika—all those who survived were collaborators."

The autobiographies of such sabra icons as Yitzhak Rabin and Moshe Dayan make only the briefest mention of the Holocaust. The Shoah had little to do with their daily lives. It was part of the life in the Diaspora which the pioneers so despised.

Jews who fought with partisans, or who took part in rebellions such as the Warsaw Ghetto uprising, were accepted because they conformed to the ideal of the fighting Jews. There was a sense in the pre-state Yishuv and later in Israel that the Jews of Europe had suffered for their lack of Zionist zeal; had they come to Palestine sooner they would not have suffered under the Nazis. Ben-Gurion complained that these Jews "did not want to listen to us," and their deaths risked sabotaging the dreams of Zionism by denying the Yishuv the human material it needed to build a state. Yitzhak Gruenbaum, a leading figure in Polish Jewry in the Yishuv, complained: "The problem with the Jews in the Exile is that they prefer the life of a beaten dog to death with honor."

The survivors were regarded as human debris, often immoral, and unwilling to adopt the pioneering Zionist ethos. The guilt among many for having lived while their relatives perished was mirrored by the repressed guilt among sabra Israelis over the failure of the Jews of Palestine to do more to try to save their brethren in Europe. Unable to deal with the recrimination and the burden of pain, most Israelis kept an unspoken bargain not to talk too much about the survivors.

Such attitudes took decades to change. The decline of the pioneering ethos and the fragmentation of the old political certainties have permitted a review of attitudes toward the Holocaust in line with the general Israeli mood of reexamining the past. Slowly Israelis have rediscovered an interest in the Diaspora. The children of the survivors began to ask questions, and the survivors themselves felt time was running out. More Hebrew-language books have been published in the past ten years touching on the Shoah than on any other subject. More and more school hours are dedicated to studying the Final Solution, and tens of thousands of teenagers go to Poland every year to visit the death camps and rediscover their family roots. More school leavers write their final history examination papers on the Holocaust than on any other subject.

There is a rush to record the testimonies of the last survivors, some of whom are the only source of information on the fate of whole Jewish communities. Yad Vashem, the Holocaust Memorial in Jerusalem, has plans to draw up as comprehensive a list as possible of the victims of the Holocaust, using computers to identify and cross-check names contained in the documents of its archives. It hopes it will eventually have a database of about five million names on record as "virtual tombstones."

The Holocaust, too, has been given the "post-Zionist" treatment by Israeli historians. Tom Segev, a noted historian and columnist in the newspaper *Ha'aretz*, described in his book on Israel and the Holocaust, *The Seventh Million*, the climate of powerlessness, ambivalence, and at times indifference among Jews in Palestine as the Holocaust was taking place.

Jewish newspapers in Palestine, he recorded, treated the reports of Jews being slaughtered as secondary to the main developments of the war. On January 13, 1942, for instance, *Ha'aretz* ran a story about Nazi atrocities in Kharkov below a report about a "great football victory" for a Jewish team in Damascus. "From a professional point of view, the newspapers missed one of the biggest stories of the century," wrote Segev.

Ben-Gurion said that Hitler's policy "puts the entire Jewish people at risk," but he also discerned an historic opportunity: the Nazis would provide a "fertile force" for Zionism. The Jewish Agency negotiated an elaborate arrangement with the Nazis to allow Jews to emigrate from Germany to Palestine with at least part of their assets. The *haavara* (transfer) agreement, as the deal was called, may have saved lives but was at odds with the boycott of the Nazis declared by American Jews. Ben-Gurion dismissed those wanting to boycott Hitler as assimilationist Jews who sought to remain in the Diaspora; the priority should be to save Germany's Jews and their assets for Zion.

Segev noted that after Kristallnacht in 1938—when German mobs destroyed Jewish homes, stores and synagogues—Ben-Gurion worried that other countries would open their doors to German refugees and divert immigrants from the Zionist project. Those who did arrive in Palestine were often regarded as too old, too urban, too middle-class, too bourgeois, to be of any use in building the country. The "Hitler Zionists" were the wrong "human material." The Jewish Agency tried to select the best immigrants and at one point it attempted to limit immigrants to those under 35 years old and demanded that they give a written commitment to work on the land.

The ambiguity of the Yishuv's response to the Nazis is illustrated by the visit to Palestine in 1933 by a correspondent for Joseph Goebbels' newspaper, *Der Angriff*. According to Segev, the writer had been invited by Jewish leaders to produce a series of articles on Zionism. Entitled "A Nazi Visits Palestine," the series was highly sympathetic to Zionism. It was deemed to be so important that *Der*

Angriff cast a special commemorative medallion with a swastika on one side and the Star of David on the other.

★

Sabon—"Soap"—was the derogatory name used by many Israelis for survivors of the Holocaust. The term was derived from the belief that the Nazis had made soap from the bodies of Jews because of a shortage of industrial fats, and sums up in a single word the contempt which sabras felt for Jews who did not live up to the heroic ideal.

The soap story originates not among the sabras, but among the survivors. German camp guards used to taunt Jews with threats to turn them into soap. The letters RIF printed on bars of soap were widely understood to be a misspelled German acronym for *Rein Jüdisches Fett*, or "Pure Jewish Fat." In fact they stood for *Reichsstelle für Industrielle Fettversorgung*, or State Center for the Supply of Fats. Macabre camp jokes included the story of a Jew who drank a bottle of cologne because he wanted to become perfumed toilet soap.

The soap story was repeated over and again until it became an accepted fact. It made its way into literature, textbooks, and Knesset speeches. "On the shelf in the store, wrapped in yellow paper with olive trees drawn on it, lies the Rabinowitz family," wrote the author, Yoram Kaniuk in his novel, *Man, Son of Dog*. Bars of RIF soap, some bought in Poland at high price, made their way to Israel and were the object of uncomfortable debate. Some tried to give them away to museums. Others buried the soap and had rabbis recite the mourner's kaddish. As recently as 1995, a Tel Aviv auction house put up for sale a bar of soap allegedly made from human fat, with an opening bid of U.S. $300, but had to withdraw it after a public outcry.

Israeli researchers ruled that the RIF story was a myth. The Nazis did experiment with making soap from human fat in Danzig, they acknowledged, but did not succeed in turning the project into industrial production. "What the Nazis did is horrendous enough; we do not need to believe the additional horrors they thought about but did not have time to realize," wrote Yehuda Bauer, one of Israeli's foremost Holocaust scholars, in a letter to the *Jerusalem Post* in 1990. "The Holocaust deniers waiting in the wings are eager to pick up any inaccuracies we may inadvertently commit, and we should not ease their 'work.'"

Sara Shner-Neshamit, a researcher at Kibbutz Lohamei ha-Getaot, never had the insult directed at her. As a former partisan fighting against the Nazis, she said she enjoyed more respect in Israel than ordinary Holocaust survivors.

Born in Poland, Shner-Neshamit studied in a Catholic school in Lithuania, took up medicine in Kovno but switched to Latin. She prepared to emigrate to Israel by studying educational psychology in Vilna, but the war broke out before she could leave for Palestine. She wandered from ghetto to ghetto and was sent to forced labor camps.

When the Germans decided to liquidate her camp, she managed to escape with some 50 other prisoners by hiding under the floorboards of a clinic where she worked as a nurse. They stayed hidden for two days as the Germans searched for the escapees. "There was a woman with a baby. I had helped her give birth in the clinic. The baby started to cry in our hiding place. It was a question of life and death for 50 people. The mother had to suffocate the baby with a pillow. Then she threw the body of the baby on to my knees. To this day I don't know how I remained normal."

The group came out after the Germans had left. Shner-Neshamit went in search of the partisans and worked among them as a nurse. After several close brushes with death, she volunteered to join the advancing Red Army in the summer of 1944, but changed her mind. "The colonel in the Red Army convinced me I had done enough. He told me something I have never forgotten: 'Your people have mostly been killed. There are very few of you left. You must stay alive and become a witness, and tell what the Nazis did to you.' I decided to become a witness."

Now aged 85 and with eight books to her name—works of history, novels, and a children's book—she continues the work of recording the past and reinforcing the memory of the Holocaust. When I met her, she was working on a book about the soap question, *No Peace, Even for the Dead*, published in 1998. In it she examines the workings of the gruesome laboratory near Danzig which began to make soap from human fat.

It had been disguised as an anatomical research facility run by one Rudolf Spanner, professor of anatomy at the Danzig Academy of Medicine. The retreating Germans tried unsuccessfully to set fire to the facility three times before the arrival of the Red Army. Polish investigators later discovered boilers for the bodies, a special pressure cooker for large bones, piles of severed heads, a furnace to dispose of superfluous body parts, large quantities of caustic soda and about 20 kilos of the resulting soap. The bodies came from the Danzig prison, where inmates were guillotined, and from the Stutthof concentration camp.

Shner-Neshamit had received a booklet by Polish investigators as far back as 1957, but Israelis' suspicion of the survivors was such that she put the material away until recently. "Why did I write a book about soap?" she asked rhetorically. Her stare hardened and she spoke deliberately. "Because anti-Semites and racists must know that the Nazis did not make soap out of Jews. They did not have enough fat on them. They made soap from the bodies of Germans killed in the euthanasia program. They also used Russians and Poles. It is a lesson of what Nazism really is. The lesson for racists is that if there should ever be another Nazi regime, this will also happen to their own families."

*

Every year at ten o'clock on the 27th of Nisan (April–May in the western calendar), the air raid sirens wail for two minutes throughout Israel. Jews stop whatever they are doing. Drivers stop their cars, even on the busiest highways. Everybody stands in reverential silence. It is a simple but powerful act of remembrance for the victims of Hitler's Final Solution. To watch a crowded street suddenly come to a halt feels as if the collective grief of the Jews has frozen time itself.

It is a moment to honor the dwindling number of survivors. It is also a time of anguish for many: the ceaseless television documentaries, newspaper articles, and songs about the Holocaust bring back the trauma which many still find difficult to bear. On Holocaust Day, volunteers set up emergency "hotlines" to provide psychological support for victims and their families, who call by the hundreds.

The official state commemorations, the lighting of torches, the laying of wreaths and the speeches are a time for leaders to repeat the lessons of the Shoah: Jews suffered a unique evil, they were slaughtered in Europe because they had no homeland, and the creation of Israel was the answer to the Holocaust, the best revenge. The world stood by and did nothing to save the Jews in their hour of darkness; Jewish refugees found the doors closed everywhere and the British, in particular, did not allow them into Palestine. The Allies, although they knew of the death camps, did not even bomb the railway leading to Auschwitz. Israel cannot rely on anyone but itself, and it must remain strong.

There is no dispute on these central tenets of Zionism. The Holocaust is the only issue on which Israel's warring factions can come together with little or no rancor, with the exception perhaps of many Ultraorthodox Jews who do not recognize the state or its commemorations. The ceremony at Yad Vashem on Holocaust Day in 1999 was typical. It began with the lighting of six memorial candles, one for each million victims, by a group including the former Knesset Speaker, Dov Shilansky, and Zerach Wahrhaftig, one of the last surviving signatories of Israel's Proclamation of Independence.

The participants read aloud the names of the dead: both relatives and members of Jewish communities in Europe. The deputy Speaker Shevach Weiss, a Labor party member and himself a Holocaust survivor, was the first to recite names, including those of his family. "Europe is a lake of frozen Jewish blood," he said. The Likud Prime Minister, Binyamin Netanyahu, and his wife Sara also took part, reading out the names of slain relatives of Mrs. Netanyahu's father, Shmuel Ben-Artzi, the only member of his family to survive.

The former Prime Minister, Yitzhak Shamir, identified his parents and two sisters, all of whom were killed in Poland. Justice Minister Tzachi Hanegbi said that he was named after his slain grandfather, Yitzhak Strausberg, who was killed in Poland. The leader of the left-wing Meretz party, Yossi Sarid, explained how his father, Yaakov Schneider, was the only member of his family to survive the war. He decided to change his name to Sarid, the Hebrew for "remnant."

Throughout Holocaust Day, ordinary Israelis recite the names of the dead as a kind of living tombstone. One year at Yad Vashem I watched families weep as they recalled the fate of their relatives. An Israeli soldier, his rifle slung on his shoulder, spoke a few words in Hebrew. "My name is Itamar Alexander Scheffer. I am named after my grandfather, Alexander Scheffer, who died because he could not defend himself. I can defend myself." His mouth trembled and he walked away.

Israeli newspapers periodically run stories about siblings miraculously finding each other after being separated more than half a century earlier. In the 1950s, there used to be a 10-minute slot on radio before the 1:30 news dedicated to families searching for their relatives' whereabouts. The author Amnon Dankner recalled how the expressions on the faces of his parents and their friends would cloud over when *Ha-Mador le-Hipus Krovim*, "The Relatives Search Spot," came on air. They were moments of despair; only a few stories had a happy ending.

The desire to replace the people lost in the Holocaust is a strong incentive for many families to have more children. I know secular

Jews who have decided to have a third baby—"an extra one for Israel"—to ensure there are more children than parents. Religious families often want six children—one for every million killed.

Yad Vashem is Israel's national shrine. Foreign dignitaries are brought here to lay wreaths, just as they would pay respect to the war dead in other countries. Israeli soldiers come to Yad Vashem as part of their general education during national service.

The development of nuclear weapons was part of Israel's determination not to permit another Holocaust, or at the very least to be able to take its enemies with it into oblivion. But in many ways Jews today face greater dangers in Israel—from terrorism, wars and the threat of Arab non-conventional weapons—than in the rest of the world, particularly in western countries which have been sensitized for the moment against anti-Semitism after the horrors of the Holocaust.

Holocaust Day is the occasion when Tel Aviv University issues its yearly report on the trends of anti-Semitism in the world. A substantial number of Israelis believe that the beast of Jew hatred is lurking just below the surface in the gentile world, waiting to rear its head at the first opportunity. It is a conviction reinforced by the reemergence of anti-Semitism in eastern Europe since the end of Communism. In 1999, the Tel Aviv researchers expressed particular concern about events in Russia which, they said, "witnessed violence against Jewish life and property, by means of arson and explosives accompanied by popular incitement, and the most severe anti-Semitic rhetoric by politicians heard in decades."

Israelis have a complex relationship with the gentile world, and with the Jewish Diaspora. Both anti-Semitism and the lack of it are perceived as threats to Jews living outside Israel. Anti-Semitism means physical danger, and vindicates the need to have a Jewish state. The integration of Jews, on the other hand, brings with it the risk of "spiritual destruction" through assimilation. In the United States, arguably the country most welcoming to Jews, the rate of intermarriage is more than 50 percent, and only a fraction of mixed couples bring up their children as Jews. This slow melting away of diaspora Jewry in western countries is commonly referred to as the "silent Holocaust" or the "second Holocaust."

In 1998, when the Tel Aviv University study found that the overall level of anti-Semitic incidents in the world had dropped for the third year running, Avi Becker, the executive manager of the World Jewish Congress office in Israel, said the situation was "good for the Jews, but bad for Judaism. [. . .] Today the challenge is really how to maintain Judaism in a positive sense, and not really to assimilate and disappear without this physical threat of anti-Semitism." More than a century earlier, Herzl put it more succinctly when he noted that "only anti-Semitism has made Jews out of us."

Israel sees itself not just as a refuge for persecuted Jews, but as a place where there is a sufficiently large critical mass of Jews (shored up by religious restrictions against intermarriage) to prevent assimilation. Where diaspora Jewry once provided crucial material support for the Jewish state, Israel now believes it can provide spiritual sustenance to Jews abroad, by exposing them to a modern society which moves according to a Jewish rhythm of sabbaths and a calendar of Jewish feasts. In its ideological foundations, Israel is the negation of diaspora. Modern Israelis now take a more sanguine view of those who have decided to remain abroad. The *yeridah* or "descent" of Israelis emigrating to the United States and elsewhere scarcely causes a murmur anymore.

However, there remains an unresolved contradiction over the future of the Diaspora. The different arms of world Jewry seem to work against each other. One seeks to preserve endangered and isolated Jewish communities in the remotest corners of the world (every year at Passover, for instance, *matzah* bread is airlifted out to needy groups). The other branch seeks to uproot Jews by encouraging them to move to Israel. Ancient Jewish communities that have disappeared by emigration to Israel are said to have been "rescued." A few years ago I was struck by the resentment of the remnant of the venerable Jewish community in Damascus as it struggled to maintain its identity. Most of its members, including the rabbi, had emigrated to Israel and a rabbi had to be brought from Turkey to slaughter meat and conduct ceremonies.

Interestingly, Herzl did not think that assimilation was an abomination. Far from it. His early idea for eliminating anti-Semitism was to eliminate Jews by mass conversion and intermarriage. In 1893 he proposed to go to Rome to approach the Pope with his scheme for a great Viennese pageant. At noon on a Sunday, Jews would go in festive procession to St. Stephen's Cathedral and convert with pride. Herzl would remain as one of the few Jews in Austria and preach conversion.

Three years later, when he published *The Jewish State*—in essence calling for the removal of the Jews by migration rather than by conversion—he still maintained that assimilation was "not discreditable"; he merely argued that it was impossible because of anti-Semitism. "We naturally move to those places where we are not persecuted, and there our presence produces persecution."

It is an irony of history that the same decaying splendor of Vienna should have produced first Theodor Herzl and, decades later, Adolf Hitler. The antidote before the poison, as Herzl's biographer, Amos Elon, put it. Herzl could not have known that anti-Semitism would take the extreme form of the Nazis, but he knew in 1896, when he published *The Jewish State*, that it was an incurable disease that could only become more acute. "Anti-Semitism increases day by day and hour by hour among the nations; indeed it is bound to increase, because the causes of its growth continue to exist and cannot be removed." He wanted to harness the power of industrialization to organize an orderly mass migration from Europe to the Jewish state; instead it was Hitler who used industrial machinery for mass slaughter.

Herzl saw the cause of anti-Semitism—a term coined in 1879 by a German anti-Jewish agitator, Wilhelm Marr, to describe antagonism to Jews based on political and racial ideas rather than the older religious hatred and persecution—in the very emancipation of Jews. The more the Jews were freed from medieval restrictions and entered the professional world, the more they aroused the hostility of middle-class Christians. Jews either rose to become capitalists, or sank to become socialist revolutionaries; they had most to lose in class conflict, said Herzl, because they "stand in the most exposed positions." Assimilation offered no solution because just as Jews were about to melt into the surrounding gentile society, a new outbreak of hostility would ensure that they rediscovered their Jewish identity.

As he feverishly drafted the manuscript for *The Jewish State*, Herzl jotted down in his diary: "The Promised Land, where we can have hooked noses, black or red beards, and bandy legs, without being despised for it. Where at last we can live as free men on our soil . . . So that the derisive cry of 'Jew' may become an honorable appellation like German, Englishman, Frenchman. In short—like that of all civilized peoples."

In his alternating bouts of despair and euphoria, Herzl tried to relax by listening to Wagner's works at the Paris Opéra. After a performance of *Tannhäuser*, he resolved that the Jewish state must construct auditoria as splendid as those in Paris. Wagner, who inspired

Herzl's vision of a prosperous and bourgeois Jewish state, also stoked the fire of Hitler's anti-Semitism. Wagner's music was performed at Nazi conventions and in the concentration camps. "Whoever wants to understand Nationalist Socialist Germany must know Wagner," wrote Hitler.

When the rise of the Nazis sent hundreds of thousands of Jews fleeing out of Germany, just one in six went to Palestine; however, they made up a substantial proportion of the new immigrants in the 1930s. "Hitler appeared and the Jews began to come," said Ben-Gurion. The German Jews became known as the *yekkes*, a term of unknown origin, and were regarded with suspicion for their wealth and refined middle-class manners. The yekkes established Israel's still blossoming café society and formed the core of what would become the Israel Philharmonic Orchestra (IPO). Not quite Herzl's Parisian opera, yet its first concert was conducted by none other than Arturo Toscanini. The IPO has to this day an unwritten rule of not playing Wagner, despite periodic attempts by some determined music lovers, including the conductors Zubin Mehta and Daniel Barenboim, to rehabilitate the composer among Israeli audiences. The orchestra did play Wagner at first, conducted by the great Toscanini himself, but the ban was imposed after Kristallnacht. When the Rishon Le-Zion Symphony Orchestra played Wagner in October 2000, the performance was interrupted by a protester wielding a loud rattle.

The IPO's unspoken ban on Wagner is the last public gesture of enmity toward Germany. Anti-German emotions can still flare, such as when it emerged that German firms had helped Iraq develop chemical weapons; once again, Israelis said, Jews face the prospect of being killed by German gas. But for the most part Germany is treated with great pragmatism. Most Israelis, for instance, have no hesitation in driving Volkswagen or Mercedes Benz cars. In 1952, Israel gave up its boycott of formal contacts with Germany and, despite violent demonstrations orchestrated by Begin's Herut party, negotiated a reparations agreement which has supplemented the income of tens of thousands of survivors and their families, and accelerated Israel's industrialization. Germany is Israel's second-largest trading partner after the United States, and military relations are also close. In the mid-1990s, Germany agreed to pay for two diesel-powered submarines for the Israeli navy and to share the cost of a third.

Hardly a day passes in Israel without some mention in the newspapers of the Holocaust, the Nazis, or Hitler. In fact Israelis seem ever more interested, perhaps obsessed, by this dark chapter of their history. A computer search of the archives of the English-language *Jerusalem Post* turns up about 1,000 articles mentioning the word "Holocaust" in 1998—more than three per day of publication—compared with about 550 five years earlier. This is a quick, unscientific survey, but it does not contradict other anecdotal evidence.

Not just in Israel, but also in western countries there seems to be a rekindling of interest in the Holocaust. In 2001, Britain observed a day of commemoration for the Holocaust for the first time. In 1998 a U.S. study showed that newspapers were featuring the Holocaust more prominently than they ever did at the height of the Final Solution through coverage of issues such as the campaign to restore Jewish assets in Swiss banks, the discovery of the Jewish roots of Secretary of State Madeleine Albright, and the controversy over Daniel Goldhagen's 1996 book, *Hitler's Willing Executioners*.

Still, Israel has been oddly aloof from the recent struggles of diaspora Jews to recover funds in dormant Holocaust-era Swiss bank accounts, and art work looted by the Nazis. I remember being surprised to find that *Ha'aretz* regularly placed the Swiss bank affair under the rubric of "Foreign News." The Holocaust, while important to Israeli identity, gives way to more pressing national issues in the lives of most Israelis. Restitution was seen as the private business of Jews abroad. The recovery of this wealth was not a priority for Israel, which regards diaspora Jewish organizations as ineffective talking shops, useful mainly to raise funds for Israel.

The imagery of the Holocaust has become part of Israel's political language, not just in its conflict with Arabs, but as a rhetorical means of abusing opponents in internal political squabbles. I have watched the children of Jewish settlers occupying hilltops in protest at the 1993 Oslo accords shouting "Nazi" at Israeli policemen sent to evict them. An Israeli historian, Professor Moshe Zimmerman, in 1995 said the offspring of settlers were "exactly like Hitler Youth." And in 1997 an Ultraorthodox columnist wrote that screening movies on board aircraft was immoral, describing the airlines as "the angel of death disguised as compassionate nurses who slaughters passengers with poison gas."

And so it goes on. So ubiquitous has this language become that some Israelis are worrying openly about the debasing of the Holocaust. It can stretch to the absurd limit of a Tel Aviv pirate radio station calling itself "Holocaust Survivors" Radio" in the vain hope that

its broadcasts of popular Greek music (no connection with the Holocaust) would not be shut down by police.

*

The exhibition halls of the museum at Kibbutz Lohamei ha-Getaot
naturally give prominence to acts of Jewish resistance in Nazi-
occupied Europe. There is a room dedicated to the Warsaw Ghetto
uprising, and other displays deal with events such as the attempt to
parachute soldiers from the Yishuv behind enemy lines to rescue
Jewish communities and gather intelligence for the Allies. It was a
doomed project. The parachutists did not save any Jews, and most of
the agents were captured and killed. Still, their mission became the
stuff of Zionist legend. The story of one of the parachutists in particular, the poet Hannah Szenes, has become immortalized in Israeli
folklore. One of her poems of the early 1940s *Walk to Caesarea*, is
among the best-known Israeli songs of mourning: "God—may there
be no end/to sea, to sand/water's splash/lightning's flash/the prayer
of man."

Ghetto Fighters' House, as the museum is known, does attempt to
place the Nazi horrors in a wider context. Yad Vashem, for instance,
portrays the British as heartlessly blocking ships laden with Jewish
refugees from landing in Palestine, but the Ghetto Fighters' House
acknowledges that Britain was left to fight Germany alone. I noticed,
too, a large board with the grim statistics of the Second World War. It
offered the estimate of a total of 55.6 million dead in Europe and
Asia, of whom 24.3 million were soldiers and 31.3 million were civilians. Of the total dead, 6.141 million were Jews. The number of dead
in Europe stood at 39.941 million. It was recognition that the vast
majority of the victims of the conflagration in Europe were non-
Jews.

Many Jews regard the Holocaust as a unique evil in the course of
world history, worse than the African slave trade or the destruction of
North American Indians. It is a unique tragedy which has befallen a
unique people, with a unique history of persecution. Understandably,
Jews tend to remember the war simply as the setting for the Holocaust, and regard Nazi ideology as being principally directed at the
extermination of the Jews. But many, many other people were murdered by the Nazis. What sets the Holocaust apart is not the number
of those killed, but the ideological imperative to wipe out the Jews as
a "race," and the obsessive thoroughness with which the genocide
was conducted. By the war's end, the Nazis had exterminated two-

thirds of European Jewry, and about four-fifths of the Jews in the
territories they occupied.

The most famous exhibit at the Ghetto Fighters' House is the bulletproof glass cubicle which protected Adolf Eichmann during the
eight months of his trial in Jerusalem in 1961. Here sat the Nazi
prince of darkness, the man who masterminded the logistics of the
Nazi machinery of death. The cubicle is a symbol of Zionism's triumph over the Holocaust. The Jewish state was born despite Hitler's
attempt to annihilate the Jews, and the Jewish state hunted down a
leading architect of the Final Solution and kidnaped him from a
street in Argentina. Eichmann's trial was not, like the Warsaw Ghetto
uprising, an act of hopeless desperation. It was the belated retribution
of history.

Every year on Holocaust Day Israeli television replays the moment
when one of the most famous witnesses, Yehiel De-Nur, fainted in
court. Born Yehiel Feiner, he survived Auschwitz and later took the
Hebraized name of De-Nur, an Aramaic word meaning "from the
fire." He wrote several books about the Holocaust under the alias of
"Ka-Tzetnik 135633," his number in the Auschwitz *Konzentra-
tionslager*, or KZ (Ka Tzet) for short. At the Eichmann trial De-Nur
gave an other-worldly description of the murder of the Jews. "...They
did not live, they did not die, in accordance with the laws of this
world. Their names were numbers. . . . They left me, they kept leaving
me, left . . . for close to two years they left me and always left me
behind . . . I see them. They are watching me. I see them . . ." Then his
body slumped to the floor.

Gideon Hausner, the Attorney-General who personally took
charge of the prosecution, later wrote that Eichmann had disconcerting eyes which "burned with a bottomless hatred." Many among the
thousands of Israelis who attended the trial saw a fearsome monster.
The Mossad operation to kidnap him in Argentina and spirit him
back to Israel had been code-named Attila. But in fact Eichmann
looked more like the stiff and fussy traveling salesman he had once
been, outwardly no different from countless middle managers, an
accountant perhaps, dressed in a dark suit. He was thin and balding,
and had a nervous tic in the corner of his mouth. "The banality of
evil," was how Hannah Arendt, the American historian and philosopher, summed it up in her book, *Eichmann in Jerusalem*. Psychiatrists
declared him normal. "More normal, at any rate, than I am after having examined him," Arendt reports one expert as saying.

Eichmann never climbed beyond the rank of an SS *Obersturmbann-*

führer, the equivalent of a lieutenant-colonel, but gained notoriety as the most senior expert in the Reich on Jewish affairs. At first he dealt with the emigration of Jews, but as the extermination gathered pace he was charged with organizing the massive logistics of transporting millions to their deaths, even denying the army the train transports which it desperately needed for the war effort.

Eichmann did not dispute the facts; he described the Shoah as "one of the greatest crimes in the history of humanity." Instead he minimized his own role, claiming to have been a small cog in the machinery of the Holocaust. He did not give orders for execution, but merely organized the mass deportation of Jews. He said he did it as efficiently as he could, because he was honor-bound to carry out his duties. "There is no blood on my hands," he told the court. He would rather have shot himself than take part in direct killings; in fact, he proposed to hang himself publicly as expiation. He said he liked Jews—even studied a bit of Hebrew and learned some prayers—but he did not express regret. "Repentance is for little children," he declared. More than one Israeli commented that Eichmann was not so much immoral as amoral. He seemed blind to the abomination that he had orchestrated. He could not see that he had done wrong.

Eichmann did not hang himself. Israel did it for him at Ramla prison on May 31, 1962. It was the first and only judicial execution carried out by the State of Israel. Eichmann walked upright to the gallows, after drinking a half-bottle of red wine and declining the help of a Protestant pastor. "After a short while, gentlemen, we shall all meet again. Such is the fate of all men. Long live Germany, long live Argentina, long live Austria. I shall not forget them." With these unmemorable final words, he was executed. His body was cremated, and the ashes were thrown into the Mediterranean to avoid creating a pilgrimage site for neo-Nazis. An anonymous grave for the man responsible for countless anonymous deaths with no graves. So worried were Israeli officials that Eichmann might be adopted as a martyr that it was not until 37 years later, in 1999, that they announced they would make public his 1,300-page long prison memoirs in a controlled "scholarly" fashion.

Peter Malkin, the Mossad agent who seized Eichmann outside his home on Garibaldi Street in Buenos Aires, where he lived under the assumed name of Ricardo Klement, was the first Israeli to converse with him in a Mossad safe house, while waiting to smuggle him on board an El Al flight. In *Eichmann in my Hands*, published in 1990,

Malkin belatedly recounted his role in the operation, noting ruefully that his long anonymity in a trade where only failures are publicized made him a "victim of my own success."

Malkin had been under orders not to speak to Eichmann, but could not contain his curiosity. He recounted the frustration of trying to understand a man who was so emotionally dead, "beyond the reach of human feeling." In their nightly conversations, Eichmann declared that he loved children, all children. He was never an anti-Semite; in fact, he was repelled by the crude hatred of some of his Nazi colleagues. He enjoyed studying Zionism, including Theodor Herzl's writings. "Haifa, ach, the view from Mount Carmel is enchanting," Eichmann told his captor, recalling his visit to Palestine before the war. "You must believe me, I was always an idealist. Had I been born Jewish, I'd have been the most fervent Zionist!" He tried to prove it by reciting a prayer which a rabbi had taught him: *Shema Yisrael, adonai elohenu, adonai ehad . . .* "Hear, O Israel, the Lord our God is one Lord . . .", the Jewish declaration of faith, recited twice a day and, among other occasions, when Jews face martyrdom for the sanctification of God's name. When Malkin told him that his own nephew, his boyhood playmate, had been killed, Eichmann seemed perplexed. He replied: "Yes, but he was Jewish, wasn't he?"

News that Eichmann had been brought to Israel was greeted with unrestrained joy. The Jews had struck back at their oppressors for the first time since the destruction of the temple. "Notice had been served that no Nazi was safe anywhere around the world," wrote Malkin. "Now, fifteen years after the war, they cringed in fear of us."

If Eichmann's arrest gave Israelis a new sense of national pride, then his trial was an occasion for national catharsis. Scores of witnesses testified about their experiences of the Holocaust. Survivors told their stories out loud, and Israelis cried openly. People could be seen gathering in the streets to listen to the latest developments. Sometimes motorists would stop, overcome by emotion. The witnesses often had little to say about Eichmann's direct conduct. Arendt records in her book that at one point Hausner submitted the diaries of Hans Frank, the former Governor-General of Poland hanged at Nuremberg as a war criminal. The defense pointed out that Eichmann's name was not mentioned once in the 29 volumes.

This did not matter much to the country, which listened with harrowed attention to the proceedings. If not a show trial, it was certainly a piece of historical theater, the national saga of Jewish

suffering played before the world. The trial was held in a large concert hall to accommodate Israeli and foreign visitors. It was broadcast
live on radio. A television camera provided footage for foreign networks even though Israel itself had no television at the time. "As I
stand before you, Judges of Israel, to lead the prosecution of Adolf
Eichmann, I do not stand alone," declared Hausner in his opening
address. "With me, in this place and at this hour, stand six million
accusers. But they cannot rise to their feet and point an accusing finger toward the man who sits in the glass dock and cry: 'I accuse.' For
their ashes were piled up in the hill of Auschwitz, in the fields of Treblinka. [. . .] Their blood cries out but their voices cannot be heard. I,
therefore, will be their spokesman."

The trial helped remove the stigma that marked the survivors. As
Avraham Tzoref told me in Kibbutz Lohamei ha-Getaot, the trial
showed that "everybody who survived was a hero, not just those who
fought in the war." Oriental Sephardi Jews, who knew little of the
Holocaust of European Jewry, were included in the process. Eichmann's warders were deliberately chosen to be Sephardi Jews, presumably for security reasons. But by the end, they, too, shared the
collective pain.

Shalom Nagar, of Yemenite extraction, was one of two warders
selected to operate the gallows that killed Eichmann. They used separate buttons. The idea was to leave doubt as to who had actually carried out the execution. In an interview with Israel Radio in 1998
Nagar said he did not know who the other warder was. At first he
had refused to be involved in the hanging, but his boss made him
watch movies about the Holocaust and he relented. Eichmann was
left hanging for three hours. "He was white, white, white. And at that
very moment, with all that was going through my head, I thought he
would eat me up. I considered him a man-eating animal," said Nagar.
"Six million is not easy for anyone to understand." The body was
wrapped in a shroud and placed on a stretcher. As a final vengeance,
Nagar recalled that the man who operated the oven to cremate Eichmann had been a survivor of the camps.

The Eichmann trial was a reproach to the rest of the world for not
doing enough to hunt down Nazi war criminals, some of whom at
the time did not even bother to adopt assumed names. But after the
trial, Israel lost interest in bringing Nazis to justice. It dedicated its
intelligence resources to fighting the enemies of the present rather
than those of the past. It sat on the sidelines, while cheering and boo-

ing the rest of the world as it grappled with the moral questions of prosecuting aged Nazi suspects decades after the atrocities were committed.

Israel was finally dragged back into the playing field of Nazi war crimes trials when U.S. authorities withdrew the citizenship of John Demjanjuk, a Ukrainian-born car worker in Cleveland, Ohio. He was accused of being the sadistic Treblinka camp guard known as "Ivan Grozny," Ivan the Terrible. Two decades after the trial of Eichmann as the godfather of the Final Solution, Israel now decided to take on a presumed monster at the other end of the Nazi chain of command, a camp guard who beat and tortured victims as they were being pushed into the gas chambers. It was an opportunity to demonstrate not only the evil of the Germans, but also the depravity of their willing collaborators in the invaded territories of eastern Europe. Unlike the Eichmann trial, however, the show trial of John Demjanjuk turned into a seven-year legal débâcle that reflected poorly on all those involved.

The bear-like Demjanjuk was stripped of his American citizenship in 1981, and was extradited to Israel in 1986 to face the charge that he was Ivan the Terrible of Treblinka where some 800,000 Jews perished. Once again, as in the Eichmann trial, the survivors came out to point an accusing finger at their tormentor. After a 17-month hearing, televised live from a converted theater in Jerusalem, Israel's district court in 1988 declared Demjanjuk guilty, and sentenced him to death "without hesitation or doubt." His pugnacious lawyer, Yoram Sheftel, was confirmed as the man Israelis loved to hate, a Jew defending a Nazi. A survivor of the Holocaust threw acid at Sheftel's face, permanently damaging one eye.

Demjanjuk's conviction rested on an identification card from the SS training camp at Trawniki in Poland (serial number 1393) as well as on contradictions in Demjanjuk's alibi. It was the emotional evidence of Treblinka survivors who recognized Demjanjuk which identified him as Ivan the Terrible and placed him in Treblinka in Poland.

The Israeli public had lost interest by the time the appeal came to court in 1989. It was at this juncture, however, that the state's case against Demjanjuk began to fall apart. With the winds of glasnost, archives in the Soviet Union were opened to western researchers. Documents on the proceedings of Soviet war crimes trials carried out between 1944 and 1961 were found to include the testimonies of more than 30 *Wachmänner* (guards) from Treblinka and other camps.

All of them identified Ivan the Terrible as a guard named Ivan Marchenko, not Ivan Demjanjuk. Moreover, German documents showed that Demjanjuk had served at the Sobibor death camp in Poland and the Flossenburg labor camp in Bavaria: they did not mention Treblinka.

With the arrival of the new evidence, the Supreme Court judges said, "doubt began to gnaw away at our judicial conscience." Demjanjuk was unanimously acquitted of being Ivan the Terrible, even though the court remained convinced that he had, indeed, been a *Wachmann*, and by definition an accessory to the Final Solution. "Wachmann Ivan Demjanjuk has been acquitted by us, because of doubt, of the terrible charges attributed to Ivan the Terrible of Treblinka," said the president of the court, Justice Meir Shamgar. "This was the proper course for judges who cannot examine the heart and the mind, but have only what their eyes see and read. The matter is closed—but not complete. The complete truth is not the prerogative of the human judge."

The case was riddled with unsolved mysteries. In his application for U.S. citizenship, Demjanjuk had given his mother's maiden name incorrectly as Marchenko, the name of Ivan the Terrible. He later explained that he had forgotten it and had used a common Ukrainian surname. He also claimed to have been a farmer in Sobibor but subsequently retracted the claim and explained that he had chosen the place at random from a map. If Mr. Demjanjuk was a *Wachmann* at Sobibor, however, none of the survivors seem to have recognized him. The defense argued that the original Trawniki document had been a Soviet forgery, yet later successfully relied on Soviet documents to save Demjanjuk from the gallows.

The court said Demjanjuk had only had a chance to defend himself against charges relating to Treblinka. A fresh trial on his possible actions at Sobibor or other camps was deemed to be unreasonable after seven years of proceedings in Israel. An unspoken problem was that any change in the terms of Demjanjuk's extradition might have provoked conflict with American courts. If Demjanjuk was not Ivan the Terrible, he would not be convicted of being merely a "terrible Ivan."

The Demjanjuk affair was a political fiasco for the Israeli government. It was an embarrassment to U.S. attempts to flush out war criminals, and a blow to Nazi-hunting organizations. Demjanjuk, although acquitted, left too many questions unanswered. The trial was, above all, a slap in the face of the Holocaust survivors. Their harrowing memories of what happened half a century beforehand were found to be all too fallible. "Gentlemen, now all the Nazis can celebrate. They will celebrate, because that murderer will continue to live out his life and I, we, the handful who are left, the pain will remain with us," said Yosef Charni, one of five Treblinka survivors who testified against Demjanjuk, amid the uproar outside the courtroom after the verdict was read. He fought back his tears as he said: "I am only a man, and sometimes I ask myself now if it is worthwhile that I should survive only to see such a thing happen in my own country."

Only the Supreme Court emerged with some integrity. Over the next two months it threw out appeals to hold a new trial. In the dead of night, a handcuffed Demjanjuk was driven to Ben-Gurion airport, flanked by elite officers of the Israeli prison service. He left for New York by business class on Israel's national airline, El Al. The last of many ironies is that Israel may unwittingly have saved Demjanjuk's life. By securing his extradition, Israel prevented his deportation to the Soviet Union. Fyodor Fedorenko, another Ukrainian-born U.S. citizen who came under war crimes investigation in the U.S. at the same time as Demjanjuk, was deported in 1984 to Moscow. Three years later, Fedorenko was executed by firing squad. He was 80 years old.

The Demjanjuk débâcle has ensured that Israel, the Jewish state born from the ashes of the Holocaust, the protector of oppressed Jews and the custodian of Jewish memory, will never again hold a Nazi war crimes trial.

★

"The Russians did it best," said Tzvika Dror. "As the Red Army advanced, witnesses pointed out Germans on the spot. They said 'He killed my father, he killed my mother' and so on. The Germans were given a summary court-martial and they were killed." Dror brandished a mock machine-gun. "Rat-tat-tat-tat! Rat-tat-tat-tat! It was the laws of war."

By the time Israel was formed, however, war criminals had to be dealt with according to legal process. Jews who collaborated with the Nazis were prosecuted in Israel, but few Israelis paid any attention to the trials.

As a kibbutz-born sabra, Dror had no direct experience of the Holocaust. His interests lay in the local history of Palestine, and the military history of the Palmach. He was married to a survivor and settled in Kibbutz Lohamei ha-Getaot. In the late 1970s he agreed to write a book on the experiences of kibbutz members. "When I interviewed people they started to apologize. One of them said 'I was in the Warsaw Ghetto but I was not a fighter.'

"I spoke to a woman who had been at Auschwitz. We met about 20 times but we never got anywhere. She had a block. It took a year and a half. Then one day she told me 'I handed over my brother to the Gestapo.' She had tried to organize work for him and sent him to the authorities to get a permit. They arrested him because he was a Jew, and she felt she killed her brother."

We sat in Dror's workroom, a hut the kibbutz had given to him where he could write his books and work on the community's newsletter. Dror was dressed in baggy jeans and a sweater, and wore black-rimmed spectacles. The walls were covered with papers, notes, pictures of the icons of the early years of the state—Ben-Gurion, Yitzhak Rabin, Yitzhak Sadeh, the first commander of the Palmach—as well as photographs of his grandchildren. Above his old computer, he had lined up several broken clocks. "I will not throw them away. They remind me that time is passing quickly," he said. Nevertheless, we sat there for hours, with the shutters closed. Dror said he was not an academic but a chronicler. He told stories. One story led to another. They went off at tangents to his main point. We seemed to be walking at random through the graveyard of Israel's past, stopping here and there to look at the inscriptions on the tombstones. We talked about the Holocaust, the kibbutz, the Arabs, the Palmach, the survivors, the founding of Tel Aviv, Lebanon—all the while consuming an odd assortment of red wine, grapefruit juice, sardines, and biscuits.

"I was born in Israel," said Dror. "My first fears were about Arabs. In 1929 I was two and a half years old. I remember my mother clutching me to her breast and running to a building when there was a rumor that the Arabs of Jenin were coming to attack us. I remember the unrest of 1936. I was terrified. My trauma, if I have one, is the Arabs, not the Poles or the Germans."

"I saw the War of Independence and how the problem of the Arab refugees started. On Passover, I saw the Arabs going past our kibbutz as they fled from Haifa in 1948. I saw the expulsion from Lod and Ramla. I saw a mother with a baby who died on the road. There were thousands of refugees."

Then we were back to discussing the Holocaust and his feelings about visiting Poland with survivors. "I am not moved by Auschwitz itself," explained Dror. "The most powerful moment, for me, is when

I go with friends to see the houses where they used to live. When I prepared my book about Kibbutz Lohamei ha-Getaot, I decided to start with how people came out of the concentration camps or from hiding in the woods and tried to go back to their homes. When they got home they found their houses taken by Polish families, if they had not been destroyed altogether. The refugees looked for another home; they needed another home. The tragedy is that their new homes [in Israel] were Arab homes."

The founders of Kibbutz Lohamei ha-Getaot debated the name of their community. One proposed to call the kibbutz Vilna, after the Lithuanian center of Jewish learning. Others protested. How could one possibly ask for a bus ticket to Vilna? Many wanted to preserve the name of the Arab village, so they called it Kibbutz Lohamei ha-Getaot Sumayriyya. The Jewish National Fund, however, ruled that joining the memory of the Warsaw Ghetto uprising with the Arab village was unthinkable, and handed down a suitable biblical name—Asher. The settlers agreed to give up Al-Sumayriyya, but would not abandon the memory of the ghetto fighters. That, after all, was the point of the kibbutz. The JNF rejoined that it was inappropriate to include the word "ghetto" in an Israeli settlement. And so the tug of war went on between those trying to preserve something of the diaspora heritage, and those wanting to impose a new Hebrew culture.

"There were orchards left behind by the Arabs," said Dror, launching into another tale. "In the early years a friend of mine was trying to irrigate them, but the water did not flow. He sat down to eat a tangerine. Suddenly a man appeared. He was an Arab who spoke a bit of Hebrew. He explained how to lay the irrigation tubes and make it work. My friend asked him how he knew. The man answered 'This is my orchard.' Do you know when my friend told me this story? Just two years ago."

Once, he said, two boys writing a project on the birth of the kibbutz for their barmitzvah wanted to know why one set of cypress trees on the kibbutz was taller than the other. Their parents did not tell them, so they went to Dror. "I told them the tall ones were planted by the Arabs to protect their orchards from the wind. The smaller ones were planted by us later. That's why they are smaller," he explained. "There is a bomb shelter next to the trees, and I said we needed the shelter because those who used to live here now live in Lebanon and they want to take revenge.

"It was 1981. I was here interviewing survivors and I looked out of the window. I saw the trees and the shelter. There is a connection between the Holocaust and the parents who did not want to tell the truth about the trees and the shelter."

One wall of Dror's room had a striking poster of two modern dancers—his daughter, Liat, and his son-in-law, Nir. It advertised a performance called *Hakira*, or "Investigation," and it reproduced two first-person accounts of interrogation: one was a Jew's account of being questioned by the Gestapo and the other was a Palestinian's experience of interrogation at the hands of the Shin Bet internal security service. The message was clear—in their treatment of Arabs, the Jews are resorting to some of the same methods adopted by the Nazis. This kind of parallel is often drawn by Palestinians, but hardly ever by Israelis.

It was getting dark. As I made to leave, I asked Dror the meaning of Hebrew phrases written with a thick felt pen on the wall of a gray metal cabinet.

They were some favorite quotations, he explained. There was Arthur Ruppin, the father of Jewish settlements such as Degania and the man who helped to negotiate the haavara agreement with Nazi Germany: "What the Arabs can give us we do not need. What we need, they cannot give us." There was an English historian: "Suffering is the housemate of history." And there was Yitzhak "Antek" Zuckerman, one of the leaders of the Warsaw Ghetto uprising and a founder of the kibbutz: "Pain, pain, pain. . . ."

★

The Jews came before dawn. They used car headlights to illuminate their way, and the villagers of Al-Sumayriyya opened fire. Muhammad Amer, known as Abu Amer, had just finished his guard duty, and had given his weapon to the next shift when the fighting started. He slipped out of the village with three other men to summon reinforcements from the Arab Liberation Army of Fawzi al-Qawkji, whose units had taken over an old British base nearby.

He saw a convoy of 40 vehicles coming up from Acre. "The soldiers in the lead vehicles wore red *keffiyehs*," he recalled. "The guard at the entrance to Al-Sumayriyya thought they were Arab reinforcements. He welcomed them by firing shots in the air, and was killed on the spot. The villagers shouted that the soldiers were disguised as Arabs, and families started to flee eastward through fields of wheat while they were being shot at." Five villagers died that morning, said Abu Amer, and within days Hagana sappers had blown up the houses of Al-Sumayriyya.

Some 800 villagers, all Muslims, had lived in Al-Sumayriyya. They grew citrus fruit, melons, bananas, cucumbers, wheat, sesame, and other crops. The village maintained its own mosque and school. Some historical sources suggest the name of Al-Sumayriyya derives from the sect of the Samaritans who lived in the area until the eighteenth century. Archaeological remains on nearby hillocks indicate that the area has been inhabited since antiquity.

Most of Al-Sumayriyya's inhabitants joined the stream of refugees in Lebanon. After wandering from village to village, Abu Amer, too, crossed the northern border to find food for the family. By his own account, it was not a particularly heroic episode. He went to the refugee center, lied about his father being killed in the war and registered himself as being responsible for a family of ten people. He stayed in Lebanon for six months, selling the supplies he received in order to make money to "have fun in Beirut." Then he heard that Israel would soon block the return of the refugees and, with the help of Druze villagers, slipped back across the border.

Abu Amer now lives in the village of Al-Makr, a few miles to the east of Kibbutz Lohamei ha-Getaot. In the distance, he can see the orchards and cypress trees of what was once Al-Sumayriyya. Although an Israeli citizen, enjoying what should be equal rights with the Jews, he can neither go back to his destroyed village nor work his family's 27 dunams of land, and has not been compensated for the loss. He is in exile within a state that claims to be democratic. There are tens of thousands of such "internal refugees" in Israel. Jews may settle in the Galilee from as far away as Minsk, but a Palestinian may not move a few miles back to his ancestral plot.

"I have almost forgotten about the village," said Abu Amer. "There is no hope of going back. They have brought Jews from abroad." Still, Abu Amer did not complain too much. He considered himself lucky. He had prospered despite the circumstances. He owned 90 head of sheep and farmed vegetables. His two sons leased out tractors and bulldozers. The family lived in a sizeable compound of two houses and a large garden. Except for the issue of land, said Abu Amer, Israeli laws are fair. Arabs even get state pensions. "The refugees in Lebanon say Israel is a criminal state. But I am here. The police will not arrest me unless I have done something wrong. I am living in my homeland. It is true that the Israelis took my land, but I can see it," he said. "In Lebanon the refugees live under Lebanese control and are oppressed."

At the age of 71, Abu Amer spoke with hindsight. Given the con-

flict of the past half-century, the days of British rule seemed a gen-
teel, idyllic period when Jewish and Arab plowmen toiled equally on
the land. "Relations with the Jews were good," recalled Abu Amer.
"We thought we were happy because we thought the Jews would
bring good business." Abu Amer understood the price that Palestinians paid for the mistakes of their leaders. "We were not educated," he
explained. "My father said most people in the village could not read."
Had the Arabs accepted the 1947 U.N. partition plan, he said ruefully,
the western Galilee, which included Al-Sumayriyya, would have
been part of an Arab state in Palestine. Instead the leaders rejected it
and the Palestinians lost everything.

Abu Amer was unusual in his readiness to forgive. He had never
been to Kibbutz Lohamei ha-Getaot. He knew the horror stories but
he did not want to go to the museum. "I do not want to see injustice," he said. Nazi Germany, he declared, "was destroyed by God for
the crime it committed against the Jews."

His sons and grandsons, and friends in the village, sat around us.
Abu Amer's younger son smoked a water pipe. These men were
brasher, more confident, more Israeli. They saw the glass not as half
full, but as half empty. They had no experience of the trauma of 1948
or of the humiliation of the refugee camps. They did not look across
the border to Lebanon, feeling grateful to have been spared the worst
of the Palestinian dispersion; instead they gazed inward at the Jews
around them, resenting the Arabs' status as second-class citizens. Arabs
in Israel, they told me, continue to be discriminated against. They get
poorer wages, less land and less water to cultivate it.

Abu Amer's eldest son, Amer, 43, said: "The Nazis committed
crimes against the Jews, and the Jews committed crimes against us.
Here they destroyed villages and threw people out; there they killed
people and put them in ovens. It's a difference of style." Every day,
said Amer, he passes Al-Sumayriyya on his way to the coastal town of
Nahariya. "When I am with my children I tell them 'This is your
grandfather's village.' I was not born there, but I have not forgotten
it." He was once hired to work at Kibbutz Lohamei ha-Getaot, but
kept quiet about his family's roots there. "I did not tell them," said
Amer. "We just discussed work. It was difficult." Silence. Everybody
hides his pain in silence.

*

The conquest and destruction of Al-Sumayriyya was the opening
shot in Operation Ben-Ami, in which the Hagana cleared the coastal

road up to the Lebanese border and linked up with an isolated kib-butz in the hill country. All the Arab villages along the road and some to the east were captured. Although the territory had been allocated by the United Nations to the Arab state, most of the Arab communi-ties were razed to ensure that the inhabitants would never return.

Operation Ben-Ami was part of an overall Hagana strategy, known as *Tochnit Dalet*, or "Plan D," to secure the areas allocated by the U.N. to the Jewish state, as well as blocks of Jewish settlements and access routes in the Arab areas beyond, before the expected onslaught of regular Arab armies. Under Plan D's operations, conducted in April and May 1948, the Hagana moved away from local "active defense" to offensive action designed to conquer and hold territory.

The ostensible purpose of Plan D was military—to clear the inte-rior of the prospective Jewish state and to establish territorial conti-nuity between major concentrations of Jewish population. In practice, by calling for "operations against enemy settlements which are in the rear of, within or near our defense lines, with the aim of preventing their use as bases for an active armed force," Plan D meant the eviction of the Arab population and the destruction of villages. The preceding months had seen a steady stream of Palestinians—usually the wealthy urban classes—leaving their homes for safer areas. But Plan D marked the start of the mass flight, caused by a mixture of war, the breakdown of Palestinian society, and outright expulsion, which continued for months.

In the weeks before the attack on Al-Sumayriyya, the mixed cities of Haifa, Tiberias, Jaffa, and Safad, as well as the all-Arab Beisan (Beit She'an today), had already fallen to Jewish forces, with only a small proportion of their prewar Arab populations left behind. Acre fell to the Hagana three days after the capture of Al-Sumayriyya. By the end of the war, some 700,000 Palestinians had fled their homes—roughly 60 percent of Palestine's prewar Arab population, and roughly 85 per-cent of the Arab population within the borders of the State of Israel. More than 400 of some 500 Arab villages within the borders of Israel were destroyed. Arab property was taken over by the state, or looted and appropriated by individual Jews.

In the 1940s the flight and eviction was known as a "transfer" of population; in modern times it is called ethnic cleansing. The leaders of the new Jewish state feared that Arabs in their midst would form a potentially hostile and dangerous "fifth column." Moreover, they wanted to ensure a permanent Jewish majority, and seized the Arabs' lands to settle Jewish immigrants. The U.N. partition plan would have left the prospective Jewish state with a large Arab minority amounting to more than 45 percent of the population. With the war, the internal Arab "problem" was conveniently eliminated in the fog of battle. Even the Bible seems to provide justification for such harshness when God tells Moses on the banks of the Jordan River:

> Speak unto the children of Israel, and say unto them, When ye are passed over Jordan into the land of Canaan; Then ye shall drive out all the inhabitants of the land from before you, and destroy all their molten images, and quite pluck down all their high places: And ye shall dispossess the inhabitants of the land, and dwell therein: for I have given you the land to possess it [. . .]. But if ye will not drive out the inhabitants of the land from before you; then it shall come to pass, that those which ye let remain of them shall be pricks in your eyes, and thorns in your sides, and shall vex you in the land wherein ye dwell. (Num. 33: 51–55)

The new Israeli state was adamantly opposed to United Nations resolutions demanding the return of refugees. For decades, Israel has maintained that the Palestinian refugees left of their own volition, smugly expecting to return home with the victorious Arabs, or as a result of evacuation orders from Arab leaders. Israel washed its hands of their plight; their fate was the responsibility of the Arab states that had caused the war and provoked their departure. But in the late 1980s a new and younger generation of Israeli historians, armed with a more iconoclastic mindset and fresh documents released by state archives in Israel and the West, began to demolish this founding myth of Israel. Benny Morris, in particular, spearheaded the reevaluation with *The Birth of the Palestinian Refugee Problem*, published in 1988. He found that the Israeli government and army deliberately evicted many of the Palestinians, encouraged and nudged others to leave, and resolved not to allow the Arabs back. The exodus was accelerated in no small part by atrocities carried out by Jewish forces.

"The Palestinian refugee problem was born of war, not by design, Jewish or Arab," Morris concluded. "It was largely a product of Arab and Jewish fears and of the protracted, bitter fighting that characterized the first Arab–Israeli war [. . .]."

Morris painted a picture of Israeli leaders who had no overall plan to force out the Arabs, but quickly exploited and accelerated their departure once the prospect of a land largely free of Arabs became a possibility.

Having shattered the myth of "voluntary" departure—there was no blanket Arab order for evacuation—Morris was accused by veteran Israeli historians of being "pro-Palestinian." But in refusing to accept the Arab notion of a preconceived Jewish master-plan to "transfer" the Palestinians to make room for Jews, Arab academics complained that Morris had not gone far enough. Indeed, some Palestinians such as Sharif Kanaana, an anthropologist at Bir Zeit University in the West Bank, wrote in his book, *Still on Vacation: The Eviction of the Palestinians in 1948*, that Morris's new history was "a lot more dangerous than the previous line of Israeli propaganda, because it is more sophisticated."

The fate of villages in the Galilee is an important piece of evidence in the debate. Communities along the western coastal road, such as Al-Sumayriyya, were destroyed, but farther inland many were allowed to remain. Nazareth was the only major Arab city to be spared mass evacuation or expulsion. To Morris, this suggests that the uprooting of Palestinians was a haphazard affair, often determined by local military conditions and the predisposition of individual commanders. To Arabs, the Galilee villages are merely the exception to the broad pattern of expulsion, caused by local constraints such as stronger international objections to the eviction of Arab Christians and internal lobbying on behalf of friendly communities, such as the Druze.

The thinking of the Yishuv's leaders in the 1930s, when Britain proposed the partition of Palestine, sheds important light on their actions in the 1940s. Ben-Gurion told Jewish Agency colleagues he accepted partition, not because he was satisfied with the size of the Jewish part of the country but on the "assumption that after we constitute a large force following the establishment of the state—we will cancel the partition of the country and we will expand throughout the Land of Israel."

He advocated the transfer of Arabs through "mutual understanding." Others said Britain should oversee the removal of Arabs. In a letter to his son discussing the 1937 Peel Commission report and its support for an exchange of populations, Ben-Gurion said he did not wish to expel the Arabs, but made clear he was ready to use military means if Arabs did not share the belief that there was "enough room" in Palestine for both Jews and Arabs. "We must expel Arabs and take their places [. . .] and if we have to use force—not to dispossess the Arabs of the Negev and Transjordan, but to guarantee our own right to settle in those places—then we have force at our disposal."

Morris acknowledged that the Yishuv's leaders may have long

thought about the transfer of Arabs, but he argued that they did not plan for it when war broke out—a contention Arabs find difficult to believe. Had there been a specific plan for the expulsion of Palestinians, Morris maintained, there should be signs of it in the cabinet minutes, military orders, and other papers of the period. He said there is no such clear-cut evidence. Instead, Morris paints a complex picture of Ben-Gurion evolving a policy of unspoken but increasingly overt expulsion in the second half of 1948. When Ezra Danin, special adviser on Arab affairs, in October 1948 floated a proposal to set up a puppet Palestinian state in the West Bank (some Israeli officials did not think the idea anathema), Ben-Gurion's view had crystallized. He replied: "The Arabs of the Land of Israel, they have but one function left—to run away."

Ben-Gurion clearly wanted to be rid of as many Arabs as possible, said Morris. "But no expulsion policy was ever enunciated and Ben-Gurion always refrained from issuing clear or written expulsion orders; he preferred that his generals 'understand' what he wanted done. He wished to avoid going down in history as the 'great expeller' and he did not want the Israeli government to be implicated in a morally questionable policy."

The debate over the Palestinian exodus would not be complete if it were not impregnated with the emotions of the Holocaust. A small example comes from an exchange in the pages of the *Journal of Palestine Studies* in 1991. When Morris pointed to the fact that more than 100,000 Arabs were left in Israel as evidence of the lack of a systematic expulsion policy, Norman Finkelstein, a lecturer in political theory and international relations at Hunter College and New York University, known for his strong criticism of Zionism, responded: "One wonders how Morris would respond if a German historian argued that the fact that roughly one half (five million) of the Jews of Nazi-occupied Europe survived the war shows that the other half wasn't victim of a 'ruthlessly efficient' and 'systematic' policy of extermination."

As more archival material becomes available, Israel's "New Historians" will certainly provoke renewed controversy over more recent events. Morris has already cast a harsh light on Israel's border wars in the 1950s. Perhaps even the Six Day War will be reexamined as a tale of unsurpassed Israeli heroism. Still, the arguments over 1948 are made with unique passion. They deal with what has been described as the "original sin" of Zionism. If 1948 was a just war, then Israel's subsequent actions, however unpleasant, were in defense of a just cause. If Israel was born morally tainted, however, then it remains for-

ever besmirched and nothing it does, especially in its conflict with
the Palestinians, is morally defensible.

★

Mahmoud Amin took just one possession when he ran away on the
morning the Jews attacked Al-Sumayriyya—the deeds to his land. He
carried the papers with him as he made his way to Lebanon with his
wife and children. He had the documents when he was taken to a
tent camp at Ain al-Hilweh, outside Sidon, "to wait until it was safe
to go home." The months of waiting gave way to years, and the tents
became concrete blocks. More than half a century after abandoning
Al-Sumayriyya, Amin is still waiting to go back to his village and
stubbornly holds on to his yellowed land deeds. They are proof of his
forcible and illegal eviction from Palestine.

Amin had been a pillar of his village, the *mukhtar*, or headman.
Today he is bitter, resentful, and suspicious. He writes down in a
black book the passport details of my researcher before agreeing to
be interviewed by her. "There have been enough books written
about the Palestinian cause to fill a whole ship, yet not one has
changed our situation. Why should anything I say to you now make
a difference?"

It is difficult to argue the point. The Berlin Wall went up and was
torn down again in the time that Amin has been waiting to go home.
The number of registered Palestinian refugees has grown from about
900,000 in 1950 to roughly 3.5 million today—2.2 million of them
outside the Israeli-occupied territories—as exiled families multiplied. The Palestinian Central Bureau of Statistics estimated there was
a total of about 8 million Palestinians in the world in mid-1998.
About one million live in Israel, three million in the West Bank and
Gaza Strip, and 2.5 million in Jordan, prompting Israeli right-wingers
to declare periodically that "Jordan is Palestine." The remaining Palestinians are dispersed in Lebanon and Syria, and across the Arab world,
and about 200,000 live in North and South America.

The Palestinians have fought the Jordanians, the Maronites, the
Syrians, the Israelis, and even among themselves to little avail. Israeli
army columns rumbled past the ruins of Al-Sumayriyya in 1982,
crossed the border into Lebanon, destroyed much of Ain al-Hilweh
on their way to Beirut and retreated again. But nothing has changed
for Amin. Israel has signed peace treaties with Egypt, and Jordan.
Even the Palestine Liberation Organization has made a partial peace
with Israel, giving up its claim to all of Palestine for a stake in the

West Bank and Gaza Strip. Many Palestinians fear that amounts to an abandonment of their claims to return to their former homes in what is now Israel. Amin despairs of ever leaving Ain al-Hilweh.

"I regret leaving my village. From that day till now I have not seen one happy day in my life," said Amin. "I have lost everything and would give anything to go back now. First the British gave away our land, then the Arabs betrayed us. Now Yasser Arafat is at the top of the betrayal list."

He went on: "My religion tells us that one day we will defeat the Jews and regain our land. I don't think I will be around to see it. I just hope that my grandchildren do. I have made sure that my grandchildren know everything about their land and that their urge to go back is as strong as mine. I have taught them that it is only there that they can find peace and self-respect, working on their own land and not living where they are not welcomed."

Amin said he has lost all four of his sons. One was killed during the civil war in Lebanon, another was accidentally shot in Ain al-Hilweh and two died of illness. Remarkably fit at the age of 75, he lives with his wife, the widow of his eldest son, and two grandchildren. By the standards of Ain al-Hilweh, he is well off. He has a simple first-floor flat in a five-story building, and works for the United Nations Relief and Works Agency (UNRWA), the only reliable employer of Palestinians in Lebanon.

The name of Ain al-Hilweh, "Sweet Spring," seems to mock the place. It is the largest refugee camp in Lebanon, a slum quarter of the coastal city of Sidon where some 40,000 people are packed into small breeze-block huts. It is just 50 miles from Al-Sumayriyya, but it might as well be on a different planet. Ain al-Hilweh likes to call itself the "capital of diaspora Palestine," but like the Palestinian Diaspora, it has been bypassed by recent history.

Ain al-Hilweh had been part of Arafat's Palestinian "state within a state," created in south Lebanon in the political vacuum of a country sliding toward civil war in the mid-1970s. Lebanon has neither the largest number nor the largest concentration of Palestinian refugees, but it became the center of guerrilla activity when Palestinian militias were expelled from Jordan in 1970. The disparate armed factions were both a catalyst for the disintegration of Lebanon and a central component of the fighting forces during the civil war. In "Fatahland," the Palestinians had their last base for autonomous operations against Israel, but they expended most of their energies fighting the Lebanese civil war and, as in Jordan, eventually lost all freedom of action.

The PLO's military power was broken by the Israeli invasion, forcing Yasser Arafat to move to Tunis. The Palestinians descended into internecine war, and the Syrians mopped up all resistance until they turned Lebanon fully into their vassal after 1991. The Palestinians, said the literary critic Ferial Ghazoul, "stand where all the swords meet: the swords of the enemies, those of the friends, and those of the brethren."

The Lebanese army controls the roads and access to the refugee camps. The dinosaurs of Palestinian Marxist radicalism, such as George Habash and Naif Hawatmeh, have been confined to impotent semi-exile in Damascus. With the signing of the Oslo accords, Yasser Arafat and much of the rickety PLO structure moved to autonomous enclaves in the Israeli-occupied territories, where the fate of the Palestinian national movement is now being decided. The refugee camps of Lebanon are no longer the frightening strongholds of international terrorism, the places where the revolutionaries of half the world came to find weapons training and spiritual strength. The swaggering gunmen with their jeep-mounted machine-guns and trendy sunglasses have melted away.

Lebanon's camps have been reduced to Palestinian ghettos, and their inhabitants are at the bottom of the social heap. Nowhere in the Middle East do Palestinian refugees enjoy complete freedom, but here they are subjected to particularly onerous restrictions. They are a Lebanese sect without a place in Lebanon's sectarian system. They are blamed by Maronites for starting the civil war, and are at best regarded with indifference by the other groups. More than half the Palestinians in Lebanon live in camps, the highest proportion of any Arab "host" country. They are regarded as foreigners, albeit with unlimited residence permits.

There are more than a few parallels here with the status of Jews in Tsarist Russia in the nineteenth century. Palestinians do not enjoy social security or health benefits from the Lebanese state. Housing is restricted. Camps destroyed by years of war have not been rebuilt. The government forbids the establishment of new camps, or building on vacant land next to the camps. It has even restricted reconstruction within the camps. The Lebanese government has begun evicting Palestinians from informal settlements which sprang up during the war years, and the threat of demolition hangs over three camps in Beirut. All manner of official and unofficial pressures are placed on Lebanon's refugees to leave, but they have nowhere to go.

Palestinians in Lebanon cannot work without official permits, given to them at the rate of only a few hundred a year. As non-

Lebanese, they are banned from several categories of work, including state, municipal, transport, and working for large foreign companies. Moreover, practicing professions such as medicine, engineering, and law is restricted to members of recognized syndicates—whose members are Lebanese. Only within refugee camps such as Ain al-Hilweh do Palestinians enjoy a degree of autonomy. It is the only place where professionals can practice.

The refugees in Lebanon are, more than elsewhere, wards of an increasingly indifferent international community. UNRWA and other aid agencies, as well as the PLO, provide a minimum of employment and services for Palestinians. But contributions were cut back in the 1990s as the PLO's coffers ran dry, and the international community concentrated on supporting the emerging Palestinian entity in the West Bank and Gaza Strip.

The blue U.N. flags which flutter above the 12 camps in Lebanon, the refugee identity papers, the temporary travel permits, the whole oppressive paraphernalia of an eternally temporary existence are, for better or for worse, symbols of Palestinian identity. Arafat is at one with Lebanese leaders on the question of keeping Palestinians as a people apart. "We utterly reject all talk of the naturalization of refugees in Lebanon as criminal," he said in late 1999.

The fate of Palestinians throughout the Arab world is subject to the whim of the countries' rulers. Kuwait was once an important center of Palestinian diaspora, a welcoming place of relative political freedom. Its oil wealth drew hundreds of thousands, including Arafat himself, who worked there as a junior civil servant in the public works department. Kuwait was the incubator of Arafat's Fatah movement, the largest faction of the PLO. But after Allied troops liberated Kuwait from the Iraqi invaders who had marched in the previous August, the Kuwaiti royal family expelled between 200,000 and 300,000 Palestinians *en masse* in revenge for Arafat's "betrayal" in supporting Iraq. Many of the deportees had been forcibly moved several times. I met some who had gone from Israel to the West Bank in 1948, from the West Bank to Jordan in 1967, moved to Kuwait in search of work, only be to be expelled back to Jordan in 1992. Some even made it all the way back to the West Bank, despite the Palestinian uprising which was still raging, deciding that Israeli occupation was better than the vagaries of Arab rule.

In August 1995, it was the turn of Libya's Colonel Muammar Gaddafi to turn on the Palestinians in his country. Thousands were summarily deported, and many were left stranded for weeks in the desert sun on the Egyptian–Libyan border. Gaddafi said it was a demonstration of the emptiness of the promises of peace offered by the Oslo accords.

When Egypt recovered the Sinai peninsula after making peace with Israel, it demanded that the border be drawn precisely along the international frontier, ignoring requests for a slight amendment to take in part of a refugee camp which had spilled over on to the Sinai side of the border. The result was that more than 5,000 people in Canada Camp on the Egyptian side were cut off from the Gaza Strip, able to communicate with relatives in Gaza only by shouting across the border fence. They were not fully "repatriated" until late 2000.

Only Jordan has given citizenship to Palestinians who came in the two waves of refugees created by the wars of 1948 and 1967. More than half the kingdom's population is Palestinian, including much of the business and professional class, and Jordan's economy has long been supported by the remittances of Palestinians living in the Gulf oil states. More than once the late King Hussein appointed a Palestinian as Prime Minister.

Jordan is a queer entity—a Palestinian state in population, which has stubbornly repressed Palestinian nationalism. The West Bank was annexed to Jordan when it was ruled by King Hussein; it was not allowed to become any sort of Palestinian state. The Black September civil war has left a legacy of suspicion. The headquarters of the *mukhabarat*, or secret police, is popularly known as *Funduq Filastin*, or the "Palestine Hotel" because of the number of Palestinians rounded up, questioned and tortured within its walls. When King Hussein announced in 1988 that he would disengage from the Israeli-ruled West Bank, where Palestinians still have Jordanian papers, the Palestinians' passports suddenly became "temporary."

The perpetual motion of the refugees, their rootless existence, their buffeting by fate, their attempt to maintain order in chaotic circumstances, are all dominant themes of Palestinian literature. One of the best-known works by the writer Ghassan Kanafani is "Men in the Sun," a short story about three Palestinians making the desert journey through Iraq to find work in Kuwait. Their tribulations along the way end in tragedy when, seeking to steal through the border, they hide inside an empty water tanker and are killed by the stifling heat as the driver is delayed by border officials teasing him about his sex life.

Palestinians have developed a healthy skepticism about friends and foes alike. The honeyed words of Arab leaders elicit only cynicism;

Palestinians have struggled as much against <u>Arab kings and presidents</u>
<u>as they have against the Jews.</u> Mureed Barghouthy, a prominent poet
who has lived in several Arab countries, addressed these lines to
Palestinian exiles:

> To every citizen there is one ruler.
> You alone are favored with twenty
> in twenty capitals.
> If you made one of them angry,
> the law would claim your head
> and if you honored one of them
> the rest would want you dead.

★

Only the demented inhabit the alleys of Deir Yassin. The psychotic
and the schizophrenic, the paranoid and the clinically depressed, are
now the owners of this warped corner of modern Israel. Sturdy but
graceful Arab houses provide solace for the mentally ill of Jerusalem.
The name of Deir Yassin has burned a hole in the Palestinian consciousness, but in Israel it has been obliterated by an act of collective
amnesia. The area is now known as Kfar Shaul, "Saul's Village." The
Arab buildings are now home to Jerusalem's main psychiatric hospital, an institution best known for identifying "Jerusalem Syndrome," a
condition whereby visitors to the Holy City unexpectedly fall prey
to bizarre religious visions. The mental delusion whereby a whole
people can preserve the memory of biblical events more than 2,000
years old and yet eradicate a centuries-old Arab history from its midst
has not yet been given a satisfactory name. Nationalism? Propaganda?
Religious blindness? Guilt? It has elements of all of these.

Arab place names often preserve the cumulative history of the
land, and have proven invaluable to scholars and archaeologists trying
to rediscover the biblical heritage of Palestine. Israeli place names, by
contrast, are frequently chosen deliberately to wipe out the Arab tradition by claiming a biblical link, or at least by imposing a new
Hebrew reality. The name of Deir Yassin, for instance, contains in it
evidence of the passage of both Christianity and Islam in Palestine:
"Deir" means "monastery," of which many were built around
Jerusalem, and "Yassin" is the name of a Muslim sheikh said to be
buried nearby.

Under British rule, Deir Yassin became a prosperous village of
stonemasons who quarried and cut limestone blocks to supply the

British-inspired construction boom in Jerusalem. In early 1948, its inhabitants had made a nonaggression pact with the Jewish neighborhood of Givat Shaul, but such local deals usually could not withstand the pressures of war. Deir Yassin's position overlooking the frequently blockaded main highway from Tel Aviv to Jerusalem made it a strategic asset, not least because the Jewish forces wanted to establish an airfield nearby.

In April 1948 the Hagana mounted Operation Nachshon, designed to open the road to Jerusalem. It was the Jews' biggest operation to date and formed the opening campaign of "Plan D." The idea was to take over a string of Arab villages controlling the high ground above the road. The Hagana's deployment of a whole brigade was unheard of for a force accustomed to fighting with formations no larger than a company. The Etzel and Lehi dissident groups in Jerusalem had not yet been integrated into the Hagana. They set out to attack the village of Deir Yassin, on the western outskirts of the city, as an unofficial component of Operation Nachshon. In honor of their joint action, the operation was code-named *Achdut*, or "Unity."

Before dawn on April 9 some 130 Jewish fighters converged on Deir Yassin from three directions. They were soon spotted by sentries. What happened over the next few hours is still the subject of controversy and has, over the decades, become enveloped in lies and myths.

According to Yehuda Lapidot, Etzel's deputy commander of the operation, the Jews were given away by a fighter who heard an Arab guard calling out "Mahmoud." He mistook it for *achdut*, and replied with the second half of the password, *lohemet*. The villagers let off the first volley of shots. As the fighting began, Lehi brought up an armored car, but it stopped at a defensive trench dug across the main road. It was supposed to broadcast a warning to the villagers over a loudspeaker, but it is unclear whether any of them heard it.

The Jewish fighters had expected the Arabs to flee, but according to Lapidot, "the Arab resistance was strong and every house became an armed fortress." Four attackers were killed and several others wounded, including senior commanders. To silence the Arabs, the Jews said they had to throw hand grenades into houses or even blow up entire buildings. When the Jews ran out of ammunition, the Palmach sent out an armored car which gave machine-gun and mortar support. All the Arab casualties, claimed Etzel and Lehi, were the result of combat.

But according to the Arabs' version, and some Jewish and foreign witnesses, the Jewish fighters conducted a wholesale massacre of the villagers, including women, children, and the elderly. Women were raped and bodies were looted. In all, more than 250 were slaughtered. This, at any rate, is the traditional horror story of Deir Yassin.

It is supported by the evidence of witnesses such as Jacques de Reynier, the Swiss delegate of the International Committee of the Red Cross, who arrived at Deir Yassin two days after the battle. In his book, *A Jérusalem Un Drapeau flottait sur la ligne de feu*, a more emotional and descriptive account than that given in his official report, he recalled the Jewish fighters in the village: "all young people, even adolescents, men and women, armed to the teeth: pistols, machine guns, grenades, and also big cutlasses, most still bloody, that they hold in their hands. A young girl, beautiful but with the eyes of a criminal, shows me hers still dripping. She carries it around like a trophy."

Inspecting the bodies in the houses, he saw that the village had been "cleaned up" with machine guns and grenades and that the survivors had been "finished with knives." Beneath some bodies he heard a noise, and found "a small foot which is still warm." He pulled out a badly injured 10-year-old girl, and said he struggled to convince the fighters that he should take her to a Jewish ambulance he had brought to Deir Yassin. De Reynier gave the number of dead as "more than 200" in his official report, and as 350 in his book—the latter figure far higher than even Arab propagandists have claimed.

Meir Pa'il, a Hagana officer, said he watched the massacre as it took place, and sent a report and photographs to Hagana headquarters, with the opening lines of Bialik's poem, "The City of Slaughter": "Arise and go now to the city of slaughter. . . ." He claimed to have seen the Jewish fighters killing anybody they found alive. At one point, he said, they took about 25 Arabs, paraded them through Jerusalem, then brought them back to Deir Yassin's quarry and shot them.

News of the massacre caused panic among Palestinians. Arab leaders had played up the massacre in the hope of strengthening Palestinian resistance, but the propaganda had the opposite effect and caused a collapse of morale. Coming in the same week as the death of Abdel-Kader al-Husseini, the only Palestinian commander who inspired any confidence in his people, it made Palestinians feel unprotected against the seemingly bloodthirsty Jews. Deir Yassin, wrote the historian Benny Morris, "had the most lasting effect of any single event of the war in precipitating the flight of Arab villagers from Palestine." It also greatly increased pressure on the Arab states to send their armies to help their Palestinian brethren, dissolving any last hope that a full-scale war might be averted the following month.

There was, after Deir Yassin, a strange and unspoken conspiracy by all, not to hide the atrocities but to exaggerate them. The Arabs miscalculated, but Etzel understood the psychological impact of Deir Yassin and broadcast on its radio station that 240 Arabs had been killed. It was, Etzel commanders later claimed, a deliberate exaggeration designed to sow fear and confusion among the Arabs. In his book, *Revolt*, the then Etzel leader Menachem Begin denied his men had carried out a massacre but recognized that "Arab propaganda" had greatly helped the Jews. "The legend was worth half a dozen battalions to the forces of Israel [. . .] panic overwhelmed the Arabs of Eretz Yisrael," he wrote. The Jewish Agency, soon to become the government of Israel, held up the massacre as evidence of the viciousness of the Revisionists, hardline opponents of the Labor Zionist leadership. It sent a cable of condolences to King Abdallah in Transjordan expressing its condemnation of the "brutal and barbaric act which is not compatible with the spirit of the Jewish people and its cultural traditions and heritage." The British, for their part, put out the story of women being raped.

To Palestinians, Deir Yassin quickly became the symbol of Jewish evildoing, proof that the Jews, despite their suffering in the Holocaust, did not have exclusive claim to the moral high ground. The story of the atrocities—and the estimate that between 240 people (the Etzel figure) and 254 (the Arabs' figure) had been killed—were repeated and often embellished over the decades. In 1987, a study by scholars at Bir Zeit University's Center for Documentation and Research, which was working on a series of monographs on each destroyed Palestinian village, cross-checked the identities of the victims of Deir Yassin with relatives living in the West Bank and concluded that the number of deaths "did not exceed 120." Whether 100 or 200 dead, said Sharif Kanaana, one of the Bir Zeit researchers, Deir Yassin was still a massacre. The figure may have been revised, but the survivors still told stories of whole families being butchered in their homes. "What kind of resistance could there have been when the other side suffered only four dead? Twenty or thirty of the Palestinians killed were fighters. The rest were killed in cold blood," said Kanaana. "About 60 of them were women, children, and very old men. Every single one of them was an atrocity."

For Kanaana, the tragedies of Israelis and Palestinians could not be compared. "There are victims and there are victimizers," he said. "There are those who are invaded and those who invade. Palestinians did not emigrate to Poland to kill Jews. The Jews came here to kill Palestinians."

In recent years, Palestinian activists have tried to turn Deir Yassin into a memorial to the Nakba. They have begun yearly commemorative gatherings at the site, and a joint group of Israelis and Palestinians is trying to raise funds to build a monument at Deir Yassin, a counterpoint to Yad Vashem, which stands on a hill nearby. In 1998 the British Foreign Secretary, Robin Cook, laid a wreath to the victims of Deir Yassin at a school in East Jerusalem founded to care for the orphaned children of the village.

Deir Yassin, said Kanaana, "is a symbol of everything that happened to Palestinians, a symbol of the Palestinian village, a symbol of people who have been driven out. It seems to represent the whole nation being destroyed."

Just before Israel's 50th anniversary celebrations, I went to Deir Yassin with Ayish Zeidan, known as Haj Ayish, who had lived in the village as a teenager. Now 65, he had settled in the West Bank village of Beitin, where he maintains Deir Yassin's stone-cutting tradition. Haj Ayish tactfully replaced his *keffiyeh* with a western-style cap and we slipped past the guards with a fib about going to see one of the doctors. We strode up the main alleyway conspiratorially. Air conditioning units ruined the texture and balance of the hand-worked stone blocks of the buildings. Hebrew signs had been bolted to walls. In one room we found Israeli workers putting the finishing touches to a large illuminated Star of David with the number "50" to commemorate Israel's jubilee. In the company of Haj Ayish it was a jarring scene.

He pointed out the main buildings: the mosque, a compound known as "the monastery," the school and the car park, where villagers once held week-long wedding celebrations outdoors. The village cemetery outside the hospital grounds was overgrown, and the tombstones were broken: a smell of wild fennel enveloped the graves. "This was my home," he said, pointing to what is now an administrative office. "Next to it is the house of Hassan al-Zeidan, a relative. He was killed with his wife and sons."

Haj Ayish had been a schoolboy during the war in 1948. "We heard shooting. My mother did not want us to look out of the window. I fled with my sister, but my mother and my other sisters could not make it. They hid in a cellar for four days and then ran away." He said he never believed that more than 110 people had died at Deir Yassin, and accused Arab leaders of exaggerating the atrocities. There had been no rape, he said. "The Arab radio at the time talked of women being killed and raped, but this is not true. I believe that most of those who were killed were among the fighters and the women and children who helped the fighters." He said the only reliable stories of murders were of the execution of about six men in a quarry—fewer than given by other accounts—and a woman who saw her husband being shot in front of her after the village had fallen.

The elevation of Deir Yassin into the embodiment of the Palestinian tragedy is peculiar. It was doubtless a brutal incident in an ugly war. A massacre, perhaps, but arguably no worse than other forgotten massacres committed by Jewish forces, including the Hagana. In newly occupied Lydda (Lod today), Benny Morris notes, Jewish forces brutally put down what was described as a "rebellion" by the town's Arabs, firing in the streets, on houses, and at the concentrations of prisoners-of-war in the courtyards of the mosques and churches. Israeli military reports put the number of Arab dead at "more than 250," compared with the estimates of between two and four Israelis killed. The deliberate expulsion of tens of thousands of Arabs from Lydda and neighboring Ramla, including the accounts of the death of refugees on the roads, makes for a greater atrocity than Deir Yassin. Israel's refusal to allow refugees to return home poses the broader and unanswered moral question. The memorial to the Palestinians would be better placed in Ramla, the original capital of Arab Palestine.

Haj Ayish, for his part, just wants a personal acknowledgment of what he has endured. "I hope that peace will prevail. Muslims, Jews, and Christians can live together. But everybody must have their rights restored. I did not sell my home or my land. I must either have compensation or be allowed to return to my home. If there is no return or compensation, there can be no peace." He wiped away a tear. "If I don't get my rights, my son will. I urge the Israelis to make peace. The strong will not remain strong forever, and the weak will not remain weak."

★

The dream of *Al-Awda*, The Return, has sustained Palestinian refugees for decades of exile. The Return is much more than a political act, a dreamed-of victory over Israel which will allow the refugees to re-enter the borders. It is a spiritual redemption, both individual and collective, when the wrongs of half a century will be put right, when the

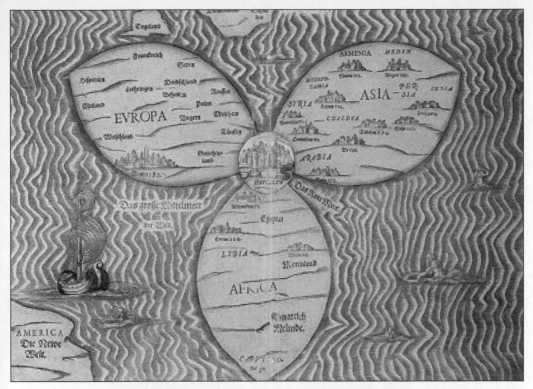

The center of the world: Jerusalem is placed at the center of this sixteenth-century map of the world in the shape of a clover leaf, by Heinrich Bunting (*above*). At the heart of Jerusalem, and at the heart of the conflict, is the platform of the Haram al-Sharif (*below*), the former site of the Jewish temple and now the location of the Dome of the Rock and the Al-Aqsa Mosque. Jews worship at the foot of one of the retaining walls—the Western Wall—where the Israeli government cleared a plaza in 1967 (*foreground*).

The cradle of religion: Jews with white *tallit* shawls pray at the Western Wall during Passover (*above left*). The Armenian Patriarch Torkom Manogian holds a torch during the Holy Fire ceremony at the Church of the Holy Sepulchre (*below left*). Tens of thousands of Muslims gather on the Haram al-Sharif for prayers during the holy month of Ramadan (*above*).

"At Basle I founded the Jewish State." Theodor Herzl (*above right*) gazing over the Rhine in Basle, during the first Zionist Congress in 1897. Two years later, Yusuf Diya al-Khalidi (*above left*), a former member of the Ottoman parliament, told him in a letter: "For the sake of God, leave Palestine in peace." Eliezer Ben-Yehuda (*below right*) dedicated his life to reviving the Hebrew language, while Khalil al-Sakakini (*below left*) established schools to instruct Arabs in the nationalist spirit.

Jaffa was the gateway to Palestine. Arab boatmen row through treacherous reefs, among them Andromeda's Rock, to carry crates of oranges to ships anchored offshore (*above*). The first Jewish settlers established Rishon Le-Zion nearby. Their main product, wine, was loaded onto camels for transport (*below*).

Britain laid the foundation for the Jewish state with the Balfour declaration. In December 1917, Hussein Bey al-Husseini (*left, holding a cane*), surrendered the city to British soldiers. In the decades that followed, the British put down repeated Arab uprisings. In the picture (*below*), a British soldier guards Arab prisoners in Jerusalem during the Arab Revolt of 1936–39.

"Circumcised Cossacks" is how Amos Oz described Israeli soldiers. These members of Ha-Shomer (*above*), an early Jewish self-defense group, dressed as Arabs and Circassians in 1907. The apogee of modern Israel's blitzkrieg doctrine came with the Six Day War. (*Left*) Major-General Uzi Narkiss (*left*), Defense Minister Moshe Dayan (*center*) and Chief of Staff Yitzhak Rabin (*right*) stride into the Old City of Jerusalem on 7 June 1967.

JERUSALEM'S JEWS DEFY ARAB SHELLS

Civilian Majority Goes About Business—Many Take Brief Shelter in Basements

Special to The New York Times.

JERUSALEM, May 23 (Delayed) —Arab shells crashed into the streets of Jewish Jerusalem sporadically—now singly, now in salvos—for the eighth day in succession today and the wind from the desert made it the hottest of the year.

Some Jews spent the day in a stifling basement just off Ben Yehuda Street, as did thousands of others in stifling basements throughout the city. Ben Yehuda Street was littered with the fragments of shop windows that had been replaced one by one since they were blown out by the great Ben Yehuda Street bombing on Feb. 22.

Nea. Zion Square telephone lines were torn down and the branches blown off a tree and draped across the sidewalk. There was a pool of blood on the sidewalk where a girl was hit by a shell this morning as she looked into the window of a dairy shop below the Jewish Public Information Office. The offices on the floor above the Public Information Office were hit yesterday.

After a salvo of mortar shells from the Old City a frail old woman, holding a little girl by the hand, came down to the basement. She sat there glaring angrily for five minutes, then muttered something in Yiddish and walked out again. Like Londoners during the Blitz the Jews of Jerusalem have to make up their minds whether they are going to take a chance and go about their business or sit safely in shelters and let their

IN PALESTINE: WAR DEVASTATION AND ARAB PRISONERS

Wreckage left in Es Sumeiriya, north of Acre, by Jewish demolition squads. The village was used by Arabs as a sniper point on the North-South Highway.

U. S. PLANE FLEET SENT TO MIDEAST

Continued From Page 1.

had not been decided whether the post would be filled.

General Hilldring accepted the appointment on April 28, but has

U. N. COUNCIL FACES PEACE QUEST ANEW

Security Group, Balked Again in Palestine Efforts, Seeks Way for Another Try

By MALLORY BROWNE
Special to The New York Times.

LAKE SUCCESS, N. Y., May 26—The United Nations Security Council pondered the next steps in the Palestine crisis tonight as it faced the final breakdown of its efforts to preserve peace in the Holy Land.

With the problem momentarily thrown back upon Washington, London, Moscow and other capitals by the Arab League's rejection of the Council's cease-fire call, the long list of futile attempts by the United Nations to avoid the war now raging in Palestine was being reviewed at Lake Success.

Just under a year and two months ago—on April 2, 1947, Britain dumped the "insoluble" Arab-Jewish conflict into the lap of the United Nations. A special session of the General Assembly convened on April 28, 1947; on May 15—exactly one year before the termination of the mandate and the outbreak of open war— the Assembly adopted the first of a string of resolutions. This initial act set up the United Nations Special Committee on Palestine.

Partition Linked to Force

After considering the majority reports of the committee, the General Assembly on Nov. 29, 1947, passed the already historic resolution containing the partition plan.

The five-nation Palestine Commission set up by this resolution set to work at the beginning of January, 1948. In less than a month

---

The Arab village of Al-Sumayriyya was captured by Jewish forces on the day Israel declared independence on 14 May 1948. Its 800 inhabitants fled, mostly to Lebanon. Their houses were demolished within days, as recorded by the *New York Times* (*above*). A year later, survivors of the Holocaust established Kibbutz Lohamei ha-Getaot, the Warsaw Ghetto Fighters' kibbutz, on the site. The children's memorial (*below*) was built next to the old Turkish aqueduct in 1981.

Exile and return: Palestinian refugees (*above*) flee Jaffa in 1948. Within a year, new Jewish immigrants from Bulgaria (*below*) had settled in the abandoned homes.

Still waiting: Palestinian refugees sit in tents at the Ain al-Hilweh refugee camp in 1951 (*above*). Five decades later, the camps have grown into chaotic cities (*below*), but millions of Palestinian exiles are no closer to returning to their homeland.

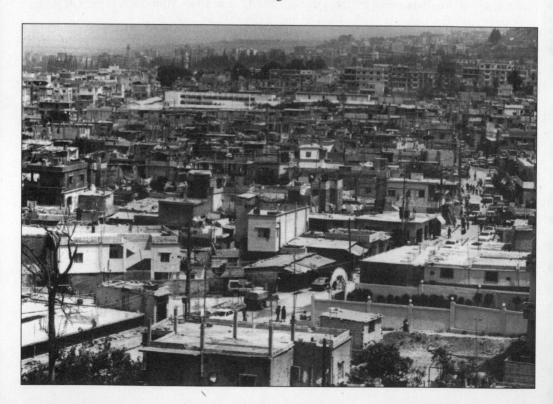

Young Jews (*above*) symbolically defy Hitler's Final Solution by carrying Israeli flags through the gates of Auschwitz, the largest Nazi concentration and extermination camp, with its mocking motto in German: "Work Makes You Free." Palestinian demonstrators (*left*) compare the Jewish state to that of the Nazis, taunting Israeli troops in Hebron by holding an Israeli flag with a swastika in place of the Star of David.

Jews meet on the dunes outside
Jaffa (*above*) in 1909 to draw lots
for their properties in the new
garden suburb which grew into Tel
Aviv (*left*), the "first Hebrew city
of modern times." Life on the
beach is the antithesis of the
religious obsession of Jerusalem.

Israeli policemen skirmish with Ultra-Orthodox Jews protesting in 1998 over the construction of a road close to an ancient burial site in Jerusalem (*above*). Election posters of Rabbi Ovadia Yosef in the 1999 elections (*below*). His Shas party, a religious movement appealing to oriental Jews disenchanted with the secular "Ashkenazi" elite, was the political phenomenon of the 1990s.

Children of war: Faris Odeh, 12, throws a stone at an Israeli tank at the Karni crossing point between Israel and the Gaza Strip (*above*). Ten days after this picture was taken on 29 October 2000, he was shot dead in a clash with Israeli troops and achieved his wish to become a *shahid*, or martyr, of the Al-Aqsa Intifada. The Palestinians are also armed, but have only light weapons. A Jewish settler (*left*) carries an M-16 rifle for protection as he takes his daughter for a Sabbath stroll in the bitterly divided city of Hebron a few days after a Jewish baby was killed and her father wounded by a Palestinian sniper in March 2001.

Would-be Islamic suicide bombers (*above*) dressed in white with mock sticks of dynamite around their waists at a rally organized by Hamas in the Jabalia refugee camp. Suicide attacks destroyed Israeli confidence in the Oslo accords in the mid-1990s and have resumed with the Al-Aqsa Intifada. But the violence has had a devastating effect on the Palestinian economy. Palestinian laborers (*below*) queue up before dawn at the Erez checkpoint in the Gaza Strip in February 2001 for a rare opportunity to work in Israel.

Under the gaze of the world: photographers jostle for the best shot of an Israeli tank crossing the border during Israel's withdrawal from Lebanon in May 2000. Israel has one of the highest concentrations of journalists, observers and aid workers in the world.

meek shall inherit Palestine, when the past will be transformed into the future. The birth of Israel has created a sort of parallel Palestinian "Zionism" of a dispersed people seeking to return to their homeland. There is a crucial difference, however. Whereas the Jews held on to the memory of the Promised Land through a centuries-old religion, the Palestinian sense of injustice is much more immediate. Palestinians were forced to abandon their lands in living memory. Like the spiritual Jerusalem which Jewish mystics believe will descend ready-made from Heaven, the many returning Palestinians envision their homes and villages waiting for them as they left them. The locks will turn with the keys which they took with them in 1948 and the doors will open to reveal their old rustic surroundings.

In Palestinian literature Palestine is often described as a lovely woman. There she will always be, waiting faithfully like a bride, calling for her sons to return. Palestine is a dream, a memory. A picture, a yellowed land deed. A name. A song. The spiritual Palestine of the exiles does not change, while the real Palestine is irrevocably transformed. For many Palestinians visiting Israel—either from the occupied territories or from abroad—the experience is disconcerting, confusing, depressing. The mind's vision of Palestine is shattered by the reality of the Jewish state: there is no earthly Palestine to fill the void. The visitor becomes even more of an exile, because the homeland of his or her dreams has vanished.

In the growing number of personal recollections by Palestinians, the moment of visiting the family house is often the most poignant. It is an irony that those Israelis most likely to live in graceful, stone-built Arab houses are educated, well-heeled, yuppies who profess the greatest understanding of the plight of Palestinians. That dreaded knock on the door—the embarrassed request of the unexpected Arab visitor: "Excuse me. My family used to live here. Do you mind if I take a look around?" can shatter liberal illusions in an instant. Some Israelis allow a cursory tour, counting the moments until the awkward visitor disappears. Others close the door in the face of the intruder, shutting out the ghost of the past, the anger and the guilt.

"I was there before you, and she will always think of me first," wrote the late Palestinian poet Rashid Husain.

> Be her husband, so what!
> I loved her before you did
> and have first place in her heart [...]
> I'll even enter your bed

on your wedding night, and come between you
though you are her bridegroom
she will embrace me, desiring me most.
I will always be between you
I'm sorry—but I was first.

Palestinian writers are trying to record the lost world before the creation of Israel. As the generation of 1948 passes away, there is a rush to preserve their memories. In *Jerusalem and I*, published in 1990, Hala al-Sakakini, daughter of the Palestinian nationalist educator Khalil al-Sakakini, described the bittersweet day when she walked back to her birthplace in West Jerusalem after the Israelis had "reunited" the city. "On Tuesday, July 4, 1967, one month after the Six Day War, my sister and I visited our house in Katamon, Jerusalem, for the first time in nineteen years. It was a sad encounter, like meeting a dear person who you had last seen young, healthy, and well-groomed and finding that he had become old, sick, and shabby. Even worse, it was like coming across an old friend whose personality had undergone a drastic change and was no more the same person."

The sisters came from Ramallah in the West Bank. From Jaffa Gate, they retraced the once familiar sights. They saw the shop of an Armenian shoe-shiner, now in ruins. Ahead was the spot where Abu Shafiq used to make delicious Arabic sweets. Gone. Mamillah Road used to be a busy shopping street, but it was now a slum. Only a shop owned by someone called Stern seemed unchanged.

They made their way past the YMCA, through the German Colony, past what used to be Sayegh's pharmacy, Dajani's grocery, Kaloti's butchery and so on until they reached Katamon. Many new buildings had been erected in empty plots. When they arrived at their old house, they noticed that the walls seemed darker. The paint on the shutters was peeling and the stairs were dirty. Al-Sakakini recalled: "what made the difference was the state of the garden. Gone was the beautiful, fragrant honeysuckle over the garden gate, gone was the jasmine shrub leaning against the house. The big adelias of many colors in front of the house were, of course, not there anymore. The garden was dry and brown."

The house had been converted into a nursery and kindergarten. That was some consolation, as their father had been fond of children. They knocked on the door, and after a while entered the living room. They heard children's voices from one of the rooms. "Two ladies appeared—one dark and the other an elderly European lady.

We addressed them in Arabic, but they seemed not to understand; so we asked them if they spoke English, but they shook their heads; so we started to talk in German and the elderly lady understood. We tried to explain: 'This is our house. We used to live here before 1948. This is the first time we see it in nineteen years. . . .'" The elderly lady was apparently moved, but she immediately began telling us that she too had lost a house in Poland, as though we personally or the Arabs in general were to blame for that. We saw it was no use arguing with her."

They went around, room by room. The house was in reasonable condition, but it was no longer home. From the veranda they looked at the former homes of the Sliheet, Sruji, and Tleel families. "We left our house and our immediate neighborhood with a sense of emptiness, with a feeling of deep disappointment and frustration," wrote Al-Sakakini. "The familiar streets were there, all the houses were there, but so much was missing. We felt like strangers in our own quarter."

*

Yasser Arafat walked into the canal house at 263 Prinsengracht in the center of Amsterdam. Millions before him had come to see the place where Anne Frank and her family had lived in hiding from the Nazis. For two years before being deported to Bergen-Belsen and killed, Anne Frank kept a diary which has become one of the best-known works of the Holocaust era. Arafat was not making an ordinary visit on March 31, 1998. The sight of his black-and-white checkered *kef-fiyeh*, always folded and draped in the shape of an outline of the map of Palestine, symbolized a tentative step by his people to acknowledge the history and suffering of the Jews.

Arafat's words after the visit were not particularly memorable. "A sad story, a very sad story," he mumbled. It ought to have been an occasion for Jews to rejoice. Here was the leader of the Palestinians recognizing in public that the Jews had been victims, and not just heartless colonizers. In doing so, the Palestinian leadership had just broken away from the ranks of the Holocaust deniers.

Instead, Arafat was met with a volley of insults. The Netherlands Israel Public Affairs Committee denounced the visit as "a cheap publicity stunt which desecrates the memory of the Jewish victims of the Holocaust." The Likud-led Israeli government dismissed it as a "gimmick," adding that Arafat should first deal with anti-Semitism in the Palestinian press.

A few months earlier the U.S. Holocaust Memorial Museum in Washington had invited Mr. Arafat to visit the museum but then declined to give him VIP status. Finally, under pressure from the State Department, it restored the VIP status. By then the damage had been done and Arafat instead chose the Anne Frank House as a place to make his gesture. Rather than being praised for setting an example to his people, Arafat was publicly humiliated. If ever there was justification for accusations that Israel and its allies abuse the Holocaust for political motives, this was it. The government of Israel, opposed to the Oslo peace accords, was fighting a short-term battle in its diplomatic war of attrition against the Palestinians, but it threw away an opportunity for reconciliation.

Arafat's visit to the Anne Frank House was, of course, a political act performed by a political leader. It was no more, and no less, sincere than the compulsory visits by countless dignitaries to Yad Vashem in Jerusalem. In 1994 there was an outcry in Israel over the refusal by the visiting Egyptian foreign minister, Amr Mousa, to pay his respects at Yad Vashem. Only after overt arm-twisting from Israel did he agree to walk through a memorial to the children who perished in the Holocaust. Four years later, here was the Israeli government resisting a voluntary attempt by the Palestinian leader to acknowledge the Holocaust.

Arafat was long presented as a new Hitler, and to a substantial number of Israelis, Hitler he must remain. The main display at Yad Vashem ends with a picture of the Mufti of Jerusalem, Haj Amin al-Husseini, and his declarations of support for the Nazis' anti-Semitic depravity.

Many Israelis harbor a visceral resentment against the Palestinians. It is not provoked just by the number of Jewish deaths the Palestinians have inflicted—Egypt has been responsible for killing far more Israelis in wars than the Palestinians did in the course of the armed struggle. It is not Palestinians' traditional denial of Israel's right to exist—Egypt, too, called for Jews to be thrown into the Mediterranean. It is not the lack of recognition—both Egypt and the PLO have signed peace accords with Israel. It is, perhaps, the Palestinians' terrorist methods which earned Arafat the comparison with Hitler. Yet it was Egypt's President Nasser who presided over the creation of the PLO. Jewish underground groups in the 1930s and 1940s, it should be noted, also resorted to bombing innocent civilians.

Egypt's late President Anwar al-Sadat had sympathized with the

Nazis as the enemy of the Arabs' British enemy, and yet he is regarded in Israel as a noble peacemaker.

The hostility to Palestinians can best be explained as a hatred bred by fear. It is not just what the Palestinians do that troubles Israel, but who they are—Palestinians—people, a people, who lay claim to the same piece of land as the Jews. A weak people who refused to disappear, just as the Jews were not wiped out by history. Israel fears the challenge which Palestinians pose to its moral legitimacy, fears losing the exclusive Jewish claim to suffering, and fears that Israel will, in turn, be forced to recognize the tragedy it inflicted on the Palestinians. It is a fear of the ghosts of the past. It is a fear that the dead body of Palestine will reappear decades after the murder, or manslaughter, depending on one's view of history.

If Hitler was the most evil in a line of oppressors in Jewish history, starting with Pharaoh, then the Palestinians have come to be regarded by many Israelis as the embodiment of the ancient Amalekites—the first, the most irreconcilable, and the eternal enemy of the Israelites. Their sin, according to the Bible, was to have blocked the way to the Promised Land and harried the Children of Israel, from the time of the exodus "when thou wast faint and weary" (Deut 25:18)until the time of King David. The Palestinians' transgression is not dissimilar: they were an obstacle to the creation of Israel and will not let it live in peace.

Even Israelis who advocate peace and territorial compromise, including those who are ready to see a Palestinian state, usually do so for pragmatic reasons. They want a border, with Israelis on one side and Palestinians on the other. Peace is not regarded as the creation of a new bond between Israelis and Palestinians but as a "separation," a divorce from a miserable enforced marriage.

There is little daily contact based on mutual respect. The relationship is one of soldier and rebel, employer and employee, ruler and subject. The middle classes on both sides do not interact freely as they do, say, in Belfast. There is no common language. There are very few mixed neighborhoods. The separation between the people, even among Jews and Israeli Arabs, is almost total. There are, for instance, hardly any mixed Israeli–Palestinian couples. At most, partners experiment with a brief romance, briefly taste the forbidden fruit (usually secretly), and then return to the safety of their own people.

I can think of no public act of reconciliation by an Israeli leader comparable to Arafat's visit to the Anne Frank House. Israeli prime ministers have not gone down to the refugee camps of Gaza to acknowledge their role in the creation of the Palestinian human misery. There has been no apology for the children killed by Israeli soldiers during the Intifada. More than seven years after the signing of the Oslo accords, Arafat has never been allowed to pray in Jerusalem.

The closest any Israeli leader has come to publicly coming to terms with the past was when the Labor Prime Minister, Ehud Barak, issued a carefully hedged expression of sorrow in October 1999. He told the Knesset: "We regret the heavy suffering that the conflict has caused, not only to us but to all the Arab nations that have fought against us, including the Palestinian people." When peace is attained, Barak said, Israel will be ready to take part in an effort to heal the wounds of war, "based on good will, friendship, and neighborliness—but not, under any circumstances, based on a feeling of guilt or responsibility for the emergence of the conflict and its results, a conflict we did not want and which we did much to prevent."

Israel thus maintains it bears no responsibility for the miseries suffered by Palestinians. The pain is, at best, the inevitable outcome of "the conflict." The fate of Palestinian refugees outside Israel or in the occupied territories hangs in uncertainty. To allow them to return is unthinkable for virtually all Israelis; at most some might be allowed to enter the West Bank and Gaza Strip, if and when a Palestinian state is declared. There has been no Israeli offer to compensate Palestinian refugees, as Jewish families and the State of Israel received compensation from Germany. All that Israel can offer is excuses—Jews who left or were forced to abandon their homes in Arab countries received no compensation for their properties. Maybe Israel will one day provide some money to rehabilitate refugees. Until then, sorry, there's nothing Israel can do. Too bad for the Palestinians if Arab rulers did not absorb the refugees.

The Palestinians, it must be said, are often their own worst enemies. Just as Arafat was deliberating on whether to visit the Holocaust Memorial in Washington, his Palestinian Authority was busy publicizing the works of the controversial French writer, Roger Garaudy, a former Marxist philosopher turned Muslim. Garaudy's claim that Jewish deaths in the Holocaust were vastly exaggerated, and that there had been no gas chambers, has earned him a conviction in a Paris court for contesting crimes against humanity. Intellectuals throughout the Arab world, distressingly silent on the abuse of freedoms in their own countries, rallied to support Garaudy's right to express his views freely. His public backers included the Palestinian telecommunications minister, Imad al-Fallouji, a former spokesman for the Islamic radical Hamas movement. Garaudy's work appeared briefly on the Palestinian Authority's Web site.

Educated Palestinians like to say that Arabs cannot be anti-Semitic because they are, themselves, "Semitic." But despite such semantic niceties, the Arab world has seen traditional Muslim contempt, or at least indifference, to non-Muslim minorities give way to the language of overt anti-Semitism borrowed from Europe. Comments denying or minimizing the Holocaust periodically appear in the Palestinian press. The first list of best-selling books in the West Bank, compiled in 1999 by a bookshop in the town of Ramallah, found that Hitler's *Mein Kampf* was in the top ten.

Cartoons in the Egyptian press depict Jews with ugly faces and hooked noses. With the Al-Aqsa Intifada, matters have become worse. Israeli groups that monitor the Arabic media regularly find appalling examples of anti-Semitic utterances, such as the columnist who wrote in Egypt's *Al-Akbar* daily early 2001: "Thanks be to Hitler, of blessed memory, who on behalf of the Palestinians took revenge in advance against the most vile criminals on the face of the earth. Although we do have a complaint against him, for his revenge on them was not enough." In the early 1990s, the store in the lobby of the Inter-Continental Hotel in Amman openly sold anti-Semitic tracts, including the notorious Tsarist forgery, *The Protocols of the Elders of Zion*, which purports to describe a vast conspiracy by Jews to dominate the world. Hidden forces, secret domination, and evil plots are staples of the rumor mill in the Arab world. This is a reflection of the authoritarian and closed nature of the regimes which, to varying degrees, rule the region. It is a sign of the deep frustration which Arabs feel in the face of the long decline of the Islamic world in its dealings with the Christian West.

Conspiracies and plots are, above all, a convenient explanation for the Arab world's failure to defeat tiny Israel. From this perspective, Israel survives not because its people are smarter or better fighters than the Arabs, but because it is a manifestation of a vast world scheme to subjugate the Arab world. The world financial system and the international media are widely believed to be entirely controlled by Jews and hostile to the Arabs.

Sex, so repressed in the Muslim world, is a frequent titillating element of conspiracy theories. At one point the Egyptian press popularized the notion that the Aids virus was invented in Israel and spread to the Arab world through a band of secret women agents sent out to seduce Arab men. Another tale was of the supposed spread of moral corruption through aphrodisiac chewing gum—made in Israel, of course. The sex scandal over U.S. President Bill Clinton's relations with Monica Lewinsky was seen as a Jewish plot to bring down the American leader who, despite being openly pro-Israeli, was said to be putting strong pressure on the then Israeli Prime Minister Binyamin Netanyahu to make territorial concessions.

The world of evil conspiracies extends to the Holocaust itself. In *Eichmann in Jerusalem*, Hannah Arendt records that a few weeks before the Eichmann trial in Jerusalem, Egypt's deputy foreign minister Hussein Zulficar Sabri told the National Assembly that Hitler had been innocent of the crime of slaughtering the Jews; he had been a victim of the Zionists, who had "compelled him to perpetrate crimes that would eventually enable them to achieve their aim—the creation of the state of Israel." I once read a variation of this theory in a Jordanian paper, which argued that the wave of anti-Semitism in Germany in the early 1990s was actually being instigated secretly by the Zionists to increase Jewish emigration to Israel.

The Middle East scholar, Bernard Lewis, concluded in his 1986 book, *Semites & Anti-Semites*, that "for most, it still seems true that despite its vehemence and its ubiquity, Arab or Muslim anti-Semitism is still something that comes from above, from the leadership, rather than from below, from the society—a political and polemical weapon, to be discarded if and when it is no longer required." But the evidence of the peace agreements of the 1990s is that hostility and hatred of Israelis and the Jews (to many Arabs the two are synonymous) is the norm. To express admiration or respect for any aspect of Israeli society is to deviate from the consensus and risk ostracism. If anti-Semitism had been imposed from the top, now it is peace which must be forced on the Arabs by their leaders. The safest way for radicals to criticize moderate Arab regimes is to attack their relations with Israel.

Among the few people to argue that Palestinians should face Israel from the moral high ground, rather than through silly name-calling, is Edward Said, a professor of English and comparative literature at Columbia University. Perhaps the most articulate critic of Arafat's signing of the Oslo peace accords, he nevertheless said in a series of articles in 1997 and 1998 that it was time for Palestinians to recognize and understand Jewish history, not least the Holocaust's impact on Israel. In Egypt's English-language *Al-Ahram Weekly*, Said complained in 1998 of "a nasty wave of anti-Semitism and hypocritical righteousness insinuating itself into our political thought and rhetoric." He continued:

> The history of the modern Arab world—with all its political failures, its human rights abuses, its stunning military incompetences, its decreasing production, the fact that, alone of all modern peoples, we have receded in democratic and technological and scientific development—is disfigured by a whole series of out-moded and discredited ideas, of which the notion that the Jews never suffered and that [the] Holocaust is an obfuscatory confection created by the elders of Zion is one that is acquiring too much, far too much, currency [. . .] I cannot accept the idea that the Holocaust excuses Zionism for what it has done to Palestinians: far from it. I say exactly the opposite, that by recognizing the Holocaust for the genocidal madness that it was, we can then demand from Israelis and Jews the right to link the Holocaust to Zionist injustices toward the Palestinians [. . .]

In June 2001, pressure from intellectuals such as Said prompted the Lebanese government to ban a conference of Holocaust revisionists in Beirut. But there is too little of this kind of critical self-examination among Palestinians. The perspective of history is to mourn what has been lost without asking whether Palestinians themselves might have helped to precipitate the disasters which have befallen them. The "international legitimacy" which Palestinians invoke, in the form of United Nations resolutions demanding Israel's withdrawal from territories it occupied in 1967, was earlier violated by the Arabs in their rejection of the 1947 U.N. partition plan. Yet nobody seems to question whether that might have been a cardinal mistake. What the Palestinians were offered in 1947 was far more generous than the truncated, dissected mini-state on offer today.

Nobody points out that the Palestinians' current maximum demands from Israel—a state in the West Bank and Gaza Strip with Jerusalem as its capital—was denied them by Arab leaders who controlled the territories until they lost them to Israel in 1967. The critique of the past is limited to denouncing the leaders' failures to defeat Israel because of cowardice, military incompetence, or collusion with the Jews. Few ask whether it could have been possible for Palestinians and the other Arabs to avoid five decades of war.

For a people raised on Article 9 of the Palestinian Charter—which maintains that "armed struggle is the only way to liberate Palestine"—the notion of Gandhi's nonviolent protest, of challenging injustice through humanity and unarmed moral power, was long ago dismissed as an absurdity.

Until Oslo, few Palestinians could question whether killing Israeli civilians was legitimate, or even politically expedient. Those who disagreed made sure to keep their views to themselves. After the accords were signed, the Palestinian Authority learned to condemn acts of violence only under extreme pressure from its Israeli "peace partners": not because killing Israelis is wrong, but because such actions could "destroy the Palestinian dream."

Unlike Northern Ireland, where every atrocity is accompanied by moral indignation on all sides, Palestinian religious leaders—whether Christian or Muslim—have remained distressingly silent in the face of the suicide bombings against Israeli civilians. Most rabbis, too, had little to say about the rivers of children's blood shed by Israeli soldiers during the Intifada. With the outbreak of the latest uprising, any hope of taking a moral stand against killing has disappeared.

In the cradle of monotheism, the land which devised the concept of one God and universal ethics, every atrocity has an excuse, a mitigating circumstance, an explanation in terms of a previous atrocity committed by the other side, in either the recent or distant past. When it comes to political conflict, priests, sheikhs, and rabbis seem incapable of standing up for the simple principle that killing is wrong. They are little more than tribal spokesmen, defending the interests of their sides.

Tellingly, among Palestinians there is no grass-roots peace movement even remotely comparable to Israel's Peace Now. Palestinians who take to the streets are those opposed to peace with Israel, not those who advocate it. The pressure on the streets is not against conflict, but against surrender.

The revisionist work of Israel's "New Historians" has become mainstream to the point where the myths of 1948 are being revised even in school textbooks. A new set of history books for state secular schools no longer claims that the Jews in 1948 were "the few against the many," but rather that Jewish forces had the upper hand in almost every battle. The books even ask Israeli pupils to put themselves in the Arabs' shoes and consider how they would have felt about Zionism.

The Palestinian Authority, however, continues to use the old Jordanian and Egyptian texts, including vitriolic sentiments against Zionism and Jews in general. The Israeli military authorities once used to edit out passages which it found particularly offensive, but these have been restored in the texts used by the Palestinian Authority. An Israeli group called Palestinian Media Watch monitors Palestinian textbooks and its findings have shocked even Israelis hardened by years of hostile propaganda. One textbook on Arab history includes the explanation: "The best examples of racism and discrimination in the world are Nazism and Zionism." Another tells pupils: "One must be careful around Jews because they are lying traitors."

When questioned, Palestinian officials plead that they have not yet had time to draw up their own textbooks. Given the anti-Israeli and anti-Jewish sentiments carried in the Palestinian media, it is unlikely that the new books will be much more sympathetic. The Oslo accords have created a limbo of half war and half peace. Inevitably, perhaps, the compilers of textbooks can be forgiven for not rushing into setting down a new official history while the future remains uncertain.

There is a more fundamental problem. Israel lived with its myths for the best part of half a century of statehood. It is now mature enough to take a more critical view of itself. The Palestinians do not even have a state of their own. How many decades will it take for them to take a more dispassionate view of themselves, and of the Israelis, whose existence is so bound up with Palestinian identity?

6

The Tribes of Israel

TEL AVIV IS a city without landmarks. It has neither the evocative beauty of Jerusalem, nor Haifa's immense vista of the Mediterranean from the Carmel. It has no architectural symbol: no Colosseum, no Tour Eiffel, no Capitol Hill. The most salient feature is Hiriya, the city's massive and fetid rubbish heap rising to a height of 85 meters on the approach route to Ben-Gurion airport. So instantly recognizable is the mound that the Tel Aviv Museum deemed it a worthy subject for an art exhibition at the end of the Millennium. When "the first Hebrew city" wants to market itself, it has little choice but to use a picture of Arab Jaffa.

Tel Aviv is not so much ugly as ordinary. Its inhabitants are contemptuous of stuffy formality, both in attire and in architecture. The "White City," as Tel Aviv was called in the 1920s and 1930s, has given way to a dominant gray. There is not much left of the original idea of Tel Aviv as a garden city. Its residential buildings may be human in scale—usually not more than four stories high—but they are tightly packed and poorly maintained. What little grace the façades once showed the world has been obliterated by a rash of signs in discordant primary colors, wrinkles of crumbling stucco, warts and moles of air-conditioning units, and matted tangles of tubes and cables falling from the roofs.

The attraction of Tel Aviv to Israelis is not its external architecture but its way of living, whether it be playing bat and ball on the sand or idling away the afternoons in the cafés, strutting down the street in the latest fashion or shuffling along in kibbutznik shorts. The city has an air of careless freedom about it, even frivolity. Greater wealth, and a lower level of ideological intensity, give Tel Avivians more time for leisure.

In many ways Tel Aviv defines itself by what it is not: it is not Jerusalem. Jerusalem is Jewish; Tel Aviv is Israeli. The contrast encapsulates many of the schisms and contradictions of Israel's society. Jerusalem is the ancient Jewish capital, the subject of longing and messianic expectations for generations of Jews in the Diaspora. Tel Aviv is the embodiment of modern Israel: confident to the point of brashness, industrious, and unapologetically new. Its very name, meaning "Hill of Spring," implies youthfulness and regeneration.

As the civic capital of Israel, it is the center of business, culture, media, and social trends. Tel Aviv paid lip service to socialism, and when that proved to be a failure, it turned to hedonism. Jerusalem stands isolated on the mountains, on the edge of the desert, introverted, obsessed with its own antiquity and the meaning of God's revelations. Tel Aviv was founded on the Mediterranean, influenced by the countries of Europe on the opposite shores, and beyond. In Jerusalem men and women cover their bodies from each other, and their heads from God. In Tel Aviv, they show off their torsos, legs, and midriffs. In Jerusalem you pray; in Tel Aviv you play. Jerusalem is built on rock. Tel Aviv rises out of sand dunes. Jerusalem is made of weathered stone. Tel Aviv is peeling plaster.

Jerusalem stands on the front line of the conflict with the Palestinians, but on the beaches of Tel Aviv one easily forgets about the troubles just a few miles inland. While Tel Aviv drifts into post-Zionist secular indifference, Jerusalem is the battleground for national-religious zealotry.

Israel's internal divisions—between religious and secular, between Ashkenazi Jews from Europe and Sephardi Jews from the Middle East, between settlers and Israelis within pre-1967 Israel, to name a few—have reached the point where they often overshadow the confrontation with the Arabs and, increasingly, determine the course of the conflict. Some Israelis have only half jokingly suggested partitioning the country between the coastland, to be called "Israel" and the mountain region, to be known as "Judea."

*

"Tel Aviv is the antidote to the whole country, to the maniacal clinging to the past, to archaeology and to the Bible," explained Michal Peleg, a friend and novelist, and an adopted daughter of Tel Aviv. "It is

the only city in the world that is always busy destroying its past. Tel
Aviv is built on sand. It wants to bury its past in the sands." She spoke
with a mixture of boastfulness and remorse. In its contempt for the
old, Tel Aviv had ruined corners of the city that, she felt, had charm,
character, and at times even beauty.

The attractive parts of Tel Aviv have to be sought out. There are
boulevards with a Parisian feel about them, with small parks separat-
ing the carriageways. Lift your eyes above the clutter at street level,
and there are delights to be enjoyed. Tel Aviv has the world's largest
concentration of Bauhaus-inspired International Style buildings,
with their clean, austere geometric combinations of cubes, rectangles
and cylinders. The Bauhaus school was strangled in its birthplace of
Germany by the Nazis, who saw its emphasis on functionalism as
"socialist" subversion. Several of the students made their way to Tel
Aviv, where they enjoyed a free hand to put their ideas into practice
in a rapidly expanding new city.

Their creations were spared the wartime bombing that ravaged
many European cities. Yet popular indifference among Israelis has
caused almost as much harm. Tel Aviv has never properly enforced
municipal regulations requiring landlords to maintain their properties. The pressure for housing meant that additional floors in humdrum style were rudely added to the lovingly designed buildings.
Façades have been ruined by unsightly plastic shutters closing off bal-
conies to gain an extra room. As air-conditioning, cable television
and other modern conveniences were introduced, it was easier to run
the cabling on the outside of the buildings.

One of the worst planning eyesores is the gray concrete Shalom
Meir tower, once the tallest building in Tel Aviv and the Middle East,
erected on the site of what had been a genuinely loved symbol of
city, the Herzliya Gymnasium, the first Hebrew high school and a
venerable Zionist educational institution. The school, named after
Herzl, was founded in 1906 to train young intellectuals "firm with
the Zionist creed at heart" and to prepare them for the Hebrew University, which had been envisioned as early as 1901 but was not established in Jerusalem until 1923.

In 1909, the gymnasium moved from Jaffa into its own new building at the heart of the new Jewish garden suburb that was to become
Tel Aviv. The school was something of a designer's folly, a two-story
edifice in *naïf* Moorish style, with a crenellated rooftop, Arabesque
windows, and an entrance flanked by columns inspired by pharaonic
Egypt. It was, said one 1973 guidebook, "an architectural monstros-

ity," yet it was Tel Aviv's beloved centerpiece. Unlike the tower, it had character, even humor. Founders of the school, or Zionist leaders who graduated from it, have given their names to many of Tel Aviv's streets.

It is only in recent years, with greater maturity and wealth, that Tel Aviv has realized it has an architectural heritage worth preserving. Yet when the city in 1998 slapped preservation orders on some 1,500 buildings, including 280 placed under "severe restrictions," many of the landowners howled in protest. The listing of a building was regarded not as a privilege, an enhancement of the value of the property, but as a liability.

Tel Aviv is far from being the worst of Israel's cities. Throughout the country, the urban landscapes are shabby, except perhaps for Jerusalem where the former mayor, Teddy Kollek, had the sense to keep a green belt around the Turkish walls of the Old City and enforce a British-era ordinance requiring all buildings to be clad in stone. Lack of means and the haste to settle immigrants doubtless contributed to shoddy town planning, but decades of ideological disregard for bourgeois concerns, such as the beauty of cities, must equally be blamed for the neglect.

Herzl would have been horrified. He conceived of the Jewish state as a thing of lofty beauty, a new Venice. He did not want simply to export the taste of Europe, but dreamed of improving on it. "We shall build in a bolder and more stately style than was ever adopted before, for we now possess means which men never yet possessed," he declared in *Der Judenstaat*. In *Altneuland*, Herzl imagined the Jewish metropolis as built around the harbor of Haifa, a "wonderful city" of palm-lined avenues, with an "immense square bordered by the high arched arcades of stately buildings" at its heart. Houses would be in the "Moorish style." He envisioned inhabitants moving comfortably on overhead electric trains. Tel Aviv has none of this, and is only now considering building a metro.

Tel Aviv preserves a faint echo of Herzl's utopia in its name. "Tel Aviv" was the title given by Nahum Sokolow, a writer and pioneer of Hebrew journalism, to his Hebrew translation of *Altneuland*. The name was meant to evoke the duality of "Old-New Land"—*Tel*, meaning "hill," conveyed a sense of "old" because of its associations with mounds of archaeological ruins, while *Aviv* with its connotations of "spring" or "renaissance," expressed the "new."

It was an odd choice of title. "Tel Aviv" appears in the Bible not as a symbol of restoration but as a place of Jewish exile. It was at "Tel

Aviv" (Tel Abib in English translations of the Bible), on the Chebar canal in Mesopotamia, that Ezekiel lived with Jewish captives and prophesied the impending destruction of Jerusalem by Nebuchadnezzar, the ruler of Babylon, as a sign of God's wrath at the "rebellious house" of Judea.

Tel Aviv grew out of Arab Jaffa, which at the turn of the century was the most cosmopolitan city in Palestine. New ideas, technologies, and immigrants washed on to this little promontory on the sandy coast of Palestine. There was a ferment of activity, with newspapers, budding industries, trading houses, hostels, and foreign consulates.

Yet Jaffa was crowded and its warrens were unhygienic. On April 11, 1909, about 60 members of a Jewish private housing society met outside the city to found a new Jewish garden suburb. A blurred photograph of the time shows the men, many of them wearing dark suits and hats, huddled on the sand as they parcel out the land through a lottery in which plot numbers and family names are etched inside sea-shells.

By the end of the year, the first houses of what became known as *Ahuzat Bayit*, "Housing Property," were completed. After some debate over a new name—some proposed titles such as *Aviva* and *Yeffefiya*, variations of "beautiful woman"—the residents settled for Tel Aviv. The head of the committee, Meir Dizengoff, was immediately known as "Mr. Mayor" (even though Tel Aviv did not gain separate municipal status until the advent of British rule) and ran the city until his death in 1936. The main avenue, with the Herzliya Gymnasium at the top, was named after Herzl. Four roads crossed it at right angles.

The founding of Tel Aviv was the other side of the coin of the pioneering work of the agricultural settlements; both were products of the Second Aliyah. For a while construction work in Tel Aviv was enveloped in the mysticism of the "religion of labor" that inspired the settlers of Degania and other kibbutzim. The cornerstone-laying ceremony for the Herzliya Gymnasium was disrupted by angry Jewish construction workers who demanded a promise that the high school would be built by Jews, and not by more skilled Arab masons. The urban construction worker was elevated to the status of a pioneering hero, the subject of proud verses. "Huge fists crouch in the sands;/Houses—houses—houses—/I sense: It is I who is caught in the branches of dawn./As a ray in my hand gleams a spade./And the unfinished suburb grins at me, laughs:/Sun, O Sun . . .", wrote the poet Avraham Shlonsky, who settled in Palestine in 1921 and worked as a builder.

Tel Aviv, however, was never meant to be part of the creation of a new Jewish working class. It was supposed to cater to wealthier urban Jews, professionals and artisans, the very people whom the pioneers were trying to transform into a laboring class. Arthur Ruppin, the godfather of Degania, was instrumental in securing financial backing from the Jewish National Fund for the construction of Tel Aviv. He told his superiors: "It is extremely important to provide good, healthy housing for the Jewish middle classes in Jaffa. I do not think that I am exaggerating when I say that the creation of a well-built Jewish quarter will present the most important step toward the economic conquest of Jaffa by the Jews."

Tel Aviv's founders had a grandiose scheme to create the first all-Jewish city in Palestine, fully autonomous, with gardens, paved streets, sanitation, and running water—almost unknown in this corner of the Turkish empire—but they could never live up to such lofty aspirations. Lack of money was a constant problem. "Most of the small houses in Tel Aviv were built without the help of an engineer or an architect," wrote Ruppin. "The builder, whether or not he knew what he was doing, concocted some sort of plan together with the man for whom he was building, who knew even less about the field. It is hardly surprising that many monstrous buildings were produced in this way, especially as the lack of money made it necessary to build as cheaply as possible."

The Herzliya Gymnasium was intended to attract well-to-do families to Palestine. The first music school was established in Tel Aviv in 1914 and the precursor of the Israel Philharmonic performed in the city in 1936. Habimah, the first Hebrew repertory theater company, which was founded in Moscow in 1917, resettled to Tel Aviv in 1931 and became Israel's national theater company. Painters such as Reuven Rubin, who became one of Israel's national painters, found work as stage designers. The country's Zionist press and the leading publishing houses based themselves in Tel Aviv, as did the leading political parties and the Histadrut, the Jewish trade union federation. Long after the capital of Israel was formally transferred to Jerusalem, most of these institutions have remained in Tel Aviv. The defense ministry, arguably the country's most important organ of state, declined to move up the mountain. Most of the foreign embassies, refusing to recognize Israel's annexation of East Jerusalem, preferred to stay by the sea in Tel Aviv.

In muddled fits and starts, improvising along the way, Tel Aviv grew from a sandswept "Little City with Few People in It," as the painter

Nahum Gutman nostalgically described it, into the center of the country's cultural and economic life. "I tell you," wrote Haim Nahman Bialik to a colleague, "the building of the earthly Jerusalem is coming about in a way that is beyond the grasp of the intellect. Every day new houses rise up out of the sand. Tel Aviv is spreading out in all directions. [. . .] The angels are building the land overnight."

The Arab heritage has been swept away. Nine out of ten of Jaffa's 65,000 or so Arabs were driven out in 1948. Today the roles of Tel Aviv and Jaffa have been reversed; the old harbor has become the playground for Tel Avivians, offering relief from the congestion of the Jewish city. The alleyways where camels and donkeys once vied for space with a multitude of porters, traders, and tourists are now enveloped in a hush of art galleries and yuppie flats. The quays bustle with visitors strolling past seafood restaurants. Old warehouses have been converted to discotheques. Arab women sometimes wander by, their quiet manner and white scarves giving them a ghostly air as they sweep past an abandoned mosque. One kosher eatery has a minaret rising incongruously above its garish plastic awnings.

The empty ground which now extends north of old Jaffa for about a mile along the beach road was once the Arab neighborhood of Manshiyyeh. Today it consists mainly of parking lots and landscaped walks. The newly restored Hassan Bey mosque rises at the far end of this barren space. It is a lonely reminder of the Arab communities that lived until half a century ago within earshot of its call to prayer.

★

The most loved places in Tel Aviv are not buildings, but coffee houses. Some are old and venerable institutions; others are places of fickle fashion. The habit was brought by the German immigrants, the *yekkes*. The Tel Aviv *beit kafeh* is not the Italian city *bar*, a place to have one's morning coffee standing up and move on. It is more like the French *café*, a place to meet and linger. In the Hebrew language, you don't *go* to your favorite coffee house, you *sit* in it.

The coffee house is where the issues of the day are debated, the rise and fall of governments are plotted, lines of poetry are conceived and the opposite sex is courted. The *beit kafeh* is an outdoor meeting place, a forum. Tel Aviv flats are small and the weather is hot for much of the year. It is easiest to meet friends at a coffee shop on the street. If you sit long enough at a coffee house in a small country like Israel, an acquaintance is bound to walk by. Kafeh Kassit, on Dizengoff

Street, was from prestate days until the 1960s the center of bohemian cultural life; here poets such as Natan Alterman, Avraham Shlonsky, Avot Yeshurun, Alexander Penn, Natan Zach, as well as all manner of hangers-on, met during the sultry evenings. Tel Avivians walked past for the thrill of celebrity spotting. As late as the 1970s, long after Kassit's heyday, one guidebook urged tourists to catch a glimpse of the owner "dozing in a chair, head on his chest, hands clasped over his imposing belly, while his unwashed, unbarbered customers languish around the tables outside."

The core of Kassit's prestate clientele was a group of poets calling itself Trask, a name of unknown origin, who were determined to make merry even in times of trouble. For Jews, they were unusually bibulous. Their symbol was "the finger," as in "giving someone the finger." "There ink and kindness flowed/A cigarette fizzled/Wonderful wines. Good poems/Dead flies in the chandelier," wrote Alterman in one of his poems.

Dizengoff Street, the city's favorite promenade, gave birth to a Hebrew verb, *lehizdangeff*, "to do Dizengoff." In the 1950s and 1960s, different cafés served different sections of society. Pinati, south of Kassit, was where veterans of the War of Independence met. Across the street was Ditza, a chess players' café. Just north of Kassit was Beitan, famous as the favorite place of Yonatan Ratosh, father of the "Canaanite" Movement which sought to create the impossible: a non-Jewish Israeli culture. Ruval was the café of choice for the bourgeoisie and became the spot to ogle well-groomed middle-class women on Friday afternoons.

As Tel Aviv spread northward, the well-heeled moved with the tide of new construction while poorer oriental Jews took over the smaller and older buildings close to Dizengoff. In the 1980s and 1990s, the artists' scene moved to Sheinkin Street and revolved around Kafeh Tamar.

On a Friday afternoon you struggle to find an outside table at Kafeh Tamar to watch the summer parade of women's navels and well-formed male torsos of soldiers on leave. The image of the "ugly Jew" of centuries past has given way to the unadorned natural beauty of young Israelis. On Sheinkin there are also the mystics who offer an alternative to a life of empty hedonism. In the space of a few minutes one afternoon, I watched a troupe of saffron-robed Hare Krishna Israelis, clanging their cymbals and chanting Hindu incantations, followed closely by an old Hasidic Jew blaring prayers from a speaker mounted on his battered car.

The quality of coffee is not the most important feature of most coffee shops. For years Israelis have cheerfully sipped an awful substance called *bots*, or "mud," a bastardization of Turkish coffee. Instead of delicately boiling and re-boiling water, ground coffee, sugar, and cardamom into a perfumed nectar, as has been done in the Levant for centuries, Israelis take a glass of hot water, throw in cheap ground coffee, stir it for a moment with sugar, and serve up the mud. As Israelis became more worldly they graduated to instant coffee. In many parts of the country the greatest luxury one can ask for is *ness*, a cup of Nescafé or other instant powder. Real sophisticates request a *cafe hafuch*, an "upside down coffee," which bears a vague resemblance to a cappuccino. In recent years there has been a proliferation of establishments offering Italian coffee, but these are still the preserve of urban trendsetters.

Similarly, only recently has there been an improvement in the quality and choice of restaurants. For all of the country's ethnic diversity and the bounty of its agricultural produce, eating in Israel has long been a miserable affair. Israeli families eat their ethnic delicacies at home, but the country as a whole has developed only a poor man's version of cooking borrowed from the Middle East and eastern Europe. The requirements of kosher food may restrict the variety of dishes, but Israel has produced nothing to rival a New York Jewish deli. Hummus and grilled meat are popular, but these dishes are rarely as sumptuous as those produced by the Arabs. Felafel, deep-fried balls of chickpea paste, is marketed abroad as the quintessential Israeli snack food, but it has been eaten by Arabs for at least two centuries. Toasted cheese sandwiches, overcooked pasta, and under-dressed Greek salad are the standard fare of the average restaurant. Cheese does not usually have a name—it is either "yellow" or "white." Despite Israel being a Mediterranean country, olive oil has only recently become commonly available at restaurants. For decades, culinary fusion and experimentation consisted of little more inventive than putting a chicken schnitzel in a pitta bread.

In the 1950s writers gave advice on how to cook during austerity, as meat was virtually nonexistent, chicken was rationed and eggs were restricted to three a week. Today, though, the newspaper columns are filled with discussions of champagne drinking, suggestions for fine wines, and where to find the best cappuccino.

I was once given a glossy coffee-table book with lavish photographs that portrayed Israel as a gastronomic south of France set in the Middle East. Yet the text admitted that Israeli chefs still face an uphill struggle among philistine Israelis:"These Jeremiahs see food as part of a long tradition of atonement and suffering."

In recent years there has been an explosion of ethnic restaurants—Japanese, Chinese, Vietnamese, Italian, French, Argentinian, Mexican, and many more. These are an affirmation not so much of the multi-faceted nature of Israeli society as of its love of globe-trotting. There has also been a proliferation of U.S.-style fast-food restaurants. The felafel must compete with the cheeseburger and the shwarma is yielding ground to the pizza.

"Americanization" denotes the complex of changes in Israel's transformation from a Jewish Sparta into a western bourgeois society. The process is bewildering to many, including both religious and old-fashioned secular Zionists who fear the erosion of cherished values. When two Israeli teenagers were killed and scores injured during a stampede at a music festival in the Negev town of Arad in 1995, President Ezer Weizman blamed the "Americanization" of Israeli youth. "We have to beware of the McDonald's, we have to beware of Michael Jackson, and we have to beware of Madonna. We need not only culture, but culture that is specifically Israeli and Jewish," he pronounced, despite the fact that the tragedy took place at a festival of Israeli music and was caused in part by the very Israeli habit of pushing and shoving.

There is no doubt that Israel loves America. Politically and militarily the United States has sustained Israel against its enemies, and culturally Israel has taken to mimicking American manners. U.S.-style personality politics, rather than the old Polish backroom dealing, has come to dominate public life. Advertisements often include slogans in English. One ad for dog food boasted that it was "eaten by American dogs."

Shopping malls are sprouting everywhere. Basketball teams have adopted cheerleaders. Israelis are among the world's most enthusiastic users of the Internet. Television was not introduced until 1968 because of resistance from Ben-Gurion, who regarded it as cultural pollution (many Israelis, especially Arabs, resorted to watching programs broadcast from neighboring Arab countries). But now the airwaves are filled with American shows. The end of the *Seinfeld* comedy series caused almost as much heartbreak in Tel Aviv as it did in New York.

Israeli parents, particularly among the secular, have taken to giving their children English-sounding names, such as Ben, Ron, Tom, Shelley, and Guy. Oddly, some of these are not specific to gender—I know both boys and girls called Ronni.

America may be palpable everywhere in Israel, but American-style service culture is notable for its absence. Israelis are often brusque, haughty and, frankly, rude. Rejection of polished diaspora manners, the contempt for the little hypocrisies that make life flow more smoothly, have turned Israel into a place where every day consists of a series of battles—against aggressive motorists, against intemperate telephone callers, against all manner of self-righteous petty officials, against elbow-wielding queue-bargers and against surly waiters, to name just a few. Merely to preserve one's self-respect, to avoid being treated as a *freier*, a sucker, is a frenzied and exhausting experience.

Israeli friends explain that this is part of Israel being a country of proud Jews, but I sense there is more to it than that. It is as if Israelis have not yet come to terms with the fact that the days of deprivation—the poverty, the ghettos, oppression, genocide, the years of austerity, the immigrant camps, the hardships of the pioneering days—are gone. There is plenty for everybody.

★

"I don't want to be American; I want to be Russian. Russians care about books and culture. We take the commercialization and the false glamor from America. But we don't have a sense of democracy. If we imported that from America along with junk food we would be better off."

Irit Linur does not so much converse as hold forth. That is what she is paid to do, originally as a columnist and later as a radio presenter. She is not just a thirty-something loudmouth, however. She has two successful novels to her name, one of which has been turned into a film.

With her thick brown curly hair, black shirt and trousers, Linur came across as younger than her 36 years when I met her in a Tel Aviv sushi restaurant. She slouched and crushed her straw with girlish enthusiasm. Her manner retained the rough edges of adolescence.

Few Israelis would accuse Linur of writing highbrow literature, despite the extravagant claims she has been known to make for her work. Both of her novels—*Two Snow Whites* and *The Siren's Song*—are love stories involving single, childless professional women with media-related jobs. Her heroines are the kind of people one would expect to meet on Sheinkin and, after Linur runs the characters though a string of disappointing suitors and heartbreak, with the odd mysterious death thrown in, they ultimately find satisfaction. Linur professes to dislike the venerable figures of Israeli literature who, in her view, lack "charm." "Nobody can be inspired by Bialik," she said.

By Israeli standards, Linur is considered to be radically feminist, but her writing is largely limited to poking fun at the conventions of courtship. Unlike better-known authors like Amos Oz, Linur does not try to impart any important political or social message. Linur is a good storyteller, an entertainer. Her concerns are domestic—love, relationships, marriage, and the modern woman—the stuff of day-to-day middle-class life anywhere in the world, set in an Israeli context. "I'm not interested in the conflict with the Arabs. We will settle it eventually," she explained.

This is not to say that she is indifferent to politics. Linur is unapologetically patriotic, waves the Israeli flag on Independence Day and thinks Israel should keep lots of tanks and missiles even if there is peace with the Arabs, "just in case." Israel, she said, "is the best country in the world." She sees the rest of the globe as inherently anti-Semitic. She refuses to have her books published in Germany.

Her world is Tel Aviv. She likes the fact that even rich people live in tasteless buildings. "When I go to Paris or London the houses are so beautiful and quaint. It's like a beautiful woman—you stare at her but you would not want to live with her. It's the flaws that attract us to people and places."

Linur, who studied psychology and philosophy at Tel Aviv University, is best known for her criticism of Israeli males. During the 1994 soccer World Cup she derided men's love of the sport. "Soccer players are the filthiest, wad-spitting, testicle-scratching athletes in the world of sport—and therefore they resemble their fans the most." Linur blames the army. "Israel is a very male-oriented, chauvinistic society because of the place of the army," she told me. "Everybody thinks very highly about retired military men. If you were a colonel, you are considered to be qualified to run for mayor of a city."

In a country where marriage and producing children is considered to be both a religious and patriotic duty, Linur once rashly pronounced that she saw no need to wed, only to find herself marrying Alon Ben-David, the military affairs correspondent of state-run Channel 1 television news. "A macho man" is how she described her spouse. Now, she said, she finds herself urging siblings to get hitched. "We are all natural *shadchanim* [match-makers]. If you see a single man, you don't want him to rot alone."

Linur and Ben-David did make one protest against tradition: having a civil wedding. This would be unexceptionable anywhere in the industrialized world, but for two Israeli Jews to do so is daring to the point of giving offense. In Israel civil weddings are impossible: the government has left personal matters—marriage, divorce, death—in the hands of religious authorities and their arcane traditions. Linur had to find a registrar in Cyprus, the Gretna Green or Reno of the Middle East, which caters to Israelis and Lebanese alike who have run into trouble with rabbis, sheikhs, or priests. Israelis who marry in Cyprus include couples of different religions (intermarriage is disallowed), those with one partner whose Judaism is rejected by the rabbis (which in their view amounts to intermarriage) or lovers whose marriage is otherwise forbidden by Jewish law (such as between a descendant of the priestly *Kohanim*, the Cohens, and a divorcee). Linur and Ben-David went to Cyprus out of choice. "I would not let the rabbis into my life," said Linur. "But it annoyed me that I had to go abroad to get married—in English at that."

Yet she agrees with the rabbis on at least one question: the aversion to Jews marrying gentiles. "I could never envision myself dating a non-Jew. Men are different enough besides being of a different religion. When I hear about mixed marriages in the United States, to me it's a silent, nonviolent genocide. It saddens me as a Jew."

Here lies the irony of the great schism between religious and secular Israelis. For all their railing against rabbinical strictures, secular Jews do not stray very far from tradition. Zionism itself borrowed the idea of the return to Zion from the daily synagogue prayers. Had the rabbis not put up a fence of regulations to preserve Jews through the centuries, there would be no Jews, secular or otherwise, and no Jewish state. Scratch the surface of a secular Israeli, a Tel Aviv psychologist once told me, and you find a traditional Jew.

*

Amnon Arieli had once been a regular Sheinkinite. He was a popular columnist and advertising copywriter, and something of a Tel Aviv celebrity. In 1984 he became a *Hozer Be-Tshuva*, one who "returns in repentance," that is, a born-again Jew. Throwing out his jeans and sandals, he donned the black suit and other accoutrements that identify him as an Ultraorthodox Jew, one of the *Haredim*, the "fearful" before God.

Today the secular world of Sheinkin Street is a strange and foreign land to Arieli. "Of course I miss it," he said, sighing, when I met him in Jerusalem, "I miss movies, theaters, concerts. I need to sit with friends and talk nonsense. I don't do it anymore, not so much because it's not allowed, but because I don't want people to see me. I don't want to harm my family through gossip."

The dark suit, he said, is a uniform, "as in the army." It says you belong to the Haredim, and it keeps you from straying from the path of the *Halacha*, or the "Way" of religious law. Dressed as he is, he can no longer linger in a café to speak to an attractive girl. For the sake of his children, he complies with a rabbinical ban on television sets. If he wants to watch a program, he has to sneak out to a friend's house like a thief.

Before it became a chic neighborhood, Sheinkin was part of a district settled heavily by Hasidic Jews. In the early years of the state, Tel Aviv had been home to about 20 different Hasidic groups. With time, though, most moved out to the neighboring town of Bnei Brak, which is isolated as far as possible from secular distractions. Those Haredim left in Tel Aviv are, for the main part, active in religious revival. Sheinkin is an important recruiting ground for the newly observant.

Becoming religious is not just a matter of discovering faith, or going to synagogue more frequently. It is a complete, root-and-branch transformation, where the minutiae of every act of daily life become subject to elaborate regulation. The secular and religious worlds must by necessity be separate. A religious Jew cannot, for instance, eat in a non-kosher household or break the Sabbath by turning on a light switch. The process can tear families apart.

Arieli's wife, Ora Morag, was a fashion designer whom he had met at a café. At first she tried to accommodate his needs, but ultimately would not join him on the road to Haredi existence. They divorced and Arieli remarried a newly religious woman, a painter, after meeting her through a matchmaker. The couple moved out of Tel Aviv to a Haredi community in the West Bank, halfway to Jerusalem. Symbolically Arieli is suspended between the two cities: he has cut himself off from the secular world of Tel Aviv, but has never been fully accepted into the cloistered world of the Haredim. "They do everything to welcome you, but you are always a stranger. They don't know where you came from. Maybe your father and mother were not even Jewish, or maybe I'm a *mamzer*"—a "bastard" born of a forbidden union who may not marry a Jew. "They are afraid that I will 'go back,'" he explained.

I met the 54-year-old Arieli in the lobby of the Holiday Inn hotel in Jerusalem. Its coffee shop was, of course, kosher. He ordered a Coca-Cola and, incongruously, recited a blessing before sipping from the nectar of American culture.

Over the years Arieli had compromised on his religious attire. His beard was close-trimmed rather than the full bush favored by the sages. He said he wears the full black suit and hat for the Sabbath and holidays, but during the working week, especially in summer, he limits himself to black trousers, a white open-necked shirt with the *tzitzit* (a small prayer shawl worn beneath) dangling loosely and a black kippa on his head. "It's simply too hot outside," he explained. "I've worn sandals all my life, but I can't wear them now. Everybody would look at me."

Speech matters too in the religious communities. "There is Hebrew and there is Israeli," he said. Most Haredim speak Yiddish among themselves, to avoid profaning the holy tongue by using it for prosaic matters, and read Hebrew with the Ashkenazi cadence, saying *sha*bbas (sabbath) and *sho*lem (peace, used as a greeting) with the stress on the first syllable, instead of sha*bbat* and sha*lom* stressed on the final syllable. At first, Arieli found his fellow Haredim all but incomprehensible, and anyone meeting him immediately knew he was a newly observant sabra. Arieli's "return in repentance" was a gradual process. His grandfather had been observant, while his father was a socialist pioneer who maintained some Jewish traditions, such as lighting candles on the Sabbath and going to synagogue during the major holidays. "My father liked *hazzanut* [cantorial music]. I hated it. It was a symbol of diaspora, a world which should pass away," said Arieli. "For him it was a connection to his family. They all died in the Holocaust."

For Arieli the change began with the birth of his first daughter. He was awestruck and felt he did not have any values to pass on to her. He read a newspaper advertisement inviting him to a gathering with Ikka Israeli, a former painter whom Arieli had known, now a rabbi. "I really wanted to meet him. I was very angry with him because he had left us. He was a traitor," recalled Arieli. He went to the appointed address, but the meeting had been canceled because of rain. Another rabbi asked him to stay for tea. They ended up speaking for five hours, and Arieli agreed to come back to study some Talmud, a book he had never opened in his life.

Slowly Arieli was drawn into Orthodox life. He started wearing a kippa at the study sessions and six months later announced to his friends that he had become religious. "It was like coming out when you are a homosexual," he recounted. "I did it on a Friday in a café in Dizengoff where my friends used to meet. One of them saw me with a kippa and asked if someone had died. When I told them I had become religious, they were very upset. I lost all my friends. Whenever I saw them we ended up arguing, so I stayed away for a year. Now they accept me. My head was full of Torah and religious things. Girls and politics did not interest me."

Arieli and his ex-wife wrote separate books about their experience. His was called *A Captive Child*, a reference to a person who is biologically Jewish but grows up in captivity (literally or figuratively) in ignorance of Jewish law. Hers was a fictionalized account entitled *One Hundred New Apples (Plus VAT)*, an allusion to a conversation with religious women who wanted to know the price of a dress but did not want to discuss money on the Sabbath, so asked for the equivalent in the price of apples.

The problems of adjustment were often bizarre. Arieli found himself storing cigarette smoke in balloons so he could inhale it during the Sabbath without breaking the proscription against lighting fires. Morag, describing her former husband as "Yonatan," recalls how she tried hopelessly to satisfy his strange wishes. She kept the kitchen kosher and assiduously prepared for the Sabbath, even cutting toilet paper into pieces in advance so that he would not have to risk doing "work" on the day of rest.

As a journalist on Haredi newspapers, Arieli ran into unexpected problems. "One day somebody gave me a picture of a synagogue and I put it in the paper. It became a big scandal because in the picture you could see the name of God on the synagogue. Something that has the name of God on it, even a newspaper, cannot be thrown away or be used for toilet paper. It was very funny."

Arieli was part of a wave of back-to-religion conversions in the 1980s involving mainly Ashkenazi intellectuals and the artistic set. Today it is mainly the less educated Sephardim who are the target of the proselytizers. Occasionally there is a noteworthy catch, such as Israel's most famous belly dancer, Bari Simone, who since her conversion has taken to sewing wedding dresses in Bnei Brak. Now going under the name of Bruria Toledano, she wrote a warning letter to 30 belly dancers, listing the names of several performers who had died, fallen ill, or otherwise suffered calamity because of their sins.

Thousands are drawn into the Haredi fold by charismatic rabbis such as Amnon Yitzhak. His sermons are not of the gentle, cerebral kind that drew Arieli, but a raw harangue. "A time will come when a secularist will walk down the street and people will say, 'Did you see? There goes a secularist!' There won't be any left. Maybe there will be one in a museum, like a fossil from a bygone age," he told one crowd.

Many secular Israeli parents consider the religious enticement of their sons and daughters as a cultlike brainwashing, yet a large amount of taxpayers' money is funneled into the religious networks, including groups seeking to recruit "repentant" Jews.

Arieli explained that Haredim have traditionally been afraid of secular Israel. But time is now on their side. "The secular are afraid because the population of religious people is growing. Next door to me there is a family with 14 children. The religious and the Arabs are competing over who has more children. I have only three children. I don't want anymore, but my wife is ashamed to go out on the streets. For the religious, having children is like a flag. We are a democratic country, and no government can exist without the religious."

★

McDonald's conquered Communist Moscow years before it was able to penetrate the defenses of the Promised Land. The fast food chain made the first breach in 1993 with a restaurant in Ramat Gan in greater Tel Aviv, and quickly pushed through with dozens of outlets throughout the country.

The humble cheeseburger became the preeminent symbol of Israel's culture war. Old-time Labor Zionists saw it as an assault upon Israeli culture, the agricultural lobby objected to McDonald's being allowed to import its own strain of potatoes, and the families of fallen soldiers objected to the gaudy presence of the golden arches next to a memorial to the dead soldiers of the Golani brigade. All this, however, was nothing compared to the enmity of the Haredim, who were affronted by the relentless spread of the non-kosher burgers, even to Jerusalem itself.

In the 1996 general election the golden arches were shown on the Labor party political broadcasts as evidence of cultural openness, affluence, and the good life. But United Torah Judaism, the main Haredi party, held up the same arches as a symbol of the poisoning of traditional Jewish values. At one point, the private Channel 2 television network banned a commercial depicting the assembly of a "virtual" McDonald's cheeseburger.

McDonald's says the individual ingredients of its products—meat, cheese, etc.—are kosher. The problem lies in the combination of beef patty with cheese, which contravenes the ban on mixing meat and dairy products on the basis of the biblical injunction: "Thou shalt not seethe a kid in his mother's milk" (Exod. 23: 19). The row was reminiscent of an incident a few years earlier, when Pepsi was forced to stop a poster campaign on the theme of the Ascent of Man from an ape to Pepsi-drinking teenagers. The religious authorities complained that the ad challenged the teachings that God created the universe just under 6,000 years ago.

Another front in the rabbis' war against the vile cheeseburger has been the desecration of the Sabbath. The Ministry of Labor periodically sends inspectors to check whether McDonald's employs Jews on Saturdays, the most profitable day for many restaurants, in defiance of a 1951 law that forbids Jews from working on the Sabbath. Needless to say, religious officials cannot themselves check whether the Sabbath is being violated, because that would involve working on the Sabbath, so they employ Druze inspectors to police Jews on the Jewish day of rest. Jewish law has remained so ossified that Jews cannot run their own modern state in their ancestral land without recourse to a *shabbes goy*, a gentile who performs tasks for Jews on the Sabbath.

Even if Israelis were to give up on cheeseburgers and driving to the beach on Saturdays, how can they obey the order not to work on the Sabbath while keeping the army on alert? Should policemen all go home? Should nobody look after power stations at the weekend? A doctor may break the Sabbath to save a life, but what about the routine running of a hospital? Many of the compromises emerging from the competition between tradition and statehood are incongruous. The state airline, El Al, does not fly on the Sabbath, and loses money while Ben-Gurion airport stays open on Saturdays to cater to foreign airlines.

The Chief Rabbinate maintains a large bureaucracy of inspection to ensure that restaurants, hotels, and even the armed forces maintain the required standards of Jewish dietary law and Sabbath observance. This work is duplicated by other armies of inspectors from the courts of the Haredi sects, who do not trust the government-backed rabbinate to do the job properly. The certificates of approval are vital for any business wanting to cater to the growing religious public, and this creates an unwieldy system that is open to abuse. Even the mighty Coca-Cola company was forced to disclose its secret formula to gain rabbinical approval.

An old adage says that more than Israel kept the Sabbath, the Sabbath kept Israel. Observance of the day of rest is a central element of

Judaism, on the strength of Moses' injunction to the Israelites gathered on Mount Sinai: "Six days shall work be done, but on the seventh day there shall be to you an holy day, a sabbath of rest to the Lord: whosoever doeth work therein shall be put to death. Ye shall kindle no fire throughout your habitations upon the sabbath day"(Exod. 35: 2–3).

The sages of antiquity defined "work" as the 39 prototypes of labor—ranging from writing to the tanning of skins—involved in erecting the Tabernacle. But the world has moved on since the times when the Israelites wandered the desert. Using electrical machinery, for instance, does not fit neatly into any of these categories, yet Orthodox Jews are told they may not open or close any electrical circuit, be it a light switch or television set, on the Sabbath.

On Friday nights, the lifts in Jerusalem's blocks of flats are switched over to a Sabbath rhythm. They continuously travel up and down, stopping at every floor, so that observant Jews can get home without violating the Sabbath by having to press an electrical button. During the Gulf War in 1991, the state set up a "silent" Sabbath radio station. Observant Jews would tune in before the Sabbath and leave their sets on. There would be no sound, except in case of an impending Scud missile attack.

Jerusalem's Institute for Science and Halacha tries to reconcile technology with tradition through ingenious devices such as the "Sabbath telephone." "There are two possible definitions of electricity," explained the institute's head, Rabbi Levi Yitzhak Halperin. "It can be like lighting a fire. For example most light bulbs give out heat and light. Otherwise, it can be like building or fixing something. Without electricity, the equipment does not work. In a sense, using electricity would be like fixing it."

So how, I asked, can you use a telephone on the Sabbath? The trick is *gramma*, an Aramaic word meaning "to cause indirectly." Rabbi Halperin explained: "Jews are not allowed to light a candle on the Sabbath or to put it out. But if a wind comes through the window and is about to blow out the candle, I am allowed to close the window." This idea of "preventing the preventer" is applied to Rabbi Halperin's Sabbath telephone. Instead of a dial, it has ten holes, each with a tiny photoelectric cell. A light flashes through every few seconds, halting a circuit which is trying to dial the number. If you place a little stick in the hole, the flash of light is blocked, the feedback mechanism is interrupted, the preventer has been prevented and the number is dialed. Was this not cheating? God's Law is perfect, replied

Rabbi Halperin. "If God left a loophole, there was a reason. We are allowed to use it."

His showroom had other marvels, such as a hospital bedside buzzer based on gramma and a Sabbath water heater. Publications issued by the institute explained the reasons for going through the trouble of installing special Sabbath technology in, say, a hospital. "The psychological effect on an observant patient who becomes aware that the Sabbath is disregarded because of his endangered status is detrimental to his recovery. The mental anguish and fear he suffers from this knowledge may be devastating."

In the West Bank settlement of Alon Shvut, I met another group of religious and engineering experts. Ezra Rosenfeld, an American-born engineer, offered what is my favorite definition of electricity. "It is like creating scent. There is a passage in the Talmud that says you are not allowed to put perfume on your clothes on the Sabbath. But if your clothes were already scented, you are allowed to add more." Armed with this ruling, his group designed an electric wheelchair for use on the Sabbath. The machine is switched on before the Sabbath, but the current flowing from the battery is not strong enough to turn the wheels. To travel, all the patient has to do is increase the current. "You see, it's like adding perfume to scented clothes," declared Rosenfeld.

Jewish law, he assured me, had the answer to the problems of modern society. "The problem is that the part of Judaism which relates to a sovereign Jewish state is, well, dusty. It did not develop for 2,000 years since the destruction of the temple."

*

Theodor Herzl had an early taste of the political power of the rabbis. He had planned to convene the founding congress of his Zionist movement in Munich, but shortly before the gathering was due to open in August 1897, he was forced to move the venue to Basle in Switzerland. The reason was the implacable opposition of Germany's rabbis to Zionism. "The aspirations of the so-called Zionists to establish a national Jewish state in Palestine contradict the messianic promises of Judaism as enunciated in the holy scripture and later religious canons. [. . .] Judaism obliges its adherents to serve the fatherland to which they belong with utmost devotion and to further its national interests with all their hearts and strength," they said in a letter of protest.

From its very inception, Zionism has been at odds with important parts of Jewish religious leadership. Zionism may have drawn inspiration from the messianic promise. But for most rabbis of the time—whether they were mystical Hasidim, their scholarly "Lithuanian" critics known as the *Mitnagdim* or "Opponents," the various strains of more modern Orthodoxy, or even the emerging Reform movement—Zionism was an abomination. The traditionalists saw the movement as an affront to God's promise of salvation, and a manifestation of modernism. At the other end of the spectrum, reform-minded Jews saw Zionism as casting doubt on their loyalty to their countries and endangering the emancipation of Jews.

In *The Jewish State*, Herzl envisioned rabbis spreading the message of Zionism through the synagogues, and leading communities of immigrants to the new homeland. By the time he wrote *Altneuland*, when the religious leadership's opposition was already apparent, Herzl was almost stridently opposed to the rabbis. He mocked anti-Zionist rabbis who declared that "Zion was everywhere but in Zion!" The main character of the novel observes that in the New Society, "religion has been excluded from public affairs once and for all."

In modern Israel, not only has religion not been excluded, but its impact has become all-pervasive. It influences the political alliances of the country. In the debate over the disposal of the West Bank, Gaza Strip, and Jerusalem, Zionist-religious groups form the most ardent opposition to concessions. In a large range of social and personal domains—whom Jews may marry, where they are allowed to go at weekends, what they are allowed to eat and, even after death, where they may be buried—the Haredim are at the forefront of attempts to tighten observance of religious law.

One of the biggest arguments over the wording of Israel's Proclamation of Independence concerned the place that should be given to God in the announcement of the rebirth of the nation. Just hours before Ben-Gurion was due to make the announcement, religious and socialist Zionist leaders were at loggerheads over whether to include a reference to the "Lord of Israel." In the end, they settled on the ambiguous "Rock of Israel."

Ben-Gurion made several other concessions to secure the acquiescence of Haredi groups in the formation of the state. They include declaring the Sabbath the state's official day of rest, a promise not to introduce civil marriage and divorce, a commitment to keep public institutions kosher and a guarantee of autonomy for religious schools. Ben-Gurion agreed, moreover, to defer the military draft for several hundred Haredi Jews studying in yeshivas.

This laid the basis for Israel's religious status quo. It was a pragmatic compromise to avoid a rift in the nation at a time when it was fighting for survival. The Haredim were regarded by the Yishuv's leaders as a relic of eastern European Jewry which should be preserved as a kind of cultural museum piece. The Ultraorthodox disagreed as a matter of dogma with the creation of a secular Jewish state and considered themselves to be living "in exile among the Jews." They had settled in Jerusalem long before the advent of Zionism. If Zionists saw in the Holocaust proof of the need for a Jewish state, many Haredim regarded the Shoah as divine punishment for the sin of Zionism and its lack of faith in God's redemption. The Haredim were nevertheless ready to deal with the reality of the state and made it their business to try to improve its Jewish character, but they never fully accepted the authority of the state and its judiciary.

The Haredim, grouped around the Agudat Israel party (founded in 1912 in central and eastern Europe), joined the religious Zionists in the first Israeli government, but the coalition was soon beset by religious disputes. In 1951, Ben-Gurion's first government was brought down by a controversy over whether Sephardi immigrants should be given a religious or a secular education. In 1952 Agudat Israel withdrew over plans to draft religious women for nonmilitary "national" service. The religious Zionists, amalgamated into the National Religious Party (NRP), remained faithful junior partners of successive Labor governments. In 1976, Prime Minister Yitzhak Rabin took delivery of new American fighter jets in a ceremony which spilled over into the Sabbath. In the ensuing row over religious desecration, the NRP abstained in a vote of no confidence tabled by Agudat Israel, prompting Rabin to dissolve the government and call an election. It was the first link in a chain of events that led to the downfall of Labor and the startling victory by Likud in 1977.

This political earthquake also marked a rebirth of religious politics. The NRP reached the peak of its electoral support and switched sides to Likud. Agudat Israel, too, reentered the government. The new Prime Minister, Menachem Begin, was more sympathetic to Jewish tradition and was hailed as the "first Jewish Prime Minister of Israel." He granted universal draft deferment for yeshiva students and increased state funding for religious institutions.

In subsequent elections, Labor and Likud were closely matched and the religious parties became king-makers, able to extract increasingly generous concessions in return for their support of one or other party. Haredi society, insulated from secular Israel by its exemption from military service, generously financed by the state and by diaspora philanthropists, and with the political muscle to preserve its position, was transformed into a vast "society of scholars." Its men now shun secular studies—television, the Internet, and even encyclopedias have been banned by the rabbis—and seclude themselves for years, even a lifetime, in their Talmudic academies. The women have become the main breadwinners, often relying on the network of religious schools to find employment as teachers.

Full-time Talmud study used to be a calling for an elite. But there are now tens of thousands of yeshiva and kollel (yeshiva for married men) students in Israel, more than in the venerable pre-Holocaust academies of eastern Europe. Some enthusiasts claim the intensity of Jewish study is higher now than at any time since the days of the sages who compiled the Talmud. The flowering of scholarship is seen by the Haredim as a "miracle," evidence of divine favor and proof that the yeshiva world has been able to stop secular erosion. Religious parties, both Haredim and the NRP, have grown in strength from holding 16 out of 120 seats in the first Knesset of 1949 to an unprecedented 27 seats in elections 50 years later.

Yet success carries the seeds of future disaster. The expanding "society of scholars" requires ever more generous state finance to support its social and learning institutions. Generations are being pauperized by their unwillingness (and inability) to work in the modern world. Haredi neighborhoods are among the poorest in the country. There are not enough jobs for rabbis, inspectors, and teachers of religious studies to employ the output from the yeshivas and kollels.

Moreover, the growth of Haredi society, its drain on state finances and the religious strictures which it tries to impose on the rest of the country have created a backlash from secular Israelis who fear their country is being turned into a theocracy and, at the very least, resent seeing their tax shekels spent on people who do not serve in the army. With their high birth rate, some estimates are that Haredim could account for 30 percent of Israel's population by the year 2023. "Good Morning, Iran," says the title of one Aviv Geffen song, reflecting the dismay of secular Israel.

Haredi parties traditionally stood aloof from the great issues of war and peace, but in recent years their supporters have become markedly right-wing on the questions of territorial concessions to the Arabs. There has been a convergence of traditionally anti-Zionist Haredim and religious Zionists who wear crocheted skullcaps.

Only the Hasidic sect of the Naturei Karta, an Aramaic title meaning "Guardians of the City," remain adamantly anti-Zionist, on the grounds that Zionism is an affront to God's will, to the point of regarding the Palestinian leader Yasser Arafat as the rightful president of all of Palestine and accepting seats in the Palestinian cabinet. The Naturei Karta were the shock troops of the Sabbath battles of the 1950s, but today their influence is insignificant.

The Lubavitcher movement, on the other hand, has become an important factor in Israeli politics. In the 1996 elections, it helped to swing the vote in favor of Likud's leader, Binyamin "Bibi" Netanyahu, with a poster campaign declaring "Bibi is Good for the Jews." Based in New York, the Lubavitchers transformed themselves from a minor Hasidic dynasty into the leading force of international Jewish revival. Known also as Habad (the Hebrew acronym for its motto "Wisdom, Understanding, Knowledge"), the Lubavitchers are more worldly and yet in many ways more bizarre than other Hasidic sects. The movement has more than 3,000 "emissaries" in over 100 countries around the world and administers a yearly budget of about $700 million. Its activities stretch from caring for Jewish children affected by the nuclear disaster at Chernobyl to winning over Jewish criminals in American prisons and offering Passover meals for Israelis wandering through Nepal. In Israel during the 1982 Lebanon War, Habad's *mitzva* ("good deed") vans followed army tanks into enemy territory to give spiritual support to the troops. Habad does not cut itself off from secular Jews, it actively seeks them out.

Habad has bewildered many Jews with its messianic pretensions. Its philosophy is that the Messiah's arrival can be willed by the faithful if they are worthy. The late Lubavitcher leader Menachem Mendel Schneerson, known simply as the Rebbe, would tell followers that the Messiah's coming was imminent, if only they would exert themselves a little bit more and perform more good deeds. Habad founded its own village in Israel, Kfar Habad, close to Ben-Gurion airport. It includes a replica of its two-story redbrick headquarters in Brooklyn, complete with lovingly reproduced stained-glass windows, cast-iron grilles, and a brass plate bearing the address, 770 Parkway.

Habad's messianic fervor began to break its moorings in 1990. While Israel panicked over the looming Gulf War and the threat of Iraqi chemical weapons, the Rebbe told followers that the cataclysm was a portent of the imminent arrival of the Messiah. There was no need to obtain gas masks or store emergency supplies because God would protect Israel.

The following year the Rebbe expressed surprise that the Messiah had not yet come. Habad responded with a massive advertising campaign, putting up posters with the words: "Prepare for the Coming of the Messiah." As the Rebbe's life ebbed away after a stroke in 1992, the movement's fervor intensified. Posters bearing a portrait of the bearded Rebbe, with his black hat and piercing eyes, began to appear first with the slogan "The Messiah is Coming," and then finally "Welcome, King Messiah." The Rebbe, however, did not reveal himself as the Messiah. He died in 1994. His movement became hopelessly divided between the messianists, who believe the late Rebbe is a kind of hidden Messiah, and the official leadership, which sees the Rebbe's death as a hiatus before the arrival of the true Messiah.

Orthodox critics fear that Habad, or at least a substantial part of it, is speeding down the road of idolatry and question whether the followers of the messianic doctrine can be considered Jews anymore. Even during the Rebbe's life, Rabbi Eliezer Schach would denounce the Lubavitcher leader as a "false Messiah," a caustic reference to past charlatans such as the seventeenth-century mystic, Shabbetai Zvi, who declared himself Messiah and gathered a huge following in the Orient and Europe before being arrested by the Ottoman Sultan and ignominiously converting to Islam.

The rivalry between the Rebbe and Rabbi Schach spilled into Israeli politics, and turned the 1988 elections into a no-holds-barred contest fought with religious amulets, vows, blessings, and counterblessings. So intense was the electioneering that Haredi parties more than doubled their representation from 6 to 13 seats. Emboldened by their strength, Haredi parties opened a new campaign in Israel's longrunning cultural war, known as "Who is a Jew?" The vexed question revolves around the central pillar of Israel, the Law of Return. The law enshrines the right of every Jew to settle in Israel and from the outset the state also welcomed people who were not Jews—the gentile spouses of Jews, as well as children and grandchildren of mixed couples. The argument was that if quarter-Jews were sufficiently Jewish to be singled out for discrimination and murder by the Nazis under the Nuremberg Laws, then they were Jewish enough to be granted refuge in Israel. More controversially, though, the Law of Return left unanswered the question of who is Jewish. Is it to be decided by Orthodox Jewish law, the *halacha*, which stipulates that only children of Jewish women and converts can be regarded as Jews? Or should it be decided by the immigrant, on the basis that anybody who calls himself or herself Jewish should have a place in Israel?

In a series of cases since the 1950s, the Supreme Court opened a gap between secular law and the halacha. This might have been an arcane dispute, were it not for the monopoly on personal law granted to the rabbis. The result is an absurd situation whereby an immigrant may be welcomed as a Jew by the state, but find that he or she cannot marry a Jew or be buried with Jews and these disadvantages can be passed on to their children.

Religious parties have consistently agitated for secular legislation to conform with the Orthodox view. In 1970, the government modified the Law of Return with the halachic stipulation that a "Jew" means a person who was born of a Jewish mother or has become converted to Judaism. There was also the non-halachic requirement that the person should not be a member of another religion. Under Orthodox Jewish law, Jewishness is a question of biology rather than belief. A person born as a Jew can never stop being a Jew even if he is, say, a Catholic priest.

This legal compromise shifted the battleground to the question of "Who is a Convert?" and, related to it, the dispute over "Who is a Rabbi?" with the right to carry out conversions. In the 1988 election the religious parties, with the Lubavitcher Rebbe at the forefront, campaigned for the Law of Return to be amended to specify that only those converted to Judaism "according to the halacha" should be registered as Jews. This would have little impact in Israel, where only Orthodox conversions were recognized, but the dispute opened up a rift between Israel and the Diaspora, especially in the United States, where non-Orthodox rabbis from the Conservative and Reform streams are dominant.

Given the low rate of immigration from western countries, the change would have had little direct impact, but the proposal symbolically impugned the Judaism of the bulk of American Jewry; if accepted, the Jewish state would be telling the biggest and wealthiest diaspora community that its form of Judaism was not Judaism at all. Outraged American communities threatened to cut off donations to Israel. In any event, Labor and Likud formed a government of national unity, and the religious amendment was dropped.

The question of the legitimacy of non-Orthodox conversions continues to plague Israeli public life, however. In the late 1990s, Reform and Conservative rabbis raised the stakes by resorting to the courts and political pressure to win recognition for conversions carried out by their rabbis within Israel.

More serious than the impact on relations with the Diaspora is the fact that Israeli governments, and their dealings with the Arabs, are often held hostage to the whims of the religious parties.

In 1990, Rabbi Ovadia Yosef, spiritual leader of the Sephardi religious party, Shas, declared that he could no longer support the "extremist, warmongering government" headed by the Likud Prime Minister, Yitzhak Shamir. He backed the Labor party's attempt to set up a rival center-left coalition, but the maneuver foundered on the opposition of two other rabbis—the nonagenarian Rabbi Eliezer Schach, spiritual leader of the Degel ha-Torah party and the Lubavitcher Rebbe, who counted two crucial supporters in the Agudat Israel party.

The Rebbe, unlike other Hasidic sages, had openly espoused the vision of a "Greater Land of Israel" ever since Israel captured the West Bank in 1967. Questioned by an Israeli reporter, the Rebbe declared he was confident the Messiah would soon come, and added that "for the few minutes until then, we need the not-one-inch policy" (of Mr. Shamir).

At a rally in Tel Aviv, Rabbi Schach launched into a diatribe against secular Israelis:

> I want to speak out without fear. There are kibbutz members today who do not know what Yom Kippur is, what the Sabbath is, what the mikveh [ritual bath] is; they have no concept of Judaism; they rear rabbits and pigs. Do they have any link with their fathers? Can such a kibbutz survive? Did their fathers eat on Yom Kippur?. . . Can these people be called Jews?

Mr. Shamir now led a center-right government, arguably the most hardline coalition that Israel had seen on the issues of settlement and peace. Two aged and rival rabbis, one of whom was contemptuous of Zionism and the other one who did not even live in Israel, had conspired to determine the course of the Middle East.

The débâcle was a humiliation for Rabbi Ovadia Yosef, who at the time still deferred to the venerable Rabbi Schach. In the 1992 elections, however, Shas joined the victorious Labor party and made its final break from Rabbi Schach, not least because the Lithuanian sage had alienated oriental Jews by saying they were "not sufficiently mature to lead, either in Torah or in national affairs."

Shas is the political phenomenon of the late 1990s. Helped by a change in election rules which encouraged fragmentation in parliament, the party went from strength to strength regardless of which government was in power, and regardless of whether Shas was in the cabinet or in opposition. In the 1999 election Shas secured an astounding 17 seats, just two seats short of the defeated Likud party.

Shas is the only Haredi party to reach beyond its religious constituency. It is not only a religious party, but also an ethnic party carrying the flag of Sephardi revival. The key to its success is its social and educational network serving poor families of oriental Jews. To maintain its ever expanding institutions, however, Shas needs to be able to extract state funds and has been involved in repeated corruption scandals. Rabbi Yosef, famous for his controversial pronouncements against women and secular Israelis, has taken over the mantle of hate figure for the Left.

Inevitably, perhaps, there has been a backlash. In the elections of January 2003, Shas declined precipitously from 17 seats to 11. The star of the campaign was a fiercely secular Shinui party, led by the former television broadcaster Tommy Lapid. At a time of intense conflict with the Palestinians, his demand that yeshiva students be drafted into the army found a strong resonance. By coming in third in the election, he could take over the religious parties' role as a kingmaker and turn the tables on the rabbis. That, at least, was his hope.

Shinui had little to say on relations with Palestinians, beyond declaring that it was to the Right of Labor and to the Left of Likud. Instead it presented itself as the champion of the Ashkenazi middle class. Lapid's slogan was "freedom of religion and freedom from religion." Describing the religious parties' extortion of state funds as Mafia-like, and their restrictions as an affront to modernity, he demanded civil marriages and public transport on the Sabbath.

Lapid, a 71-year-old survivor of the Holocaust whose father died in the Mauthausen death camp, seemed to dislike oriental Jews almost as much as the rabbis. He told one Israeli interviewer: "If we let the East European Ghetto and the North African ghetto take over, we will have nothing to float on. We will blend into the Semitic region and be lost within a terrible Levantine dunghill."

Such views elicited an outraged response. Rabbid Yosef lumped Shinui and Meretz, the Left-wing secular party, as a common enemy. "These are evil ones. They cannot abide our Torah. Let there be a thistle in their eyes, let them go deaf, that they may not hear," he said.

Sephardi Jewry had been preeminent in Palestine until the nine-

teenth century. Its proud heritage harked back to the Golden Age of
Muslim-ruled Spain—known to Jews as Sepharad—before the Jews
were expelled at the end of the Christian *Reconquista* in 1492 and
spread through much of the Mediterranean world. Sephardim like to
point out that it was their medieval forebears who devised the Cab-
bala, whose esoteric and mystical teachings form a central part of
Ashkenazi Hasidic thought. Although favored by the Turkish authorities, Sephardim in Palestine steadily lost ground to the new arrivals
from eastern Europe. The British established separate chief rabbis for
Ashkenazim and Sephardim, an arrangement maintained by Israel.
"Sephardi" has become synonymous with oriental Jews, although
strictly speaking many Jews who immigrated from the rest of the
Middle East are not descended from Spanish Jews, and many
Sephardim came from European countries such as Italy and the
Balkans. Some prefer to describe oriental Jews in Israel as
Mizrahiyim, or "Easterners," which carries political as well as religious
connotations.

The Jews who arrived from Middle Eastern countries in the 1950s
and 1960s were, for the most part, poverty stricken and poorly educated. Oriental Jews who wanted to study the Talmud had to do so in
Ashkenazi yeshivas, and the first generation of Shas leaders emerged
from the "Lithuanian" educational system. Habad, too, was particularly active among oriental immigrants. Oriental Jews share with
Ashkenazi Haredim, especially the Hasidic sects, the belief in prayers
at the tombs of sages, faith in charms, and the power of the righteous
to cure illnesses and perform miracles. Both regard their background
in the Diaspora with pride and both feel excluded from centers of
power long dominated by the Labor-inspired, Ashkenazi-dominated
secular elite.

Many Sephardim put up pictures on their walls of both the Lubavitcher Rebbe and Baba Salli, a Moroccan sage who died in Israel in
1984 and is buried in the Negev town of Netivot.

Mizrahiyim make up roughly half of Israel's Jewish population.
Their electoral power cannot be ignored by any party. Yet oriental
Jews have spent much of their time trying to find their place in
Ashkenazi-run Israeli society. At first they voted for the Labor party,
drifted with the years toward the National Religious Party, then
strongly supported Likud and finally rallied around Shas in the 1990s.
Oriental Jews never went through the emancipation experienced by
European Jews, and never developed the same cultural rift between

religious and secular. They emerged from Muslim societies where religion and state were not separate as in Europe. Mizrahiyim are both more respectful of religion than secular Ashkenazi Jews, and more tolerant of secularism than Ashkenazi Haredim.

The Baghdad-born Shas leader, Rabbi Yosef likes to wear oriental finery of the office of Sephardi Chief Rabbi which he once held. At his weekly Saturday night gatherings in Jerusalem, when he holds forth on religious issues of the day, he is surrounded by oriental Jews dressed in the black suits and hats of Ashkenazi Haredim. Few images better sum up the dislocation of Sephardi Jews in Israel than the sight of oriental Jews engaged in religious revival in the costume of the shtetls, the eastern European Jewish hamlets.

★

The old central bus station in south Tel Aviv was crowded, noisy, and smelly, and its replacement in 1993 by a new multistory facility nearby did not come a moment too soon for Israel's hard-pressed commuters.

Yet with the passing of the old station, a piece of Israeli culture has also gone. The bus station was partly the country's transportation nerve center, and partly oriental souk. Little stalls selling fried food, sweets, clothing, and much more crammed the pavement around the bus lanes. Engine fumes mingled with the smoke of grilled meat, creating a distinctive smog. Above all there was the noise—the rattle of buses, the honking of horns, the bustle of passengers, loud oriental music played through underpowered speakers, and traders who shouted "Three cassettes for ten shekels!"

The bus station was the breeding ground for a new style of oriental underground music. *Muzika Mizrahit*, known condescendingly as "bus station music" or "cassette music," was not aggressive like its British contemporary, punk rock. There were no harsh electronic sounds, no abusive lyrics. Its words were not about anger, protest, or anarchy. Bus station music was a poor man's crooning about the age-old theme of unrequited love. It borrowed from Arabic, Turkish, Greek, Italian, French, and Spanish music, and blended these elements into sentimental and pathos-filled songs.

Israel's poorer and marginalized oriental Jews have often been compared to American blacks, but in many ways they are more similar to hillbillies. With its cheap synthesized sounds muzika mizrahit is a kind of Hebrew country-and-western. One expert describes the genre as having a "dramatic schlock-pop sound." Much of it sounds as if it is being played by a cheap wedding band. In fact, the music did originate from bands playing at the marriages and bar mitzvahs of oriental Jewish families.

Muzika mizrahit singers were long shunned by mainstream Israeli record companies. Radio stations refused to play their songs. It was not considered cool or avant-garde, but embarrassing. Oriental musicians resorted to recording their performances and distributing the cassettes at street markets, especially at the Tel Aviv bus station. The king of muzika mizrahit was born Zohar Arkabi of a Yemenite immigrant family in Rishon Le-Zion, but changed his name to the more Ashkenazi-sounding Argov. He had been a child cantor at his family's local synagogue, and emerged in 1977 as a popular singer with an emotional, nasal voice. It was just at the time when Mizrahiyim carried the Likud party to power. Argov broke into the mainstream in 1982 with his saccharine love song, *Ha-Perah Be-Gani* ("The Flower in My Garden").

Fame set him on a self-destructive path of drugs and alcohol. Friends recounted how Argov would visit them first in a Mercedes, then a cheaper Japanese-made Subaru, then a taxi, and finally by bus. The end came in 1987 when, at the age of 32, he hanged himself in a police cell in Rishon Le-Zion after being arrested on drugs charges.

The indifference of the musical establishment toward Argov became a symbol of the wider Ashkenazi contempt for Mizrahiyim. Later Argov became the subject of a highly popular play and film, books, and at least two television documentaries. In 1999, Rishon Le-Zion decided to honor him by naming one of its streets after the "king," but when councillors protested that immortalizing a drug addict would set a bad example, the city settled on naming the street "The Flower in My Garden."

Over the years muzika mizrahit has moved out of ghetto-like radio programs on "Mediterranean Music" into the mainstream. Moreover, the next generation of East–West fusion bands are the rage, but their works, while popular, are not yet part of the accepted musical canon of Israel. On Memorial Day for Israel's fallen, the songs on the radio are distinctly European even though many, perhaps most, of the dead are Mizrahiyim.

Avihu Medina, the best-known oriental songwriter who composed many of Zohar Argov's songs, is scathing of the "Bolshevist" Ashkenazi musical establishment. "I feel the prejudice every day, all day," he said. "All I have to do is turn on the radio. I don't hear my songs all day, all week, all month. I can say I am one of the greatest songwriters in Israel. A newspaper did a survey and found I was the third most popular songwriter. A year ago they did another survey of which songwriters get most air play, and I was number 52."

I met Medina at his home in Petach Tikva, part of the greater Tel Aviv sprawl. It was a modest bungalow with simple furniture. A keyboard and two guitars occupied a corner of the living room. Medina wore a blue T-shirt and jeans, and kept his hair short, like a former soldier. He explained that the Yemenites, as a sign of mourning for the destruction of the temple, used only drums and rhythm instruments. Medina learned how to play the guitar on a kibbutz where, as he put it, "I learned to be an atheist." He regularly won prizes in Mizrahi music festivals, often with patriotic lyrics such as "Don't be afraid, Israel, because you are a young lion, and when the lion is roaring everybody is afraid."

Medina's anger at the exclusion of oriental-style music boiled over after the 1973 Yom Kippur War, in which he served as a tank commander and was captured on the Egyptian front. "I came back from the war and wrote two songs which won second and third prize in the [Mizrahi] festival, but I did not hear them on the radio. I went to the radio station and asked why they were not playing them. They said 'They are not Israeli, they are oriental.' I thought I was going crazy. I was ready to die for the country. I was barely alive when I came back from the war and somebody who came from Poland 20 years earlier suddenly tells me I'm not Israeli. I was the third generation to be born in Israel, but if you want to be an Israeli, you have to come through Warsaw. After that incident I recognized the prejudice, the apartheid. I still feel it very strongly."

The oriental style was not always anathema to Israel's cultural establishment. In the prestate days of Israel there was a cultural movement to adopt Middle Eastern patterns of music, speech, and architecture as part of abandoning the Diaspora in Europe and trying to merge with the new Levantine surroundings. The growing conflict with the Arabs, culminating in the war of 1948, the influx of European Jews, and the contempt for "primitive" oriental immigrants conspired to move cultural tastes away from Arabic influences. Jews were now trying to be the flag-bearers of the western world in the Middle East. Singers of oriental extraction, especially Yemenite women, were popular as long as they did not stray too far from European conventions. A bit of eastern warbling was pleasingly exotic, but anything too oriental was unacceptable.

Yemenite Jews, Medina reminded me, arrived in Palestine in substantial groups as early as 1881, before the first Zionist settlers. They have as strong a claim to the country as any descendants of Ashkenazi pioneering families. The Yemenites were driven by the belief that the Messiah was about to appear, rather than by Zionist nationalism. They interpreted a passage from the Song of Solomon, "I will go up to the palm tree" (S. 7.8), as meaning Yemenites will "go up" (the same verb in Hebrew means to "ascend" to the Holy Land by making *aliyah*) in the year of the palm, *tamar* in Hebrew, whose letters in numerology are equivalent to the year 1880. A slightly different process yielded the year 1882.

A host of factors—for example, the departure of the first Yemenite families, rumors that Baron Rothschild was about to buy up tracts of land to give away to Jews and the greater ease of access to Palestine after the Ottoman occupation of Yemen and the opening of the Suez Canal—resulted in a large-scale migration. By the turn of the century, there were between 2,000 and 3,000 Yemenite immigrants in Jaffa and Jerusalem. By the time the Jewish state was declared, there were about 28,000 Yemenites in the country.

Oriental Jews emigrated to Palestine at a greater rate than European Jews, even in the romantic pioneering days of the Second Aliyah. By the eve of the First World War, oriental Jews made up a third of the Jewish population of Palestine although they accounted for, at most, just 8 percent of world Jews. The Yemenites were the largest and most united group, but there were also contingents from Bukhara, Georgia, Iran, Afghanistan, Iraq, Kurdistan, Syria, and North Africa.

The Yemenites endured great suffering in the Holy Land. Unlike the other Jewish communities supported by donations from the Diaspora, they had no wealthy patrons. Many lived in caves in the Kidron Valley outside the walls of Jerusalem and also worked as laborers in the earliest Zionist settlements, such as Rishon Le-Zion and Rehovot, where there are still Yemenite quarters.

At the end of 1910, the recently formed Palestine office of the Jewish National Fund sent out an emissary to convince more Yemenites to immigrate. The Yemenites were the Jewish peasantry that the Russian Zionists so ardently wanted to become. They built the Land of Israel as stonemasons, builders, and farm hands, but they did not sing about it to the world and their contribution was easily forgotten. Their story commands at most a footnote in mainstream Israeli history books.

★

"I had a baby brother. My father said he died when he was one year old but we have never been to his grave," recounted Avihu Medina. "He fell off his bed and bumped his head. My mother took him to hospital. Four days later they said he died. There was no funeral. I don't know if his death is the truth or a lie."

Hundreds, perhaps thousands, of Yemenite families have similar stories to tell about children who mysteriously disappeared in the 1940s and 1950s. Half a century later, nobody can tell them exactly what happened. Israeli experts tend to attribute the disappearance to administrative chaos in the hospitals where many children of immigrants died of malnutrition and disease after the arduous journey to Israel.

The loss is an unresolved trauma for the community. Stoked by a long-felt sense of injustice at the hands of the Ashkenazim, it has given rise to a widespread belief: that the Yemenite babies were kidnaped by government authorities, sold for adoption to Ashkenazi families, often to American Jews, and some were even used for medical experiments. The Labor establishment, the theory holds, knew all about the kidnapings and has covered up the truth to this day. The disappearance, say some Yeminite activists, is "the worst crime in the history of the Jewish people since the selling of Joseph to the Ishmaelites." Some call it their own "Holocaust," and what's worse, claim that it was perpetrated by other Jews. The sinister interpretation is supported by the emergence every once in a while of someone claiming to have rediscovered a long-lost child or sibling.

Nothing better distils the anger, resentment, pain, and bewilderment of the Mizrahiyim than the story of the lost Yemenite children. Medina himself claims to have met two such "stolen children." One of his recent songs, *Uvi'arta* ("You Shall Purge"), derives from the biblical injunction: "If a man be found stealing any of his brethren of the children of Israel, and maketh merchandise of him, or selleth him; then that thief shall die; and thou shalt put evil away [purge] from among you" (Deut. 24: 7).

Rage has turned to violence. In 1994 there was a shoot-out in Yehud between police officers and followers of Uzi Meshulam (called "rabbi" by his devotees although the Chief Rabbinate maintains he was never ordained) who had been a leading voice in the

campaign against the government's "cover-up." Meshulam's deten-
tion for five years turned him into a Yemenite martyr, and his follow-
ers were blamed for an unproven series of attacks, including the
murder of a senior prison officer. His followers speak of the "Ashke-
Nazis" and wear the yellow Star of David. One eatery in the town of
Rosh Ha'ayin run by a pro-Meshulam supporter is called the "Sold-
Yemenite Children Restaurant": its menu includes "One boy, $5,000;
One girl, $4,500."

After the birth of Israel, the Yemenites were the first of the Jewish
communities in the Middle East to be transplanted *en masse* to Israel.
About 48,000, virtually the whole community, were airlifted in early
1949 with the tacit approval of Yemen's rulers. The Yemenites' messianic expectations were cruelly dashed by the encounter with the
secular, socialist Zionist movement that had just triumphed over the
Arabs.

The Yemenites were regarded by sabras as strange, exotic creatures.
Their robes and dark skin gave them the appearance of being part of
a new biblical Exodus. One newspaper at the time described the
Yemenites as "a fabulous tribe, one of the most poetic of the tribes of
Israel." For Ben-Gurion, the sight of Jewish doctors caring for sick
and emaciated Yemenites amounted to "the birth pangs of the Messiah."

In March 1950, Jews in Iraq were allowed to leave on condition
that they left behind their possessions and renounced their citizenship. Under Operation Ezra and Nehemiah, more than 120,000 Iraqi
Jews were airlifted to Cyprus and then brought by ship to Israel. Jews
from North Africa also began to stream in, although the flow of
Moroccan Jewry, the largest of the Maghreb communities, did not
peak until the late 1950s and early 1960s.

As Jews came from dozens of countries, the Jewish population of
about 650,000 more than doubled between 1948 and 1951. It was seen
as a massive "rescue" from anti-Semitism, both of the European and
Arab varieties, although in many cases the Jews faced no imminent
danger. The rush bore little resemblance to Herzl's vision of a rigidly
ordered migration to avoid "serious disturbances," both in the old
countries and in the new homeland. Conditions in Israel's immigrant
camps were miserable. Epidemics were not uncommon. One member
of the Zionist Executive complained: "It is not an exaggeration to say
that the conditions were better in the refugee camps in Germany, after
the war." Some officials were struck by the irony of "Jews keeping
other Jews in camps." Many worried that the camps bred laziness,

degenerates, and "counterrevolutionaries." But for all the muttering within the government about the "poor human material" pouring into the country, no leader dared to turn off the taps of mass migration.

European and oriental Jews were subjected to similar indignities in the camps, but the Ashkenazi immigrants fared better. Being the first arrivals, European Jews received the best of the abandoned Arab houses. Soon oriental Jews formed a disproportionate number of the residents of immigrant camps, and of the later *ma'abarot*, or transition camps, where there were no communal dining halls and residents arranged much more of their domestic lives. Immigrants could go out to work, and children attended school. Many ma'abarot were placed on the edge of towns, or became towns in their own right. Although the ma'abarot were an improvement, there was not enough work to go around.

Many European immigrants had families already living in Israel who could help them integrate, and in time a considerable number received reparations from Germany. In the autumn of 1949, writes Tom Segev in *The First Israelis*, the Polish government gave permission for the country's Jews to emigrate and the Israeli authorities secretly resolved to give them privileged treatment. In the minutes of the meetings of the Jewish Agency, officials argued that "a good many of us are of the same tribe" as the Poles. One declared: "It will be a blessing to the country. [. . .] That's why I suggest we give them priority in housing. The Polish Jews have been living well. For them, the camps are much harder than for the Yemenites, for whom even the conditions in the camps mean liberation."

In those days learned academics argued that the "primitive mentality" of the newcomers should be understood as similar to that of children, the retarded, and the mentally disturbed. In 1950, *Ha'aretz* published what would become a notorious diatribe against North Africans. "The primitiveness of these people is unsurpassable. They have almost no education at all, and what is worse is their inability to comprehend anything intellectual. As a rule, they are only slightly more advanced than the Arabs, Negroes, and Berbers in their countries. It [their education] is certainly even lower than that of the former Palestinian Arabs. [. . .] Many of them suffer from serious eye diseases, as well as skin and venereal diseases. I have yet to mention robbery and theft. Nothing is safe from this anti-social element, no lock is strong enough. [. . .]"

Ben-Gurion was not immune to such prejudices. Segev quotes an article by Ben-Gurion from 1954 in which he explained that "in the past few hundred years the Jews of Europe have led the nation, in both quantity and quality." They were the "leading candidates for citizenship in the State of Israel," and this was the significance of the Holocaust. "Hitler, more than he hurt the Jewish people, whom he knew and detested, hurt the Jewish State, whose coming he could not foresee. He destroyed the substance, the main and essential building force of the state. The state arose and did not find the nation which had waited for it." In the absence of the nation, Israel had to bring the Jews of the Arab countries, said Ben-Gurion.

*

On the road from Ashkelon to Beersheva, the town of Sderot brashly announces its existence with a large billboard displaying a picture of a pleasant-looking girl with the words SDEROT—A BEAUTY OF A PLACE.

It was put up after Miri Bohadna, a daughter of Sderot, was crowned Miss Teen Israel in 1995. The slogan is an act of supreme confidence, chutzpah even, for a community that at the turn of the Millennium was ranked second from the bottom of the socioeconomic index among Jewish towns in Israel, lower even than several Arab communities.

Sderot grew out of a ma'abara tent camp established in 1951 as part of a chain of settlements designed to contain infiltration from the Gaza Strip. For years it had no electricity or running water. It was at first populated by Jews from Iran and Kurdistan, and from the mid-1950s by North Africans, mainly from Morocco. Sderot is typical of the "development towns" in the Negev. The desert was Ben-Gurion's brave new frontier, the Jewish state's strategic hinterland. It was supposed to be fertilized by the toil of oriental immigrants, and bloom with their sweat. The patriotic photographs of the 1950s show immigrants arriving in ma'abarot and new towns in dramatic monochrome, often shot from a low angle looking upward to highlight the thrust, determination, hope and heroism of the times, the stuff of living poetry.

Today, however, the cities in the desert represent the marginalization of its inhabitants, especially oriental Jews. The industries founded in the 1950s are being forced to close down, and there is little to replace them. A few of these new towns, such as the port of Ashdod, have been successes, but many are unemployment black spots. The term "Development Town" has become a euphemism for underdevelopment.

The statistics for 1997 show that development towns had an

unemployment rate of 12.7 percent, sharply higher than the national figure of 7.7 percent and nearly double the 6.4 percent rate of Tel Aviv. Mizrahiyim who make up most of the population of development towns are the vast majority of prison inmates. Many more Ashkenazim than Sephardim go to university and work as doctors, lawyers, and top managers. Overall, on average they earn one and a half times more than Sephardim. In Sderot, the average monthly wage is about NIS (Israeli shekels) 3,000, roughly a third of the national average. In a country of immigrants, Sderot has a negative migration rate, meaning that anybody given a chance will leave town, usually for Tel Aviv.

Tippex, a band that emerged from Sderot to become one of the best-known bands of the 1990s, mocks development towns built by ministerial fiat, in a song entitled "Dust Heights."

Sderot has, of late, developed an abundance of musical talent, becoming the crucible of at least half a dozen popular bands fusing elements of eastern and western sounds. Its inhabitants like to compare Sderot to, well, Liverpool, the birthplace of the Beatles. There is no Cavern Club for fans to crowd into; instead those hoping to be discovered as the stars of the future rehearse after school hours in bomb shelters.

Nobody can explain precisely what drives Sderot's musical renaissance. What is certain, however, is that the central figure is Haim Uliel. Greeting me at his home in a pair of shorts and a white T-shirt, he hardly looked the part of the patriarch of Israel's new musical genre, arguably the first authentic Israeli sound. He used to hear Moroccan and Arabic music played in his father's café, but found it embarrassing. When he started out in a local band, they played Led Zeppelin covers. Over time, however, he found himself increasingly comfortable in the oriental style. Uliel's Moroccan-style band, Sfatayim, or "Lips," made its mark in 1990. Its success inspired another group, Renaissance, whose trio sing exclusively in Moroccan Arabic. Then there was Tippex, known in English as Tea-Packs, led by Kobi Oz, the former keyboard player of Sfatayim.

Uliel has never left Sderot. "I know that if I had gone to Tel Aviv I would have been ten times more successful," he said. "I don't know why I love this place." In his living room, with black leather furniture arranged precisely, if starkly, within the whitewashed walls, Uliel played a track from his latest CD. "From Morocco to Zion," an oriental chant over complex drum rhythms, was an ode to the fortitude of his parents' generation. Uliel spoke of Morocco as a paradise lost, a place where almost every Jewish family had money, land, and "two or three Arab servants in their house." His comments brought to mind a poem by Erez Biton about the fate of Zohara al-Fasia, one of many musicians and singers who had been famous in the Arab world before coming to Israel.

> Zohara Al-Fasia
> Singer at the court of Muhammad the Fifth in Rabat in Morocco.
> They say of her that when she sang,
> Soldiers fought with knives
> To carve their way through the crowd
> To touch the hem of her dress
> To kiss the tips of her fingers
> To lay down silver riyals as a sign of thanks.
>
> Zohara Al-Fasia
> Today you can find her
> In Ashkelon, in Block 3, beside the welfare office
> The smell of remains of sardine tins on a wobbly three-legged table
> Stained regal carpets on a Jewish Agency bed
> Staring, in a dressing gown,
> For hours in the mirror
> At cheap garish makeup
> And when she says: Muhammad the Fifth is the apple of our eye
> At first you don't understand.

Uliel's parents immigrated to Israel in 1954. "They came to the ma'abara in Sderot just as the town was being established. There were just a few huts." His father, like most of the men, found seasonal work in the kibbutzim. There was not enough employment to go around for the population of about 3,000 immigrants. Those with skills left; the rest languished in poverty. Frustration exploded in 1956, one month after the end of the Sinai campaign. Water to Sderot had been cut off, except for one tap, because the municipality had not paid its bills. When the man who paid out the dole fell ill and did not turn up on the appointed day, a mob shouting for "water and bread" burst into the employment office and burned it down. Uliel's father was among the leaders of the riot. "My father said that if there is no work in Sderot, why do you need an employment office?" said Uliel.

The riot, said Uliel, was the beginning of "the war." Three years later, Moroccans rioted in Wadi Salib, a slum that had once been an

Arab quarter of Haifa. In the early 1970s, a militant group of oriental Jews calling themselves the Black Panthers, after the movement of black Americans in the late 1960s, agitated for better conditions for Sephardim. Golda Meir, demonstrating the disconnection from reality in the dying days of the Labor government, could only comment that the Black Panthers were "not nice boys." Even after its crushing defeat in 1977, Labor remained haughty.

Mizrahiyim remain staunch Likud voters, even though Labor's policy of redirecting money from West Bank settlements to the development towns would benefit many oriental Jews. According to Uliel, many Moroccans' political outlook may be conservative on social issues but it is moderate on the questions of war and peace. But still the resentment lingers. "You don't vote for Likud because you hate the Arabs," he explained, as if stating the obvious. "You vote for Likud because you hate the Labor party."

The mutual incomprehension between oriental immigrants and the Labor establishment in the early decades of the state is captured in *Tarnegol Kapparot*, "Sacrificial Chicken," a novel by Eli Amir published in 1983. In the story of an immigrant youngster who leaves a kibbutz to return to the ma'abara, in defiance of the prevailing pioneering ideal, Amir expresses much of the frustration he experienced when he arrived in Israel from Baghdad in 1950, at the age of 12.

The book opens with the main character, Nuri, a teenager recently arrived from Iraq, catching a bus to an assembly point where kibbutz representatives select immigrants to join their communities. As the hopefuls line up, trying to be chosen by the most desirable kibbutzim, Nuri has a flashback of his first encounter with Israel—being sprayed with DDT:

No sooner had we arrived in Lod than the disinfectors were upon us, sprayer in hand. The white dust stung my eyes and made me want to cry and shout out: "I'm not a diseased fruit! What are you doing to me?" Then suddenly I saw my father, arrayed in his best suit ready to greet the longed-for bride, the land to which he turned three times a day—and now his blue-striped suit was speckled with white patches [...] he was so perplexed and helpless that I wanted to weep for what they had done to my father.

It has long been said that Israel loves immigration, but hates immigrants. In the 1950s many sabras complained of oriental immigrants living for free at the expense of the state. In the early 1990s the tables were turned with the flood of immigrants leaving the wreckage of the Soviet Union. It was the turn of veteran Israelis, among them many Sephardim, to grumble about the burden of absorbing the "Russians."

Sderot's population more than doubled from about 10,000 to 23,000 in the 1990s. "Sderot used to be like a large family," muttered Uliel. "You could look at a child's face and know who his parents were." Now, Uliel complained, Sderot has lost its character. "You cannot integrate that many people," he said. "You now hear people standing in line at a bank swearing at the new immigrants. Moroccans have started leaving their wives and taking up with Russian women. The government has brought people who have no idea of what religion is. On Shabbat they have barbecues. It looks kind of strange. For forty years on Yom Kippur nobody has traveled, and suddenly now there are cars on the roads."

*

A muffled piano melody filtered through the front door of the flat. I lingered on the landing outside for a moment, then knocked. The musical spell was abruptly broken. A woman with a shock of dyed blond hair—too blond—greeted me with a sunny smile.

Natasha Gnatovskaya was the housekeeper, and musical companion, of Edith Kraus, an accomplished concert pianist who had suffered a stroke five years earlier. Gnatovskaya had herself been an acclaimed pianist in her native Ukraine, but like other immigrants, she and her husband, a fellow musician, were still scraping a living doing cleaning jobs.

Theirs was a common story of the vast *aliyah* from the Soviet Union in the 1990s. Supremely qualified professionals found themselves doing menial and underpaid work, and many never regained the prestige they had enjoyed as doctors, musicians, engineers, or scientists. Nearly half the suicides in Israel in the 1990s were committed by immigrants from eastern Europe.

Gnatovskaya had one consolation, however: Kraus was as much of a soul mate as an employer. Kraus was born in Vienna of Czech parents. Gustav Mahler was her great-uncle on her father's side. In 1949 she arrived in Israel from Prague with her husband and her two-year-old daughter. She gave music lessons in Givatayim, now part of Greater Tel Aviv, while her husband worked in a factory and later tried his hand in the textile business. "He started selling neckties. It would have been astonishing if it had gone well. Nobody wears a necktie in Tel Aviv," she said. Kraus shrugged off the difficulties of readjusting to life in Israel. "We did not expect a paradise," she said.

Kraus particularly enjoyed playing works by Viktor Ullmann and Pavel Haas, composers who, like her, had been at Theresienstadt. Unlike Kraus, however, they were murdered at Auschwitz in 1944. Kraus moved to Jerusalem after her husband's death in 1984, but she continued to work for many years, making her last recording just before her stroke in 1993. Despite Kraus's illness, Gnatovskaya was full of admiration for her talent. "When I heard her play it sounded like somebody playing at the age of 20," she said.

The women made an odd couple. One the vivacious, if slightly bewildered, new immigrant. The other a central European *grande dame* whose aristocratic manners had not been eroded either by her three-year passage through the Nazi "model" concentration camp at Theresienstadt, or by decades of living among abrasive Israelis, or by the stroke that had partly paralyzed her.

Gnatovskaya came to Israel from Kharkov in the Ukraine in 1991, at the height of the influx of immigrants from the Soviet Union. One popular joke at the time was that any Soviet immigrant not carrying a violin case was probably a pianist. Gnatovskaya was one of those not carrying a violin case. She had been teaching at Kharkov's musical academy, and performed in concerts abroad. More than 700,000 Jews from the former Soviet Union have emigrated to Israel since 1990, in the biggest wave of *aliyah* since the upheaval of Mizrahiyim in the 1950s.

Unlike the early immigrants, today's "Russians" have come to a developed western economy. They were not dumped in tent camps, but housed in flats or hotels, given living allowances, tax breaks to buy appliances, and free Hebrew tuition. None of this amounts to luxury, but it is unheard-of generosity when compared with the conditions of penury which Moroccans and others had suffered. Even so, said Gnatovskaya, nothing was easy. "The country is very small, and there are many musicians who came to Israel. There are a lot of musicians who are not very good, but you cannot just come in and throw them out to make room for people from outside," she explained in broken Hebrew with a thick Russian accent. "My first job was like everybody else—cleaning. I did not imagine that we would have to do this kind of work. No language, no contacts with Israelis, no advice, no help. Half a million immigrants, and all are like sheep."

Unlike many of the Soviet immigrants who would have preferred to make their new homes in western Europe or the United States but found the way barred, Gnatovskaya, at the urging of her husband, chose to settle in Israel: he considered those who went to Germany as "people without principles" who care only about money. She went on: "I don't want to be looked at as a pauper sneaking into somebody's pocket. Here, if anyone on the bus shouts 'stinking Russian' at me I can tear off their head. Here I have the right to do it. In Germany I don't."

If the Sephardim were offended by the ungodliness of Israel in the 1950s, the Russians generally find the country oppressively religious for their assimilated taste. They are frequently humiliated by Orthodox rabbis' doubts over their Jewishness. There have been cases of Russian immigrants dying as Jews in terrorist attacks, only to be refused burial in a Jewish cemetery because of suspicions that they might be goyim. More than once, the rabbis have circumcised corpses of Russian immigrant men before burying them. A steady trickle of Russians has flowed out of Israel, with Canada being one of the favorite destinations.

The Russians in Israel have become, arguably, the most volatile and important group of swing voters in Israeli politics. In a country where voting patterns are highly rigid, the Russians helped to sweep to power Labor in 1992, Likud in 1996, Labor in 1999, and Likud again in 2000. It took Sephardim a whole generation to make their political weight felt, while the Russians successfully fielded their own political party, led by the former Soviet dissident Natan Sharansky, who first entered the cabinet in 1996, just five years after the start of the Russian influx. The Russians have been pulled in every direction. Right-wingers want them to help populate the West Bank, left-wingers see them as a secular bulwark against religious encroachment, strategists regard them as a weapon in the demographic battle with the Arabs, economists calculate their importance as human capital, while sports enthusiasts hope they will help improve Israel's dismal performance in international sporting contests. To some extent, all have been disappointed; the majority of Russians have been too preoccupied by problems of daily living to concern themselves with the great national questions.

The arrival of the Soviet immigrants was nevertheless a momentous turn of events for Israel. If the fall of the Berlin Wall allowed the two sides of Germany to be reunited, it also permitted Israel to rediscover the Ashkenazi Diaspora left in the Russian lands, the birthplace of pioneering Zionism. On November 9, 1917, the *Times* reported two events side by side. One was a brief note carrying the text of the

Balfour Declaration; the other was news of the rise of the Bolsheviks in the Soviet Union. Under the headline COUP D'ETAT IN PETROGRAD, the paper reported that "The extreme wing of the Petrograd Soviet, under the leadership of the pacifist, agitator Lenin, announces that it has deposed the Provisional Government of M. Kerensky. . . ."

One item recorded the promise of the Jewish state, the other the promise of "an immediate democratic peace" under Communism. Communism and Zionism had been competing ideologies among Russian Jews, but at the end of the twentieth century the former has collapsed while Zionism has triumphed. No more proof is needed than the exodus of Russian Jewry to Israel.

★

Ben-Gurion airport at 20:45 on May 24, 1991. It was a Friday night. An El Al jumbo jet landed on the tarmac and taxied to a halt in front of a throng of soldiers, officials, and journalists. The plane was marked with large letters spelling out CARGO.

Moments later, the doors opened to reveal the precious shipment: hundreds of shy, bewildered, and bedraggled Ethiopian Jews. A boy waved effusively. Old men in white robes shuffled down the steps, clinging to the rail. A blind woman was led down by a child. Many were barefoot. It was a scene drawn from the biblical Exodus, except that these Jews did not walk through the Red Sea but were carried aloft over it, a feat that for many of the immigrants was almost as miraculous.

They had no possessions except for some who clutched plastic bags. Israeli soldiers rushed up the steps to help the frail. Many still had stickers on their foreheads, placed there by Israeli officials trying to identify family groups to be airlifted out of Addis Ababa. The reception committee lost all dignity and swamped the new arrivals. In the crush of people, I felt something touch my hand. It was a little Ethiopian boy grasping my fingers and grinning. "Shalom," he said.

The scene was played out just a few months after Israel had been powerless as Iraq rained Scud missiles on its cities during the Gulf War. Here, finally, was something to cheer about. It was a moment of wonder for all Israeli Jews; Zionism was proving its role as a refuge. For the first time in history, declared the Prime Minister, Yitzhak Shamir, black people were being transported not to slavery, but to freedom.

The arrival of the Ethiopian Jews, calling themselves *Beta Israel* (House of Israel) was part of the same realignment of the post-Cold-

War world that brought the Russians. As the Soviet Union collapsed, its Ethiopian client, the Marxist dictator Mengistu Haile Mariam, lost the civil war. With rebel troops closing on Addis Ababa, Israel secured permission to airlift Ethiopian Jews who had been waiting in the capital for a chance to escape the looming chaos. It was a small window of opportunity, opened with the help of American diplomatic pressure and some strategically placed bribes totalling about $30 million. In short, Israel ransomed the Ethiopian Jews at the cost of about $2,000 each.

Some two dozen aircraft—El Al airliners, military transporters, and even an Ethiopian Airlines plane—ferried about 15,000 Beta Israel in a continuous air bridge lasting just over a day under the code-name of "Operation Solomon." Addis Ababa's airport was turned for that time into an extension of sovereign Israel. No visas were required to leave; all you needed was approval from Israeli officials on the ground who had the power to decide who was a Jew and who was not. The logistics experts calculated that by stripping the aircraft to the bare minimum (some planes had only a carpet of mattresses to accommodate the passengers) and by estimating that the average underfed Ethiopian weighed much less than Israelis, they would be able to carry an unprecedented number of passengers. The jumbo I saw carried 1,068 passengers, a record for the aviation books.

Like the Yemenites who arrived more than four decades earlier, the Ethiopians were regarded as a fascinating and romantic tribe of Israel. The folklore of the Beta Israel claims the community descended from the Jewish followers of Menelik, revered in Ethiopian legends as the son of the union between King Solomon and the Queen of Sheba, and the founder of the Ethiopian royal house. They are called "Falashas" by other Ethiopians, a term meaning "Wanderers" or "Strangers." Once commonly used, the name is now considered derogatory.

The Beta Israel follow a form of religion based on biblical injunctions rather than rabbinical teaching. The existence of Ethiopian Jews was known to the twelfth-century Jewish traveler, Benjamin of Tudela, and his contemporary, the Arab geographer Idrisi. In the sixteenth-century, Rabbi David ibn Zimra issued a ruling that the Falashas were "of the seed of Israel, of the Tribes of Dan." Christian missionaries wrote extensively about the Falashas and tried to convert them, but it was not until the end of the nineteenth century that the rest of the Jewish world took an active interest in the well-being of the Beta Israel, in large part as a reaction to the activities of the missionaries.

Once Israel was established, a pro-Falasha movement brought a group of Ethiopian children to study Hebrew, receive a Jewish education and return to Ethiopia to spread the knowledge. Israeli leaders, however, were opposed to any mass immigration: bureaucratic correspondence in 1949 and 1950 quoted in Tom Segev's *1949: The First Israelis* includes letters from officials saying they were "horrified" by reports that the Falashas might be brought in. One complained that "these people's ways are not much different from those of the Abyssinians," that "intermarriage is common among them" and that they include "a large number of people with venereal diseases."

Ethiopian Jews trickled into Israel at a rate of no more than a few dozen a year until the late 1970s. With the downfall of the Emperor Haile Selassie, there were growing demands from Ethiopians in Israel and their supporters among American Jews for the Falashas to be brought to Israel. In 1973, Rabbi Ovadia Yosef, then the Sephardi Chief Rabbi, issued the crucial ruling that "the Falashas are Jews, whom it is our duty to redeem from assimilation, to hasten their immigration to Israel, to educate them in the spirit of our holy Torah, and to make them partners in the building of our sacred land."

Menachem Begin was more sympathetic to the Ethiopian Jews than his predecessors, and in 1979 pledged to speed up their immigration. Israel had been able to bring a small number of Jews in exchange for providing weapons to the Marxist regime, but disclosure of the deal in 1978 ended the arrangement. From 1980, the Mossad set up a clandestine route through Sudan. Pushed by oppression, and pulled by news of the clandestine passage to Israel, the stream of Ethiopian Jews turned into a flood heading northward. Under pressure from the United States, Sudan permitted an airlift of about 8,000 Beta Israel under Operation Moses, which was interrupted by premature publicity. It was not until the fall of Mengistu that the remaining Jews could join their relatives in Israel.

"Half of my dream was fulfilled," said Tamir Tamiat, a teacher born in the northern Gondar region of Ethiopia who was brought to Israel as a 16-year-old boy in Operation Moses, "I always dreamed that I would find the temple in Jerusalem as it was described in the Bible. When I came I saw that it was destroyed. The dream was not reality."

The Ethiopians did not suffer the indignities of being sprayed with DDT or having their sidecurls cut by the sabras, but there were other humiliations. First there was the demand by the Orthodox establishment that Ethiopians undergo a symbolic circumcision and perform

a ritual immersion as a "renewal of Judaism"; in other words, the rabbis doubted the Jewishness of Ethiopians. Many rabbis refuse to
marry Ethiopians, and resist any attempt officially to recognize
Ethiopian *kessim* or priests. In 1995, it emerged that Israeli health
authorities routinely discarded all blood donated by Ethiopians
because of the perceived risk of infection with HIV.

The more than 60,000 Ethiopian Jews in Israel are still the poorest
and least educated of the immigrants. They are most likely to be languishing in "temporary" caravan parks far away from other population centers or in slum-like neighborhoods. More than 10 percent of
Ethiopian children who came in Operation Moses drop out of
school. Ethiopian Jews do not have the numerical power of either the
Sephardim or the Russians. Their skin color immediately sets them
apart from the rest of society. A growing number have made it into
university, but as the society polarizes, slogans such as "Death to the
Whites" have begun to appear on the walls of some Ethiopian neighborhoods. The Tel Aviv bus station is the gathering place for
Ethiopian youngsters where some pass the time drinking, stealing, or
doing drugs.

Those who can afford it spend weekend nights at Soweto, a club
on Tel Aviv's beachfront. The hall shakes with the reggae beat of Bob
Marley. Walls are covered with psychedelic pictures of the Jamaican
idol and Haile Selassie, the "Conquering Lion of the Tribe of Judah,"
who is regarded by Rastafarians as God incarnate. It was late on a
Friday night when I went to the Soweto club. Most of the revelers
had already gone home. A few teenagers studied their own dancing
moves in front of mirrors. The pounding rhyme of Bob Marley's
song, "Iron Lion Zion," washed over me, but suddenly, listening to
them in Israel, they took on a strange and new meaning.

The Zion of Bob Marley is not Israel, but Ethiopia, and his children of Israel are not the Jews, but blacks. It was like seeing a familiar
figure in a distorting mirror. The name of the club . . . Marley's
lyrics . . . These Ethiopian teenagers were being transported back to
Africa. They were not so much a part of the Jewish people who had
come home to their Promised Land, as part of the world's black
Diaspora.

★

Operation Solomon was not the end of the Ethiopian Diaspora.
Soon after the 1991 airlift was over, it emerged that remote commu-

nities of Beta Israel had been left behind. Moreover, Israel faced the dilemma of what to do about the thousands of so-called *Falas Mora*, clansmen of Ethiopian Jews who had converted to Christianity and were hoping to join relatives in Israel. Their link to Judaism is tenuous, and, as one relative brings another, there is potentially no end to the number of Ethiopians who could claim citizenship in Israel.

Throughout the world there are countless people claiming, like the Ethiopian Jews, to be members of the "Lost Tribes" of Israel—the ten tribes which the Bible says were dispersed when the northern kingdom (which split from the southerners after the death of King Solomon) was destroyed by the Assyrians.

Dozens, perhaps hundreds of far-flung groups counting tens of millions of people claim to descend from the ten tribes. They include the Pathans, a clan of Sunni Muslim warriors straddling both sides of the Afghani–Pakistani border and numbering around 15 million people. Some Ibo of Nigeria, a mostly Christian people of nearly 20 million, have been turned down in their attempt to immigrate as descendants of Israelites. Research in the late 1990s showed that the Lemba of southern Africa, who claim to be Jews, had a particularly high percentage of a DNA marker known as the "Cohen Gene."

The discovery of lost tribes is endlessly fascinating to Jews. Some Israelis, such as a group called *Amishav* (My People Returns), actively seek out lost tribes and organize their immigration. In the early 1990s the group arranged the conversion to Judaism by members of the Shinlung tribe on the Indian–Burmese border and helped them emigrate to Israel.

If Ben-Gurion had once argued that Israel should admit anyone crazy enough to call himself Jewish, today's Israeli leaders are worrying about how to keep out the impoverished masses of the world. The influx of tens of thousands of non-Jews among Russian immigrants—between 10 and 50 percent of the immigrants, depending on who is making the estimate—has already reopened the arguments over who is a Jew. There are growing demands for the Law of Return to be tightened. In a column in the *Jerusalem Report* magazine calling for a restriction of immigration, the author Ze'ev Chafets asked: "Who Isn't a Jew?"

The mass migration of the early 1990s has all but drained the reservoir of Jews in distress. Observers have started to talk of the "End of *aliyah*." Zionism's task of rescuing Jews is more or less complete. What is left is the well-integrated Jewish population of the western

world, especially the United States, whose six million Jews still out-
number the Jewish population in Israel. The largest Jewish city in the
world is not Tel Aviv, but New York.

Israeli immigration officials talk of convincing these successful
Jews that while they may not be in physical danger, they face a life of
"spiritual distress" because of growing assimilation. Some Israeli leaders have even ventured to suggest that more than Israel needs American Jewry to survive, American Jews need the link to Israel to
preserve their identity. Fewer than 2,000 American Jews make their
way to Israel every year. They are usually the politically or religiously
committed, or the misfits. Many return to the United States within a
few years.

In *Altneuland*, Herzl predicted that Jews who had migrated to
America would pick themselves up once again and move to Palestine. Nearly a century later, however, most American Jews would
rather live in a climate of tolerance, democratic freedom, and capital-
ism, even at the cost of assimilation. Given Israel's chronic conflict
with the Arabs, interfering rabbis, and overbearing government, the
Land of Opportunity is more attractive than the Promised Land.

7

The Curse of Peace

THE APACHE HELICOPTERS appeared over the Mediterranean in broad daylight. They fired their missiles toward Gaza's shore for more than an hour, blasting away at bases of the Palestinian security forces, the Fatah movement's offices, and even the skiffs of the pathetic Palestinian "navy."

This attack, on a scale unseen in the years of Palestinian autonomy, was Israel's retribution for the lynching of two Israeli reserve soldiers by a Palestinian mob in the town of Ramallah just a few hours earlier on October 12, 2000. It was much more than revenge, however. It was a display of impotent rage; a public admission of failure. Seven years after signing the Oslo accords, Israel was throwing its military might at its "peace partner." Just a few weeks earlier, Israel had regarded the Palestinian security forces as vital allies in containing the "enemies of peace." Now they were the enemy.

From his office on the Gaza beachfront, Yasser Arafat looked out over the sea as the Israelis sent him what amounted to a blunt warning that all he had painstakingly achieved from the day in 1991, when the Palestinian delegation at the Madrid peace talks stood up to speak with its own voice, could be lost. Arafat's embryonic "state"— with its trappings of ministries, security forces, flags and international airport—could be crushed at a moment's notice.

And yet Arafat's lieutenants found the Palestinian "President" strangely serene, even elated. "It was like he was back in the old days in Beirut," said one aide. "The President looked out and shook his head. The security men urged the President to leave. But he replied: 'I challenge you all to stay. I will stay.' We all stayed. He continued working at his desk and made telephone calls to find out what was going on. Some missiles struck a few hundred yards away from the office. Within minutes thousands of people came to defend the building as human shields, but we begged them to go home."

At the time of the attack, Arafat was meeting the United Nations' special envoy, Terje Larsen. "The whole building was shaking. Larsen was terrified and he wanted to go to his armored car," said one Arafat aide, laughing, as we drank coffee in a room on the first floor of Arafat's office later that night. "We are not scared. The Israelis are more powerful than us. They can start the war, but only we can decide when to end it—and if there is a war it will only end in Tel Aviv." Until that night, the violence that had engulfed the West Bank and Gaza Strip for the previous fortnight might have been another (albeit more intense) spasm of the sort that has punctuated the "peace process" as it shuddered forward. Arafat had previously been accused by Israel of failing to do enough to stop violence. With the helicopter raid, Arafat was firmly identified as the moving force behind the violence.

Despite the repeated efforts of the international community to prevent a spiral of bloodshed, Israelis and Palestinians became locked in the dreadful and seemingly inescapable confrontation that became known as the Al-Aqsa Intifada. The Palestinian uprising quickly evolved from the ritualistic rage of stone-throwing riots into the bloody chaos of a communal war, with guerrilla-style attacks, terrorist carnage, Israeli reprisal raids and the full-scale military reinvasion of Palestinian cities. Its consequences are impossible to predict. Will the revolt escalate into a wider war, sucking in neighboring Arab countries, ultimately carrying the risk that weapons of mass destruction will be used? Or is it the last bloodstained confrontation before both sides exhaust themselves and accept the inevitability of a negotiated compromise?

At the time of writing, in February 2003, more than two years after the start of the uprising, there is no sign of the fires of hatred burning themselves out. It has become increasingly difficult to give an accurate number of victims of the conflict. Different groups give slightly different figures. B'tselem, the Israeli human rights group, has counted more than 2,500 dead between the start of the Intifada and the end of January 2003. These include 1,834 Palestinians killed by Israelis, and 669 Israelis killed by Palestinians. Palestinian groups put the number of Palestinian dead at around 2,000.

The uprising propelled the Middle East back to the age of utter mutual hostility that had supposedly been overcome by the 1993 Oslo accords and the establishment of Palestinian autonomy that brought

Arafat back to his homeland. Anti-Israeli rhetoric, often outright anti-Semitism, rose through the Arab world as Arab satellite television beamed images of the struggle for Palestine directly to individual homes. In Israel, meanwhile, those calling for the "transfer" of Palestinians have gained an audience among Jews with their message that the only way to get rid of terrorism is to get rid of the Palestinians.

Israelis have felt a degree of personal fear that was supposed to have been banished by the creation of the Jewish state. Palestinians, in turn, have been subjected to repressive measures unseen since the start of the occupation in 1967, while the infrastructure and institutions of their future state have been progressively destroyed by Israel.

Far from ending the century of conflict between Jew and Arab, the Oslo accords seem merely to have brought the war back home after it had been pushed beyond Israel's borders for five decades. In the attempt to establish Palestinian self-rule, the West Bank has become "Lebanonized" into a bewildering patchwork of Israeli and Palestinian cantons, with a proliferation of armed groups including Jewish settlers and a constellation of Palestinian factions.

In Lebanon, and earlier in Jordan, the Palestinians created a kind of "state-within-a-state" and helped to precipitate a chaotic civil war. With the defeat of Ehud Barak in the Israeli election in 2001, Ariel Sharon and Yasser Arafat, the two main protagonists of the 1982 Lebanon war, now septuagenarians, came face to face again in the glare of international attention. As in Beirut in 1982, Arafat has been repeatedly besieged by Israeli forces only to survive another day. Suicide bombings, a tactic first devised in Lebanon, have become appallingly commonplace, carried out by men and women, adults and teenagers alike. The sight of Israel's withdrawal from south Lebanon earlier in the year, after nearly two decades of occupation, may have emboldened many Palestinians into thinking that they too can inflict enough pain on Israel to make it withdraw from the territories occupied in 1967. The Palestinians, admittedly, have nothing like the RPGs, artillery and tanks they possessed in Lebanon. But they have enough weaponry to ensure that, for the first time since Israel took the West Bank and Gaza Strip in 1967, the Jewish state has been forced repeatedly to resort to using heavy weapons such as tanks, helicopter gunships and even jets.

There has been a process of brutalization as the conflict has dragged on. The first phase of the Intifada was dominated by mass revolt, with the *shebab*, or Palestinian youth, manning the barricades and throwing stones at Israeli positions. These clashes produced some of the most powerful, iconic images of the Al-Aqsa Intifada, such as the David-and-Goliath scene of Faris Odeh, a 12-year-old boy, throwing stones at an Israeli tank in the Gaza Strip. Despite warnings from his school, beatings from his father and entreaties from his mother not to go out and throw stones, Faris was determined to become a martyr or *shahid*. He obtained his wish when he was shot dead at the Karni crossing point ten days after the famous photograph was taken. Muhammad al-Durrah, a boy the same age, has become another symbol even though he had no intention of becoming a martyr, or *shahid*. The heart-wrenching, unwatchable footage of his death on September 30, 2000 shows him cowering in terror as his father tries vainly to shield him from the bullets of Israeli soldiers engaged in an exchange of fire with Palestinian gunmen. His name has become the inspiration for songs and poems across the Arab world.

The Al-Aqsa Intifada quickly evolved into something more akin to the old armed struggle, with road ambushes and mortar firing in the occupied territories, and suicide bombings against civilians in Israel. Driving on the roads of the West Bank and Gaza Strip at night has become nigh impossible. Isolated settlements in the Gaza Strip have been heavily targeted by Palestinians. There have been recurring exchanges of machine-gun, mortar, and tank fire across the valley between Gilo, a large Jewish neighborhood in the annexed eastern half of Jerusalem, and Beit Jala, a Christian village outside Bethlehem.

Suicide bombings on civilians in Israel have brought the fear of being killed in the course of the most mundane activities: going to school, doing the shopping or stopping to relax with a cup of coffee. Here too there have been dreadfully vivid images—charred buses, the distraught faces of revelers whose night out has been ripped apart by a bomb, or the sight of Ultra-Orthodox volunteers picking through wreckage and sniffing objects to seek out shreds of human remains for later burial.

Israel has responded with measures ranging from erecting defensive concrete screens on particularly exposed roads, to imposing collective punishments on Palestinians, such as "closures" that restrict the movement of Palestinians in and out of their cities, the destruction of hundreds of houses and oppressive curfews in towns under occupation. The Palestinian Red Crescent Society reported that between the end of June 2002 and the end of January 2003 the town of Nablus had spent 3,944 hours under curfew, compared with 1,384 hours without curfew. A whole people has been pauperized and survives on the charity of the outside world. Thousands of acres of agricultural land and orchards have been ripped up, including that universal symbol of peace, the olive tree.

Israel has used overwhelming firepower to try to silence those who fire on Israeli targets, and blasted away buildings associated with Palestinian security forces—the same forces that Israel demands should take action against "terrorists." Israel's policy of "targeted killings"—called "assassinations" by Palestinians—had claimed the lives of 86 alleged terrorist activists and masterminds, as well as about 42 bystanders by January 2003. The killing of Salah Shehadeh, the head of Hamas' military wing, during an air raid on Gaza in July 2002 may have been the biggest scalp claimed by Israel, but it was also its biggest blunder. The use of a bomb dropped by an F-16 onto a building in a built-up part of the Gaza Strip claimed the lives of 15 civilians.

Beginning at the end of 2001, Israel changed tactics and staged ever deeper and harsher incursions into Palestinian territory. They culminated in March 2002 with Operation Defensive Shield, a month-long rolling reinvasion of the major Palestinian cities that was the biggest Israeli military operation since the Lebanon war two decades earlier. Human rights groups said there was evidence of war crimes committed by Israeli forces during the raids, particularly during the battle and partial destruction of the refugee camp in Jenin.

The fighting was reminiscent of the siege of Beirut, when Sharon and Arafat last confronted each other. But this time, Sharon held back from sending Arafat into exile. His Palestinian Authority, flawed as it may be, has legitimacy at home and abroad. Two decades after Beirut, the Palestinians are fighting on their own soil.

In early 2003, Israel was in control of most cities of the West Bank and staged periodic raids into the Gaza Strip. Israeli forces have destroyed all buildings in Arafat's compound in Ramallah, except one housing his private offices. The Palestinian leader became a prisoner in a jail of rubble. The erection of a "security wall"—really a series of walls, fences and other defenses—was begun around Palestinian areas the previous summer, eating away at more Palestinian land, to try to keep the suicide bombers out.

Israel may have displayed its overwhelming military superiority over the Palestinians, but as of February 2003, it was still constrained politically and had failed to impose calm by force of arms. Israel cannot kill or exile Arafat, nor can it annex the West Bank and Gaza Strip. Its military campaign consists of raids, reprisals and containment.

Grim, bloody, and frightening as the fighting has been, the confrontation remains, at the time of writing, a war of attrition. The aim of Arafat and Sharon is principally to weaken the political will of the other and to remove him from power.

★

How did it all go so wrong? How did the hope engendered by that handshake between Arafat and Yitzhak Rabin on the South Lawn of the White House turn to despair? The Oslo peace accords have been killed by a thousand cuts. My notebooks from the years that followed the signing ceremony are filled with the details of massacres, suicide bombings, riots, killings, gun-battles, and the assassination of Rabin himself. There was the callousness of the Israeli government in its treatment of Palestinians, its relentless confiscation of occupied land even as it negotiated peace, the chronic unreliability of Arafat and the chaotic authoritarianism of his rule, the cynical use of violence and the fanaticism of the politics of religion. The letter and spirit of the Oslo accords have been repeatedly violated on all sides—the Palestinian media kept up a steady stream of anti-Israeli incitement, while Israel declined to release prisoners it had promised to set free; Arafat did not wholeheartedly stop terrorism, but with the expansion of settlements and the refusal to carry out further "redeployments," Israel seemed reluctant to end the occupation. The list is long.

In the bittersweet years of peace negotiations between 1993 and 2001, Israeli civilian casualties seemed to increase the more Israel made concessions, while Palestinians were subjected to suffocating security measures and economic strangulation. In many ways terrorism became worse and the occupation became more stifling the longer the "peace process" went on. Palestinian standards of living collapsed as a result of Israeli security restrictions and punishments. Nobody was able to savor the "fruits of peace" for very long. Peace became a curse.

The Israeli–Palestinian "Declaration of Principles" negotiated in secret in Oslo and signed in Washington in 1993 were ground-breaking in their time, but they offered no definitive solution to the basic conflict between Israel and the Palestinians. The well-meaning but vague declarations about resolving differences only by peaceful means proved a poor anchor in the storms of extremist violence.

In the 1978 Camp David accords, Israel and Egypt set out the core principle for peace—a full Israeli withdrawal from Sinai—and agreed on the modalities in subsequent negotiations. Oslo, however, set down only the initial modalities—the withdrawal of Israeli forces from most of Gaza and an area around Jericho, a "phased redeployment" from unspecified chunks of territory in the West Bank, and a timetable for future agreements. The Palestinians were granted autonomy for five years. But Oslo gave no indication of how a permanent peace would be reached. The most difficult issues—the status of Jerusalem, the borders of the Palestinian "entity" (and related issues such as control of water), the fate of settlements and the future of refugees—were all left to be dealt with in a future final status agreement. The step-by-step approach was an implicit threat that Israel could halt or even reverse the process.

Oslo was deliberately ambiguous. It hinted at a future Palestinian state, but left enough unsaid for Labor to be able to present it as no more than the autonomy proposal agreed in principle by the Likud government at Camp David fifteen years earlier. Israel gave Palestinians a "down payment"—in the form of recognition for the PLO and withdrawal from Gaza and Jericho—but the final "cost" was left unresolved. It was like agreeing to the sale of a house, but having the new owner move into a room with the final price yet to be agreed.

The idea was to build up trust. Instead, the grinding pace of negotiations, with each side fearing that a small concession now would mean a major surrender in the final status talks later, created growing suspicion. The vagueness of the Oslo accords meant they became hostage to extremists on both sides who, believing they had been betrayed, set out to destroy the deal and already in 1994 set in motion the cycle of attack and reprisal.

The most disconcerting and heartbreaking aspect of the Al-Aqsa Intifada is the way it broke out so soon after Israel unveiled its proposals for a permanent peace. The Palestinians, having long complained about Israel's foot-dragging in the negotiations, saying the delays were stoking Palestinian frustration, balked when Israel presented the most generous proposal it had ever put on the table.

For three weeks in July 2001, U.S. President Bill Clinton brought Ehud Barak and Yasser Arafat to Camp David to negotiate a final and permanent peace accord, the culmination of years of the Oslo process. Clinton hoped to crown his presidency by recreating the magic of Jimmy Carter's mediation between Israel and Egypt that resulted in the Camp David accords of 1978. Instead, Clinton unwittingly lit the fuse that led to the collapse of the Oslo accords, whose signing he had presided over at the White House seven years earlier. Politicians, diplomats, and academics will argue for years to come about what went wrong at Camp David. Was it poor negotiating tactics, a clash of personality, Israeli attempts at trickery, or a Palestinian refusal to give up the myths of the struggle?

By the end of the summit Israel had suggested as a "basis for discussion," but not formally proposed, handing over about 91 percent of the West Bank, and compensating the Palestinians with territory in the Negev desert equivalent to 1 percent of the West Bank. On the last day, the sides concentrated on negotiating the emotionally charged issue of sharing Jerusalem, which Israel had hitherto regarded as its indivisible capital. The main proposal was for Palestinians to be given sovereignty over the outer Arab neighborhoods of Jerusalem, and "functional autonomy" in the inner neighborhoods. There were also proposals for Palestinian sovereignty in two of the Old City's four quarters. The Temple Mount would remain under Israeli sovereignty but with Palestinian "permanent custodianship" over the Haram al-Sharif. It was, by Israeli standards, a stunning concession, but the Palestinians turned it down. According to a Palestinian newspaper account, Arafat's defense of the Islamic holy places brought tears to the eyes of the Palestinian delegation as he rejected Clinton's pressure with the words: "Do you want to come to my funeral? I will not give up Jerusalem and the holy places." Dennis Ross, the U.S. special envoy, placed a less honorable, different emphasis on these events, saying that during the arguments over the Temple Mount Arafat had rejected outright its holiness to Jews, to the point of claiming that the Jewish temple had not been built in Jerusalem but in Nablus.

Clinton clearly put the blame for the breakdown on Arafat, and praised Barak for his courage in breaking the taboos of Israeli politics. The Palestinians retort that the Israeli offer was merely a "sugar-coated" fraud. The figure of 91 percent of the occupied territories may sound impressive, but Palestinians contend the true figure was somewhat lower because Israel had excluded from its calculations Jerusalem, the former no-man's land, and a slice of the Latrun salient that had been incorporated into Israel at the end of the 1967 war. Moreover, the settlement blocks, military access roads, and early warning stations meant the West Bank would be split up into three separate "cantons."

The Palestinians hardly budged from their demand for a complete Israeli withdrawal from the territories occupied in 1967, including East Jerusalem. They believed they had already shown flexibility by agreeing to border adjustments to account for settlement blocs, on condition that Israel offered an equal amount of land or equal quality as compensation, a 1:1 ratio and not 1:9. In the Old City, the Palestinians agreed to Israeli sovereignty in the Jewish Quarter. The "Wailing Wall," that is the immediate praying area, would be in Israeli hands, but the rest of the western retaining wall of the Haram al-Sharif would be Palestinian. Moreover, overall sovereignty over the sacred mount had to be Palestinian. The other explosive issue, the fate of Palestinian refugees, was hardly broached before Camp David collapsed in acrimony.

According to the account given a year after Camp David by Robert Malley, a special assistant to Clinton on Arab-Israeli affairs, and Hussein Agha, a writer on Palestinian affairs, it was an opportunity missed "less by design than by mistake, more through miscalculation than through mischief."

Barak had pressed for an early summit on the basis of all-or-nothing, warning Palestinians that the alternative to agreement was confrontation. Barak's abrasive manner did not help. The man nicknamed "Napoleon" by his own Israeli colleagues because of his imperious manner declined to meet one-to-one with Arafat, or even join a three-sided meeting including Clinton. Barak approached the negotiation as he might one of his old commando operations—moving by stealth, then striking quickly and unexpectedly with overwhelming force.

In the run-up to the summit, Barak had done everything to look and sound tough. He at first neglected the Palestinians and tried to pursue abortive negotiations with Syria. When he turned to the Palestinian issue, he declined to carry out a partial redeployment promised by the previous government of Benjamin Netanyahu, and even retracted a promise to hand over three villages near Jerusalem to the Palestinians. Precisely because he was prepared to make a momentous concession on the final accord, Barak did not want to waste his ammunition with small steps along the way.

When he struck with his offer, the Palestinians appeared to have been caught unprepared and suspected a trap. Arafat, suspicious of Barak's hawkish posturing, had always been reluctant to go to Camp David. He had asked for more "preparation," as Palestinians said they feared that a failure would lead to an explosion. Arafat had asked for a "safety net" in the form of an American guarantee that the long-postponed interim redeployment would be carried out if the talks failed, but Barak insisted on a high-wire, take-it-or-leave-it negotiation. Clinton was aware of the risks, but nevertheless supported the Israeli view.

The Palestinians knew that back home, opinion was increasingly critical of the terms negotiated by Arafat in the Oslo accords and the negotiators feared a backlash if they were seen to "surrender" on issues of principle. A year after Camp David, Abu Mazen recalled the pressure the Palestinian team faced from Israel and the United States: "We felt as if we were in a prison."

The Palestinians infuriated the Americans and Israelis by failing to produce any clear counterproposals to Israel's steadily improving offers. At one point, according to Malley and Agha, Clinton rebuked Arafat: "If the Israelis can make compromises and you can't, I should go home. You have been here fourteen days and said no to everything. These things have consequences; failure will mean the end of the peace process . . . Let's let hell break loose and live with the consequences."

Barak subsequently claimed that Arafat never intended to reach a peace settlement, accusing him of secretly planning Israel's demise while stringing along Israeli and western leaders. "What they want is a Palestinian state in all of Palestine. What we see as self-evident, two states for two peoples, they reject. Israel is too strong at the moment to defeat, so they formally recognize it. But their game plan is to establish a Palestinian state while always leaving an opening for further 'legitimate' demands down the road," he said in an interview in June 2002 seeking to rebut the Malley-Agha account.

After Camp David broke up in failure, Clinton tried to pick up the pieces of his mediation. In late September, sensing that trouble was about to break out, Clinton called Arafat to tell him that he was about to issue a bridging proposal that would improve the offer at Camp David. But the genie of Jerusalem had been let out. It created a volatile atmosphere of religious passion and political cynicism. It was only a matter of time before violence would be ignited. Ariel Sharon, the leader of the Likud opposition party, provided the spark for the explosion that, ironically, propelled him to power. He marched on to Jerusalem's Haram al-Sharif on September 28, 2000 to demand that Israel should never give up the Temple Mount to Arafat and his henchmen. Wearing dark glasses, Sharon allowed himself a moment of buffoonery when he told a television crew that far from provoking Palestinians, he had come seeking "peace."

Sharon was accompanied by a train of about 1,000 police officers. To Palestinians the "visit" looked more like an invasion than a tourist excursion. Reasoning that Sharon could only have been given such heavy police protection with Barak's express approval, they quickly rose up to "defend" Al-Aqsa against Sharon's political assault, and

Israel's heavy-handed police killed four Palestinians during rioting at Friday prayers a day after the visit.

The Al-Aqsa Intifada was born. The nationalist conflict between Israelis and Palestinians now took on the semblance of holy war. One can debate whether Arafat, as the Israelis claim, deliberately detonated the violence, or whether the Intifada was a spontaneous outburst that was turned into a mass uprising by the trigger-happy response of Israeli soldiers. Reading the public statements of the time, there is a sense of foreboding and evidence that both sides expected an imminent confrontation. Palestinian leaders said they would fight for Jerusalem, while the Israeli army, which had long feared an outbreak of Palestinian violence should the Camp David talks collapse, issued repeated warnings of a harsh response.

In previous clashes in 1996 and 2000, Palestinian riots had already turned into gun battles involving Palestinian forces. The army was determined that the Palestinians should not succeed, as the Israelis saw it, in exerting diplomatic pressure through violence.

In the first three months of the uprising, B'Tselem, Palestinians paid the heaviest price. B'Tselem, an Israeli human rights group, lists 279 Palestinians killed, almost all of them civilians, compared with 41 Israelis dead, about a third of whom were members of the security forces. The televised death of Muhammad al-Durrah and the televised lynching of the two Israeli soldiers in the first days of unrest had the effect of inflaming emotions on both sides. A commission of inquiry headed by U.S. Senator George Mitchell issued a report in May 2001 that avoided issuing blame to either side, or better said, found fault with both.

> . . . we have no basis on which to conclude that there was a deliberate plan by the PA [Palestinian Authority] to initiate a campaign of violence at the first opportunity; or to conclude that there was a deliberate plan by the GOI [Government of Israel] to respond with lethal force. However, there is also no evidence on which to conclude that the PA made a consistent effort to contain the demonstrations and control the violence once it began; or that the GOI made a consistent effort to use non-lethal means to control demonstrations of unarmed Palestinians. Amid rising anger, fear, and mistrust, each side assumed the worst about the other and acted accordingly.

There is little doubt that, once the Intifada had started, Arafat sought to exploit Palestinian anger and even stoke it with inflammatory broadcasts on his radio and television stations. Palestinian television broadcast Friday prayer sermons such as one from Shaikh Ibrahim Ma'adi, who declared in June 2001: "Blessed are the people who strap bombs onto their bodies or those of their sons." Arafat walked a tightrope between the fury of his people and the frustration of Israel. The uprising carried great dangers, but also opportunities.

At the age of 71, Arafat regained a twinkle in his eye. Arafat had until then looked increasingly dejected, with his lower lip trembling from suspected Parkinson's disease and his military fatigues looking even more absurd hanging on the frame of a frail old man. The popularity of the man who went by titles such as "The President," "The Symbol," was fast declining. He was stuck in a kind of Palestinian "bantustan," leopard-spots of autonomous areas scattered through territories still controlled by the Israeli army. Thanks to the Al-Aqsa Intifada, however, Arafat regained for a while some of his former authority. He was now working with the grain of his frustrated people; he could no longer be accused of being an Israeli quisling.

For some time, Israel's attempt to use overwhelming force, the death of so many young Palestinians, and the blame placed on Sharon for sparking off the Intifada, helped to sweep away criticism of Arafat's behavior at Camp David. Robin Cook, the British Foreign Secretary who crossed the lines into Gaza the night of the first Israeli helicopter attack, was struck by Arafat's presence. "He was very focused, very resolute, very courageous," recounted Cook.

In the Arab world, crowds of protesters took to the streets to declare their support for the Palestinians. Some even demanded another "war" with Israel. The kings, princes, and presidents of the Arab world were hostages of the Palestinians and put up a show of unity. At an emergency Arab summit in Cairo, the first full summit since the Gulf War, they denounced Israel, criticized the West, and quickly opened up their money purses once more to support Arafat. "The anger of the Arab world is a strong card for the Palestinians," said one senior Palestinian envoy.

Behind the sound and fury of the Intifada, negotiations between Israel and the Palestinians struggled on. In December 2000, Bill Clinton threw a last roll of the dice by issuing his "parameters" for peace. Under this bridging proposal, the Israelis would withdraw from between 94 to 96 percent of the West Bank and would receive the equivalent of between 1 and 3 percent in territorial compensation—equivalent to a total of 97 percent. The balance of 3 percent would be accounted for by the "safe passage" route between the West Bank and Gaza Strip under Palestinian control. The Israeli withdrawal would be phased, Palestine would be "non-militarized," and an international force would be deployed to provide reassurance.

He proposed a division of Jerusalem on the basis that what is Jewish should be Israeli, and what is Arab should be Palestinian. At the core, the Haram al-Sharif would be under Palestinian sovereignty, with the Western Wall under Israeli sovereignty. There would also be a form of words recognizing the sacredness to Jews of the "Holy of Holies" lying somewhere beneath the Haram al-Sharif, a contention that the Palestinians rejected. Palestinian refugees would have a right of return to their "homeland," but their access to Israel would be subject to Israeli sovereign decisions—an artful way of saying Israel would take no more than a symbolic number. All refugees would receive compensation and assistance from the international community.

The Israelis agreed with reservations. After a delay, Arafat also agreed but his response was so hedged with conditions that, to some U.S. officials, it was a "No." In January 2001, Israeli and Palestinian negotiators convened in Taba and reported coming very close to a final accord. One finesse to the Palestinian demand for the "right of return" of refugees was a proposal to settle refugees in a part of Israeli territory that would then be annexed by the Palestinian state under the land swap arrangements. By then, however, Barak had called early elections and was effectively a lame duck prime minister. Arafat did not go the extra mile, maybe not even an inch, to save the Labor government. In February, Ariel Sharon was elected by a large majority with an explicit commitment to repudiate the offers made at Camp David and Taba. Had Arafat foreseen that this would be the inevitable consequence of the crisis he was stoking?

Perhaps Arafat thought that the rise of Ariel Sharon, whose reputation as the man responsible for the massacres of Palestinians in Beirut in 1982 made him repugnant to many abroad, would give Palestinians extra international leverage. But the cost to Arafat was the loss of an Israeli negotiating partner, of an American president whose concern for peace in the Middle East was manifest until his last day in office. Such a combination was unlikely to recur soon.

Many Palestinians were beyond caring. The word "Intifada" carries the sense of "shaking off." Many Palestinians felt a sense of release from the world's expectation that they should behave as if they were at peace with Israel, despite the fact that it continued to expand settlements, restricted the movement of Palestinians, took the lion's share of water, and generally continued to treat Arabs with arrogance. "The first Intifada was to force the Israelis to the negotiating table," explained one Palestinian colleague, "This Intifada is to get rid of occupation."

★

The distant, crackling voice of Motta Gur has an electrifying quality, even now, decades after he radioed Israel's High Command with the momentous news. "*Har ha-Bayt be-yadeynu . . . Har ha-Bayt be-yadeynu . . . .*" "The Temple Mount is in our hands . . . the Temple Mount is in our hands . . . ." It is a day seared into Israeli consciousness, the miraculous climax of an extraordinary war, when even the most secular of Jews could not help but feel that God was smiling upon them. In six days in 1967, the Israelis were propelled from the depths of anxiety about an imminent Holocaust, to the soaring heights of fulfillment of the prophetic promise to restore Jerusalem to the Jews.

The recording of Gur's famous message is replayed yearly on the radio on the anniversary of the Six Day War, known as "Jerusalem Day." The clipped words of the man who led Israel's paratroopers into the Old City are part of the collection of symbols of Israel's finest moment, a fleeting time of clarity and certainty, when all of the country agreed on what was right and what was wrong. A well-known photograph of the period shows a helmeted defense minister, Moshe Dayan, striding purposefully up the Via Dolorosa from Lion's Gate, flanked by Yitzhak Rabin, the Chief of Staff, and Major-General Uzi Narkiss, the commander of the central front. Another picture captures the army rabbi, Shlomo Goren, triumphantly blowing the *shofar*, the ram's horn, at the Kotel, which would henceforth lose the appellation of "Wailing Wall." It was now the object of rejoicing. The most loved image of that unique day, still sold as postcards on street corners throughout Israel, is the iconic picture of battle-hardened paratroopers holding their helmets and looking up, awe-struck, at the ancient Herodian stonework of the wall. Proud but humble victors, not wailing worshippers; soldiers doing God's work.

"We have returned to the holiest of our sites, and will never again be separated from it. [. . .] We have come not to conquer the holy places of others, nor to diminish by the slightest measure their religious rights, but to ensure the unity of the city and to live in it with others in harmony," Dayan declared that day. Minutes earlier, he had observed the centuries-old tradition of Jews slipping handwritten supplications to God in between the cracks of the wall. His read: "May Peace descend upon the Whole House of Israel."

It was not to be. Imperceptibly at first, the great victory of the Jews in 1967 was transformed into prolonged and debilitating military occupation. In contrast with 1948, the Palestinians for the most part stayed in their towns and villages. Israel inherited a large and resentful Palestinian population. The Arab states' defeat of 1967 crystallized the revolutionary Palestinian guerrilla groups. In Israel, victory energized a Jewish national-religious movement that would become increasingly militant.

A whole century of the Arab–Israeli conflict is symbolized most powerfully by the struggle to control the Temple Mount, or the Haram al-Sharif. This flattened hillock with a trapezoid esplanade measuring roughly 475 yards long by 300 wide is a piece of holy real estate so sensitive that Cold War strategists used to envisage a global nuclear conflagration being sparked by some dispute on the Temple Mount.

Moshe Dayan was only too aware of the explosive potential of Jerusalem's holy places falling into Israeli hands. He took a far-reaching decision: the Israeli flag would be removed from the Dome of the Rock, Israeli soldiers would be withdrawn from the Haram al-Sharif and the army Rabbinate's offices on the sanctuary would be closed. Day-to-day control of the Muslim holy places would be restored to Muslim religious authorities. Dayan insisted only on the right of Jews to visit the site of what had once been their destroyed temple—but not to pray there.

"I was convinced that precisely because control was now in our hands, it was up to us to show broad tolerance, so rare an attitude among the regimes of the preceding decades and centuries," wrote Dayan, in *Story of My Life*. "We should certainly respect the Temple Mount as an historic site of our ancient past, but we should not disturb the Arabs who were using it for what it was now—a place of Muslim worship."

This show of magnanimity helped to avoid inflaming the wider Muslim world. It also served to fend off international pressure when Israel set about annexing East Jerusalem as part of its "eternal and indivisible" capital, and initiated a hard-nosed policy of population engineering. Israel made little secret of its desire to increase the number of Jews to preserve the Jewish "majority" and reduce—or at least control—the number of Arabs in the city. Israel used the full range of bureaucratic and planning measures to do so.

Dayan was helped immeasurably by rabbinical tradition, which forbids Jews from ascending to the Temple Mount—let alone praying there. The rabbis say the destruction of the temple has not altered the holiness of the ground. Because Jews today are considered to be in a state of ritual impurity which can be cleansed only with the ashes of a red heifer, which no longer exists, they may not violate the temple's area. Given the uncertainty over where precisely the "Holy of Holies" stood, the whole Haram al-Sharif is forbidden. The Chief Rabbinate ruled in 1967 that "we shall be faulted, God forbid, in breaking a most severe prohibition regarding the desecration of this holy place." Religious tradition, one senses, had a large element of political wisdom enshrined within it.

For some Israelis, however, the perpetuation of the ban was, and remains, the cause of mourning, a stain on Israel's national honor and a contradiction of God's will. Like the exiles who built the Second Temple when they returned from Babylon, they demanded that today's Israelis should build the Third Temple.

General Uzi Narkiss recounted shortly before his death in 1997 how the army rabbi, Shlomo Goren (a future Chief Rabbi) had approached him with a chilling proposal on the day Israel captured the Old City. "Now is the moment to put 100 kilogrammes of explosives into the Mosque of Omar [Dome of the Rock] so that we may be rid of it once and for all," said Rabbi Goren. The rabbi implored the general to seize a moment that would never appear again, but he was brusquely warned by Narkiss that he would be jailed if he persisted.

Decades later, Rabbi Goren kept up pressure for Jews at least to be allowed to pray on the Temple Mount. He published a ruling that certain carefully chosen parts of the esplanade were accessible to Jews because they were not part of the ancient temple enclosure. For years, Jewish militants have played cat-and-mouse with the police and Muslim guardians, slipping into the Haram al-Sharif dressed as tourists and mumbling a prayer before being bundled off.

This would all be a cultural oddity were it not for the deadly violence that the Temple Mount can ignite.

On October 8, 1990, a group of devotees of the "Temple Mount Faithful" provoked fierce rioting by thousands of Palestinians when they tried to ascend to the Haram al-Sharif to lay the "foundation stone" of the new temple. They were stopped by police, but in the clashes that followed, 17 Palestinians were killed by security forces on the esplanade and another was killed in the Old City. The blood-soaked T-shirts of the "martyrs" of that day are on display in the small museum at the Haram al-Sharif. Guides still point out the scars on the marble cladding of the Dome of the Rock left by Israeli bullets.

Four days after the massacre, I watched in astonishment as thousands of Jews at the Western Wall danced in frenzied circles with Torah scrolls to celebrate Simhat Torah, the feast of the "Rejoicing of the Torah." It may be a sign of fortitude for Jews to celebrate their festivals in the face of adversity; but to dance with abandon a few yards from where another people have suffered calamity seemed to display only callousness.

In 1996, three years after the signing of the Oslo accords, the Likud Prime Minister Binyamin Netanyahu disregarded the advice of the intelligence services and gave his approval for the opening of an archaeological tunnel running from the Western Wall to the Via Dolorosa, along the base of the Temple Mount. "Without exaggerating, we are touching the rock of our existence," he declared.

For Palestinians, the tunnel meant the Israelis were "touching" their holy sites and altering the status of Jerusalem. The violence that followed permanently changed the rules of the Intifada. Instead of the old stone-throwing riots, Palestinian security forces now joined in. More than 70 Israelis and Palestinians were killed in this foretaste of the Al-Aqsa Intifada.

If Palestinians are so quick to rise up in defense of Al-Aqsa it is not just because of religious zeal. It is also because they have good reason to be suspicious of Israeli intentions. In 1984, Israeli security forces uncovered a plot by a group of Jewish settlers, known as the Jewish Underground, to blow up the mosques on the Temple Mount. The year before, a group of seminary students had been caught preparing to dig under the mount, using an ancient passageway, to hold a Passover service by the ruins of the temple. There were rumors that they planned to establish a subterranean "settlement" and negotiate for prayer rights on the Temple Mount.

In 1969 a crazed Australian Christian tourist set fire to the Al-Aqsa mosque and destroyed the famous wooden pulpit donated by Saladin. In 1982, an unstable Jew opened fire on a Muslim guard at the Dome of the Rock. The list of incidents goes on.

All this may not be directly the work of the Israeli government, but Palestinians have little reason to trust the authorities. Within days of taking over the Old City, Israeli bulldozers cleared more than 100

Arab families from the Mughrabi neighborhood in front of the Western Wall to create a plaza for Jewish worshippers. Despite Dayan's
pledge to preserve holy places, two mosques were knocked down.

If you look across the little domes and rooftops of the Muslim
Quarter in the Old City, you see ever more blue-and-white Israeli
flags marking houses that have been bought up by the settlement
movement with the tacit support of the Israeli government. Is it a
coincidence that most of these acquisitions seem to encircle the Temple Mount?

In the refurbished Jewish Quarter (where Arabs are excluded by
law) you can buy a large poster depicting an aerial view of Jerusalem
with a model of the Temple superimposed on the spot where the
mosques now stand. In one of the alleyways, the Temple Institute spe-
cializes in manufacturing the precious implements, vessels, and gar-
ments to be used in the rebuilt temple.

Other Muslim holy sites in the West Bank have been steadily taken
over by Jews. The tombs of Abraham in Hebron, Joseph in Nablus,
and Samuel just outside Jerusalem—all Muslim mosques before
Israel's occupation—have been wholly or partly converted into Jewish synagogues with the knowledge and cooperation of the Israeli
military authorities.

Under the Oslo accords, Israel retained control of several religious
sites: Rachel's Tomb in Bethlehem, Joseph's Tomb in Nablus, and the
Cave of the Patriarchs in Hebron. This meant an Israeli military presence (and a settler presence in Hebron) in the heart of these Arab
cities. Whenever trouble erupts, these religious outposts become the
convenient and inevitable focus of Palestinian violence. The area
around Rachel's Tomb is constantly littered with rocks. Joseph's Tomb
turned into a veritable death trap during the troubles in 1996 and
2000. In the most recent uprising, it was overrun by Palestinians and
set on fire, but it was rebuilt on Arafat's orders. In revenge for the helicopter raids of October 2000, Palestinians in Jericho set on fire a
synagogue built over an ancient Jewish prayer site with a 1,300-year-
old mosaic floor depicting a ram's horn, a palm branch, and a menorah with the words *Shalom Al Yisrael*, "Peace be unto Israel."

Theodor Herzl thought that the power of holy sites could be harnessed for universal humanism. In *Altneuland*, he fantasized about
building a great Peace Palace in Jerusalem where "international con-
gresses of peace-lovers and scientists" would be held. Instead, holy
sites and political violence are intimate friends in Palestine. The first
anti-Jewish riots broke out in 1920, during the Muslim feast at Nebi

Musa, the supposed tomb of Moses. The names of Hebron, Bethlehem, Jerusalem, and Shechem may resonate with ancient holiness, but
these cities strung out along the spine of the mountains of the West
Bank have become places of bloodshed. The holy places of Palestine
are the lightning rods of the conflict between Jews and Arabs, attract-
ing and concentrating the full fury of the national and religious contest for the land. In a region where sacred texts are also tribal
histories, holy sites are symbols of each side's historical claim to the
land. The God of the real Middle East is a jealous one.

★

By night the Jewish children sleep behind sandbagged windows
while automatic gunfire crackles in the alleys near Abraham's tomb.
By day they make merry in the playground, oblivious to the fact that
they live on the front line of the Al-Aqsa Intifada.

In the somber streets of Israeli-controlled Hebron, Arabs spit at the
sight of Israeli jeeps and soldiers look at you through the sights of a
gun. Tension here is such that Palestinians in the first year of the
Intifada were forced indoors by curfews lasting months, with only a
few hours a week to buy essentials.

In these poisonous surroundings, the last thing I expected to find
as I visited the cluster of white stone-clad blocks of flats of Avraham
Avinu in October 2000 was the sight of bicycles scattered carelessly
and children playing in huts erected for Sukkot, the Feast of
Tabernacles.

In the world of Jewish settlers, the baby carriage is as much an
instrument of political struggle as the assault rifle. The presence of a
defenseless child represents rootedness, a flesh-and-blood claim to
the land, a demonstration of faith in God's promise to protect the
Jews, despite the threats and tribulations of the present, and to restore
them to their ancestral land.

Life on Israel's frontier is a family activity. In a world where
somber and earnest bearded men carry their guns even to the grocery store, where settlements are built in laager-like concentric circles for protection, there is something surreal about the sight of an
Orthodox woman wandering by dreamily, pushing her children in a
pram. Dressed in bright knitted hair coverings, faded long jeans, skirts
and trainers, these women look like a cross between a Victorian
matron and a sixties hippie.

Where the settler women go, the Israeli state is sure to follow. Jewish families and children require housing, schools, clinics and the pro-

tection of the army. Even the most banal domesticity acquires political, even messianic significance. The ideal here is not the kibbutzniks' religion of manual labor in the fields, but housework. Every day spent in the Land of Israel, every diaper that is changed, every daily prayer that is recited, is a step toward the redemption and the creation of the holy Kingdom of Israel.

Israelis are outraged by the fact that Palestinian children are allowed to risk death by throwing stones at Israeli soldiers. Here in Hebron, Jewish children are also part of a dangerous political game. In March 2001, a ten-month-old baby girl, Shalhevet Pass, was killed in Hebron by a Palestinian sniper as she was being pushed in her stroller by her father, who was seriously wounded. Settlers responded by rampaging repeatedly in Arab neighborhoods, burning cars and buildings. In the following few days, five children—Arabs and Jews— were killed by guns and bombs.

If there is one clear political objective of the chaotic conflict that has become the Al-Aqsa Intifada, it is the Palestinians' determination to make life hell for Jewish settlers in the hope of eventually driving them out of the West Bank. Settlers are most exposed on the roads, but several communities have been infiltrated by Palestinian gunmen slipping though the perimeter fence, bursting into family homes and killing anyone they can find.

Unlike the Jewish settlement fortresses on the hilltops of the West Bank, the settlers in Hebron live in a valley in the heart of the Arab city. They are often exposed to direct gunfire from surrounding hills in the Palestinian sector.

"The army have a big machine-gun on the roof, and at first the children were frightened by the sound. But they got used to it when we explained it was our army. Now they laugh," said Michel Cohen, a 40-year-old teacher wearing the black skullcap of the highly devout. "We must be careful, but not scared. God is our keeper," he added, tapping on the flimsy Sukkot huts. "If He decides that we should go to these huts made of plywood we should not be afraid. We are happy. It teaches us to believe that we are correct. The Romans, the Turks and the British could not stop us. The Jews will live here forever."

The Hebron settlers feel vindicated in their warnings that peace with "terrorists" was impossible. David Wilder, the spokesman for the Hebron settlers and virtually the only person willing to speak to foreign journalists, said: "We brought every politician and general to show them the places from where we would be shot at. Everything we predicted has come true. Some places come under fire from three directions. It was all obvious and inevitable Israel will have to take back most of the land it gave to Arafat."

The Hebron enclave is a point of constant friction. The hatred is palpable. A few streets away from the Avraham Avinu neighborhood, Palestinians gathered around a shop that had been struck a few days earlier by Israeli gunfire and rockets. The metal shutters looked as if they had been ripped with a can opener. "It is not written anywhere in the Bible or Koran that there will be peace between Jews and Arabs," said Hijazi al-Shyoukhi, a 55-year-old lawyer. "They believe this is the Land of Israel. We believe it is an Islamic land from where the Prophet Muhammad ascended to Heaven. You cannot make peace with this religious conflict."

Security experts and Left-wing Israelis at times talk of removing the Hebron settlers because they cannot be defended effectively. But these outposts are the spiritual and ideological fountainhead of the religious Zionist settlement movement. "If we were to leave it would mean acquiescing to terrorist blackmail. If you have to leave every place that is exposed, you would have to leave the whole state of Israel," said Wilder. With Palestinians periodically opening fire on Jerusalem's neighborhood of Gilo, the settlers claim there is now no difference between living in the settlements or in Israel proper, between "political" settlements and "security" settlements. All of Israel is a settlement.

Alone among the cities of the West Bank, Hebron has a permanent presence of settlers in the heart of the Arab city. A string of Jewish enclaves juts defiantly into the souk. As Wilder predicted, the Israeli army has reoccupied much of the West Bank, and the Arab part of Hebron has been no exception. Several Arab buildings on the road linking the Hebron enclaves with the main settlement of Kiryat Arba on the outskirts of the city have been demolished to give the settlers safer access.

This remains the sharp end of the conflict. Hebron, King David's first capital, is the mother of Jewish settlements. Its pioneers have become the aristocracy of Israel's powerful and purposeful national-religious movement. Its veterans have spread to the four corners of the West Bank to found new settlements and fight new battles. As God promised to Abraham, the settlers of Judea and Samaria have multiplied to become as numerous as the stars and the grains of sand.

In less than four decades, the settlers have grown from a handful of early visionaries in Hebron to between 160,000 and 200,000 people (depending on who is counting) living in scores of communities in 2002. These continue to grow, under friendly Likud governments or hostile Labor ones, whether the peace talks are going well or badly. The Oslo accords brought the construction of a network of new roads and bypasses around Palestinian towns, a sure sign that Israel had no intention of relinquishing the whole of the West Bank. The relentless expansion of settlements, with the weekly confiscation and expropriation of Palestinian land, is for Palestinians a powerful indication of the hollowness of Israel's honeyed words of peace.

★

It all began with a meal. In the spring of 1968, several months after the end of the Six Day War, Arab homes in Hebron were still bedecked with the white flags of surrender. A group of Orthodox Jews led by Rabbi Moshe Levinger rented out the modest Nahar al-Khalid Hotel in Hebron, also known as the Park Hotel, and held a Passover seder in the "city of the Patriarchs." It was an explosive act of ordinariness that would open the way to the settlement of the biblical Judea and Samaria and give birth to an entirely new political ideology.

About 60 people took part, a "Who's Who" of the future settlement leadership. Many thought they would be evicted by the army within a few days, but some participants, like Rabbi Levinger himself, had come to stay. A lorry pulled up and unloaded his family's washing machine, refrigerator, and bookshelves. The settlers declared they would never leave, and have remained in Hebron ever since.

"That seder is the most cherished memory of my life. It was a very emotional thing. We had the feeling we were making history. When it became known that Israelis had returned to Hebron it was like an electric shock for the Israeli public. It was like we had reached the moon," recalled Eliakim Haetzni who, despite being a secular lawyer, is one of the most outspoken ideologues of the settlement movement.

"These people were religious. They started cleaning to make the kitchen kosher. They took over and turned the place upside down. They burned their bridges behind them and took their households along. They put up *mezuzot* [parchment with scripture affixed to the doorposts of Jewish homes] and an *eruv* [a suspended wire to create a symbolic 'wall' within which objects may be carried on the Sabbath]. They did it with such an air of assuredness, as if they were on Allenby Street in Tel Aviv. I looked on and saw a power whose extent I could not foresee. It is as if you had a car and discovered it had an extra gear. Secular Israel did not realize what had slowly grown in its womb."

According to Haetzni, the Arabs of Hebron were so terrified that the Israelis would slaughter them to avenge the 1929 massacre that they were grateful the Jews had only come to live in the city. "You have no idea what wonderful relations we had with the Arabs," recalled Haetzni wistfully. "They were guests at the weddings of my children, but not anymore." By Haetzni's own account, it was cordiality imposed by force. The terrified Palestinians played along with the Israelis for as long as they believed them to be invincible. After the Yom Kippur War, relations began to deteriorate. Only a new demonstration of Israeli resolve to remain in the territories could restore quiet, said Haetzni. Autonomy for Palestinians, yes, but only after Israel annexes Judea and Samaria. If conflict with the Arabs is inevitable, then so be it; it's part of life as a Jew in the gentile world.

The conflict, said Haetzni, is as much between Jews as between Jews and Arabs. It is ultimately about whether Israelis want to be proud Jews or "some hybrid thing called Israelis . . . a rabble with an army." For Haetzni, Israelis who demand peace with the Arabs are hopeless dreamers. "They want to form a new nation with the Arabs. But they have a problem, because the Arabs do not want them. They are more and more Islamic, and more and more Palestinian. Zionism created a conscience among Arabs who call themselves Palestinian. It's a son born out of wedlock. It happens to the best families."

If Rabbi Levinger is the father of the settlement movement, then the German-born Haetzni is its godfather. Zionism, to him, has to remain in constant movement to survive. Like a spinning top, it will topple over if it stopped; the source of energy is settlement.

Haetzni and Levinger first helped to orchestrate the resettlement of the Ezion Bloc south of Jerusalem by the "children" of the settlers who had been driven out of the area by the Arab Legion in 1948. Secured with the eventual approval of government, the venture was a stepping stone to the major objective: the "illegal" return to Hebron.

Soon after the war there had emerged the "Land of Israel Movement," a broadly based group demanding the retention of all conquered territories. It included old-style right-wingers who bemoaned even the loss of Transjordan, Labor stalwarts and a generous number of worthies such as Isser Harel, the legendary first head of the Mossad and Natan Alterman, the foremost poet of his generation. Israel at the time was elated by victory. It felt invincible and was mesmerized by the historic heartland falling into its grasp. Zionism meant, after all, the return to Zion. The Zion of the Bible was not Tel Aviv, Rishon Le-Zion, or Degania; it was the holy places of Jerusalem, Bethlehem, Hebron, and Nablus. All these were now in Israel's hands. The political question of the day was not whether the land should be settled, but how much of it should be populated with Jews.

The Arabs responded to their defeat with intransigence. The status of the territories was left in limbo. Israeli ministers opted for a compromise plan—an internal Israeli compromise—to retain large chunks of the West Bank for security reasons while using the rest to negotiate peace with Jordan.

Except for East Jerusalem and a band of territory around the city, the West Bank and Gaza were not annexed formally but were instead subjected to a creeping *de facto* annexation. The land was opened up to extensive settlement by Jews, its water resources were harnessed for Israel's benefit, and its Arab population exploited as a source of cheap labor. Settlers enjoyed the privileges of Israeli civil law while Palestinians around them languished under military rule.

In 1968, the Passover guests in Hebron were pushing an open door. The government, Rabbi Levinger recalled, "did not say yes, and did not say no" to his Hebron action. Ben-Gurion himself, although out of power, had given a nod and a wink to the settlers. The military authorities looked the other way and even gave them a few weapons for protection.

Caught between the growing agitation of the Arabs and the fear of public opprobrium if the settlers were removed, the government struck another internal Israeli bargain: the settlers could remain in Hebron, but would be housed out of sight in the compound of the military governor. In March 1970, the government succumbed to demands for a Jewish return to Hebron and announced the establishment of Kiryat Arba, a settlement on the outskirts of the city, the Hebron equivalent of Jewish Upper Nazareth above Arab Nazareth.

The tactics of the Hebron settlers were to be repeated again and again. A surprise settlement, usually of a place of religious symbolic power, followed by declaration of intent to stay and negotiations with the government over a "reasonable" compromise. The settlers would always take what was offered, on the basis that it was a permanent gain, and press for more. These were devastatingly effective "salami tactics."

The settlers ably tapped into popular emotions, and exploited the divisions among ministers. The government never found the inner resolve to halt the encroachment. To deny the settlers would be to deny Israel's own mythologized history. If Jews have a right to live in Israel, *a fortiori* they have a right to settle the West Bank. What was so different between the actions of the settlers, and those of the pioneers of yesteryear who carried out similar "illegal settlement" in the face of opposition from the British authorities? Israel's pre-1967 borders include swathes of territory beyond the 1947 U.N. partition borders, yet these "occupied" territories are recognized internationally as part of Israel proper. For many Israelis, the war of 1967 was as legitimate as the War of Independence, and the Arabs lost the land as a result of their own aggression.

As he planned his Hebron venture, Haetzni said he was surprised to find that, after 19 years of independence, secular Israelis had all but lost the pioneering spirit which they sang about in their patriotic tunes. The only motivated *halutzim* (pioneers) were now to be found in the national-religious camp, which had been galvanized by the "miracle" of 1967. In particular, the Jewish scholars at the Merkaz ha-Rav yeshiva became the torch-bearers of the new religious Zionist militancy.

The yeshiva had been founded by the first Ashkenazi Chief Rabbi of Palestine, Avraham ha-Cohen Kook. In contrast with most religious authorities of the time, who believed that the redemption of the Jews would have to await the appearance of the Messiah, Rabbi Kook saw the Balfour Declaration and the Zionist movement as part of God's work, and *atchalta de-ge'ula*, the "beginning of redemption." He cast the secular, socialist Zionists in the role of God's unknowing emissaries.

After the death of the elder Rabbi Kook in 1935, Merkaz ha-Rav passed into the hands of his son, Rabbi Zvi Yehuda ha-Cohen Kook. In the 1950s it grew into the center of the nationalist interpretation of religion, which saw the state and the army as holy, a further stage in God's plan, a manifestation of the divine presence in Zion. Unusually for a yeshiva, Markaz ha-Rav turned Israel's Independence Day into a religious holiday. The faults of the state were "details" to be redressed in due course, not a reason to shun the Zionist enterprise as sinful, as most Ultraorthodox rabbis had done. The younger Rabbi Kook compared the development of Zionism to the construction of the temple:

Our sages explain that all of the material used in the building of the Temple became sanctified only after it was set into place. We build with the secular, and sanctify afterward. [. . .] Just as the stones used in building the Temple were not sanctified, so too the building of Eretz Israel is accomplished by every segment of the nation of Israel; by the righteous, and by the less righteous.

On Independence Day of 1967, Rabbi Kook stood up in the study hall of his yeshiva and gave a speech which his disciples came to see as a veritable prophecy. He said a great blessing was about to descend upon Israel and that Israel's task was not yet complete. He recalled how, when the United Nations voted to partition Palestine into a Jewish and an Arab state, he could not bring himself to join the celebrating crowds because portions of Eretz Israel had been given into "foreign hands."

"They have parted my land!" cried the rabbi, repeating the reproach to the gentiles in the book of Joel (Joel 3:2). He went on:

And where is our Hebron?! Do we forget this?! And where is our Shechem?! Do we forget about this?! And where is our Jericho?! Do we forget about this too! And where is our other side of the Jordan?! Where is each block of earth?! [. . .] Is it in our hands to relinquish any millimeter of this?! God forbid!

As the rabbi spoke, Egyptian divisions were already rumbling into Sinai in the countdown to war. Three weeks after his outburst, Hebron, Shechem, Jericho, and the other cities of the West Bank had fallen to the Israeli armed forces. Some of the paratroopers who captured the Old City had been Merkaz ha-Rav students, and within minutes of Israeli forces taking the Western Wall a military jeep was sent out to bring Rabbi Kook to the holiest site in Judaism.

Rabbi Kook taught that settling all of Eretz Israel was a positive religious commandment. "Greater Israel," the union of the occupied territories with Israel, is known in Hebrew as *Eretz Israel ha-Shlema*—the "complete" Land of Israel. Giving up land was a sin so serious that it ranked alongside idolatry, unchastity (including incest and adultery), and murder—sins for which Jews should choose martyrdom rather than commit. His ideology created a young and energetic cadre of activists who were totally committed to the settlement of Judea and Samaria, a right-wing vanguard that filled the pioneering role once adopted by the kibbutz movement. Rabbi Kook's philosophy deeply influenced the whole of Israel's right-wing camp.

Merkaz ha-Rav became a kind of Jewish missionary order dedicated single-mindedly to the cause of settling the land. Yet the absolute sacredness bestowed upon the land meant that, sooner or later, these visionaries would come into conflict with the state, and rabbinical law would clash with civil law.

In Rabbi Kook's philosophy, the state was also part of the divine plan for redemption and its leaders should be honored as "the judge that shall be in those days" (Deut. 17: 9). What to do when the state failed to follow God's will to settle the land? The conundrum was resolved by according to the state a conditional holiness. The state was the means of settling the land, as opposed to the traditional Zionist view of settling the land as a means of creating the state. Jewish statehood was merely the vehicle for reclaiming the land. Any attempt by the state to prevent Jews from settling the land was therefore deemed to be illegitimate; any such government orders would be "null and void, like the dust of the earth," ruled Rabbi Kook.

This was only one step removed from accusing ministers and governments of betraying God's manifest will if they give up territory or even restrict settlement.

The crisis of the Yom Kippur War in 1973 and the territorial concessions of the 1978 Camp David accords led to the crystallization of what political scientists call Israel's "radical right," a broad nationalist front dedicated to preserving Israel's territorial gains, by illegal means if necessary.

Merkaz ha-Rav abjured violence. In the earliest settlement ventures in Gush Ezion and Hebron, the devotees of Rabbi Kook believed they were simply showing the way to a confused nation, taking the action that ministers knew was right but feared to carry out. But over the decades the settlement movement became radicalized by a series of confrontations with successive governments over their territorial concessions, and by the growing militancy of Palestinians among whom the would-be pioneers had implanted themselves.

Gush Emunim, the "Bloc of the Faithful," was founded in 1974 by graduates of Merkav ha-Rav to press for extensive Jewish settlement and bring about a grand movement for national spiritual "reawakening." Its members were alarmed by the disengagement agreement whereby Israel withdrew from a slice of Egyptian territory, and Gush Emunim campaigned ardently against similar concessions on the Golan Heights. More important, it fully backed a campaign by veterans from Hebron to give up their studies and "close the Talmuds," turning their energies to establishing a new Jewish settlement in Nablus, the biblical Shechem.

The tactics employed by the campaign to establish "Elon Moreh," named after the place near Shechem where Abraham built an altar upon entering Canaan, were a hybrid of the Palmach's illicit settlement activities of the 1930s, and the civil disobedience of the American civil rights movement. Seven times the movement harnessed thousands of Israelis to establish illegal settlements in the Samarian hills, only to be evicted by the army. In the end Yitzhak Rabin caved in and allowed a small group of settlers to live in the Qadum military camp near Nablus until the government had decided on the matter. It was another Hebron-style compromise that granted the settlers their first foothold in the northern part of the West Bank.

Gush Emunim saw the election of Menachem Begin in 1977 as the realization of its political dreams, heralding the annexation of the occupied territories. But Begin startled his supporters by keeping a tight check on settlements during the negotiations that led to the Camp David accords with Egypt, under which Israel agreed to give up all of the Sinai and grant autonomy to Palestinians.

The peace process with Egypt polarized the country. The nationalist Right mustered its forces to prevent the withdrawal from Sinai, while the embryonic Peace Now movement emerged from a 1978 petition by more than 300 reserve officers who told Begin: "A government that would prefer to establish settlements beyond the Green Line over the ending of the historical conflict and extension of normal international relations in our region would prompt us to ask questions regarding the correct path of our country."

Gush Emunim resorted to the now familiar game of cat-and-mouse with the army to slip into settlements scheduled for evacuation. Yamit, a secular town of sun and sea built by Labor, to which Begin had once promised to retire to write his memoirs, was turned into a religious ghetto. As residents took handsome payoffs to move out, Gush Emunim's faithful moved in to prevent the abandonment of territory that was belatedly declared to be "holy." In a heightened atmosphere of religious frenzy, Rabbi Moshe Levinger advocated an exemplary act of suicide but was overruled by a collective rabbinical decision.

The final act was played out in April 1982 on the rooftops of Yamit, where a hard core of protesters barricaded themselves against soldiers who painstakingly removed them one by one despite the bricks being thrown at them. Followers of Rabbi Kahane ensconced themselves in a bomb shelter with explosives, ammunition, and cyanide capsules. They threatened to kill themselves, and were only coaxed out by Rabbi Kahane himself, who was flown in from the United States.

Army bulldozers and sappers razed Yamit, including its memorial to fallen Israeli soldiers. With only hours to go before the arrival of the Egyptians, the last protesters gathered at the ruins to rend their clothes in mourning and pray that Yamit would be rebuilt.

The settlers' gloom over the loss of the settlements in Sinai masked what would become a major government-led expansion of settlements in the West Bank itself to "compensate" for the concessions made to Egypt. This drive would not be led by the highly motivated activists of Gush Emunim, but by planners creating dormitory satellite towns within commuting distance of Tel Aviv and Jerusalem. Financial incentives, houses with gardens and amenities such as swimming pools—not religious devotion—were the key to drawing out thousands of Israelis from their cramped flats in the big cities. This was pioneering through suburban sprawl.

Camp David, like Oslo, set in motion a spiral of violence between Jewish settlers and Palestinians in the West Bank. Then, as now, extremists on both sides formed an unspoken alliance to destroy the peace agreement.

In the spring of 1979, Rabbi Levinger's American-born wife, Miriam, led a group of women and children from Kiryat Arba to the center of Hebron where, clambering up a ladder propped on the back of a lorry, they took over Beit Hadassa. The government did not allow their menfolk to join them, but eventually permitted a procession of men to hold a Sabbath evening meal with their wives.

In May 1980, a group of chanting men was ambushed outside Beit Hadassa by a three-man Fatah squad armed with assault rifles and hand grenades. The attackers killed six Jews before making their getaway. The attack, one of the bloodiest carried out in the West Bank since the start of the occupation more than a decade earlier, came at a time of growing Palestinian militancy. A few months earlier, another settler had been killed in Hebron. Riotous protests and the stoning of settlers' cars had become increasingly frequent. Vigilante-style retaliation by Jews was common as well.

The settlers believed their security had been forsaken by the defense establishment. A group of plotters known as the "Jewish Underground" resolved to exact revenge by striking at those whom it held ultimately responsible for the attacks—the leaders of the National Guidance Committee, a PLO-backed umbrella group formed to oppose the Camp David accords.

They selected five of the leaders, including prominent West Bank mayors, whose cars would be booby-trapped with bombs designed to maim rather than kill. The operation was mounted after the 30-day period of Jewish mourning but was only a partial success. Two mayors—Bassam al-Shak'a of Nablus and Karim Khalaf of Ramallah—were crippled. One of the targets was saved because he was abroad, another was spared because his dog scared away the attackers. The bomb meant for the fifth victim blinded an Israeli army sapper.

In July 1983, in retaliation for the stabbing of a settler in Hebron, Underground members disguised in Palestinian headscarves threw a grenade and fired assault weapons at students from the Islamic College in Hebron, killing three and wounding more than 30. A year later, the group was finally rounded up by the Shin Bet as it prepared to commit its most brutal act yet—the bombing of five Arab buses full of passengers in revenge for similar attacks on Israeli buses.

Oslo, like Camp David, exposed and deepened the rift within Israeli society, to the point where the assassination in 1995 of the Israeli prime minister, Yitzhak Rabin raised fears of a Jewish "civil war." Such a prospect has receded with the start of the latest Palestinian uprising, although the settlers have embarked on a new campaign of "illegal" settlement. There is a grim equilibrium in the politics of Israel: making peace with Arabs means strife among the Jews, while war with the Arabs restores a certain unity.

The late Ehud Sprinzak, Israel's best-known expert on right-wing extremism, argues that these acts of Jewish terrorism were not the work of the fringe, but a reflection of the mainstream of settlers. "The idealistic people who began in 1968 to settle Judea and Samaria did not go there with violent intentions. None of them expected to become vigilantes, terrorists, or supporters of terrorism," he wrote in his 1991 book, *The Rise of the Radical Right.* "Yet within twelve years the combination of messianic belief and a situation of continual national conflict with a built-in propensity for incremental violence resulted in extra-legalism, vigilantism, selective terrorism and, finally, indiscriminate mass terrorism."

⋆

The early morning news woke me with a jolt. ". . . more than 20 Arabs have been killed in the Cave of the Patriarchs," said the radio announcer: ". . . reports that it was carried out by a Jewish resident . . . the army is investigating . . . additional reinforcements have been sent to Hebron . . . ."

I drove with a colleague to Hebron along a route that was by now familiar because of the multiplying incidents in the "Elder Sister" of Jerusalem. Through damp patches of winter fog, we left the Old City of Jerusalem and Mount Zion behind us, passed the Monastery of Mar Elias on the southern edge of the city, glimpsed the volcano-like hill of Herodion in the undulating Judean desert, drove past Rachel's Tomb and crossed a semideserted Bethlehem. We placed a *keffiyeh* on the dashboard to ward off stone-throwers as we skirted the Deheisheh refugee camp, then promptly hid it away and put on our best broken Hebrew to get through Israeli army checkpoints. About an hour after setting off, we crept into eerie, menacing Hebron.

Even from the fragmentary first reports, we understood that what had happened in the city was a new kind of carnage unseen in the previous six years of the (first) Intifada. At that time, in 1994, the Intifada's grim routine of soldiers shooting stone-throwers had been almost replaced by a low-level guerrilla campaign of shootings against soldiers and settlers. This was different: a religious Jew had massacred devout Muslims at prayer in a sacred place in the holy month of Ramadan. It was the first step in turning the political struggle for the West Bank into something resembling a holy war.

In contrast to his ban on Jewish prayers on the Temple Mount, Moshe Dayan relented to pressure to allow Jews to pray in Hebron's Cave of Machpelah, known to Arabs as the Ibrahimi mosque. This is the reputed burial place of Abraham, Isaac, and Jacob as well as of their wives. Dayan was determined to remove the "shameful ban" on Jews ascending beyond the seventh step leading to the shrine. Over the years, private prayers became prayer meetings, prayer meetings need books and, step by step, the settlers carved out part of the site as a synagogue.

The inexorable expansion of Jews in the Cave of Machpelah was a microcosm of the settlers' inexorable colonization of the West Bank. Where the old Zionist pioneers spoke of "another dunam, another goat," the new breed of religious settlers worked on the basis of another synagogue, another settlement. Prayer became a highly political act. At the Ibrahimi mosque, friction grew. An explosion was only a matter of time.

Any account of how the handshake of peace at Oslo turned into the battles of the Al-Aqsa Intifada must dwell on the events in Hebron on that Friday, February 25, 1994. The vagaries of the Muslim and Jewish calendars had ensured that the Jewish feast of Purim coincided with Ramadan, the Muslim holy month of fasting. The alignment of dates was an ill omen.

Before dawn that day, Baruch Goldstein, an American-born doctor living in the settlement of Kiryat Arba on the outskirts of Hebron, entered the Cave of Machpelah. He was dressed in an army uniform and was carrying a Galil assault rifle, the Israeli version of the AK-47. One of the Muslim guardians later recalled how Goldstein had pushed him aside with the butt of his rifle and made his way into the main chamber of the complex, the Isaac Hall, where hundreds of Muslim worshippers were praying. Goldstein opened fire on the faithful as they bowed on the ground for the *sajdah*, the ritual prostration. Amid cries of *Allahu Akbar!*, "God is Great!," the panic-stricken crowd desperately scurried for cover behind marble pillars and the tombs of Isaac and Rebecca. Goldstein killed 29 people and wounded many more, emptying and reloading three full magazines of bullets, before being overpowered and bludgeoned to death. Witnesses later recalled how there was so much blood on the ground that they slipped as they tried to get out.

When I arrived in Hebron that morning I made my way to the Al-Ahli hospital, a half-built building on a hilltop. The crowd parted as the victims were brought in ambulances, on friends' shoulders, on the bonnets of cars. The wards were on the brink of chaos. One man lay dead on the floor of an office, blood pooling around his head. Doctors struggled to cope with the waves of dead and injured. First came the victims of the massacre, then those shot in riots on the streets of Hebron in clashes between Palestinians and Israeli soldiers, and finally those hurt in the mêlée as they tried to extricate the casualties and bring them to hospital. Nearly as many people were killed outside the mosque as inside it. One bloody clash took place outside the hospital itself where, for some reason, a squad of soldiers had decided to make a provocative appearance.

Staff quickly lost track of their bloodstained victims as relatives whisked the dead away for a quick burial. It took weeks to compile a reliable list of massacre victims. Harbi Abu Sbeh, a 26-year-old man lying in bed with an ashen face and quivering lips whispered the question everybody in Hebron wanted to ask, the question that continues to be asked: "They are talking about peace. But what kind of peace is this?"

The Israeli army saturated Hebron with soldiers to contain the Palestinians' rage. When an Arab carries out an attack, the army usually wastes little time in demolishing the house of the perpetrator's family. His whole community is frequently placed under punitive curfew. But now, faced with an atrocity carried out by a Jew, the

Israeli army demonstrated the skewed morality of the occupier: it placed the Arab city under curfew while providing escorts for convoys of Jewish settlers who wanted to drive out of Kiryat Arba. As with everything else in the West Bank, there is one law for Jews and another for Arabs.

Outside Beit Hadassa, a Jewish settlement enclave in the heart of Hebron, there was no sign of remorse, of guilt or horror at the murderer whom the settlers had produced. On the contrary. "He should have killed 500," muttered one Jewish woman in a long skirt and headscarf. She was walking with her two children dressed in fancy costumes for Purim. One was a pirate, with an eyepatch. Nothing, not even mass murder on their doorstep, would stop the carnival.

For many of Hebron's Jews, the massacre was a reenactment of the Purim story contained in the Scroll of Esther, which recounts how the Jews of Persia were saved from a plot to exterminate them. To the settlers, the Arabs are the embodiment of the evil vizier, Haman, who schemed to wipe out the Jews of Persia. Goldstein took on the role of Mordecai, the Purim hero who destroyed the Jew-killers. After the massacre, the story soon spread among the settlers that the good doctor Goldstein, who had so often dipped his hands in Jewish blood as he tried to save victims of terrorist attacks, had by his self-sacrificing act saved the community from a looming plot by Hebron's Arabs to massacre the Jews.

"It's a holy war," said Aryeh Bar-Yosef, a 36-year-old theology student. "I hope that there will be many more Jews like Baruch Goldstein who will kill the last of the Arabs. Not only them, all the enemies of Israel." It was a quick step to turn Goldstein from hero to saint. His "temporary" grave in the settlement of Kiryat Arba became a pilgrimage site, complete with a cabinet for prayer books and hagiographic works such as *Baruch Ha-Gever*, a play on words meaning both "Baruch the Man" and "Blessed be the Man," which also has connotations of "Hero." It took the Israeli authorities six years to muster the courage to demolish the shrine-like trappings at the site.

Goldstein, a supporter of the late American extremist Rabbi Meir Kahane, believed that the Palestinians were the embodiment of gentile evil, a "cancer" that should be excised by throwing all Arabs out of the country. By his act of desperation, he may have thought he was saving Jews from the disaster of the government's accommodation with the Palestinians, whom Goldstein regarded as the modern-day incarnation of the Nazis.

Liberal Israelis were horrified. For the author, Amos Oz, the settlers were no better than the Islamic fundamentalist groups that had emerged in the Arab world. The settlers, he wrote, were "Hizbollah with skullcaps." Prime Minister Yitzhak Rabin denounced Goldstein as "a foreign implant" and an "errant weed." He formally banned the Kahane-inspired groups, Kach and Kahane Chai. But he refused to bow to pressure from several cabinet ministers and academics for the Jewish enclaves in Hebron to be eradicated.

Hebron makes a mockery of its own name. *Hevron* in Hebrew and *Al-Khalil* in Arabic are derived from similar words meaning "Friend," because Abraham, with whom the city is intimately associated, was God's "friend." But Hebron is a city of hatred fired by religious extremism.

For Jews, Abraham is the first patriarch of the Israelites, who received God's promise that his seed would be as numerous as the stars and would inherit the land of Canaan. To live in Hebron is to be watered by the fountain of Jewish history. For Arabs, Abraham is the first Muslim. Islam is the pure faith as received by Abraham and unsullied by the subsequent "lies" of Judaism and Christianity. Just about every Arab in Hebron can quote the Koranic passage: "*ma kaana ibrahimu yahudiyyan wa-la nasraaniyyan wa-laakin kaana haniifan musliman wa-ma kaana min al-mushrikiina . . .*" (3:67)—"Abraham was neither Jew nor Christian. He was an upright man, one who had surrendered himself to Allah [i.e. a Muslim]. He was no idolater . . . ."

Hebron is haunted by the ghosts of massacres in God's name. In 1929 more than 60 Jews were slaughtered by Arab mobs in the brutal climax of a long dispute over the control of Jerusalem's Western Wall, the *Kotel*. On Yom Kippur of the previous year, Jews had erected a screen at the wall to separate male from female worshippers. British police removed the screen, but Muslim religious authorities, who formally owned what they called the Al-Buraq wall and adjacent passageway, presented the move as the first step toward a Jewish takeover of the Al-Aqsa mosque.

The Mufti launched a campaign for the "defense" of Muslim holy places. Building work was begun on the top tier of the wall, and Jewish worshippers below were harassed by the banging of cymbals and by animals being driven through the alleyway. Jewish leaders, who had in the past tried to "buy" the wall, demanded that the wall be expropriated by the British government and permanently handed over to the Jews.

In August 1929, thousands of Jews marched in Tel Aviv chanting "The Wall is Ours!" The following day hundreds of members of the right-wing Betar youth group marched to the Kotel and raised the Jewish flag. Muslims responded a day later, streaming down from the Al-Aqsa mosque at the end of Friday prayers and burning Jewish holy books at the wall. Fully-fledged Arab riots broke out in Jerusalem the following week and spread to the rest of the country. At the end of a week-long orgy of violence, 133 Jews and 116 Arabs had been killed.

Hebron's Jewish community, about 600 mostly non-Zionist pious Jews who had lived in Hebron for centuries under Turkish rule, had refused protection by the Hagana, trusting the friendship of their Arab neighbors. There were notable cases of Arabs who hid and protected Jewish families against the mobs, which sometimes included their own relatives. But these were not enough to stop the carnage.

Today's Hebron settlers remember only the killers. In their eyes, all of Hebron's Arabs are tainted by the sin of their fathers and uncles, a perception scarcely helped by the fact that Palestinians themselves have never expressed remorse. On the contrary, the three Arabs who were hanged by the British in Acre for their part in the murders were turned into the heroic martyrs of Palestinian nationalist poetry and folk songs, some of which are still heard at weddings today. "They are three heroes who faced their deaths like lions," said one song. "O Jewish one, do not rejoice over their fate. And remember that, while Arab youths did not have any weapons except for their clubs and you had your modern gun, you kept complaining that they were stronger and the aggressor . . . ."

Among today's Jewish settlers, the 1929 massacre is a byword for Arab barbarity. A room in the basement of Beit Hadassah, a block of flats on the site of what was a clinic in 1929, has been turned into a shrine to the murdered victims. There are pictures of burned holy books and injured children.

The settlers, a tiny minority living in a resentful Arab city, believe that another massacre will take place the moment the Arabs sense they have the power to carry it out. The Palestinians, on the other hand, believe that within every armed settler lurks a would-be Goldstein.

★

Exactly forty days after Baruch Goldstein's massacre, at the end of the Muslim period of mourning, Raed Zakarne, a 25-year-old Palestinian Islamic militant, blew himself up in a car bomb which he detonated next to a crowded Israeli bus in the town of Afula. He killed seven Israelis and an Arab woman passenger, and wounded more than 50 others, including children traveling home after school.

Charred nails, used by the bomber as additional shrapnel, littered the street, mixing in with pools of blood and broken glass. As lorries carried away parts of the wreckage, orange municipal street-cleaning vans used high-pressure water hoses to wash down the scene. Later in the evening, about 200 people gathered at the site. They shouted: "Death to the Arabs!" and "Goldstein! Goldstein! Goldstein!"

A week after the Afula attack, a man with a pipe bomb strapped to his body boarded a bus in the town of Hadera and blew himself up, killing five passengers and injuring more than 30 others. Mosques in the Gaza Strip broadcast a message from the bombers: "We have killed many of the sons of pigs and monkeys, and wounded dozens to avenge our martyrs in Hebron."

The attacks were not isolated incidents of retaliation, but the start of a sustained campaign of suicide bombings that would have a devastating political impact, destroying Israelis' confidence in peace while embarrassing Arafat and undermining his authority.

Hamas, the Palestinian Islamic fundamentalist movement, imported Hizbollah's tactics from Lebanon. But instead of striking at military installations, Hamas bombed "soft" civilian targets. Public buses were the favorite. For all of the words written about the deadly new sophistication of the "martyrdom operations," and the resources poured in by Israeli, American, and (sporadically) Palestinian authorities to foil them, suicide attacks are a brutally primitive form of guerrilla warfare. They are an admission that the only way the Palestinians can reliably deliver a bomb is by sending a young man to blow himself up with the device.

Hamas (an acronym for *Harakat al-Muqawama al-Islamiyya*, or the Islamic Resistance Movement, which spells the Arabic for "zeal") filled the political space left by the PLO as it moved toward the path of a diplomatic settlement. With the first Intifada at its height in 1988, the PLO tried to capitalize on the rebellion by declaring independence, recognizing Israel's right to exist and "renouncing" terrorism. The move was the first step on the diplomatic road to Oslo. But the Intifada was also the stimulus for the radicalization of the Muslim Brotherhood in Palestine, part of the wider movement for Islamic revival founded in Egypt in 1928. As Arafat declared that the PLO charter was *caduc*, a French term meaning "lapsed," the newly formed

Hamas distributed its own covenant refashioning the PLO's old revolutionary slogans into Islamic language.

Where the PLO covenant said that "armed struggle is the only way to liberate Palestine," Hamas's charter declared: "There is no solution to the Palestinian Problem except by Jihad [holy war]. The initiatives, options, and international conferences are a waste of time and a kind of child's play." Instead of the PLO charter's assertion that Palestine "is an indivisible part of the Arab homeland," Hamas affirms that "the land of Palestine is an Islamic *waqf* [trust] upon all Muslim generations till the day of Resurrection." Instead of denouncing "Zionism and imperialism," Hamas castigates "the unbelievers."

The charter quotes at length from Koranic verses and other Islamic writings, such as the passage from a *hadith* or saying of the Prophet:

> The Last Hour will not come until the Muslims fight against the Jews and the Muslims kill them, and until the Jews hide themselves behind a stone or a tree, and a stone or a tree says: "Muslim or Servant of Allah there is a Jew behind me; come and kill him . . . ."

Hamas leavens its Islamic themes with European anti-Semitism. It quotes the forged *Protocols of the Elders of Zion* as proof of Zionism's evil plot to take over first Palestine, then the whole of the land between the Nile and the Euphrates, and eventually the rest of the world. The Jews were the instigators of the First World War, which led to the destruction of the Islamic caliphate, and set up the United Nations as a means of ruling the world.

Hamas's language may be different, but the message is the same as that of the old PLO: Israel must be destroyed, Palestine must be redeemed by force and there is no room for compromise over a single square inch of land. There is an important difference, however, on the nature of a future liberated Palestine. Hamas wants to create an Islamic society, and believes that the PLO's vision of a secular state is a blasphemy.

For many years, these ideological differences were subsumed into the daily organization of the first Intifada. The factions called rival strike and memorial days, and sometimes clashed, but for the most part each faction respected the other's "activities." The PLO made little attempt to prevent Hamas from imposing more conservative social norms; it was a brave woman who would walk in Gaza without a veil.

Hamas claims much of the legacy of Palestinian struggle, presenting itself as the instigator of the Intifada in 1987 and the direct heir of Sheikh Izz al-Din al-Qassam, the first leader of armed Palestinian resistance in the 1930s.

Yet Hamas's resort to armed force was a novelty. Until the outbreak of the Intifada, the Muslim Brotherhood most of the time shied away from armed confrontation with the Israeli authorities. As the Israelis tried to suppress the PLO and other nationalist factions, the religious movement was allowed to operate largely unhindered.

The Muslim Brotherhood stuck to its orthodox view that it first had to bring up an "Islamic generation" through education and social work as the necessary prelude to "jihad." Islamic Jihad was created in the 1980s as a reaction to the Muslim Brotherhood's policy of cooperation. Once Hamas took up the armed struggle, however, it was by far the most capable of the militant groups. Where the PLO factions depended on funds from Arab states channeled through their "national" institutions, Hamas drew its strength from its network of schools, nurseries, clinics and, above all, mosques.

The first Intifada maintained a philosophy of enraged mass action. It encouraged stone-throwing riots, strikes, and civil disobedience but largely avoided armed attacks. Guns, when they were used, were usually turned against "collaborators." The Intifada waned during the months of siege-like curfews imposed by the Israelis in the West Bank and Gaza Strip during the crisis over Iraq's invasion of Kuwait in 1990 and 1991. When the Gulf War started, the housebound Palestinians cheered the sight of red comet-like balls of fire—Iraq's Scud missiles—streaking toward Tel Aviv.

Negotiations with Israel gathered pace after the war and the Madrid peace conference in October 1991. As the PLO gradually stood back from the violence, Hamas's attacks intensified. At first Hamas attacked Jewish settlers, and then armed soldiers in the West Bank—both considered to be more than legitimate targets by the bulk of Palestinians. Suicide bombings against military targets were tried even before the Goldstein massacre, but were usually little more than explosive suicides.

The Hebron massacre was the turning point. Hamas and Islamic Jihad began to bomb civilian buses within Israel proper. Whether Goldstein's massacre was the cause, or merely the pretext, for Hamas's new brutality has never been clear. In part, the new tactics may simply have been the result of new expertise. In December 1992, Israel "temporarily" deported more than 400 Hamas and Islamic Jihad activists to Lebanon in reprisal for a series of attacks that culminated in the abduction and murder of an Israeli border policeman.

The expulsion became snarled up in legal objections. When the buses were finally sent across the northern border, the Lebanese authorities resolved not to allow them to enter. The deportees were left stranded in a tent camp between Israeli and Lebanese lines, and until international pressure forced Israel to repatriate them within a year, they became a constant symbol of the callousness of Israel's actions. The first contingent returned just days before the signing of the Oslo accords, and Israeli intelligence agencies have long suspected that they brought back new bomb-making skills learned from Hizbollah members who visited the deportees' camp.

The honor of dying for Palestine, the pain they could inflict on Israel, and the certainty of Paradise with its forbidden pleasures of alcohol and virgins, drew young men to volunteer for "martyrdom" operations. Sometimes recruits would be made to lie in graves to become used to the idea of their death. They left behind video recordings explaining their actions.

I once asked Sheikh Abdallah Shami, a leader of Islamic Jihad in the Gaza Strip, why, rather than sending young men to sacrifice themselves, he did not volunteer to kill himself. "You don't understand," he replied. "The young people are full of fire. They would criticize me for taking their place."

After a particularly bloody spate of attacks in 1996, the suicide bombers came under intense pressure from the Palestinian Authority and went more or less dormant until the Al-Aqsa Intifada. The uprising elevated the suicide bombers to the status of heroes; they were the Palestinians' strategic weapon against a more powerful Israel, a bomb "guided" by a disposable human being to challenge Israel's high-tech weaponry, striking in the heart of Israel and imposing what Palestinians regarded as a "balance of terror."

The Palestinian Authority formally condemned suicide attacks against civilians, and Fatah militants at first concentrated on attacking Israeli targets within the West Bank and Gaza Strip. But by early 2002, the Al-Aqsa Martyrs' Brigade, an offshoot of Arafat's Fatah movement, was turning its hand to suicide attacks within Israel, particularly after Israel's liquidation of its leader, Raed Karmi. The group also brought the innovation of using women, who are less likely to draw attention, as suicide bombers.

The wider Islamic world was divided by suicide bombings. Some Muslim authorities regarded it as a form of suicide, and therefore banned by Islamic law. Many more, however, endorsed the methods as a legitimate form of struggle against Israeli occupation. The Saudi ambassador to London, Ghazi Algosaibi, outraged Jews when he penned a poem on the front page of the *Al-Hayat* daily praising suicide bombers as martyrs who "died to honor God's word."

At the end of 2002 the Palestinian Authority sought to negotiate a ceasefire with militant factions. However, Hamas would not agree to a complete cessation, and refused to recognize the distinction between attacks in Israel and the occupied territories. Hamas was ready to offer, at most, a pact to avoid killing civilians if Israel did likewise, and stopped arresting Palestinians and blockading their towns. It said, however, that settlers would not be considered "civilians." Abdel-Aziz Rantisi, one of Hamas's main ideologues, said: "Our position is against ending the resistance. Operations inside Israel will continue."

★

Yitzhak Rabin had rarely looked so relaxed as on the night of November 4, 1995.

About 100,000 people turned out to hear him speak at Tel Aviv's Kings of Israel Square. It was a display of confidence in the ultimate victory of peace after a dreadful period of suicide bombings, settler campaigns of disobedience, and right-wing protests.

Hopelessly out of tune, Rabin sportingly joined the rest of the rally's participants in singing the "Song of Peace." It had been banned from the airwaves when it came out after the Six Day War, but was now adopted as an anthem by the supporters of Oslo. "Let the sun rise, light up the morning," went the lyrics. "It will not return those whose candle has been blown out. Nor will it return those buried in the dust with bitter tears. Sing out. Sing the song of peace."

Rabin made an unambiguous pledge to seek peace with the Palestinians and called on Israelis to forswear violence: ". . . it is violence which undermines the foundations of Israeli democracy. We have to denounce it, we have to spit it out, we have to isolate it . . . ."

As if in response, a few minutes later three shots rang out as Rabin walked to his car, which was waiting at the back of the stage. Yigal Amir, a 27-year-old Jewish religious extremist and a law student at the University of Bar-Ilan, had slipped through the sloppily secured cordon of the "sterile" zone around Rabin and fired three rounds from his 9mm Beretta pistol at pointblank range. Two dum-dum bullets found Rabin's back, while the third wounded a bodyguard.

Someone shouted that the shots were just blanks. But the Prime Minister was fatally wounded and died in hospital.

Despite threats to his life, which the Shin Bet assumed came from Palestinians, Rabin had refused to wear a bulletproof vest. A bloodied sheet of paper was retrieved from the pocket of his jacket with the words to the "Song of Peace." Within days, nearby pavements were smooth with wax from countless memorial candles, while the walls became steadily covered with graffiti bearing the guilt-stricken confessions of left-wing Israelis who felt they had not done enough to defend peace and stand up for the Prime Minister.

President Bill Clinton's choked words of grief—*Shalom Haver*, "Goodbye Friend"—became the motto of Israel's traumatized peace camp. At the signing of the Oslo accords in Washington, Rabin had been moved to quote a verse from the kaddish, part of the daily Jewish prayers: "He who creates peace in His high places, may He create peace for us and for all Israel; and say Amen." Little more than two years later, it was his son who recited the kaddish, now as a mourning lament, at the Prime Minister's graveside in Jerusalem. In death, Mr. Rabin achieved a final diplomatic triumph, bringing to Jerusalem King Hussein of Jordan, who returned to the city for the first time since losing the western half of his kingdom in 1967; President Hosni Mubarak of Egypt, who had never set foot in the Jewish state in his 15 years as leader; as well as ministers from Qatar, Oman, and Mauritania who had no diplomatic relations with Israel.

Fourteen years after Anwar al-Sadat paid with his life for making peace with Israel, Rabin was assassinated for seeking an accommodation with the Palestinians and giving up the biblical heartland whose conquest he, as Chief of Staff in 1967, had masterminded.

Hamas's suicide bombings had shattered Israeli morale, and helped to isolate the Prime Minister. If during the Intifada Palestinians had suffered the bulk of the casualties, now it was Jews who were overwhelmingly paying the price of "peace." In the same way as the Left had broken the spirit of Menachem Begin by protesting about the death toll in Lebanon, the Right kept a protest vigil outside Rabin's home in Jerusalem with a running tally of the Jews killed by terrorists. Jewish extremists, incensed by territorial concession and Palestinian attacks, held Prime Minister Yitzhak Rabin responsible for the deaths of Jews and for handing over sacred land. At right-wing demonstrations, crass placards depicted Rabin as a Nazi and as a man shaking the bloodstained hand of Arafat.

Amir had reached the conclusion that the Prime Minister could be killed under *din rodef*, the Jewish "law of the pursuer." This extreme thesis, which is believed to have been discussed "theoretically" in some right-wing yeshivas, held that Rabin was a *rodef*, a person pursuing another with intent to kill, and should be killed before he did any harm. In court hearings, a smirking Amir said he had acted alone but "maybe with God's help." Amir was not a settler, but shared the beliefs of the national-religious movement and studied at a religiously inspired university.

Amir, his brother Haggai, and a friend, Dror Adani, are reported to have discussed several plans to kill Rabin, including using a sniper rifle or pouring nitroglycerine into the plumbing of Rabin's home to cause an explosion. Amir had tried on three earlier occasions to shoot Rabin at public functions but failed, either because the Prime Minister canceled his appearance (on one occasion due to a double suicide bombing) or because he could not get close enough. Israeli newspapers reported that among Amir's possessions were a copy of Frederick Forsyth's assassination thriller, *The Day of the Jackal*, and of *Baruch Ha-Gever*, "Baruch the Hero," extolling Baruch Goldstein.

Within days of the assassination, Rabin's foreign minister and fellow Nobel prize winner, Shimon Peres, took power. He ordered the army to withdraw from Palestinian cities. Oslo was to be made permanent and irreversible. Amir would not be allowed to win.

One by one, Jenin, Tulkarm, Kalkiliya, Nablus, Bethlehem, and Ramallah were handed over to the Palestinian "police." The Israelis often retreated at night to reduce the risk of clashes with Palestinian crowds. Palestinians would wake up to a "liberated" city with their colors flying from the rooftops and flock to the abandoned military bases. Some revisited the newly whitewashed cells where they had been jailed. Elections were held for the Palestinian "parliament," and Arafat was elected "President" with overwhelming public support.

As well as being the visionary of the Oslo accords, Peres (once a territorial hardliner) also wanted to be, like Rabin, "Mr. Security." Rabin had always said that Israel would "seek peace as if there were no terrorism, and fight terrorism as if there were no peace."

Around nine in the morning on January 5, 1996, a cell-phone rang in a bare concrete house in the Gaza Strip. When Yihya Ayyash took the call, the telephone exploded, blowing off part of his head. As Hamas's master bomb-maker, Ayyash would doubtless have appreciated the elegance of the device that dispatched him. Israel made little secret that it was behind the assassination. Ayyash was the first and greatest hero of Hamas's armed wing. His name and surname were both derived from the Arabic verb "to live," yet he was a purveyor of death. In the two years that the 29-year-old Ayyash was on the run as the Shin Bet's most-wanted man, his bombs were credited with having killed some 50 Israelis.

However brilliant the liquidation of "The Engineer" may have been tactically, it was in many ways a strategic blunder. The response of Hamas, and the smaller Islamic Jihad group, was swift and devastating. Suicide bombers carried out four deadly attacks in the space of two weeks, killing more than 50 Israelis.

Peres, never a favorite with the Israeli electorate, had tried to capitalize on the popular sympathy for Rabin by calling an early election. Now the bombers ruined his attempt to consolidate his power, and brought down another Israeli Prime Minister. Neither the emergency "Summit of the Peacemakers" called in Sharm Al-Sheikh to express international support for Peres, nor Israel's ill-fated bombardment of South Lebanon in May 1996 (during which it killed about 100 Lebanese refugees at a United Nations base in Qana), could save Peres from defeat.

Binyamin Netanyahu, the young and telegenic Likud party leader, came to power promising to be tough on Arafat and make sure that the Palestinians kept their commitment to fight terrorism. But Netanyahu, the man who once compared Rabin to Chamberlain, now had to confront the reality of Oslo. For all of the international frustration with the Likud leader, it was none other than Netanyahu who handed over most of Hebron, the "City of the Patriarchs," to the Palestinians. And it was Netanyahu who reluctantly agreed to a further stage of redeployment of troops from the West Bank. In doing so, he lost political allies on the Right. He was eventually forced to call early elections in 1999 and was trounced by the Labor party's Ehud Barak. Yet Mr. Barak, despite his aura as Israel's most decorated soldier and the political heir of Yitzhak Rabin, managed to hold the reins for less than two years before he, too, lost political allies, saw his peace policy collapse, and lost power.

Clearly, Oslo has aggravated the chronic instability of Israel's political system which gives smaller parties—especially the religious factions—disproportionate power in making and breaking governments.

In January 2003, Ariel Sharon succeeded where three previous prime ministers failed—he was reelected to office. Palestinian violence—which had unmade Peres, Barak, and contributed to Rabin's murder—drove Israeli voters back into the arms of Likud. Arafat may have hoped that Sharon's inability to halt attacks on Israelis would bring about his downfall. Instead violence destroyed the Israeli peace camp. The unexpected legacy of Oslo is the unprecedented influence that Palestinians can wield over Israel's political system—a power that they understand only imperfectly. When Arafat signed the Oslo accords, he never fully made the transition from revolutionary to statesman. He lost the trust of most Israelis, and of a large number of his own people.

*

Gaza's central prison was painted an innocent white. The Palestinian flag fluttering from the roof took the place of the Star of David, while a stout wall replaced the flimsy fence of Israeli occupation days. Large billboards advertising Pepsi, 7-Up, and locally made ice-cream screened the prison from view, as if to mock Gazans into believing that Palestinian authoritarian rule could be masked with the illusion of wealth and consumer culture.

Some things at the central prison took longer to change, however. Within a year of the Palestinian takeover, there reemerged the same line of women in headscarves standing outside a side entrance, waiting to be allowed to see their jailed sons. "When the Israelis were here we came to visit our brothers. And now when the Palestinians are here we still come to the jail," said 38-year-old Sahira Abul-Saroya, squatting in the shade as she cradled a baby. "They arrested my 19-year-old brother 48 days ago. They beat him badly."

For a fleeting moment, between the departure of the last Israeli guards and the arrival of the first Palestinian forces, the prison tasted the air of freedom. On that day in May 1994, you could simply wander in, as if to contemplate the archaeological ruins of a departed civilization.

For days, thousands of people lined the main road from the Rafah crossing point to welcome the arrival of the Palestinian security forces. The old Intifada graffiti had been replaced by welcoming messages and colorful murals of the "Ship of Return" carrying the Dome of the Rock and other symbols of Palestinian nationalism. Sometimes the picture was artfully fashioned from the Arabic letters for *Filastin*.

Inside the prison, Palestinian activists, some of them former inmates, were holding the keys until the uniformed contingent could take over. They were happy to show visitors around. The Israelis had cleaned the place up, but in one cell of the adjacent courtroom there were still the names of prisoners scrawled with a burned piece of orange peel. Twenty-five inmates, I was told, used to be packed in a cell three yards deep by two wide. "They should turn this place into a museum, for the children to see what happened during 27 years of occupation," said Nafez, a veteran who had been jailed here three times.

The men were full of hope. One recalled his trial: "I told the judge that one day we would rule ourselves. One day we will change places; that I would be the judge and he would be the prisoner," recounted Muhammad al-Ghazzawi.

At the main fence outside, a lone Israeli soldier casually ducked stones thrown by children returning from school. "I don't want them to leave," explained one child. "Who will we throw stones at when they're gone?"

The boy's words carried more truth than he imagined. The days of revolt of the first Intifada were brutal, but exhilarating. It gave Palestinians a sense of purpose, of power, of grasping destiny in their own hands. The enemy was obvious: Israel.

The half-peace negotiated at Oslo, leading to a half-freedom in Gaza and the West Bank, confused the picture. Palestinians did not have a fully-fledged state, but they no longer had the soldiers directly occupying their towns. The Palestinian Authority stood in this ambiguous middle ground, demanding independence but struggling to live up to its commitment to restrain those ready to use weapons to get it. Yasser Arafat became part Palestinian liberation leader, part Israeli vassal.

Israel made no secret of what it expected from the Palestinians. In 1993, just before signing the Oslo accords, Rabin explained: "The Palestinians will be better at [establishing internal security] than we were, because they will allow no appeals to the Supreme Court and will prevent [groups like] the Association for Civil Rights in Israel from criticizing the conditions there. [. . .] They will rule by their own methods, freeing, and this is most important, the Israeli soldiers from having to do what they will do."

For decades Arafat represented the aspirations of a whole people. Now he had to twist and turn to balance the competing demands of his exasperated people and his ambivalent Israeli peace partners, and usually upset both. The gates of Gaza's prison reflected this strange ambivalence. At times of security cooperation with Israel, the cells filled with Islamic suspects, many of them veterans of Israeli jails. At times of confrontation, such as during the Al-Aqsa Intifada, they emptied out as Palestinian factions united against Israel.

When Israel liquidated Yihya Ayyash, the bomber was given a hero's funeral by tens of thousands of Palestinians in Gaza and the Palestinian Authority bemoaned the loss of the "martyr." Arafat, who only weeks earlier had removed his *keffiyeh* during a condolence call to Rabin's widow in Tel Aviv, now set out to make a condolence visit to the Hamas spokesman, Mahmoud al-Zahhar, himself a frequent inmate of Arafat's prisons.

But when Hamas embarked on its revenge bombings, Arafat's security forces cast their net far and wide. The attacks reached such intensity that they were about to ruin Arafat's diplomatic game.

All of a sudden, after the carnage of 1996, Hamas became strangely dormant. Apart from a short spate of attacks in the summer of 1997, there was almost total silence from the bombers until the Al-Aqsa Intifada, regardless of whether the peace process was "stalled" in the Netanyahu years or made "progress" under his Labor successor, Ehud Barak. The release of Sheikh Ahmad Yassin in October 1997—in exchange for two Mossad agents arrested in Jordan after a botched assassination attempt against a Hamas political leader—may have had a moderating influence.

The Palestinians have long complained, with some justification, that Hamas was being manipulated by Jordan (supposedly Israel's best friend in the Arab world) to undermine the Palestinian Authority. But the accession of King Abdallah to the throne in Jordan in 1999 seemed to make it more difficult for Hamas to operate freely in Amman. The major factor seems to have been Arafat's cooperation with Israeli security forces, with the direct involvement of the CIA. Ramadan Shallah, the leader of Islamic Jihad, once complained in apologetic tones: "Regrettably, Arafat has so many intelligence services in the self-rule areas that if you open your window, preventive security peeps in; if you open your door, the presidential security service comes in; if you go out to your garden, you bump into military intelligence; and if you go out to the street, you come across general intelligence."

As Rabin predicted, the Palestinian security forces operated with even fewer legal niceties than the Israelis. Civilian judges were routinely ignored, security courts condemned people to death with little semblance of due process. Torture was common. In the first four years of self-rule, more Palestinians died in Palestinian prisons than in Israeli ones.

In addition to the "enemies of peace," as Israel called those who continued to wage armed attacks, Palestinian prisons also held "enemies of Arafat." Critics, sometimes members of Arafat's own legislature and students at Bir Zeit University, were locked up for being too vociferous in their denunciations of his semidictatorship. Some journalists have been detained merely for broadcasting the proceedings of the elected Palestinian council, or even for not reporting prominently enough sycophantic praise heaped on Arafat.

Several prominent human rights activists in Gaza who long fought against Israeli abuses—such as Eyad Sarraj, a Gaza psychiatrist, and Raji Sourani, a prominent lawyer—have been repeatedly arrested and harassed. In 1996, Sarraj spent a week in jail after telling the *New York Times*: "People are intimidated. There is an overwhelming sense of fear. The regime is corrupt, dictatorial, oppressive. I say this with sadness, but during the Israeli occupation I was 100 times freer." At the time many felt that Sarraj had overdone his criticism, but soon enough such comments became commonplace.

In a climate of both confusion and authoritarian rule, Edward Said, the Columbia University academic, described Arafat's regime as bearing "the lineaments of an unappetizing marriage between the chaos of civil war in Lebanon and the tyranny of Saddam Hussein's Iraq."

It took a long time for the international human rights machinery to pay attention to what was being done by the Palestinian security forces. The Palestinians had for so long been the victims of the Israelis that it was difficult to begin to think of them as oppressors. The New York–based Human Rights Watch, in its 2000 annual report, stated: "Arbitrary detention without charge or trial, torture and ill-treatment during interrogation, grossly unfair trials, and restrictions on freedom of association and expression continued."

Arafat has permitted a façade of democracy. The Palestinian legislative council, elected at the same time as Arafat, has debated and complained about corruption, lack of accountability, waste of public funds, and the need for the rule of law. Arafat, however, has largely ignored his "parliament" and has left legislation he does not like, to gather dust on his desk. Arafat regards himself as a Palestinian patriarch, a father figure who demands respect and occasionally produces a stick to keep his unruly clan in line. Husam Khader, one of the locally bred Fatah activists from Nablus who once objected to Arafat's move to impose his choice for Speaker of the council, recounted a quintessentially Arafatesque response to the challenge: "He called me over during a council meeting and pulled my head down by the ear. He kissed me on the left cheek, and then bit me on the right."

Arafat created a fiefdom in his own image. He obsessively controlled all the finances, all appointments, down to minute details such as deciding on civil servants' applications for holidays and travel per diems. Arafat's day was spent signing endless sheets of paper with the colored pens he kept in a sleeve pocket. Meetings were held in the dead of night, as if he were still presiding over an underground movement. Ministers had competing and overlapping tasks. This controlled chaos frustrated rational planning, but its main aim was to fragment the power of rivals and to keep control in Arafat's hands. Personally an ascetic, Arafat was widely blamed for permitting a system of patronage and corruption. With its bloated civil service and security forces, the Palestinian Authority became the main dispenser of jobs and privileges in the Gaza Strip. In the days of the armed struggle, Arafat used Arab funds to buy allegiance and create relations of dependence. In his would-be state, it was the donations of the Western world that propped up Arafat and his system.

With his return to Gaza, the mystique of Arafat wore off. Palestinians know better than most the faults of the strange, physically unassuming man who, some quip, speaks Arabic almost as poorly as he does English, and who has become visibly weakened.

"Arafat should have stayed outside in Tunis. Instead he should have appointed an interim authority accountable to him. It would have been better," said Haider Abdel-Shafi, president of the Red Crescent Society in the Gaza Strip when I went to see him in 1998, before the latest Intifada. The Palestinian Authority, he said, was a joke and should have been separated from the broader PLO leadership.

Abdel-Shafi, a founding member of the PLO, is respected in the Gaza Strip as a figure of principle. He had been the chief negotiator at the Madrid peace conference, but resigned in protest at the parallel negotiating process that took place behind his back in Oslo. The deal which Arafat signed, he said, had been a mistake. It fooled the world into thinking that the Palestinian problem had been resolved and took international pressure off Israel.

The Palestinian Authority argued that real democracy can only come about after independence. But for Abdel-Shafi, the only hope for Palestinian independence was to set up a model democracy that would inspire greater support at home and sympathy abroad. "Progress can only be achieved through a democratic change. We need an organized society to exploit whatever potential we have. We need to put the Palestinian house in order," said Abdel-Shafi speaking before the latest Intifada. "I think it will be difficult for that to happen under Arafat."

At the time only a minority of prominent Palestinians were willing to express such sentiments publicly. Most Palestinians grumbled about corruption and ineptitude, but seemed to accept the Palestinian Authority's argument that real democracy could only come about after independence. It was not until the disaster of Israel's incursion into the West Bank in April 2002 that Arafat came under serious pressure to change his ways.

Palestinians used to relieve their frustrations by telling jokes at Arafat's expense. One tells of a donkey that blocked the way of a car carrying top Palestinian leaders. One tried to drag the donkey away but it stubbornly stayed on the road. The other tried to throw stones but failed to move it. Finally Arafat got out of the car and whispered in the donkey's ear and the beast immediately trotted away.

"What did you say to the donkey?" asked the ministers.

"I offered him a job in the Palestinian Authority," replied the President.

For a few years under Palestinian autonomy, during the lull between the two Intifadas, life in Gaza gradually adopted an air of normality. Women could walk once more without a veil and not fear harassment by Islamic radicals. The long beachfront came back to life with families relaxing on the sand and restaurants for those fortunate enough to have jobs and disposable income.

Donkey carts mixed on the streets with businessmen carrying portable telephones. Roads were improved. There was even a short-lived building boom of office blocks and flats, but many have been left half completed. A belly-dancing club sprang up on the seafront offering sad, unerotic shows to thin audiences of men, mostly security personnel. The political graffiti defying Israeli soldiers was replaced by anodyne messages such as "The Hassan family welcomes the respected guests and congratulates the groom, Ibrahim."

And yet even in 1998, the slow-simmering frustration was palpable. I went to see Muhammad Abu Sisi, the father of Hatem Abu Sisi, the 16-year-old boy who was the first *shahid* to be killed in the Intifada of the 1980s. A street is named after him in the Jabalya refugee camp, the largest in Gaza, where the Intifada broke out in December 1987.

Abu Sisi was dressed in a white robe and white skullcap, and had the thin beard of a devout Muslim. A faded picture of the Dome of the Rock hung on his bare concrete wall, alongside two photographs of Hatem, the eldest son of his six children. "Hatem was a good boy. He was my favorite," said the father. "He was smart."

He told me the Intifada had been a huge waste of blood. Had it not forced the Israelis out of Gaza, and brought a Palestinian government? I asked. "What Palestinian government?" he retorted. "The Jews are still the government. Are you stupid? If you go just outside Gaza you will see Israeli soldiers. This thing they call peace is nonsense. It's *kalam fadi* [empty words]."

For many Gazans like Abu Sisi, the Gaza Strip is divided between those "inside" who lived under occupation, and those who came to rule from "outside"—Yasser Arafat and the rest of the exiled leadership of the PLO. "Those who came from outside did not do anything for us. They are corrupt. They came here poor and now they own villas. The Palestinian Authority is *zift* [Lit. tar; useless]." They came here as guards of the Israelis.

"I hope God will bring a storm and get rid of these pagans, both the Israelis and the Palestinians. We're waiting for God. God created us, and God will blow it up."

Even in these days of calm, everyone knew the struggle was not over. Shopkeepers and restaurant owners did a lively trade. But they knew it was not yet time to take down their embroidered maps of Palestine with the words: "For those who were martyred for the land of sad oranges. . . .And to those who have not been martyred yet."

★

The sun rose through the haze of dawn. The ground was still in dark twilight, but it was already alive with the groan of cars on their way to Erez, the gateway from the Gaza Strip to Israel. Thousands of people streamed toward the blood-orange sun in their battered Peugeots. Headlights glowed in the dust kicked up by wheels, shoes and the charcoal fires of stall-holders offering workers sustenance before the day's labor on the other side of the frontier.

Palestinian police officers stopped the traffic just short of the border. The workers—all men, many of them clutching small black plastic bags of food and other necessities—quickly shuffled along the last few hundred yards of a covered and fenced passageway. It opened up into more than two dozen lanes, each with a metal cage protecting an Israeli officer who checked the workers' permits. Turnstiles clattered constantly while armed soldiers paced between the lines of workers.

This human cattle enclosure represented, for Gaza, the days of plenty. It was the symbol of an economic boom—a herd of sullen day laborers doing Israel's heavy and dirty work. These workers considered themselves lucky to have jobs. A permit to work in Israel has been as valuable as any possession in Gaza, a guarantee of livelihood for a whole extended family.

Erez is Gaza's aorta. If the number of workers pumped out through Erez increases, Palestinian economic life quickens; if Israel clamps down, Gaza goes into spasm. During the Al-Aqsa Intifada, the Israelis tried rubber bullets, machine-guns, bombardment, and assassination. Their last hope of restoring control was that the economic agony of their blockade of Palestinian enclaves would, in the end, convince Palestinians to give up their uprising.

Since the signing of the Oslo accords, the rest of the Arab world, the intellectuals in particular, earnestly tried to hold the line against cultural or economic contacts with Israel. The Arabs' suspicion of the peace process was summed up by an Egyptian cartoon depicting an Israeli soldier trading in his uniform for a businessman's suit on his way to conquering the Arab world. For Palestinians, though, economic cooperation with the Jewish state is not a question of debate, but one of necessity. One of the most profitable Palestinian ventures has been the casino complex in Jericho established to attract Israeli gamblers. Before the Al-Aqsa Intifada, a growing number of Israeli bargain-hunters had begun to venture across the border of the West Bank to buy food and goods from Palestinians. An unspoken source of income has been the organized theft of Israeli cars, many of which are resprayed light blue and driven by none other than the Palestinian police.

In 1990, fully a third of Gaza's workforce had jobs in Israel. Earnings in Israel, and remittances from Gazans abroad, accounted for more than half the Strip's gross national product while Gaza's agricultural production, especially of oranges, steadily declined. Most Palestinian workers in Israel are employed as builders—in Tel Aviv, in the booming Israeli satellite towns and even in the Jewish settlements which gnaw away daily at what little is left of Arab Palestine. It is a sign of the utter dependence of Palestinians on the Israeli economy that, for the past three decades since Israeli occupation of the West Bank and Gaza Strip, the Jewish state has been built largely by Palestinian hands. In some cases the Gazans work as farm hands, picking crops from the lands once owned by their families.

All other economic activity in Gaza is a consequence of what happens in Erez and the other checkpoints around the Gaza Strip. Trade in and out of the Strip is held hostage by Israeli security restrictions. I have watched lorryloads of fruit and vegetables rotting in the sun because of Israeli soldiers' refusal to let them pass. Even when the goods can be exported, they must be unloaded from Gazan trucks and reloaded on to Israeli vehicles.

Within the Strip, the Israeli army controls strategic crossroads and routes, mainly to protect the few thousand settlers who occupy about a quarter of the total area of the Gaza Strip and take the lion's share of the water resources. As the Palestinian uprising has dragged on, whole tracts of agricultural land have been bulldozed and homes demolished along large swathes of the Gaza Strip to create free-fire zones for the army to protect the fence with Israel, the Jewish settlements in Gaza and the key roads.

Arafat built a fully equipped international airport near Rafah, but for four years it was a white elephant. The Israelis would not let it operate for fear of losing control over the passage of people and goods in Gaza. It finally opened in 1998, and Palestine Airways was able to move from its place of exile in Port Said in Sinai to Gaza, serving seven regional destinations with a fleet of three aircraft. With the uprising, this too has been repeatedly closed down. Even when it operated, however, the Israelis remained in charge in the back rooms. At the southern end of the Strip, Egypt imposes onerous restrictions on the passage of Palestinians, who must be escorted by police even if they simply want to go to Cairo airport.

"Liberated" Gaza is an enormous open prison. Size: 28 miles long, and between three and eight miles wide. Population: 1.04 million stateless Palestinians, two-thirds of whom are refugees. Gaza, the biggest Palestinian city, sees itself as the capital of the emerging Palestinian state. But for the moment it is little more than a refined Bantustan, a form of government abolished by the South Africans in the early 1990s and reinvented by the Israelis in the 1993 Oslo accords— with the agreement of the Palestinians and the blessing of the international community.

Yet for Arafat, Gaza is the kernel of statehood. It was the seat of Haj Amin al-Husseini's ill-starred All-Palestine Government, established under Egyptian auspices in 1948 and abolished by Cairo in 1952. It was the birthplace of the Intifada. Gaza is the only part of Palestine to which nobody has laid claim. Unlike the West Bank, which was annexed by Jordan, the Gaza Strip was ruled as a kind of Palestinian reservation by Egypt; it was kept at arm's length from Cairo. For Israelis, Gaza does not arouse the same religious and emotional intensity as the West Bank. In contrast with the reoccupation of the West Bank cities in 2002, Israeli forces feared getting bogged down in the heart of the Gaza Strip. Instead they controlled the edges and limited themselves to deep armored raids into the cities to round up suspects and exact retribution.

Gaza has been continuously inhabited for more than 3,000 years. It was born as a strategic staging post on the Via Maris, the Mediterranean highway of antiquity. Gauze fabric is believed to have originated in Gaza, hence its name. The Bible says Samson perished in Gaza while destroying the temple of the Philistines, who gave their name to Palestine and today's Palestinians. Gaza was the reputed burial place of the Prophet Muhammad's grandfather, and the birthplace in the eighth century of Al-Shafi, founder of the Shafi'ite school of Islamic jurisprudence.

Little of this venerable history is still visible in the dreary streets of Gaza. It is no longer an entrepôt of the Mediterranean, and has lost its strategic importance as the gateway between Africa and Asia. Gaza is a cul-de-sac, an appendix that nobody wants. Its railway runs from nowhere to nowhere: the tracks were ripped up by the Israelis to raise high fences around their army camps.

Arafat used to predict fondly that Gaza would become the Singapore of the Middle East. But even in the days of "peace," it was a brave investor who came here.

When I first arrived in the Middle East, there was virtually nothing to mark the border of the Gaza Strip. Erez did not appear on Israeli maps. Ever since Israel occupied the West Bank and Gaza Strip in 1967, the territories have been regarded as "administered" rather than "occupied." They were not legally annexed to Israel, but the cartographers did not dare draw the border. Only recently, after Oslo, have the frontiers reappeared on the maps.

At the height of the first Intifada, unwary Israeli drivers could stray into a Gaza riot. With the succession of security crises and the establishment of Palestinian autonomy, Israel adopted ever more stringent security measures at Erez. The border that has always existed in the minds of Israelis and Palestinians began to appear on the ground in the form of ever more numerous and larger army roadblocks.

Erez has become an international border passage, with a parking area, inspection sheds for vehicles, computers to verify identities, and even a separate terminal for foreigners, diplomats, U.N. staff, and Palestinian VIPs. Although the Palestinians do not formally constitute a state, the Israelis demand to see passports, and search bags.

The unilateral policy of "separation" between Israel and the Palestinian areas has broken up Palestinian communities. The Gaza Strip has been severed from the West Bank, while the West Bank has been cut off from East Jerusalem. From the mid-1990s, a whole lexicon developed to describe the restrictions. "Separation" means that only those with work permits and special passes may go to Israel. This became the norm even at times of calm. "General Closure" signifies that nobody may enter Israel from the West Bank and Gaza Strip. "Internal Closure" means that even travel between Palestinian towns within the West Bank is forbidden. A journey through the West Bank that takes an Israeli an hour or two on bypass roads can take Palestinians a whole day through checkpoints, side tracks and a succession of taxis. The restrictions, going by names such as "Closure" and "Internal Closure," were brought in to stop the suicide attacks of the 1990s, but became even more oppressive with the Palestinian uprising. Many are the tales of tragedies, such as the death of the sick unable to reach a hospital in time, caused by the obduracy of teenage soldiers manning the checkpoints. At one point the Israeli government floated the idea of building a long bridge between the two sides, but soon abandoned the notion as prohibitively expensive. In October 1999, six years after the signing of the Oslo accords, Israel finally allowed the opening of "safe passage" routes between Gaza and the West Bank through Israeli territory, but even this limited connection was severed as a result of the Al-Aqsa Intifada.

Closure may stop workers going to jobs, but the determined terrorist can often get through. Closure is, first and foremost, a political tool. It is a means of demonstrating to a nervous Israeli public that the security establishment is "doing something" about terrorists, and it is a means of reminding the Palestinian Authority that Israel retains the whip hand. To understand why Palestinians never fully embraced the Oslo accords, one need look no further than the economic and social impact of Israel's policy of "separation" and "closure."

In 1996, there were 121 days of general closure—one third of the year—causing a loss of more than 18 percent of GNP to the West Bank, and nearly 40 percent in the Gaza Strip. In the first years of Palestinian autonomy, between 1993 and 1996, Palestinian economists estimate that the real gross national product per capita fell by between a quarter and a third, despite the fact that the international community was pumping hundreds of millions of dollars a year into the Palestinian economy to support the peace process. The total losses caused by all restrictions in the four years amounted to about $2.8 billion, nearly twice the amount disbursed by foreign donors.

With the improvement of (Israeli) security, the closure was steadily eased. The first nine months of 2000 had seen the greatest economic activity in five years and the Palestinian economy was undergoing a modest boom. But the outbreak of the Al-Aqsa Intifada has been met with what the U.N. describes as the most draconian movement restrictions since the start of the occupation in 1967.

A report by the office of the U.N. Special Coordinator in the Occupied Territories found that in the period between October 1, 2000 and January 31, 2001—a period of 123 days—there had been 93 days of closure. This was compounded by severe restrictions *within* the Palestinian territories. In the Gaza Strip, Israeli forces repeatedly cut off the roads between the three main cities—Gaza, Khan Yunis, and Rafah.

By the end of the first year of the Al-Aqsa Intifada, a survey by the Palestinian Central Bureau of Statistics found that 14 percent of households had lost their usual source of income, and a further 48 percent reported losing more than half their usual income.

The Palestinian Economic Council for Development and Reconstruction reported that unemployment had more than quadrupled to 51 percent, while the Palestinian Gross National Product fell by about 37 percent. In January 2003, a report by Christian Aid, a British charity, found that nearly three-quarters of Palestinians were living below the U.N. poverty line of $2 a day, while a quarter of all children were anemic. If the Oslo accords failed to deliver security to the Israelis, they patently failed to deliver economic prosperity to impoverished Palestinians, whose GNP per capita is about one-tenth that of Israelis.

It is equally true, however, that the Intifada, and the Israeli security response to it, have had a devastating impact on Palestinian livelihoods. However much Israeli actions may be criticized, those who wage the Intifada and decide on its tactics also bear heavy responsibility for the pauperization of Palestinian society. Even in good times, when more workers were allowed into Israel, the increased income barely kept up with the Gaza Strip's population growth—more than 4 percent a year compared with Israel's 2 percent. The Palestinian population in the West Bank and Gaza Strip stands at about three million, and is projected to rise to 7.4 million by 2025. Adding the million or so Israeli Arabs, there are about four million Arabs within the boundaries of the old mandate of Palestine, compared with about five million Jews.

The Palestinians have traditionally regarded population growth as a strategic tool in the struggle against Israel. The wombs of Palestinian women, leaders liked to say, were the Palestinians' "biological weapon." I remember one cartoon showing a Palestinian mother

crying over the body of her son who had been killed by Israeli soldiers while in her belly she carried a fetus clutching an AK-47.

The evidence of this demographic explosion is seen throughout
Gaza, where every street seems to be a playground. The sight of a
foreigner passing by will instantly attract a swarm of curious and
boisterous kids. Half of the population is aged 14 or younger. Two-
thirds are younger than 25. These are the "Children of the Stones,"
the young rioters whose uprising hounded the Israelis out of most
of the Gaza Strip. They now hope to complete the job, helped by
their older cousins with guns and bombs. In the first Intifada, as
now in the second, the revolt was taken not only as a challenge
to the Israeli oppressor, but as a reproach to a whole generation
of indifferent Arabs, best captured by the late Syrian poet, Nizar
Qabbani:

> Like mussels we sit in cafés
> one hunts for a business venture
> one for another billion
> and a fourth wife
> and breasts polished by civilization.
>
> One stalks London for a lofty mansion
> one traffics in arms
> one seeks revenge in nightclubs
> one plots for a throne, a private army,
> and a princedom.
>
> Ah, generation of betrayal
> of surrogate indecent men,
> generation of leftovers,
> we'll be swept away
> —never mind the slow pace of history—
> by children bearing rocks.

* * *

To begin to understand Palestine, you must head into the hills of
Al-Diffeh al-Gharbiyyeh, the West Bank. Find the stone houses of the
villages, pass the wells and valleys known to the writers of the Bible,
watch the Palestinian women in dresses embroidered with the symbols of their tribal histories and watch the peasants labor around
olives planted on slopes terraced since time immemorial.

Here is the stuff of Palestinian memory; these are the images of its poetry. The writings of exiled Palestinians speak most emotionally about the distinctive aroma of the *za'atar*, the wild thyme that grows here; the particular flavor of their grandmother's *mansaf*, a dish of boiled mutton and rice in yoghurt sauce; the succulence of the figs; the simple grace of the stone houses with their internal vaulted ceilings; the sincere hospitality of Palestinian families; the warm familiarity of their religious rituals; the untutored wisdom of their proverbs and the natural spirituality of the local Arabic dialect. The *fellah*, the Palestinian peasant, is the exalted symbol of national identity, the keeper of the land and the guardian of the memory of the Lost Paradise of Palestine.

In the Gaza Strip, in the camps of Lebanon, in the cafés of London and Paris, Palestinians bemoan their destroyed villages in the coastal plain, but the world of the Palestinian peasant lives on in the rugged hills of the West Bank. Ruled by Turkish, British, Jordanian, and Israeli occupiers, the villagers of the West Bank have resolutely stayed on their land. If the exiles speak of *Al-Awda*, "The Return," then the West Bank villagers think of *sumud*, "steadfastness," a conscious self-preservation, a holding on to the land and tradition at all costs, a kind of stubborn passivity. The fellah on the West Bank may not be able to influence global events, but he can refuse to disappear. Fadwa Tuqan, a poet from Nablus, put it thus:

> Enough for me to die on her earth
> be buried in her
> to melt and vanish into her soil
> then sprout forth as a flower
> played with by a child from my country.
> Enough for me to remain
> in my country's embrace
> to be in her close as a handful of dust
> a sprig of grass
> a flower.

Gaza may be the land of the sad oranges, but the West Bank is the land of the olive tree, the quintessential symbol of sumud. It represents both continuity with the Mediterranean cultures that have passed over these hills, and the distinctive Palestinian identity of local peasants.

During the struggles between Israelis and Palestinians, the Israeli army has regularly uprooted olive trees as a form of punishment. Jewish settlers like to replace them with fast-growing conifers as testament to their claim to the land.

The West Bank is not quaint like Tuscany. Its hills are often rocky and bleak. The fellah is usually too poor nowadays to build anything more than a bare breeze-block hut. Yet the minaret of a village mosque lends an overall grace even to the most humdrum of villages.

In contrast, there is little of aesthetic value that the Israelis have built in the West Bank. Jewish settlements do not merge with the hills, but rudely cut off their tops. The settlers' houses stand out, glaring with white walls and red roofs, parodies of Swiss chalets. They are usually arranged in concentric rings around the hilltops, a modern circling of the wagons. The Israelis have vandalized the landscape of their own beloved biblical patriarchs.

The main road of the West Bank runs along the spine of the mountains, from Hebron to Jenin, twisting through the hills. At one point it opens into a wider vale. On the left there are two mountains, separated by a cleft leading westward down to the coast. These are Mount Ebal and Mount Gerizim, the symbols of God's curse and blessing respectively and the old center of Palestine, visible to ancient travelers both from the sea and from across the Jordan. Between the two lies the city of Nablus, close to the site of the biblical Shechem. This is the historical crossroads of the West Bank. Well-watered and fertile, Nablus has long considered itself the capital of the region. Indeed until the mid-nineteenth century it was the most important city in Palestine, the center of olive oil production and the manufacture of soap.

The opening up of Palestine to world trade allowed the coastal plain to develop. Jaffa gained ascendancy through the export of cash crops such as cotton and oranges. Meanwhile European intrigues in the Holy Land turned Jerusalem into the political capital, a role it has kept under the British and the Israelis.

But in many ways the story of Palestine begins in Nablus. The Bible recounts how Abraham first came to Shechem when he arrived in the Land of Canaan and built an altar in the "plain of Moreh." In antiquity the mountain range of Judea and Samaria preserved the ancient Hebrews from assimilation into the Canaanite, Philistine, and Greek cultures of the plains. In modern times the West Bank has been the barrier protecting Palestinians from being swallowed up by the Jewish state.

The kasbah of Nablus, with its maze of dark passageways, is a subversive's paradise. During the first Intifada a tranquil market day here could turn instantly into a battle between Israeli soldiers and stone-throwing youth, the *shebab*. The Palestinians almost always had the upper hand. The city market no longer boasts the finest goods from Europe and Syria—in the 1850s a British visitor, Mary Eliza Rogers, reported finding "Manchester prints, Sheffield cutlery, beads, and French bijouterie, very small mirrors, Bohemian glass bottles for narghiles, Swiss hand-kerchiefs . . ."—but it remains by far the liveliest of Palestine's Arab souks.

The Old City of Jerusalem has become commercialized with souvenir shops. The souk of Hebron, as the frontier of the war between Jewish settlers and Palestinians, is eerily deserted. Ramallah is too new to have a kasbah. In Nablus, however, you feel you are getting closer to the old Syrian centers of Damascus and Aleppo. There are Turkish steam baths and an Ottoman clock tower with an ode to Sultan Abdel-Hamid II written in a flourish of Arab calligraphy.

This is the domain of the handcart. Poke your head through the dark doorways in the kasbah and you will find men working around a vat of olive soap. An old Arab apothecary is indicated by the mummified carcass of a crocodile. The alleys are redolent of cumin and cardamom, saffron, and pepper. Lentils, beans, chickpeas, and nuts erupt out of coarse sacks. Little stalls sell bags of licorice juice. Nablus makes Palestine's finest *knafeh*, a sweet made of layered semolina and cheese drenched in syrup. During the month of Ramadan this gastronomic bounty is redoubled, and strolling through the souk during the daylight hours of fasting becomes an exquisite torture.

Nablus is known to Palestinians as the "Mountain of Fire" because of the ardor of its nationalism. There is a rebelliousness about the place that is recorded as far back as the secession of the northern kingdom of Israel after King Solomon's death and successive revolts by the Samaritans against the Byzantines. In more modern times, Nablus was the center of the revolt of Arab peasants against Muhammad Ali's Egypt in 1834, and has been prominent in almost all of the upheavals of the Palestinian struggle against Zionism.

★

For Palestinians today, however, the real political and economic capital of the West Bank is Ramallah. However much they may shout it from the roofs, East Jerusalem is not the capital of the Palestinian state: it is Ramallah. Gaza may be the seat of President Arafat's office, but most Palestinian ministries are either based in Ramallah, or have offices in the town. Ramallah is home to the Palestinian broadcaster, two newspapers, and many writers and artists. It even boasts a music conservatory. Since December 2001, when Israel began to target Arafat himself, the Palestinian leader has lived and worked amid the flattened remains of his compound in Ramallah.

During the years of normalization before the Al-Aqsa Intifada, dollar stores, world food restaurants, and cafés sprang up. In the summer the main park offers children's entertainment and live music. There were hotels, public swimming pools, cinema clubs, and Internet cafés. At weekends the center was jammed with traffic. Girls in tight jeans mixed with women in white peasant's veils. Valentine's Day became increasingly popular with young Palestinians here. Ramallah is bourgeois, secularized, cosmopolitan. It is home to the most famous Palestinian university, Bir Zeit.

In parts of Ramallah you are as likely to hear English spoken as Arabic. And even when they speak Arabic, well-heeled teenagers (sometimes called *Kit-Kat* because of their partiality to imported chocolate) mix the language with generous portions of American slang. Herein lies the source of the city's buzz—the umbilical link with *Amerka*, the United States. Sons and daughters of Ramallah form one of the largest Arab communities in the United States, and they have brought back money, skills, and education. There are more of the city's original families in America than in Ramallah. "How far is Ramallah from Palestine?" is a joke common among exiles.

Families used to quip that it is easier for a person from Ramallah to go to *Amerka* than to Jerusalem. Since Israel sealed off Jerusalem from the rest of the West Bank, this has become literally true for many residents. As Arab East Jerusalem has steadily withered on the vine, Ramallah has blossomed.

"Jerusalem is not going to be the capital. I am realistic. Since this is going to be the *de facto* capital, you have to start planning for it," said Ibrahim Abu Lughod, a professor of political science at Bir Zeit who returned to Palestine in 1991 after many years spent teaching at the Northwestern University in Chicago. "The future of Jerusalem is part of the future of the conflict. As long as there is inequality in power, nothing is going to happen to Jerusalem except a slow death. We've failed in our effort to revive it."

Arab East Jerusalem is being slowly strangled by the noose of Israeli checkpoints preventing movement between the city and the West Bank. School classes are dwindling, hospitals have trouble bringing in medical staff and theaters struggle to fill seats as West Bankers are banned from the city.

The first signs of life appear a few yards outside the Al-Ram checkpoint on the road to Ramallah. It is the most convenient meeting point for Jerusalemites and West Bankers. A succession of wedding halls has appeared to cater to divided families.

At first sight, Ramallah is an odd candidate for the capital. In a land crammed with religious and historical symbols, Ramallah has no claim to past greatness. It is an upstart, with its origins as a Christian agricultural village founded in the sixteenth century. The buildings which architects are desperately trying to save from disappearing under the urban sprawl were villas erected only in the 1920s. Ramallah has no baggage of history, and this may have been its blessing. It is, in a sense, the Palestinian equivalent of Tel Aviv, where a modern life can be started and experimented with.

Under the impact of emigration abroad, the influx of refugees and migration from surrounding villages, Ramallah has become a mixed town, yet has managed to retain a secular atmosphere. It provided sanctuary for many middle-class families fleeing Jaffa, Ramla, and Lod, refugees who proved to be among the most dynamic of Palestinians as they wandered through the world.

Ramallah became famous as a summer resort town in Jordanian times, a place of happy memories. At times of conflict, it dedicates itself to nationalist politics. With the outbreak of fighting in 1996, and the Al-Aqsa Intifada, Ramallah's name has featured prominently in the catalog of bloody incidents. Israel's security services came to regard Ramallah not only as the Palestinian political capital, but also "the capital of Palestinian terrorism." A briefing paper lists 32 major terrorist incidents—including the assassination in October 2001 of the hardline Israeli tourism minister Rehavam Zeevi—emanating from groups in the city. The city's political consciousness may have been stirred by a tradition of education. The Quakers established schools and clinics early on. Bir Zeit University (which Palestinians fondly describe as their own Harvard) became the first full-fledged Palestinian university in 1975.

Its head, Hanna Nasir, was deported in 1974 and did not return for 19 years. The university was repeatedly closed by the Israeli military authorities—the last time from January 8, 1988 until April 29, 1992. As the Intifada raged, teaching continued in impromptu classes held in offices and houses in Ramallah. Bir Zeit provided much of the intellectual leadership of the Intifada. Its academics, such as Hanan Ashrawi, a professor of English literature, were later prominent in the negotiating team that went to Madrid and subsequently bargained with the Israelis and Americans.

But if Bir Zeit provided the impetus for dialogue and peace negotiations with Israel, it quickly turned against much of what Oslo came to stand for. Its academics are among the most outspoken critics of corruption, nepotism, and the negotiating tactics of the Palestinian Authority. The West Bank's intellectual and cultural elite centered in Ramallah vocally demanded both liberation and democracy, and got neither. In February 2000—after students stoned the visiting French Prime Minister, Lionel Jospin, for denouncing Hizbollah—the Palestinian security forces encircled the campus, hauled students out of their dormitories and threw them behind bars.

Emile Ashrawi, a musician and photographer, now perhaps better known as Hanan Ashrawi's husband, explained the wild swings of emotion caused by Oslo. "There is an Arabic saying here that someone fasted and fasted, and instead of breaking the fast with a big meal he ate an onion. We suffered and suffered, and what did we get? An onion."

★

The Basilica of the Annunciation looks like a rocket that is about to take off from the ramshackle center of Nazareth. It is visible from every corner of the city, but from the outside at least, it imposes itself brutishly on the architecture of Jesus' hometown. The church, though, is the pride of the city and especially of the Franciscans who are the "custodians" of Roman Catholic sacred sites in the Holy Land. Built over the grotto venerated as the site where the Angel Gabriel told Mary that she would give birth to the Son of God, the interior of the current church is boldly modern. Its bare concrete structure is softened by mosaics and panels of artwork donated from communities as far away as Venezuela and Japan, representing the universality of the Church of Rome.

It is the largest church in the Middle East and its fortresslike architecture fits its position as a bastion of embattled Christianity in the Levant. Nazareth's importance to the Christian world meant the city was spared the wholesale eviction of Arabs experienced in Jaffa, Haifa, Lod, and Ramla. After 1948 Nazareth became the largest Arab city in Israel, a sanctuary for the remnant of Palestinians in the country, an Arab "capital" in a Jewish state.

Work on the new basilica began in 1955, at a time when Arabs in Israel, although considered to be citizens, lived under martial law and required permits to travel through the country. Palestinians in Israel were treated collectively as dangerous subversives, an Arab fifth column in the bosom of the Jewish state. At the same time they were cut off by the rest of the Arab world because they were regarded as suspiciously Israeli. They lived in a democracy, but were subject to military rule between 1948 and 1966. They were denied both their Palestinian identity and membership of Israeli society.

Palestinian Israelis, or Israeli Arabs, depending on one's preferred terminology, were reconnected with their Palestinian cousins in the West Bank and Gaza Strip after Israel's victory of 1967. But the million or so Israeli Arabs, who make up about one-fifth of the country's population, remain a kind of lost tribe of the Palestinian people, abandoned in the no-man's-land of the conflict between Israel and the Arabs, between their nationality and their identity. With the years the Arabic spoken by Palestinian Israelis has become peppered with Hebrew words.

The late Emile Habibi, in his allegorical novel *The Strange Events in the Disappearance of Said Abu al-Nahs al-Mutasha'il,* coined the term which has come to describe the surreal status of Israeli Arabs: *al-Mutasha'il,* "The Pessoptimist," made by combining *mutasha'im* (pessimist) with *mutafa'il* (optimist).

"When I go abroad it makes for a lot of confusion," said Adeeb Daoud, an architect living in Nazareth. "If I say I'm a Palestinian they think I live in the West Bank. If I say I'm Israeli they think I'm Jewish. I once went to Egypt and they thought I was a Yemenite Jew. You always have to explain your identity."

His father and mother were born in the now destroyed village of Iqrit, a Christian Maronite village on the border with Lebanon. His family quietly cherished Israel's Independence Day, usually detested by most Israeli Arabs, because it was the one day a year that Iqrit's villagers were allowed to return to the ruins of their homes. "When I was a boy we were not allowed to go to Iqrit," said Daoud. "But Independence Day was a day of freedom. All the closed military zones were opened for the day. You could go to Iqrit and cry over your village on the day that Israelis celebrate Independence Day."

Iqrit has become a *cause célèbre* for Israeli Palestinians. The village was not destroyed in the heat of battle, but as a result of cold postwar calculations about Israel's desire to have a strip of territory near the border clear of Arabs. The villagers were told they were being evacuated temporarily in November 1948 and, despite promises that they would return, Iqrit was demolished on Christmas Eve in 1951.

Only the blue-domed church of the Virgin Mary was left standing. "This church was God's witness to the terrible crime committed by Israel," said Aouneh Sbeit, a folk poet and a spokesman for Iqrit's campaign to return and rebuild the village. Here, among the icons of the Greek Catholic chapel, Iqrit's families gather for Christmas and Easter ceremonies, funerals and the occasional wedding. Iqrit's priest died years ago, so the parishioners must borrow the services of a churchman from other Arab Christian communities in the Galilee. Only the dead can go back: in 1972, Israel allowed the villagers to bury their dead in the village.

About 500 people lived here at the end of British rule. The surviving inhabitants, their descendants and dependants now number thousands of people scattered throughout Israel. In 1995, the government offered to allow only some of the villagers to return and retake part of their former lands, but the community rejected the proposal as insufficient.

Jewish communities also protested. "If they allow them to come back, thousands of people from other villages will also want to return," said Avi Krampa, head of the regional council and a resident of Shomera, a few hundred yards away from Iqrit. Did he not feel any remorse about taking over other people's land? "I feel very, very good. I don't feel guilty. I don't think that Jewish people should feel guilty about living in Israel."

Israel's Declaration of Independence solemnly pledges that the Jewish state "will foster the development of the country for the benefit of all its inhabitants; it will be based on freedom, justice and peace as envisaged by the prophets of Israel; it will ensure complete equality of social and political rights to all its inhabitants irrespective of religion, race or sex; it will guarantee freedom of religion, conscience, language, education and culture . . . ." The hard statistics, however, paint a story of systematic discrimination against Israel's Arab population. No matter what improvements Arabs may have enjoyed in their standards of living, health, and education, their achievements are far outstripped by those of Jews.

Arabs make up about 20 percent of the Israeli population, but in 1999 the government acknowledged that they held just 5 percent of civil service jobs. There were only 70 Arabs among the 3,386 officials in the four most senior ranks, while Arabs were overrepresented in low-paid untenured jobs. Since the establishment of the state, no Arab citizen has been appointed to the position of director-general or even deputy director-general in a government ministry. An Arab judge served for a year on Israel's Supreme Court, and was replaced by a Jew.

In 1997, the Israel Electric Corporation admitted it had just five Arabs and "a number of Druze and Circassians" in its staff of more than 10,000 people. Because electricity generation and distribution was seen as a strategic industry, each applicant had to undergo a security evaluation.

Arab municipalities account for 12 percent of the population, but in the early 1990s received less than 3 percent of the local government budget. A greater proportion of Arabs than Jews lives under the poverty line. Arab schools receive less money than Jewish schools. Of the Arabs who do go to university, only 0.5 percent receive government jobs (compared with 15 percent for Jewish graduates) and 10 percent become drivers, waiters, and hold other blue-collar jobs (compared with 3 percent of their Jewish counterparts).

Many jobs and benefits are reserved for veterans of the Israeli army, and by mutual consent, Israeli Arabs do not serve. Advertisements offering construction or other services regularly tell prospective clients that the company uses only *Avodat Ivrit*, a pioneering-era slogan meaning "Hebrew Labor." It is usually translated into English as "army veterans," which means the same thing: Jews only.

Druze and Bedouin are drafted into the army as part of Israel's attempt to divide and rule by maintaining distinct ethnic identities among non-Jews. The Druze, in particular, have developed a mixed reputation for bravery in battle and brutality in their treatment of Palestinian civilians. In the 1990s a small but growing number of Christian and Muslim Arabs were volunteering to serve in the Israeli army, seeking to stake their claim for equality in Israeli society by demonstrating that they share the burden of defending the state. But there was a countercurrent among Druze youngsters who complain that they are still discriminated against. A growing number are refusing to serve in the army.

The allocation of land is perhaps the most emotive of injustices. In the first three decades of statehood, the area farmed by Jewish farmers almost doubled, while that worked by Arabs shrank significantly. New towns are built for Jews, while Arabs face all manner of building restrictions. Nazareth and other Arab communities lost lands so that the state could establish the new, Jewish-dominated Natzeret Illit or "Upper Nazareth" on the heights above the Arab city. It does not take long to see which Nazareth receives the bigger share of state funds.

In 1976, a general strike called to protest about the mass expropriation of Arab land in the Galilee turned violent: six Arabs were killed and many others were injured in clashes with security forces. Since then, "Land Day" has become a yearly rallying point for Israeli Arabs, a time to assert national identity.

Palestinians in the West Bank and Gaza Strip have belatedly started to hold Land Day demonstrations in solidarity with the "Palestinians of 1948." In 2000, moreover, three Druze municipalities in Israel added their voices to the commemorations for the first time. The gradual normalization of relations between Israel and the Palestinians during the Oslo process brought attempts to establish greater equality for Israel's Arab citizens. On March 8, 2000, the Supreme Court ruled that it was illegal for the state to allocate land exclusively to Jews, upholding a complaint by an Arab couple who had been prevented from building a home in the Jewish settlement of Katzir. The decision was a blow to a basic pillar of the Zionist venture—that land acquired for Jews by the state should remain in Jewish hands in perpetuity. Months later, with passions running high over the Palestinian uprising across the border in the West Bank, the Jewish residents were mounting an effective rearguard action against admitting Arabs.

But as in the West Bank, the "progress" did not prevent Israeli Arabs from violently expressing their frustration when the Al-Aqsa Intifada broke out. There were short-lived, but unprecedented riots throughout Israeli Arab communities. The Israeli police killed 13 Israeli Arabs, and Jewish mobs from Upper Nazareth descended on the Arab city, killing two. It seemed that the Israelis had also concluded that the true identity of Israeli Arabs was not Israeli but Arab. The overreaction of the security forces destroyed the belief in the possibility of equality for Arabs. Despite an eve-of-election apology by Ehud Barak, he had lost the Arabs' crucial support and lost the election. In the 2003 elections, a parliamentary committee banned two Israeli Arab parliamentarians, Azmi Bishara and Ahmed Tibi, from running in the campaign on the grounds that they supported the enemies of Israel. However, the decision was overturned by a Supreme Court ruling.

For years nationalist politics among Palestinians in Israel revolved around the Communist party, the only joint Jewish-Arab party, which espoused equality for Arabs and a two-state solution to the Palestinian problem. Alongside Nazareth's crosses and church spires there fluttered the red flag, even after the collapse of Communism in the Soviet Union.

"Here we shall stay . . ." wrote Tawfiq Zayyad, the late poet and veteran Muslim-born Communist mayor of Nazareth,

> . . . Like a brick wall upon your breast
> And in your throat
> Like a splinter of glass, like spiky cactus
> And in your eyes
> A chaos of fire
>
> Here we shall stay
> Like a wall upon your breast
> Washing dishes in idle, buzzing bars
> Pouring drinks for our overlords
> Scrubbing floors in blackened kitchens
> To snatch a crumb for our children
> From between your blue fangs

Some Palestinians in Israel openly identified with the PLO, and left the country to join the armed struggle abroad. But for the most part, the central demand was equality with Jews rather than their eradication. For all their sympathy for Palestinians in the West Bank and Gaza Strip, few Palestinians in Israel express allegiance to Yasser Arafat or show any desire to live under his rule.

In 1998, Azmi Bishara, one of a new crop of nationalist activists, took the simple but preposterous step of running for election as the first Arab Prime Minister of Israel. Right-wing Jews were predictably outraged at his chutzpah and tried to rush through a bill requiring the Prime Minister of Israel to be Jewish. The response of many Arabs was equally telling. As Bishara toured the country ahead of the 1999 general election, Arab rivals and supposed friends alike tried to convince the upstart professor of philosophy to stand down. His campaign was denounced by other Israeli Arab leaders as "irresponsible," "political suicide," a "waste of Arab votes" and, by splitting the traditional Arab–Zionist Left alliance, they said, it would be a gift to the Likud party. Even Yasser Arafat was known to be upset.

Bishara knew he had no chance of victory, but he was fond of comparing his campaign to that of Jesse Jackson in the United States. He argued that the change in Israel's electoral system, which now provided separate ballots for Prime Minister and for parliament, gave Arabs an opportunity to place their grievances on the mainstream agenda. Bishara hoped to garner enough support to deny either the Labor or Likud candidate an outright victory, to force a second round of elections and, in return for his support for one or other side, to extract political concessions.

In the end, though, Bishara withdrew on the eve of the first round of voting and gave Labor's leader Ehud Barak a clear run to defeat the incumbent, Binyamin Netanyahu. The power play had failed, but in a sense Bishara had made his point—to expose the contradiction between Israel as a Jewish state and Israel as a democracy.

Bishara's political makeup contains a strange combination of elements. Although an Israeli, he was a long-time professor at Bir Zeit in the West Bank. Although running to become Prime Minister of Israel, he did not think Israeli Arabs should enlist for the Israeli army. He demanded the end of discrimination against Israeli Arabs, but believed it was impossible within the Zionist state. And although a Palestinian by identity, he no longer believes in the now-standard Palestinian demand—an independent state in the West Bank and Gaza Strip.

"Life here is full of contradictions," Bishara told me, puffing on one of his favorite cigars in his office in Nazareth. "The people are Arabs, Palestinians, but they yearn to be equal Israeli citizens. You will never get equality with the Jews. You are cheating yourself if you think you can be equal—unless you convert to Judaism."

In late 2001, he had his parliamentary immunity stripped to face charges of supporting terrorist organizations after two controversial speeches. In the first, in August 2000, he had hailed Israel's withdrawal from Lebanon as a "victory" for Hizbollah that gave him "the first taste of victory since the Six Day War and produced a spark of hope." A year later in Syria, he is said to have called on Arabs to "enlarge the sphere of resistance."

When I spoke to him in 1998, he said that partition, the two-state solution, should be abandoned. Instead there should be a single Israeli-Palestinian "binational state," with separate legislatures but a common parliament. This would deal with the problem of having to uproot Jewish settlers in the occupied territories, and of accommodating the aspirations of the Arabs within Israel. It would mean abandoning the cherished notions of exclusive national states.

The quest for equality, to be assimilated as Israelis, would only lead to fragmentation among the Arabs, a step backward. "If you lose national identity, you will not become Swedish. You will become Christian, Druze, and Muslims. It would be pre-national." As if to prove his point, activists of the Islamic movement were camped on an empty lot across the street from his office to demand the construction of a vast new mosque at the foot of the Basilica of the Annunciation.

The dispute caused the worst rift between Christians and Muslims in the city in living memory, complete with sectarian riots at Easter 1999. Christians saw the demand as a deliberate "provocation," an attempt by Muslims to rob them of their claim to the holiness of Nazareth. Muslims responded that the site was next to an Islamic shrine, and in any case there was a shortage of mosques in Nazareth. After granting approval for the mosque, the Israeli government stopped work on the site in January 2002 amid warnings by the Vatican that the mosque, if constructed, would form a "cancer" in the relations between the Vatican and Jews.

Islamic groups emerged in Israel in the 1990s. The first Islamic Parliamentarian, Abdulmalik Dehamshe, was elected to the Knesset in 1996, at the same time as Bishara. He immediately made his presence felt by giving his inaugural speech in Arabic and successfully demanding that a mosque be established within the Knesset building. As a lawyer representing Palestinian inmates from the occupied territories, he had been a Communist sympathizer in the 1960s and 1970s. But after serving seven years in jail for membership of Fatah, he became an observant Muslim and represented, among others, Sheikh Ahmad Yassin, the spiritual leader of Hamas.

Christians in Palestine have traditionally identified themselves principally as Palestinians. Fully integrated into Arab culture, they played a prominent role in the early agitation against Zionist settlement and the subsequent armed struggle. George Habash, the "Father of Hijacking," and Naif Hawatmeh—both Christians—headed radical Marxist factions that were once among the most determined opponents of Israel. But today Christians are an embattled minority within the Arab minority.

There were about 150,000 Christians in Palestine in 1947, accounting for nearly 13 percent of the country's Arab population. As the first Arab–Israeli war broke out, wealthier Christian families were among the first to leave and by the end of the conflict about 50,000 Christians became refugees as part of the Arab exodus from Palestine. Christians were not always evicted as systematically as Muslims, especially in the Galilee. Israeli government figures show that in 1949,

Christians made up a disproportionate 21 percent of the roughly 150,000 Arabs who remained in Israel.

Christians, mainly Greek Orthodox followed by Roman Catholics, today make up about 11 percent of Israel's non-Jewish population, faring better than their co-religionists in the West Bank and Gaza Strip, where they form a mere 2 percent of the population of the emerging Palestinian state. In Bethlehem, the churches have taken to tolling their bells in a sign of mourning when Christian girls marry Muslims.

In Jerusalem, Christians declined from about 29,000 under British rule in 1944, to roughly 15,000 under Jordanian rule in 1966 to about 10,000 today under Israeli control. "My fear is that in 15 years, Jerusalem and Bethlehem will become a Walt-Disney-type Christian theme park, a place for Christians to visit to see where Christians worshipped long ago," said George Carey, the Archbishop of Canterbury, when he visited the Middle East in 1992. "I want Christians to be able to come here and see living Christianity."

It has become customary to attribute the decline in the number of Christians to Israeli oppression. Certainly the conflict over Palestine (especially the turmoil in the West Bank and Gaza Strip), bureaucratic policies designed to reduce Arab numbers in Jerusalem, the whole series of Israeli security measures as well as policies giving preferential treatment to Jews have done little to encourage Christians to stay on. But this is only part of a complex picture. The difficulties which Christians are facing apply equally, and probably in larger measure, to Palestinian Muslims. Yet Muslims show greater fortitude. Christians throughout the Middle East are in trouble, from Iraq's Chaldeans to the Copts of Egypt. The attempt to carve out a Christian state in Lebanon ended in abject failure and a terrible civil war.

As an educated, middle-class sector of the population, Christians throughout the region struggle against two demographic enemies— a lower birth rate than Muslims and a higher rate of emigration. Christians leave in greater proportion because it is easier for them to do so—they have the education, skills, and family members abroad to help them gain entry and settle in a new country. Christians began leaving the country in the last century and the popularity of foreign names—George, Albert, Jimmy, etc.—is living testament to the affinity that they feel with the wider Christian world.

★

Plaintiff Number 11, Su'ad Srour al-Meri, recalled the day on Friday, September 17, 1982, when the Phalangists came to the Sabra

and Shatila camps in Beirut. She told the court in her written testimony:

> They lined us up in the living room and they started discussing
> whether or not to kill us. Then they lined us up against the wall and
> shot us. Those who died died; I survived with my mother. My broth-
> ers Maher and Ismail were hiding in the bathroom. When they [the
> soldiers] left the house, I started to call my brothers' names; when one
> of them replied I knew he wasn't dead. My mother and my sister
> were able to escape from the house, but I was not able. A few
> moments later while I was moving, they [the soldiers] came back,
> they said to me, "You're still alive?" and shot me again. I pretended to
> be dead. That night I got up and I stayed until Saturday. I pulled
> myself along crawling into the middle of the room and I covered the
> bodies. As I put out my hand to reach for the water jug they shot at
> me immediately. I only felt a bullet in my hand and the man started
> swearing. The second man came and he hit me on the head with his
> gun; I fainted. I stayed like that until Sunday, when our neighbor
> came and rescued me.

Su'ad was fourteen at the time of the massacre. She lost her father,
three brothers, (aged 11, 6, and 3) and two sisters (18 months and 9
months). Hers was one of many accounts of horror from the massacre of hundreds, perhaps thousands of Palestinians. A bullet was still
lodged in her spine, and she walked with crutches. In June 2001, she
traveled to Brussels as representative of 23 Palestinian and Lebanese
plaintiffs who lodged a civil action against the man they held responsible for the atrocities: Ariel Sharon, the Israeli Prime Minister, who
was Defense Minister at the time of the Israeli invasion of Lebanon.
"I've waited impatiently for this day," Su'ad told journalists.

Seizing on a Belgian law giving its courts "universal jurisdiction"
to try war crimes wherever they may take place, the plaintiffs accused
Sharon and three other senior officers at the time of the Lebanon war
of acts of genocide, crimes against humanity, and crimes against persons and goods protected by the 1949 Geneva Conventions.

More than half a century after the Nuremberg trials, and forty
years after Israel's Eichmann trial, the lengthening arm of international human rights law had reached the point where it was now
challenging a serving Israeli prime minister. Ariel Sharon, according
to the plaintiffs, was now to be ranked alongside the former Yugoslav
president Slobodan Milosevic, the Chilean dictator Gen. Augusto

Pinochet, and other rogues of the world. In the Belgian legal system, Sharon found himself in the same position as Hissène Habre, the former dictator of Chad, and Hashemi Rafsanjani, the ex-president of Iran, who were the subject of similar human rights lawsuits.

A few days before the Sharon case was presented in Brussels, a Belgian court convicted two Rwandan nuns and two others for their part in a massacre of about 7,000 ethnic Tutsis during the 1994 genocide.

But in 2002, the case against Sharon suffered several blows. In January, the former Phalangist warlord, Elie Hobeika, was killed by a car bomb in Beirut amid reports that he was ready to testify in the Sharon case.

The following month the International Court of Justice, which deals with disputes between states, ordered Belgium to rescind an arrest warrant for Adbulaye Yerodia Ndombasi, the former foreign minister of the Democratic Republic of Congo, on charges of war crimes and genocide for allegedly inciting a bloodbath against ethnic Tutsis in 1998. The court ruled that the minister enjoyed immunity as a serving minister at the time, and experts saw the decision as blunting Belgium's "universal jurisdiction" and sounding the death knell for the case against Sharon and other leaders.

In June, the Belgian appeals court ruled that the suit against Sharon "is not admissible because of the principle of Belgian law that crimes committed in other countries cannot be prosecuted in Belgium unless the author or presumed author has been found in Belgium." Campaigners to have Sharon indicted were cheered by moves in parliament to pass an "interpretative law" that would overturn this restriction. The "interpretation" was approved by the Belgian Senate in January 2003 and had to be passed by the House of Representatives. However, Sharon may avoid trial because the law would still require that cases be somehow linked to Belgium, and would preserve the state immunity of serving heads of state. Israel's legal establishment at first dismissed the Sharon lawsuit as a political stunt, asking why no leader of the Phalangists, who actually did the killing, had been named in the lawsuit. Chibli Mallat, the Lebanese lawyer organizing the legal challenge, said the complaint is also aimed at "all other persons, whether Lebanese or Israeli, whose responsibility will be established during the events of the investigation." In any case, he argued, Sharon's "command responsibility" was the most serious charge.

Israel's Belgian lawyer, Michele Hirsch, who played a central role in securing the convictions in the Rwandan nuns case, fought a rearguard battle to convince the judges that they had no jurisdiction over the Sabra and Shatila affair. Hirsh argued that, as in the Rwandan case, the suspects had to be in Belgium. Moreover, she claimed, the question of the 1982 massacres had already been the subject of a judicial inquiry by an Israeli commission headed by the Supreme Court president, Judge Yitzhak Kahan.

In the findings issued in February 1983, the commission dismissed Sharon's defense that he could not have foreseen that the Phalangists would have carried out mass murder when they were sent in by Israel supposedly to "mop up" Palestinian fighters.

The Israeli judges said "no prophetic powers" were needed to realize the danger of allowing the Phalangists to enter the Palestinian area days after the assassination of their leader, Bashir Gemayel. The commission ruled that Sharon bore indirect, but personal responsibility "for having disregarded the danger of acts of vengeance and bloodshed by the Phalangists against the population of the refugee camps, and having failed to take this danger into account when he decided to have the Phalangists enter the camp." Moreover, Sharon was deemed responsible "for not ordering appropriate measures for preventing or reducing the danger of massacre as a condition for the Phalangists' entry into the camp."

The commission sidestepped the question of whether Israel was in Lebanon as an occupying force, and therefore under the formal obligations of the laws of war, but said Israel could not avoid the issue. It said:

> . . . it should also not be forgotten that the Jews in various lands of exile, and also in the Land of Israel when it was under foreign rule, suffered greatly from pogroms perpetrated by various hooligans; and the danger of disturbances against Jews in various lands, it seems evident, has not yet passed. The Jewish public's stand has always been that the responsibility for such deeds falls not only on those who rioted and committed the atrocities, but also on those who were responsible for safety and public order, who could have prevented the disturbances and did not fulfill their obligations in this respect.

The Israeli cabinet accepted the report. Sharon was forced to resign as defense minister, but remained within the government as a minister without portfolio. Ever since then, Sharon has maintained that he bears no responsibility for what happened. He spent two decades fighting libel lawsuits in Israel and America, with little success, against journalists who wrote what he claimed were "fabrications."

He continues to maintain that the invasion of Lebanon was one of the most justified in Israeli history, and that the defeat of the PLO in Lebanon forced the Palestinian leadership to the discussion table to negotiate peace—even though he disagrees with the accords that emerged from the talks.

Now, even if he wins in Belgium, Sharon may yet spend years fending off war crimes suits against himself. Deep in his heart, Sharon might not have been surprised to hear that a human rights lawsuit was filed against him. In his autobiography, *Warrior*, Sharon notes how he told cabinet colleagues that approving the Kahan Commission report would mean endorsing the notion that the Israeli government had been guilty of mass murder. He recalled telling them: "If you accept the conclusions of the Kahan Commission you will be branding the mark of Cain on the foreheads of the Jewish people and on the State of Israel with your own hands."

Throughout his career as a soldier and politician, Sharon, known simply as "Arik," felt that his daring and visionary plans were constantly obstructed by others, be they incompetent generals, jealous political rivals, spineless ministers, or untrustworthy foreigners. In 1973, when the then Major-General Sharon left the army after he had been passed over for promotion to the top job, his friend Uri Dan predicted: "Those that do not want Sharon as chief-of-staff will see him as defense minister. Those that do not want him as defense minister will see him as prime minister."

The prophecy came true, but it took Sharon nearly two decades and the Al-Aqsa Intifada to rehabilitate himself in the eyes of Israelis after the Sabra and Shatila massacre. For years he was the loose cannon on the Right of Israeli politics. As housing minister in the Likud government in the early 1990s, Sharon, the man known as "the bulldozer," dedicated his considerable energy to expanding Jewish settlements in the West Bank and Gaza Strip.

He liked to claim he knew how to defeat terrorism, if only leaders had the political courage to do what was needed. Always an outsider, Sharon enjoyed the devoted following of core admirers, who greeted him with shouts of "Arik—King of Israel." But as much as Sharon could bring out passionate support, he also repelled a substantial proportion of Israelis.

Then, around 1996, Sharon appeared to change. As he was given senior positions in the Netanyahu government, first as national infrastructure minister and then as foreign minister, Sharon seemed to calm down. He became less abrasive and blustering, more of an Israeli elder statesman. "Has Ariel Sharon gone soft?" asked the *Jerusalem Report* in 1997. A year later, newspapers started wondering whether Sharon would turn out to be a "peacemaker," a figure like Moshe Dayan who went from being a security hawk to a dove in the peace negotiations with Egypt. The man who used to argue that "Jordan is Palestine" was given a warm reception in Amman. Sharon's expertise was central to the 1998 Wye River talks with Palestinians that agreed on a further stage of Israeli withdrawal from the West Bank. Slowly, the image of Sharon as the monster of Sabra and Shatila was dissolving into the earlier pragmatic Sharon who had ordered the dismantling of the Yamit settlement in Sinai under the terms of peace with Egypt.

When Binyamin Netanyahu lost the 1999 elections, Sharon was elected Likud leader. As a septuagenarian, he was regarded as something of a stand-in leader while the Likud party princes fought it out for supremacy. But then came the debacle of the Camp David talks in July 2001, and Sharon's visit to the Haram al-Sharif that sparked off the Intifada. Nobody will ever know why Sharon embarked on such a provocative act. Israel was awash in talk of possible Palestinian violence. Did he deliberately want to spark an explosion?

The most common explanation is prosaic: Sharon feared being outflanked on the Right by a resurgent Binyamin "Bibi" Netanyahu, who was showing signs of returning to the political fold. What better gesture than to take a stand on the indivisibility of holy Jerusalem? It may be banal, but one should not underestimate the importance of petty political rivalries on Israel's momentous questions of war and peace. Likewise, Barak's refusal to stop the visit may have been the outcome of a mixture of fear of being outmaneuvered on the question of Jerusalem, and the knowledge that Barak had a better chance of winning the election against Sharon than against Netanyahu. Sharon, one of the last of the generation of Israeli fighting fathers, can thank the Intifada that he detonated for sweeping him to power.

Many of those who voted for Sharon may have hoped for the return of the old Arik of Beirut, who would respond to every bullet with a missile and put the Palestinians back in their place. The Arab world denounced the rise to power of the man they called "The Butcher of Beirut," but Sharon moved cautiously at first. Sharon may have defended his actions in the Lebanon war, but he seemed to learn the need for consensus among the Israeli public in waging military operations. The risks of divisions became even more apparent with the assassination of Yitzhak Rabin, whom Sharon had served as adviser on terrorism in the 1970s.

Sharon established a broad government of national unity, putting Labor figures in key positions. Binyamin Ben-Eliezer became defense minister and Shimon Peres became foreign minister—one Labor minister to fight the Intifada, and the other to defend Israel's actions to the world. Sharon, the champion of "Greater Israel" and the man who said any territorial compromise would result in more terrorism, now said he was ready to make "painful compromises" for peace if the Palestinians would give up violence. In 1990, Sharon had a shouting match with the ultrahawkish Likud prime minister, Yitzhak Shamir, at a Likud party meeting during a row over Shamir's minimal diplomatic steps in negotiating the Palestinian issue with the U.S. and Egypt. Now he speaks of the possibility of a Palestinian state being established. In contrast with Barak, who negotiated with the Palestinians virtually to the last day of his government, Sharon has declined to resume talks on a permanent status, imposing demands such as a seven-day period of quiet before talks could begin. In any case his notion of a Palestinian state is of a rump territory consisting of about half the territory of the West Bank, instead of the equivalent of 97 percent that Labor was prepared to offer.

For several months, Sharon's methods for suppressing the Intifada were little different to those of his predecessor, who had already resorted to using helicopters, gunships and tanks, imposing closures and uprooting of trees. Sharon, the general who led the famous Unit 101 into the Gaza Strip for counterinsurgency operations in the 1950s, seemed as hamstrung as the outgoing general, Ehud Barak, the much-decorated commando who, dressed as a woman, assassinated Palestinian leaders in Beirut in the 1970s.

Then toward the end of 2001 flashes of the old Sharon returned. Rather than negotiate a deal with Arafat, he tried to make the Palestinian leader "irrelevant," besieging him in his headquarters and threatening to send him back into exile. By then, however, Israelis were feeling so embattled that the Labor minister acquiesced in such measures, insisting only that Arafat not be personally harmed.

The Labor party, fearing punishment at the ballot box, remained in government until October 2002. It summoned up the courage to revert to its pro-peace platform, electing a new leader in the form of Amram Mitzna, a former general who advocated a resumption of talks with Palestinians and, if necessary, unilateral "separation" from the occupied territories.

Israelis, however, were not to listen to this message. In the campaign for the general elections in January 2003, Sharon was hurt by allegations that a controversial $1.5 million contribution to the Sharon family breached party funding laws. His televised explanation was abruptly taken off the air by a judge who deemed the appearance to be a partisan attack on Labor. Yet Likud rose from 19 to 38 seats in the 120-seat Knesset. The Labor party was trounced, falling from 25 seats to 19, while the dovish Meretz party slumped from 10 seats to 6. The defeat of the "peace camp" was best exemplified by Yael Dayan and Yossi Beilin, the leading doves of the Labor party who defected to Meretz only to find they did not win a seat.

At the time of writing in February 2003 it was still unclear what kind of coalition Sharon would be able to put together. He made clear his preference for another government of national unity with Labor, but Mitzna was adamant that he stay out of a coalition with Likud and would instead try to rebuild the party as a "fighting opposition."

In a political spectrum that has shifted sharply to the Right, Sharon now presented himself as a centrist. He had two months earlier fended off a leadership challenge from Bibi Netanyahu, who set himself up as the champion from the Right, demanding the expulsion of Arafat and offering only autonomy for Palestinians. In May of 2002, Sharon, the man who once said any concession to Palestinians would only invite more terrorism, stood against his own party's central committee, which voted a motion declaring that "No Palestinian state will be established west of the Jordan." In Israel and abroad, Sharon came to be regarded as the sane, moderate voice of the Likud party. In private conversations with diplomats and world leaders, he dropped hints that he was the man who could make peace with the Palestinians once he had secured a period of calm and neutralized Arafat. For as long as the uprising continues, Sharon's claim to want a political settlement with the Palestinians will never be seriously challenged.

Even for a country like Israel, where old politicians are constantly recycled, Sharon has made an extraordinary comeback. The "mark of Cain" that was the Lebanon War has been effaced by the bloodshed of the Al-Aqsa Intifada and turned the old warrior into a would-be "man of peace." Yasser Arafat's greatest achievement in more than two years of the Palestinian uprising was to rehabilitate Ariel Sharon.

*

There is something both macabre and farcical about the photograph of Yasser Arafat lying on a hospital cot, grim-faced, giving blood for the victims of the September 11 attacks in America. Throughout the previous year of the Palestinian uprising, Arafat had been accused by Israel of fomenting terrorism, or at least of harboring terrorists. As a student in the 1950s, Arafat had sent a petition written in blood telling the Egyptian government "Don't Forget about Palestine." Now with his own blood the Palestinian leader was desperately trying to send American leaders the message: "I am not a Terrorist."

A day earlier, immediately after the destruction of the World Trade Center and the other attacks, Arafat had ordered his security forces to quell Palestinian crowds spontaneously celebrating the disaster that had befallen America. They tried to stop news of the rallies from spreading, to the point of confiscating film and threatening cameramen. Arafat immediately sent his condolences to the American people, saying: "It's an unbelievable disaster. It is touching our hearts. It is very difficult to explain my feelings. God help them, God help them." When the displays of anti-American passions embarrassed the Palestinian leadership, Arafat moved quickly to send a positive television counterimage with his blood-giving session.

Arafat was determined not to repeat his error of more than a decade earlier, when he disastrously threw in his lot with Saddam Hussein after Iraq's invasion of Kuwait. Now, as Washington demanded to know who was with America in the "war against terrorism" and who was against, Arafat elected to stay on the right side of President George W. Bush. The Palestinian leadership knew that for several weeks before September 11, the Bush administration had been preparing to "engage" once more in the Middle East with a major speech to the United Nations and a possible meeting between the U.S. president and the Palestinian leader.

In the first six months of the presidency, Bush's aides had made clear he had no intention of becoming personally involved in the details of Israeli-Palestinian peace talks as Bill Clinton had done until his last day in office. President Bush, officials said, could not match Clinton's personal fervor and in any case it was better not to risk his prestige unless there was a good chance of a successful mediation. In fact, some White House aides suggested Clinton's attempt to force the peace may have precipitated the violence. The direct involvement of the president, they explained, was the "last shot" in the diplomatic arsenal and should be saved for when it would be most effective. The office of Clinton's special envoy to the Middle East was folded back into the State Department. If there was an early priority in the Middle East for the Bush administration it was Iraq.

During his election campaign President Bush had declared his commitment to Israel's security and, like others before him, spoke of his desire to move the U.S. embassy to Jerusalem. The State Department under Colin Powell was more critical. It issued periodic rebukes of Israeli actions, such as the demolition of Palestinian homes. In June 2001, Powell endorsed the idea of international monitors to help supervise a ceasefire, a move that Israel has repeatedly rejected.

With the U.S. stepping back from the Arab-Israeli dispute, it was left largely to a succession of Europeans to try to hold the ring around the combatants. Figures such as Javier Solana, the European Union foreign policy supremo; Lord Levy, special envoy of the British Prime Minister; and a succession of European foreign ministers maintained a constant flow of visits that became known as "relay diplomacy." They believed that the presence of foreigners provided "a dose of aspirin" to keep down the temperature of the conflict, while they waited for America to administer the cure. A surprisingly active role was played by Germany, despite the baggage of its Nazi history. In June 2001, Joshka Fischer, the German foreign minister, was in his hotel on the Tel Aviv beachfront when a suicide bomber blew himself up at a discotheque nearby, killing himself along with 21 Israeli teenagers. Outraged, Fischer said he went to see Arafat in Ramallah after the bomb and "banged my hand on the desk to demonstrate the seriousness of the situation." Threatening to cut off European aid to the Palestinians, he extracted a public declaration of a ceasefire from Arafat, dictating changes to the statement, but like other truces it was short-lived.

The September 11 attacks forced the Bush administration to reassess its policy in the Middle East, just as it was doing everywhere else. Sharon hoped that after September 11 the world at large would be more sympathetic to Israel's own "war on terrorism." But as so often in the past, the unexpected crisis gave Arafat a new lease of life, a chance to reshuffle a poor hand of cards in the hope of finding an elusive ace.

The Intifada had been stuck in a bloody and debilitating cycle that suffocated Palestinian society and was weakening the Palestinian Authority, both at home and abroad. Western countries had criticized Israel's use of "excessive force," but Palestinian attacks on Israeli civilians were sullying the Palestinian case. Any hopes Arafat may have had that the Intifada would bring substantial Arab support proved to be in vain. Arab capitals, wanting to avoid an escalation with Israel,

were long on rhetoric and short on material or diplomatic assistance
for the Palestinians. "Arafat is like an abandoned dog," one Palestinian
journalist told me. Behind the scenes some Arab leaders tried to
moderate Palestinian actions for fear that the unrest could spill into
the region. After all, popular fury against Israel and America could
easily turn to hatred of the "betrayal" of Arab governments that failed
to support the Palestinian cause.

Washington now needed the support of Arab and Muslim states,
not only to help in the hunt for al-Qa'ida activists, but more important, to fend off accusations that the forthcoming war in Afghanistan
was a war against Islam. In return, the Arabs now demanded action to
address the Israeli-Palestinian conflict.

In a series of seemingly coordinated moves, the Bush administration leaked the news that it would have launched a new Middle East
initiative in September, had the attacks on America not taken place.
On the day the reports appeared, Bush confirmed that he supported
Palestinian statehood. "The idea of a Palestinian state has always been
a part of a vision, so long as the right of Israel to exist is respected,"
Bush told reporters after meeting congressional leaders. A Palestinian
state had long been the implied destination of the Oslo framework,
and had been advocated openly by President Clinton a few months
earlier, but the idea had never been previously endorsed by a Republican president.

President Bush's remark, so seemingly casual, was seen as an important change of direction by some Arabs. A columnist writing in the
Lebanese daily *al-Nahar* said the statement amounted to an American
version of the Balfour Declaration, which established a Jewish homeland. But in London, an editorial in the pan-Arab daily expressed
skepticism. "Did we have to lose the lives of six thousand innocent
Americans and a hundred billion dollars before Bush Jr. 'mumbled'
these few vague words about a Palestinian state?" the paper asked.

In Jerusalem, there was alarm that Israel would, as Sharon put it, be
made to "pay the price" of building America's coalition against Bin
Laden. Sharon responded with a misjudged appeal to Washington: "I
call on the Western democracies and primarily the leader of the free
world, the United States: do not repeat the dreadful mistake of 1938,
when enlightened European democracies decided to sacrifice
Czechoslovakia for a 'convenient temporary solution.' Do not try to
appease the Arabs at our expense—this is unacceptable to us. Israel
will not be Czechoslovakia." The White House quickly made clear its
anger at the implicit accusation that Bush, the leader of the one

country that has resolutely stood by Israel politically and militarily, was acting as a latter-day Neville Chamberlain, who had appeased Hitler. "Those comments made by the prime minister are unacceptable in the president's opinion," said the White House spokesman bluntly. One European foreign minister recalled: "Bush was furious. He may not know much history, but he certainly knew about Czechoslovakia."

Such intemperate language between Israel and its most important protector had not been heard for at least a decade, since President Bush's father was in the White House. Then, as in 2001, the cause of the rupture was Washington's attempt to build a coalition in the Islamic world and to force political concessions from Israel. During the 1991 Gulf War, the elder Bush demanded that Israel refrain from retaliating against repeated salvos of Scud missiles fired by Iraq at the Jewish state for fear that Israel's involvement would upset the military alliance. A few months after the defeat of Iraq, Bush rewarded his Arab allies by compelling the reluctant Israeli prime minister, Yitzhak Shamir, to attend the Madrid peace conference. As relations between Washington and the Shamir government deteriorated over Israel's settlement policy, Washington froze $10 billion worth of loan guarantees. Israel has long been regarded by the U.S. as a "strategic ally." But in 1991 it was treated as a strategic liability. The same seemed to be happening after September 11, 2001.

With Sharon on the defensive and his coalition in turmoil, Yasser Arafat was effectively rehabilitated in the West when, after a year of diplomatic isolation, he was invited to Downing Street by Tony Blair, the British prime minister who was acting ever more as America's alter ego in Europe. Arafat repaid Blair with a public repudiation of Osama bin Laden's claim to be fighting on behalf of the Palestinians. "The Palestinian cause is a just one . . ." said Arafat, "There can be no mix between our just cause and objectives, and methods that are unjust like the terrorist acts and killing of civilians that happened recently in the United States." As he took his leave, Arafat flashed a V-for-Victory sign and gave a broad grin that summed up his delight. The Houdini of the Middle East appeared to have staged another of his great political escapes. "The Old Man," as Arafat was sometimes known, flipped to reposition himself with the swiftness and precision of a young gymnast. Or so it seemed.

Throughout the Intifada, Arafat had adopted a laissez-faire attitude to Palestinian violence. Now that he needed calm, the more extreme factions and even many within his own Fatah movement would not

easily submit to Arafat's diplomatic imperatives. Indeed, some probably set out deliberately to sabotage them.

Two days after Arafat's appearance in London, gunmen from the
Popular Front for the Liberation of Palestine assassinated the hardline
tourism minister, Rahavam Zeevi, in supposed retaliation for Israel's
assassination of their own leader, Abu Ali Mustafa, several months
previously. Earlier in the week Zeevi, who advocated the "transfer" of
Palestinians from the occupied territories and routinely called militants "vermin" that should be eliminated, had announced his resignation from the government because Sharon was, in his view, going
soft. Indeed, the night before the murder Sharon had announced he
would personally lead peace negotiations with the explicit aim of
creating a Palestinian state within certain "red lines" including Israeli
control of Jerusalem.

Zeevi's murder marked the first time in decades of conflict that
Palestinians had killed an Israeli cabinet minister. The last high-profile
assassination attempt, against the Israeli ambassador to London,
Shlomo Argov, resulted in Israel's invasion of Lebanon in 1982. Telling
ministers that "the era of Arafat is over," Sharon ordered the army to
enter deep into several Palestinian cities in an operation that left scores
dead over the following days and weeks. Despite the casualties, and the
international attention drawn by the damage done to Bethlehem in
the run-up to Christmas, Sharon was retaking the political high
ground. He accused Arafat of being the Palestinian version of Osama
bin Laden. The dominant issue of Middle East diplomacy, for months
to come, was no longer Sharon's unwillingness to make peace, but
Arafat's credibility. As if to underline Israel's accusation of Arafat's
"double-talk," a day after the Zeevi assassination Israeli forces killed a
senior leader of the Tanzim, the grassroots militia of Arafat's own Fatah
movement that had been prominent in the Intifada. Atef Abayat was
killed with a booby-trap bomb placed in his car. Senior Israeli officials
were quick to point out that Arafat had assured foreign envoys that
Abayat, on the top ten list of Israel's most-wanted men, had been
arrested and was in a Palestinian jail. "Arafat informed the Europeans
that Abayat was under arrest in Bethlehem. A few hours later we killed
him," said a senior Israeli military intelligence officer. "He wandered
around Bethlehem freely. Today Europeans are very critical of Arafat."

At the United Nations General Assembly in New York in November, President Bush refused even to shake hands with Arafat, who had
been a regular visitor to the Clinton White House. Bush told the
assembly in a speech that he was working "toward a day when two

states, Israel and Palestine, live peacefully together within secure and recognized borders." But he added the warning: "Peace will only come when all have sworn off, forever, incitement, violence, and terror."

A little more than a week later, with Arafat starting to round up Islamic suspects, Colin Powell launched his long-delayed peace initiative, saying "It's time—no it's past time—to end this terrible toll on the future." He adopted unusually tough language to demand that Palestinians stop violence, and that Israel end its "occupation," a term hitherto used only rarely by Washington. To demonstrate his seriousness, he appointed a special envoy, Anthony Zinni, a retired Marine Corps general, to broker a ceasefire. He made clear that Arafat had to take the first step: "Get that ceasefire in place, and other things start to happen. Without that ceasefire, we are all still trapped in the quicksand of hatred," said the Secretary of State.

Powell's initiative, in preparation for several months, was dead almost from the moment it started and, in retrospect, marked a turning point in the Israeli government's policy toward Yasser Arafat. Far from soothing the combatants, the arrival of Gen. Zinni coincided with a new escalation. In the first two days of December 2001, Islamic extremists staged a double suicide bombing that killed 10 Israelis and wounded 170 in a busy Jerusalem pedestrian precinct, as well as a suicide bombing on a bus in Haifa that killed a further 15 Israelis. It was, Hamas said, retaliation for Israel's assassination of a prominent Hamas militant, Mahmoud Abu Hanoud, in a missile strike a week earlier. The Palestinian Authority declared a "state of emergency" and began rounding up more than 100 Hamas and Islamic Jihad suspects. But in contrast with the Islamists' careful avoidance of confrontation with Arafat's forces during a major round-up in 1996, Hamas leaders defied the Palestinian Authority, accusing it of "trying to become Israel's protector." Islamic militants rioted and exchanged fire with Palestinian security forces.

The Sharon government was not impressed and embarked on a campaign to weaken Arafat personally. The cabinet declared that "the Palestinian Authority is an entity that supports terrorism, and must be dealt with accordingly."

As Israel visited retribution on the various Palestinian security arms—the very bodies that are supposed to be arresting the militants—Israeli helicopters opened fire noisily and spectacularly on Arafat's helipad, destroying helicopters that had long been grounded months earlier by the Israelis. Bulldozers tore up the runway at Gaza airport, which Arafat had already been banned from using. Helicopters rocketed a building in the compound of Arafat's offices in Ramallah, about 50 yards away from the Palestinian leader. Ten days after the Tel Aviv and Haifa attacks, 10 Israelis were killed in an ambush on a bus in the West Bank. Sharon sent his tanks into Ramallah. One pointed its barrel directly at Arafat's offices about 150 yards away. Sharon's government declared Arafat to be "irrelevant," yet it dedicated itself to maximizing the political and diplomatic pressure on the Palestinian leader. Arafat became a prisoner in Ramallah, unable to fly abroad or even to go to attend Christmas celebrations in Bethlehem.

Facing demands for action from the U.S., Europe and the United Nations, Arafat appeared on Palestinian television on December 16 and issued his strongest call for calm since the start of the Intifada. "I renew the call to completely halt all activities, especially suicide attacks which we have condemned and always condemned." A few days later, as gun battles between Palestinian forces and Islamic groups left six dead and more than 70 injured in the worst case of inter-Palestinian fighting in seven years, Hamas announced it would suspend mortar attacks and suicide missions inside Israel "until further notice." This left open the option of attacking Israeli targets in the occupied territories.

The announcement was followed by the quietest three weeks since the start of the uprising. Arafat finally appeared to have changed strategy, but rather than seize the moment the international community became distracted by a crisis between India and Pakistan that, if allowed to escalate, could lead to war and even a nuclear cataclysm. Just as Israeli ministers began to ask whether it might be possible to renew the dialogue with the Palestinians and Zinni returned to the region to kick-start security talks, Israeli commandos seized a ship laden with weapons, including Katyusha rockets, in the Red Sea. Israel maintained the weapons were being sent to the Palestinian Authority by Iran and accused Arafat of planning to terrorize Israeli cities. On January 9, 2002, the ceasefire was broken. Two Hamas gunmen slipped into an Israeli army outpost on the border between the Gaza Strip and Egypt, killing four soldiers during a short, sharp fight before being killed themselves. The army retaliated by bulldozing about 50 homes in the Rafah refugee camp. Four days later, Israel resumed the policy of "targeted killings" with a roadside bomb that killed Raed Al-Karmi, the leader of the Al-Aqsa Martyrs' Brigade in Tulkarm. "The so-called ceasefire is a joke and is canceled, canceled, canceled," said the militia in a leaflet. "Revenge is coming." As the cycle of violence spun with a new hellish pace, the Al-Aqsa Martyrs' Brigade took the lead in carrying out ambushes and suicide attacks, including the first suicide bombing by a woman.

By the end of January, Washington accepted Israel's account of the Karine-A incident, President Bush accused Arafat of "enhancing" terrorism rather than fighting it and Washington officials let it be known that they were reconsidering their ties with the Palestinian Authority. The United States was turning its back on Arafat. The Palestinian leader would have to do more than stage another blood-giving stunt. Now his own life was at risk.

*

Beirut was dressed like a bride, with its bright lights, freshly painted façades and glistening new hotels. The Arab summit in March 2002 was supposed to be the city's great political celebration, a rejoicing over the reconstruction of the country after the quelling of the civil war and the withdrawal of Israeli forces from the south of the country. It was supposed to be a moment of reconciliation as well, a time when Iraq would be welcomed back to the Arab fold and when the Arabs would adopt a Saudi-inspired plan to make a joint offer of peace with Israel.

Instead the party guests—the kings, princes, sheikhs, life presidents or their ministerial appointees—arrived in acrimonious mood, not helped by the torrential downpour that soaked the city. Yasser Arafat, the best man, was prevented by Israel from leaving Ramallah to attend the summit. King Abdallah of Jordan and President Hosni Mubarak of Egypt also stayed away. They were supposedly protesting about the treatment of the Palestinian leader, but according to the rumors swirling around Beirut, they either feared assassination or had taken umbrage because Saudi Arabia had stolen the diplomatic limelight. In all, about half the Arab leaders were absent.

As at many weddings, old resentments burst out. President Emile Lahoud and the prime minister, Rafiq Hariri, bickered in public over who should meet the dignitaries at the airport. And despite the speeches supporting the Intifada and denouncing the "criminal" actions of Israel, the Lebanese hosts delivered a public snub to the embattled Palestinian leader by refusing to allow him to address the summit by live satellite video link-up. Lebanese officials said they feared Israel would tamper with the broadcast. Instead of seeing Mr. Arafat, the leaders of the Arab world might be confronted by none other than Ariel Sharon.

As the Palestinian delegation walked out in fury, claiming it was a deliberate plot by Lebanon and Syria to undermine the Palestinian leadership, Arafat delivered his speech live on Al-Jazeera television, seeking to address Arabs over the heads of their leaders.

The summit limped on, with Crown Prince Abdallah, Saudi Arabia's effective day-to-day ruler, making a rare direct appeal to Israelis: "The use of violence, for more than fifty years, has only resulted in more violence and destruction, and the Israeli people are as far from security and peace, notwithstanding their military superiority and despite efforts to subdue and oppress. Peace emanates from the heart and mind, and not from the barrel of a cannon, or the exploding warhead of a missile."

The following day, the Arabs adopted a declaration offering, in essence, a comprehensive peace in exchange for a comprehensive Israeli withdrawal. If Israel retreats from all territories occupied in 1967 and allows the establishment of a Palestinian state with East Jerusalem as its capital, the Arabs declared, then they would be ready to "consider the Arab-Israeli conflict ended, and enter into a peace agreement with Israel, and provide security for all the states of the region" as well as "establish normal relations with Israel in the context of this comprehensive peace."

In behind-the-scenes arguments, the Arabs watered down Prince Abdallah's original offer of "full normalization" with Israel, and fudged the "Right of Return" of Palestinian refugees, saying there should be a "just solution" to their plight in accordance with U.N. General Assembly resolution 194. The summit also supported Lebanon's claim that Israel still controls a slice of its territory known as the Shebaa farms, even though the United Nations says Israel has withdrawn completely from Lebanon.

For all the fuss, the Beirut Declaration was completely unoriginal. "Land for peace" has been the basis of all peace negotiations between Israel and the Arabs since the 1978 Camp David accords. The novelty lay in presentation. The Arabs collectively—including radicals such as Iraq, Syria and Libya—endorsed the idea of peace and tried to engage Israeli doves. It was a far cry from the 1967 Khartoum summit, convened immediately after Israel's victory in the Six Day War, when the Arabs issued the "Three No's"—no peace, no negotiations and no recognition of Israel.

Such was the despair over events in the Holy Land, after a series of harsh incursions by Israeli forces into Palestinian cities and refugee camps, that the Beirut declaration was welcomed in Arab and western capitals as offering renewed hope for the Middle East. In October, President George W. Bush had spoken of his "vision" of a Palestinian state; now Arabs replied with what amounted to their own "vision" of peace with Israel. Together, Washington, D.C., and the Arabs were painting the "horizon" of peace to draw Israel and the Palestinians away from violence. But even before the colors were dry, the canvas was already being splattered with the blood of innocents.

★

Surveying the dining hall at the Park Hotel, the maître d'hôtel. Maxim Elkrief, was pleased with his arrangements for the Passover seder. He decided to go back to the kitchen to give final instructions to the waiters and cooks catering for roughly 250 guests, mostly elderly. As Elkrief made to go, a large explosion turned his careful dinner arrangement into a hellish scene of blood, screaming and destruction.

"At first I thought the blast had occurred outside, in the parking lot," he recalled. "But soon I realized all the windows had been blown out. It was hard for me to understand what was happening. I saw people lying on the floor. Guests were screaming. Severed arms, legs and a head were all over the place. Tables were smashed and the upholstery was torn out of chairs. It was so pretty, with crisp white tablecloths and flower arrangements, and then everything turned black."

A day later, as hotel staff washed bloodstains off the floor, two tables were still set with matzah, wine bottles and uneaten entrées, all covered with dust and glass shards. Holding his 18-month-old son, Avriel, at his wife's bedside in hospital, Shlomo David said: "I was joining my wife and son at our table. I managed to say 'happy holiday' to someone at the neighboring table, and then there was a huge explosion. I saw my wife and son fly in the air and then everything went dark. I called out to them but there was no response. I continued groping for them in the darkness, until I found them both. . . . We jumped through the back door into the swimming pool."

Netanya, a seaside town chosen as a retirement home by many retirees, particularly English-speakers, has experienced more than its fair share of bombings in the previous eighteen months. The Passover bomb, however, was the most shocking atrocity it had yet seen. The mood was venomously anti-Palestinian. "What is this government waiting for? It should take them all out," shouted one young man outside the hotel as he returned from prayers with a prayer shawl over his shoulder.

It was the bloodiest in a spate of bombings and shootings. Hamas said it was "a clear message to our Arab rulers that our struggling people have chosen their road and know how to regain lands and rights in full, depending only on God." There was no doubt that Israeli retribution would come.

The events of the following weeks marked the transition point where Arafat slipped from being unwilling to stop Palestinian attacks to being unable to do anything about them. Arafat made a half-hearted, conditional ceasefire offer the day after the Netanya attack, but Israel's tanks were already on the move.

Before dawn on March 29, three separate columns of tanks and armored vehicles entered Ramallah and surrounded Mr. Arafat's headquarters. Snipers took up position on nearby buildings as armored bulldozers smashed through several points of the perimeter wall and gates of the British-built compound.

In the afternoon, after sporadic exchanges of fire, armored vehicles moved into the compound and soldiers poured in through a large gap in the wall punched by a bulldozer. A tank fired a smoke shell to mask troops as they moved in, and heavy machine-guns raked the upper windows to keep Palestinian fighters away. Arafat and his entourage were penned into a single building of the compound.

It was the start of Operation Defensive Shield, Israel's largest military operation since the Lebanon war two decades earlier, involving the mobilization of more than 20,000 reserve soldiers. It involved the rolling invasion of most Palestinian cities in the West Bank, from where suicide bombers have been slipping across the long and open border into Israel.

Ariel Sharon said Israel had sought a ceasefire and wanted peace. It had restrained itself in the face of Palestinian attacks in the previous fortnight, to no avail. "All we have received in return was terrorism, terrorism and more terrorism," said Sharon. "No sovereign nation would tolerate such a sequence of events." Sharon regained popularity, after his approval ratings had slipped earlier in the year because of his apparent paralysis. The peace movement had been stirring back into life, with some 200 reserve officers signing a petition that they "will not continue to fight beyond the 1967 borders in order to dominate, expel, starve and humiliate an entire people." But as the call-up was issued, there were few protests. Most Israelis, including advocates of Israeli withdrawal, believed there was no choice but to fight terrorism. Behind the sense of unity, in a war that many Israelis regarded as one of "survival," there were intense disputes over what form the military action should take.

Sharon declared: "Israel will act to crush the Palestinian terrorist infrastructure, in all its parts and components, and will carry out comprehensive activity to achieve this goal. Arafat, who has established a coalition of terror against Israel, is an enemy and at this point he will be isolated." Israeli officials gave warning that Arafat could soon be sent back into exile. Sharon was already on record as bemoaning his decision not to order the liquidation of Arafat during the siege of Beirut in 1982 and, more recently, expressing regret that assured the U.S. that Arafat would not be harmed or deported.

Labor members of the cabinet mounted a rearguard defense against demands that Arafat should be expelled. The heads of the intelligence services also advised restraint. "Chairman Arafat can do much more damage abroad than where he is under siege," said a senior Israeli security source. "He will go all over the world presenting himself as a pacifist, and some leaders will believe him."

Within hours of the start of the Israeli operation, Ayat Akhras, a teenage Palestinian girl, was the first to exact revenge by blowing herself up at the entrance to an Israeli supermarket in a suburb of Jerusalem, killing two Israelis. In a video statement released by the Al-Aqsa Martyrs' Brigade, she mocked the "slumbering" Arab leaders and declared: "The Intifada will continue until victory."

By the third day of Israel's Operation Defensive Shield Israel's tanks were entering other cities in the West Bank and, despite more suicide attacks, international opinion was turning in favor of Arafat. Large anti-Israeli and anti-American demonstrations were breaking out across the region by Arabs roused to anger by televised scenes of war and the hourly reports—sometimes true and sometimes false—of civilians being killed. European countries called for Israel to halt its operation. The Pope, in his Easter message, said: "It seems that war has been declared on peace. But nothing is resolved by war. It brings only greater suffering and death."

Dreadfully serious as the situation had become, it was also surreal. Arafat found himself in the strange position of being "isolated" in his ruined headquarters, but still able to make telephone calls around the world. On Al-Jazeera television he made a melodramatic pronouncement: "They want to arrest me, send me into exile or kill me. But I tell them no. I want to be a martyr, a martyr, a martyr.... Please God, let me taste martyrdom." Israel, however, gave public assurances that

he would come to no harm. Over the next month, the army passed
water and food to Arafat's entourage. The supplies, said the army,
included 13,000 pitta breads, 420 cans of hummus, more than 100
kilograms of cheese and hundreds of kilograms of coffee, sugar and
tea.

In a bizarre turn of events, a group of about 50 international
activists holding white flags marched with their hands in the air or
with interlocked arms into the semi-destroyed compound, ignoring
warning shots from bewildered Israeli soldiers. A delighted Arafat
hugged and kissed his visitors. "What is important for me is not what
I am facing," he told a television crew that slipped in. "For me this is
not the first time. . . . But the most important thing is what our people are facing day and night."

★

Sharon waited the end of the Easter holiday before ordering the
invasion of Bethlehem. Israeli forces had been there twice before, but
had always avoided Manger Square, the main plaza outside the
Church of the Nativity. This time, on April 2, they had no such
qualms. Attack helicopters fired on gunmen in the square and alleyways around the ancient church built on the site of Jesus' birth.

It was no secret that the Israelis would come into Bethlehem. For
days, transporters had been carrying scores of tanks and armored personnel carriers past the walls of the Old City of Jerusalem to mass
them near Rachel's Tomb. A day before the attack, Hanna Nasser, the
mayor of Bethlehem, recalled the damage caused by two previous
incursions in terms of lives lost, infrastructure destroyed, tourist-
based economy ravaged. "This one is going to be worse," he predicted. "But no matter what Sharon destroys, he cannot destroy the
will of the people. This is the end of Sharon. He will never give security to his people. Nobody can stop a person ready to give up his soul
to attack another."

There was a tense, menacing air about the place. An alleged collaborator had been killed earlier in the morning. Palestinian fighters in
fatigues and black bandanas had swaggered in the square opposite the
Bethlehem Peace Center, built on the site of the former Israeli police
station as part of the Millennium renovations. "This is our church
and mosque. This is our land," said one fighter, calling himself Abu
Badr, armed with an M-16 rifle. "We are waiting for them. Let them
come and we will see what happens. They are cowards. They do not
dare come out of their tanks."

In any event, Israeli forces had no problem slicing through the thin resistance of Palestinian fighters. As we entered Bethlehem on a rain-swept day, there was nobody to be seen except soldiers in tanks and armored personnel carriers. The voices of a dozen sheikhs calling the Muslim faithful to prayer rose through the streets but no one responded. People did not even dare peek out of their windows to see. Pictures of Palestinian "martyrs," in defiant pose with their weapons, peeled from the walls. Doubtless there would be more pictures to add in the days ahead.

Around 3 P.M., Palestinian gunmen shot off the locks to the Franciscan convent attached to the church and burst in. By the end of the day some 200 people—militiamen, policemen, civilians, priests, nuns and (briefly) five Italian journalists—were besieged in the basilica. "They did not damage anything and seemed respectful of the church," said one of the journalists. The foreigners were later evacuated in a convoy of diplomatic vehicles, leaving the gunmen and clergy besieged within.

It took another day for the rest of the world to appreciate the drama around one of Christianity's holiest shrines. Reached by mobile telephone, Ibrahim Abayat, a leader of the Al-Aqsa Martyrs' Brigade, which has claimed responsibility for suicide bombings and shooting attacks, said: "The situation is very difficult here. The tanks and armored personnel carriers are in Manger Square. The soldiers are besieging the church. We have wounded inside the church." Israel was furious by what it saw as the cynical use of churches by the gunmen. However, Michel Sabbah, the Latin patriarch of Jerusalem and the head of the Roman Catholic church in the region, said the gunmen had been given sanctuary. "The basilica is a place of refuge for everybody, even fighters, as long as they lay down their arms," said Sabbah, "We have an obligation to give refuge to Palestinians and Israelis alike."

Israel said it would not attack the church. But in the weeks that followed, there were periodic exchanges of fire. Israeli snipers killed several Palestinians in and around the church. With rotting bodies placed in a crypt, the stench of the dead mingled with the smell of the unwashed human mass. Those within slept under shared blankets. When the food ran out, they survived on a thin soup made from a strange assortment of grass and leaves from the garden. To add to one of the Holy Land's most surreal scenes, the Israelis hoisted loudspeakers over the square to subject those within to loud music and ear-splitting noise as a form of psychological warfare. Those inside responded by ringing the church bells.

On the second day of the invasion, journalists ventured into the alleys of the old city. We followed the trail of devastation along a street named after Pope Paul VI, who had visited Bethlehem in 1964. We inched forward on foot, some with helmets and others just with scarves, uncertain whether to walk down the middle of the street or use the scant cover provided by pillars and doorways.

The only sound was that of gushing water—little fountains all along the street where Israeli armored vehicles had ripped off water pipes as they passed by. The rivulets merged with the driving rain, washing around the debris of urban warfare—a yellow car with its end sheared off, remnants of Molotov cocktails, gas masks, broken glass and brass bullet casings, smashed masonry, a hole in the road where a bomb appeared to have exploded and even the broken door of an Israeli armored vehicle.

We froze every time shots rang out. An Israeli patrol darted by, menacing, but seemingly uninterested in journalists. Matters were not helped when a Palestinian who approached us dressed in the white vest of a rescue worker turned out to be a wanted fighter trying to slip out of the city with foreigners.

Down one alleyway we found the metal door to a house shot through like a colander. An elderly Arab woman emerged from another doorway, crying in Arabic *Mat! Mat!* (Dead! Dead!). A man beckoned to us and led us through a room that served as a grocer's shop and into the next room, used as a bedroom and kitchen. There we found Sumayya Abda lying on the floor, a 64-year-old woman dressed in a long purple velvet dress, with her white headscarf drenched in blood. Next to her lay her son, Khaled, 37, who ran the shop. Their faces were puffy and contorted, like a Francis Bacon painting. They carried no arms.

The bodies had been there since the previous morning. Nobody had cleaned or moved the corpses. It was as if the evidence of the tragedy had been deliberately left undisturbed until someone from the outside world could witness and record this moment, a footnote in the agony of the Holy Land. One of Sumayya's sons, Sameh, stood next to the bodies, speaking in broken English as if translating for his elderly mother. He pronounced their names and ages slowly, so that we journalists could note them down accurately. The paraphernalia of the lost lives surrounded the bodies—a radio, a stove, cheap wardrobes, a picture of Jerusalem's Dome of the Rock, posters of local martyrs and even a small portrait of Iraq's President Saddam Hussein.

According to neighbors, Sumayya had refused to open her door—
or did not open it fast enough—when the soldiers demanded to be
let in. One could trace the trajectory of bullets or grenade fragments
between the little holes in the door and the pockmarks on the
vaulted ceiling of the room, ripping out two lives somewhere in
between.

In the mosque next door we found another body, a middle-aged
man who had died after being wounded. He still had a drip in his
arm. Who was he? A group of women shrugged, then one said: "Abu
Yusef, I think. He is a member of the Palestinian police. He is not
from here. He is from Jenin." In this conflict, it was becoming harder
to disentangle fact from fiction. Had there been a street battle here, or
were these deaths wanton murder? We did not have much time to
find out. Bursts of gunfire rang out and we retreated, leaving the
bodies as footnotes to a history of tragedy. At least some of their
names had been recorded.

★

In the uproar over the sieges in Ramallah and Bethlehem, scant
attention was paid at first to the trickle of Israeli casualties coming
from the north of the West Bank, in Jenin. An Israeli captain died on
April 3. The next day the Israelis lost a major, a lieutenant and a staff
sergeant. Three more died on April 6, and a further two soldiers were
killed two days later. It was becoming apparent that the real war was
being fought in Jenin, which had a fierce reputation as the "capital"
of Islamic suicide bombers—fully 23 of the roughly 100 suicide
bombers of the Al-Aqsa Intifada had come from Jenin and the
refugee camp.

Then on April 9 Israel suffered its worst military blow—the death
of 13 soldiers killed in a well-organized ambush in the alleys of
Jenin's refugee camp. According to Israeli reports, a patrol ventured
into a courtyard between two houses and was attacked by a suicide
bomber. At the same time, booby traps were detonated all around.
When reinforcements rushed in, they were cut down by the bullets
fired by Palestinian gunmen.

All this was taking place away from the eyes of the world. For
about a week, humanitarian workers could not recover the corpses
on the streets or bring assistance to civilians caught in the fighting.
Medical staff said they were shot at every time they tried to venture
out of the hospital. Journalists were resolutely kept out of Jenin, and
could only watch from a distant hilltop as tanks and helicopter gun-

ships carried out their business. Palestinian spokesmen raised a clamor that Israeli forces had "massacred" Palestinians and dug mass graves to hide the bodies, while the families of the dead soldiers complained bitterly that Israel was being too squeamish in its operation and was putting soldiers' lives at risk. "They decided to send soldiers to die instead of planes so everything will look good on CNN," the father of one soldier told an Israeli radio station.

The Israeli government insisted there were no atrocities, but that it had fought a "fierce battle" against determined terrorists. The vast majority of Israeli military fatalities—23 out of 29 killed in Operation Defensive Shield—died in Jenin. But the army fed the massacre theory by saying initially that 100 or more Palestinians had been killed and by suggesting it would bury the bodies in a remote site in the Jordan Valley. Amid Israeli fears of a propaganda disaster, Nahum Barnea, an Israeli columnist, wrote: "If Israel does not find some way to give them a dignified burial, the bodies will bury Israel."

It was only on April 15 that most foreign journalists were able to slip into the refugee camp to see what had taken place. Whole sides of houses had been sheared off by Israeli bulldozers, exposing the contents of homes like children's doll's houses. The totality of the destruction of the Hawashin neighborhood shocked even hardened correspondents. An area roughly 400 yards by 400 yards had been pounded, blasted and ground to rubble by tanks, helicopters and bulldozers. The objects of daily life—toilet paper, shoe boxes, crockery, chairs and clothes—littered the ground. The overpowering, sickly smell of the dead seeped from under the rubble. Burnt body parts lay strewn in one house, while another man lay buried to his head and shoulders under the debris of a destroyed building. Near another cluster of five bodies, grotesquely charred and twisted, one resident stood with his eight-year-old son. "We hate the Israelis more now," said Jamal Mohammed. "This child has seen what happened. Now he will hate the Israelis."

An investigation by Human Rights Watch, a human rights group based in New York, found there was prima facie evidence that Israel had committed war crimes and other violations of the Geneva Conventions. The destruction of the Hawashin neighborhood, where the ambush of Israeli soldiers had taken place, might count as "wanton" destruction. The catalogue of alleged abuses included unlawful killings, some summary executions, indiscriminate shooting, using Palestinian civilians as human shields, denying civilians access to medical care and generally failing to protect the camp's population of about 14,000.

But, crucially, the group said it could only confirm 52 dead Palestinians—more than half of them suspected militiamen—and did not expect the figure to rise substantially because of the low number of missing people, some of whom might have been arrested. This was far lower than the figure of 500 or more dead quoted by Palestinian spokesmen. "Human Rights Watch found no evidence to sustain claims of massacres or large-scale extra-judicial executions by the IDF in Jenin refugee camp. However, many of the civilian deaths documented by Human Rights Watch amounted to unlawful or willful killings by the IDF. Many others could have been avoided if the IDF had taken proper precautions to protect civilian life during its military operation, as required by international humanitarian law," said the report.

The Palestinians could not decide whether to treat events at Jenin as an atrocity—a new Sabra and Shatila—or as an act of military heroism: a new Karameh. Yasser Arafat opted for both, describing Jenin as "Jeningrad" while at the same time demanding an international investigation into the "massacres."

★

A long convoy of armor-plated vehicles snaked its way through the deserted streets of Ramallah and pulled into Yasser Arafat's ruined compound. Men armed with submachine-guns jumped out, standing between the Israeli soldiers on the rooftops and Palestinian gunmen inside. Colin Powell, the U.S. secretary of state, emerged from one of the vehicles as he embarked on one of his more unusual diplomatic encounters. Instead of the palaces and executive offices that he normally frequented as secretary of state, the former general came to a building bearing all the scars of war.

Although besieged, Arafat won a victory on that Sunday, April 14. Powell's arrival demonstrated that the road to peace and stability in the Middle East still runs through Arafat's office. The Palestinian leader had broken out of his siege isolation by doing little more than wait for the outrage to grow. Despite the threats to send him into exile, Arafat remained under the protection of the American eagle. Sharon has been firing at Arafat's feet, but was not allowed to raise his aim.

From the start of Operation Defensive Shield, Israeli officials had asked themselves how much time they would have to conduct their raids before being forced to stop by international pressure. The answers coming out of Washington, D. C., were contradictory. President George W. Bush, speaking two days after the Israeli incursions began, seemed to give Ariel Sharon carte blanche. "I can understand why the Israeli government takes the action it takes," said the President at his ranch in Texas. "Their country is under attack. Every day there has been a suicide bombing." In a speech at the White House four days later, his tone had changed noticeably. President Bush still blamed Arafat for the crisis, saying: "The situation in which he finds himself is largely of his own making. He's missed his opportunities and thereby betrayed the hopes of the people he's supposed to lead." But now Bush added an unambiguous call for Israel to stop its operation. "To lay the foundations of future peace, I ask Israel to halt incursions into Palestinian-controlled areas and begin the withdrawal from those cities it has recently occupied."

Colin Powell seemed to take a roundabout route to Israel. Raising Arab suspicions that he was deliberately giving Israel more time, he did not reach Jerusalem until nearly two weeks after the start of Operation Defensive Shield, having traveled first to a succession of Arab countries and to Madrid. "Don't you think it was more important to go to Jerusalem first?" asked King Mohammed VI of Morocco. When Powell did reach Israel, Israeli military operations were still in full swing despite several more U.S. calls for a withdrawal "without delay."

It was a forlorn mission for Powell, who left without achieving a ceasefire and felt undermined by White House comments describing Sharon as a "man of peace." By the end of April, though, the U.S. was able to take the edge off the crisis. Israeli tanks gradually pulled back to the outskirts of Palestinian cities. The siege on Arafat's office was lifted on May 2, after he agreed to jail six prominent wanted men under the supervision of American and British "wardens." The prisoners were: the four alleged killers of Israel's tourism minister Rehavam Zeevi; Ahmed Saadat, the leader of the Popular Front for the Liberation of Palestine, which ordered the assassination; and Fouad Shubaki, a close adviser to Arafat accused of bankrolling the Karine A arms shipment.

A few days later, foreign mediators succeeded in resolving the siege of the Church of the Nativity, but not until after an embarrassing diplomatic contretemps. The Israelis and Palestinians seemed to have reached agreement to send some of the gunmen into exile in

Italy, but Rome objected and said it had not been consulted. In the end, 13 militants were sent to Cyprus, where they were admitted as "guests" in a hotel, living in legal limbo. As the priests cleaned up the fifth of the siege and reconsecrated the church, the European Union argued for days before agreeing which European countries would take in the exiles and what their legal status would be.

The external monitoring of the Palestinian jail in Jericho, to stop Arafat's "revolving door" policy in dealing with security prisoners, was an unusual act of micromanagement for a U.S. administration that had come to power seeking to stay out of the morass of the Middle East. It was also a new departure for Britain, which had not played such a direct role since the end of its mandate on Palestine. The monitoring was an important signal to Israel that international intervention, far from benefiting only Palestinians, can also serve to give reassurance to Israel. The experiment was, nevertheless, fraught with danger in a country where Palestinian mobs have taken regularly to storming prisons to free inmates. Nobody who saw the image of a Palestinian man showing off his bloodstained hands to a crowd after the lynching of two Israeli soldiers in a Ramallah police station at the start of the Intifada in October 2000 can underestimate the risks.

The Israeli army claims to have achieved important military gains during Operation Defensive Shield, including the arrest or killing of a dozen of the most wanted militants and the capture of large amounts of arms, ammunition and explosives. There were also propaganda gains in the discovery of documents linking the Palestinian leadership more closely to militants, even though there was no smoking-gun paper showing that Arafat had ordered specific suicide bombings. But it did not take long for Hamas to rise up once more, with a suicide bombing in Rishon Le-Zion on May 8 which killed 16 people in a billiard hall.

News of the carnage reached Sharon just as he was meeting Bush in Washington, D. C., where he was said to be coming under growing pressure to negotiate with Arafat. As Sharon cut short his visit, he had to decide once more how far he could push his military response. Israel mobilized for invasion of Gaza, of the kind it had carried out in the West Bank. However, the tanks were held back at the last moment, ostensibly because Arafat was rounding up members of Hamas.

Sharon had, for the moment, reached the limits of his security response. The generals feared that entering the Gaza Strip, where militants had had weeks to prepare their defenses, would repeat the bloodbath of Jenin on a larger scale. With an economy suffering from the impact of the Intifada, Israel could ill afford a mass mobilization of reserves that a reoccupation of Gaza would need. Moreover, Sharon did not want to antagonize the United States, whose patience had been tested during Operation Defensive Shield, as it mulled plans to call an international conference.

All eyes turned on what President Bush would say. After weeks of intense fighting within the administration, and lobbying by Europeans, Arabs and Israel, President Bush stepped up to the lectern of the Rose Garden on January 24, 2002, to make his first detailed policy pronouncement on the Middle East. It started as a carefully calibrated speech: "For the sake of all humanity, things must change in the Middle East. It is untenable for Israeli citizens to live in terror. It is untenable for Palestinians to live in squalor and occupation." It did not take long, however, for Bush to drop his bombshell:

> Peace requires a new and different Palestinian leadership, so that a Palestinian state can be born. I call on the Palestinian people to elect new leaders, leaders not compromised by terror. I call upon them to build a practicing democracy, based on tolerance and liberty. If the Palestinian people actively pursue these goals, America and the world will actively support their efforts. If the Palestinian people meet these goals, they will be able to reach agreement with Israel and Egypt and Jordan on security and other arrangements for independence. And when the Palestinian people have new leaders, new institutions and new security arrangements with their neighbors, the United States of America will support the creation of a Palestinian state whose borders and certain aspects of its sovereignty will be provisional until resolved as part of a final settlement in the Middle East.

Bush seemed to adopt Sharon's view of causes of the crisis and of the solution: get rid of Arafat. Palestinian statehood was not a right, but a privilege to be conferred for good democratic behavior. The Palestinians were to be held to a far higher standard of democracy than any other Arab regime. And even then, they would obtain a neutered kind of freedom, a state with temporary borders and its independence circumscribed by security agreements with Israel, Jordan and Egypt. The Palestinian leadership had to fall in with the "war on terrroism" or face isolation.

Nabil Shaath, one of the Palestinian chief negotiators, contrived an optimistic response: "The music of the speech was bad, the lyrics were not that bad." The "lyrics" were in the buried detail of the speech. If Palestinian violence subsided, Bush said Israel should release frozen funds, withdraw its forces to positions held before the start of the Intifada and freeze settlements. "Ultimately," said Bush, "Israelis and Palestinians must address the core issues that divide them if there is to be a real peace, resolving all claims and ending the conflict between them. This means that the Israeli occupation that began in 1967 will be ended through a settlement negotiated between the parties, based on U.N. Resolutions 242 and 338, with Israeli withdrawal to secure and recognize borders." He said a permanent peace agreement could be reached by June 2005. The American view that the territories captured in 1967 were "occupied" rather than "disputed"—implying that the pre-1967 border is the basis for future negotiation—and America's commitment to a three-year timeline to statehood were real, but distant gains for the Palestinians.

President Bush's speech crystalized the disparate calls for "reform" from Israel, the outside world and Palestinians themselves. However, the term meant different things to each side: Israel, and seemingly also Bush, understood reform to mean that Arafat should be removed from power, or at least sidelined. European countries interpreted it as a call to prepare Palestinian institutions for statehood within three years.

Arafat himself saw "reform" as a means of reasserting his authority. Although he had survived Sharon's onslaught, he was now a shadow of his former self. He had gained some prestige during the siege of his office by his readiness to stand fast against the Israelis. But it was an ephemral popularity. When the Israeli operation was finished, Arafat's failures were apparent in the rubble of his headquarters, the devastation of the cities, the bereavement of every family and the impoverishment of all Palestinians. All the suffering had brought Palestinians no closer to liberation. Arafat had neither made peace nor waged a successful war.

When Arafat emerged from a month in captivity to make a victory tour around Ramallah, he drew small crowds of well-wishers. The bargain he had struck to secure his own freedom stuck in the throat of many Palestinians, who regard militant fighters as heroes. "Arafat paid a high price for his freedom," said one shopkeeper in Ramallah. "The Israelis lifted the closure around his compound, but it remains imposed on all Palestinians. We cannot move anywhere outside the town."

A few days later, during a visit to the West Bank, Arafat was given a cool reception in Jenin and avoided entirely the "Jeningrad" refugee camp. A dais had been prepared amid the rubble, but his security chiefs sensed an ugly mood among the people. In an interview on CNN, Arafat distanced himself from suicide bombings, suggesting they were the handiwork of "international powers." It was not an attitude likely to endear him to the Islamic militants who led the fight against the Israelis in Jenin. The "Symbol" who said he was ready to be "martyred" by Israel feared a Palestinian bullet.

In a speech to the Palestinian legislative council in May, Arafat admitted: "No nation ever marched to freedom without mistakes." One council member shouted: "You have to correct the mistakes." But Arafat made only vague promises. After Bush's speech, he announced presidential and legislative elections for early 2002. Under pressure from Palestinians, he pushed though a Basic Law—a kind of constitution—that had been left on his desk for years. The cabinet was slimmed down from 31 to 21 ministers. A new finance minister, Salam Fayyad, was brought in to sort out the mess of Palestinian accounting and keep donors happy, while a new interior minister, Abdel-Razzaq al-Yahya was given nominal charge of reorganizing the myriad Palestinian security forces, but they remained as ineffective—or deliberately passive—as ever. A proposed new Palestinian constitution, that would appoint a "prime minister" to take over day-to-day running of Palestinian affairs, was revived but moved forward only slowly.

Few believed Arafat would really change his ways, except under intense pressure. The Palestinian leadership tried to use the reform process as a weapon against Israel, saying it was impossible to press ahead with political, financial and security reforms while Israel's suffocating security measures remained in place. The elections were cancelled on the grounds that the registration of voters and the balloting process would be impossible while Israel remained in the cities of the West Bank.

Under Egyptian and European sponsorship, his lieutenants negotiated desultorily with other factions to seek a joint ceasefire with Israel, or at least a pact not to target civilians inside Israel. Abu Mazen, a senior Oslo negotiator, said in December 2002 that all Palestinian militant groups should agree to a "pause" to avoid giving Israel a pretext to seize "what remains of our fledgling state." Saying what had previously been almost unthinkable, he said it was time to "reassess the Palestinian struggle and seize the political rewards of the sacrifices endured by the people so that they don't have to go on forming an endless column of martyrs, prisoners and invalids." But despite the general sense of exhaustion among Palestinians, the cease-fire talks went nowhere.

Israel's reoccupation of Palestinian cities, the construction of security walls, fences and ditches seemed slowly to reduce the tempo of suicide bombings. Israel's top brass began to float the idea in early 2003 that the "worst is over," even though the conflict maintained its grim routine of shootings, bombings, retaliation, arrests and assassinations. Between 40 to 70 Palestinians were being killed per month. Arafat's office was besieged several more times after Operation Defensive Shield, most recently in September 2002, but the Palestinian leader was spared each time.

Foreign envoys came and went through the rubble of his headquarters and through Sharon's offices in Jerusalem as the outside world tried to draw up a "road map" to turn Bush's "vision" into reality. This was managed by the "Quartet"—the grouping of America, the European Union, the United Nations and Russia. They drew up a complex joint document setting out the minutiae of reciprocal steps toward a ceasefire, Israeli withdrawal from areas it had reoccupied, a settlement freeze and the resumption of peace talks. This seemed like much "process" to replace the lack of "peace." The publication of the "roadmap" was repeatedly delayed, and the Israeli election of January 2003 forced another postponement.

By the start of 2003, there seemed no obvious end to the war of slow and painful attrition. Sharon's reelection promised more of the same, while Arafat's cancelation of his election signaled little change on his part. Change, if it came, would probably be the results of events farther east, in Iraq.

★

"Yasser Arafat is not of this world. He sees himself as a mythological figure. He doesn't deal with day-to-day issues of running a government but floats above, riding on the myths of the Right of Return and Jerusalem," said Shlomo Ben-Ami, the former Israeli foreign minister, trying to explain the mystery of Arafat.

More than a year after being voted out of office, Ben-Ami, who negotiated fruitlessly with Arafat and his lieutenants, still seemed baffled by the Palestinians' reluctance to take what was being offered to them. The Labor government, operating without a majority, had offered more than any Israeli government could conceivably offer, including more than nine-tenths of the West Bank, a division of Jerusalem, Palestinian sovereignty over most of the Temple Mount, and symbolic gestures on Palestinian refugees. What more could they want? And yet Arafat walked away. Palestinians respond that their firm stand was justified. After all, Israel substantially improved its offer in the six months between the Camp David and Taba negotiations.

Having made the conceptual leap of recognizing Israel and accepting autonomy under the Oslo accords, Arafat has hardly budged since. In the interim phase of Oslo, he accepted what most Palestinians regard as humiliating terms. But when it came to agreeing to a permanent solution, Arafat stuck by the absolutes of "international legitimacy: complete Israeli withdrawal from the West Bank and Gaza Strip, the evacuation of settlements, East Jerusalem and the Old City as the capital of Palestine, (with the concession of some rights for Jews in the Jewish Quarter and part of the Western Wall), and the Right of Return for refugees to Israel.

Ben-Ami's only explanation is that Arafat was simply incapable of reaching a pragmatic, rational settlement with Israel. He may speak of a two-state solution, but cannot accept the consequences—a state for the Jews, with no Right of Return of Palestinians to Israel, and recognition that the Temple Mount is sacred to Jews as well as to Muslims. The Palestinians were not seeking conciliation, but vindication of their claims. The way Ben-Ami put it, permanent peace would mean the end of the road for the Palestinian revolution. The man who kept the Palestinian movement alive by perpetual motion would have to come to rest. Palestine, the great Arab cause, would become an insignificant statelet; Arafat the symbol would become mere man, an old man. "It is not possible to reach agreement with Arafat," concluded Ben-Ami, shaking his head.

There are not many Israeli leaders who are as dovish and as thoughtful as Ben-Ami, and his name was once touted as a possible future prime minister of Israel. One can argue over the merits of Israel's offer, and the justice of Palestinian claims. But the disillusionment of Ben-Ami with the whole negotiation experience is a testament to Arafat's failure of leadership. In a situation where Israel holds most of the cards, peace negotiations between Israel and the Palestinians are as much a negotiation among Israelis. Arafat has lost Israel's peace camp and succeeded in driving Israelis into the arms of Ariel Sharon. Other leaders who made peace with Israel had to find the means to win the trust of ordinary Israelis. Egypt's President Anwar Sadat visited Jerusalem and addressed the Knesset in person and Jordan's King Hussein went down on his knee to apologize to the parents of a girl who had been killed by a Jordanian soldier. But in the popular Israeli view Barak offered peace and Arafat responded with the Intifada.

Arafat himself seemed to have a flash of realization in June 2002, after the disaster of Israel's Operation Defensive Shield, when he told an Israeli interviewer that he belatedly accepted the Clinton parameters set out 18 months earlier. It was a rare implicit admission by Arafat that all that had happened since the outbreak of the Intifada had been a terible mistake. But by the time he reached this belated conclusion, it was too late. Israelis had lost faith in him. Up to the outbreak of the uprising, Oslo had gradually but fundamentally changed Israeli opinions. A combination of negotiations and, yes, periodic outbursts of unrest, had convinced Israelis that there was no solution but a substantial withdrawal from the occupied territories and the creation of a Palestinian state. The Likud party, under its often reviled leader Binyamin Netanyahu, formally abided by a narrow interpretation of the terms of Oslo and presided over the retreat of Israeli forces from most of Hebron, the "elder sister" of Jerusalem. Hardly anyone on the Right spoke any more of a "Greater Land of Israel." Even Ariel Sharon said he favored the creation of a Palestinian state. The issue between Left and Right is not whether territory should be given up, but how much Israel can hang on to. The difference is no longer one of principle, but of degree. In many ways this remains true today. Opinion polls show most Israelis would accept the creation of a Palestinian state. The fundamental question for Israelis is the credibility of the Palestinians in general, and of Arafat in particular.

It is only a small step from Ben-Ami's pessimistic belief that Arafat cannot make peace to the widespread Israeli view that Palestinians as a whole do not want peace. That the unprecedented violence of the Al-Aqsa Intifada should have broken out within weeks of unprecedented Israeli concessions has revived the deep-seated fear that the Palestinians will be satisfied with nothing short of the destruction of Israel. The anarchic armed violence has stirred deep fears even in a country as powerful as Israel. Some Israelis remembered the "war of the roads" in 1947, others drew parallels with the Arab Revolt of 1936–1939. One article in the liberal daily *Ha'aretz* spoke of the Palestinians' "One Hundred Year Intifada."

If the first stone-throwing Intifada had provoked intense soul-searching among Israelis, the wholesale use of arms in the Al-Aqsa

Intifada caused a sense of betrayal among many Israelis who had dared to believe in the promise of peace. A minority have plucked up the courage to say that it is time to abandon the settlements. For most Left-wing Israelis, however, Arafat's words of peace and reconciliation, the signed agreements to resolve disputes by peaceful means, were all lies. "There is nobody to negotiate with. We are stunned by the hatred of the Palestinians," one liberal Israeli journalist friend complained. "The Palestinians are not after peace. They want to get rid of the Jews."

It is a dangerous hopelessness, because it leads many Israelis to the idea that the Palestinians are a people not to be negotiated with, but to be crushed. If peace is something that only the Messiah can bring, then why bother seeking an accommodation with the Palestinians? Concessions will make no difference to the Palestinians, and will only endanger Israel. If there has to be a fight with irreconcilable enemies, then Israel might as well fight from a position of territorial strength. Such arguments have long been popular on the Right. Liberal and Left-wing Israelis are now adopting them too. "The Right was right," is the refrain from many Israelis. The risk is that an exasperated Israel will, sooner or later, resort to extreme measures.

Some on the far Right in Israel, including members of the lunatic fringe of the Sharon government such as the late Rehavam Zeevi, believe that the way to get rid of the problem is to get rid of the Palestinians with a "transfer," voluntary or otherwise, of Arabs. Opinion polls in the first half of 2002 showed that fully 40 percent of Israeli Jews favored the "transfer" of Palestinians to other countries. In April, Effi Eitam, a religious ultra-nationalist former brigadier who looks forward to the day when Arabs will no longer inhabit the land, was elected to lead the National Religious party and was admitted to the cabinet. The idea of a mass expulsion, of finishing off the job started in 1948 is inconceivable short of a general Middle East war breaking out. The succession of wars since 1948 proves even such a despicable step would offer no respite. In any case, the world would not stand for it. In 1999, NATO went to war with Yugoslavia to stop ethnic cleansing. Nevertheless, in a situation of prolonged bloodshed and mayhem, the appeal of extremist ideologies among Jews could increase, leading to more active vigilante and "underground" groups. Another Goldstein-like atrocity is a constant danger, particularly if the Sharon government is ever cajoled back into negotiations.

Increasingly, Israelis speak openly of ridding themselves of the Palestinian Authority. But for all the delight it would bring to the settlement movement, it is far from certain that most Israelis have the stomach for a full-fledged occupation of the Palestinian areas. Incursions into Palestinian cities have proven to be comparatively easy for Israeli forces, but a permanent occupation would be a different matter. On the Left, some Israelis now advocate a unilateral "separation." Israeli troops would withdraw to a new line and leave the Palestinians to sort themselves out. Critics say the move threatens even worse chaos, and without negotiations Palestinian claims will remain unresolved. Moreover, creating a separation line raises the awkward political question of where the border should run.

The option being most actively canvassed in the Israeli government is deposing Yasser Arafat—either by assassinating him, sending him into exile, or letting him wither into an "irrelevance"—in the hope that a more accommodating leader will emerge. According to the Hebrew daily *Maariv*, as early as 2000 before the collapse of the Oslo accords the Shin Bet intelligence agency prepared an assessment of Arafat under the title: "Arafat—an asset or a burden." Overturning years of intelligence opinion in favor of Arafat, the Shin Bet is reported to have concluded that Israel would be better off without him. "Since Arafat has no specific serious or distinct successor, the standing of the Palestinian leadership in the world is expected to weaken greatly," *Maariv* reported. "The new leader would depend on the support of Arab and international leaders. The influence of Egypt and Jordan on the Palestinians would become much stronger. The new leadership would be more pragmatic, less religious, younger, and more open to compromise."

The truth is that nobody in Israel can guarantee that what would follow would be any better than Arafat. A combination of Arafat's own chicanery, and Israel's assassination of senior Palestinians over the decades, has ensured that there is no obvious successor to the Palestinian "president." The Palestinian Authority consists of one chief and many Indians. Most of the Palestinian figures who have risen to prominence are reviled by Palestinians as corrupt, inefficient, or dictator-like secret policemen.

"Removing Arafat is not a solution," said Shimon Peres, serving as foreign minister in the Sharon government in December 2001, "It could create an alternative that is much worse and bring Hamas and Islamic Jihad down on us." Marwan Barghouthi, the 42-year-old leader of the Tanzim militia from Mr. Arafat's own Fatah movement, which has been at the center of much of the fighting during the Al-Aqsa Intifada, would have a chance of establishing himself as a populist leader, should he emerge from Israeli prison after his arrest during Operation Defensive Shield.

Even before Israel's threats to oust Arafat, the issue of the Palestinian succession has been a burning question as the Palestinian leader has become visibly weakened. In the rest of the Arab world, the passing away in recent years of such veterans as President Hafez al-Assad of Syria, King Hussein of Jordan, and King Hassan II of Morocco has not fundamentally changed their respective countries, or the region. But in many ways Arafat remains the embodiment of the Palestinian cause. There is nobody else who can represent the history of the Palestinian movement, and embrace both refugees and Palestinians in the occupied territories.

There is a succession process, of sorts, under the terms of the draft Basic Law for the Palestinian autonomous areas. The Speaker of the Palestinian legislative council, Ahmed Qreia, known as Abu Alaa, a senior negotiator throughout the Oslo process, would lead the Palestinian Authority for 60 days while new elections are held. Another senior negotiator, Mahmoud Abbas, known as Abu Mazen, is often tipped as a possible leader. He is part of the historical PLO leadership, and a moderate in negotiations with Israel. But he is short of charisma, and in these days of inflamed emotions he may be regarded as too accommodating with the Zionist "enemy."

The late Faisal Husseini, the well-liked former head of the PLO in Jerusalem, died of a heart attack in Kuwait in May 2001. His successor, Sari Nusseibeh, an intellectual from another notable Jerusalem family, is a leading dove. A prominent spokesman at the time of the first Intifada, Nusseibeh has resurfaced after years away from the limelight. He is one of the very few prominent Palestinians to have uttered anathemas such as criticizing the Intifada as a mistake and accepting boldly that most Palestinian refugees will never return to Israel. But the uproar caused by the ultra-pragmatism of the urbane Oxford—and Harvard—educated professor of philosophy may rule him out as a leader of the Palestinian movement.

Many Palestinians would favor a collective leadership to take over from Arafat. This may prevent disintegration, but is likely to lead to paralysis. In any scenario, the heads of the myriad Palestinian security services will have a crucial say in who emerges as leader. Jibril Rajoub, the once powerful head of Preventive Security in the West Bank, has been discredited among militant Palestinians for surrendering hundreds of Palestinians after his headquarters in Beitounia, near Ramallah, came under ferocious attack by Israeli forces during Operation Defensive Shield. His counterpart in Gaza, Muhammad Dahlan, resigned in 2002 but remains influential. As veterans of Israeli jails, Dahlan and Rajoub are fluent Hebrew speakers. Their readiness to arrest Islamic activists in the past make them the sort of people Israel would like to "do business" with. But even these kingmakers have doubts. "The alternative to Arafat is 1,000 Tanzim who will compete over who can commit more terror attacks against Israel," Dahlan once said.

What is almost certain is that if Arafat is removed by Israel, any pragmatist that might emerge would be regarded as a stooge and "collaborator" with Israel. In the end, through gritted teeth, Israel will probably find that continuing to deal with Arafat's lieutenants, if not the Palestinian leader himself, is its only option. The best Israel can hope for is that he will hand over some power to a "prime minister," but he is unlikely to satisfy himself with a purely ceremonial role. Prime ministers in other Arab countries all play second fiddle to their presidents, kings or emirs. Although losing popularity, Arafat remains the Palestinians' historic leader, who led the armed struggle and peace negotiations, and who can transcend the divisions of the West Bank, Gaza Strip, and refugees. If Arafat cannot make peace, it may be that nobody else will be able to do so for a generation.

The indispensability of Arafat only magnifies the seriousness of his errors. Israel may have portrayed him as the cynical mastermind behind the uprising. But more than Arafat's supposed strategy of violence, his greater fault may be the lack of any strategy, political or military. Having failed to win over the Israeli public, Arafat is also increasingly distant from his own people. Corruption, lack of democracy, inefficiency have weakened his position. None of these are as damaging as his failure to make real headway toward ending the occupation and establishing a Palestinian state.

Arafat hardly prepared his public for the notion of a pragmatic solution, never engaging in a discussion over what would constitute an acceptable deal. Preferring to avoid divisive issues, for example, whether to abandon the "Right of Return," Arafat has instead told Palestinians for eight years that the day was quickly approaching when a Palestinian child would raise the Palestinian flag over the churches and mosques of Jerusalem. Those who don't like the idea, he said, could "go and drink the water of the sea in Gaza." This was the sum total of his political discourse on the future shape of a Palestinian state. Arafat's was not a vision of the future, but an unrealistic promise to right the wrongs of the past. As a result there was never much excitement or zeal among the Palestinians about building their own state. When the time came to compromise, Palestinians cried "Betrayal!."

Having failed to enunciate a clear and achievable peace policy, Arafat has also proven to be an inept leader of the confrontation. Arafat seems to have stumbled and improvised his way through the Al-Aqsa Intifada. In the same way as he remained passive during the negotiations at Camp David, Arafat did nothing to stop or at least direct the uprising for more than a year. Moderates criticize Arafat for allowing the Intifada to create such damage to Palestinian livelihoods and political standing, without any achievements to show for the suffering. "What we have is not a popular Intifada," said Nusseibeh. "It is a series of violent acts led by a small group of people. The majority are not involved." Hardliners, however, denounce Arafat for supposedly submitting to Israeli and American demands to stop the uprising in return for empty promises of talks. "The Intifada will continue until independence," declared Marwan Barghouthi, the Tanzim leader. The Intifada has become inchoate, an expression of rage. Like the Arab revolt of 1936 and the first Intifada of 1987, the uprising could end up turning Palestinians against each other. "This Intifada is a rebellion against both Israel and Arafat," is how one Palestinian colleague put it. "Ordinary Palestinians ask themselves 'What have we achieved? Is this going to be another defeat to be added to the long list of defeats?'"

Many Palestinians thought they could mimic the tactics of Hizbollah in forcing Israel to leave south Lebanon by inflicting enough pain on Israel. Indeed, Israel has suffered significantly higher casualty rates during the Intifada than it did during the last years of the occupation of south Lebanon. Despite the superiority of the Israelis, nearly 200 members of the security forces have been killed in the Intifada. Nevertheless, the tactics adopted during the Intifada show that Palestinian militants drew the wrong lesson from Lebanon.

Hizbollah's violence succeeded because it was carefully calibrated to achieve a clear political objective, and its fighters were disciplined. Hizbollah's policy of concentrating its attacks on Israeli and allied forces in south Lebanon, rather than on staging cross-border raids into Israel, sent a message to Israel that it has a border to which it can withdraw. In contrast, Palestinian militants have utterly failed to draw a distinction between civilian and military targets, between occupied territories and Israel. They have often chosen "soft" targets such as civilians in Israel and settlers. Suicide bombings in Israel only send

Israel the message that it has no choice but to keep fighting the Palestinians, because any easing up would only make it easier for the militants to attack Israel. The distinction between Arafat's Fatah movement and Islamic groups has become blurred. The former supposedly concentrates on targets in the occupied territories, the latter stages suicide operations in Israel. At times, though, the factions have operated together.

Many Palestinians say the Intifada is a message to Israel that its agony will not end until it withdraws from the occupied territories. But the methods chosen by Palestinians seem instead to convince most Israelis that they can never be trusted. The tactics of chaos and anarchy may make it more difficult for Israel to crush the Intifada because it has no central organization. But they also render the West Bank and Gaza Strip well-nigh ungovernable for Arafat himself when he attempts to restore calm, as he did at the end of 2001.

As of February 2003, Arafat has shown himself to be the great survivor of the Middle East. He has lived through assassination attempts, three military sieges, his expulsion from Jordan and Lebanon after placing himself at the center of two chaotic civil wars, and even a plane crash. Over and beyond his extraordinary luck, part of the reason for Arafat's survival lies in the importance of Palestine in the mind of Arabs and the conscience of the West. At times of disaster, somebody has usually stepped in to help salvage something of the Palestinian cause.

After 1970, Syria and Lebanon helped the PLO reestablish itself in Beirut. In 1982, the United States brokered a deal for the PLO to withdraw from Beirut under the protection of foreign forces. In 1983, it was once more Saudi Arabia's intervention that stopped the Syrian-backed rebels from crushing Arafat and his loyalists during their last stand in Tripoli. After the fiasco of the 1991 Gulf War, it was Israel's Labor government that revived the fortunes of Yasser Arafat in 1993 with the Oslo accords. In 2002, it was the U.S. that once again saved Arafat from Sharon's wrath.

In the mythologized history of the Palestinian revolution, survival against the odds amounts to victory, another stage in the march to Jerusalem. But a man like Arafat, who too often feels immune from the consequences of his errors, can make a dangerous leader. In Jordan and Lebanon, the Palestinians suffered disaster. Arafat could yet lead Palestinians to another political and humanitarian tragedy. With his black-and-white keffiyeh draped over his head in the shape of Palestine, Arafat is both the problem and the solution to the agony of

Palestine. Palestinian intellectuals speak of the need for an Israeli equivalent of South Africa's F. W. de Klerk, who ended apartheid, to take an historic and brave decision to end a quarter of a century of military occupation in the West Bank and Gaza. But Arafat, alas, is no Palestinian equivalent of Nelson Mandela, a figure of reconciliation and moral stature, a man capable of instilling pride and patience in his own people yet finding the words and gestures to assuage the fears of the frightened oppressor.

Arafat started his political life as a would-be Palestinian Joshua who would take the land by force of arms. He may turn out to be a kind of Palestinian Moses, leading his people to the brink of statehood, but unable to enter the Promised Land.

8

Among the Nations

BILL CLINTON CUT an imperial figure as he rose to the podium of the Knesset. Only an American president could bring the members of this most raucous of parliaments to such a reverential hush. Here, after all, was the embodiment of the country that does more than any other to preserve the state of the Jews with money, arms, and diplomatic protection.

When he delivered his address, however, Clinton sounded more like a pilgrim than Caesar. He spoke of peace, of the patriarchs and the prophets of the Bible, and of America's admiration for Israel. "For decades, as Israel has struggled to survive, we have rejoiced in your triumphs and shared in your agonies," said Clinton. "In the years since Israel was founded, Americans of every faith have admired and supported you. Like your country, ours is a land that welcomes exiles—a nation of hope; a nation of refuge."

Israel was a model democracy, he said, and every American president since Truman had been committed to Israel's survival. The President enumerated his offerings to Israel: a promise to maintain the level of military and civilian aid, privileged access to American high technology, military equipment such as F-15 and F-16 fighters, as well as generous help to develop Israel's own antimissile shield, called the Arrow.

He cursed the gods of violence. "So long as Jews are murdered just because they are Jews, or just because they are citizens of Israel, the plague of anti-Semitism lives, and we must stand against it," declared the President. There was the augury for peace and "the promise of a Sabbath afternoon not violated by gunfire."

And at the end, Clinton made his declaration of faith before the assembly of Israel. The President recounted how he and his wife had first visited Israel 13 years earlier, when, as an out-of-office former governor, he made a religious trip with his pastor. "We visited the holy sites. I relived the history of the Bible, of your scriptures and mine. And I formed a bond with my pastor. Later, when he became desperately ill, he said he thought I might one day become President, and he said [. . .] 'If you abandon Israel, God will never forgive you.' He said it is God's will that Israel, the biblical home of the people of Israel, continue forever and ever."

The Knesset broke into a standing ovation. It had never witnessed anything like it. The Christian fundamentalists who come to express solidarity with Israel have usually been regarded as useful allies, but cranks. Now the President of the United States, the most powerful country in the world, declared that America's support for Israel was nothing less than a divine ordinance.

Peace in the Middle East was Clinton's one foreign policy obsession, commanding his time until his last day in office, even as he was about to be engulfed once more by scandals over the gifts, political favors, and the granting of questionable eleventh-hour presidential pardons.

Clinton has long been hailed in Jerusalem as the most pro-Israeli of American presidents. In an unexpected way, Clinton's devotion to the region also made him the most pro-Palestinian of American presidents. It was Clinton who brought Yasser Arafat through the front door of the White House, whereas previous presidents had prevented him even from visiting the United Nations in New York.

In 1998, four years after his momentous Knesset speech, Clinton returned to the Middle East. This time, however, he was at odds with the Israeli government led by the Likud leader, Binyamin Netanyahu, who was stalling the process of territorial concessions. Clinton made no appearance at the Knesset, and it was the Palestinians' turn to savor their moment of emotional symbolism.

To the horror of many Israeli government ministers, the American President flew by helicopter to Gaza international airport and formally opened it. Two vast flags—one Palestinian and one American—fluttered side by side. Clinton gave America's blessing to Palestinian aspirations for statehood and said they should regard America as their friend. "For the first time in the history of the Palestinian movement, the Palestinian people and their elected representatives now have a chance to determine their own destiny on their own land," declared

Clinton. A photograph shows Yasser Arafat clutching Clinton's hands to his breast, seemingly in a gesture of eternal gratitude.

Even as the Al-Aqsa Intifada raged during his final months in office, Clinton clung to the hope of negotiating the end to a century of conflict between Zionism and Arab nationalism, of completing the task begun with the signing of the Oslo accords at the South Lawn of the White House in 1993 at the start of his presidency.

As he packed up his belongings and prepared to move into retirement in January 2001, Clinton found time to pen an open letter to the Israelis and Palestinians. Explaining that none of the many questions he had dealt with mattered more to him than the fate of Israel, Clinton told the Israelis not to despair in the face of the Palestinian uprising. "Do not draw the wrong lessons from this tragic chapter," he urged them. "The violence does not demonstrate that the quest for peace has gone too far—but that it has not gone far enough. And it points not to the failure of negotiations—but to the futility of violence and force. The alternative to a peaceful settlement never has been clearer; it is being played out before our very eyes."

In his letter to the Palestinians, Clinton adopted a more severe, even admonishing tone. He acknowledged the "daily humiliations" faced by Palestinians, and understood their anger. But he went on: "Nothing you have accomplished has been accomplished through violence, and nothing will be. It will only be accomplished through peace and negotiations. Now, more than ever, is the time for courageous leadership. For courage is not only, or even mainly, measured in struggle. It is measured in the ability to seize historic opportunities."

By then, Palestinians had lost all hope in Clinton. His public admonishing of Yasser Arafat after the failure of the Camp David summit, and the intensified anti-American mood caused by the Al-Aqsa Intifada, meant that the warmth of Clinton's visit to Gaza had dissipated. Palestinian newspapers hailed the end of the Clinton administration as "the end of the era of the Jewish lobby."

Clinton gave his first interview as a private citizen to Israel's Channel Two television. The interviewer said, gushingly, that Clinton must be "lonely" and should "leave everything behind and come to Israel to be with us." Clinton let slip that one of his first postpresidential projects was to learn Hebrew.

Few other presidents may share Clinton's devotion to Israel, but this is a question of degree rather than principle. In many ways the Clinton Presidency distills modern America's relationship with the

Jewish State. There is a powerful, visceral commitment to the survival and welfare of Israel, and a struggle to reconcile this support with the American strategic interests in the Arab world. Even if Jews strongly prefer Democratic presidents and Arabs lean toward the Republicans, the question transcends party affiliation; there have been Democrats like Jimmy Carter who hectored Israel and Republicans like Ronald Reagan who considered Israel to be a "non-Nato ally."

A cold strategic calculation would favor American support for the Arabs, who are more numerous than the Jews and who control most of the world's oil reserves as well as the access routes to the Suez Canal. This means that American support for Israel, while unshakeable, is not unconditional. Most American presidents, Clinton included, prefer to deal with Israeli leaders ready to make territorial compromises with the Arabs. It is no surprise that Clinton's relationship with Yitzhak Rabin, Shimon Peres, and Ehud Barak was much closer than with Binyamin Netanyahu.

Arabs, and many other critics of Israel, blame American support for Israel on the pernicious effect of the all-powerful "Jewish lobby" in America, especially on Congress. President George Bush, Sr., at the time of his battle of wills with Yitzak Shamir, himself once complained that he was "one lonely guy . . . against something like a thousand lobbyists on the Hill." American Jews, it is true, are generous political donors and active campaigners on behalf of Israel. In a few states such as New York, Jews form a significant proportion of voters.

But Israel's lobbyists could not succeed by political and economic force alone. They can only win by striking a deeper chord in the American psyche. To the religiously minded, like Clinton, Israel is a manifestation of God's will on earth. To liberals Israel is an example of democracy surviving in a harsh environment. To conservatives, it is a country of admirably tough people who do what is necessary to protect their vital interests. American Protestant groups had advocated "zionism" with a small "z" long before Theodor Herzl founded the Zionist Movement, while America's founding fathers found inspiration for their quest for freedom in the stories of the biblical Israelites fleeing Pharaoh.

The influence of Jews results from their integration into American society, their prominence as an educated and successful group that can shape opinion. America sees Israel as an image of itself, a country born of the power of a compelling idea of "freedom" and built on the romance of "pioneers" with a God-given destiny. Critics of both America and Israel may add that the two countries are settler societies that share the guilt of displacing the indigenous inhabitants from their lands. All the money of Arabs cannot compete with the ability of Israel to present itself as the embodiment of American values of democracy and freedom in a region ruled by despots.

Henry Kissinger, the former Secretary of State, wrote that "Israel is dependent on the United States as no country is on a friendly power." Its leaders resorted to intransigence to preserve a semblance of dignity in its "one-sided relationship" with Washington, and feared that any sign of weakness would only provoke more demands. "It takes a special brand of heroism to turn total dependence into defiance; to insist on support as a matter of right than as a favor [. . .]" Kissinger wrote in *Years of Upheaval*. "Israel affects our decisions through inspiration, persistence, and a judicious, not always subtle or discreet, influence on our domestic policy."

At the end of the First World War President Woodrow Wilson endorsed the creation of a "Jewish Commonwealth" in Palestine, despite his philosophy that native populations "are not to be bartered about from sovereignty to sovereignty as if they were chattels, or pawns in a game." His own commission of inquiry, sent out to ascertain the views of the inhabitants of "Syria" after the war, issued a report ridden with gloom about the likely impact of Zionism.

The two commissioners, Henry King and Charles Crane, said they had set out with abundant literature on Zionism and with "minds predisposed in its favor." But having seen the situation in the region, they were struck by the depth of Arab opposition to Zionism and concluded that the Zionist program of Jewish statehood could not be achieved without "the gravest trespass" on the rights of Arabs, and could only be imposed by force of arms. The commission recommended that Syria, including Palestine and Lebanon, remain united as a single Arab territory ruled by the Hashemite Prince Faisal.

In those days of innocence when America was not yet seen by the Arabs as an imperialist demon, the commission found that a large majority of the Arabs it had spoken to wanted America, rather than Britain or France, to accept the mandate to rule the region. This preference, they said, was the result of "the unselfish aims with which she [America] had come into the war; the faith in her felt by multitudes of Syrians who had been in America; the spirit revealed in American educational institutions in Syria [. . .] their belief that America had no territorial or colonial ambitions, and would willingly withdraw when the Syrian state was well established." Needless to say, the King–Crane report was quietly ignored.

It is difficult these days to imagine that America was not always the Jewish state's most loyal friend. The bounty of economic help, the lonely defense of Israel in the United Nations and the Herculean diplomatic effort of trying to untangle the knot of the Arab–Israeli conflict are all comparatively recent developments.

President Harry Truman recognized Israel as the *de facto* authority in the territories it occupied, just 11 minutes after the end of the British mandate in May 1948. But had it been left up to his Secretary of State, George Marshall, Israel would probably not have been born. The United States voted in favor of the partition of Palestine at the United Nations in 1947, but the State Department recoiled once violence broke out and sponsored an attempt to place Palestine under U.N. trusteeship.

Emotionally symbolic as Truman's gesture of recognition may have been to Jews, it was not America that ensured the survival of Israel during those critical early months, but the Soviet Union. Zionist officials and Soviet diplomats busily schemed to defeat Washington's attempt to suspend the partition of Palestine. In contrast with Washington's *de facto* recognition of the Jewish state in May 1948, Moscow was first to acknowledge Israel *de jure*. And most important, while the United States imposed an arms embargo, it was the delivery of aircraft and weapons through Communist-ruled Czechoslovakia, with the blessing of the Soviet Union, that allowed Israel to defeat the Arab armies in 1948.

Few issues better illustrate the cynicism of world diplomacy than the sanctimony that has accompanied many countries' shifting alliances in the Middle East.

Israel was the product of a rare moment of entente between the United States and the Soviet Union. Both agreed that after the horrors of the Second World War, the Jews should have their own state in Palestine, regardless of what the Arabs might say.

With the start of the Cold War, however, Israel drifted toward Washington and several of the Arab states allied themselves to Moscow. Having initially armed Israel, Czechoslovakia became Egypt's quartermaster with a large weapons deal in September 1955, accelerating the spiral of events toward the Suez Crisis the following year.

France may be regarded these days as one of the most pro-Arab countries in Europe, but in the 1950s Paris took up the role of Israel's best ally, supplying tanks and fighter aircraft. Egypt's President Gamal Abdel-Nasser was then the main backer of the Algerian rebellion against French rule, and Paris decided that the enemy of its Egyptian enemy must be its friend.

It was France—not Britain and its Balfour Declaration—that first promised to restore Jewish independence in Palestine. "Rightful Heirs of Palestine!" said a proclamation issued by Napoleon to the Jews in 1799, as he advanced through Palestine. "[...] Hasten! Now is the moment, which may not return for thousands of years, to claim the restoration of civic rights among the population of the universe which had been shamefully withheld from you for thousands of years."

The proclamation was dated Jerusalem, but Napoleon never reached the holy city, having been ignominiously turned back at the gates of Acre by its Turkish defenders supported by a British naval squadron.

In the 1950s, France provided the impetus for Israel's nuclear weapons program by helping to build the nuclear reactor at Dimona just as, decades later, France would become instrumental in the development of Iraq's nuclear program.

Nasser's nationalization of the Suez Canal drew Britain into a conspiracy with France and Israel. Eight years after the British were hounded out of Palestine by the Jews, the respective armed forces plotted to attack Egypt. Israel invaded Sinai to give Britain and France a pretext to "intervene." But President Dwight Eisenhower, infuriated by this final spasm of old world colonial intervention and fearing that it would upset Washington's policy of drawing the Arabs into the anti-Soviet "Baghdad Pact," forced the anti-Nasser allies to withdraw. Eisenhower threatened to cut off all aid to Israel.

Israel fought the Six Day War with French arms but without French support. Charles de Gaulle, who had withdrawn from Algeria, banned the sale of weapons to Israel on the eve of the Six Day War and subsequently tilted increasingly toward the Arabs.

By then, though, Washington's relationship with Israel was warming quickly. In the latter years of the Eisenhower presidency relations with Israel improved, and with the election of the Democrats they underwent a transformation.

John F. Kennedy was the first American president to guarantee Israel's security, and he sold Hawk anti-aircraft batteries to Israel in 1962. Lyndon B. Johnson, who prevaricated in the build-up to the Six Day War because of America's commitment to Vietnam, later sold fighter jets to Israel.

The Yom Kippur War deepened the United States' involvement in the Middle East. The U.S. carried out an emergency airlift of military supplies that helped Israel turn the tide of the war, but then prevented the Jewish State from crushing Egypt's Third Army. The U.S. could not countenance the defeat of its Israeli ally, but it could not permit the humiliation of Egypt either.

This strategy, as well as Henry Kissinger's shuttle diplomacy, yielded the Disengagement Accords with Egypt and Syria and ultimately prepared the way for the Egyptian–Israeli peace treaty of 1978, under Jimmy Carter. After Camp David, the U.S. provided Egypt with aid almost as enormous as that given to Israel—about $2 billion a year compared with $3 billion for Israel. The United States, despite its support for Israel, or perhaps because of it, established itself as the only broker of peace in the region.

It was Ronald Reagan who, seeing the world starkly divided into communists and anticommunists, formally elevated Israel as America's "strategic ally" only months before it invaded Lebanon. But the Gulf War of 1991, conducted by President George Bush, showed that far from being an ally, Israel was a strategic embarrassment when it came to projecting U.S. military power in the Arab world.

It seemed for a while as if the transformation of the world after the collapse of Soviet Communism and the crisis in the Gulf would weaken the long friendship between America and Israel, built up during the years of the Cold War when Israel was seen as a western bastion against Soviet expansionism. Bush lost the election, however, and the relationship between Israel and America was not put to the test for years to follow. Bill Clinton was the fortunate heir of the Oslo accords, which fell into his lap in his first year in office. The agreement had been negotiated without American involvement, but after hosting the signing ceremony, Clinton effectively became the guardian of the peace deal between Israel and the Palestinians. He tried hard to push the accords forward, but Clinton let slip what might have been a unique opportunity to resolve the Arab-Israeli question.

★

The day after the September 11 attacks, George W. Bush gathered his national security team to discuss how America would wage the war on terrorism. Intelligence reports immediately identified Osama bin Laden as the man responsible for the atrocities, but senior figures in the administration were already thinking far beyond al-Qa'ida. "Why shouldn't we go against Iraq?" they asked.

If the Bush administration had one priority in the Middle East when it came to office in January 2001, it was not the Israelis and Palestinians, but the unfinished business with Saddam Hussein. Donald Rumsfeld, the Defense Secretary, and Paul Wolfowitz, his deputy, had been among the signatories of an open letter in 1998 urging Bill Clinton to adopt "a comprehensive political and military strategy for bringing down Saddam and his regime."

Now, at the moment of America's agony, they argued that the war on terrorism should include not only terrorists such as bin Laden, but also state sponsors of terrorism, with Saddam at the top of the list. The hawks were temporarily overruled; Bush said Americans expected bin Laden to be dealt with first. But the decision only postponed the moment of reckoning in Iraq. Indeed, the swift defeat of the Taliban encouraged the belief that American power could also effect "regime change" in Iraq.

America's new doctrine of "preemptive" action against the threat of weapons of mass destruction owes much to the experience of Israel. For American conservatives, the Israeli attack on the Osiraq nuclear complex near Baghdad in 1981 is the best example of why Washington should be able to remove threats even if they do not pose an imminent danger. Had the Israelis not bombed the reactor, Saddam Hussein might by now have the first nuclear bomb in the Arab world. Israel always had to worry about how America would respond to its actions; that is a concern that the Bush administration does not have.

It's unclear whether the Bush administration is also studying the lessons to be drawn from Israel's failures. Israel's attempt to impose "regime change" in Lebanon, for instance, went horribly wrong. The Israelis went in to cheers from Lebanon's Shi'ites, and soon found themselves at the receiving end of their suicide bombers. Israel also learned that public support for a war of choice, rather than a war of necessity, can be brittle. Failure in these cases does not elicit fortitude, but rather polarization and protests that sap a country's will to continue a costly war, as happened to America over Vietnam and to Israel in Lebanon.

In the Gulf War of 1991, Israelis liked to argue that the crisis was a conclusive repudiation of the claim that the central problem of the Arab world is Zionism. The invasion of Kuwait had nothing to do with Israel, or with the expropriation and dispersal of Palestinians. It was about despotism and greed, a dispute between ruling elites that differ only in degrees of authoritarianism. This time, however, Israelis like to think that America's war on terrorism and Iraq is, in fact, the same war that Israel has waged for decades against Palestinian militants and Arab despots.

America's solution for the Arab world—the democratization of the Palestinian Authority, Iraq and ultimately of the rest of the Arab world—has floated among Israelis for years. Figures such as Binyamin Netanyahu and Natan Sharansky argued that Israel could not make peace with Syria and the Palestinians until they and other regimes became democracies that could be trusted not to resort to war and conflict to resolve their differences. It seemed a recipe for endless procrastination until the settlement of the occupied territories had been made permanent.

It is arguable that, for the foreseeable future, any true democracy in the Arab world would throw up an Islamist regime that is more militant on the Palestinian question than the autocratic regime it might replace. Arab leaders are, in general, far more cautious than their populations when it comes to demands for action to stop the oppression of Palestinians. For the most part, they are also likely to be less anti-American than their people.

America, in the view of most Arabs, is guilty of a galling "double standard." One country, Israel, contravenes one U.N. Security Council resolution after another concerning the occupation of territory by force, yet receives nearly $3 billion a year in military and civilian aid from Washington, D.C. This is the largest grant by the U.S. to any country, amounting to roughly $500 per Israeli, more than the total GNP per capita of many African countries struggling to obtain relief from crushing international debts.

Another country, Iraq, contravenes U.N. resolutions arising from its invasion of Kuwait, yet still languishes a decade after the liberation of Kuwait under the most comprehensive sanctions regime devised by the international community, resulting in poverty, disease and premature death for all but the richest Iraqis.

Saddam is denounced for oppressing his own people, but the daily bloodletting in Israel and Palestine is all but forgotten. In his State of the Union address in January 2003, President Bush declared that "the gravest danger in the war on terror, the gravest danger facing America and the world, is outlaw regimes that seek and possess nuclear, chemical, and biological weapons." He barely mentioned the issue that concerns Arabs most closely, saying: "In the Middle East, we will continue to seek peace between a secure Israel and a democratic Palestine."

For many Arabs it is a perversion of justice that Israel should be regarded as a key ally of Washington when it is armed with nuclear weapons and the missiles to carry them, that it rejects the Nuclear Proliferation Treaty and declares that the Fourth Geneva Convention does not apply to its occupation of the West Bank and Gaza Strip. In contrast, Iraq faces war because it has not disarmed of weapons of mass destruction.

America has well-polished arguments to rebut such accusations: in contrast with the clear obligations placed by the U.N. on Iraq, Israel's withdrawal from the occupied territories should be accompanied by recognition of the Jewish state within secure and recognized borders. Israel is a victim of terrorism, and has a right to defend itself. Israel may be the largest recipient of America aid, but Egypt is the second largest beneficiary.

But these arguments do not dispel the deeply held belief among many Arabs that America, the greatest power in the world, wields its power unfairly. To many Arabs, America's pernicious influence is all pervasive: its military power fragments the Arab nation, its money corrupts Arab rulers and its social manners pollute Islam. In this climate of heightened resentment, anyone who can humiliate or stand up to America is regarded as a hero to a substantial number of Arabs.

The war on terrorism, the campaign against Saddam and the Israeli-Palestinian conflict could merge into one. In making Iraq the next major target of America's "war on terrorism," Bush runs the risk of intensifying the terrorists' war against America. It is also clear that popular anger over Palestine has helped both Osama bin Laden and Saddam Hussein draw support in their campaigns against America.

Bin Laden's terrorist network was born out of his resentment at America's presence on the holy soil of the Arabian peninsula, and none of the September 11 hijackers were Palestinian. But such is the power of Palestine that he invokes its name to justify his war on America. Bin Laden's network, now partly destroyed by the success of U.S. military action in Afghanistan, calls itself the World Islamic Front for Jihad Against Jews and Crusaders. In a video message issued shortly after the September 11 attacks, Bin Laden hailed the way America was "struck by God Almighty." America's suffering, said Bin Laden, "is only a copy of what we have tasted" over decades of humiliation. He evoked the plight of children dying in Iraq and tanks rolling through Palestinian towns, and concluded with the rallying cry: "As to America, I say to it and its people a few words: I swear to

God that America will not live in peace before peace reigns in Palestine, and before all the army of infidels depart the land of Mohammad, peace be upon him. God is the Greatest and glory be to Islam."

In November 2002, Bin Laden's allies carried out a double attack on Israeli holidaymakers in Kenya as part of an international campaign against tourists. Three Israelis, including two children, and at least ten Kenyans were killed when suicide bombers detonated a car bomb and devastated the lobby of the Paradise Hotel. Minutes earlier, gunmen fired two missiles at an Israeli charter aircraft taking off from Mombasa airport, missing it by a few feet. Binyamin Netanyahu, the former Israeli prime minister, said this kind of attack on commercial airliners is likely to affect other countries. "It always starts with Israel, but it never ends there," he said.

Saddam, for his part, likes to present himself as the new Saladin who will liberate Jerusalem. He stages military parades of volunteers supposedly ready to give up their lives for Palestine. More important, Saddam has tried to stoke the fire of Intifada by paying the families of suicide bombers $25,000, while the families of other "martyrs" receive $10,000.

If and when America goes to war, Saddam may try to fire his remaining missiles at Israel in the hope of drawing it into conflict. In contrast with 1991, when Iraq used only conventional warheads, Saddam may feel he has nothing to lose by arming his last missiles with chemical or biological weapons, or by sending pilots on suicide missions to attack Israeli cities with nonconventional weapons.

Israel has not taken the threat lightly. For more than a decade Israelis have been issued with gas masks and instructions on how to protect their homes. In January 2003, Israel hurriedly tested its Arrow anti-missile defense, which was deployed alongside updated U.S. Patriot missiles, which performed badly during the 1991 Gulf War.

A question mark remained over whether Israel would respond if attacked. Many in the Israeli establishment believed Israel had lost some of its deterrent power by not responding to Saddam's Scud missile attacks in 1991. But twelve years later, Sharon is likely to weigh up some factors: if the casualties of an attack are light, Israel is likely to hold back in order not to upset American operations; but if there are mass casualties, Sharon may not be able to resist demands for stern action, and perhaps even retaliation in kind. Even then, he would have to consider whether revenge would bring any benefits in a war designed to remove Saddam from power.

The victory of the first Bush administration in the Gulf War of

1991 put radical Arab nationalism on the defensive, imposed a Pax Americana on the Gulf, and forced the PLO to take a pragmatic step to salvage the organization. It was the essential precursor to the 1993 Oslo accords.

The second Bush administration has spoken of exploiting the overthrow of Saddam to spread democracy through the Middle East and exert pressure on other rogue states. But as it seeks to create a new Middle East, it has said little about what it intends to do about the old problem of the Middle East, the Israeli-Palestinian dispute. After dealing with his father's unfinished business in Iraq, will George W. Bush also try to complete the business of peace started by his father with the 1991 Madrid peace conference? Or will Ariel Sharon be able to seize the moment of a war with Iraq to impose his own "regime change" on the Palestinians and send his old foe Yasser Arafat into exile?

★

A faded blue flag hangs above an old Arab house outside the Old City of Jerusalem. It was once a sentinel on no-man's-land between the Israeli and Jordanian ceasefire lines, but today it is dwarfed by large hotels that Israel is erecting on the waste-ground to erase the traces of the division of the city.

Known as MAC (Mixed Armistice Commission) House, the U.N. building had been a place for Israeli and Jordanian military officers to meet under the auspices of the United Nations Truce and Supervision Organization, the first-ever U.N. peace-keeping mission and now one of the most pointless.

These days MAC House serves no useful function. It is merely a run-down office for U.N. staff who have no ceasefire line to monitor. The frontier that divided Jerusalem in 1948, when UNTSO was deployed, has long since been shifted by force of Israeli arms down to the Jordan Valley.

The official rationale for UNTSO is now "to support other U.N. peace-keeping missions." This amounts to diplomatic-speak for artificial job creation. The real purpose is political—to keep the blue U.N. flags flying on the old "seam" of Jerusalem and on Government House (the seat of the old British government on the Hill of Evil Counsel); to demonstrate the continuing presence of the U.N. in Jerusalem.

The flags are a symbol of the world's enduring and obsessive interest in Israel—a reminder that the United Nations, when it decided to partition Palestine in 1947, intended to maintain Jerusalem as a *corpus separatum*, a separate body to be run directly by the U.N.. Today MAC House stands as a reproach to Israel for the annexing of East Jerusalem in 1967.

Most countries, apart from a few Central American countries, take a similar view and have kept their embassies in Tel Aviv. American presidential candidates issue promises to move the U.S. embassy to Jerusalem, but once in office they find a thousand reasons why it is not feasible just at the moment.

Most Israelis would like MAC House to be bulldozed. For Palestinians, the U.N. flag in Jerusalem provides hope for their claim to statehood with Jerusalem as their capital. If in 1947 Jews danced in the streets to rejoice at the partition vote by the General Assembly, Israel today regards the body as contemptibly anti-Israeli and even anti-Semitic. And where the Palestinians and the other Arabs furiously rejected the partition vote as illegitimate, today they regard the U.N.'s battery of resolutions as the foundation of "international legitimacy" for their cause.

Israel got off to a bad start with the U.N. in September 1948, when the Lehi underground group assassinated Count Folke Bernadotte, the U.N.'s peace mediator in Palestine, who proposed reallocating the Negev region from the Jewish state to the Arab state and placing Jerusalem under Arab sovereignty.

Every year the General Assembly passes more than a dozen resolutions critical of Israel, and the Arabs have seized on every U.N. forum—from economic development to women's rights—to harangue Zionism. "If Algeria introduced a resolution declaring that the earth was flat and that Israel had flattened it, it would pass by a vote of 164 to 13 with 26 abstentions," Abba Eban, a former Israeli foreign minister, once remarked. Sometimes Israel secured a mere two votes in its favor—its own and that of the United States.

However much it may rail against the ignorance and bias of the outside world, Israel cannot escape the fact that it derives its legitimacy from international treaties and documents. The Balfour Declaration is, for Israel, a covenant with the temporal powers of the world to establish a modern Jewish state. The declaration was approved at the Allies' conference at San Remo in 1920, and incorporated in the Mandate on Palestine conferred upon Britain by the League of Nations in 1922. An act of imperialism created the embryo of Israel, but in this regard the Jewish state is no more artificial than the Arab states which were also carved out by the Allies after the First World War.

Ever since Herzl lobbied the chanceries of Europe to secure a charter for the Jewish colonization of Palestine, the Jewish and Palestinian questions have been in large part in the hands of the nations of the world. The U.N. partitioned Palestine to create a Jewish state as an act of expiation for the Holocaust. Sooner or later, it will recognize the independence of Palestine as atonement for the suffering and injustice which was inflicted on the Palestinians.

Palestinians make a distinction between the original U.N. of 1947, when it was dominated by the large powers, and the U.N. of the 1970s, when it swelled with newly decolonized countries. The Palestine Liberation Organization enjoys a status at the U.N. that is a shade below that of full statehood, while for decades Israel was a pariah excluded from the vital regional groupings (it only joined the Western European and Others Group in 2000).

In 1974, Arafat secured an invitation to address the U.N. General Assembly despite the objections of the United States. Standing at the podium in New York, with the holster of his handgun showing below his green fatigues (the weapon itself had been left behind), Arafat chastised the old U.N. "The General Assembly partitioned what it had no right to divide—an indivisible homeland. When we rejected that decision, our position corresponded to that of the natural mother who refused to permit King Solomon to cut her son in two when the unnatural mother claimed the child for herself and agreed to his dismemberment," he declared.

Appealing directly to the heads of Third World liberation movements who packed the hall, Arafat said: "I am a rebel and freedom is my cause." He urged Israelis to "turn away one by one from the illusory promises made to them by Zionist ideology," and offered Jews the prospect of a united, secular, and democratic Palestinian state. "Today I have come bearing an olive branch and a freedom fighter's gun," concluded Arafat. "Do not let the olive branch fall from my hand."

A year after Arafat's appearance, the General Assembly passed a resolution equating Zionism with racism; Israel was consigned to the same outcast status as South Africa under apartheid. But in a measure of the fickleness of the United Nations' pronouncements, the resolution was repealed in 1991 as soon as the balance of power shifted in the U.N. following the fall of the Berlin Wall and the Gulf War. Most of the ex-Communist countries quickly restored relations with Israel, both as a means of signaling their break with the past and as a route to befriending the U.S. African countries, which had severed relations in 1973 in response to the Israeli army's crossing of the Suez

Canal into the African continent, started sending ambassadors back to Tel Aviv. In the 1990s, Israel's foreign ministry struggled to find enough diplomats to fill new posts.

With the outbreak of the latest Palestinian uprising, the mood at the United Nations once again became hostile to Israel. Within days of the start of the Intifada, the Security Council condemned Sharon's "provocation" in going to the Al-Aqsa compound and "acts of violence, especially the excessive use of force against Palestinians, resulting in injury and loss of human life." Three weeks later, the U.N. Human Rights Commission passed a resolution deploring Israel's "measures which constitute war crimes, flagrant violations of international humanitarian law, and crimes against humanity."

The low point came in August 2001, with the United Nations' World Conference Against Racism, Racial Discrimination, Xenophobia, and Related Intolerance. The Arabs sought to revive the old "Zionism is Racism" accusation with texts in the draft declaration that denounced Israel as "a new kind of apartheid" and decried "the emergence of racial and violent movements based on racism and discriminatory ideas, in particular the Zionist movement, which is based on racial superiority." Elsewhere, there were attempts to play down the Nazi Holocaust of the Jews as one of several "holocausts" with a lower case "h," part of a spectrum of horrors that include "the ethnic cleansing of the Arab population in historic Palestine." A group of Arab lawyers in Durban distributed pamphlets depicting Israelis with hooked noses and blood dripping from their fangs. So vulgar was this propaganda attack that Mary Robinson, the U.N. human rights commissioner, a Roman Catholic, responded with a Kennedyesque declaration of solidarity: "I am a Jew."

The American and Israeli delegations walked out in disgust. In the end, it was left to the European countries to dilute the final text to remove language overtly critical of Israel, but which acknowledged the "plight" of Palestinians.

Any self-respecting world statesman will, at some point, try his or her hand at Middle East peace-making. Jerusalem and Gaza have become as important "capitals" on the diplomatic circuit as any in Europe. And given the hypersensitivity of both Israelis and Palestinians, few high-level visits pass off without incident.

In my years in Jerusalem, Bill Clinton was prevented from visiting the Old City in 1994 because the Israelis and the Palestinians could not agree on who should accompany him to the disputed holy sites. The President of the United States could only gaze out of the window of his suite in the King David Hotel across to the ramparts of the holy city.

Two years later President Jacques Chirac of France did walk through the alleys of Jerusalem, but publicly berated his Israeli security guards for being too aggressive and threatened to fly home. In 2000, his Prime Minister, Lionel Jospin, was pelted with stones by Palestinians at Bir Zeit University after accusing Lebanon's Hizbollah group of "terrorist acts." Britain's Foreign Secretary, Robin Cook, had his dinner with the Prime Minister abruptly canceled in 1998 after he had the temerity to meet Palestinians near a controversial new Jewish neighborhood in anexed East Jerusalem.

No visit to the Holy Land can have been as emotionally charged as the Pope's pilgrimage in March 2000. He kissed two bowls of earth, one presented by Israeli officials and the other by Palestinians, each side trying to earn his spiritual—and political—blessing for their position. The Pope tiptoed around controversies such as the question of whether the Vatican could have done more against the Holocaust, and a dispute between Muslims and Christians in Nazareth. He prayed in the Grotto of the Nativity in Bethlehem, and visited the Deheisheh refugee camp where he declared that "the Palestinian people have the natural right to a homeland."

Israelis waited with trepidation. Before the visit Amos Oz recalled that his relatives "turn their eyes away every time they walk past a church." The first papal visit by Pope Paul VI in 1964 was remembered in Israel more as an insult than an honor. The Pope had nipped across the border from Jordan for a day's visit, and did not utter the word "Israel."

Six decades earlier, when Herzl went to seek the "spiritual consent" of the Vatican in 1904, Pius X told him bluntly that since the Jews had not acknowledged Jesus, the Vatican could not acknowledge the Jewish people or the Zionist movement. Herzl explained that he was only interested in the "profane" earth of Palestine, and would favor extraterritoriality for holy places. He invoked the desperate plight of the Jews, but it was all in vain. "We pray for the Jews," said Pius X. "May their minds be enlightened [. . .] if you come to Palestine and settle your people there, we shall keep churches and priests ready to baptize all of them."

But nearly a century later, in the Jubilee year of the Church of Rome, the roles were utterly changed. Now Pope John Paul II begged forgiveness (although he denied the Church's responsibility) for the sins of Christians against the Jews through the ages. At the

Western Wall in Jerusalem, he adopted the Jewish form of supplication and slipped a note between the massive stone blocks, which read: "We are deeply saddened by the behavior of those who in the course of history have caused these children of yours to suffer and, asking your forgiveness, we wish to commit ourselves to genuine brotherhood with the people of the Covenant."

The Pope, who as Karol Wojtyla had seen the war in Poland and the impact of the Holocaust first hand, mesmerized many Israelis and brought the glimmer of hope that the millennial rivalry between Judaism and Christianity might, just might, be overcome.

He visited Yad Vashem's Hall of Remembrance, where an eternal flame glows in memory of the six million killed, three million of them in the pontiff's native Poland. Sever Plotzker, one of the Israeli journalists there, reported in *Yediot Ahronot*: "I am willing to swear that when I looked at the movement of his trembling lips yesterday in the dark Hall of Remembrance in Jerusalem, I saw him whispering *kaddish*."

*

When Palestine suffers, the American Colony Hotel comes to life. At the first sign of political trouble, pilgrims and tourists stream out of Israeli hotels while journalists pour into the American Colony, pleading for a room. As the tourist coaches disappear, the car park fills with journalists' cars. The wealthier television networks have bullet-proof vehicles. Others have plastic windows to fend off stones. Most make do with rock-proof plastic windows and improvised "PRESS" and "TV" signs.

At times of crisis the Colony is a place for journalists to rekindle friendships with their far-flung colleagues. Its courtyard and bar are abuzz with old war stories, bad jokes, and the exchange of snippets of information. Ibrahim, the barman, knew the trysts and foibles of many of those who had been coming over the previous decade and more, but was as always the model of discretion.

The "colony" was established by American Christians in the nineteenth century as a place of good works in Jerusalem. Now the American Colony is a place for the Palestinian elite and expatriates. Brass plaques name the famous visitors—Graham Greene, John Le Carré, and Peter Ustinov.

A former Pasha's palace, the American Colony is tucked away close to the old ceasefire line. Nothing that Israel has built nearby can rival the intimate atmosphere of an evening spent in the inner courtyard of the American Colony, with its little fountain splashing at the foot of soaring palm trees and the ocher stone draped in bougainvillaea.

Jerusalem is already home to one of the world's biggest resident contingents of foreign correspondents, and many more come when there is a crisis. The journalists are but a small part of the veritable army of observers, monitors, chroniclers, members of international organizations, charity workers, activists, researchers, and adventurers who swarm around Israelis and Palestinians. In many ways, Jerusalem is already an "international city."

Israelis and Palestinians conduct their quarrel under bright stage-lights; their fight is political theater. A stone can hardly be thrown in Jerusalem without somebody capturing it on camera. I have watched a dozen photographers and cameramen crowding around a single stone-thrower or Israeli soldier. Israelis and Palestinians have instinctively learned the art of speaking in sound-bites.

As the world watches, often confused, the partisans of Israel and the Palestinians conduct their arguments with vehemence, bombarding newspapers with outraged letters, accusations of bias, or the offers of exclusive "briefings" on the situation.

The causes of the Israelis or of the Palestinians, counting a few million people each, have an extraordinary ability to inspire loyalty abroad. The Jews are seen by their supporters as uniquely sinned against; sympathizers of the Palestinians see the Jews as uniquely sinning.

In none of the other chronic conflicts of the world can news agencies set the "Urgent" bells ringing regularly with a bulletin of a single Israeli or Palestinian killed in a clash. Most of those who die in this conflict still have their names recorded. No death in Africa, Asia—or even in the rest of the Middle East—receives as many column inches as a person killed in the Holy Land. The genocide of Rwanda has faded from memory, the war raging in Chechnya hardly registers as a blip on the news agencies, yet the roughly 2,000 or so people killed since the start of the Al-Aqsa Intifada command obsessive attention.

Why does the world—why do we journalists—pay so much attention to events in this corner of the world?

The usual reason given is the geopolitical importance of the Middle East. The mix of oil, the Suez Canal, large armies, and nuclear weapons means that statesmen become involved, and journalists follow close behind. The close involvement of the United States serves to reinforce the priority given to coverage of the Middle East.

Moreover, the Arab–Israeli conflict is easier to cover than most.

Access is easy. There are no remote jungles to penetrate or dilapidated airports to brave. A journalist from London or New York can arrive on the spot of any incident within hours of its taking place. There is usually no overt censorship, even though both sides exert pressure on journalists. The combination of fast-working Israeli media, a dense network of Palestinian journalists and "fixers," and the presence of a large body of international journalists in Jerusalem generates an unstoppable flow of "news."

Both sides are usually happy to speak and, even with the gun battles of the latest uprising, the conflict between Israel and the Palestinians is safer to cover than most wars.

Small atrocities in Israel can attract more coverage than a large atrocity elsewhere because they can be instantly reported. Israelis complain of the world's "double standard" in the intensity of scrutiny it gives to Israel's actions, while ignoring abuses in the Arab world. Fair or not, this is the price that Israel must pay to be able to call itself "the only democracy in the Middle East."

The truth is that most Israelis would far prefer the overwhelming attention of the world to none at all. There is an unmistakable boast in the Israeli dictum, "Jews is News." The former editor of the *Jerusalem Post*, David Bar-Illan, used to write a popular weekly column in which he poured vitriol on foreign correspondents' (anti-Israeli) bias, ignorance, mistakes, and over-simplification. Palestinians, too, complain frequently and bitterly about the quality of foreign reporting. Time and again, I am asked by Palestinians how it is that Jews manage to control the world's media and it is almost impossible to convince them otherwise.

Israel and the occupied territories receive a disproportionate amount of attention for similar reasons that western news organizations dedicated so much coverage to South Africa under apartheid; the Israelis are seen as a "white" European people whose actions, brutality, bravery, successes, and fiascos are of natural interest to western audiences. Events here are also of concern to many in the Third World because of the perception that the Palestinians' struggle is the last great anticolonial cause.

Remove for a moment the biblical imagery and with it the argument over who has the historical "right" to the land, and free yourself from the emotions of the Holocaust: Israel then begins to look much more like European settler colonial regimes established elsewhere in the world. Had Herzl succeeded in founding the Jewish State in Uganda in 1904, would it have turned into a Jewish South Africa, with a white population resorting to military and administrative oppression to keep the restive natives at bay? Or would it be considered an island of liberal democratic values in a dark continent?

Herzl himself was aware of the dangers, saying he wanted to create a new Venice rather than another Boer state. Tellingly, in *Altneuland* he waxes lyrical about how scientific research being carried out in the New Society may result in a cure for malaria that would, in turn, permit the further colonization of Africa.

In reality, one cannot escape from the fact that the Jewish state was established in Palestine, that Jews have an historical connection to the country, and that the Holocaust did happen. The argument is whether these factors justify Israel's treatment of the Palestinians, and whether Palestinians are justified in the methods that they have employed.

All this does not fully explain the West's enduring interest. I think there is a deeper, cultural source. The struggle between Israel and the Palestinians is a grand epic whose symbols are familiar. Most people in the West will know something of the Bible, the Crusades, anti-Semitism, and the Holocaust. In an era when television can report live from the biblical cities of Jerusalem, Bethlehem, and Hebron, few can have missed the David-and-Goliath scenes of Palestinians using simple slings to hurl stones at the Israelis.

The conflict over the Holy Land—or Israel, or Palestine—is a vast story of tragedy and redemption. It is a tale of larger-than-life characters. Yasser Arafat's *keffiyeh* and Moshe Dayan's eye-patch are instantly recognizable. There is a constant moral tension about the place—the survival of the ancient amidst the new, the superposition of the religious and the profane, the sullying of the spiritual with the brutal, the discordance between epic heroism and pettiness. This attempt to reconcile the earthly Jerusalem with the heavenly Jerusalem makes the country compelling and tragic.

The creation of Israel, and its conflict with Palestinians, is a saga that seems to start with Abraham and is still unfolding before our eyes. It is as if we were still witnessing the sibling rivalries of the Bible. We feel outrage at Cain for the murder of Abel. We are torn between the rights of Ishmael, Abraham's first-born, and Isaac the true son born of Sarah. We witness Jacob's deception in taking Esau's birthright, and watch in wonder at the magnanimity of Joseph toward his treacherous brothers.

Epilogue

SOON AFTER the signing of the Oslo accords, Shimon Peres had few illusions about the problems of making peace and of disentangling Israel from the occupied territories. "You can turn eggs into an omelette, but it is very difficult to turn an omelette into eggs," he explained in his office in Jerusalem. "What we are trying to do is to turn an omelette into eggs."

Peres should know. In a previous incarnation, before becoming the leading dove of Israeli politics and negotiating the peace accords with the Palestinians, Peres had been one of the greatest friends in government of the Gush Emunim settlement movement in the 1970s. The purpose of settlement is to make it more difficult, almost impossible, for an Israeli government to withdraw from the territories. Now he was struggling with the consequences.

Look at the map of the West Bank and Gaza Strip today and you soon realize what a scrambled mess the occupied territories have become. Palestinian cities and autonomous enclaves splattered here and there, Jewish settlements sprinkled everywhere, connected together with matted strings of Israeli-controlled roads.

Is there a solution? Oslo provided a path toward a two-state solution, Israel and Palestine side by side. It was the same philosophy that inspired the U.N. partition resolution in 1947. Many of the same problems remain. Anyone who has dealt with the problem since the 1930s has quickly discovered there is no obvious way to separate Arab and Jew in Palestine. Despite the mass exodus of Palestinians in 1948, Arabs today still make up about one-fifth of Israel's population. Since 1967, successive Israeli governments have settled a large number of Jews in the captured territories, further mixing the populations.

In the absence of a demographic or geographical dividing line, the line that has the greatest chance of ensuring stability is a political and historical one—Israel's pre-1967 borders. There is an international consensus that the lands captured in 1948, including those beyond the 1947 U.N. partition line, are properly Israel's, while the territories captured in 1967 should be considered occupied. The settlements in the West Bank and Gaza Strip are illegal in virtually everybody's reading of international law. Not everyone likes the idea of partition—many among both Israelis and Palestinians will feel their resulting states will be geographical runts. Extremists on both sides claim all the land between the Jordan River and the Mediterranean for themselves.

Nevertheless the pre-1967 line, described as the borders of Auschwitz by the former Israeli foreign minister Abba Eban, is the only boundary on which there is any hope of achieving a negotiated agreement. It is the starting point for any solution. Withdrawal from the occupied territories is the core demand of the majority of Palestinians, and is accepted by a substantial number of Israelis. A majority of Israelis could be won over if Israel had credible assurances that withdrawal would end a century of conflict, with no outstanding Palestinian claims. Such a deal would be regarded as a "fair" deal by the majority of the Arab world, and the international community. Nelson Mandela likes to say that the end of apartheid liberated not only the blacks, but also the whites of South Africa. A withdrawal from the West Bank and Gaza Strip, with a deal on Jerusalem, would liberate Israel from accusations of being an "occupier." It may also free Palestinians and Israelis alike from a debilitating victim complex.

There are undeniable security reasons for Israel to retain the West Bank—the mountains form a "wall" against aggressors to the East, protect Israel's narrow coastal plain and provide vital early warning positions. From Israel's perspective, it is better to fight a future war in the Jordan Valley than from the foothills near Ben-Gurion airport. This has to be balanced against the risks of continuing the conflict. In the past decade, more Israelis have died within Israel and the occupied territories than trying to defend the borders. Despite the fury in the Arab world over the treatment of Palestinians, no Arab armies have been mobilized to threaten Israel. A permanent peace accord under which the Palestinians sign away all claims to Israel is not a guarantee of peace, but should make it more difficult for a future irredentist Palestinian state to find Arab allies.

Security arrangements can be devised—early warning stations, demilitarization of the Palestinian state, access routes for Israeli forces in times of crisis, and the deployment of a tripwire international force in the Jordan Valley. In conditions of peace, as a further guarantee, Israel and Palestine could be bound into the NATO system of alliances and partnerships.

The basic principle of the two-state solution is that in return for Palestinian recognition of Israel in its boundaries before 1967, Israel gives up what it captured after 1967. Even the issue of Jewish settlement can be addressed if Israel cedes to Palestine territory to compensate for settlement blocks that stay within the Jewish state. The central debate in Israel is this: Is an Israeli withdrawal likely to stop a future war? Or will it merely make Israel weaker when that war inevitably comes? Egypt's Anwar Sadat understood his task was to convince Israelis that the answer to the first proposition is "Yes." Now the Palestinian uprising is pushing them toward the view that peace is impossible. At the time of the first Intifada, Albert Agazarian, a Palestinian historian, encapsulated the problem of the Arab-Israeli dispute as follows: "Israel is holding us by the throat and choking us. What's worse, it can't let go." Little has changed since then. The task for Palestinians is to find a way of telling Israel it is safe to let go.

The problem is that the dispute between Israel and the Palestinians is not just about territory; it's about historical legitimacy. The conflict goes much deeper than the events of 1967; it is about the consequences of the war of 1948, the creation of Israel, and the dispersion of the Palestinians. The problem is not just Israel's military occupation of Palestinians, but also the dispossession of Palestinians and the Jewish millennial claims to the Promised Land.

Even if Israel were prepared to withdraw from all of the territories occupied in 1967, which it is not, each side would retain emotional historical claims on the other. In the case of Israel it is the connection with the biblical heartland of "Judea and Samaria." For Palestinians, it is the "right of return" for the refugees exiled from what is Israel today. There is a trade-off here: Israel gives up its claim to Hebron, Bethlehem, and Nablus, while the Palestinians give up the Right of Return to Jaffa, Ramle, Lod, and Haifa. That is the logic of the two-state solution: Israel for Jews, Palestine for Arabs.

And what of Jerusalem? It should not be an object of contention, but strive to become a symbol of peace and reconciliation. This means retaining some kind of unity of the city, and making an exception to the strict "land-for-peace" formula. The profane parts of Jerusalem can be apportioned to the Israeli and Palestinian states. The Israeli municipal boundaries are man-made, designed to separate

Jerusalem from the West Bank rather than unite its people, and there is no reason not to change its borders.

The Old City is the irreducible core of the matter. The solution here will require imagination and, above all, good will. Under the 1947 partition plan, an enlarged Jerusalem was supposed to be a "corpus separatum," a separate body, that would be run by the international community. A similar idea, an international body that would include Islamic countries, could be applied to the walled city, or if necessary, just to the sacred mount comprising the Haram al-Sharif and the Western Wall. I personally like the idea of leaving the mount without sovereignty, merely dividing up administrative functions. It would be a "sovereignty of God," a kind of modern-day holy of holies that testifies to the indivisibility and mystery of the single God to whom Muslims, Jews, and Christians all pray.

All this does not entirely resolve Shimon Peres's omelette problem. How will the state of Palestine be linked to the millions of Palestinians remaining in Israel and Jordan? This question may affect the stability of the region. Political scientists speak of one day establishing a supranational structure, perhaps a confederation, encompassing Israel, Palestine, and Jordan. This might ease problems of national identity for the Palestinians spread across three countries. The economic benefits are obvious—Israel wants economic integration in the Middle East, the Palestinians need access to markets in Jordan and Israel, while Jordan needs access to the Mediterranean. In other words, the Palestinian question has to be solved not only by partition of the British mandate of Palestine, but also by a reintegration of the larger pre-1921 British-ruled Palestine.

There is nothing extraordinary about the above. Establishing a Palestinian state in the territory occupied by Israel in 1967 is the basis of the "parameters" spelled out by Bill Clinton in January 2001. That Israel and the Palestinians could not reach an agreement when a deal seemed so close at hand may be a crying matter for a generation to come. I suspect that an agreement between Israel and the Palestinians, whenever it happens, would not look very different. The sooner it happens, the fewer lives will be lost.

In the imbalance of power between a regional power and a stateless people, Israel can win wars, but it cannot bomb the Palestinians into becoming reconciled with the Jewish state. Striking at the Palestinians is like punching at sand; they are too weak to be defeated in the conventional sense of the word. The Palestinians, on the other hand, cannot impose a military solution on Israel but can inflict

agony on Israel. As the September 11 attacks show, an attacker determined to kill himself is almost impossible to stop and can cause disproportionate damage armed with nothing more than a knife. Israel
can offer inducements or issue threats, it can contain and repress
Palestinians, but peace and calm have to be granted by the Arabs.
Neither the exodus of Palestinians in 1948 nor their occupation in
1967 have ensured peace for Israel. In an age of missiles and weapons
of mass destruction, war poses enormous risks. Israel's only guarantee
of peace, then, is acceptance by the Arabs, and the key to acceptance
is reaching a convincing agreement with the Palestinians.

The situation creates a lopsided negotiation between Israel and the
Palestinians. The strongest side must make the most tangible concession: land. The Israelis want peace and the end of violence; the Palestinians do not want peace for its own sake, but that ill-defined quality
of "justice." Palestinians believe they made the historic compromise
in 1993 with the Oslo accords by recognizing Israel and giving up
more than three-quarters of the former British mandate of Palestine.
This helps to explain the infuriating Palestinian negotiating tactic of
saying "No" to everything at Camp David that was not a full Israeli
withdrawal from the West Bank, Gaza Strip, and East Jerusalem.

In all its other negotiations with Arab states—Egypt, Jordan, and
even the failed negotiations with Syria—Israel understood the bargain. The Jewish state would have to give up all the land occupied in
1967 in return for peace. That Israel should demand to haggle over
the fate of the occupied territories amounts, in Palestinian eyes, to an
Israeli policy of "What's mine is mine, what's yours we share." Even
Lebanon, which allowed Hizbollah to wage a guerrilla war for years,
has secured a full Israeli withdrawal without ever recognizing Israel's
legitimate right to exist. Why should Palestinians, the people who feel
most directly aggrieved by Zionism, be different? Why should they
accept anything less than "international legitimacy"? Under the terms
of U.N. Security Council Resolution 242, which asserts "the inad-
missibility of the acquisition of territory by force," Israel's occupation
of territories in 1967 is illegitimate. Why, ask the Palestinians, should
Israel expect to hold on to any part of the occupied territories?

In seven years of talks, the Israelis always made one concession too
few in Palestinian eyes, while Israelis always suspected the Palestinians
of negotiating in bad faith. Israelis wonder where Palestinian demands
will stop. The West Bank? Jerusalem? Jaffa? The destruction of Israel?

Interviews with senior negotiators at Camp David carried by
Israeli and Palestinian newspapers about a year after the summit illus-

trate the gulf of perception. "The feeling was that they were constantly trying to drag us into some sort of black hole of more and more concessions without it being at all clear where all the concessions were leading, what the finishing line was," recalled Shlomo Ben-Ami the Israeli foreign minister at the time, in an interview with *Ha'aretz*. About two months earlier, Abu Mazen told *Al-Ayyam*: "When they say 'We offered you 95 percent,' I'm asking 'Why not 100 percent?' When they are saying 'Almost full control of Jerusalem,' [I'm asking] 'Why wouldn't control be in full?'"

The negotiation is ultimately about who was right and who was wrong. Ben-Ami said he felt Palestinians were trying to "humiliate" Israel with their demand of every inch of the 1967 lands. Abu Mazen believes that to accept anything less than the "relative justice" of the occupied territories would be degrading.

After Clinton's departure from the White House, America's attempts to salvage the peace process concentrated more on the "process" than on the substance of "peace." Oslo was already a phased, step-by-step accord. With the breakdown of Oslo, a commission headed by Senator George Mitchell proposed in May 2001 a set of smaller steps that each side should take, such as declaring a ceasefire, observing a "cooling off" period and making confidence-building gestures. These included, controversially, a complete freeze in Jewish settlements. All this would then lead to a resumption of negotiations. When the Mitchell process failed, the CIA Director, George Tenet, devised in June an even smaller set of steps for each side to take in order to achieve a ceasefire. When that failed, the Israelis and the Palestinians negotiated even further "understandings" about how to begin the Tenet process.

Truces came and went. For both Sharon and Arafat, remaining in the fight was preferable to the risk of a humiliating disengagement. For Sharon, opening talks would amount to giving Arafat a "prize for violence." For Arafat, halting the uprising entirely, without any gain except the vague prospect of more uncertain negotiations, would be taken by many Palestinians as a betrayal of the sacrifice of hundreds of martyrs, and so Arafat would risk a civil war. It is time to look once more at the other end of the process, and identify what negotiations will lead to. This may give each side a stronger incentive to respect a ceasefire.

Many believe that only partial agreements are possible for the foreseeable future. Clinton suggested returning to the interim redeployment promised by Israel under the 1998 Wye River accord but never carried out. His veteran former envoy to the Middle East, Dennis Ross, said the sides could go further by negotiating first an agreement on establishing a Palestinian state, and security arrangements for Israel. The emotional questions of the Right of Return and Jerusalem would then be left for a later stage. A similar logic seems to inform President George Bush's notion in June 2002 of creating a Palestinian state with "provisional" borders.

The experience of Oslo is that partial agreements ultimately lead to conflict. In any case, an interim deal may not be palatable to either side. Many Israelis will regard a partial solution as surrendering concrete assets in exchange for worthless promises from Arafat. As long as issues remain outstanding, Israelis fear, Palestinians will have an excuse to return to violence. Palestinians, for their part, will fear the interim may become permanent, and the outstanding issues such as Jerusalem and the "right of return" will be ignored forever.

Only the promise of internationally recognized statehood for Palestinians, and of lasting peace for Israelis with guarantees of no further Palestinian claims against the Jewish state, may be a strong enough incentive to compromise and step back from the conflict. The ideal solution would be for Arafat and Sharon to negotiate a permanent accord secretly, through an Oslo-style back-channel. Given Arafat's historic role in the Palestinian movement and Sharon's credibility on the nationalist Right, the two old foes would be best placed to reach an historic accord. A secret channel would insulate the leaders from the public day-to-day pressures of fighting the Intifada and would circumvent the endless failures of step-by-step measures. Admittedly, with Sharon declaring Arafat to be "irrelevant," it is difficult to see the two men even starting negotiations, let alone reaching a permanent agreement.

In the autumn of 2001, Shlomo Ben-Ami, now out of office, proposed an alternative: strong international pressure to compel the two sides to reach an accord. He advocated convening an international conference presided over by the United States, Europe, Russia, the United Nations, and key Arab countries. It would be a second round of the Madrid conference. Its aim would not be to negotiate a new peace agreement, but to implement the parameters already set down by President Clinton in 2001.

For an Israeli to invite the world to join the negotiations is revolutionary. Israel has for many years tried to avoid international conferences and maneuvered to ensure that the United States, its greatest ally, retains the monopoly on Middle East mediation. Palestinians have long tried to "internationalize" the conflict by bringing in other would-be mediators in the hope of exerting pressure on Israel. But Arafat ultimately accepts the central role of the United States as the only country that has an impact on Israel. Now Ben-Ami wants to turn to the tables, by harnessing international pressure to make Palestinians accept the deal that they had previously turned down.

Each side would be able to present the conference as an attempt by the world to crack the whip against the other recalcitrant side. Given the Palestinians' demand for "international legitimacy," a conference involving other Arabs would provide diplomatic cover for Arafat to take the final step. An immediate problem, of course, is that Labor is no longer in government, and Sharon is adamant that the previous proposals are dead. "The peace plan offered to Arafat at Camp David has never been offered before by any prime minister and will never be offered again by any prime minister, including me," said Sharon emphatically at the end of 2001. The other problem is that the last time the world tried to impose a solution—with the U.N. 1947 partition resolution—it was a disaster.

Nevertheless, I think there is scope for the world to declare clearly what constitutes a fair deal. It would salvage something from the collapse of the Oslo accords, and provide a firm rallying point for those in both camps who seek an accommodation. The main operative United Nations resolutions—242 and 338—provide an unsteady legal anchor for the peace process. They are more than a quarter of a century old and could usefully be updated. For instance, these resolutions make no mention of Palestinian statehood, or even of Palestinians. In Security Council Resolution 242 of 1967, the key land-for-peace provision, Palestinians are alluded to not as a people but as a problem. A secondary phrase affirming the need "for achieving a just settlement of the refugee problem" appears sandwiched ignominiously between the need to guarantee freedom of navigation through international waterways, and a call to establish demilitarized zones between Israel and Arab states.

Resolution 1397 of March 2002, "Affirming a vision of a region where two states, Israel and Palestine, live side by side within secure and recognized borders," did little more than enshrine Bush's vague "vision." It did not say what Palestine should look like.

The outside world has been intimately bound up with the affairs of Palestine and Israel ever since Britain issued the Balfour Declaration. That the question remains unresolved more than half a century after the original U.N. partition resolution is a stain on the international community. The quarrel between Israel and the Palestinians is one of many factors—but an important one—poisoning relations between the West and the Islamic world. As the September 11 terrorist attacks in America show, the Middle East is not a distant place that can be safely left to its own devices. Anybody with a grudge against America, against the West, or against pro-western regimes can seize the issue of Palestine to rally enraged supporters. To resolve the agony of Palestine, to deny it as a source of incitement for extremists, would be a major victory of the "war against terrorism."

Chronology

c. 1900–1800 B.C.E.	Jerusalem mentioned as Rushalimum in Execration Texts
c. 1200 B.C.E.	Emergence/arrival of "Israelites" in Canaan. Archaeological record murky
587–586 B.C.E.	Nebuchadnezzar destroys first Jewish temple
538 B.C.E.	Exiles return to rebuild Second Temple
332 B.C.E.	Alexander the Great conquers Palestine
164 B.C.E.	Judah Maccabee leads revolt against Seleucid rule and liberates Jerusalem
63 B.C.E.	Palestine falls under Roman influence. Pompey captures Jerusalem and appoints Hyrcanus II as High Priest
c. 7–6 B.C.E.	Birth of Jesus
70 C.E.	Second Temple destroyed when Roman legions put down the First Revolt
135 C.E.	Second Revolt led by Bar-Kochba is crushed. Jews banned from Jerusalem
200–499 C.E.	Palestinian and Babylonian Talmuds compiled
336 C.E.	Constantine completes building of Holy Sepulcher to underline the Roman empire's adoption of Christianity
c. 570 C.E.	Birth of Muhammad
638 C.E.	Omar Ibn al-Khattab conquers Jerusalem
692 C.E.	Dome of the Rock is completed by Caliph Abdel-Malik
1099	Crusaders capture Jerusalem. Godfrey de Bouillon becomes first Latin ruler
1187	Saladin defeats Crusaders at Battle of Hattin
	Saladin recaptures Jerusalem. Al-Aqsa mosque is rededicated
1260	In the battle of Ayn Jalut the Mamelukes defeat the Mongol hordes of Hulagu and complete the eviction of the Crusaders
1537–41	Jerusalem is walled during the reign of Suleiman the Magnificent

1798	Napoleon campaigns in Egypt and Palestine. He is turned back at Acre the following year
1831–40	Ibrahim Pasha, the Ottoman governor in Egypt, takes control of Palestine, and puts down major uprising centered in Palestine
1853–56	Crimean War
1867	Mark Twain visits Palestine
1881–82	Wave of pogroms against Jews in Russia after Tsar Alexander II is assassinated. Start of first Zionist immigration, or *aliyah*. Rishon Le-Zion founded in 1882
1896	Herzl writes *Der Judenstaat* after Dreyfus affair
1897	First Zionist Congress in Basle launches program to resettle Jewish people in Palestine
1898	Herzl visits Palestine
1902	Herzl writes *Altneuland*
1904–14	Second Aliyah, with large proportion of socialist pioneers, settles in Palestine in the wake of fresh pogroms in Russia
1905	Nagib Azoury publishes *Le Réveil de la Nation Arabe*, predicting a future conflict between Zionism and Arab nationalism
1908	Palestinian delegates to Ottoman parliament issue warnings of Jewish takeover
1910	Kibbutz Degania founded
1911	*Filastin*, a major Palestinian newspaper, is launched in Jaffa
1914	First World War begins. Turkey allies itself to Germany and Central powers
1916	Sharif Hussein of Mecca declares Arab Revolt, supported by Britain, which promises to support creation of Arab kingdom based in Damascus
1917	British government issues Balfour Declaration supporting Jewish national homeland in Palestine. General Allenby enters Jerusalem
1918	First World War ends. Allies carve up Middle East and Britain takes Palestine.
	Palestinian delegates to General Arab Congress declare Palestine to be part of southern Syria
1920	Year of the first Nakba, or catastrophe. Prince Faisal evicted from Damascus by French troops. In general turmoil, Arabs attack Tel Hai and Yosef Trumpeldor is killed. Riots at Nebi Musa. San Remo conference assigns mandate for Palestine to Britain. First Palestinian National Congress demands independence for Palestine
1920	Hagana formed
1921	Arab riots in Jaffa
1929	Countrywide Arab riots. 250 killed, including 60 Jews in Hebron
1935	Sheikh Izz al-Din al-Qassam killed by British troops as he leads first armed uprising against British rule
1936–39	Arab Revolt rages across the country. The Hagana cooperates

with British forces to quell the unrest after rebels take control of most of the inland towns and, briefly, even Jerusalem

1937   Etzel (Irgun Tzva'i Leumi), a Jewish underground group, is formed in reaction to Arab Revolt. Peel Commission recommends partition of Palestine into a Jewish and Arab state incorporated into Transjordan. Both sides reject the proposal

1939   Britain issues White Paper promising an independent Arab-ruled Palestine within ten years, and restricts Jewish immigration and land purchase. Within months, the Second World War breaks out

1940   Lehi (Lohamei Herut Israel) formed as breakaway after Etzel declares truce

1942   British turn back Rommel at Al-Alamein

1944   Etzel declares anticolonial revolt against Britain

1945   Second World War ends with millions of people, including Jews, uprooted. Hagana joins Jewish revolt against British in Palestine and backs "illegal" immigration of Jews

1947   Britain hands over problem of Palestine to U.N., which votes to partition Palestine into a Jewish and an Arab state, with Jerusalem as an international city

1947–48   Fighting breaks out immediately. As Jewish forces gain upper hand, Palestinian exodus begins. Israel declares statehood when British mandate ends on May 14, 1948, and repels invasion by combined Arab armies.

1948   Short-lived "All Palestine Government" is established in Gaza under Egyptian auspices in September. Transjordan responds by convening a Palestinian congress to denounce the Gaza "government" and call for the unity of the two banks of the Jordan

1949   Egypt, Lebanon, Transjordan, and Syria sign armistice agreements with Israel

1949–56   Constant infiltration of Palestinian *fedayyin* leads to escalating campaign of Israeli crossborder reprisals

1956   In secret accord with Britain and France, Israel invades Sinai in October, giving European powers excuse to "intervene" and retake Suez Canal, which had been nationalized by Gamal Abdel-Nasser. But operation ends in fiasco when United States forces allies to withdraw

1959   Yasser Arafat founds Fatah movement in Kuwait

1964   First Arab summit in Cairo in January decides to establish the Palestine Liberation Organization. The Palestine National Council meets for the first time in Jerusalem in May, under leadership of Ahmad Shukayri

1965   Fatah carries out first armed attack in January

1967   In Six Day War in June, Israel captures Sinai, West Bank, and Golan Heights. East Jerusalem is annexed. Dayan says he is "waiting for telephone call," but Arabs respond with intransigence at Khartoum summit

1968 Palestinian militias, supported by Jordanian forces, make a surprising stand at Karameh in Jordan in March when Israel mounts raid in reprisal for a landmine that strikes a bus carrying students

1969 Yasser Arafat takes over Palestine Liberation Organization

1970 Palestinian militias expelled from Jordan in "Black September"

1972 PLO members, using the code name Black September, kill 11 Israeli athletes at Munich Olympics

1973 Yom Kippur War breaks out in October with a surprise attack by Egypt and Syria. With American military airlift, Israel defeats attackers

1974 Golda Meir resigns within months of winning election and hands over to Yitzhak Rabin. Yasser Arafat invited to address U.S. General Assembly

1975 Civil war in Lebanon. Palestinians ally themselves to Muslim leftists against Christian Right

1977 Political revolution in Israel as Likud takes power. Sadat visits Jerusalem

1978 Camp David accords signed in Washington

1979 Egyptian–Israeli peace treaty

1982 Israel evacuates settlement of Yamit in Sinai in April, but invades Lebanon in June. Arafat leads PLO leadership into exile in Tunis after two-month siege. Phalangist allies massacre Palestinians at Sabra and Shatila refugee camps in Beirut in September

1987 Palestinian uprising, known as the Intifada, breaks out in Jabalya refugee camp in the Gaza Strip in December

1988 Arafat declares Palestinian statehood at Algiers meeting of Palestine National Council. Says he renounces terrorism

1990 Iraq invades Kuwait. As U.S.-led forces mass in Saudi Arabia, Iraq offers to "link" withdrawal from Kuwait to Israeli withdrawal from occupied territories

1991 Iraqi forces retreat from Kuwait in February. About 300,000 Palestinians expelled from Kuwait. In recognition of Arab states' support in anti-Iraq coalition, U.S. convenes Madrid peace conference in October. Palestinians take part, but only as part of Jordanian-Palestinian delegation

1992 Labor leader Yitzhak Rabin wins election on promise to pursue peace. Deports 400 Islamic militants in response to increased attacks by Hamas and Islamic Jihad

1993 Oslo accords signed in Washington after secret negotiations between Israel and PLO

1994 Baruch Goldstein, a settler, massacres 29 Palestinians praying in Hebron's Cave of the Patriarchs, or the Ibrahimi Mosque. Hamas responds with a campaign of suicide bombings. Nevertheless, Israeli troops withdraw from Gaza and Jericho, and Yasser Arafat returns to Palestinian soil

1995   Yitzhak Rabin assassinated by right-wing religious Jew, Yigal
        Amir. His successor, Shimon Peres, presses ahead with the
        withdrawal from major cities in the West Bank

1996   Arafat wins presidential elections in January. But Israel kills
        bomb-maker Yihya Ayyash. Hamas and Islamic Jihad respond
        with a new wave of bombings in February and March. Israeli
        army bombards South Lebanon in April to silence Hizbollah
        Katyusha rocket attacks, but shelling of a U.N. base with the
        death of about 100 villagers causes international uproar. Shi-
        mon Peres loses the June election to the Likud leader,
        Binyamin Netanyahu. Israel opens archaeological tunnel at
        base of Temple Mount, provoking riots and first gun battles
        between Israeli and Palestinian forces in September

1997   Netanyahu agrees to withdraw from four-fifths of Hebron in
        January, leaving a wedge of Israeli-held territory to defend
        about 500 settlers in the center of the city. The following
        month he gives go-ahead for construction of a new Jewish
        neighborhood in East Jerusalem, sparking protests, riots, and
        international criticism

1999   Netanyahu defeated by Labor party's Ehud Barak, who prom-
        ises to pull out of Lebanon and make peace with the Palestini-
        ans by the following year

2000   Army withdraws from South Lebanon "Security Zone" in
        May. Camp David summit in July fails to reach "final status"
        agreement between Israel and Palestinians. In September, Ariel
        Sharon visits Al-Aqsa mosque, sparking Al-Aqsa Intifada

2001   In elections in February, Barak is defeated. Ariel Sharon
        becomes Prime Minister, and forms a government of national
        unity. After September 11 terrorist attacks on America, Presi-
        dent George Bush supports Palestinian statehood and his
        administration launches new peace mediation. But escalation
        in violence isolates Palestinian Authority. Sharon declares Arafat
        to be "irrelevant" and besieges him in Ramallah.

2002   Israeli commandos capture a ship laden with weapons from
        Iran bound for the Palestinian Authority in January and three-
        week ceasefire is broken. President Bush accuses Arafat of
        enhancing terrorism, but European countries try to revive
        peace negotiations the following month as some 200 Israeli
        reserve officers sign petition declaring they will not serve in
        the occupied territories. Arab summit in Beirut in March
        offers Israel peace if it withdraws from occupied territories.
        But a suicide bomb in a hotel in Netanya provokes Operation
        Defensive Shield, Israel's largest military strike since the
        Lebanon war. Yasser Arafat is besieged by Israeli forces in his
        headquarters in Ramallah but is released in May after intense
        mediation. In June President George W. Bush calls on Palestini-
        ans to choose new leadership not "compromised by terror,"

and Arafat calls elections. In response to continued Palestinian attacks, Israeli forces establish permanent security control of most Palestinian cities in West Bank and stage deep raids in the Gaza Strip. Diplomatic "Quartet" delays publication of "Roadmap" for ceasefire and resumption of negotiations for a permanent accord by 2005.

2003   Ariel Sharon reelected Prime Minister in January. United States steps up preparations for war in Iraq.

Bibliography

Biblical quotations are drawn from the Authorized King James Version, unless there was compelling reason to quote a more modern version.

Quotations from the Koran are drawn from:

The Koran (trans. J. N. Dawood), Penguin Classics, 4th edn., Penguin Books, London, 1974

I have found the following Web sites useful in keeping track of developments and as starting points for research:

The Daily Telegraph: http://www.telegraph.co.uk

BBC: http://news.bbc.co.uk/hi/english/world/default.stm

The New York Times: http://www.nytimes.com

The Washington Post: http://www.washingtonpost.com

Yahoo: http://dailynews.yahoo.com/full_coverage/world/israeli_palestinian_conflict/

Ha'aretz daily: http://www3.haaretz.co.il/eng/htmls/1_1.htm

The Jerusalem Post daily: http://www.jpost.com/

Palestine Report: http://www.jmcc.org/media/reportonline/report.html

Israel Ministry of Foreign Affairs: http://www.israel.org/mfa/home.asp

Israel Central Bureau of Statistics: http://www.cbs.gov.il/engindex.htm

Palestinian National Authority: http://www.pna.net

Palestine Central Bureau of Statistics: http://www.pcbs.org

United Nations on Question of Palestine: http://www.un.org/Depts/dpa/qpal/index.html

Bir Zeit University web site links: http://www.birzeit.edu/links/index.html

Palestinian Development Infonet (via Mc Gill University): http://www.arts.mcgill.ca/MEPP/mepp.html

Amnesty International: http://www.web.amnesty.org

Human Rights Watch: http://www.hrw.org

The Middle East Media Research Institute: http://www.memri.org/

Palestinian Media Watch: http://www.pmw.org.il/

B'Tselem, The Israeli Information Center for Human Rights in the Occupied Territories: http://www.btselem.org

The Jerusalem Report Magazine: http://www.jrep.com/

More academic information can be obtained from the following sources:

Dinur Center of Research in Jewish History, The Hebrew University, Jerusalem: http://www.hum.huji.ac.il/dinur/links/texts.htm

The Jewish Virtual Library: http://www.us-israel.org/index.html

Journal of Palestine Studies: http://ipsjps.org/html/journal.html

Palestine-Israel Journal: http://www.pij.org/

The Palestinian Academic Society for the Study of International Affairs: http://www.passia.org/

GENERAL SOURCES

Al-Udhari, Abdallah (trans. and ed.), *Modern Poetry of the Arab World*, Penguin Books, London, 1986

Amichai, Yehuda, Poems of Jerusalem and Love Poems: a Bilingual Edition, The Sheep Meadow Press, Riverdale-on-Hudson, 1988

Birman, Abraham (ed.), *An Anthology of Modern Hebrew Poetry*, Abelard-Schuman, London, 1968

Carmi, T. (ed. and trans.) *The Penguin Book of Hebrew Verse*, Penguin Books USA, New York, 1981

Dankner, Amnon and Tartakover, David, *Eyfo hayinu umah 'assinu* (Where we were and what we did: An Israeli lexicon of the fifties and the sixties), Keter, Jerusalem, 1996

Darwish, Mahmoud, *The Music of Human Flesh* (trans. Denys Johnson-Davies), Heinemann, London, 1980

Darwish, Mahmoud, *Victims of a Map* (trans. Abdullah al-Udhari), Al Saqi Books, London, 1985

Elon, Amos, *The Israelis: Founders and Sons*, Sphere Books, London, 1972

Elon, Amos, *Herzl*, Holt, Rinehart & Winston, New York, 1975

Encyclopedia Judaica CD-Rom edition, Judaica Multimedia (Israel) Ltd, text copyright Keter, Jerusalem, 1997

The New Encyclopedia Britannica in 32 volumes, 15th edition, Encyclopedia Britannica Inc., 1990

Friedman, Thomas L., *From Beirut to Jerusalem*, Anchor Books, Doubleday, New York, 1989

Gilmour, David, *Dispossessed: The Ordeal of the Palestinians*, Sphere Books, London, 1983

Grossman, David, *The Yellow Wind* (trans. from the Hebrew by Haim Watson), Bantam Dell, New York, 1988

Hattis Rolef, Susan (ed.) *Political Dictionary of the State of Israel*, Macmillan, New York, 1987

Herzl, Theodor, *The Diaries of Theodor Herzl* (ed. and trans. Marvin Lowenthal) Dial Press, New York, 1956

Herzl, Theodor, *The Jewish State*, Dover Publications, New York, 1989

Herzl, Theodor, *Old New Land* (trans. Lotta Levensohn), Marcus Weiner, New York, 1997

Jayyusi, Salma Khadra (ed.), *Modern Arabic Poetry: An Anthology*, Columbia University Press, New York, 1987

Jayyusi, Salma Khadra (ed.), *Anthology of Modern Palestinian Literature*, Columbia University Press, New York, 1992

The Jerusalem Post on CD Rom 1990–June 1997, Silver Platter International, N.V.

Johnson, Paul, *A History of the Jews*, Weidenfeld & Nicolson, London, 1987

Kepel, Gilles (trans. Anthony F. Roberts), *Jihad: The Trail of Political Islam*, I. B. Tauris, London, 2002

Khalidi, Rashid, *Palestinian Identity: The Construction of Modern National Consciousness*, Columbia University Press, New York, 1997

Khalidi, Walid, *Before Their Diaspora: A Photographic Record of the Palestinians 1876–1948*, Institute for Palestine Studies, Washington DC, 1984

Kimmerling, Baruch and Migdal, Joel S., *Palestinians: The Making of a People*, Harvard University Press, Cambridge, Mass., 1995

Morris, Benny, *Righteous Victims: A History of the Zionist–Arab Conflict, 1881–1999*, John Murray, London, 1999

New Oxford Annotated Bible CD Rom, Version 2, Oxford University Press, Oxford, 1991

Oz, Amos, *In the Land of Israel* (trans. from the Hebrew by Maurie Goldberg-Bartura), Fontana Paperbacks, London, 1983

Penueli, S.Y. and Ukhmani, A. (eds) *Anthology of Modern Hebrew Poetry, Vol. 2*, Institute for the Translation of Hebrew Literature and Israel Universities Press, 1966

Sachar, Howard M., *A History of Israel: From the Rise of Zionism to Our Time*, Alfred A. Knopf, New York, 1979

Sachar, Howard M., *A History of Israel Volume II: From the Aftermath of the Yom Kippur War*, Oxford University Press, Oxford, 1987

Said, Edward, *The Question of Palestine*, Vintage Books, New York, 1992

CHAPTER I: A SMALL COUNTRY WITH A BIG HISTORY

A Handbook for Travellers in Syria and Palestine, John Murray, London, 1868

Baedeker, Karl (ed.) *Palestine and Syria: Handbook for Travellers*, Karl Baedeker, London, 1898

Ben-Arieh, Yehoshua and Davis, Moshe (eds.) *Jerusalem in the Mind of the Western World, 1800–1948*, Praeger, Westport, Conn., 1997

Cook's Tourist's Handbook for Palestine and Syria, Thomas Cook & Son, London, 1891

Roberts, David and Bourbon, Fabio, *The Holy Land: Yesterday and Today*, The American University in Cairo Press, Cairo, 1996

Treves, Frederick, *The Land that Is Desolate: An Account of a Tour in Palestine*, Smith, Elder, London, 1912

Twain, Mark, pseud. (Samuel Langhorne Clemens) *The Innocents Abroad*, Electronic Text Center, University of Virginia Library

CHAPTER 2: ONE GOD, MANY RELIGIONS

Al-Tabari, *The History of al-Tabari (Volume XII) The Battle of al-Qadsiyyah and the Conquest of Syria and Palestine* (trans. and annotated by Yohanan Friedmann), State University of New York Press, New York, 1992

Armstrong, Karen, *A History of God: The 4,000 Year Quest of Judaism, Christianity and Islam*, Ballantine Books, New York, 1993

Armstrong, Karen, *Jerusalem: One City, Three Faiths*, Ballantine Books, New York, 1997

Avi-Yonah, M., "The Economics of Byzantine Jerusalem," in *The Israel Exploration Journal*, 8, 1958

Bahat, Dan and Sabar, Shalom, *Jerusalem: Stone and Spirit: 3000 Years of History and Art*, Matan Arts Publishers, Tel Aviv, 1997

Ben-Arieh, Yehoshua, *Jerusalem in the 19th Century: Emergence of the New City*, Yad Izhak Ben-Zvi, Jerusalem, 1986

Ben-Arieh, Yehoshua, *Jerusalem in the 19th Century: The Old City*, Yad Izhak Ben-Zvi, Jerusalem, 1984

Benvenisti, Meron, *City of Stone: The Hidden History of Jerusalem* (trans. from the Hebrew by Maxine Kaufman Nunn), University of California Press, Berkeley, 1996

Cohn-Sherbok, Lavinia and Dan, *A Short Reader in Judaism*, Oneworld, Oxford, 1996

Elon, Amos, *Jerusalem City of Mirrors*, Little, Brown, Boston, 1989

Eusebius, *The History of the Church*, revised edn, Penguin Books, London, 1989

Eusebius, *The Life of the Blessed Emperor Constantine* (A revised translation, with prolegomena and notes, by Ernest Cushing Richardson) electronic edition from Christian Classics Ethereal Library at Calvin College, http://www.ccel.org/

Fairuz, *Zahrat al-Madain* (Flower of Cities), A. Chahine & Fils, Beirut

Flusser, David, in collaboration with R. Steven Notley, *Jesus*, The Magnes Press, The Hebrew University, Jerusalem, 1997

Fulcher of Chartres, *Chronicle of the First Crusade* (trans. Martha Evelyn McGinty), University of Pennsylvania Press, Philadelphia, 1941

Glassé, Cyril, *The Concise Encyclopedia of Islam*, Stacey International, London, 1989

Goodman, Philip, *The Passover Anthology*, The Jewish Publication Society, Philadelphia and Jerusalem, 1993

Grant, Michael, *The History of Ancient Israel*, Phoenix, London, 1997

Haggadah (trans. from the Hebrew by Harold Fisch), Koren, Jerusalem, 1996

Hammer, Reuven, *The Jerusalem Anthology: A Literary Guide*, The Jewish Publication Society, Philadelphia and Jerusalem, 1995

Hodgson, Marshall G, *The Venture of Islam: Conscience and History in a World Civilization, Volume One: The Classical Age of Islam*, University of Chicago Press, Chicago, 1974

The Holy Qur'an (text, translation and commentary by Abdullah Yusuf Ali), new revised edn, Amana Corporation, Washington DC, 1989

Johnson, Paul, *A History of Christianity*, Penguin Books, London, 1976

Josephus, Flavius, *The Works of Flavius Josephus* (trans. William Whiston), T. Nelson & Sons, Edinburgh, 1880

Le Strange, Guy (trans.) *Palestine under the Moslems: A Description of Syria and the Holy Land*, AMS Press, reprinted 1990

Maalouf, Amin, *The Crusades through Arab Eyes* (trans. Jon Roshschild), Al Saqi Books, London, 1984

Murphy-O'Connor, Jerome, *The Holy Land: An Archaeological Guide from Earliest Times to 1700*, Oxford University Press, Oxford, 1986

Peters, F. E. *Jerusalem: The Holy City in the Eyes of Chroniclers, Visitors, Pilgrims, and Prophets from the Days of Abraham to the Beginnings of Modern Times*, Princeton University Press, Princeton, New Jersey, 1985

Prior, Michael and Taylor, William (eds) *Christians in the Holy Land: The World of Islamic Festival Trust*, London, 1994

Rahman, Fazlur, *Islam*, 2nd edn, University of Chicago Press, Chicago, 1979

Rock, Albert, *The Status Quo in the Holy Places* (trans. Vincent Gottwald), Holy Land Publications, Jerusalem, 1989

Romann, Michael and Weingold, Alex, *Living Together Separately: Arabs and Jews in Contemporary Jerusalem*, Princeton University Press, Princeton, New Jersey, 1991

Runciman, Steven, *A History of the Crusades*, Penguin Books, London, 1991

Schiller, Eli, *Sefer Z'ev Vilnay* ('Zev Vilnay's Jubilee Volume), Ariel Publishing House, Jerusalem, 1984, reproducing T. Canaan's "Mohammedan Saints and Sanctuaries in Palestine," *Journal of the Palestinian Oriental Society*, 4 (5), 1924

Saldarini, Anthony, *Jesus and Passover*, Paulist Press, New Jersey, 1984

Shanks, Hershel (ed.) *Ancient Israel: A Short History from Abraham to the Roman Destruction of the Temple*. Prentice-Hall, Englewood Cliffs, New Jersey, 1995

Silk, Dennis (ed.) *Retrievements: A Jerusalem Anthology*, Keter Publishing House Jerusalem, Jerusalem, 1977

Smith, George Adam, *The Historical Geography of the Holy Land*, reprint by Ariel Publishing House, Jerusalem, 1966 (first published by Hodder & Stoughton, 1894)

Steinsaltz, Adin, *The Essential Talmud* (trans. from the Hebrew by Chaya Galai), Basic Books, New York, 1976

Storrs, Ronald, *Orientations*, Nicholson & Watson, London, 1943

Vilnay, Zev, *Legends of Jerusalem*, The Jewish Publication Society of America, Philadelphia, 1973

Waugh, Evelyn, *Helena*, Penguin Books, London, 1963

Wilkinson, John, *Jerusalem Pilgrims before the Crusades*, Aris & Phillips, Warminster, 1977

CHAPTER 3: EVERY MAN UNDER HIS VINE

Al-Sakakini, Khalil, *Kazeh ani, rabotai* (Such am I, Oh World: Diaries of Khalil al-Sakakini), (trans. from the Arabic by Gideon Shilo), Keter, Tel Aviv, Israel, 1990

Alterman, Natan, *Selected Poems* (trans. Robert Friend), Hakibbutz Hameuchad, Israel, 1978

'Amud HaEsh – Perakim BeToldot HaTzionut (Pillar of Fire—Chapters in the His-

tory of Zionism), Shikmona, in conjunction with the Israel Broadcasting Authority, Jerusalem, 1982

Baratz, Joseph, *A Village by the Jordan: The Story of Degania*, Ichud HaBonim, Tel Aviv, 1960

Ben-Gurion, David, *Memoirs*, World Publishing, New York, 1970

Ben-Yehuda, Eliezer, *ha-Mavo ha-Gadol* (Prolegomenon) (trans. from the Hebrew by Scott Bradley Saulson), thesis, D.Litt. Et Phil. Semitic Languages, University of South Africa, November 1985

Bialik, Nachman Hayyim, *Complete Poetic Works of Hayyim Nachman Bialik* (trans. from the Hebrew, Vol. 1, edited and introduced by Israel Efros), The Histadruth Ivrith of America, New York, 1948

Dayan, Moshe, *Living with the Bible*, William Morrow, New York, 1978

Dayan, Shmuel, *Pioneers in Israel* (introduced, edited and arranged by Yael Dayan, trans. from the Hebrew by Sidney Lightman), World Publishing, Cleveland and New York, 1961

Freiman, Aharon Mordechai, *Rishon Le-Tzion*, 1906–7, copy available at Rishon Le-Zion museum.

Gur, Batya, *Murder on a Kibbutz*, Harper Perennial, New York, 1995

Hertzberg, Arthur (ed.) *The Zionist Idea*, Atheneum, New York, 1979

Levontin, Zalman David, *Le-eretz avoteynu* (To the land of our fathers), 2nd edn, Eytan, Shoshani, Tel-Aviv, 1923/24 (taf resh peh dalet)

Mandel, Neville J., *The Arabs and Zionism before World War I*, University of California Press, Berkeley, 1976

Ma'oz, Moshe (ed.) *Studies on Palestine during the Ottoman Period*, esp. Ch. 20, "The Political Awakening of the Palestinian Arabs and their Leadership toward the End of the Ottoman Period" by Yehoshua Porath, Magnes Press, Jerusalem, 1975

St. John, Robert, *Tongue of the Prophets, The Life Story of Eliezer Ben Yehuda*, Doubleday, Garden City, New York, 1952

Schiller, Eli (ed.) *Yafo Va'Atareyha* (Jaffa and its sites), a collection of articles in the Kardom series (March–April 1981), published by Ariel, Jerusalem

Shalev, Meir, *The Blue Mountain* (trans. from the Hebrew by Hillel Halkin), Harper Collins, New York, 1991

Shva, Shlomo and Ben-Amotz, Dahn, *Eretz Tzion, Yerushalayim* (Land of Israel and Jerusalem), Zmora Bitan Modan, Tel-Aviv, 1973

Uris, Leon, *Exodus*, Bantam Books, New York, 1986

Wilensky, Moshe (music), Mohar Yehiel (lyrics), *The Negev Lullaby*, Israel, c. 1950

Ya'ari, Avraham, *The Goodly Heritage* (trans. Israel Schen), Jewish Agency at the Jerusalem Post Press, 1958

Ya'ari, Avraham, *Zichronot Eretz Israel* (Memories of the Land of Israel) Part 2, Massada, Ramat Gan, Israel, 1974

CHAPTER 4: THE HUNDRED YEARS WAR

Allon, Yigal, *The Making of Israel's Army*, Sphere Books, London, 1971

Antonius, George, *The Arab Awakening: The Story of the Arab National Movement*, Lebanon Bookshop, Beirut, 1969

Barnea, Amalia and Aharon, *Mine Enemy: The Moving, Hopeful, Friendship of Two Couples—Israeli and Arab* (trans. from the Hebrew by Chaya Amir), Grove Press, New York, 1986

Black, Ian and Morris, Benny, *Israel's Secret Wars: A History of Israel's Intelligence Services*, Grove Weidenfeld, New York, 1991

Collins, Larry and Lapierre, Dominique, *O Jerusalem*, Steimatzky, Jerusalem, 1995

Dayan, Moshe, *Story of My Life*, Sphere Books, London, 1977

Dayan, Moshe, *Breakthrough, A Personal Account of the Egypt–Israel Peace Negotiations*, Weidenfeld & Nicolson, London, 1981

Dayan, Yael, *Israel Journal, June 1967*, McGraw-Hill, New York, 1967

Dayan, Yael, *My Father, His Daughter*, Weidenfeld & Nicolson, London, 1985

Gal, Reuven, *A Portrait of the Israeli Soldier*, Contributions in Military Studies, No. 52, Greenwood Press, New York, 1986

Glubb Pasha, *A Soldier with the Arabs*, Hodder & Stoughton, London, 1957

Gowers, Andrew and Walker, Tony, *Yasser Arafat and the Palestinian Revolution*, Corgi, London, 1991

Hersh, Seymour M., *The Samson Option: Israel, America and the Bomb*, Faber & Faber, London, 1991

Herzog, Chaim, *The Arab–Israeli Wars: War and Peace in the Middle East from the War of Independence through Lebanon*, Vintage Books, New York, 1984

Horovitz, David (ed.) *Yitzhak Rabin: Soldier of Peace*, Peter Halban, London, 1996

Kimmerling, Baruch, *Zionism and Territory: The Socio-Territorial Dimensions of Zionist Politics*, Research Series No. 51, Institute of International Studies, University of California, Berkeley, 1983

The King-Crane Commission Report, 1919, available through http://www.hri.org/docs/king-crane/introduction.html

Lawrence, T. E., *Seven Pillars of Wisdom*, Penguin Books, London 1962

Le Carré, John, *The Little Drummer Girl*, Pan Books, London, 1984

Lewis, Bernard, *What Went Wrong? The Clash Between Islam and Modernity in the Middle East*, Weidenfeld & Nicolson, London, 2002

Oren, Michael B, *Six Days of War: June 1967 and the Making of the Modern Middle East*, Oxford University Press, Oxford, 2002

Ostrovsky, Victor and Hoy, Claire, *By Way of Deception*, St. Martin's Press, New York, 1991

Rabin, Yitzhak, *The Rabin Memoirs*, Steimatzky, Bnei Brak, Israel, 1979

Rubin, Barry, *Revolution until Victory: The Politics and History of the PLO*, Harvard University Press, Cambridge, Mass., 1994

Rubinstein, Danny, *The Mystery of Arafat* (trans. Dan Leon), Steerforth Press, South Royalton, Vermont, 1995

Schattner, Marius, *Histoire de la droite Israelienne: de Jabotinsky à Shamir*, Editions Complexe, Bruxelles, 1991

Schiff, Ze'ev and Ya'ari, Ehud, *Israel's Lebanon War* (ed. and trans. Ina Friedman), Simon & Schuster, New York, 1984

Schiff, Ze'ev and Ya'ari, Ehud, *Intifada* (ed. and trans. Ina Friedman), Simon & Schuster, New York, 1989

Schölch, Alexander, *Palestine in Transformation: Studies in Social, Economic and Political Development* (trans. William C. Young and Michael Gerrity), Institute for Palestine Studies, Washington, DC, 1993

Sharon, Ariel with Chanoff David, *Warrior: The Autobiography of Ariel Sharon*, Steimatzky, Bnei Brak, 1989

Shipler, David, *Arab and Jew: Wounded Spirits in a Promised Land*, Times Books, New York, 1986

Shlaim, Avi, *The Politics of Partition: King Abdullah, the Zionists and Palestine, 1921–1951*, Oxford University Press, Oxford, 1990

Teveth, Shabtai, *The Cursed Blessing: The Story of Israel's Occupation of the West Bank*, Random House, New York, 1970

Teveth, Shabtai, *Moshe Dayan: The Soldier, the Man, the Legend*, Quartet Books, London, 1974

Tuchman, Barbara, *Bible and Sword: How the British Came to Palestine*, New York University Press, New York, 1956

Van Creveld, Martin, *The Sword and the Olive: A Critical History of the Israeli Defense Force*, Public Affairs, New York, 1998

Wallach, John and Janet, *Arafat: In the Eyes of the Beholder*, Heinemann, London, 1990

CHAPTER 5: VICTIMS OF VICTIMS

Anti-Semitism Worldwide, Annual Report, Tel Aviv University, available through http://www.tau.ac.il/Anti-Semitism/annual-report.html

Arendt, Hannah, *Eichmann in Jerusalem: A Report on the Banality of Evil*, Faber & Faber, London, 1963

Begin, Menachem, *The Revolt*, Steimatzky, Jerusalem, 1977

Dawidowicz, Lucy S. *The War against the Jews 1933–45*, Penguin Books, Harmondsworth, 1987

De Reynier, Jacques, *Rapport de M. Jacques de Reynier, chef de la delegation du Comité international de la Croix-Rouge en Palestine, sur les combats de Deir Yassin (Jérusalem)*, 13 April 1948, International Committee of the Red Cross, Geneva

De Reynier, Jacques, *A Jérusalem Un Drapeau flottait sur la ligne de feu*, Éditions de la Baconnière, Neuchâtel, Paris, 1950

Dror, Tzvika, *Dapei Edut* (Testimonies of Survival), Hakibbutz Hameuhad Publishers, Tel Aviv, Israel, 1984

Finkelstein, Norman, Rejoinder to Benny Morris, article in *Journal of Palestine Studies XXI*, No 1 (Autumn 1991), pp. 61–71

Gilbert, Martin, *The Holocaust: The Jewish Tragedy*, Fontana, London, 1987

Hanania, Ray, *Deir Yassin: Arab & Jewish Tragedy in Palestine*, USG Publishing, Illinois, 1998

Hausner, Gideon, *Justice in Jerusalem*, Nelson & Sons, London, 1966

Kanaana, Sharif, *Still on Vacation? The Evictions of the Palestinians in 1948*, Bir Zeit University, 1987, available through http://www.birzeit.edu

Kanafani, Ghassan, *Men in the Sun and Other Palestinian Stories* (trans. from the Arabic by Hilary Kilpatrick), Heinemann, London, 1978

Khalidi, Walid (ed.) *All that Remains: The Palestinian Villages Occupied and Depopulated by Israel in 1948*, Institute for Palestine Studies, Washington, DC, 1992

Lewis, Bernard, *Semites & Anti-Semites*, W.W. Norton, New York, 1986

Lynd, Staughton, Lynd, Alice and Bahour, Sam (eds) *Homeland: Oral Histories of Palestine and Palestinians*, Olive Branch Press, New York, 1994

Malkin Peter Z. and Stein, Harry, *Eichmann in My Hands*, Warner Books, New York, 1990

Morris, Benny, *The Birth of the Palestinian Refugee Problem 1947–1949*, Cambridge University Press, Cambridge, 1987

Morris, Benny, *1948 and After: Israel and the Palestinians*, Clarendon Press, Oxford, 1994

Said, Edward, "A Desolation and they call it Peace," article in *Al-Ahram Weekly* No. 383, 25 June–1 July 1998, available through http://www.ahram.org.eg

Sakakini, Hala, *Jerusalem and I, A Personal Record*, Economic Press, Amman, 1990

Schechtman, Joseph B., *The Mufti and the Fuehrer: The Rise and Fall of Haj Amin el-Husseini*, Thomas Yoseloff, New York, 1965

Segev, Tom, *The Seventh Million: The Israelis and the Holocaust* (trans. Haim Watzman), Hill & Wang, New York, 1993

Shner-Neshamit, Sara, *No Peace, Even for the Dead*, Kibbutz Lohamei ha-Getaot, 1998

Szenes, Hannah, *Walk to Caesarea* (trans. from the Hebrew by Ziva Shapiro), Caesarea, 1942

Wasserstein, Bernard, *Vanishing Diaspora: The Jews in Europe since 1945*, Penguin Books, London, 1997

Wistrich, Robert S., *Anti-Semitism: The Longest Hatred*, Methuen, London in association with Thames Television International PLC, 1991

CHAPTER 6: THE TRIBES OF ISRAEL

Ahroni, Reuben, *Yemenite Jewry: Origins, Culture and Literature*, Indiana University Press, Bloomington,

Alterman, Natan, *'Ir Ha Yona* (The City of the Dove), HaKibbutz Hame'uhad, Tel Aviv, Israel, 1972

Amir, Eli, *Tarnegol Kapparot* (Sacrificial Chicken), Am Oved, Tel Aviv, Israel, 1984

Ariel Quarterly, The Israel Review of Arts and Letters (Jerusalem), 99–100, 1995

Arieli, Amnon, *Tinok Shenishba* (A Captive Child), Am Oved, Tel Aviv, 1996

Bialik, Chaim Nachman, *Selected Poems*, bilingual edn (trans. Ruth Nevo), Dvir & the Jerusalem Post, Jerusalem, 1981

Biton, Erez, *Minha Maroka'it* (A Moroccan Offering), 'åEqed, Tel Aviv, Israel, 1976

Biton, Erez, *Na'na'* (Mint), 'Eqed, Tel Aviv, Israel, 1979

Hoffman, Edward, *Despite All Odds—The Story of the Lubavitch*, Simon & Schuster, New York, 1991

Hoffmitz, Laible, *The Other Side of Israel: The Story of Development Towns*, Bloch, New York, 1978

Kark, Ruth, *Jaffa: A City in Evolution 1799–1917*, Yad Izhak Ben-Zvi Press, Jerusalem, 1990

Klorman, Bat-Zion Eraqi, *The Jews of Yemen in the Nineteenth Century: A Portrait of a Messianic Community*, E.J. Brill, Leiden, 1993

Landau, David, *Piety and Power: The World of Jewish Fundamentalism*, Hill & Wang, New York, 1993

Linur, Irit, *Shtei Shilgiot* (Two Snow-Whites), Zmora Bitan, Tel Aviv, 1993

Meir, Yosef, *HaTnu'a HaTzionit ViYhudei Teyman* (The Zionist Movement and the Jews of Yemen), Sifriat Afikim, Tel Aviv, Israel, 1982–83 (Hebrew date, taf shin mem gimal)

Morag, Ora, *Me'a Tapuhim Hadashim (Kolel Ma'am)*, [One hundred new apples (plus VAT)], Alpha/Zmora Bitan, Tel Aviv, 1989

Nini, Yehuda, *Teyman VeTzion* (Yemen and Zion: the Political, Social and Intellectual/Spiritual Background to the First Immigration from Yemen) HaSifria HaTzionit, Jerusalem, Israel, 1981–82. (Hebrew date, taf shin mem bet)

Ruppin, Arthur, Memoirs, Diaries, Letters (ed. Alex Bein, trans. Karen Gershon), Weidenfeld and Nicolson, London and Jerusalem, 1971

Segev, Tom, *1949: The First Israelis*, The Free Press, New York, 1986

Shkhor, Ilan, *The Dream that Turned into a Metropolis: The Birth and Growth of Tel-Aviv, the First Hebrew City in the World* (Hebrew title: HaHalom), Avivim Publishers Ltd, Tel Aviv, Israel

Shva, Shlomo, *'Ir Kama* (Rising from the Sands. Tel Aviv: The Early Days) Zmora, Bitan, Israel, 1989

CHAPTER 7: THE CURSE OF PEACE

Abu-Amr., Ziad, *Islamic Fundamentalism in the West Bank and Gaza: Muslim Brotherhood and Islamic Jihad*, Indiana University Press, Bloomington, 1994

Ashrawi, Hanan, *This Side of Peace, A Personal Account*, Simon & Schuster, New York, 1995

Barghouthy, Abdellatif, "Arab Folksongs and Palestinian Identity," *Journal of Mediterranean Studies*, Vol 6, No 1: 147–172, 1996, The University of Malta

Butt, Gerald, *Life at the Crossroads: A History of Gaza*, Rimal Publications, Nicosia, 1995

The Complaint against Ariel Sharon, available from Mall Law Offices web site, http://www.mallat.com/articles/comp.htm

Charter of the Islamic Resistance Movement (Hamas) of Palestine (trans. Muhammed Maqdsi), *Journal of Palestine Studies XXII*, No 4 (summer 1993), pp. 122-134

Diwan, Ishac and Shaban, Radwan, A., *Development Under Adversity: The Palestinian Economy in Transition*, Palestine Economic Policy Research Institute (MAS) and the World Bank, 1998

Erased in a Moment: Suicide Bombing Attacks Against Israeli Civilians, Human Rights Watch. October 2002

Habibi, Emile, *The Strange Events in the Disappearance of Said Abu'l-Nahs al-Mutasha'il*, first published in Arabic 1974, 3rd edn Hebrew trans. by Anton Shammas, Mifras, Haifa, 1986

The Impact on the Palestinian Economy of Confrontations, Mobility Restrictions and

Border Closures, 1 October 2000–31 January 2001, Office of the United Nations Special Coordinator in the Occupied Territories (UNSCO), Gaza, 25 February 2001, available from: www.arts.mcgill.ca/MEPP/ unsco/unfront. html

Kahan, Yitzhak, et al, *Report of the Commission of Inquiry into the events at the refugee camps in Beirut, 8 February 1983,* available through Israel Ministry of Foreign Affairs web site, http://www.israel.org/mfa/go.asp?MFAHoigno

Kook, Tzvi Yehuda ha-Cohen, *Torat Eretz Israel: The Teachings of Harav Tzvi Yehuda HaCohen Kook,* ed. Shlomo Aviner (trans. from the Hebrew by Tzvi Fishman), Torat Eretz Yisrael, Jerusalem, 1991

Losing Ground: Israel, Poverty and the Palestinians, Christian Aid report, January 2003

Oz, Amos, *Israel, Palestine and Peace,* Vintage, London, 1994

Qabbani, Nizar, *Children Bearing Rocks,* available through http://hanthala. virtualave.net/poetry22.html

Qleibo, Ali H., *Before the Mountains Disappear: An Ethnographic Chronicle of the Modern Palestinians,* A Kloreus Book, 1992

Rapaport, Era, *Letters from Tel Mond Prison: An Israeli Settler Defends His Act of Terror* (ed. William B. Helmreich), The Free Press, New York, 1996

Rogers, Mary Eliza, *Domestic Life in Palestine,* Kegan Paul International, London, 1989

Roy, Sara, *The Gaza Strip: The Political Economy of De-development,* Institute for Palestine Studies, Washington, DC, 1995

Said, Edward, *Peace and its Discontents: Gaza–Jericho 1993–1995,* Vintage, London, 1995

Said, Edward, *The Politics of Dispossession: The Struggle for Palestinian Self-Determination 1969–1994,* Vintage, London, 1995

Segal, Haggai, *Dear Brothers: The West Bank Jewish Underground* (trans. from the Hebrew by I.B.R.T, Jerusalem), Beit-Shamai, Israel, 1988

Sharon, Ariel, with David Chanoff, *Warrior: The Autobiography of Ariel Sharon,* Simon & Schuster, New York, 1989

Sprinzak, Ehud, *The Ascendance of Israel's Radical Right,* Oxford University Press, New York, 1991

Tsimhoni, Daphne, *Christian Communities in Jerusalem and the West Bank since 1948: an Historical, Social and Political Study,* Praeger Publishers, Westport, Conn., 1993

CHAPTER 8: AMONG THE NATIONS

Butt, Gerald, *The Lion in the Sand: The British in the Middle East,* Bloomsbury, London, 1995

Fromkin, David, *A Peace to End All Peace: Creating the Modern Middle East 1914–1922,* Penguin Books, New York, 1991

Kissinger, Henry, *Years of Upheaval,* Little, Brown, Boston, 1982

Quandt, William B., *Peace Process: American Diplomacy and the Arab–Israeli Conflict since 1967,* The Brookings Institution, Washington, DC; University of California Press, Berkeley and Los Angeles, 1993

Shepherd, Naomi, *The Zealous Intruders: From Napoleon to the Dawn of Zionism—*

The Explorers, Archaeologists, Artists, Tourists, Pilgrims and Visionaries Who Opened Palestine to the West, Harper & Row, San Francisco, 1987

Shepherd, Naomi, *Plowing Sand: British Rule in Palestine 1917–1948*, John Murray, London, 1999

Sherman, A. J., *Mandate Days: British Lives in Palestine 1918–1948*, Thames and Hudson, London, 1997

Wasserstein, Bernard, *The British in Palestine: The Mandatory Government and the Arab–Jewish Conflict 1917–1929* (2nd edn), Blackwell, Oxford, 1991

Weizmann, Chaim, *Trial and Error*, Harper & Brothers, New York, 1949

Index